P9-DBP-043

Workbook/Laboratory Manual to accompany

MOTIVOS DE CONVERSACIÓN

SECOND EDITION

Workbook/Laboratory Manual to accompany

MOTIVOS DE CONVERSACIÓN
ESSENTIALS OF SPANISH

SECOND EDITION

Eduardo Neale-Silva
Professor Emeritus, University of Wisconsin, Madison

Robert L. Nicholas
University of Wisconsin, Madison

María Canteli Dominicis
Iona College

Gustavo Medina

Random House 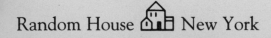 New York   This is an EBI book

Second Edition

9 8 7 6 5 4 3 2 1

Copyright © 1988 by Newbery Award Records, Inc., a subsidiary of Random House, Inc.

All rights reserved under International and Pan-American Copyright Conventions. No part of this book may be reproduced in any form or by any means, electronic or mechanical, including photocopying, without permission in writing from the publisher. All inquiries should be addressed to Newbery Award Records, Inc., 201 East 50th Street, New York, N.Y. 10022. Published in the United States by Newbery Award Records, Inc., and simultaneously in Canada by Random House of Canada Limited, Toronto. Distributed by Random House, Inc.

ISBN: 0-394-36506-2

Manufactured in the United States of America

Drawings by Axelle Fortier

TABLE OF CONTENTS

PREFACE

This Workbook/Laboratory Manual is designed to accompany *Motivos de conversación, Essentials of Spanish,* second edition. It is thematically coordinated with the chapters of the student text, presenting practice materials in two preliminary lessons (*Preliminares*) and eighteen regular lessons. Numerous exercise types, from controlled to communicative, are provided. Because of the unique lesson organization of *Motivos de conversación,* these exercises allow students to use the new vocabulary and grammar at the beginning of each lesson. New illustrations and dialogues that differ from those in the text have been especially created to reenter and review text material.

Each chapter of the Manual is divided into two sections.

The Workbook

The Workbook includes a variety of written exercises covering vocabulary usage, grammatical structures, guided composition, translation, and other writing activities. Personalized questions and exercises appear at each lesson's end to allow students more freedom of expression. Answers to all but the open-ended exercises are given in the Answer Key.

Each Workbook chapter follows this format:

Gráficos: vocabulary exercises based on the vocabulary lists and dialogues in the Gráficos section of the text
Grámatical esencial: structural exercises based on the grammar points presented in the corresponding section of the text
Para repasar: short review of select grammar topics from previous lessons
Comunicación: exercises providing a synthesis of the vocabulary and grammar of the chapter.

The Laboratory Manual

The tape program that accompanies *Motivos de conversación* is intended to develop pronunciation, listening comprehension, and speaking skills. It is also meant to give students a sense of the variety of ways in which Spanish is spoken in Latin America and Spain. Many new listening passages have been written for the tape program, and open-ended exercises are included so that students can answer personalized questions. The Answer Key contains the dictations and the answers to those structural exercises for which answers are not given on the tape.

Each lesson of the Laboratory Manual follows essentially the same format as the Workbook, except that the Laboratory Manual contains a section on pronunciation not found in the Workbook and does not contain the *Para repasar* section found in the Workbook.

An additional feature of the Workbook/Laboratory Manual for this edition is the Glossary of Grammatical Terms. Students will find the Glossary to be a useful reference tool as they study the text's grammar explanations. Grammatical terms used in the text are defined clearly in English, and bilingual examples are given where appropriate.

vii

GLOSSARY OF GRAMMATICAL TERMS

The following glossary presents brief definitions of grammatical terms. A knowledge of these terms will help you better understand the grammatical explanations offered in *Motivos de conversación, second edition*

ACTIVE VOICE   A sentence is in the active voice if the subject acts upon an object: *He* (subject) *bought the car* (object). **Él compró el coche.**

ADJECTIVE   An adjective expresses a quality or characteristic of a person, event, or thing: *a big house, a responsible person;* **una casa** *grande,* **una persona** *responsable.*

ADVERB   A word or phrase has an adverbial function if it qualifies or limits a verb, an adjective, or another adverb: *He returned rapidly.* **Volvió** *rápidamente. She is very nice.* **Es** *muy* **simpática.**

AGENT   This term refers to the person or entity that performs the action in a passive voice construction: *The door was closed by Mary.* **La puerta fue cerrada por María.**

AGREEMENT   This refers to the grammatical relationship between a subject and a verb or between an adjective and a noun. In the phrase *yo* **hablo** the subject and the verb agree: both are first person. In the phrase **casas grandes** the noun and the adjective agree: both are plural.

ANTECEDENT   This is the name given to the noun or noun-equivalent to which something refers: *Of all these presents the ones on the table are the best.* The antecedent of *the ones* and *the best* is *presents.*

ANTONYM   A word opposed in meaning to another: *alive ≠ dead;* **vivo ≠ muerto.**

ARTICLE   This refers to either of the two words *a* or *an* (**un/una**), the indefinite articles, and *the* (**el, la**), the definite articles.

AUXILIARY   A verb used in combination with another verb to form a tense or mood: *He has gone out* (present perfect). **Él** *ha* **salido.** *I am not working* (present progressive). **No** *estoy* **trabajando.** Two common auxiliary verbs are *to have* (**haber**) and *to be* (**estar**).

CARDINAL NUMBERS   These are the numbers *one, two, ten, fifty-two*, etc., as opposed to the ordinals (*first, second, tenth*).

CLAUSE   There are two kinds of clauses: (a) an independent clause, which can stand alone because it contains both a noun and a verb; (b) a dependent clause, which acquires meaning only in association with an independent (main) clause. Example: *He spoke* (main clause) *after the president arrived* (dependent clause). **Habló después de que llegó el presidente.**

COMMAND   A verb form that is used to give orders. Familiar commands relate to **tú** and **vosotros,** whereas formal commands are associated with **Ud.** and **Uds.** These are direct commands: *Come* (**Venga, Ven**), *Eat* (**Coma, Come**), etc. Indirect commands are introduced by *let/que*: *Let him/her enter.* **Que entre él/ella.**

COMPARATIVE   The form of an adjective that establishes a comparison by stating a higher or lesser degree of a quality: *He is taller (shorter) than John.* **Él es** *más alto (más bajo) que* **Juan.**

CONDITIONAL   A verb form that expresses possible or potential actions: *I would go.* **Yo** *iría.*

TO CONJUGATE   To give all the inflected forms of a verb within each tense: *I speak, you speak, he speaks* (**hablo, hablas, habla**), and so on.

ix

CONJUGATION The totality of inflected forms that a verb can have: *I come, she comes, coming, they have come,* etc. In Spanish all verbs belong to one of three groups: **-ar** or first conjugation (**hablar, preparar**), **-er** or second conjugation (**comer, vender**), and **-ir** or third conjugation (**escribir, vivir**).

CONJUNCTION A word or phrase that links together words, phrases, or clauses: *John and Mary;* **Juan y María.** *He waited **until** the train arrived.* **Esperó *hasta que* llegó el tren.**

DECLARATIVE STATEMENT A sentence that makes an affirmation or declaration (not a question).

DEMONSTRATIVE An adjective or pronoun that points out something: *that tree, this one; ese* **árbol,** *éste.*

DIMINUTIVE A word that implies small size or the decreased importance of persons, things, or events: *Johnny,* **Juanito;** *birdie,* **pajarito.**

DIPHTHONG A combination of a strong vowel (**a, e, o**) and a weak vowel (**i, u**) with the stress on the strong vowel, or a combination of two weak vowels with the stress on the second weak vowel (**ai, ou, ei, oi; ui, iu**).

DIRECT OBJECT The person or thing identified by asking the question *who/what?* + main verb or *who/what?* + *is/are* + past participle. *He buys the hat.* **Compra *el sombrero.*** *What does he buy? What is bought? → The hat* (direct object).

FEMININE Term applied to all Spanish nouns representing the female gender either literally or grammatically. **Universidad, hermana,** and **casa** are feminine in Spanish. See *gender.*

FUTURE A tense that expresses what is yet to come, expressed in English with *will* and *shall: I will (shall) do it.* **Lo haré.**

GENDER A grammatical term used to divide nouns into categories. Spanish nouns belong to two genders: masculine and feminine.

GERUND The name often given to the present participle, the verbal form ending in *-ing* in English (*entering, coming*) and in **-ndo** in Spanish (**entrando, viniendo**).

IDIOM A set expression (group of words) peculiar to a language (*in spite of, at random, it's raining cats and dogs*) and that cannot be translated literally.

IMPERATIVE See *command.*

IMPERFECT A past tense in Spanish that expresses a continuing or a repeated action: *He was walking (used to walk).* **Andaba.** See *preterite.*

IMPERSONAL CONSTRUCTION One whose subject is *it: It is important.* **Es importante.** *It must be so.* **Debe ser así.**

INDICATIVE See *mood.*

INDIRECT COMMAND A command referring generally to third persons and containing the word *let /que: Let him enter.* **Que entre él.**

INDIRECT OBJECT The person or thing identified by asking *for what/whom?* or *to what/whom?* something is done. *I gave Mary the money. To whom did I give the money? → To Mary* (indirect object). *I bought the present for Louise. For whom did I buy the present? For Louise* (indirect object).

INFINITIVE The form of a verb introduced in English by *to: to sing, to sell, to come.* In Spanish this form of the verb ends in **-ar, -er,** or **-ir** and is listed as the main entry in Spanish dictionaries: **cantar, vender, venir.**

INFINITIVE The form of a verb introduced in English by *to: to sing, to sell, to come*. In Spanish this form of the verb ends in **-ar, -er,** or **-ir** and is listed as the main entry in Spanish dictionaries: **cantar, vender, venir.**

INTERROGATIVE This term refers to words and sentences that ask a question: *Who is she? ¿Quién es ella? When did she come? ¿Cuándo llegó? What? How? Where?* etc. *¿Qué? ¿Cómo? ¿Dónde?* etc.

INTONATION This refers to the rise and fall in pitch of the voice in speech.

INTRANSITIVE Intransitive verbs are verbs whose action stops with itself and is not directed toward anything else: *Fish swim.* **Los peces** *nadan. All animals die.* **Todos los animales** *mueren.*

MASCULINE Term applied to all Spanish nouns representing the male gender either literally or grammatically. **Pan, hombre,** and **tren** are masculine in Spanish. See *gender*.

MOOD The name given to several groups of verb forms; for present purposes, two moods are contrasted here: (a) indicative mood, comprising five tenses (present, imperfect, preterite, future, conditional) and (b) subjunctive mood, comprising two tenses (present subjunctive, imperfect subjunctive). The indicative denotes actions or states conceived as facts, whereas the subjunctive conveys commands, possibilities, wishes, etc.

NEUTER A term applied to words or constructions that are not associated with either masculine or feminine gender. In Spanish the demonstrative pronouns **esto, eso, aquello** are neuter.

NOMINALIZATION This term refers to words or phrases (adjectives, articles, demonstrative and possessive pronouns, etc.) that substitute for nouns: *the only one* (**el único**), *the blue ones* (**los azules**), *these* (**éstos**), etc.

NOUN A word denoting an object, person, or event: *newspaper, lawyer, competition;* **periódico, abogado, competencia.** A proper noun is a capitalized name in English.

OBJECT PRONOUN A pronoun that can be a substitute for a direct object noun (*me, you, him, her, it, us, you, them*) or for an indirect object noun (*to me, to you, to him, to her, to it, to us, to you, to them*). In Spanish: **me, te, le/lo/la, nos, os, les/los/las.**

ORDINAL NUMBERS Numerals that point out an order or series: *first, second, third,* etc.

ORTHOGRAPHIC CHANGES Also called spelling changes. They are dictated by the need to preserve the original sound of a verb: **llego > llegué; saco > saqué; comienzo > comencé.**

PASSIVE VOICE A construction in which a thing or person is acted upon by an agent. *The examinations are corrected by Mr. Suárez.* **Los exámenes son corregidos por** *el señor Suárez.*

PAST PARTICIPLE The form of a verb that expresses a completed action or state: *seated, sung;* **sentado, cantado.** The past participle is the second component of all perfect tenses: *he has gone, she had written;* **ha** *ido,* **había** *escrito.* See *perfect forms*.

PERFECT FORMS Compound forms (there is one for each simple form) that combine the verb *to have* (**haber** in Spanish) and a past participle: *I have (had, will have, would have,* etc.) *finished;* **he/haya (había/hubo/hubiera, habré, habría,** etc.) **terminado.**

PERSON Each verb in a given tense has six forms that indicate the person involved in the action of the verb: singular (one person): *I* (first person), *you* (second person), *he, she, it* (third person); plural (more than one person): *we* (first person), *you* (second person), *they* (third person).

PLUPERFECT The name given to a tense that combines the imperfect of the auxiliary verb **haber** and a past participle: *I had gone out.* **Yo** *había salido.*

POSSESSIVE A word (adjective or pronoun) that indicates ownership: *my house, their son, a friend of mine; mi* **casa,** *su* **hijo, un amigo** *mío.*

PREPOSITION A part of speech that connects a word (noun, verb, etc.) to other words: *a cup of milk, she came with him;* **una taza** *de* **leche, vino** *con* **él.** Other prepositions: *to, in, for, on, at, over, from, by,* etc.; **a, en, para, por, sobre,** etc.

PREPOSITIONAL PRONOUN A pronoun that follows a preposition: *with her, for him, against me;* **con** *ella,* **para** *él,* **contra** *mí.*

PRESENT PARTICIPLE The verb form that ends in *-ing* (*coming, doing*) in English and **-ndo** (**cantando/haciendo**) in Spanish.

PRETERITE A past tense in Spanish that expresses an action viewed as completed. *He came.* **Vino.** *I did not see it.* **No lo** *vi.* See *imperfect.*

PROGRESSIVE FORMS Combinations of the verb *to be* (**estar**) and a present participle: *We are working* (present progressive). **Estamos trabajando.** *We were working* (past progressive). **Estábamos trabajando.**

PRONOUN A word that takes the place of a noun: *they, us,* etc.; **ellos, nosotros,** etc.

PROVISO CLAUSE A clause that stipulates a precondition: *I will do it provided that you pay me.* **Lo haré** *con tal de que me pagues.*

RECIPROCAL A pronoun applied to constructions expressing a mutual relationship. *They see each other.* **Se** *ven. They talk to one another.* **Se** *hablan.*

REFLEXIVE PRONOUN The six pronouns used with the six persons of a reflexive verb (**me, te, se, nos, os, se**).

REFLEXIVE VERB A verb whose action is initiated by a subject and is received by the same subject: *I prepare myself.* **Me preparo.**

RELATIVE PRONOUN A word that relates a person or thing to a following statement: *The boy who entered the house is my nephew.* **El muchacho** *que* **entró en la casa es mi sobrino.** Other relatives: *that, when, where, which,* etc.; **quien, lo que,** etc.

RESULTANT STATE CONSTRUCTION A combination of *to be* (**estar**) + participle, used to express the state or condition resulting from an action. *The book is written in Spanish.* **El libro** *está escrito* **en español.**

SENTENCE A statement with a subject and a verb expressing a complete thought: *Ann came.* **Ana vino.** *I bought a new suit.* **Compré un traje nuevo.**

SEQUENCE OF TENSES The relationship between the tense of the main clause and the tense of the dependent clause: **Le pido** (present indicative) **que no venga** (present subjunctive).

STEM The infinitive minus its **-ar/-er/-ir** ending. Also called the root. **Habl-** (root), **-ar** (ending).

STEM-CHANGING VERB Name given to Spanish verbs that change **e > ie, o > ue, e > i** or **o > u** in the root in stressed syllables in certain tenses: **mueren, pidió.**

STRESS   The greater emphasis placed on a given syllable, whether it bears a written accent or not.

SUBJECT   The word or words denoting the person, thing, or event about which something is said: *Robert works here.* **Roberto** trabaja aquí. *Traveling is fun.* **El viajar** es **divertido.**

SUBJECT PRONOUN   A pronoun that can take the place of a noun subject: *I, you, he (she, it), we, you, they.*

SUBJUNCTIVE   See *mood.*

SUFFIX   A letter or syllable added to the end of a word: *kindly, birdie;* **amable**mente, **pajar**ito.

SUPERLATIVE   A form of an adjective or adverb that denotes the highest degree of a particular quality: *the most beautiful flower;* la **flor** más **hermosa.**

SYLLABICATION   This refers to the dividing of words into syllables: **es-pe-cial-men-te.**

SYNONYM   A word that has the same meaning as another: *simple = plain, rich = wealthy;* **sencillo =** fácil, rico = adinerado.

TENSE   Sets of verb forms (six in each tense) that express present, past, or future time. Spanish has seven simple tenses, made up of simple verb forms: *I buy,* **compro;** compound tenses have two or more verbs: *I have bought,* **he comprado.**

THIRD-PERSON VERBS   Spanish verbs that are generally used in the third-person singular or the third-person plural: **Me gusta el libro. Le interesan los viajes. Os encanta la televisión.**

TRANSITIVE   Transitive verbs are verbs whose action is directed toward a person or thing (direct object): *He opened the book.* **Abrió el libro.** *He sold the house.* **Vendió la casa.**

VERB   The part of speech that expresses the occurrence of an action or the existence of a state or condition: *he spoke, they will come, she is;* habló, vendrán, es. Some verbs are regular (they take a fixed set of endings); others are irregular (they deviate from the normal pattern of endings).

VOICE   See *active voice* and *passive voice.*

P R E L I M I N A R E S 1
WORKBOOK

Nombres y personas

Sara: Hola, me llamo Sara. ¿De dónde eres tú?

Pablo: Soy de Miami y me llamo Pablo. ¿Cómo se llama la profesora?

Sara: Se llama Patricia Valdés García. Es de Nueva York.

Pablo: Mi amigo también (*also*) es de Nueva York.

A. *Diálogo*. Study the drawing and the dialogue and answer the following questions.

1. ¿Cómo se llama la estudiante?

   _____

2. ¿De dónde es el estudiante?

   _____

3. ¿Cómo se llama la profesora?

_____

4. ¿Es la profesora de Miami?

_____

5. ¿De dónde es el amigo de Pablo?

_____

B. *¿Cómo se llama...?* Write the English form of the following Spanish names.

1. Carlos _____   5. Pedro _____

2. Ana _____   6. Alicia _____

3. Juan _____   7. Juana _____

4. Ricardo _____

El alfabeto y los cognados

A. *El alfabeto*. Write the Spanish letter that corresponds to each of the following.

1. zeta _____   7. i griega _____   13. eñe _____

2. be _____   8. hache _____   14. ge _____

3. che _____   9. elle _____   15. te _____

4. cu _____   10. eme _____   16. equis _____

5. jota _____   11. ere _____   17. ve doble _____

6. ese _____   12. erre _____   18. ele _____

B. *Cognados*. Write the Spanish form of the following English words. Try to use the correct definite article—**el** or **la**—before each one.

1. democracy _____   4. communism _____

2. class _____   5. socialism _____

3. person _____

Asking Questions

Rewrite these statements as questions.

1. Sí, María Luisa es de México.

   _____

2. El estudiante americano se llama Carlos.

   _____

3. Sí, la profesora colombiana es inteligente.

   _____

4. Sí, la educación es importante.

   _____

5. Sí, el senador de California es famoso.

   _____

Saludos y conversaciones

Answer the following questions.

1. Buenos días. ¿Cómo te llamas?

   _____

2. Hola. ¿Eres de los Estados Unidos?

   _____

3. Buenas tardes. ¿Cómo está Ud.?

   _____

4. Buenos días. ¿De dónde eres?

   _____

5. Buenas noches. ¿Es Ud. el profesor de la clase de español?

   _____

PRELIMINARES 1
LABORATORY MANUAL

Nombres y personas

A. *Diálogo*. You will hear a dialogue twice. First listen carefully and try to understand the gist of the ideas. The second time, repeat each sentence after the speaker. Imitate the speaker as closely as possible.

Miguel: ...   Miguel: ...

Carlos: ...   Carlos: ...

Miguel: ...   Miguel: ...

Carlos: ...

B. Answer the questions based on the dialogue in A. Repeat the correct answer during the second pause.

1. ...   2. ...   3. ...

C. *En clase*. Answer each question by using the following cues. You will hear each question twice. Repeat the correct answer during the second pause.

1. Alicia   2. Guatemala   3. Madrid   4. cubano   5. Nueva York

Pronunciación

<u>The Spanish Vowels</u>

Spanish **a** sounds approximately like the *a* in the English word *father*. Listen and repeat.

a   da   la   ama   sala   casa

Spanish **e** sounds approximately like the *e* in the English word *they*. Listen and repeat.

e   de   me   Elena   elemento   Venezuela

Spanish **i** sounds approximately like the *i* in the English word *marine*. Listen and repeat.

| i | mi | ti | Silvia | Lima | Misisipí |

Spanish **o** sounds like the *o* in *Coca*, but without the glide of *Cola*. Listen and repeat.

| o | lo | yo | oro | todo | modo |

Spanish **u** sounds like the *u* in *Julie*. Listen and repeat.

| u | tú | su | uno | luna | mucho |

Here are a few words that are not in your Laboratory Manual. Repeat them after the speaker.

| 1. ... | 3. ... | 5. ... | 7. ... | 9. ... | 11. ... |
| 2. ... | 4. ... | 6. ... | 8. ... | 10. ... | |

Repeat these sentences after the speaker.

1. Ana es norteamericana.

2. Es buena amiga de Carmen.

3. Elena es de México.

Here are a few sentences that are not in your Laboratory Manual. Repeat them after the speaker.

4. ...   5. ...   6. ...

The Spanish Alphabet

Pronounce the letters of the Spanish alphabet in groups of three after the speaker.

| 1. a b c | 3. f g h | 5. l ll m | 7. p q r | 9. u v w |
| 2. ch d e | 4. i j k | 6. n ñ o | 8. rr s t | 10. x y z |

Cognados

Listen to the following words in English, then say the corresponding Spanish cognate. Repeat the correct answer.

1. ...   2. ...   3. ...   4. ...   5. ...   6. ...

Asking Questions

You will hear four sentences. Each sentence will be repeated twice. Restate each one as a question. Repeat the correct answer during the second pause.

1. ...   2. ...   3. ...   4. ...

Comunicación

A. *Diálogo*. You will hear a dialogue that contains answers to the following questions. First read the questions. Then listen to the dialogue and try to understand the gist of the ideas. Listen a second time for the answers to the questions. After you have written your answers, the speaker will say them. Repeat the correct answers after the speaker.

1. ¿Cómo se llama la profesora?

   _____

2. ¿De dónde es ella?

   _____

3. ¿De dónde es Antonio?

   _____

4. ¿De dónde es la amiga de Antonio?

   _____

5. ¿Cómo se llama la amiga de Antonio?

   _____

B. *Dictado* (Dictation). You will hear a series of statements twice. Complete the following sentences by filling in the appropriate words from the statements. Repeat the correct answer after you hear it.

1. Carlos es de _____.

2. ¿Es _____ el profesor García?

3. ¿_____ la amiga de Carlos?

4. El estudiante de Bolivia _____.

5. El actor se llama _____.

₧RELIMINARES 2
WORKBOOK

Me gusta/te gusta/le gusta

A. *Los deportes* (Sports). Write a sentence telling whether you like or don't like the following activities.

1. el tenis

   _____

2. el vólibol

   _____

3. el fútbol

   _____

4. el béisbol

   _____

B. *Preguntas* (Questions). Write the question you would ask your friend to find out if he or she likes the following things.

1. las matemáticas

   _____

2. la universidad

   _____

3. la clase de español

   _____

4. la filosofía

   _____

C. Now write down how you would tell your friend what you think your professor feels about these things.

1. la música moderna

   _____

2. las discotecas

   _____

3. las comedias de la televisión

   _____

4. el teatro

   _____

El calendario

A. *Este* (This) *mes*. Look at this month's calendar and complete the following sentences according to the days and numbers you see. Write out the numbers.

MODELO: Hoy es miércoles, el veinte y cuatro de junio.

1. Hoy es _____.

2. Si hoy es _____, mañana es _____.

3. Ayer fue (*Yesterday was*) _____.

4. El próximo (*next*) domingo es _____.

5. El último (*last*) día del (*of the*) mes es _____.

B. *Las estaciones*. Complete the following sentences with the name of the appropriate season.

1. Si es enero, es _____.

2. Si es noviembre, es _____.

3. Si hoy es el 25 de julio, es _____.

4. Si mañana es el primero de abril, es _____.

Las matemáticas

A. Answer the following problems. Spell out the numbers.

1. 2 + 7 = _____

2. 10 − 8 = _____

3. 14 + 15 = _____

4. 31 − 30 = _____

5. 22 + 3 = _____

B. Complete the following sequences logically. Spell out the numbers.

1. 20, 23, 26, _____

2. 2, 4, 6, 8, _____

3. 29, _____, 25, _____, 21

4. 21, 22, 24, 27, _____

5. 5, _____, 15, _____,

   25, _____

6. 13, 14, _____, 16, _____,

   18, _____

Interrogaciones

¿Quién es, de dónde es y cómo es? Describe the people in the drawings by making a statement about them based on the drawings, the maps, and the following words. Write your opinion of what they are like—**importante, sentimental**, etc.

1. el presidente

   _____

2. la actriz

   _____

3. el profesor

   _____

4. yo

   _____

5. mi (my) amigo/a

   _____

Comunicación

A. *¡Hola y adiós!* Express in Spanish.

1. Hello, what's up?

_____

2. Nothing new. And you?

_____

3. So-so. See you tomorrow.

_____

4. See you later.

_____

B. *Preguntas*. Create questions that could be answered by the following statements.

1. Es de Guantánamo.

_____

2. Sí, las dos profesoras de Chile son muy inteligentes.

_____

3. Es un amigo de California.

_____

4. ¡Es un profesor imposible!

_____

5. Me llamo _____.

C. *(No) Me gusta(n)*. Indicate whether you like or dislike the following. Use complete sentences.

1. el invierno

_____

2. las tragedias

_____

3. la televisión en español

_____

4. la ópera

_____

5. los deportes

_____

PRELIMINARES 2
LABORATORY MANUAL

Me gusta/te gusta/le gusta

¿Te gusta o no te gusta? Repeat these expressions of like or dislike after the speaker.

1. ...   2. ...   3. ...   4. ...   5. ...   6. ...

Pronunciación

Spanish ch, ll, ñ; k, w, h, q

Spanish **ch** is considered a single letter and sounds just like the *ch* in the English word *church*. Listen and repeat.

champán   chocolate   mucho   Chile

Spanish **ll** is also considered a single letter and in most parts of the Spanish-speaking world is pronounced as a strong [y] sound. Listen and repeat.

me llamo   se llama   ella   Guillermo

Spanish **ñ** sounds like the *ni* in the English word *onion*. Listen and repeat.

niño   enseña   señorita   señor

The letters **k** and **w** appear in Spanish only in words of foreign origin; **h** is always silent; and **q** is always followed by a silent **u**. The **qu** combination is pronounced as a hard [k] sound. Listen and repeat.

kilómetro   wagneriano   hache   Honduras   Albuquerque   Quito   quien

El calendario

A. *¿Qué día es mañana?* You will hear the name and calendar number of a day of the week. State the name and number of the following day. Repeat the correct answer during the second pause.

MODELO: Hoy es lunes, el veinte y tres. → Mañana es martes, el veinte y cuatro.

1. ...   2. ...   3. ...   4. ...   5. ...   6. ...

B. *¿Qué estación?* You will hear the name of a month. State what season it would be in the Northern Hemisphere. Repeat the correct answer during the second pause.

MODELO: febrero → Si es febrero, es invierno.

1. ...   2. ...   3. ...   4. ...   5. ...

Las matemáticas

A. *Dos más dos son cuatro.* You will hear a series of mathematical statements. Complete each one, then repeat it. Repeat the correct answer after the pause.

1. ...   2. ...   3. ...   4. ...   5. ...

B. *Más números.* You will hear a list of numbers. State the numbers you get by adding four to each one. Repeat the correct answer during the second pause.

1. ...   2. ...   3. ...   4. ...   5. ...

Interrogaciones

You will hear a statement twice. Use **cómo, dónde, qué,** or **quién** to ask a question that would be answered by that statement. Repeat the correct answer during the second pause.

MODELO: Elena es inteligente. → ¿Cómo es Elena?

1. ...   2. ...   3. ...   4. ...   5. ...

Comunicación

A. *Diálogo.* You will hear a
dialogue between two
women in the drawing.
First read the following
questions, then listen to
the dialogue and try to
understand the gist. Listen
a second time and then
answer the questions.
Repeat the correct answers
after the speaker.

1. ¿Quién es la señora?
2. ¿De dónde es la profesora?
3. ¿Le gusta Nueva York?

4. ¿Cómo se llama la estudiante?
5. ¿Le gusta Nueva York también?

B. *Dictado.* You will hear a series of sentences twice. Use the second pause to write down
exactly what you hear.

1. _____

2. _____

3. _____

4. _____

5. _____

L E C C I Ó N   U N O
WORKBOOK

Gráficos

A. *El primer* (first) *día de clase.* Complete the following paragraph by writing in the names of the articles or persons numbered in the drawing, along with the appropriate definite article (**el, la**).

Hoy es el primer día de la clase de español. (1) _____ Tolón contesta las

preguntas de Luis, (2) _____ de Nueva York. (3) _____ usa

(4) _____ y (5) _____. Luis estudia (6) _____ y pregunta

sobre Sudamérica. La profesora pronuncia los nombres de los países (*countries*) de

Sudamérica. Luis usa (7) _____ y (8) _____. La profesora usa

(9) _____. (10) _____ de español está (*is*) en (11) _____.

(12) _____ está en (13) _____.

B. *En la clase de hoy*. Study the drawing again, read the dialogue, and answer the
questions that follow.

Profesora Tolón: Luis, ¿estudia usted español en casa (*at home*)?
           Luis: Sí, estudio en casa y en la biblioteca.
Profesora Tolón: Pronuncia bien el español. ¿Estudia el libro todos los días (*every
                day*)?
           Luis: Sí, todos los días. Me gusta mucho.
Profesora Tolón: ¡Qué bueno (*How nice*)!

1. ¿Quién enseña la clase de español hoy?

      _____

2. ¿Dónde estudia Luis?

      _____

3. ¿Cómo pronuncia Luis el español?

      _____

4. ¿Estudia Luis el libro todos los días?

      _____

5. ¿Le gusta el libro?

      _____

6. ¿ Contesta Luis en español o (*or*) en inglés?

      _____

Gramática esencial

1.–3. Gender and Plurals of Articles and Nouns

A. *En la clase*. Write the appropriate definite and indefinite article for each of the following
nouns.

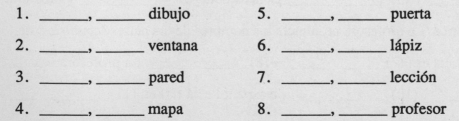

1. _____, _____ dibujo   5. _____, _____ puerta

2. _____, _____ ventana   6. _____, _____ lápiz

3. _____, _____ pared   7. _____, _____ lección

4. _____, _____ mapa   8. _____, _____ profesor

NAME_____ DATE_____ CLASS_____

B. *¿El o* (or) *un?* Complete the following sentences with an appropriate definite or indefinite article. More than one answer may be possible. Follow the model.

MODELO: La amiga de Carlos trabaja en una universidad.

1. _____ profesora Tolón entra en _____ clase de español.

2. _____ amigo de ella habla con _____ estudiante de Colombia.

3. En _____ clase el estudiante practica y prepara _____ lección.

4. _____ joven de Tejas conversa con _____ amigo de _____ clase.

5. _____ profesor Gómez no es _____ profesor interesante.

C. *El plural.* Make the following phrases plural where possible. Follow the model.

MODELO: un papel de la alumna → unos papeles de las alumnas

1. un dibujo en la pared

_____

2. la profesora de la Argentina

_____

3. el lápiz de Tomás

_____

4. una lección en el cuaderno

_____

5. una universidad en la ciudad

_____

4. Agreement and Position of Adjectives

A. *¿De dónde es?* Complete the following sentences with the correct indefinite article and form of the adjective.

MODELO: Es una profesora inglesa. (inglés)

1. ¿Es _____ señor _____? (español)

2. No es _____ amiga _____.   (francés)

3. Es _____ alumno _____.   (colombiano)

4. La silla es _____ silla _____.   (italiano)

5. Es _____ profesor _____. (mexicano)

B. *¿Cómo es?* Complete the following sentences with the correct definite article and form of the adjective.

MODELO: ¿ Es <u>el</u> joven <u>inteligente</u>? (inteligente)

1. _____ clase es muy _____. (interesante)

2. ¿No es _____ clienta _____? (generoso)

3. _____ lección es _____. (importante)

4. ¿Es _____ _____ profesora de español? (sentimental)

5. ¿Es usted _____ profesor _____? (famoso)

5.–6. Subject Pronouns and Present Tense of **-ar** Verbs

A. *¿Quién hace...?* Rewrite these sentences according to the model.

MODELO: Juana Tolón trabaja en la universidad. → Ella trabaja en la universidad.

1. Alex entra y contesta el teléfono.

_____

2. Julia y tú no trabajan hasta mañana.

_____

3. Sí, Roberto y Joaquín hablan mucho.

_____

4. Elena y Alina usan el libro de Cándido.

_____

5. Fermina no prepara la lección hoy.

_____

6. Tú y yo no usamos el mapa.

_____

B. *¿Qué hacen?* Rewrite these sentences, using the verbs given in parentheses.

1. Yo no trabajo mucho por la mañana.

   (estudiar) _____

   (practicar)_____

2. ¿No estudia usted aquí?

   (entrar) _____

   (enseñar) _____

3. Ellas no practican con el profesor López.

   (conversar)_____

   (hablar) _____

4. Julia, mamá y yo usamos el mapa de Madrid.

   (preparar)_____

   (estudiar) _____

5. En la clase nosotros estudiamos.

   (preguntar)_____

   (contestar) _____

C. *¡Cómo hablan!* Form statements from these elements. Follow the model.

   MODELO: Miguel / conversar / con Susana → Miguel conversa con Susana.

   1. ellos / hablar / por la mañana y por la noche

   _____

   2. tú y yo / no / contestar / en inglés

   _____

   3. nosotros / también / pronunciar / las palabras nuevas

   _____

   4. ¿cuándo / conversar / tú / con el profesor de matemáticas?

   _____

5. ella / no / usar / la palabra / «no»

_____

6. vosotros / practicar / el francés / mucho / por la mañana

_____

7. ustedes / sólo / contestar / en español

_____

Para repasar

Tres amigos. Complete this dialogue by writing the missing words.

Graciela: Buenas tardes, Patricia. ¿Cómo _____?

Patricia: Así así. No hay _____ de nuevo.

Graciela: ¿Y cómo está tu (_your_) amigo americano?

Patricia: Muy bien, _____.

Graciela: ¿De _____ es él?

Patricia: Es _____ San Antonio.

Graciela: ¿Y cómo _____ llama él?

Patricia: Se _____ Robert. Aquí está.

Graciela: Hola, Robert. Yo _____ Graciela.

Robert: ¡Hola!

Graciela: ¿_____ gusta Guadalajara?

Robert: Sí, me _____ mucho. Es muy bonita (_pretty_).

Comunicación

A. *El primer día*. Tomorrow is the first day of Spanish class. Express the following conversation in Spanish.

1. Hi, Alicia. How are you?

   _____

2. Good afternoon, Richard. Fine, thanks. And you?

   _____

3. Very well, thanks. When is (*es*) the first day of the new Spanish class?

   _____

4. Tomorrow. Aren't you practicing for (*para*) the class?

   _____

5. Tomorrow? Impossible! I work tomorrow.

   _____

6. Where do you work? Here?

   _____

7. Yes. I teach English in the afternoon.

   _____

8. Really? Why (*Por qué*) don't you speak with the Spanish professor?

   _____

9. Good idea! (*¡Buena idea!*) Thanks, Alicia.

   _____

B. *En el trabajo* (At work). Form questions that can be answered by the following statements.

1. No, no uso lápiz y papel en el trabajo.

   _____

2. Hablamos varias lenguas.

   _____

3. Sí, también hablamos alemán.

_____

4. A veces conversan en francés.

_____

5. Mario contesta el teléfono.

_____

6. Sí, ellos pronuncian muy bien el español.

_____

C. *(No) Me gusta.* Name five things you like or dislike about your Spanish class using the following verbs. Follow the model.

MODELO: contestar → (No) Me gusta contestar en español.

1. usar

_____

2. estudiar

_____

3. entrar

_____

4. conversar

_____

5. practicar

_____

Now use the same verbs to state whether you actually do or do not do the activities you listed in 1–5. Follow the model.

MODELO: (No) Contesto en español.

6. _____

7. _____

8. _____

9. _____

10. _____

D. *Sólo tú.* Answer the following questions about yourself.

1. ¿Conversas mucho en español?

_____

2. ¿Usas lenguas extranjeras (*foreign*) en la clase? ¿En casa (*At home*)?

_____

3. ¿Cuándo practicas para la clase?

_____

4. ¿Hablas varias lenguas? ¿O (*Or*) sólo hablas inglés?

_____

5. ¿Preparas la lección por la mañana o por la noche?

_____

6. ¿Con quién hablas cuando entras en la clase?

_____

7. ¿A veces contestas el teléfono en español?

_____

LECCIÓN UNO
LABORATORY MANUAL

Gráficos

A. *Cosas de la clase*. You will hear a series of words on the tape. Repeat each one, and then say the plural form. Repeat the correct answer during the second pause.

1. ...   2. ...   3. ...   4. ...   5. ...   6. ...   7. ...   8. ...

B. *Yo en la clase*. Using the cues you will hear, tell what you are doing. Repeat the correct answer during the second pause.

MODELO: practicar español → Practico español.

1. ...   2. ...   3. ...   4. ...   5. ...   6. ...   7. ...

C. *Elisa y la profesora Juárez*. You will hear a series of statements made by Elisa or Professor Juárez. You will hear each statement twice. Circle the letter of the sentence that you associate most closely with each statement.

1. a. La profesora no usa el bolígrafo.

   b. Elisa habla con la profesora.

   c. Hay muchos dibujos en la pared.

2. a. Elisa entra en la clase.

   b. La profesora trabaja mucho.

   c. A veces ella practica con Mario.

3. a. No usamos los cuadernos.

   b. Le gusta enseñar español.

   c. Ella habla con los alumnos.

Pronunciación

Accentuation

Words ending in a vowel, **n**, or **s** are normally stressed on the next-to-last syllable. Listen and repeat.

Sacramento   Virginia   Carmen   Dolores

Words ending in any other consonant besides **n** or **s** are normally stressed on the last syllable. Listen and repeat.

Ecuador   Trinidad   Portugal   Paraguay

Here are a few words that are not in your Laboratory Manual. Repeat them after the speaker.

1. ...   2. ...   3. ...

If a word ends in a vowel, **n**, or **s** but is not stressed on the next-to-last syllable, the word must carry a written accent mark. Listen and repeat.

Santa Bárbara   México   nación   inglés   América   Málaga

If a word ends in a consonant other than **n** or **s** but is not stressed on the last syllable, that word must also carry a written accent mark. Listen and repeat.

Cortázar   Cádiz   imbécil   azúcar   Gómez

A. You will hear these words twice. Underline the stressed syllable.

MODELO: compañero → compañero

1. famoso   3. José   5. Isabel   7. Portugal   9. Chile

2. Honduras   4. contestan 6. profesor   8. francés   10. Francia

B. You will hear these words twice. Write in an accent mark if necessary.

1. Acapulco   3. Panama   5. americano   7. terminar   9. dificil

2. Carmen   4. explosion 6. America   8. Hernandez

Diphthongs

A strong vowel (**a**, **e**, or **o**) and a weak vowel (**i** or **u**) join to form a single syllable. This combination is called a *diphthong*. Listen and repeat.

baile   auto   veinte   estudia   bien   gracioso

Two weak vowels together also form a diphthong. Listen and repeat.

ciudad   triunfo

If an **i** or a **u** carries a written accent, it does not form a diphthong. Listen and repeat.

María   dúo

Here are a few more examples that are not in your Laboratory Manual. Listen and repeat.

1. ...   2. ...   3. ...

Two strong vowels together do not form a diphthong. Listen and repeat.

Rafael   Bilbao

C. You will hear these words twice. Underline the diphthongs (four words contain no diphthongs).

MODELO: estudia → estud<u>ia</u>

1. día 2. autor 3. diurno 4. Rafael 5. fraile 6. treinta 7. Mindanao 8. dúo

Linking

In spoken Spanish, words are linked or joined with each other according to several principles.

Link a final consonant and an initial vowel. Listen and repeat.

San Antonio   Los Ángeles

Link a final vowel and a different initial vowel. Listen and repeat.

Pablo es profesor.   Escriba usted.

Link a final vowel and the same initial vowel. Listen and repeat.

Es una alumna.   Escribe en español.

D. Listen as the following sentences are read twice. Show which words should be linked, as in the model.

MODELO: Es un estudiante popular.

1. Rodolfo no es generoso.

2. Cecilia es amiga de Enrique.

3. Mateo es un nombre masculino.

4. Antonio es de Buenos Aires.

5. El comercio es importante.

Gramática esencial

1.–3. Gender and Plurals of Articles and Nouns

A. First repeat the model sentence, then substitute the cue words that are given on the tape and repeat the entire sentence. Repeat the correct answer during the second pause.

MODELO.   El alumno habla español. (profesora) → La profesora habla español.

1. a. ...   b. ...   c. ...   2. a. ...   b. ...   c. ...   3. a. ...   b. ...   c. ...

B. You will hear a sentence using the singular form of a noun. Repeat the sentence using the plural form. Repeat the correct answer during the second pause. Follow the model.

MODELO: No uso el cuaderno. → No uso los cuadernos.

1. ...   2. ...   3. ...

C. Repeat the same steps with this model sentence.

MODELO: Rosa no conversa con una amiga. → Rosa no conversa con unas amigas.

1. ...   2. ...   3. ...

4. Agreement and Position of Adjectives

First repeat the model sentence, then substitute the cue words that are given on the tape and repeat the entire sentence. Repeat the correct answer during the second pause.

MODELO: Hablo con un profesor famoso. (profesoras / mexicano) →
           Hablo con unas profesoras mexicanas.

1. a. ...   b. ...   c. ...   2. a. ...   b. ...   c. ...

5.–6. Subject Pronouns and Present Tense of -ar Verbs

A. First repeat the model sentence, then substitute the cue words that are given on the tape and repeat the entire sentence. Repeat the correct answer during the second pause.

MODELO: Tú contestas en español. (yo) → Yo contesto en español.

1. a. ...   b. ...   c. ...   3. a. ...   b. ...   c. ...

2. a. ...   b. ...   c. ...   4. a. ...   b. ...   c. ...

B. You will hear a sentence. If it is singular, change it to plural, and vice versa. Follow the model. Repeat the correct answer during the second pause.

MODELO: Yo estudio por la noche. → Nosotros estudiamos por la noche.

1. ...   2. ...   3. ...   4. ...   5. ...

Comunicación

A. *Compañeros de clase*. You will hear the **Texto** from page 30 of your textbook. First, listen carefully and try to follow the gist of the ideas. Then you will hear the **Texto** again followed by questions read twice. During the first pause, answer the question. During the second pause, repeat the correct answer.

1. ...   2. ...   3. ...   4. ...   5. ...

B. You will hear a series of questions based on the information below. Listen carefully and circle the letter of the correct answer. For the last question, write your own answer.

Universidad Central					
Alumno: Jorge Guzmán			Semestre: Primero		
Número	Sala	Nombre	Día	Hora	Profesor
31	20	Geometría	Lunes	7-8	Castro
25	8	Español	Lunes	9-11	Tolón
11	4	Inglés	Viernes	1-2	Klein
24	16	Filosofía	Martes	3-4	Borges
20	7	Drama	Jueves	7-9 PM	Bennett

1. a. La profesora Tolón enseña la clase de español.

   b. El profesor Klein enseña la clase de filosofía.

   c. El profesor Bennett enseña la clase de inglés.

2. a. Él estudia en la Universidad de California.

   b. Ella practica español en la universidad.

   c. Jorge Guzmán estudia en la Universidad Central.

3. a. La profesora Tolón enseña por la noche.

   b. El profesor Bennett enseña por la noche.

   c. Ella enseña en la sala número veinte y uno.

4. a. Sí, usa el libro de geometría.

   b. No, usa el libro de inglés.

   c. No, usa el libro de filosofía.

5. a. El señor Klein y los alumnos conversan en inglés.

   b. La profesora Borges no habla inglés.

   c. Ellas estudian matemáticas el lunes por la mañana.

6. _____

C. *Dictado*. You will hear a short paragraph about Profesora Tolón. During the first pause, write each sentence in the space provided. During the second pause, check what you wrote.

_____

_____

_____

_____

_____

_____

D. *Sólo tú*. You will hear a series of questions about yourself. You will hear each question twice. Answer in complete Spanish sentences. No answers will be given on the tape.

1. _____

2. _____

3. _____

4. _____

5. _____

LECCIÓN DOS
WORKBOOK

Gráficos

A. *Un hotel del centro*. Complete the following paragraphs by writing in the names of the items numbered in the drawing along with the appropriate definite article.

Cuando visito (*I visit*) Buenos Aires me gusta comer en (1) _____ Córdoba

del Hotel León. Allí, en el centro de la ciudad, hay de todo— (2) _____

Colón, (3) _____ de flores, (4) _____ Cortefino, (5) _____

francés y (6) _____ Internacional. No hay casas ni (*nor*) edificios de

apartamentos. Y me gusta usar (7) _____ y (8) _____ para (*to*) visitar

a mis amigos en otro barrio.

Hoy sólo como (9) _____ de jamón y queso y bebo (10) _____.

Necesito comprar regalos para mis amigos, pero me gusta mucho leer (11)

_____ y no tener que mirar (12) _____.

B. *De un barrio al otro*. Read the dialogue and answer the questions that follow.

Eugenio: ¿Qué hay, Fausto? ¿Qué haces hoy?
Fausto: Necesito visitar a unos clientes del barrio Perón.
Eugenio: ¿En tu coche nuevo?
Fausto: ¡Imposible! Mi amigo Alejandro tiene mi coche hoy.
Eugenio: ¿Verdad? Pues, ¿por qué no tomas el metro de la plaza Arrabal?
Fausto: No me gusta usar el metro. Es muy caro. ¿No hay un autobús en la calle del hotel Colima?
Eugenio: Sólo hay autobús por la tarde. Pero en la calle Florida hay muchos taxis buenos y baratos.
Fausto: No es una mala idea. A ver si hay un taxi allí. ¿Vienes también?
Eugenio: No, gracias. Tengo un millón de cosas que hacer (*a million things to do*) aquí en el centro. Y tengo un cliente—el viejo Molina—que desea vender su almacén.

1. ¿Qué necesita hacer Fausto hoy?

   _____

2. ¿Quién tiene el automóvil nuevo de Fausto?

   _____

3. ¿Es barato usar el metro?

   _____

4. ¿Hay autobuses en la calle del hotel por la mañana?

   _____

5. ¿Dónde hay taxis buenos y baratos?

   _____

6. ¿Viene Eugenio con Fausto?

   _____

7. ¿Qué desea hacer el viejo Molina?

   _____

Gramática esencial

7. More on the Definite Article

A. *En el centro*. Complete these sentences. Follow the model.

MODELO: El viejo Molina habla _____ cliente. (a) →

El viejo Molina habla al cliente.

1. ¿Cuándo abren las puertas _____ almacén? (de)

2. Los dependientes _____ tiendas Florinda son muy malos. (de)

3. En la galería Ochoa hay muchos cuadros _____ Perú. (de)

4. En el bar del hotel Crillón hay jugo de naranja _____ Florida. (de)

5. Él vende muchas cámaras _____ clienta francesa. (a)

6. Pero no vende cámaras _____ hombres alemanes. (a)

B. *Conversación en el café*. Write the appropriate definite article as needed.

1. No me gusta discutir _____ política de _____ Américas.

2. _____ bar del café es muy bonito.

3. Nos gustan _____ noticias de _____ periódico.

4. _____ camareros (*waiters*) no necesitan discutir con _____ clientes, ¿verdad?

5. _____ vino es de Italia, pero _____ leche es de _____ Estados Unidos.

6. _____ viejo Molina desea comer una hamburguesa.

8. Possessive Adjectives

A. Express in Spanish.

1. my car _____

2. her clients _____

3. his letters _____

4. your (polite, sing.) news _____

5. our camera _____

6. your (familiar, sing.) neighborhood _____

7. my newspapers _____

8. their clerks _____

B. Complete each sentence using **su** or **sus** as appropriate. Then rewrite the sentence using an alternate format for clarification. Follow the model.

MODELO: No necesito <u>su</u> cámara. (*her*) → No necesito la cámara de ella.

1. No me gusta _____ reloj. (*his*)

   _____

2. Deseo comer en _____ casa. (*their*)

   _____

3. A veces ella discute mucho con _____ clientes. (*her*)

   _____

4. _____ vinos son malos y caros. (*Your, [polite, pl.]*)

   _____

5. _____ apartamento es pequeño pero muy bonito. (*her*)

   _____

9. Present Tense of **-er** and **-ir** Verbs

A. Write the appropriate form of the verb in parentheses.

1. Por la mañana yo (comer) _____ un sándwich de queso y (beber)

   _____ un vaso grande de leche en casa.

2. Mis amigos (leer) _____ el periódico y (discutir) _____ las

   noticias.

3. Ahora nosotros (vivir)_____ en un apartamento en el centro, pero tú

   (vivir)_____ en una casa en el barrio Miramar.

4. Vosotras (vender) _____ regalos baratos y caros.

5. A veces entras en un café y (escribir) _____ cartas a tus amigos de los

   Estados Unidos.

B. Write the appropriate ending for each verb stem.

   1. ¿En qué barrio viv_____ vosotros?

   2. El señor Molina escrib_____ unos editoriales fantásticos.

   3. ¿Qué periódico le_____ tú?

   4. Nosotros no com_____ en el restaurante Goya.

   5. (Yo) no discut_____ la política.

   6. ¿Cuándo abr_____ ellos los almacenes?

   7. ¿Y dónde viv_____ tu amiga francesa?

10. Irregular Present Tense Verbs: **hacer, decir, tener, venir**

A. Change the verb according to the new plural subject.

   MODELO: Miguel no tiene un apartamento caro.

   (Juan y Rosa) → Juan y Rosa no tienen un apartamento caro.

   1. Yo no tengo un carro nuevo. (ustedes)

      _____

   2. ¿Y tú qué haces en el centro? (vosotros)

      _____

   3. A veces, el cliente viene por la mañana. (los dependientes)

      _____

   4. Digo que el metro es muy práctico. (los jóvenes)

      _____

   5. En el periódico dice que el presidente viene a nuestro barrio hoy. (los alumnos

      mexicanos)

      _____

B. Complete these sentences with the correct present indicative form of the verb in parentheses.

1. (decir) (Yo) _____ que no me gusta la cerveza alemana.

2. (venir) ¿Vosotros no _____ al restaurante con nosotros?

3. (hacer) Nosotros _____ los sándwiches.

4. (tener) El bar _____ vinos de la Argentina.

5. (venir) ¿Cuándo _____ tú a comer en casa?

6. (decir) Las clientas _____ que el jamón es caro.

7. (venir) Yo no _____ aquí mucho, pero tú

   _____ todos los días.

11. Numbers 20–1.000.000

Complete the following sentences by spelling out the numbers in Spanish.

1. Hay (22) _____ apartamentos en su edificio.

2. Tenemos (80.000) _____ pesos en el banco central.

3. El coche sólo tiene (1776) _____ kilómetros.

4. ¿Verdad que hay (100) _____ cuadros en su casa?

5. Ellos viven en la calle (105) _____ del barrio Colón.

6. Las noticias dicen que hay (1.000.000) _____ de

   automóviles en Los Ángeles.

Para repasar

A. Unscramble these elements and construct logical sentences. Make any changes or additions that are necessary.

1. el alemán / conversar / y / la francesa / en español

   _____

2. de la universidad / trabajar / le gusta / en / la biblioteca

   _____

3. el lunes / catorce / es / hoy / marzo

_____

4. no / el invierno / en Nueva York / me gusta

_____

5. ¿estudiar / los alumnos / cuándo / de la profesora Valle?

_____

B. Change these nouns and adjectives to the plural, adding the correct definite article.
Follow the model.

MODELO: ciudad / francesa → las ciudades francesas

1. bolígrafo / caro

_____

2. español / romántico

_____

3. mapa / interesante

_____

4. silla / nueva

_____

5. almacén / barato

_____

6. noticia / importante

_____

C. Change these plural nouns and adjectives to the singular. Follow the model.

MODELO: Hablan de los profesores españoles. → Hablan del profesor español.

1. Vienen de los almacenes caros.

_____

2. Tomo los autobuses en las plazas centrales.

_____

3. Preguntan a los dependientes nuevos.

_____

4. Contestan a las clientas japonesas.

_____

5. Hablan de las noticias de hoy.

_____

Comunicación

A. You are traveling in Mexico with your cousin who speaks very little Spanish. Express in Spanish these sentences you or she may have to use.

1. I need a map of the city.

_____

2. Sometimes she likes to drink coffee in the afternoon.

_____

3. They are coming to the hotel tomorrow.

_____

4. Do you have a bar in the hotel?

_____

5. I don't have my car today. I take the subway.

_____

6. No, I don't like to argue with my clients.

_____

7. Let's see if they have a newspaper there.

_____

8. Do you live in a house or an apartment?

_____

9. Is there a good restaurant here?

_____

10. There are many pretty paintings in the store.

_____

B. Form questions that could be answered by the following statements.

1. Deseo comer en el restaurante del hotel.

_____

2. Dice que no le gusta el centro.

_____

3. Sí, tenemos un regalo para la dependienta.

_____

4. Hago el café por la mañana.

_____

5. Sólo necesitamos un reloj práctico y barato.

_____

6. Hay muchos taxis en la plaza Morales.

_____

C. Answer the following questions and share your responses with the class.

1. ¿Desea vivir en una casa o en un edificio de apartamentos?

_____

2. ¿Quién hace el desayuno (*breakfast*) en su casa?

_____

3. ¿Por la mañana le gusta beber café?

_____

4. ¿Viene a clase todos los días?

_____

5. ¿Cuántos (*How many*) estudiantes hay en su clase de español?

_____

6. ¿Discute las noticias de hoy con sus amigos?

_____

7. ¿Escribe muchas cartas a sus amigos que viven en otras ciudades?

_____

8. ¿En qué tiendas le gusta comprar regalos caros?

_____

LECCIÓN DOS
LABORATORY MANUAL

Gráficos

A. You will hear a series of words. Repeat each one, and then say the singular form. Repeat the correct answer during the second pause.

1. ...   2. ...   3. ...   4. ...   5. ...   6. ...

B. You will hear a series of sentences. Each sentence will be read twice. Circle the letter of the word you associate most closely with each sentence.

1. a. bancos   b. almacenes   c. carros

2. a. las tiendas   b. el periódico   c. el barrio

3. a. casas   b. regalos   c. coches

4. a. una dependienta   b. un edificio   c. un cuadro

Pronunciación

Spanish b, v, d, g, j

Spanish **b** and **v** are pronounced exactly the same, but they both have two sounds, depending on their positions. At the beginning of a word, after a pause, and after **m** or **n** they have a hard (explosive) sound, almost like the *b* in the English word *boy*. Listen and repeat.

buenas noches   invitación   nombre   barrio   venir   vaso

In all other positions, particularly between vowels, **b** and **v** have a soft (fricative) sound. Listen and repeat.

escribo   trabajamos   joven   nuevo

Spanish **d** has a hard sound at the beginning of a word, after a pause, and after **n** or **l**. Listen and repeat.

decir   domingo   el diálogo   cuando   grande   el dibujo

In all other positions, and particularly between vowels, **d** has a soft sound similar to the *th* in the English word *this*. Listen and repeat.

edificio   periódico   usted   cuadro

Spanish **g** has a hard sound at the beginning of a word, after a pause, and after **n**. Listen and repeat.

lengua   gasolina   gramática   inglesa

The **g** between vowels is softened considerably. Listen and repeat.

digo   pregunta   me gusta   bolígrafo

Before the vowels **e** and **i**, Spanish **g** resembles a harsh *h* sound, as in the English word *history*. Listen and repeat.

página   Gibraltar   general   geografía

The hard **g** sound before **e** and **i** is written as **gu** in Spanish. Listen and repeat.

guitarrista   guerra   Guillermina

Spanish **j** appears primarily before the vowels **a**, **o**, and **u** and sounds just like the **g** before **e** and **i**. Listen and repeat.

jamón   jugo   Jorge   San Juan

A. Repeat these sentences after the speaker.

1. Diego es un amigo uruguayo.
2. Don Jaime es un ingeniero argentino.
3. Juliana es de San Jacinto.
4. La abuela de Víctor vive en un barrio bonito.

B. Draw a slash through the underscored letters (b̲, y̲, d̲, g̲) when they should be pronounced as soft (fricative) sounds.

1. sabemos	4. vivir	7. tengo	10. Gloria
2. también	5. buenos días	8. amigo	11. Diego
3. barbero	6. perdón	9. luego	12. Guillermo

C. Explain briefly what you must remember about the underscored letters in these words.

1. guitarra _____

2. viernes _____

3. Jorge _____

4. <u>d</u>on<u>d</u>e _____

5. a<u>d</u>iós _____

Gramática esencial

7. More on the Definite Article

A. First repeat the model sentence, then substitute the cue words that are given on the tape and repeat the entire sentence. Repeat the correct answer during the second pause.

MODELO: Miguel habla a <u>los hombres</u>. (dependiente) →
Miguel habla al dependiente.

1. ...   2. ...   3. ...   4. ...

B. Repeat the same steps with this model sentence.

MODELO: Elena y Federico conversan del <u>Perú</u>. (la Argentina) →
Elena y Federico conversan de la Argentina.

1. ...   2. ...   3. ...   4. ...

8. Possessive Adjectives

A. You will hear a series of sentences. Change the article to the appropriate possessive adjective. Follow the model. Repeat the correct answer during the second pause.

MODELO: Conversamos del barrio. →
Conversamos de nuestro barrio.

1. ...   2. ...   3. ...   4. ...   5. ...   6. ...

B. You will hear a series of questions. Each question will be asked twice. Be sure to use a possessive adjective in each answer. Repeat the correct answer during the second pause.

MODELO: ¿Es americano el coche de Juan? → Sí, el coche es americano.

1. ...   2. ...   3. ...   4. ...   5. ...

9. Present Tense of -er and -ir Verbs

A. First repeat the model sentence, then substitute the cue words that are given and repeat the entire sentence. Repeat the correct answer after the speaker.

MODELO: Yo como mucho queso. (tú) → Tú comes mucho queso.

1. ...   2. ...   3. ...   4. ...

B. Answer these questions negatively. Repeat the correct answer during the second pause.

MODELO: ¿Vives en el barrio Colón? → No, no vivo en el barrio Colón.

1. ...   2. ....   3. ...   4. ...

10. Irregular Present Tense Verbs: hacer, decir, tener, venir

A. First repeat the model sentence, then substitute the cue words that are given on the tape and repeat the entire sentence. Repeat the correct answer after the speaker.

MODELO: ¿Qué hacemos nosotros aquí? (yo) → ¿Qué hago yo aquí?

1. ...   2. ...   3. ...

B. Repeat the same steps with this model sentence.

MODELO: Mi cliente no dice mucho. (yo) → Yo no digo mucho.

1. ...   2. ...   3. ...

C. Repeat the same steps with this model sentence.

MODELO: ¿No vienes tú por la tarde? (Uds.) → ¿No vienen Uds. por la tarde?

1. ...   2. ...   3. ...

D. Repeat the same steps with this model sentence.

MODELO: No tenemos café colombiano. (tú) → Tú no tienes café colombiano.

1. ...   2. ...   3. ...

11. Numbers 20–1.000.000

You will hear some math problems in Spanish. You will hear each one twice. Circle the letter of the correct answer.

MODELO: Veinte más veinte son cuarenta.

a. 20   b. 35   (c.) 40

1. a. 150   b. 400   c. 600

2. a. 3.000.000   b. 2.500   c. 33.000

3. a. 61   b. 62   c. 72

4. a. 30   b. 36   c. 90

5. a. 90 dólares   b. 200 pesos   c. 120 pesos

Comunicación

A. *Laura escribe a su amiga.* You will hear the **Texto** from page 50 of your textbook. First, listen carefully and try to follow the gist of the ideas. Then, you will hear the **Texto** again, followed by some questions. You will hear each question twice. During the first pause, answer the question. During the second pause, repeat the correct answer.

1. ...   2. ...   3. ...   4. ...   5. ...

B. *Dictado.* You will hear a series of sentences twice. During the first pause, write each sentence in the space provided. During the second pause, check what you wrote.

1. _____

2. _____

3. _____

4. _____

C. *Artículos de regalo.* You will hear a series of questions based on the drawing. Listen carefully and circle the letter of the correct answer. For the last question, invent your own answer.

1. a. Sí, tienen relojes caros.

   b. No tienen relojes.

   c. Tienen muchos relojes.

2. a. Sí, la cámara es barata.

   b. Pues, el reloj es alemán.

   c. Sí, la cámara es alemana.

3. a. No, tienen una rebaja de vinos chilenos.

   b. Hay muchas cosas chilenas en la tienda.

   c. Hoy sólo hay relojes y cuadros.

4. a. No venden cuadros en la tienda.

   b. Sólo venden cuadros de Chile.

   c. Sí, venden cuadros modernos también.

5. _____

D. *Sólo tú.* You will hear a series of questions about yourself. You will hear each question twice. Answer them in complete Spanish sentences. No answers will be given on the tape.

   1. _____

   2. _____

   3. _____

   4. _____

LECCIÓN TRES
WORKBOOK

Gráficos

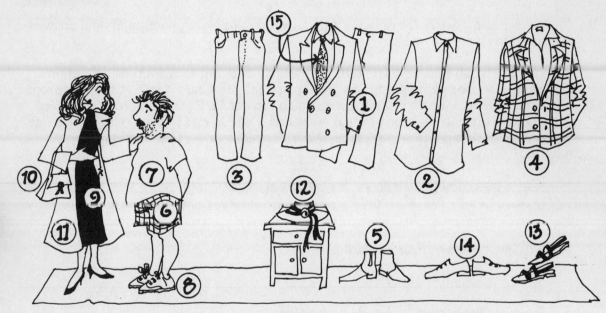

A. *¿Qué lleva Benicio a la fiesta?* Complete the following dialogue between Cati and her husband by writing in the names of the articles numbered in the drawing, along with the appropriate definite article where needed.

Benicio: No voy a la fiesta. No soy tonto, Cati, estoy muy gordo.

Cati: Ay, Benicio. No deseo discutir. ¿Qué vas a llevar?

_____(1) y _____(2) nueva

o _____(3), _____(4) y

_____(5)?

Benicio: No, no. Estoy muy cómodo con mis _____(6),

_____(7) y _____(8).

Cati: Tienes cinco minutos, Benicio. Yo estoy lista (*ready*).

Benicio: Estás preciosa con tu _____(9) rosado de seda,

_____(10), _____(11) y

_____ (12). Es fácil para una persona alta y delgada lucir (*to look*) bien.

Cati: Gracias. Es mi vestido favorito. No llevo la falda, la blusa y _____ (13) porque es una fiesta muy importante.

Benicio: ¿Sí? Pues voy a buscar los calcetines y _____ (14). Voy a llevar el traje, ¡pero no _____ (15)!

Cati: Ay, Beni, ¿por qué no la corbata?

Benicio: Bueno, si estás incómoda, acepto llevar la corbata. Tú ganas (*win*).

Cati: Gracias, Beni. Te pago con mi corazón (*heart*).

B. *Un hombre listo*. Study the drawing again, read the following paragraph, and answer the questions that follow.

Benicio, el esposo (*husband*) de Cati, no gasta mucho dinero cuando va de compras. No usa tarjetas de crédito porque no desea pagar interés. Claro que le gusta llevar ropa nueva y elegante, y no ropa vieja, manchada o incómoda. Es un hombre listo y sólo compra ropa cuando los precios están rebajados. Cuando está hablando de la ropa que va a comprar, siempre (*always*) pregunta a la dependienta:—¿Cuál es el precio rebajado?

1. ¿Gasta poco dinero cuando va de compras el esposo?

   _____

2. ¿Por qué no usa tarjetas de crédito?

   _____

3. ¿Le gusta llevar ropa incómoda y manchada?

   _____

4. ¿Cuándo compra él ropa?

   _____

5. ¿Qué pregunta a la dependienta cuando está comprando ropa?

   _____

6. Benicio es alto y delgado, ¿verdad?

   _____

7. ¿Qué ropa lleva Benicio hoy?

   _____

NAME_____ DATE_____ CLASS_____

8. ¿Qué ropa lleva él a la fiesta?

_____

Gramática esenclal

12. More Irregular Present Tense Verbs: **estar, ser, dar, ir**

Complete the following sentences with the form of the verb in parentheses that corresponds to the subject.

1. Elena Ruiz _____ una fiesta mañana, ¿verdad? (dar)

2. ¿Dónde _____ la casa de Elena? (estar)

3. No tengo idea. Yo no _____ a la fiesta. (ir)

4. ¿Por qué? Elena _____ muy simpática. (ser)

5. Mariela y yo no _____ (ir) porque nosotros _____ (estar) incómodos con Elena y sus amigos.

6. Pero ellos _____ muy simpáticos. (ser) Yo _____ amigo de ellos. (ser)

7. Ellas te (*you*) _____ una invitación. (dar)

8. Ricardo y Mario _____ una fiesta mañana también. (dar)

9. ¿A qué fiesta _____ tú? (ir)

10. Yo _____ a la fiesta de Ricardo y Mario. (ir) Si deseas ir, su casa _____ en la calle Nieves. (estar)

13.–14. **Ser** Used to Express Identification, Origin, Material, and Possession; **estar** Used to Express Location

Complete the following sentences with the correct form of **ser** or **estar** to show identification, origin, material, possession, or location.

1. Ella _____ dependienta de la tienda Macy's.

2. Las blusas rebajadas allí _____ del Japón.

3. Y esa falda negra, ¿_____ de seda o _____ de algodón (*cotton*)?

Lección 3: Workbook 51

4. ¿Pero dónde _____ los grandes almacenes de la ciudad?

5. El suéter rojo _____ de una famosa diseñadora (*designer*) cubana.

6. Nosotros _____ clientas del Almacén El Encanto.

7. Claro que vosotras _____ de Madrid, pero hay muchas dependientas que

   _____ de Sevilla.

8. Los nuevos abrigos no _____ del Canadá.

9. ¿_____ tú clienta de Marcia? Yo _____ clienta de ella también.

10. Yo _____ aquí porque quiero comprar sandalias.

15. Ser and estar with Adjectives

A. Complete these sentences by writing the correct form of **ser** or **estar** as appropriate.

1. El vestido de Alina no _____ blanco, _____ amarillo.

2. Las camisas nuevas de Pancho _____ manchadas y él _____ muy

   triste.

3. Yo _____ enferma y no voy de compras hoy.

4. Claro que la dependienta _____ ocupada. ¡Todos los precios

   _____ rebajados!

5. Ella _____ joven, pero _____ cansada todas las mañanas.

6. ¿_____ cara la ropa en el Almacén Patiño?

7. Nosotros _____ muy contentos porque hoy compramos ropa nueva.

8. ¿Quieres ir al centro si no _____ ocupado ahora?

9. Tú _____ muy simpática. Me gusta ir de compras contigo (*with you*).

10. Yo no _____ rico, pero tengo toda la ropa que necesito.

B. Complete each sentence with the correct form of **ser** or **estar** according to the cue.

1. Él _____ un jóven muy rico. (*He always has money to buy clothes*).

2. Tú _____ cansado. (*You've been working hard all day at the store*).

3. Nosotros _____ jóvenes. *(We're both 11 years old.)*

4. Alicia _____ una persona triste. *(She's always crying about her bad luck.)*

5. Los viejos Godoy _____ enfermos. *(They complain constantly about aches and pains.)*

6. Ud. _____ muy enferma hoy, ¿verdad? *(You just caught a nasty cold.)*

7. Jorge _____ simpático. *(He's a very pleasant salesperson.)*

8. Los precios _____ rebajados. *(Those clothes are on sale today.)*

9. Vosotras _____ muy altas. *(You are very tall.)*

10. La blusa y la falda _____ caras y yo no _____ rica. *(The clothes are expensive, and I'm not rich.)*

11. Juan y Cecilia _____ enamorados. *(They're in love.)*

12. ¿Cómo _____ ella? *(You wonder what your boss is really like.)*

C. Express the following sentences in Spanish. Remember the different meanings conveyed by **ser** and **estar.**

1. She's a very difficult client.

   _____

2. They're comfortable jeans, but they're not reduced in *(de)* price.

   _____

3. The blouse is reduced, but it's not (made of) silk.

   _____

4. It's easy to use a credit card.

   _____

5. The boots are from Canada and they are in the new department store downtown.

   _____

6. I'm happy when I'm buying new clothes.

   _____

7. He looks young in his shorts.

_____

8. I'm not rich, tall, or thin!

_____

16. Present Participles and Progressive Forms

A. Change the following sentences to the present progressive form.

MODELO: Hoy no trabajo. → Hoy no estoy trabajando.

1. Sofía no compra ropa nueva.

_____

2. Emilio gana mucho dinero.

_____

3. No buscamos botas de vaquero.

_____

4. Doy el dinero al dependiente.

_____

5. Tú pagas con tarjeta de crédito.

_____

6. Los Godoy gastan mil dólares en el Almacén Ruiz.

_____

7. Tú discutes el precio de todo.

_____

B. Answer the following questions using the present progressive tense.

MODELO: ¿No compras la blusa de seda? →
          No, no estoy comprando la blusa de seda.

1. ¿Trabaja Lisa en el Almacén Marroquí?

_____

2. ¿Escribe una carta la señorita González?

_____

3. ¿Vendemos regalos elegantes?

_____

4. ¿Miran Uds. los nuevos vestidos de Europa?

_____

5. ¿Bebes un vaso de leche en la cafetería?

_____

6. ¿No lee Elena los precios de la ropa?

_____

7. ¿Hablamos nosotros de las nuevas modas (*fashions*)?

_____

Para repasar

Hablando de Ud. Tell about yourself by answering these questions in Spanish.

1. ¿Qué hago yo hoy?

_____

2. ¿Qué tomo por la mañana?

_____

3. ¿Dónde vive mi mejor (*best*) amigo/a?

_____

4. ¿Qué periódico leo?

_____

5. ¿Qué deseo comprar hoy?

_____

6. ¿Qué me gusta comer por la noche?

_____

7. ¿Qué hacen mis padres (*parents*)?

_____

Comunicación

A. You're buying a present for a female friend, and you're talking to the saleslady at the department store. Express the following conversation in Spanish.

1. I am looking for something (*algo*) pink or white for my friend.

_____

2. Doesn't she wear blue or green?

_____

3. Well, she's very sad today. Pink and white are cheerful (*alegre*) colors, true?

_____

4. Yes, but the important thing is the feeling (*el sentimiento*) and, of course, the price.

_____

5. Agreed. But I'm not rich. How much is the white silk blouse?

_____

6. It's reduced from $200 to $150. It's pretty, isn't it?

_____

7. Yes. Will you lend me (*Me presta*) $100?

_____

8. Young man/lady, Patina is a big department store, and I am very busy. We sell clothing, but we don't lend money.

_____

B. Form questions that could be answered by the following statements.

1. Sí, estamos pagando con una tarjeta de crédito.

_____

2. Son muy incómodas las sandalias.

_____

3. ¡Claro, llevo una camiseta al concierto!

_____

4. Pobre sí soy, pero tonto no soy.

_____

5. Ella está cansada.

_____

6. Damos la fiesta el sábado 25.

_____

7. Estoy buscando mis calcetines.

_____

8. No llevo la camisa roja porque está manchada.

_____

C. *Sólo tú.* You're out on a shopping spree. Describe five articles of clothing you are looking for.

MODELO: Estoy buscando un bolso negro.

1. _____

2. _____

3. _____

4. _____

5. _____

D. Finish each sentence with a form of **ser** or **estar** as appropriate and one of the following words or phrases: **cansados / incómoda / cliente de Marcia / de _____** (*a place*) **/ puertorriqueños / listo / negro / de _____** (*someone*).

1. Nosotros _____.

2. La ropa _____.

3. Mi amiga _____.

4. Los zapatos _____.

5. El dependiente y Uds. _____.

6. Tú y yo _____.

7. El vestido _____.

8. La tarjeta _____.

LECCIÓN TRES
LABORATORY MANUAL

Gráficos

A. You will hear groups of three words repeated twice. During the first pause, say the word that is not related to the other two. During the second pause, repeat the correct answer.

1. ...　　2. ...　　3. ...　　4. ...　　5. ...　　6. ...

B. *La ropa*. You will hear a series of sentences. Repeat each one, then state it in the plural. Repeat the correct answer after the speaker.

MODELO: La camisa está manchada. → Las camisas están manchadas.

1. ...　　2. ...　　3. ...　　4. ...　　5. ...

C. You will hear a series of statements. You will hear each statement twice. Circle the letter of the best rejoinder to each.

1. a. Es un joven gordo.
   b. Elena está cansada.
   c. Compro unos pantalones nuevos.

2. a. ¿Por qué no lavas la camisa?
   b. ¿No acepta tarjetas de crédito?
   c. ¿Qué está buscando aquí?

3. a. Busco una falda roja.
   b. Gracias. Eres una buena amiga.
   c. Es una chica triste, ¿verdad?

4. a. Es cara pero me gusta mucho.
   b. Está rebajada de veinticinco dólares.
   c. Está rebajada de quince dólares.

Pronunciación

<u>Spanish r</u>

When **r** appears between vowels in Spanish, it sounds like the letters *d* and *t* in *Betty had a bit of bitter butter*. Listen and repeat.

eres   naranja   cuarenta   claro   periódico

If **r** appears before a consonant, imagine that a slight [e] sound is present between the **r** and the consonant. Listen and repeat.

largo   acuerdo   carta   verde   corbata

At the end of a word, **r** is pronounced with less force and is slightly less audible. Listen and repeat.

prestar   ir   suéter   ayer   a ver

<u>Spanish rr</u>

The **rr** is pronounced as a strong trill. You need to arch your tongue. Let the tip of your tongue rest loosely just behind the upper front teeth while you puff out air to make the tip of your tongue flip up and down. Listen and repeat.

turrón   marrón   ferrocarril   corro   tierra

You also pronounce the sound **rr** when a single **r** appears at the beginning of a word or a phrase or after the letters **l** or **n**. Listen and repeat.

Rosa   Ricardo   Enrique
el reloj   en realidad   un radio

A. Repeat these sentences after the speaker.

1. Raúl recibe recomendaciones de Ramón.
2. Don Ricardo es de Puerto Rico.
3. La guitarra es de Rita Martínez.

B. You will hear a series of words. You will hear each word twice. Repeat the word and circle the letter that you think it contains.

1. r / rr   3. r / rr   5. r / rr   7. r / rr
2. r / rr   4. r / rr   6. r / rr   8. r / rr

Gramática esencial

12. More Irregular Present Tense Verbs: **estar, ser, dar, ir**

A. First repeat the model sentence, then substitute the subject given on the tape and repeat the entire sentence. Repeat the correct answer during the second pause.

MODELO: La chica está contenta. (tú) → Tú estás contento.

1. ...   2. ...   3. ....   4. ...   5. ...

B. Repeat the same steps with this model sentence.

MODELO: Yo soy listo. (la chica) → La chica es lista.

1. ...   2. ...   3. ....   4. ...   5. ...

C. First repeat the model sentence. Then substitute the two cues that are given and repeat the entire sentence. Repeat the correct answer after the speaker.

MODELO: Yo doy dinero. (Elena / blusa) → Elena da una blusa.

1. ...   2. ...   3. ....   4. ...   5. ...

D. Repeat the same steps with this model sentence.

MODELO: Yo voy a la tienda. (tú / almacén) → Tú vas al almacén.

1. ...   2. ...   3. ....   4. ...   5. ...

13.–14. **Ser** Used to Express Identification, Origin, Material, and Possession; **estar** Used to Express Location

A. First repeat the model sentence, then substitute the cue words that are given on the tape and repeat the entire sentence. Repeat the correct answer during the second pause.

MODELO: Yo soy de México. (Miguel) → Miguel es de México.

1. ...   2. ...   3. ....   4. ...   5. ...

B. During the pause, answer these questions negatively. Always begin by saying **No, amigo**. Repeat the correct answer after the speaker.

MODELO: ¿Eres de Miami? No, amigo, no soy de Miami.

1. ...   2. ...   3. ....   4. ...   5. ...   6. ...   7. ...   8. ...

15. **Ser** and **estar** with Adjectives

Change the meaning of each of these statements by changing the verb to either **ser** or **estar**. Repeat the correct answer during the second pause.

1. ...   2. ...   3. ....   4. ...   5. ...

16. Present Participles and Progressive Forms

First listen to the model sentence, then change the verb to the present progressive and repeat the entire sentence. Repeat the correct answer during the second pause.

MODELO: Ella no compra la camisa. → Ella no está comprando la camisa.

1. ...   2. ...   3. ....   4. ...   5. ...

Comunicación

A. *Dos amigas van de compras.* You will hear the **Texto** from page 69 of your textbook. Listen carefully and try to follow the gist of the ideas. Then you will hear the **Texto** again, followed by some questions. You will hear each question twice. During the first pause, answer the question. During the second pause, repeat the correct answer.

1. ...   2. ...   3. ....   4. ...   5. ...   6. ...

B. You will hear a series of questions based on the drawing. You will hear each question twice. During the first pause, answer the question. During the second pause, repeat the correct answer. For the last question, invent your own answer.

TARJETA AZUL

NOMBRE CLIENTE: LUIS PÉREZ TOLÓN

NÚMERO DE CUENTA: 000-213-8886

COMPRA	DÍA	TIENDA	MERCANCÍA	PRECIO
1112	8/7	TIENDA CHÉVERE	2 CAMISAS	$ 49,00
1113	29/7	ALMACÉN PULIDO	PANTALONES	$118,00
1114	30/7	ALMACÉN PULIDO	CHAQUETA	$250,00
1115	31/7	CASA DE SEDA	CALCETINES	$ 18,00
1116	31/7	MODA FINA	BLUSA	$ 75,00

BALANCE ANTERIOR: $1.875
BALANCE TOTAL: $2.385
PAGO MENSUAL: $116
LÍMITE DE CRÉDITO: $2.000

---

1. ...   2. ...   3. ....   4. ...   5. ...   6. ...

7. _____

C. *Dictado.* You will hear a short paragraph about Luis. During the first pause, write each sentence in the space provided. During the second pause, check what you wrote.

_____

_____

_____

_____

_____

_____

D. *Sólo tú.* You will hear a series of statements about yourself. Indicate whether each is true or false by saying, **Sí, estoy de acuerdo** or **No, no es verdad.**

1. ...   2. ...   3. ....   4. ...   5. ...   6. ...

LECCIÓN CUATRO
WORKBOOK

Gráficos

A. *Aquí viene la familia.* Complete the following paragraph by writing in the names of the articles or persons numbered in the drawing, along with the appropriate definite article where necessary.

La abuela Tina y Rosa, su hija, están comprando comida (*food*) y regalos para los

niños Paco y Rosita. Ellos vienen esta tarde con su mamá Leticia, que es hija de la

abuela Tina y hermana de Rosa. La abuela Tina trae _____ (1)

y _____ (2) de _____ (3) y

_____ (4). La tía Rosa trae una _____ (5)

para Rosita y un _____ (6) para Paco, su sobrino. Tienen prisa

porque la tía Rosa oye un _____ (7) y sabe que es necesario ir

al aeropuerto. La abuela Tina no va al aeropuerto. Ella va a casa a poner la mesa para la

cena. En _____ (8) de una tienda, ella ve

_____ (9), _____ (10),

_____ (11) y una _____ (12) de vino.

Desea comprar un _____ (13) nuevo para la visita, pero decide

comprar _____ (14).

B. *Rosa tiene prisa.* Study the drawing again, read the dialogue, and answer the questions that follow.

Abuela Tina:	¿Traes el regalo para Leticia?
Tía Rosa:	Sí, y traigo la muñeca y el sombrero para los niños.
Abuela Tina:	Dime, ¿cuándo tienes que ir al aeropuerto?
Tía Rosa:	Bueno, es casi hora de ir (*time to go*). Oigo el avión.
Abuela Tina:	Ay, hija. Yo sé que tienes prisa. Pero hazme un favor.
Tía Rosa:	Claro, mamá. ¿Qué deseas?
Abuela Tina:	Por favor, lava (*wash*) el mantel antes de ir (*before going*). Está manchado.
Tía Rosa:	Lo siento (*I'm sorry*), mamá, pero tengo que salir en cinco minutos. ¿Por qué no pones el mantel nuevo?
Abuela Tina:	Es una buena idea, hija.

1. ¿Quién trae el regalo para Leticia?

_____

2. ¿Adónde tiene que ir la tía Rosa?

_____

3. ¿Qué oye la tía Rosa?

_____

4. ¿Qué sabe la abuela Tina?

_____

5. ¿Por qué es necesario lavar el mantel?

_____

6. ¿Por qué no va a lavar el mantel la tía Rosa?

_____

7. ¿Qué va a hacer la abuela Tina?

_____

Gramática esencial

17. Irregular Present Tense of conocer, saber, oír, poner, salir, traer, ver

A. Complete the following sentences with the correct form of the verb in parentheses.

1. ¿ _____ tú al esposo de Leticia? (conocer)

2. Yo no _____ quién es. (saber)

3. Leticia _____ a los niños de Costa Rica. (traer)

4. ¿ _____ Ud. el precio del pan? (saber)

5. Sí, yo _____ (ver) el aeropuerto, pero no _____ (oír) el avión.

6. Ellos _____ de San José por la mañana. (salir)

7. Nosotros no _____ a la sobrina de Leticia. (conocer)

B. Rewrite these sentences, using the subjects given in parentheses.

1. Tú pones el mantel y yo pongo los cubiertos.

(ella/Uds.) _____

(nosotros/ellas) _____

(vosotros/él) _____

2. ¿Cuándo sale el avión de Santiago?

(su esposo) _____

(Elena y yo) _____

(tú y Raimundo) _____

3. Ellas traen manzanas de la frutería.

(Yo) _____

(Vosotras) _____

(Tú) _____

4. Veo una muñeca en la vidriera.

(tú) _____

(ellos) _____

(nosotros) _____

5. ¿No oyes a los nietos?

(ustedes) _____

(ella) _____

(nosotros) _____

18. Uses of the Preposition **a**

Supply **a** where needed and make the necessary contractions.

1. Conozco ____ Buenos Aires muy bien.

2. ¿Cuando vemos ____ los hijos de Alina?

3. Ellos tienen ____ tres niños y una niña.

4. Sí, conocemos ____ el hermano de Enrique.

5. ¿Por qué no vamos ____ ir ____ Venezuela?

6. ¿No vas ____ traer flores, Enrique?

7. Ella conoce ____ la tía Rosa, pero no conoce ____ la abuela Tina.

8. Voy ____ ir de compras mañana.

9. Tenemos ____ dos sobrinos en Miami.

19. Idioms with **hacer** and **tener**

A. Answer the following questions using an **hacer** idiom.

1. ¿Qué tiempo hace en los Andes?

_____

2. ¿Hace calor en Tejas en el verano?

_____

3. Cuando hay una tormenta (*storm*), ¿hace calor o hace mucho viento?

_____

4. ¿Hace sol en Acapulco en el verano?

_____

5. ¿Qué tiempo hace en la primavera y en el otoño en su ciudad?

_____

B. Complete the following sentences with a **tener** idiom.

1. En invierno la abuela Tina siempre _____.

2. Está vieja. _____ 82 _____.

3. Si no sale la tía Rosa para la farmacia, _____ ir tú.

4. Traemos jugo para los niños porque _____.

5. Tú _____. Ellos salen hoy de Panamá y no mañana.

6. Nosotros _____ comer porque

_____.

7. A él no le gusta estudiar. No _____ de ir a la biblioteca.

8. _____ porque el avión sale en cinco minutos.

20. Affirmative Familiar Commands

Rewrite the following sentences as familiar affirmative commands.

MODELO: El padre mira las fotografías. → ¡Mira las fotografías, padre!

1. La tía Rosa bebe el vino.

_____

2. La abuela Tina escribe una carta.

_____

3. Siempre dices la verdad.

_____

4. La abuela hace ejercicio todos los días.

_____

5. La tía Rosa va al aeropuerto ahora.

   _____

6. Elena pone el mantel.

   _____

7. Lorena trae los platos.

   _____

8. Luis viene por la tarde.

   _____

9. Tú tienes paciencia, mamá.

   _____

10. Lorena lava los vasos.

   _____

Para repasar

Complete the following paragraph with **ser** or **estar** as appropriate.

Andrés _____ (1) un buen amigo de mi familia. Él _____ (2) de Santo

Domingo, pero ahora _____ (3) de vacaciones en Nueva York. _____ (4)

fácil gastar mucho dinero en las tiendas y restaurantes cuando una persona

_____ (5) viajando. Hoy Andrés usa su tarjeta de crédito porque

_____ (6) pobre. Él _____ (7) esperando (*waiting for*) una carta de sus

padres con un cheque. Nosotros _____ (8) en el Hotel Plaza. _____ (9)

un hotel caro y muy bonito. Andrés _____ (10) con nosotros. Mañana vamos a

Filadelfia. Allí _____ (11) la casa de sus tíos Carlos y Mónica. Ellos

_____ (12) en Europa, pero su prima Elisa _____ (13) en casa. Vamos

por (*by*) avión a Filadelfia aunque (*even though*) _____ (14) caro y nosotros no

_____ (15) ricos.

Comunicación

A. *Una sorpresa.* Miguel's parents are arriving from Colombia, and he's getting his apartment ready for their visit. Express the following conversation in Spanish.

1. Why do you have to go to the fruit store?

     _____

2. I need to buy flowers for the house. My parents leave Medellín today.

     _____

3. Are they bringing your brothers and sisters?

     _____

4. They are bringing my older brother and my younger sister.

     _____

5. How old is she?

     _____

6. She's nine months old and is learning to walk now.

     _____

7. Is their visit (*visita*) a surprise?

     _____

8. Yes, it's a surprise. They don't know I'm married!

     _____

B. *Por favor...* Use the familiar affirmative forms of the following verbs to tell your little brother or sister six things he or she ought to do.

MODELO: beber → Por favor, ¡bebe el jugo de naranja!

1. (escribir) _____

2. (ir) _____

3. (poner) _____

4. (salir) _____

5. (venir) _____

6. (?) _____

C. *Sólo tú.* Use the following expressions with **tener** to tell about yourself.

1. Hoy tengo que _____

2. No tengo ganas de _____

3. Tengo razón porque _____

4. Tengo mucha prisa porque _____

5. Tengo _____ años.

D. Now use the same expressions to tell about your Spanish instructor.

1. _____

2. _____

3. _____

4. _____

5. _____

LECCIÓN CUATRO
LABORATORY MANUAL

Gráficos

A. You will hear a series of words. Repeat each one, and then say the masculine form of the word. Repeat the correct answer during the second pause.

1. ...   2. ...   3. ...   4. ...   5. ...   6. ...   7. ...

B. You will hear a series of sentences. You will hear each sentence twice. Circle the letter of the phrase you associate most closely with each sentence.

1. a. Él es su esposo.

   b. Él es primo de Lola.

   c. Ella es tía de Juanito.

2. a. Su sobrino trae flores.

   b. No está casada.

   c. Conoce al esposo de Leticia.

3. a. Los nietos están en su casa.

   b. Sé dónde está la farmacia.

   c. Ella es la tía de ellos.

4. a. Hay una sorpresa en la vidriera.

   b. Tía Rosa, hazme un favor.

   c. Rosa tiene prisa y no va a la farmacia.

Pronunciación

Before **a**, **o**, and **u**, Spanish **c** has a hard [k] sound. Listen and repeat.

    Caracas   cuarto   cómoda   muñeca

Before **e** or **i**, Spanish **c** actually has two pronunciations: it is pronounced like *th* in the English word *thing* in most parts of Spain, but like the sound [s] in the English word *hiss* in Hispanic America. These tapes will generally use the Hispanic American pronunciation. Listen and repeat.

    cenar   farmacia   César   sucio

The hard [k] sound before **e** and **i** is written as **qu** in Spanish. Listen and repeat.

    máquina   vaquero

Spanish **x**

In Spanish, **x** before a consonant is pronounced like the [s] sound in the English word *hiss*. Listen and repeat.

    expresión   excelente   explicación   excusa

When **x** appears between vowels, it sounds like the English *gs* or *ks* combination. Listen and repeat.

    exigente   exótico   examen   existencia

Spanish **z**

Spanish **z** appears before the vowels **a**, **o**, and **u**, but not before the other vowels. Like **c** before **e** or **i**, it has two pronunciations, but since the *ss* sound is used in most of the Spanish-speaking world, this is the pronunciation used on these tapes. Listen and repeat.

    manzana   tiza   marzo   diez

A. You will hear a series of words. You will hear each word twice. Repeat each one and circle the letter or letters you think the word contains.

    1. que / qui   3. c / z   5. ce / que   7. r / rr

    2. cu / ca   4. g / x   6. ch / c   8. que / ce

B. Explain briefly what you must remember about pronunciation of the underscored letters in these words.

    1. <u>qu</u>esadilla _____

    2. e<u>x</u>cursión _____

3. cerebro _____

4. Enrique _____

5. exageración _____

6. zoología _____

Gramática esencial

17. Irregular Present Tense of **conocer, saber, oír, poner, salir, traer, ver**

A. First repeat the model sentence, then substitute the cue words given on the tape and repeat the entire sentence. Repeat the correct answer during the second pause.

MODELO: Yo conozco a Rosa. (tú) → Tú conoces a Rosa.

1. a. ...   b. ...   c. ...

MODELO: Tú sabes el nombre de la farmacia. (ella) →
Ella sabe el nombre de la farmacia.

2. a. ...   b. ...   c. ...

MODELO: ¿Usted no ve los platos en la vidriera? (ella) →
¿Ella no ve los platos en la vidriera?

3. a. ...   b. ...   c. ...

MODELO: ¿Tú oyes el avión? (Ellos) → ¿Ellos oyen el avión?

4. a. ...   b. ...   c. ...

MODELO: Nosotros no ponemos el mantel. (Ella) → Ella no pone el mantel.

5. a. ...   b. ...   c. ...

MODELO: Ella siempre trae sorpresas. (yo) → Yo siempre traigo sorpresas.

6. a. ...   b. ...   c. ...

MODELO: Ahora nosotros salimos de la frutería. (tú) → Ahora tú sales de la frutería.

7. a. ...   b. ...   c. ...

B. Form questions in response to the statements that you hear. Begin each question with **¿Cuándo?**. Repeat the correct answer during the second pause.

MODELO: Pongo la mesa ahora. → ¿Cuándo pones la mesa?

1. ...   2. ...   3. ...   4. ...   5. ...

18. Uses of the Preposition **a**

A. First repeat the model sentence, then substitute the cue words given on the tape and repeat the entire sentence. Be sure to include the word **a** if the cue words require it. Repeat the correct answer during the second pause.

MODELO: Traigo <u>las flores</u>. (los tíos) → Traigo a los tíos.

1. ...   2. ...   3. ...   4. ...   5. ...   6. ...

B. During the pause, answer the questions on the tape negatively. Be sure to include the word **a** if necessary. During the second pause, repeat the correct answer.

MODELO: ¿Ayudas a tu hermana? → No, no ayudo a mi hermana.

1. ...   2. ...   3. ...   4. ...   5. ...   6. ...

19. Idioms with **hacer** and **tener**

A. You will hear a series of questions formed with **tener**. You will hear each sentence twice. Answer negatively using the cues you see. Repeat the correct answer after the speaker.

MODELO: ¿Tienes hambre? (sed) → No, tengo sed.

1. salir a caminar   3. la frutería   5. manzanas

2. sueño   4. 30 años   6. calor

B. For each statement that you hear, create a question with **hacer** to which that statement is a logical rejoinder. You will hear each statement twice. Repeat the correct answer during the second pause.

MODELO: Sí, porque es verano. → ¿Hace calor?

1. ...   2. ...   3. ...   4. ...   5. ...

20. Affirmative Familiar Commands

You will hear a series of statements. Give the affirmative familiar command form of each statement. Repeat the correct answer during the second pause.

MODELO: Yo tengo paciencia. → ¡Ten paciencia!

1. ...   2. ...   3. ...   4. ...   5. ...   6. ...   7. ...

Comunicación

A. *La familia es lo primero.* You will hear the **Texto** from page 92 of your textbook. First, listen carefully and try to follow the gist of the ideas. Then you will hear the **Texto** again, followed by questions. You will hear each question twice. During the first pause, answer the question. During the second pause, repeat the correct answer.

1. ...   2. ...   3. ...   4. ...   5. ...   6. ...

B. You will hear a story related to the drawing. Then you will hear series of statements based on the story and drawing. Listen carefully and circle the letter of the answer that best completes each statement.

1. a. va de compras

   b. pone la mesa

   c. trae una sorpresa

2. a. oyen las noticias

   b. ponen una botella de vino

   c. ven un mantel manchado

3. a. que su hermana y su mamá no salen de compras mucho

    b. que hoy es martes

    c. que Paco saca buenas notas

4. a. café con leche

    b. al esposo de Leticia

    c. un jamón

5. a. oyen a su mamá y a su tía hablar de la sorpresa

    b. ven a su tío hablar de las noticias

    c. salen con su abuela a la farmacia

6. a. no pone flores en la mesa

    b. tiene mucha prisa

    c. tiene razón

C. *Dictado*. You will hear a short paragraph about the family. During the first pause, write each sentence in the space provided. During the second pause, check what you wrote.

    _____

    _____

    _____

D. *Sólo tú*. You will hear a series of statements about yourself. Indicate whether each is true or false by saying **Sí, tengo ganas** or **No, no tengo ganas.**

    1. ...   2. ...   3. ...   4. ...   5. ...

LECCIÓN CINCO
WORKBOOK

Gráficos

A. *Una casa cómoda.* Complete the following dialogue between Lilia and her architect by writing in the names of the articles numbered in the drawing, along with the appropriate definite or indefinite article where needed.

Arquitecto: Este apartamento es perfecto, ¿verdad, Lilia?

Lilia: Bueno, es un poco pequeño, pero es práctico. Es difícil trabajar y

después tener que limpiar, cocinar, pasar _____ (1)

en casa...

Arquitecto: A ver, a ver. Es una casa muy cómoda. Aquí tiene una

_____ (2) grande con

_____ (3). Es fácil poner

_____ (4), _____ (5) y

_____ (6) en la sala. En la cocina hay un

_____ (7) moderno,

_____ (8) y _____ (9).

A ver... ¿qué más?

Lilia: Pues, ¿no hay _____ (10)? ¿Y son grandes el

_____ (11) y _____ (12)?

Arquitecto: Claro que sí. Y en el dormitorio, además de

_____ (13), hay _____ (14)

y espacio para _____ (15) o

_____ (16) y _____ (17)

y _____ (18). Y hay dos

_____ (19).

Lilia: Pero no necesito dos cuartos de baño. Cuando llego a casa desconecto

_____ (20), cocino y ceno y miro la televisión

para descansar. ¡No voy a limpiar dos baños!

Arquitecto: Bueno, pues no limpie, no lave, no pase la aspiradora. ¡No diga más!

Lilia: ¿Cómo? ¿Qué dice?

Arquitecto: Lilia, por favor, lea el periódico de hoy. Es muy fácil encontrar (*to find*)

una buena sirvienta.

Lilia: ¿Sirvienta? Pero eso (*that*) es caro, ¿no?

Arquitecto: No, no es caro. Con un apartamento pequeño, es muy barato tener una

sirvienta.

B. *Una mujer ocupada.* Study the drawing again, read the following paragraph, and
answer the questions that follow. (Some questions refer to the dialogue in A.)

Lilia tiene un trabajo muy exigente. Por la mañana llama a sus clientes por teléfono.
Después abre, lee y contesta las cartas. Por la tarde usa la máquina de escribir para
hacer su reporte de ventas. A veces sale a cenar con sus clientes más importantes.
Cuando llega a su casa por la noche no tiene ganas de hacer nada, y así necesita un
apartamento cómodo y fácil de limpiar. ¿A quién le gusta llegar a un apartamento sucio?

1. ¿Cómo es el trabajo de Lilia?

_____

2. ¿Qué hace Lilia por la mañana en el trabajo?

_____

3. ¿Para qué usa ella la máquina de escribir?

_____

4. ¿Le gusta a ella tener que limpiar la casa cuando llega del trabajo?

_____

5. ¿Qué hace ella para descansar?

_____

6. Según (*According to*) el arquitecto, ¿es caro tener una sirvienta?

_____

Gramática esencial

21. Polite Commands; Negative Familiar Commands

A. Read the following statements, then write the polite command form for the person(s) being addressed.

MODELO: Ud. habla con los clientes. → ¡Hable Ud. con los clientes!

1. Ud. come en la cocina.

_____

2. Ud. abre el periódico ahora.

_____

3. Uds. dicen que el apartamento no está sucio.

_____

4. Ud. hace la cama todos los días.

_____

5. Ud. pone un sofá en el dormitorio.

_____

6. Ud. sale sin pasar la aspiradora.

_____

7. Uds. compran una lámpara nueva.

_____

8. Uds. vienen a ver el apartamento.

_____

9. Ud. ve su nueva casa.

_____

10. Ud. llama a sus clientes.

_____

11. Ud. busca un escritorio práctico.

_____

B. Now give the negative polite command form of these sentences.

MODELO: Ud. grita en la calle. → ¡No grite Ud. en la calle!

1. Uds. oyen las noticias por la mañana.

_____

2. Ud. cruza la calle sin mirar.

_____

3. Ud. apaga la lámpara.

_____

4. Uds. no dan mil pesos por el sillón.

_____

5. Ud. trae una cómoda muy moderna.

_____

6. Uds. van a otra tienda mañana.

_____

C. Complete these sentences with the negative familiar command forms of the verb in parentheses.

1. (lavar) No _____ los platos en el fregadero.

2. (salir) No _____ si el cuarto está sucio.

3. (decir) No _____ eso (*that*).

4. (leer) No _____ mi carta.

5. (buscar) No _____ una casa en el barrio Miramar.

22. Demonstrative Adjectives and Pronouns

A. Complete the following sentences with the appropriate demonstrative adjective or pronoun.

1. (*That*) _____ apartamento está sucio. ¿Por qué no vemos (*this one*)

_____?

2. (*This*) _____ cocina es muy pequeña y (*that one [distant]*) _____

es pequeña también.

3. (*Those*) _____ lámparas están rebajadas. ¿Están rebajadas (*these*)

_____ lámparas?

4. ¿Por qué está tan caro (*this*) _____ escritorio? (*That one*) _____

es más nuevo.

5. ¡(*These*) _____ camas son incómodas! ¿Cómo son (*those [way over*

there]) _____ camas?

6. Lo siento, pero (*that*) _____ sofá está manchado. Traiga (*that one [way*

over there]) _____, por favor.

B. Express in Spanish, using the appropriate demonstrative adjective or pronoun.

1. I want to buy this one (**estante**), but I want to see that one too.

_____

2. I like this one (**cocina**), if that one isn't reduced.

_____

3. Don't wash this (plate), wash those over there!

_____

4. Those (rugs) are expensive, but this one is inexpensive and very pretty.

_____

5. Please don't use this one (**teléfono**); use that one over there.

_____

23. Telling Time

A. Answer the following questions using the cues given in the drawings.

1. ¿A qué hora sale Lilia para el trabajo?

_____

2. ¿A qué hora llega la sirvienta a limpiar la casa?

_____

3. ¿A qué hora llama Lilia por teléfono a los clientes?

_____

4. ¿A qué hora come su sándwich hoy?

_____

5. ¿A que hora llega ella a su apartamento?

_____

6. ¿A qué hora ponen su programa favorito?

_____

7. ¿A qué hora terminan las noticias?

_____

Para repasar

¡A despertar, Lilia! Complete the following paragraph as though you were Lilia and just waking up. Use **hacer** and **tener** as necessary.

Hoy _____ (1) frío y sólo _____ (2) ropa de verano.

_____ (3) que ir al Almacén Robles a comprar un suéter. No _____ (4)

ganas de trabajar. Pero _____ (5) que a ver unos clientes a las once en punto.

La verdad es que _____ (6) un trabajo muy exigente. Creo que las mujeres de

hoy _____ (7) una vida muy dura. ¡Ah, _____ (8) una idea! Si

_____ (9) buen tiempo más tarde, digo en la oficina que _____ (10)

que llevar a mi sobrino al doctor y salgo a caminar por el centro.

Comunicación

A. *Una fiesta.* You're giving your first party in your new apartment, and you have hired Lupe to help with the preparations. Express the following conversation in Spanish between you and Lupe.

1. What time is it, Lupe?

_____

2. It's almost five, miss. Anything else?

_____

3. Five in the afternoon? My friends arrive at six!

_____

4. Please, don't shout, miss. I have to vacuum and that's all (**eso es todo**).

_____

5. No, Lupe, don't vacuum the rug. Wash these plates and clean the kitchen.

_____

6. The kitchen is not dirty. Look!

_____

7. You're right. Well, go to the store right now and buy more flowers like these.

_____

8. I'm sorry, but I have to rest. Please don't be so demanding.

_____

B. *Hablando de apartamentos*. Form questions that could be answered by the following statements.

1. No, el apartamento sólo tiene tres dormitorios.

_____

2. No, no vayan al apartamento después de las cinco de la tarde.

_____

3. Sí, éste tiene sala, comedor y dos baños.

_____

4. Esta cocina es eléctrica, ¡pero el lavaplatos es usted!

_____

5. No llames por teléfono. Mejor ve en persona.

_____

6. Busque un apartamento en la colonia Martí.

_____

7. La clienta viene a las dos en punto.

_____

C. *Sólo tú.* You have volunteered to do any house chores that your roommate wants you to do for one day. Using the verbs in parentheses as cues, express in Spanish the commands that your roommate is likely to give you.

1. (cocinar)

_____

2. (limpiar)

_____

3. (traer)

_____

4. (lavar)

_____

5. (poner)

_____

6. (ir)

_____

7. (prestar)

_____

LECCIÓN CINCO
LABORATORY MANUAL

Gráficos

A. *Las cosas de la casa.* You will hear a series of words. Repeat each one and then say the plural form. Repeat the correct answer during the second pause.

1. ... 2. ... 3. ... 4. ... 5. ... 6. ... 7. ... 8. ... 9. ... 10. ...

B. You will hear a series of requests. You will hear each one twice. Circle the letter of the statement you associate most closely with each.

1. a. La alfombra está sucia.

   b. El teléfono está en la sala.

   c. Uso el sillón cuando descanso.

2. a. Diga que no estoy en casa.

   b. El cuarto de baño está muy sucio.

   c. Por favor, limpie la cocina.

3. a. Cenamos en un restaurante mañana.

   b. Cuando llego a casa, descanso.

   c. Tengo que hacer la cama ahora mismo.

4. a. No tiene ganas de cocinar.

   b. Tenemos mucho calor.

   c. No, gracias, prefiero mirar la televisión.

Pronunciación

Intonation Patterns

Most declarative statements in Spanish rise in intonation up to the first stressed syllable and hold steady until the last stressed syllable of the sentence; then the tone drops noticeably. For example:

La señorita no sabe quién es la profesora.

A. Repeat the statements you will hear. Imitate the intonation patterns of the speakers.

1. Yo sé que Juan no viene.

2. Isabel trae los platos a la mesa.

3. Mercedes no oye las noticias.

4. No sale hoy con los amigos.

5. Todos trabajamos en casa.

Interrogative statements in Spanish rise in intonation up to the first stressed syllable and hold steady until the last stressed syllable; then the tone goes up once more. For example:

¿Conoce Albuquerque la señora Moreno?

B. Repeat these questions after the speakers.

1. ¿Ud. no sabe que Carmen es mi prima?

2. ¿Es necesario acompañar a tu tía Margarita?

3. ¿Son Pedro y María los hijos de Ramón?

4. ¿Por qué no sales de casa ahora?

5. ¿Por qué no compran Uds. la ropa en los almacenes?

When you hear the number cue on the tape, say each of the following statements aloud. Use the appropriate intonation pattern. After you have read each statement or question, wait for the speaker to say it. Then repeat the sentence, imitating the speaker as closely as possible.

1. ¿Sabe Ud. que Juan es mi nieto?

2. No traemos los periódicos para Uds.

3. Don Tomás es el abuelo de Enrique.

4. ¿Por qué no sales de casa ahora?

5. ¿No compran Uds. la ropa en los almacenes?

D. The following questions and statements will be read twice. Repeat each one and then check the appropriate space to indicate whether the sentence is declarative or interrogative.

	Declarative	Interrogative
1.	_____	_____
2.	_____	_____
3.	_____	_____
4.	_____	_____
5.	_____	_____

Gramática esencial

21. Polite Commands; Negative Familiar Commands

A. Listen to the following sentences, then change the verb to the appropriate polite command. Repeat the correct answer during the second pause.

MODELO: Me gusta comer en la cocina. → Pues, ¡coma en la cocina!

1. No tengo ganas de hacer la cama.

2. Traemos un sillón.

3. Abro las ventanas por la mañana.

4. Necesito hablar con el cliente.

5. Voy a la casa.

6. Pagamos con tarjeta de crédito.

7. Digo la verdad.

8. Ponemos el estante en la sala.

B. Now you will hear a series of sentences. You will hear each sentence twice. Use the negative familiar command form to tell the speaker not to do the action described in each sentence. Repeat the correct answer during the second pause.

MODELO: Hago la cama. → ¡No hagas la cama!

1. ...   2. ...   3. ...   4. ...   5. ...

22. Demonstrative Adjectives and Pronouns

A. First repeat the model sentence, then substitute the cue words and repeat the entire sentence. Repeat the correct answer during the second pause.

MODELO: Lavo este plato. (vaso) → Lavo este vaso.

1. sofá   4. apartamentos

2. silla   5. cuartos de baño

3. teléfono

B. Repeat the same steps with this model sentence.

MODELO: Yo limpio este apartamento, pero aquél no. (habitación) →
            Yo limpio esta habitación, pero aquélla no.

1. dormitorio   4. máquina de escribir

2. cómoda   5. sala

3. televisor

23. Telling Time

You will hear the speaker make a statement that includes a reference to time. Under each clock write the letter of the sentence to which each clock refers.

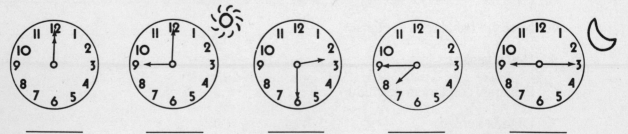

_____   _____   _____   _____   _____

Comunicación

A. *Felisa y Julián buscan un piso.* You will hear the **Texto** from page 111 of your textbook. Listen carefully and try to follow the gist of the ideas. Then you will hear the **Texto** again, followed by questions. You will hear each question twice. During the first pause, answer the question. During the second pause, repeat the correct answer.

1. ...   2. ...   3. ...   4. ...   5. ...

B. *Villa Dorada.* You will hear an advertisement for the sale of a house read twice. Then you will hear a series of incomplete statements based on the advertisement. Each statement will be followed by three choices for completing that statement. Provide an original answer for the last question.

1. a.   b.   c.

2. a.   b.   c.

3. a.   b.   c.

4. a.   b.   c.

5. a.   b.   c.

6. _____

C. *Dictado.* You will hear a short paragraph about your dream apartment. During the first pause, write each sentence in the space provided. During the second pause, check what you wrote.

_____

_____

_____

_____

D. *Sólo tú.* You will hear a series of questions about yourself. You will hear each question twice. Answer in complete Spanish sentences. No answers will be given on the tape.

LECCIÓN SEIS
WORKBOOK

Gráficos

A. *Una cena para muchos*. Complete the following paragraph by writing in the names of the articles or persons numbered in the drawing, along with the appropriate definite article.

Rubén y Fausto preparan para esta noche una cena para sus amigos. Rubén fue al

supermercado y compró varias cosas—_____ (1),

_____ (2), _____ (3) y un

_____ (4). Fausto salió temprano por la mañana y en la

pescadería (*fish store*) compró _____ (5) y

_____ (6). En la frutería compró

_____ (7), _____ (8) y

_____ (9) para hacer _____ (10) de

frutas. Después hizo _____ (11) de mariscos para sus amigos

que no comen carne. En el mercado, Rubén subió al Café París y desayunó café con

leche y varios _____ (12) con _____ (13).

Luego comió _____ (14) negros en casa de tía Rosa. Después

comió un poco de _____ (15) frito en la Cafetería Tin-Tin.

Ahora toma una taza de _____ (16) sin

_____ (17). Él dice que está a dieta pero, ¿quién cree eso?

B. *Una dieta especial.* Study the drawing again, read the dialogue, and answer the
questions that follow.

Fausto: ¿Desayunaste, Rubén?
Rubén: Sí, pero no comí casi nada. Un café y unos panecillos con mantequilla.
Fausto: ¿Dónde comiste?
Rubén: Pues, fui al Café París. ¿Tienes el cuchillo?
Fausto: Aquí está. ¿No fuiste por la casa de tía Rosa?
Rubén: Claro que sí. Ella hizo unos frijoles muy ricos.
Fausto: ¿No compraste helado para postre?
Rubén: No. Hice otra paradita (*little stop*).
Fausto: ¿Dónde más fuiste?
Rubén: Bueno, subí a la Cafetería Tin-Tin para comer tostadas de dieta.
Fausto: ¿Y?
Rubén: Y comí medio (*half*) pollo frito con papas fritas.
Fausto: ¿Y ahora qué estás tomando? ¿Vino?
Rubén: No. Solamente tomo una taza de té sin azúcar.
Fausto: Comprendo. ¡Sólo haces dieta cuando estás en casa!

1. ¿Qué tipo de ensalada hizo Fausto?

    _____

2. ¿Con qué frutas hizo Fausto la ensalada?

    _____

3. ¿Qué utensilio usó (*used*) Fausto cuando hizo la ensalada de frutas?

    _____

4. ¿Qué otros utensilios hay en la cocina?

    _____

5. ¿Qué tipo de sopa hizo Fausto?

    _____

6. ¿Qué comió Rubén para el desayuno?

_____

7. ¿Qué hizo Rubén después de visitar a la tía Rosa?

_____

8. ¿Qué comió Rubén con el pollo frito?

_____

9. ¿Compró Rubén helado para el postre?

_____

Gramática esencial

24. The Preterite Tense

Write the correct preterite form of the verbs given in parentheses.

1. (correr / comprar) Yo _____ al supermercado y _____ helado.

2. (subir / beber) Después Fausto y yo _____ al Café París y _____ un café.

3. (gastar) Él _____ poco dinero, pero yo _____ mi último (*last*) peso.

4. (llegar / decidir) Sus amigos _____ tarde porque _____ tomar una copa en un bar primero (*first*).

5. (buscar / llegar) Yo _____ un vino blanco francés, pero _____ a la cena con un vino tinto (*red*) argentino.

6. (comer / terminar) Nosotros _____ a las 9:00 y _____ con el postre a las 11:00.

7. (creer) ¡Por cierto, ellos no _____ el cuento (*story*) de la dieta!

8. (salir) Ellos _____ a las 12:00.

25. Irregular Preterites: **hacer, venir, dar, ir, ser**

A. Complete the following story with the correct preterite form of the verbs in parentheses.

El sábado pasado nosotros (dar) _____ (1) una cena magnífica. (Venir) _____ (2) muchos amigos de la escuela y del trabajo. Mariela (venir) _____ (3) con su novio y él (hacer) _____ (4) una paella deliciosa. Rodolfo y yo (hacer) _____ (5) una ensalada de mariscos. Alicia nos (dar) _____ (6) una botella de champán. Pedro y su hermano (ir) _____ (7) al supermercado primero y (comprar) _____ (8) un vino francés. ¡Tú y tu amiga (venir) _____ (9) tan tarde! Lo siento. (Ser) _____ (10) una noche inolvidable (*unforgettable*).

B. Rewrite these sentences, using the correct preterite form of the verbs.

1. Haces una sopa deliciosa.

   _____

2. Rubén, Carlos y Fausto son buenos amigos.

   _____

3. Vengo con unos amigos.

   _____

4. Elena también da unas fiestas muy bonitas.

   _____

5. ¿Y vosotros por qué no venís esta noche?

   _____

6. Vamos a casa de Paquín a comer camarones.

   _____

26. Shortened Adjectives

Complete the following sentences with the correct form of the adjectives given in parentheses.

1. (bueno) Rubén fue un _____ amigo.

2. (malo) Por cierto, él es un _____ cocinero (*cook*).

3. (primero) El _____ plato que cocinamos fue pescado.

4. (primero) Las _____ manzanas este año vinieron de Washington.

5. (malo / grande) Pues si el bistec está _____ , no es un _____ problema.

6. (grande) Ellos comieron en un _____ restaurante en Las Lomas en una sala _____.

7. (bueno) Las cenas en esa casa siempre fueron _____ y elegantes.

8. (bueno) Me dicen que no son _____ amigos.

27. Por and para Contrasted

Complete the following sentences by writing **por** or **para** as needed.

1. Fausto corrió _____ por la calle Ortíz _____ buscar más fruta.

2. Buscó una gran sandía _____ varias tiendas _____ la cena.

3. _____ las seis tiene que pasar _____ la casa de su tía.

4. Ella tiene un plato que hizo _____ él _____ la tarde.

5. _____ mucho tiempo esperó ver al dueño de la frutería.

6. —Doy cien pesos _____ una sandía fresca, señor Veloz.

7. _____ la ventana, Fausto vio una sandía perfecta.

8. —No vendo ésa, Fausto. Es _____ mi esposa.

9. —Bueno, _____ doscientos pesos está en venta.

10. —Muchas gracias _____ la sandía, señor Veloz.

Para repasar

A. *¿Qué hora es?* Write out the time in Spanish.

1. _____

2. _____

3. _____

4. _____

5. _____

6. _____

B. Subtract 30 minutes from each of the times you wrote above and write the new times.

MODELO: Las dos y media menos treinta minutos son las dos.

1. _____

2. _____

3. _____

4. _____

5. _____

6. _____

Comunicación

A. *El vegetarianismo*. Express in Spanish the following dialogue about food between you and your best friend.

1. "I didn't eat those chops. I am a vegetarian (**vegetariano/a**)!"

   _____

2. "But in Spain you ate and drank everything (**de todo**)."

   _____

3. "Well, that was in the summer of 1985. Now I don't eat beef, pork, lamb, or chicken."

   _____

4. "Did you give your cookbooks (**libros de cocina**) to Albert for that reason?"

   _____

5. "Yes. He and Rafaela went to Paris to study with a great chef. They learned to cook very well."

   _____

6. "How nice! I don't like to cook. I only like to eat!"

   _____

B. *Preguntas*. Form questions that could be answered by the following statements.

1. No fui al supermercado, fue Alberto.

   _____

2. La tía Rosa fue cocinera. Dio clases de cocina.

   _____

3. Ayer hice una comida rica con pescado, camarones y papas.

   _____

4. Vinimos temprano para la cena en casa de Rubén.

   _____

5. Sí, él y yo fuimos buenos amigos por varios años.

   _____

C. *Sólo tú*. Use the preterite form of the verbs in parentheses to tell something about yourself.

1. (hacer)

   _____

2. (dar)

   _____

3. (ser)

   _____

4. (ir)

   _____

5. (venir)

   _____

LECCIÓN SEIS
LABORATORY MANUAL

Gráficos

A. You will hear a series of words. Repeat each one, and then say the singular form of the word. Repeat the correct answer during the second pause.

1. ... 2. ... 3. ... 4. ... 5. ... 6. ... 7. ... 8. ... 9. ... 10. ...

B. You will hear a series of sentences. You will hear each sentence twice. Circle the letter of the phrase you associate most closely with each sentence.

1. a. ¿Adónde fuiste?

   b. ¿Qué comiste?

   c. ¿Por qué subiste?

2. a. Compró comida para la cena.

   b. Subió al dormitorio.

   c. Comió huevos con tostadas.

3. a. ¿Compraste pescado y camarones?

   b. Por eso salí a comprar aceite.

   c. Hice huevos rancheros con frijoles.

4. a. Compraron helado con frutas frescas.

   b. Tomaste una cucharita de aceite de pescado.

   c. Comí cafe con leche y tostadas.

Pronunciación

A. Repeat these words after the speaker. Note that items 9–12 do not contain diphthongs.

1. baile	5. también	9. María
2. auto	6. gracioso	10. dúo
3. veinte	7. ciudad	11. Rafael
4. estudia	8. triunfo	12. Bilbao

B. Repeat these short sentences after the speaker. The diphthongs are underscored. Be particularly careful with them.

1. Alicia es una muchacha italiana.

2. Diego es mi amigo uruguayo.

3. Carmen Miura no habla inglés.

4. Maité viene con Juan.

5. El señor Siqueiros vive en la Ciudad de México.

Gramática esencial

24. The Preterite Tense

A. First repeat the model sentence, then substitute the cue words that are given on the tape and repeat the entire sentence. Repeat the correct answer during the second pause.

MODELO: Yo corrí al supermercado. (tú) → Tú corriste al supermercado.

1. ...   2. ...   3. ...

B. Repeat the same steps with this model sentence.

MODELO: Nosotros gastamos poco dinero. (tú) → Tú gastaste poco dinero.

1. ...   2. ...   3. ...

C. Repeat the same steps with this model sentence.

MODELO: ¿Subisteis vosotras al Café París? (Uds.) → ¿Uds. subieron al Café Paris?

1. ...   2. ...   3. ...

D. Repeat the same steps with this model sentence.

   MODELO: Yo no leí los precios. (tú) → Tú no leíste los precios.

   1. ...   2. ...   3. ...

E. Repeat the same steps with this model sentence.

   MODELO: Rubén buscó papas fritas. (nosotros) → Nosotros buscamos papas fritas.

   1. ...   2. ...   3. ...

25. Irregular Preterites: **hacer, venir, dar, ir, ser**

A. You will hear a set of questions. During the first pause, answer them negatively. During the second pause, repeat the correct answer.

   MODELO: ¿Hiciste café con leche? → No, no hice café con leche.

   1. ...   2. ...   3. ...   4. ...   5. ...   6. ...

B. You will hear a series of questions. Each question will be followed by a cue. During the first pause, answer the question, using the cue given and the appropriate preterite form of the verb. During the second pause, repeat the correct answer.

   MODELO: ¿Qué hizo Fausto por la mañana? (ir al supermercado) →
             Fue al supermercado por la mañana.

   1. ...   2. ...   3. ...   4. ...   5. ...   6. ...

26. Shortened Adjectives

Form new sentences by changing the position of the adjective. Follow the model. Repeat the correct answer during the second pause.

   MODELO: Rubén es un amigo bueno. → Rubén es un buen amigo.

   1. ...   2. ...   3. ...   4. ...   5. ...

27. **Por** and **para** Contrasted

You will hear a series of sentence fragments. During the first pause, form complete sentences by inserting **por** or **para** as needed and the cues given. During the second pause, repeat the correct answer.

MODELO: Este pescado es... (la cena). → Este pescado es para la cena.

1. ...la calle
2. ...el supermercado hoy
3. ...varios días
4. ...el martes
5. ...sus amigos
6. ...hacer sopa de polla
7. ...una sandía

Comunicación

A. *Una típica comida española.* You will hear the **Texto** from page 128 of your textbook. Listen carefully and try to follow the gist of the ideas. Then you will hear the **Texto** again, followed by questions. You will hear each question twice. During the first pause, answer the question. During the second pause, repeat the correct answer.

1. ... 2. ... 3. ... 4. ... 5. ... 6. ... 7. ...

B. *El mercado Único.* You will hear a short story and a series of questions based on the story and drawing. Both will be read twice. Listen carefully and circle the letter of the answer that best completes each statement. Provide an original answer for the last question.

1. a. Venden el aceite Napoleón a quince pesos por botella.

   b. No fue rebajado.

   c. Graciela no compró aceite.

2. a. un kilo de frijoles negros por dos pesos

     b. un kilo de frijoles blancos por veinticinco pesos

     c. un kilo de frijoles negros por cincuenta pesos

3. a. Sí, tienen sopa de cebolla.

     b. No, no venden sopa.

     c. Sí, tienen sopa de pollo y de guisantes.

4. a. Gastó dos pesos.

     b. Gastó diez pesos.

     c. Gastó cinco pesos.

5. a. No buscó chuletas de cerdo.

     b. Buscó cuatro chuletas.

     c. Buscó camarones.

6. a. Vino de Kansas.

     b. Vino de Toluca.

     c. No vino maíz hoy.

7. _____

C. *Dictado.* You will hear a short paragraph about food. During the first pause, write each sentence in the space provided. During the second pause, check what you wrote.

_____

_____

_____

_____

_____

D. *Sólo tú.* You will hear a series of statements about yourself. Complete each one as it applies to you.

1. ... 2. ... 3. ... 4. ... 5. ... 6. ...

LECCIÓN SIETE
WORKBOOK

Gráficos

A. *Una sorpresa para Paulina.* Complete the following dialogue between Paulina and Silvia by writing in the names of the items numbered in the drawing, along with the appropriate definite or indefinite article where needed.

Silvia: Lo siento Paulina, pero mi hija no puede ir.

Paulina: ¿No puede o no quiere? ¿Prefiere estar en casa y jugar a las cartas o mirar

una telenovela? Ésas son cosas de viejos.

Silvia: No, no es eso, Paulina. Yo no quiero ser una persona anticuada (*old-

fashioned*). Y no lo soy. Ahora mismo Luisita está aquí mirando

el televisión (1) de Los Caníbales. ¿Sabes que Celia

Salvaje es _una cantautora_ (2)?

Paulina: ¿Los Caníbales? ¡Es mi conjunto favorito!

Silvia: Pues, mi canción favorita de ellos es «Loco de amor».

Paulina: De noche, cuando duermo, sueño con (*I dream about*) el muchacho que toca

la guitarra (3) principal.

Silvia: ¿Micaelo? Yo prefiero al que toca _la batería_ (4). Cuando

salgo en el carro siempre pongo _la grabadora_ (5) de ellos

en _los casetes_ (6).

Paulina: Bueno, y Luisita, ¿qué piensa?

Silvia: Luisita ahora no puede hablar. En este momento puso (*put*)

el disco (7) en _el tocadiscos_ (8) y lo

oye con _audífonos_ (9). Mira, Paulina, ella tiene una cita

para ir a bailar con Rodolfo el sábado y por eso no quiere ir al concierto.

Paulina: Ah, comprendo. Pues mire, tengo dos _bolletos_ (10) y

la invito (*I invite you*) entonces.

Silvia: ¡Fantástico! El Grupo Equis. Hoy tocaron muchas de sus canciones por

la radio (11).

B. *Un sueño* (dream) *musical.* Read the following paragraph, and then answer the questions.

Paulina sintió mucha sorpresa al hablar con la mamá de su mejor amiga. ¡Piensen Uds.! Una mujer de 40 años y le gustan Los Caníbales. Esa noche Paulina soñó con Micaelo otra vez (*again*). Pero esta vez él bailó con Silvia y un coro cantó «Loco de amor». Paulina y los otros fanáticos aplaudieron y cuando terminaron de bailar, Micaelo guiñó un ojo (*winked*) a Silvia y dijo: —No seas tímida. Vuelve pronto.

1. ¿Qué sintió Paulina al hablar con Silvia? ¿Por qué?

   Paulina sintió mucha sorpresa. Ella no pensó una mujer de
   guarante años le gustan Los Caníbales

2. ¿Con quién soñó Paulina?

   Paulina soñó con Micaelo

3. ¿Con quién bailó Micaelo en el sueño de Paulina?

   Micaelo bailó con Silvia en el sueño de Paulina

NAME _____ DATE _____ CLASS _____

4. ¿Qué canción cantaron en el sueño?

   "Loco de Amor" cantaron en el sueño

5. ¿Qué instrumentos tocan los miembros del grupo Los Caníbales?

   Los Caníbales tocan las guitarras y las baterías

Gramática esencial

28. Stem-changing Verbs

A. *Decisiones, decisiones*. Complete the following sentences with the present tense form of the verb in parentheses.

1. (querer) Mira, yo no ___*quiero*___ ir a ver esa película.

2. (preferir) ¿___*Prefieres*___ tú alquilar una y verla (*watch it*) en casa?

3. (pedir) Entonces llamo por teléfono y ___*pido*___ «Morir en Venecia».

4. (volver / poder) Bueno, si los niños ___*vuelven*___ temprano, todos ___*pueden*___ ver la película con ellos.

5. (pedir) ¿Por qué no esperamos a ver qué ___*piden*___ los niños?

6. (entender / pedir / dormir) Es que tú no ___*entiendes*___, mi amor. Si nosotros no ___*pedimos*___ un vídeo ahora, yo ___*duermo*___ una siesta.

7. (almorzar / pensar) Cuando tú ___*almuerzas*___ tarde, siempre tienes sueño. Yo ___*pienso*___ que es mejor almorzar temprano.

B. Express in Spanish.

1. If it rains or snows, the children play in the recreation room.

   Si llueve y nieva, los niños juegan en el salón de recreo.

2. Don't they prefer to watch videos on the television?

   No prefieren a ver los videos en el televisor

Lección 7: Workbook 111

3. Well, the picture starts in a half hour, and I can't find the tickets!

Mira, la película comienza en demi hora, y no puedo encontrar los boletos

4. I'll be back in a minute. I think they are in the dining room.

5. No, here they are. We can leave now.

29. Polite Command Forms of Stem-changing Verbs

Answer the following questions according to the model.

MODELO: ¿Pido una canción romántica? → Sí, pida una canción romántica.

1. ¿Pensamos en la ganga de la tienda de vídeos?

Si, piensa en la ganga

2. ¿Vuelvo al salón de recreo mañana?

Vuela

3. ¿Jugamos a las cartas con los amigos?

juga

4. ¿Pedimos boletos para el concierto de Los Caníbales?

Pida

5. ¿Sirvo algo de comer después del concierto?

Sirva

30. Present Participle of Stem-changing Verbs

Change the verbs in the following statements to the present progressive tense.

MODELO: Los cantantes duermen. → Los cantantes están durmiendo.

1. Piden un disco de Los Caníbales.

Estan pidiendo

2. No servimos comida ahora.

   No estamos sirviendo _____

3. Muere la actriz de la telenovela.

   Está muriendo _____

4. Duermo una siesta en el sillón.

   Estoy durmiendo _____

5. El cantante repite su canción favorita.

   Está repitiendo _____

31. Stem Changes in the Preterite

Complete the following story with the correct preterite form of the verbs given in parentheses.

Graciela, la cantante principal del conjunto, dice que siempre tiene hambre. Por ejemplo, ella dice que ayer casi (morir) _murió_ (1) de hambre. Los otros miembros del conjunto (pedir) _pidieron_ (2) sándwiches antes de ir al club. Cuando llegaron al club, el dueño (servir) _sirvió_ (3) una gran cena. Claro que Graciela siempre llega tarde y esta vez (dormir) _durmieron_ (4) mucho antes de ir al concierto. La verdad es que ella (preferir) _prefirió_ (5) dormir y no comer. Después del concierto, en el club ellos no (servir) _sirvieron_ (6) absolutamente nada y Graciela (volver) _v
olvió_ (7) al hotel sin comer.

32.–33. Direct Object Pronouns and Position of Direct Object Pronouns

A. Write the direct object pronouns that correspond to these noun objects.

   MODELO: Cantó <u>la canción.</u> → La cantó.

1. Vendiste los casetes.

   _____ los vendiste _____

2. No pidieron un disco compacto.

   _____ No lo pidieron _____

3. Tocaste la guitarra muy bien.

   _____ La tocaste muy bien _____

4. No encuentro las entradas.

   _____ No las encuentras _____

5. Alquilé una película.

   _____ La alquilé _____

6. Vimos a Elisa y a María en el concierto.

   _____ Las vimos en el concierto _____

7. Vendimos una grabadora a mitad de precio.

   _____ La vendimos a mitad _____

8. ¿No encontraron el lugar?

   _____ no lo encontraron _____

9. Prefirieron una película de horror.

   _____ La prefirieron _____

10. Enciendo el televisor a las 9:00.

    _____ Lo enciendo a la nueve _____

B. First convert the noun in parentheses to the corresponding direct object pronoun. Then choose the correct placement for it from among the options indicated. Add any accent marks that may be necessary.

MODELO: (los boletos) _____ compro _____ en la farmacia _____. →
         Los compro _____ en la farmacia _____.

1. (la cantante) _____ oímos _____ ayer _____.

2. (la canción) ¡_____ pide _____ tú _____!

3. (Silvia) ¿Por qué no _____ llamamos _____ hoy _____?

4. (el televisor y el radio) _los_ vamos a ver _____ en la tienda _____.

5. (los billetes) _____ estoy pidiendo _____ por _____ carta.

6. (las guitarras) _____ me gusta _____ tocar _____.

7. (yo) Uds. _____ pueden _____ encontrar _____ en el café.

8. (la ciencia ficción) _____ yo _____ no _____ encuentro muy interesante.

9. (los conciertos) ¿_____ no _____ van _____ a dar _____ aquí?

10. (el tocadiscos) ¡_____ compren _____ en _____ esa tienda!

Para repasar

La vida artística. Complete the story with the preterite form of the verbs in parentheses and the corrrect form of **por** or **para** as necessary.

Los fanáticos (aplaudir) _____ (1) mucho a su cantante favorita

cuando ella (salir) _____ (2) del hotel. Todo el mundo (venir)

_____ (3) al centro _____ (4) verla.

Celia (ir) _____ (5) corriendo _____ (6)

la plaza San Quintín _____ (7) encontrar un taxi y así poder

escapar de los fanáticos. Cuando (dar) _____ (8) el dinero al

taxista (*cab driver*), él le (hacer) _____ (9) dar su autógrafo y

dijo: —Adiós, señorita, (ser) _____ (10) un gusto

_____ (11) mí llevarla en mi taxi.

Comunicación

A. *¡Qué bueno!* In a contest, your best friend has won a day with Patricia, his favorite rock star. Imagine that you are talking to him about it and express the following conversation in Spanish.

1. When does your day with Patricia begin?

_____

2. It begins at 3 sharp. I can't wait.

_____

3. Does she understand Spanish?

_____

4. Yes, she understands it. But what do I do with her?

_____

5. Ask if she prefers a great meal or if she plays cards or if . . .

_____

6. If she plays cards? I can't believe that! How much does it cost to go to the Club Paraíso?

_____

7. It's expensive, but I think it is good.

_____

8. What can we talk about? I want to ask if she has a boyfriend.

_____

9. Don't be silly. It's better if you only talk about the weather.

_____

B. Form questions that could be answered by the following statements.

1. Lo pedí a mitad de precio.

_____

2. Lo siento. No lo servimos aquí.

_____

3. Lo encontré en el salón de recreo.

_____

4. Por favor, vuelvan ustedes a las siete en punto.

_____

C. *Sólo tú.* Write five sentences telling about what you and your friend(s) did the last time you went out together. Choose from among the verbs given to tell about your experience. Use them in the preterite tense.

ir	pedir	comenzar	tocar	no poder
preferir	costar	encontrar	bailar	volver

1. _____

2. _____

3. _____

4. _____

5. _____

LECCIÓN SIETE
LABORATORY MANUAL

Gráficos

A. You will hear a series of short sentences. Restate each sentence using the appropriate verb form for the new subject given in the cue. You will hear the correct answer after the second pause.

MODELO: Miguel puede comprar el casete. (yo) → Yo puedo comprar el casete.

1. el coro
2. Silvia y Paco
3. la cantante

4. tú
5. nosotros

B. You will hear a series of verbs. You will hear each verb twice. Circle the letter of the word you associate with each.

1. a. la telenovela   b. el disco   c. las cartas

2. a. los fanáticos   b. la grabadora   c. el casete

3. a. una película   b. una cita   c. una siesta

4. a. el salón de recreo b. el tocadiscos   c. la ganga

5. a. el audífono   b. el amor   c. el boleto

6. a. la ciencia ficción b. la canción   c. el vídeo

7. a. el bajo   b. el frío   c. el billete

Pronunciación

Spanish p, t, k

The Spanish sounds [p] and [k] (as in **ca, que, qui, co, cu, kilo**) are explosive consonants. The [p] and [k] sounds, although less explosive, are very similar to their English counterparts. The Spanish **t**, however, is quite different.

The Spanish **t** is pronounced with the tip of the tongue against the *upper teeth* and not against the upper gums, as is the case with the English *t*.

tenis	todo	tímido
tanto	temprano	cita
tocadiscos	batería	cantar

The Spanish **t**, in contrast with the English *t*, is never fused with a following **r**. To pronounce the **tr** combination correctly in Spanish, imagine that there is a "little" **e** in between the letters: **tres** (t^eres), **tren** (t^eren).

trabajo	treinta	tráfico
teatro	encontrar	otros
actriz	cuatro	traje

Gramática esencial

28. Stem-changing Verbs

A. First repeat the model sentence, then substitute the cue word that is given and repeat the entire sentence. Repeat the correct answer during the second pause.

MODELO: Puedo ir al concierto. (ellas) → Pueden ir al concierto.

1. ...   2. ...   3. ...

B. Repeat the same steps with this model sentence.

MODELO: ¿No piensas cantar esa canción? (usted) → ¿No piensa cantar esa canción?

1. ...   2. ...   3. ...

C. Repeat the same steps with this model sentence.

MODELO: Pides el nuevo vídeo. (yo) → Pido el nuevo vídeo.

1. ...   2. ...   3. ...

D. Repeat the same steps with this model sentence. Remember to change both verbs this time.

MODELO: Ella puede bailar, pero no quiere. (yo) → Puedo bailar, pero no quiero.

1. ...   2. ...   3. ...   4. ...

29. Polite Command Forms of Stem-changing Verbs

You will hear a series of short negative sentences. You will hear each sentence twice. Use the sentence to form a negative polite command as demonstrated in the model. Repeat the correct answer during the second pause.

MODELO: No pienso en esa película. → ¡No piense Ud. en esa película!
              No pensamos en esa película. → ¡No piensen Uds. en esa película!

1. ...   2. ...   3. ...   4. ...   5. ...

30. Present Participle of Stem-changing Verbs

First listen to the model sentence, then change the verb to the present progressive and repeat the entire sentence. Repeat the correct answer during the second pause.

MODELO: No pido música moderna. → No estoy pidiendo música moderna.

1. ...   2. ...   3. ...   4. ...   5. ...

31. Stem Changes in the Preterite

You will hear a series of questions. During the first pause, answer the sentence negatively, using the cues given. Repeat the correct answer during the second pause.

MODELO: ¿Serviste el almuerzo al conjunto? (ella) →
              No, ella sirvió el almuerzo al conjunto.

1. Luisita   2. nosotros   3. la cantante   4. Rubén   5. ellas

32.–33. Direct Object Pronouns and Position of Direct Object Pronouns

A. You will hear a series of sentences. You will hear each sentence twice. Replace the direct object noun with a direct object pronoun. Repeat the correct answer after the speaker.

MODELO: Pedí una película de ciencia ficción. → La pedí.

1. ...   2. ...   3. ...   4. ...   5. ...

B. You will hear a series of questions. You will hear each one twice. Answer affirmatively, replacing the direct object noun with the correct direct object pronoun. Repeat the correct answer after the speaker.

MODELO: ¿Puedes pedir la canción? → Sí, puedo pedirla.

1. ... 2. ... 3. ... 4. ... 5. ...

C. You will hear a series of affirmative commands. During the first pause, respond to each one with a negative command, and remember to change the position of the direct object pronoun. Repeat the correct answer during the second pause.

MODELO: ¡Sírvala! → ¡No, no la sirva!

1. ... 2. ... 3. ... 4. ... 5. ...

Comunicación

A. *Una conversación telefónica.* You will hear the **Texto** from page 151 of your textbook. First, listen carefully and try to follow the gist of the ideas. Then you will hear the **Texto** again, followed by questions. You will hear each question twice. During the first pause, answer the question. During the second pause, repeat the correct answer.

1. ... 2. ... 3. ... 4. ... 5. ...

B. *Los Caníbales vuelven.* You will hear a series of questions based on the drawing. Listen carefully and circle the letter of the correct answer. For the last question, invent your own answer.

IOS CANÍBALES
¡SÓLO UN CONCIERTO!
JUEVES, 30 de JULIO
CLUB FUGAZZI.
Bon PUNTO

BOLETOS $8. De venta en: Café Alcatraz, Club X, El château, Café Delia o pídalos por teléfono al 88-21-21. Las canciones más populares del año: «Loco de amor» y «Muero sin vivir».

1. a. Van a cenar a las ocho.

   b. La tocan a las ocho.

   c. El concierto comienza a las ocho.

2. a. No los encontré.

   b. Los encuentro en varios lugares.

   c. Los pido al 88-20-20.

3. a. Sólo cuestan ocho pesos.

    b. No puedo pagar ocho pesos.

    c. Los venden por siete pesos.

4. a. Pido pollo frito para llevar.

    b. Pido un vídeo.

    c. Pido boletos para el concierto de Los Caníbales.

5. a. «Loco sin tu amor» y «Duermo sin morir»

    b. «Loco de amor» y «Muero sin vivir»

    c. «Muero de amor» y «Loco que no muere»

6. _____

C. *Dictado.* You will hear a short paragraph about **Los Caníbales**. During the first pause, write each sentence in the space provided. During the second pause, check what you wrote.

_____

_____

_____

_____

_____

D. *Sólo tú.* You will hear a series of questions about yourself. You will hear each question twice. Answer in complete sentences. No answers will be given on the tape.

    1. ...   2. ...   3. ...   4. ...   5. ...   6. ...

L E C C I Ó N   O C H O
WORKBOOK

Gráficos

A. *En el gimnasio* (gym). Complete the following dialogue between Ramón and Héctor by writing in the names of the articles or persons numbered in the drawing, along with the definite article when necessary.

Ramón: Hombre, ¡qué _____ (1)! ¿Por qué no te peinas? ¿Y

por qué tienes esa venda (*bandage*) en _____ (2)?

Héctor: ¿Qué dijiste, Ramón? ¡Tienes _____ (3) muy grande

y _____ (4) muy pequeña!

Ramón: Está bien, chico. Pero sécate y nos vamos, ¿no? Ya te bañaste, ¿verdad?

Héctor: Sí, pero ¿trajiste aspirinas, Ramón?

Ramón: Traje dos en el bolsillo. ¿Por qué?

Héctor: Porque todo me duele (*hurts*)—_____ (5),

_____ (6), _____ (7),

_____ (8) y, más que nada,

_____ (9).

Ramón: ¿No te sientes bien?

Héctor: Por el momento, no. Es que cuando me despierto temprano y hago ejercicio

por la mañana, me siento mal.

Ramón: Pero te acostaste temprano anoche, ¿no? ¿Y dormiste bien?

Héctor: Sí, me acosté a las 9:30.

Ramón: ¡Qué suerte (*What luck*)! Yo no cerré _____ (10)

hasta las cuatro de la mañana.

B. *Un joven moderno*. Study the drawing again, read the following paragraph, and answer the questions that follow.

Todos los días al despertarse, Héctor corre al gimnasio, hace sus ejercicios, se baña, se afeita, se seca con una toalla , se pone la ropa y sale para el trabajo. Los sábados, cuando tiene más tiempo, se baña con su jabón importado de España. Después, todavía mojado, pasa mucho tiempo delante del (*in front of*) espejo, y se peina... y se peina... y se peina... La última (*last*) vez que vine con él, le dije:—¡No lo creo, Héctor! ¡Una hora de ejercicio y dos horas de vanidad!

1. ¿A dónde va Héctor después de despertarse todos los días?

_____

2. ¿Qué hace allí y para dónde sale después?

_____

3. ¿Con qué se baña Héctor los sábados?

_____

4. ¿Qué hace Héctor delante del espejo?

_____

5. ¿Por qué se enojó con Héctor su amigo?

_____

Gramática esencial

34. Reflexive Constructions

A. Complete the following sentences by looking at the corresponding drawing and expressing what one person is doing to another.

MODELO: Mamá seca a Lolita.

1. _Eduardo afieta a Candi_ hoy.

2. _Mamá levanta a Lolita_ por la mañana.

3. _____ anoche a las siete.

4. _____ temprano.

5. Antes de ir al trabajo _____ .

6. A la hora de cenar _____ .

7. _____ para la escuela.

8. _____ para desayunar.

B. Now use the reflexive forms of the same verbs in the preterite to state that the following persons did the same things. (Each numbered sentence that follows corresponds to the sentence with the same number in A.)

1. (yo)

_____

2. (Pancho y Rita)

_____

3. (Jorge)

_____

4. (Héctor y tú)

_____

5. (Marcia y yo)

_____

6. (Vosotras)

_____

7. (yo)

_____

8. (tú)

_____

35. Position of Reflexive Pronouns

Complete these sentences by writing the reflexive pronoun that corresponds to the word given in parentheses and inserting it in an appropriate space. Add any accent marks that may be necessary.

MODELO: (tú) _____ siempre _____ acuestas _____ tarde. → Siempre te acuestas tarde.

1. (ustedes) ¿Por qué no _____ quieren _____ sentar

_____ aquí?

2. (ella) Dicen que _____ ella _____ siente _____ bien.

3. (ellas) No _____ lavan _____ las manos sin jabón.

4. (Paco y Alfredo) _____ están sentando _____ a ver

_____ el vídeo ahora.

5. (él) _____ levantó _____ con _____ un gran dolor

(*pain*) de cabeza.

6. (nosotros) _____ sentimos _____ débiles _____ por el

calor.

7. (usted) _____ con esta toalla _____, por favor.

8. (yo) _____ canso _____ cuando _____ trabajo mucho.

36. Irregular Preterites: **decir, traer; poner, querer; poder, saber; estar, tener**

A. Complete the following sentences with the preterite form that corresponds to the verbs given in parentheses.

1. Nelson (decir) _____ que él no (traer)

_____ su traje de baño (*bathing suit*).

2. —Pues nosotros sólo (traer) _____ los de nosotros. ¿No

(poder) _____ tú comprar uno en la tienda?

3. ¡Él lo (estar) _____ pensando un momento y se (poner)

_____ unos pantalones cortos ridículos!

4. Por eso, nosotros no (querer) _____ ir a la playa (*beach*)

con él.

5. Al fin (*Finally*), yo (tener) _____ que darle (*give him*)

veinte pesos.

6. Aun así (*Even so*), él no (querer) _____ comprarse un traje

de baño nuevo.

7. Nosotros (estar) _____ discutiendo por mucho tiempo.

8. Y todos los muchachos (decir) _____ :—No es posible

discutir con Nelson.

9. En ese momento, nosotros (tener) _____ que volver a la

ciudad.

B. Rewrite these sentences, using the plural form of the verbs.

1. Yo no estuve en La Habana ese año.

_____

2. Pero tú supiste que ella fue en marzo, ¿verdad?

_____

3. ¿No quisiste ir con ella?

_____

4. La verdad es que no pude ir.

_____

5. Ella pudo ir sin problemas, ¿no?

_____

6. Tuvo que ir por México primero.

_____

7. ¿Y trajo ella mucho equipaje (*luggage*)?

_____

8. No, ella sólo estuvo de vacaciones por una semana.

_____

37.–38. Indirect Object Pronouns and Positions of Indirect Object Pronouns

Complete the following sentences with the indirect object pronoun that corresponds to the pronoun in parentheses.

1. La señorita (*him*) _____ compró una toalla.

2. El doctor (*us*) _____ hizo un examen.

3. ¿No (*you, fam. sing.*) _____ miró la nariz y la oreja?

4. (*Me*) _____ tocó la cara y los dedos del pie.

5. (*Them*) _____ habló a los otros doctores de nuestra situación.

6. (*you, pol. sing.*) ¿No _____ trajo nada para el dolor?

7. ¿Qué (*you, fam. sing.*) _____ dio?

8. No (*her*) _____ habló hasta las 11 de la noche.

Comunicación

A. *Preguntas del médico.* You are going to your doctor for your annual physical exam. Answer these questions using the cues given.

1. ¿A veces se siente débil? (si no dormirse temprano)

_____

2. ¿Se cansa fácilmente? (si levantarse temprano)

_____

3. ¿Puede tocarse la nariz con el dedo del pie? (si sentarse/poder hacerlo)

_____

4. ¿Se despierta por la noche? (sólo si llamarme por teléfono)

_____

5. ¿Puede pagarme ahora? (si no enojarse primero)

_____

B. *De vacaciones*. Form questions that could be answered by the following statements.

1. Estuvimos en un hotel entre Tulúm y Playa del Carmen.

_____

2. La verdad es que no quise ir a Cancún.

_____

3. Pude bañarme en el mar (*sea*) todos los días.

_____

4. Para la cena trajeron unos camarones bastante grandes.

_____

5. Traje dos novelas de ciencia ficción.

_____

6. No sé. Las puse en un estante el primer día y no las leí.

_____

C. *Un día especial*. Use as many of the following verbs as possible to write a short paragraph describing one of your days off: **acostarse, afeitarse, alegrarse, despertarse, dormirse, ponerse, sentirse, vestirse.** Feel free to use other verbs reflexively to complement your story.

_____

_____

_____

_____

_____

_____

LECCIÓN OCHO
LABORATORY MANUAL

Gráficos

A. *El cuerpo.* You will hear a series of words. Repeat each one, and then say the plural form. Repeat the correct answer during the second pause.

1. ...   2. ...   3. ...   4. ...   5. ...   6. ...   7. ...   8. ...

B. You will hear a series of sentences. You will hear each sentence twice. Circle the letter of the phrase you associate most closely with each sentence.

1. a. Me gusta el jabón francés.

   b. ¿Trajiste una almohada?

   c. Estuve entre las sabanas por quince horas.

2. a. ¿Te despertaste a las siete?

   b. Me acosté sin sábanas.

   c. ¿Nelson le gritó?

3. a. ¿Se seca con una sábana?

   b. ¿Me dormí rápidamente?

   c. ¿Te despertaste con sueño?

4. a. Estuve gritando por dos horas.

   b. Me peino ya.

   c. Me sentí como una mujer nueva.

Pronunciación

<u>Spanish ll, y</u>

In most of Spain and in some parts of Latin America, **ll** is generally pronounced as *ly*. Repeat after the speaker.

cuchillo   ellas   llamarse   llorar   toalla

In most of Latin America and in some parts of Spain, **ll** is generally pronounced as *y*, similar to the *y* in the English word *yes*. Listen and repeat.

llover   sillón   llegar   ayudar   mantequilla

calle   panecillo   yo   yanqui   mayo

A. Repeat these sentences after the speaker.

1. No llevo tortillas en el bolsillo.
2. Maribel vive en Marbella.
3. Ellos son los Padilla.
4. Ella no llega hasta mayo.

Gramática esencial

34.–35. Reflexive Constructions and Position of Reflexive Pronouns

A. You will hear a series of sentences. Change each one to make it reflexive. Repeat the correct answer during the second pause.

MODELO: Despierto a las niñas. → Me despierto.

1. ... 2. ... 3. ... 4. ... 5. ... 6. ...

B. You will hear again the answers from the preceding exercise. After you hear each one, use the cue given to express a new sentence in the preterite. Repeat the correct answer after the speaker.

MODELO: Me despierto. (a las seis) → Me desperté a las seis.

1. con un jabón francés
2. en cuanto llegamos a casa
3. gritando
4. por el centro
5. en el espejo
6. sin peinarse

C. You will hear the speaker use a reflexive verb to express a wish. During the first pause, respond to the wish with a formal command. Repeat the correct answer during the second pause.

MODELO: Quiero acostarme. → ¡Acuéstese!
          No quiero afeitarme. → ¡No se afeite!

1. ...   2. ...   3. ...   4. ...   5. ...

36. Irregular Preterites: **decir, traer; poner, querer; poder, saber; estar, tener**

A. First repeat the model sentence, then substitute the cue words that are given on the tape and repeat the entire sentence. Repeat the correct answer during the second pause.

MODELO: Estuvimos en La Habana. (yo) → Estuve en La Habana.

1. ...   2. ...   3. ...

B. Repeat the same steps with this model sentence.

MODELO: Traje el jabón y las toallas. (él) → Trajo el jabón y las toallas.

1. ...   2. ...   3. ...

C. Repeat the same steps with this model sentence.

MODELO: Tuve que peinarme. (tú) → Tuviste que peinarte.

1. ...   2. ...   3. ...

D. You will hear a series of sentences in the present tense. During the first pause, change the sentence, using the following cues and the preterite form of the verb. Repeat the correct answer during the second pause.

MODELO: Él dice eso. (ayer) → Él dijo eso ayer.

1. anoche   5. ayer

2. por la mañana   6. el domingo

3. para el almuerzo 7. a las cuatro

4. el sábado

37.–38. Indirect Object Pronouns and Position of Indirect Object Pronouns

A. You will hear a series of sentences. During the first pause, rephrase the sentence using the indirect object given in the cue. (Remember that there are sometimes several possible placements for an indirect object pronoun, and so the answers you hear are not always the only correct ones.) Repeat the answer during the second pause.

MODELO: Traes unos discos. (le) → Le traes unos discos.

1. te   2. le   3. nos   4. les   5. le   6. me   7. les

B. You will hear the following sentences on the tape. During the first pause, restate each one, adding the appropriate indirect object pronoun for the cue given. Repeat the correct answer during the second pause.

MODELO: Puse la toalla para él. → Le puse la toalla.

1. para ellos   2. a Héctor   3. a nosotros   4. a Alicia   5. a mí

Comunicación

A. *Gestos del mundo hispánico.* You will hear the **Texto** from page 169 of your textbook. First, listen carefully and try to follow the gist of the ideas. Then you will hear the **Texto** again, followed by incomplete statements based on it. You will hear each statement twice. Circle the letter of the phrase below that best completes each one.

1. a. haciendo gestos con la cara, la cabeza y las manos.

   b. con toallas y jabón.

   c. vistiéndonos elegantemente.

2. a. la mano en la boca.

   b. dinero en la mano de los amigos.

   c. la palma de la mano hacia arriba antes de mover los dedos.

3. a. levantamos las manos por encima de la cabeza.

   b. levantamos las piernas y bailamos.

   c. nos acostamos.

4. a. bajamos del autobús.

   b. bajamos los brazos y las manos inmediatamente.

   c. subimos al Café París.

5. a. abrimos la boca y gritamos.

   b. nos sentamos.

   c. levantamos el dedo índice y el pulgar casi juntos.

B. *El extraterrestre*. You will hear a series of statements based on the drawing. You will hear each statement twice. Circle C if the statement is true (**cierto**) or F if the statement is false (**falso**).

1. C / F   3. C / F   5. C / F

2. C / F   4. C / F   6. C / F

C. *Dictado*. You will hear a short paragraph about **el extraterrestre**. During the first pause, write each sentence in the space provided. During the second pause, check what you wrote.

_____

_____

_____

_____

_____

D. *Sólo tú*. You will hear a series of questions about yourself. You will hear each question twice. Answer in complete Spanish sentences. No answers will be given on the tape.

1. ...   2. ...   3. ...   4. ...   5. ...

LECCIÓN NUEVE
WORKBOOK

Gráficos

A. *Recuerdos de mi niñez* (childhood). Complete the following composition about Mateo's childhood by writing in the names of the articles numbered in the drawing, along with the appropriate definite or indefinite article where needed.

De niño, yo vivía con mis padres y mi hermana en La Habana, la capital de Cuba. Yo

adoraba ___*la playa*___ (1). En Navidad íbamos de excursión a

Guanabo, en ___*el campo*___ (2) norte de la isla. Nosotros no éramos

fanáticos de ___*las montañas*___ (3) o de ___*la nieve*___ (4);

el único esquí que había era esquí acuático.

Esa Navidad mis padres no querían ir a Guanabo y fuimos a Yucatán, México, a

ver _____ (5) de los mayas. Hicimos un viaje especial a

Chichén Itzá, uno de los grandes centros culturales de los mayas.

Lo que más me gustaba era _____ (6) del Adivino (*Wizard*) y _____ (7) de Cuculcán. Dos veces al año, al brillar (*to shine*) el sol sobre los escalones (*steps*) de la pirámide, la gente veía la sombra (*shadow*) de una enorme _____ (8).

B. *Dos hermanos recuerdan.* Study the drawing again, read the following dialogue between Mateo and his sister, and answer the questions that follow.

Isabel: ¿No recuerdas que yo no quería hacer ese viaje con ustedes a Yucatán?
Mateo: No estoy de acuerdo. Éramos Mamá y yo los que no queríamos hacer ese viaje.
Isabel: Estás loco, Matito. Tú insistías (*insisted*) con Papá en que querías ir.
Mateo: No, Isabel. Mamá y yo no veíamos cómo íbamos a pasar dos semanas en ese calor de Yucatán, pero fue un viaje increíble. Siempre recuerdo esos tristes templos de Chichén Itzá donde sólo vivían los espíritus (*spirits*) de los mayas. No había nadie.
Isabel: Tienes razón. Ahora sí recuerdo que yo era la que más quería ir a Yucatán. También recuerdo que no me sentí muy bien en ese viaje. No me gustaba el calor.
Mateo: Ya ves. ¡Tienes mala memoria!

1. ¿Quién no quería hacer el viaje a Yucatán?

   _____

2. ¿Por qué no quería ir Mateo a Yucatán?

   _____

3. ¿Era Chichén Itzá un centro azteca?

   _____

4. ¿Quién vivía en los templos de Chichén Itzá?

   _____

5. ¿Quién era la persona que más quería ir a Yucatán?

   _____

6. ¿Por qué se sintió mal Isabel en ese viaje a Yucatán?

   _____

Gramática esencial

39.– 41. The Imperfect Tense

A. Change the meaning of the following sentences by changing the verb to the imperfect tense.

1. Viajo mucho a Yucatán.

   _____

2. No creemos los cuentos (*stories*) de los mayas.

   _____

3. ¿Vas a Uxmal?

   _____

4. Soñamos con ir a Mérida un día.

   _____

5. Ponen una película sobre (*about*) las playas del Caribe.

   _____

6. Mateo describe los templos y las pirámides.

   _____

7. Les gusta Chichén Itzá.

   _____

8. Paso los días visitando las ruinas.

   _____

9. Charlamos del Templo de Tulúm.

   _____

10. Almuerzas camarones de la costa, ¿no?

    _____

B. *Punto de vista.* Complete the following paragraph with the appropriate imperfect form of the verb in parentheses.

En mi familia (haber) _____(1) cinco personas: papá, mamá, mi

hermana Cristina, la tía Ana Loli y yo. Ana Loli (ser) _____(2)

aeromoza (*flight attendant*). Ella (ir) _____(3) a muchos países

del mundo. Una vez el avión (ir) _____(4) lleno (*full*) de

pollos. Los pollos (ir) _____ (5) en jaulas (*cages*)

pero varios de ellos salieron de las jaulas y Ana Loli los puso en el baño del avión

porque con las plumas ella no (poder) _____(6) (ver) nada.

Otras veces ella me llevaba a México. Cuando (ir) _____(7) en

el avión (ver) _____(8) muchas zonas arqueológicas. Cuando

yo le preguntaba si ella (preferir) _____(9) las ruinas de los

mayas o de los aztecas, me (contestar) _____(10) que para ella

todas (ser)_____(11) iguales (*the same*). —Una ruina es una

ruina, (decir) _____(12) ella. Ella no (ver)

_____(13) la diferencia entre una ruina y la otra. ¡En mi

opinión (haber) _____(14) mucha diferencia entre ellas!

42. Preterite and Imperfect Tenses Contrasted

A. Express in Spanish, using the preterite or the imperfect tense as needed.

1. We used to travel to Bariloche every winter.

   _____

2. My parents and I would ski, but Lili would read books about archeology.

   _____

3. One night Lili thought we were angry with her.

   _____

4. She got up and left crying.

   _____

5. I knew that she liked hot chocolate (**chocolate caliente**).

_____

6. I brought her a big cup of hot chocolate at 10:00.

_____

7. When she fell asleep, I was thinking that she was a sad little girl.

_____

B. Complete the following paragraph by writing the appropriate preterite or imperfect tense of the verb given in parentheses.

El año pasado (*I went*) _____(1) a Guatemala de vacaciones.

En Tikal (*I saw*) _____(2) una enorme pirámide. (*It had*)

_____(3) un gran número de escalones (*steps*). Dos jóvenes

americanos (*were looking at*) _____(4) los escalones. Les (*I*

asked) _____(5) qué (*they were doing*)

_____(6) y me (*they told*) _____(7)

que (*they wanted*) _____(8) subir la pirámide, pero que (*they*

were [*had*]) _____(9) miedo. Les (*I asked*)

_____(10) cuántos años (*they were* [*had*])

_____(11). Cuando me (*they answered*)

_____(12), (*I began*) _____(13) a reír.

Les (*I explained*) _____(14) que (*I was* [*had*])

_____(15) 65 años y que (*I came*)

_____(16) a Tikal todos los años para subir las pirámides.

43. Gustar

Express the following paragraph in Spanish.

I love archeology, and I don't like sports. Those soccer championships don't interest me. They seem so ordinary to me. The thing that delights me is to travel and see the ruins of an ancient civilization (**antigua civilización**). There it seems that I can feel the spirit (**el espíritu**) of the inhabitants. It interests me to learn how (**cómo**) they lived. I love to dream about ancient civilizations!

¡No me gustan los deportes!

_____
_____
_____
_____
_____
_____
_____
_____
_____
_____

Para repasar

Un viaje a Sudamérica. Answer the following questions.

1. ¿Por qué me dijiste que no te gustaba viajar?

_____

2. ¿No estuviste en quince países el año pasado?

_____

3. ¿No tuviste que ir a La Paz también?

_____

4. ¿A qué otras ciudades fuiste?

_____

5. ¿Nos trajiste una alfombra del Perú?

_____

6. ¿Entónces por qué no la pusiste en la sala?

_____

Comunicación

A. *Recuerdos del pasado*. Complete the following sentences according to your own experiences. Give the appropriate preterite or imperfect form of the verbs in parentheses. No answers will be given for any element of these sentences except the verb forms.

1. Me (encantar) _____ el lugar adonde nosotros (ir)

   _____ de vacaciones el año pasado.

2. La primera vez que yo (viajar) _____ solo(a), me (parecer)

   _____ que _____.

3. Yo siempre (soñar) _____ con hacer un viaje

   _____.

4. La última vez que (ir) _____ de viaje, me (hacer falta)

   _____.

5. Cuando (ser) _____ niño(a), me (interesar)

   _____ mucho _____ .

B. *Después del viaje*. Using the cues given and the preterite or imperfect tense of the verb, make statements about the countries you visited last summer. Add any additional words you wish to complete the thought.

   MODELO: México / parecer / ser / país / tener / muchas culturas →
   México me pareció ser un país que tiene muchas culturas.

1. interesar / saber / vivir / gente / Cuba

   _____

2. Brasil / parecer / país / precios / exorbitante

   _____

3. encantar / sangría / España

   _____

4. hacer falta / conocer / habitantes / Nicaragua

   _____

5. no / gustar / noticias / el periódico / Chile

   _____

LECCIÓN NUEVE
LABORATORY MANUAL

Gráficos

A. You will hear a series of infinitive phrases on the tape. For each one, give the **yo** form of the imperfect. Repeat the correct answer during the second pause.

1. ...　　2. ...　　3. ....　　4. ...　　5. ...　　6. ...　　7. ...　　8. ...

B. You will hear a series of statements. You will hear each statement twice. Circle the letter of the word or sentence that you associate most closely with each situation.

1. a. el gol   b. los fanáticos   (c.) la pirámide

2. a. Cuba   (b.) Venezuela   c. el Brasil

3. (a.) Iba al estadio todos los sábados.

  b. Había un templo allí.

  c. Íbamos mucho a la costa.

4. a. Éramos cinco en la familia.

  (b.) No le gustaba la nieve.

  c. Veía la nieve que había en el estadio.

C. You will hear the following paragraph twice. During the first pause, write the missing words. During the second pause, check what you wrote.

A mí no me _____gustaban_____ (1) las montañas. Por eso, en el verano,

_____iba_____ (2) a las playas del Caribe o

_____visitaba_____ (3) a mis tíos que _____vivían_____ (4) en

Yucatán. Allí _____vivía_____ (5) una pirámide que me

_____interessaba_____ (6) mucho. _____Evva_____ (7) la pirámide

del Adivino.

Pronunciación

<u>Spanish **n**</u>

A. Spanish **n** is pronounced as **m** when it is followd by **b, v, f, m,** and **p,** whether it appears within one word or between two words. Listen and repeat.

One Word	Between Words
enfermo	un poco más
conveniente	don Fernando
inmediatamente	en vez de ir
invierno	un momento
inmenso	un perro
conversación	un brazo

B. Repeat these sentences after the speaker.

1. En verano prefiero un buen vaso de sangría.
2. En verdad creo que necesito un pequeño descanso.
3. Estando en Francia decidí residir un mes en París.
4. En momentos como éste esas inversiones no son tan buenas como tú crees.
5. Recibí una carta en verso de un viejo amigo que vive en Filadelfia.
6. Está algo enfermo y por eso se siente un poco infeliz y triste.

Gramática esencial

39.– 41. The Imperfect Tense

A. You will hear an infinitive and a pronoun. During the first pause, use the imperfect form of the verb to form a phrase. Follow the model. Repeat the correct answer during the second pause.

MODELO: viajar / yo → yo viajaba

1. ...   2. ...   3. ....   4. ...   5. ...   6. ...   7. ...   8. ...

B. You will hear a model sentence. Substitute the cue words that are given in the manual and say the entire sentence, making the necessary changes. Repeat the correct answer during the second pause.

MODELO: Yo charlaba con Nora y tú saludabas a Tito. (Elena / los niños) →
          Elena charlaba con Nora y los niños saludaban a Tito.

1. Alberto / nosotras
2. nosotros / la tía Luci
3. yo / Juanito
4. tú / ellas
5. ustedes / ellos

C. You will hear a series of sentences. For each one, change the verb to the imperfect and say the entire sentence. Repeat the correct answer during the second pause.

MODELO: Soy romántico. → Era romántico.

1. ...   2. ...   3. ....   4. ...   5. ...   6. ...   7. ...   8. ...

42. Preterite and Imperfect Tenses Contrasted

A. You will hear a series of sentences. During the first pause, change the verb from the preterite to the imperfect. During the second pause, repeat the correct answer.

1. ...   2. ...   3. ....   4. ...   5. ...

Now change the verb from the imperfect to the preterite. Repeat the correct answer during the second pause.

6. ...   7. ...   8. ....   9. ...   10. ...

B. First complete the following paragraph by circling the appropriate preterite or imperfect form of the verbs in parentheses. Then listen to the tape and check your answers.

Ayer, cuando (fui/iba) a las ruinas, (busqué/buscaba) la pirámide del Adivino, pero no la (encontré/encontraba). ¿Qué (fui/iba) a hacer? (Supe/Sabía) que la pirámide (estuvo/estaba) allí, pero no (supe/sabía) el lugar exacto. Le (pregunté/preguntaba) a uno de los habitantes si no (tuvo/tenía) un mapa. Él me (miró/miraba) y me (dijo/decía) que sí. Me (llevó/llevaba) con él por una avenida entre las ruinas. (Caminamos/Caminábamos) un rato y (entramos/entrábamos) en una gran tienda con un millón de cosas—ropa, comida, muebles. ¡No (pude/podía) creerlo! Y allí me (vendió/vendía) un mapa a un precio exorbitante.

43. Gustar

A. You will hear a series of sentences. During the first pause, substitute the cue you hear for the verb in the sentence. Follow the model. Repeat the correct answer during the second pause.

MODELO: Me gusta la arqueología. (interesa) → Me interesa la arqueología.

1. ...   2. ...   3. ....   4. ...   5. ...

B. You will hear a series of questions containing **gustar** and similar verbs. During the first pause, answer the question negatively. Repeat the correct answer during the second pause.

1. ...   2. ...   3. ....   4. ...   5. ...   6. ...

Comunicación

A. *Dos leyendas y dos nombres*. You will hear the **Texto** from page 188 of your textbook. First, listen carefully and try to follow the gist of the ideas. Then you will hear the **Texto** again, followed by some incomplete statements based on it. You will hear each statement twice. Circle the letter of the phrase below that best completes each statement.

1. a. hablaban de una tribu donde sólo había mujeres.

   b. hablaban francés.

   c. hablaban sólo en un templo.

2. a. la madre iba a la playa.

   b. la madre la criaba.

   c. la niña la llevaban a la Florida.

3. a. no sabían qué otro nombre darle.

   b. no había mujeres.

   c. recordaron a las amazonas de la mitología griega.

4. a. la gente llevaba bikinis.

   b. la fuente estaba en la isla de Biminí.

   c. en Biminí había un mapa.

5. a. él ya era un poco viejo.

   b. él tenía sólo quince años.

   c. encontró a dos amazonas en el barco.

B. *¿Un accidente?* You will hear a news report about a plane. You will hear the report twice, followed by some questions. During the first pause, answer the question. Repeat the correct answer during the second pause.

1. ...   2. ...   3. ....   4. ...

C. *Sólo tu*. You will hear a series of statements about yourself. Circle C if the statement is true (**Cierto**) or F if the statement is false (**Falso**).

1. C   F   3. C   F   5. C   F   7. C   F

2. C   F   4. C   F   6. C   F

LECCIÓN DIEZ
WORKBOOK

Gráficos

A. *La lección de manejar*. Complete the following talk by a driving instructor by writing in the names of the articles numbered in the drawing, along with the appropriate definite article where needed.

Antes de salir por _____(1) es importante para el buen

_____(2) hacerse varias preguntas sobre su coche. ¿He

examinado el _____(3), _____(4) y

_____(5)? ¿He visto si _____(6) y

_____(7) están en buenas condiciones? ¿Están limpios o sucios

_____(8)? ¿He ajustado (*adjusted*)

_____(9) y _____(10) para estar

cómodo? Si usted desea manejar, ¿ha comprendido que es importante manejar con cuidado? No es solamente una cuestión de encender el coche con

_____(11), salir de prisa, parar y saber aparcar. La verdad es

que manejar es una responsabilidad pública y por eso se encuentran ustedes hoy aquí en

esta clase.

B. *Un estudiante perdido* (lost). Study the drawing again, read the following dialogue, and
answer the questions that follow.

Martín y el señor Quevedo hablan por teléfono.

Martín: He venido de la colonia Rosas y estoy en frente de la gasolinera en la
esquina de la calle Gloria.
Sr. Quevedo: Mire, Martín. Le he dicho que doble a la derecha en la segunda glorieta
después del cine Pedral. ¿Lo ha hecho?
Martín: La verdad es que no recuerdo si doblé a la derecha o a la izquierda.
Sr. Quevedo: ¿Pasó por el Banco de la Industria y el supermercado Oriente?
Martín: Sí, ésos sí los he visto.
Sr. Quevedo: Muy bien. Entonces, si ahora está en el garaje en la esquina de la calle
Gloria, tome la avenida Insurgentes todo derecho hasta el bulevar Cinco
de julio. Allí, doble a la izquierda. Entonces cruce el parque y en el
primer semáforo después del parque doble a la derecha. A una cuadra
(*block*) de esa señal nos encuentra.
Martín: Perfecto. Lo veo a las cinco.
Sr. Quevedo: ¿A las cinco? ¿Pero si sólo son las tres?
Martín: Bueno, señor Quevedo, es que he venido caminando. ¡Ayer salí a
manejar y me pusieron dos multas!

1. ¿De dónde ha venido Martín?

_____

2. ¿De dónde llamó Martín?

_____

3. Después del cine Pedral, ¿dónde tiene que doblar Martín?

_____

4. ¿Ha visto Martín el banco y el supermercado?

_____

5. ¿Qué tiene que hacer Martín en el primer semáforo después del parque?

_____

6. ¿Ha comprendido Martín las direcciones del señor Quevedo?

_____

7. ¿Por qué no viene en coche Martín?

_____

Gramática esencial

44.– 45. The Perfect Tenses and Irregular Past Participles

A. Use the correct form of the present perfect tense of the verb in parentheses to form a complete sentence.

MODELO: (salir) Martín / del parque → Martín ha salido del parque.

1. (examinar) ¿usted / las llantas?

    ¿Ha usted examinado las llantas?

2. (no entender) María Luisa / las direcciones

    María Luisa no ha entendido las direccionnes

3. (recibir) ¿tú / una multa?

    ¿Tú has recibido una multa?

4. (salir) ¿de dónde? / tantos peatones

    ¿De dónde han tantos peatones salido?

5. (traer) ustedes / la camioneta

    Ustedes han traido la camioneta

6. (no chocar) tú y yo / con la señal

    Hemos no chocado con la señal.

7. (dejar) ¿por qué? / vosotros / el carro / en la autopista

    Porqué vosotros habéis dejado el carro en la autopista

B. Restate the following sentences by changing the verb to its pluperfect form.

MODELO: No vi la acera. → No había visto la acera.

1. El otro chófer no puso los frenos.

   El otro chófer no había puesto los frenos

2. Nosotros no le dijimos nada al policía.

   Nosotros no le habíamos dicho nada al policía

3. Murieron tres peatones en el accidente.

   Habían muerto tres peatones en el accidente.

4. Tú no abriste la lata de gasolina.

   Tú no habías abierto la lata de gasolina.

5. Tú y Magali volvisteis por la carretera del norte ese día.

   Ustedes habían vuelto por la carretera del norte ese día.

6. Laura hizo un viaje en la camioneta por la mañana.

   Laura había hecho un viaje en la camioneta por la mañana

7. Ellas me escribieron una carta con las direcciones.

   Ellas me había escrito una carta con las direcciones

C. Express in Spanish.

1. He had prepared the sign.

   El había preparado el letrero.

2. She hadn't seen the accident.

   Ella no había visto el choque

3. They had put a traffic light in the corner .

   Ellos habían puesto una semáforo en la esquina.

4. The bus driver had drunk too much wine.

   El chófer había tomado demasiado vino.

5. Fifteen persons had died on the highway.

   Quince personas habían muerto en la carretera.

46.– 47. Two Object Pronouns and **se** with Direct Object Pronouns

A. Replace the direct object noun with a pronoun in each sentence.

MODELO: Ella me compra la camioneta a mí.→ Ella me la compra.

1. Él le puso el aceite al carro.

   El se lo puso.

2. Tú nos compraste los faros a nosotros.

   Tú se nos compraste

3. Pablo y Maritsa me trajeron el letrero a mí.

   Pablo y Maritsa me lo trajeron.

4. Ellas no te dieron las llaves.

   Ellas no te las dieron.

5. Por favor, enséñenos las ruedas.

   Por favor, nos las enseñen

6. El peatón me puede explicar las direcciones.

   El peatón me las puede explicar.

B. Replace the direct object noun with a pronoun in each sentence.

MODELO: Le di las llaves a Felipe. → Se las di.

1. Felipe les trajo la camioneta a los tíos.

   Filipe se la trajo

2. Ellos la vendieron a una sobrina.

   Ellos se la vendieron.

3. ¿No le compraste tú unas llantas nuevas a tu prima?

   ¿No se las compraste tu a tu prima?

4. No, les di unas llantas nuevas a mis primos.

   no, se las di a mis primos.

5. Pero nosotros no quisimos aceptar las llantas.

    Pero nosotros no las quisimos aceptar.

6. Entonces, yo le compro unas llantas a Elena.

    Entonces yo se las compro.

C. Complete each sentence in Spanish and rewrite it using the words given in parentheses.

1. El policía desea *(give it [f.] to us)*.

    El policía desea una multa. Él nos la desea.

2. El conductor no quería *(sell it [m.] to him)*.

    El conductor no quería vender el motor
    Él no se lo quería vender

3. Por cierto, Elena dijo: *(I'll buy it [f.] from you)*.

    Por cierto, Elena dijo: Voy a comprar la goma de tú.
    Voy a comprártela

4. El policía dijo: *(I can't bring it [m.] to you)*.

    El policía dijo: No puedo traer el camión a usted.
    No puedo traérselo

5. Por favor, *(Don't explain it [m.] to me)*.

    Por favor, no me lo expliques

Para repasar

A. Replace the object nouns in the following sentences with the correct direct or indirect object pronoun.

1. Yo había visto al policía en el bulevar.

    Yo lo había visto en el bulevar

2. Pero no vi la señal.

    Pero no la vi.

3. Cruzamos la avenida con cuidado.

    Cruzamos la con cuidado

4. Tuvimos que comprar un carro nuevo.

    Tuvimos que lo comprar

5. Claro que venden esos coches a precio rebajado.

Claro que los venden a precio rebajado

B. Express in Spanish.

1. Please don't invite me. I don't have the car that day. We lent it to Luis.

Por favor no me invites. No tango el coche esa dia.

nosotros lo prestamos a Luis.

2. She told me that they didn't turn left. The truth is that they didn't read the road signs carefully.

Ella me dijo que no volveron a la izquierda.

La verdad es no leieron las senales con cuidado

3. Perhaps they didn't explain the truth to me and didn't tell it to her.

Puedo ser no me explicieron la verdad y no

se la dijieron

Comunicación

A. *¿Has visto el mapa?* Study the map on page 156 and answer the questions.

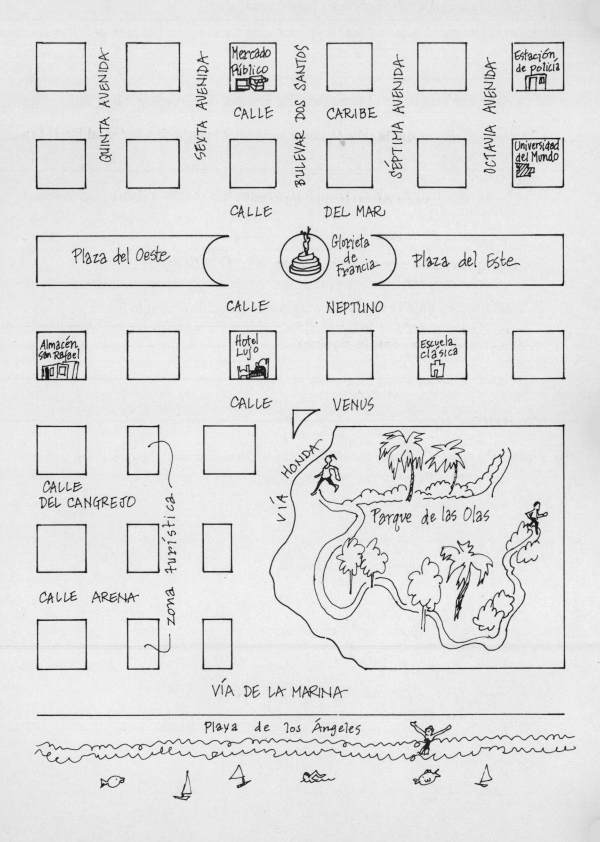

QUINTA AVENIDA

SEXTA AVENIDA

Mercado Público

CALLE

BULEVAR DOS SANTOS

CARIBE

SÉPTIMA AVENIDA

OCTAVIA AVENIDA

Estación de policía

Universidad del Mundo

CALLE   DEL MAR

Plaza del Oeste   Glorieta de Francia   Plaza del Este

CALLE   NEPTUNO

Almacén San Rafael

Hotel Lujo

Escuela clásica

CALLE   VENUS

VÍA HONDA

Parque de las Olas

CALLE DEL CANGREJO

zona turística

CALLE ARENA

VÍA DE LA MARINA

Playa de los Ángeles

1. Si soy un peatón y he venido del mercado público a la estación de policía, ¿cuántas calles he cruzado?

   _____

2. ¿Qué calles he cruzado si he venido caminando del Hotel Lujo a la playa?

   _____

3. ¿He tenido que cruzar la calle Venus para ir del Almacén San Rafael al Hotel Lujo?

   _____

4. ¿Entre qué calles han puesto la zona turística?

   _____

5. ¿Entre qué vías he encontrado el Parque de las Olas (*Waves*)?

   _____

6. Si usted ha manejado de la Universidad del Mundo al Hotel Lujo por la Octava Avenida, ¿dónde y cómo ha doblado?

   _____

B. Form questions that could be answered by the following statements.

1. Ese año habíamos ido al Brasil.

   _____

2. No había estado en Manaus antes.

   _____

3. El mapa y los boletos se los di a Felipe.

   _____

4. Ellos habían dejado las llaves en el hotel.

   _____

5. Sí, Ana María ya le había escrito la carta de Río.

   _____

6. No hemos visto São Paulo todavía.

   _____

C. *Sólo tú*. You have been out on an excursion touring a town. Use the following verbs and their perfect forms to express what you have done or events that have happened to you.

1. manejar

   _____

2. cruzar

   _____

3. ver

   _____

4. dirigirse a

   _____

5. explicar

   _____

6. decir

   _____

7. volver

   _____

LECCIÓN DIEZ
LABORATORY MANUAL

Gráficos

A. You will hear a set of phrases with infinitives. Say each one, changing the infinitive to the first person singular form of the present perfect tense. Repeat the correct answer during the second pause.

1. ...   2. ...   3. ....   4. ...   5. ...   6. ...   7. ...   8. ...

B. You will hear a series of statements or questions twice. Circle the letter of the best response to each.

1. a. He visto el Bulevar Olímpico.

   b. ¿Ha apagado los faros?

2. a. El peatón ha cruzado la calle.

   b. Ud. ha hecho un viaje largo.

3. a. No he tenido tiempo de verlo.

   b. He examinado las llantas con cuidado.

4. a. Sí, he dicho que tiene que aparcar en la otra esquina.

   b. No, no he comprendido las instrucciones.

C. You will hear a series of sentences. You will hear each one twice. Circle the letter of the word or phrase most closely associated with each sentence.

1. a. las llantas   b. el volante   c. los faros

2. a. el cine   b. el choque   c. el bulevar

3. a. el cine   b. la glorieta   c. la carretera

4. a. Ha parado.   b. Ha doblado.   c. Ha chocado.

Pronunciación

<u>Spanish **h**</u>

Spanish **h** is always silent. Remember that the combination **ch** is considered a separate letter in the Spanish alphabet: **a, b, c, ch, d.** Repeat these sentences after the speaker.

1. ¿Cuantos habitantes hay allí ahora?
2. Ese hombre es un hipócrita sin honor.
3. Esa historia habla de Holanda.
4. Hay hambre ahora en la hacienda.
5. Hoy hablaré con Hortensia Hernández.

Gramática esencial

44.– 45. The Perfect Tenses and Irregular Past Participles

A. You will hear a series of phrases. During the first pause, repeat the phrase with the present perfect form of each verb, according to the subject pronoun. During the second pause, repeat the correct answer.

MODELO: doblar a la derecha / yo → Yo he doblado a la derecha.

1. ...   2. ...   3. ....   4. ...   5. ...   6. ...   7. ...   8. ...   9. ...   10. ...

B. First repeat the model sentence, then substitute the cue words that are given on the tape and repeat the entire sentence. Follow the model. Repeat the correct answer during the second pause.

MODELO: Yo he manejado a la gasolinera. (él) →
Él ha manejado a la gasolinera.

1. ...   2. ...   3. ....

Repeat the same steps with this model sentence.

MODELO: Nosotros hemos salido sin gasolina. (yo) → Yo he salido sin gasolina.

4. ...   5. ...   6. ...

Repeat the same steps with this model sentence.

MODELO: Elena no ha perdido la llave. (ustedes) → Ustedes no han perdido la llave.

7. ...   8. ...   9. ...

C. First repeat the model sentence with the pluperfect verb, then substitute the subject given on the tape and conjugate the verb accordingly. Repeat the correct answer during the second pause.

MODELO: Yo había preparado el letrero. (él) → Él había preparado el letrero.

1. ...   2. ...   3. ....

Repeat the same steps with this model sentence.

MODELO: Yo no había pedido más gasolina. (tú) → Tú no habías pedido más

gasolina.

4. ...   5. ...   6. ...

Repeat the same steps with this model sentence.

MODELO: ¿Habías bebido tú antes de manejar? (yo) →
          ¿Había bebido yo antes de manejar?

7. ...   8. ...   9. ...

D. You will hear a series of sentences in the present perfect tense. Restate them using the pluperfect form of the verb. Repeat the correct answer during the second pause.

MODELO: Yo he abierto la puerta del camión. →
          Yo había abierto la puerta del camión.

1. ...   2. ...   3. ....   4. ...   5. ...   6. ...

46. Two Object Pronouns and **se** with Direct Object Pronouns

A. You will hear a series of sentences. During the first pause, replace the direct object noun with the corresponding object pronoun. Repeat the correct answer during the second pause.

MODELO: Elena me aparcó el coche. › Elena me lo aparcó.

1. ...   2. ...   3. ....   4. ...   5. ...

B. You will hear a series of affirmative commands. During the first pause, make them negative, placing the object pronoun before the verb. During the second pause, repeat the correct answer.

MODELO: Démelo. → No me lo dé.

1. ...   2. ...   3. ....   4. ...   5. ...

C. You will hear a series of sentences. During the first pause, substitute direct and indirect object pronouns for their corresponding nouns. Remember to substitute **se** for the indirect object pronoun **le**. During the second pause, repeat the correct answer.

MODELO: Le doy el mapa al chófer. → Se lo doy.

1. ...   2. ...   3. ....   4. ...   5. ...

Comunicación

A. *Una señorita policía inspecciona coches*. You will hear the **Texto** from page 209 of your textbook. Listen carefully and try to follow the gist of the ideas. Then you will hear the **Texto** again, followed by some incomplete statements based on it. You will hear each statement twice. Circle the letter of the word or phrase that best completes each statement.

1. a. apague los faros primero.

   b. déme veinte pesos y no le pongo una multa.

   c. aparque aquí, fuera de la carretera.

2. a. hacia la autopista.

   b. hacia la derecha y hacia la izquierda.

   c. para doblar a la derecha.

3. a. las llaves del coche.

   b. flores para la señorita policía.

   c. el carnet de manejar.

4. a. el joven no sabe manejar.

   b. debe invitarlo al cine.

   c. debe ponerle una multa al joven.

B. *Para llegar a la playa*. A short account of Alberto's walk through town based on the map will be read twice, followed by five questions. As you listen to the story, mark down Alberto's route on the map. Then you will hear some questions based on the story. You will hear each question twice. During the first pause, answer the question. During the second pause, repeat the correct answer.

1. ...   2. ...   3. ....   4. ...   5. ...

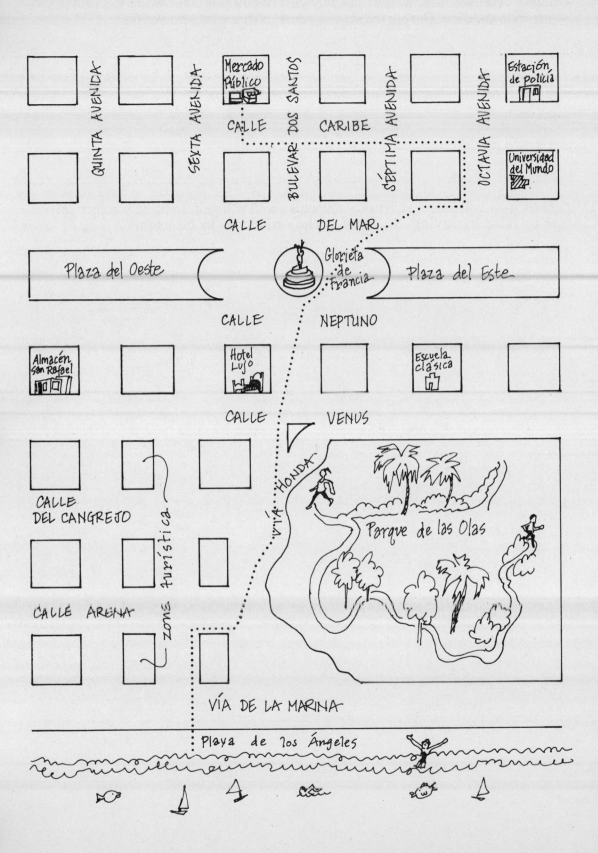

C. *Dictado*. You will hear a short story by **la señorita policía**. During the first pause, write each sentence. During the second pause, check what you wrote.

_____

_____

_____

_____

_____

D. *Sólo tú*. You will hear a series of statements about yourself. Indicate whether each is true or false by saying, **Sí, lo he hecho** or **No, no lo he hecho.**

1. ...   2. ...   3. ....   4. ...   5. ...

LECCIÓN ONCE
WORKBOOK

Gráficos

A. *Un viaje famoso.* Complete the following account of the departure of Christopher Columbus (**Cristóbal Colón**) to find a new route to the Indies. Write the names of the articles numbered in the drawing, along with the appropriate definite or indefinite article where needed.

_____(1) celebra el famoso viaje de Colón. Están reunidos

(*gathered*) _____(2) Isabel, las autoridades—con el alcalde y el

gobernador—y Colón y sus hombres. Hay _____(3) y

soldados (*soldiers*) montados a _____(4). El pueblo viste su

_____(5) y lleva _____(6). Algunos

llevan _____(7). Todos desean que Colón pueda encontrar una

nueva ruta a la India. Quieren que su país entre en una nueva época (*era*) de gran riqueza (*riches*). Claro que no saben que Colón va a encontrar un nuevo mundo.

B. *¿Una conversación histórica?* Study the drawing again, read the dialogue, and complete the statements that follow according to the dialogue.

Reina Isabel: Me sorprende que sigas buscando la ruta a la India.
Colón: Sigo buscándola porque quiero que España entre en una nueva época de riqueza.
Reina Isabel: Me alegro de que puedas viajar con tres carabelas (*caravels*)—la Niña, la Pinta y la Santa María—y no sólo una.
Colón: Sí, es mejor, pero me molesta que su Majestad venda (*sell*) sus joyas (*jewels*) para pagar esta expedición.
Reina Isabel: Es el deber (*duty*) de una reina. ¿No desean los españoles tener el país más fuerte de Europa? Sin riqueza, no es posible.
Colón: Quiero que su Majestad celebre este viaje con el pueblo de España. Hay un nuevo mundo más allá del horizonte y yo lo voy a encontrar. ¡Isabel y España son una en su gloria!

1. Colón busca

   _____.

2. Colón quiere que España

   _____.

3. Isabel se alegra de que

   _____.

4. A Colón le molesta que

   _____.

5. Colón quiere que Isabel

   _____.

Gramática esencial

48. Indirect Commands

Use the following statements to create indirect commands.

MODELO: Ella quiere comer pastel y ellos quieren comer helado. →
Pues que coma ella pastel y que coman ellos helado.

1. Antonio quiere saludar al locutor.

   _____.

2. Ellas no quieren conocer al gobernador.

_____.

3. Él no desea llegar al desfile hasta la una.

_____.

4. Las autoridades no quieren mirar el desfile.

_____.

5. Lucinda desea invitar a Mario a la fiesta de cumpleaños.

_____.

6. Pero ella no quiere poner tantas velas en el pastel.

_____.

49.– 51. Subjunctive Mood

A. Complete the following sentences with the correct indicative and subjunctive forms of the verbs in parentheses.

1. (desear, hablar) Yo _____ que tú

_____ con el alcalde de la ciudad.

2. (querer, comer) Mis padres _____ que nosotros

_____ la comida cubana.

3. (desear, vivir) Elena _____ que yo

_____ en Miami.

4. (querer, invitar) ¿No _____ usted que lo

_____ al desfile?

5. (desear, traer) Él _____ que ellas no

_____ la carroza.

6. (querer, conocer) A propósito, yo _____ que ustedes

_____ las tradiciones hispánicas.

B. Complete the following sentences with the correct present subjunctive forms of the verbs in parentheses.

1. Quiero que ustedes (buscar) _____ los trajes, pero no

   quiero que el desfile (comenzar) _____ sin nosotros.

2. Deseamos que tú (llegar) _____ un poco temprano y que

   (dirigir) _____ la primera carroza.

3. Sin embargo, no queremos que ustedes (pensar) _____ que

   se pueden ir después del desfile. Queremos que (volver)

   _____ para comer una cena típica.

4. A propósito, ¿tú quieres que yo (pedir) _____ una mesa en

   el restaurante Versailles? Me alegro de que tú (almorzar)

   _____ con nosotros hoy.

5. Y no quiero que ustedes se (dormir) _____ en la mesa. ¡Yo

   sé a qué hora se acostaron anoche después de la fiesta!

52. Subjunctive with Verbs of Volition (Will)

A. Use the subject noun or pronoun and the verb in parentheses to create a new sentence that contains the subjunctive.

MODELO: Vienes al desfile. (yo / querer) → Quiero que vengas al desfile.

1. Ellos sólo hablan en español. (yo / desear)

   _____

2. Compramos carne aquí. (usted / preferir)

   _____

3. Tú y yo conversamos en inglés. (ella / manda / no)

   _____

4. Alejandro fuma en el café. (ellos / no permitir)

   _____

5. Entro en la heladería con Ana. (Papá / no dejar)

_____

6. No tomes más sangría. (yo / recomendar)

_____

7. ¿Habláis con el locutor? (ella / aconsejar)

_____

8. Describimos el desfile. (ellos / pedir)

_____

B. Form sentences using these words in the order given. Add any other words that may be necessary. Remember that **que** should be the first word of each dependent clause.

1. nosotros / querer / la reina / venir / al desfile

_____

2. el pueblo / pedir / la banda / tocar más música

_____

3. la reina / desear / el pueblo / ya no / celebrar / su cumpleaños

_____

4. las autoridades / aconsejar / el alcalde / no / gastar / el dinero / así

_____

5. los refugiados / preferir / todos / vivir / en una cultura bilingüe

_____

6. sin embargo / el gobernador / mandar / todo el mundo / hablar / un solo idioma

_____

53. Subjunctive with Verbs of Emotion

Complete the following sentences with the appropriate form of the verb given in parentheses.

1. (traer) Me alegro de que tú me _____ mantecado.

2. (gustar) Esperamos que a ustedes les _____ el helado de mango.

3. (tener) Temo que ellas ya no _____ helado de piña.

4. (molestar) Ella siente que a ti te _____ el humo (*smoke*).

5. (permitir/fumar) Nos molesta que ustedes _____ que los clientes _____ en la heladería.

6. (servir) Me gusta mucho que él _____ un pastel de guayaba (*guava*).

7. (conocer) Sentimos que ustedes no _____ las tradiciones hispánicas.

Para repasar

Express in Spanish.

1. The cake? I had given it to her.

   _____

2. But she had promised it (the cake) to Julia and her brother.

   _____

3. We had explained it to them.   We had made the cake for the party.

   _____

4. They had not understood that.

   _____

5. But I've already brought the candles for him.

   _____

6. I went back to the bakery, but they had already closed it.

   _____

7. Fortunately (**Por suerte**), Ramón had brought a lot of *mantecado*.

   _____

Comunicación

A. *Un candidato político.* As a Hispanic candidate for political office, you are giving a speech before a group of supporters. Complete the speech with the correct indicative or subjunctive forms of the verbs in parentheses.

Me alegro de que todos ustedes (sentir) _____(1) la

importancia de una cultura bilingüe y multicultural. Me molesta que nosotros los

hispanos (tener) _____(2) que dejar la cultura y el idioma que

tanto han contribuido a la creación de este gran país. Pero primero, quiero que ustedes

(comprender) _____(3) que es una situación compleja. Como

somos tantos y de tantos países diferentes, pido que ustedes me (aconsejar)

_____(4). Por mi parte, no temo que las altas autoridades de

este país se (sorprender) _____(5) de que nosotros les (pedir)

_____(6) la ayuda económica y los derechos (*rights*) que son

parte de nuestra herencia. Sin embargo, pido que ustedes me (permitir)

_____(7) el tiempo necesario para hacer estos cambios

(*changes*). Espero que nosotros (poder) _____(8) crear (*create*)

un nuevo mundo.

B. *Mandatos políticos.* During your political campaign, you are constantly asked for advice and help from different groups or persons. Write five indirect commands for the following persons using the verbs in parentheses.

MODELO: el presidente / abrir → ¡Que el presidente abra los ojos!

1. el alcalde / gastar

   _____

2. el pueblo / pedir

   _____

3. el gobernador / mandar

   _____

4. todos / aprender

   _____

5. las escuelas / enseñar

_____

C. *Sólo tú*. Use the following verbs to express your feelings about your friends, family, city, or country.

1. gustar

_____

2. alegrarse de

_____

3. esperar

_____

4. molestar

_____

5. temer

_____

6. sorprender

_____

LECCIÓN ONCE
LABORATORY MANUAL

Gráficos

A. You will hear a series of sentences using the present subjunctive. First repeat the sentence. Then after you hear the cue, create a new sentence with that cue. Repeat the complete sentence after you hear it.

1. ...   2. ...   3. ...   4. ...   5. ...   6. ...

B. You will hear a series of statements twice. Circle the letter of the best response to each.

1. a. Le sorprende que no sigamos esas tradiciones.

   b. Desean que celebres la fiesta con ellos.

2. a. ¿Te molesta que yo llegue tan temprano?

   b. ¿Quieres que conozca a tus primos?

3. a. Quiero que aprendas español.

   b. Me alegro de que puedas venir.

Pronunciación

Stress in Word Pairs

Circle the letter of the word that is the same as the one you hear. Each word will be repeated twice.

1. a. practiqué   b. practique   5. a. continué   b. continúe
2. a. me casé   b. me case   6. a. está   b. ésta
3. a. busqué   b. busque   7. a. habló   b. hablo
4. a. llegué   b. llegue   8. a. viajó   b. viajo

Gramática esencial

48. Indirect Commands

You will hear a series of sentences. During the first pause, repeat the sentence, then change it to an indirect command. During the second pause, repeat the correct answer.

MODELO: Ella quiere invitar a Ana. → Pues, que invite a Ana.

1. ...   2. ...   3. ...   4. ...   5. ...   6. ...   7. ...

49.– 51. Subjunctive Mood

A. You will hear a series of short sentences. During the first pause, add the phrase **yo quiero** and change the verb to the present subjunctive to create a new sentence. During the second pause, repeat the correct answer.

MODELO: Aprendes dos idiomas. (yo quiero) →
          Yo quiero que aprendas dos idiomas.

1. Comemos helado.   2. Vive aquí.   3. Dices la verdad.

B. Follow the same steps with this model sentence.

MODELO: Celebran el día. (deseamos) → Deseamos que celebren el día.

1. Trae mantecado.   2. Ya no vienen.   3. Discuten con el alcalde.

C. Follow the same steps with this model sentence.

MODELO: Buscan una carroza. (¿quieres?) → ¿Quieres que busquen una carroza?

1. Llega temprano   2. Vuelven de La Paz.   3. Pido mantecado o piña.

D. You will hear a series of sentences. Respond to each one using the present indicative, as in the model. Repeat the correct answer after the speaker.

MODELO: Quieren que yo dirija el desfile. → Entonces yo dirijo el desfile.

1. ...   2. ...   3. ...   4. ...   5. ...

52. Subjunctive with Verbs of Volition (Will)

A. Combine the cues given to form a sentence in the subjunctive mood. Follow the model. Repeat the correct answer after the speaker.

MODELO: celebrar tu cumpleaños / Deseamos que tú... →
          Deseamos que tú celebres tu cumpleaños.

1. hacer / Quiero que Uds. lo… *hagan*

2. hablar / Preferimos que Ud. no… *hable*

3. gastar demasiado / Mando que ellos no…

4. pedir / No permitimos que tú lo…

5. volver ahora / ¿No dejas que ella… ?

6. comer eso / Aconsejan que él no…

B. First you will hear a statement of volition, and then you will hear a pronoun. During the first pause, use the pronoun as the subject of a dependent clause to form a new sentence containing the subjunctive. Repeat the correct answer during the second pause.

MODELO: Queremos traerlo. (ellos) → Queremos que ellos lo traigan.

1. …   2. …   3. …   4. …   5. …   6. …

53. Subjunctive with Verbs of Emotion

A. First repeat the model sentence, then substitute the infinitive cue for the verb in the main clause to create a new subjunctive sentence. Repeat the correct answer during the second pause.

MODELO: Me gusta que me traigas pastel. (alegrarse de) →
           Me alegro de que me traigas pastel.

1. …   2. …   3. …   4. …   5. …

B. You will hear a series of sentences and cues. During the first pause, combine them to form a sentence in the subjunctive mood. Follow the model. Repeat the correct answer during the second pause.

MODELO: La reina no trae al alcalde. (yo / esperar) →
           Yo espero que la reina no traiga al alcalde.

1. El alcalde no viene al desfile. (nosotros / alegrarse de)
2. La carroza llega tarde. (ella / sentir)
3. Las autoridades no me conocen. (yo / temer)
4. Allí no venden mantecado. (Paco / molestar)
5. Los refugiados hablan inglés. (nosotros / alegrarse de)

Comunicación

A. *La Virgen de la Guadalupe*. You will hear the **Texto** from page 229 of your textbook. Listen carefully and try to follow the gist of the ideas. Then listen to the **Texto** again, followed by some incomplete statements based on it. You will hear each statement twice. Circle the letter of the phrase that best completes each statement.

1. a. la reina del desfile del Día de la Raza.

   b. la patrona de México.

2. a. que construyan una iglesia en honor de la virgen.

   b. que el obispo dirija un desfile en honor de la virgen.

3. a. que no tengan rosas para ella.

   b. que no hagan lo que ella ha pedido.

4. a. la independencia de Puerto Rico.

   b. la fiesta de la Virgen de Guadalupe.

5. a. que se celebre la fiesta de la Virgen.

   b. que la gente traiga dólares a la Basílica de Guadalupe.

B. *¡Español en ocho semanas!* You and your family have just moved to Buenos Aires, and you're trying to encourage everyone in the family to learn Spanish as soon as possible. Read the advertisement below and listen to the questions on the tape. Listen carefully and circle the letter of the correct answer. For the last two questions, write your own answers.

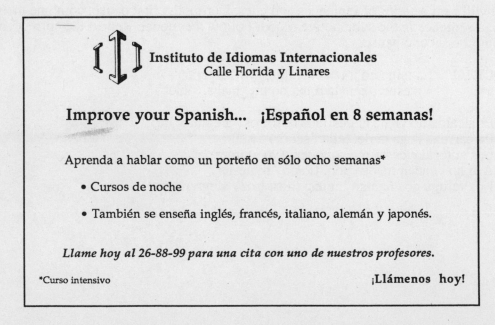

I I Instituto de Idiomas Internacionales
Calle Florida y Linares

Improve your Spanish...   ¡Español en 8 semanas!

Aprenda a hablar como un porteño en sólo ocho semanas*

- Cursos de noche

- También se enseña inglés, francés, italiano, alemán y japonés.

Llame hoy al 26-88-99 para una cita con uno de nuestros profesores.

*Curso intensivo   **¡Llámenos hoy!**

1. (a.) ocho semanas   3. (a.) en las calles Florida y Linares

    b. ocho meses   b. en la avenida Porteña

2. (a.) llame hoy   4. a. compre unos libros de español

    b. escriba una carta   (b.) haga una cita con uno de los profesores

5. _____ *No me aconsejo* _____

6. _____ *Si quiero que* _____ *P 278*

C. *Dictado.* You will hear a short paragraph about Hispanics in the United States. During the first pause, write each sentence. During the second pause, check what you wrote.

_____ *Muchas personas sientan que todos* _____ *solos equales*

_____ *En realaedad hay un* ^grande *cultaras hispanicas* ____

_____ *Alos hispos molesta* _____ *piensas asi*

_____

_____

D. *Sólo tú.* You will hear a series of statements about people you know. Use the verbs below to create a sentence in the subjunctive mood that expresses how you feel about each statement.

MODELO: Mi familia habla dos idiomas. →
                 Me gusta que mi familia hable dos idiomas.

1. sorprender   3. sentir   5. esperar

2. alegrarse de   4. molestar

LECCIÓN DOCE
WORKBOOK

Gráficos

A. *Una pequeña crisis.* Study the drawing and the dialogue and answer the questions that follow.

La madre:	Miguelito, quiero que seas un niño bueno.
La doctora:	No creo que tenga nada serio, señora. Quiero que le dé unas píldoras en caso de infección.
El doctor (a la doctora):	Es probable que no haya penicilina aquí. ¿Quiere usted que vaya al otro consultorio?
El enfermero:	Es necesario que estés quieto, Miguelito. (A la mamá) Señora, quiero que sepa que esto les pasa a muchos niños.
El paciente:	Mamá, quiero que me traigas un mantecado.
La madre:	¡Dios mío, pero que niño tan mimado (*spoiled*)!

1. ¿Cómo quiere la madre que sea su hijo?

   Quiere que él sea un niño bueno.

2. ¿Cree la doctora que el paciente tenga algo serio?

   No cree la doctora que el paciente tenga algo serio

3. ¿Qué tiene que darle a Miguelito la madre?

   La madre tiene que darle unas píldoras

4. ¿Hay penicilina en el consultorio?

   No hay penicilina

5. ¿Qué quiere el enfermero que sepa la madre?

   Quiere que sepa que esto les pasa a mucho niños

6. ¿Qué quiere Miguelito que le compre su mamá?

   Quiere que le compre un montecado

7. ¿Es Miguelito un niño mimado?

   Sí, es un niño mimado

B. Match the medical advice from the numbered list with the appropriate illness, symptom, or medication from the lettered list, and write the correct number in the blank.

1. Es probable que le den uno si se siente muy nervioso.
2. Es probable que haya algunas aspirinas en el baño.
3. Es necesario que vaya al gastroenterólogo.
5. Le pido que tenga más cuidado con la presión arterial.
4. Quiero que sepa que tiene que dejar de fumar.
6. Es importante que esté al tanto (*aware of*) de todo lo que coma y beba.

_____4_____ a. el cáncer   _____2_____ d. la jaqueca

_____1_____ b. el calmante   _____5_____ e. el ataque al corazón

_____6_____ c. la alergia   _____3_____ f. la úlcera

Gramática esencial

54. Irregular Present Subjunctives: **dar, estar, ir, saber, ser**

A. Respond to the following statements by writing a request in the subjunctive mood using the pronoun in parentheses. Follow the model.

MODELO: Vas al hospital. (yo) → Yo quiero que vayas al hospital.

1. Él es doctor. (tú)

   Quieres que él sea doctor

2. Hay varios dentistas en el consultorio. (nosotros)

   Queremos que haya varios dentistas en el consultorio

3. El paciente está tranquilo. (ustedes)

   Quieren que el paciente esté tranquilo

4. Ellas saben que tienen pulmonía. (la doctora)

   La doctora quiere que sepan que tienen pulmonía

5. Tú das sangre hoy. (ella)

   Ella quiere que tú des sangre hoy

6. Vamos a comprar pastillas para la tos. (la enfermera)

   La enfermera quiere que vayamos a comprar pastillas para la tos

B. Rewrite these words as sentences, using the order given. Make any changes and additions that may be necessary. Don't forget **que** before the verb in the subjunctive.

   Quiero
   Quieres
   Quiere
   Queremos

   Quieren

1. aconseja / yo / estar / en el hospital / una semana

   Aconseja que esté en el hospital una semana

2. no creemos / ser / gripe

   No creemos que sea gripe

3. les pido / no / me / dar / esas horribles gotas para la nariz

   Les pido que no me dén esas horribles gotas para la nariz

4. prefieren / tú / saber / la verdad / sobre tu enfermedad

   Prefieren que tú sepas la verdad sobre tu enfermedad

5. la doctora Valdés / manda / yo / ir / a un especialista

   La doctora Valdés

6. no creo / haber / una cura / contra ese virus

   _____

55. Forms of the Present Perfect Subjunctive

Respond to the following questions with the cue given and the present perfect subjunctive.

MODELO: ¿Han estado enfermos los abuelos? (Sí, siento…) →
Sí, siento que hayan estado enfermos.

1. ¿Han visto ellas la herida del paciente? (Sí, sentimos…)

_____

2. ¿Ha sufrido papá un ataque al corazón? (Sí, temo...)

_____

3. ¿Ha salido del consultorio la doctora? (Sí, me alegro...)

_____

4. ¿Ha tenido ella cáncer antes? (Sí, nos sorprende...)

_____

5. ¿Le han puesto una inyección a la niña? (Sí, espero…)

_____

56. Subjunctive with Verbs of Disbelief, Doubt, and Denial

Complete these sentences with the correct form of the verb given in parentheses.

1. (ser) La paciente no cree que nosotras _____ doctoras.

2. (saber) ¿Por que niegan que tú _____ la verdad?

3. (ir) Creo que sus pacientes _____ al hospital.

4. (dar) ¿Cree Ud. que ellos me _____ las gotas hoy?

5. (pedir) No dudan que ella _____ calmantes a los enfermeros.

6. (ir) ¿Por qué dudan ustedes que yo _____ al doctor?

7. (ser) Niegan que la herida _____ muy seria.

8. (ir) No estoy segura de que los padres _____ a la farmacia esta tarde.

9. (estar) Dudo que ella _____ en este hospital.

10. (haber) No negamos que _____ buenos médicos en esa clínica.

11. (ser) No dudo que tú _____ una paciente muy difícil.

12. (haber) Niego que él _____ tomado esas píldoras.

57. Subjunctive with Impersonal Expressions

Rewrite these words as sentences, using the order given. Make any changes or additions that may be necessary.

1. es preciso / la paciente / cuidarse / mucho

   _____

2. pero / es probable / ella / no / hacerlo

   _____

3. pues / es lástima / ellos / dejarla sola

   _____

4. es mejor / ella / aceptar / responsabilidad / por su salud

   _____

5. es cierto / ella / tener / cuidarse

   _____

6. es verdad / todos / querer / ayudarla

   _____

7. ¿Es posible / nosotros / visitarla?

   _____

58. Comparatives and Superlatives

A. Express the following comparisons and superlatives in Spanish.

1. (*as deep as*) Elsa dice que esta herida es _____ la otra.

2. (*as many hours as*) No piensa que la enfermera trabaje

   _____ el médico.

3. (*less expensive than*) Las aspirinas genéricas son _____ las otras.

4. (*most important*) Esta medicina es _____ de todas.

5. (*more than*) Ella se cuida _____ yo.

6. (*the most intelligent*) Ella opina que el doctor Ramírez es

   _____ del consultorio.

7. (*as new as*) Estas píldoras son _____ ésas.

8. (*the cheapest*) Esta farmacia es _____ de la ciudad.

9. (*fewer problems than*) En todo caso, yo tengo _____ Elsa

   y los médicos me interesan (*less than*) _____ a ella.

B. Using the verb **tener**, write equal comparisons with **tanto/a/os/as**.

   MODELO: yo / fiebre / ella → Yo tengo tanta fiebre como ella.

   1. estos pacientes / dolor / aquéllas

      _____

   2. ese médico / enfermeras en su consultorio / tú

      _____

   3. nosotras / píldoras / la farmacia

      _____

   4. Ud. / jaquecas / yo

      _____

C. Express in Spanish.

   1. (*the largest*) El hospital San Martín es _____ de toda la isla.

   2. (*the best*) Eso no quiere decir que sea _____.

   3. (*the oldest*) Es _____ de todo el Caribe.

   4. (*the oldest*) Pero un día llevé a mi hija _____ al hospital

      porque tenía gripe.

5. (*the smallest*) Tenían el consultorio _____ que jamás (*ever*) había visto.

6. (*the worst*) Y el servicio fue _____.

7. (*good*) Sin embargo, había una enfermera muy _____.

8. (*large, bad*) Ella me dijo que aunque (*although*) el hospital era

_____, los doctores eran muy

_____.

9. (*smaller, better*) Creo que en general un hospital _____ es

_____.

10. (*best, big*) Por eso, llevé a mi hija a la clínica Cinco de Mayo; es

_____ clínica de la ciudad aunque no es muy

_____.

Para repasar

Express in Spanish.

1. Alberto asks that I buy him pills for his allergy every week.

   _____

2. Nobody believes he has a serious problem.

   _____

3. His doctor advises him not to take them.

   _____

4. But Alberto orders that we bring him those pills.

   _____

5. I want him to stop taking them.

   _____

Comunicación

A. *Recomendaciones médicas*. You are a doctor giving advice to a patient who has been very ill in the hospital but is now ready to go home. Complete the following paragraph with the correct present subjunctive forms of the verbs given in parentheses.

Creo que Ud. (poder) _____(1) volver a casa hoy. Pero dudo

que Ud. (volver) _____(2) a tener tan buena salud como antes.

Lo más importante es que (cuidarse) _____(3). Es preciso que

(comenzar) _____(4) una nueva dieta. También es importante

que (encontrar) _____(5) un deporte que le (gustar)

_____(6) y que lo (practicar) _____(7)

todos los días.

Es necesario que (dormir) _____(8) ocho horas todos los días

y que sólo (comer) _____(9) las comidas de la lista que le he

dado. No puedo permitir que Ud. (beber) _____(10) alcohol,

pero es posible que (tomar) _____(11) una copa de vino a la

semana solamente.

Dudo que Ud. (sentirse) _____(12) bien durante los primeros

días en casa, pero no quiero que (molestarse) _____(13) por

eso.

Hoy quiero que primero (llevar) _____(14) la receta a la

farmacia. Es probable que allí le (pedir) _____(15) su tarjeta de

seguro (*insurance*) médico.

Señor Cruz, estoy segura de que Ud. va a mejorarse (*to get better*). Si le duele algo,

deseo que me (llamar) _____(16). Lo más importante es que

(tener) _____(17) fe (*faith*) en el futuro y que no (perder)

_____(18) el sentido de humor.

B. *Sólo tú*. Identify the following items in your life.

1. your most difficult class

   _____

2. your best friend

   _____

3. the worst restaurant in town

   _____

4. the best movie you have seen this year

   _____

5. the youngest / oldest person in class

   _____

6. the largest and smallest cities in your state

   _____

LECCIÓN DOCE
LABORATORY MANUAL

Gráficos

A. You will hear a series of sentences. After each one, repeat the sentence, changing the noun to the feminine form. Make any other necessary changes for gender agreement. Repeat the correct answer after you hear it.

1. ...   2. ...   3. ...   4. ...   5. ...

B. You will hear a series of sentences. After each one, repeat the sentence, changing the noun to the plural. Pluralize the verb if needed. Repeat the correct answer after you hear it.

1. ...   2. ...   3. ...   4. ...   5. ...

C. You will hear a series of statements. You will hear each one twice. Circle the letter of the sentence that you associate most closely with it.

1. a. No creo que haya aspirinas.

   b. Quiero que vayan al dentista.

   c. Creo que están en el hospital.

2. a. No dejen que me ponga una inyección.

   b. Es necesario que estés quieto.

   c. Tengo mucha fiebre.

3. a. Me mordió mi hermana.

   b. Ahora está en el hospital.

   c. Quieren que les den pastillas para la tos.

4. a. Quiero que me traigan mantecado.

   b. Quiero tomar aspirinas y dormir.

   c. Quiero que busques la receta para el pastel de piña.

Pronunciación

The Auxiliary **haber**

A. The forms of **haber** do not receive heavy stress in the spoken language. For this reason, you may miss them in ordinary conversation with a native speaker of Spanish. This is particularly true of the forms **he, has,** and **ha.** Since the h is silent, these forms can easily be absorbed by stressed syllables; thus "new" and longer syllables seem to appear. In other cases, **he, has,** and **ha** seem to disappear completely. Listen and repeat.

1. Él ha ido. (Elaído.)
2. No he entendido. (Noentendido.)
3. Tú has hablado. (Túasablado.)

B. Repeat these sentences after the speaker.

1. Él ha venido hoy.
2. ¿Lo has visto?
3. No lo he explicado.

4. Nunca he entrado allí.
5. ¿Ha hablado él?

Gramática esencial

54. Irregular Present Subjunctives: **dar, estar, ir, saber, ser**

You will hear a series of sentences. During the first pause, change the verb in the sentence to the subjunctive and combine it with the phrase **es necesario que** to create a new sentence. During the second pause, repeat the correct answer.

MODELO: Ella va al dentista. → Es necesario que ella vaya al dentista.

1. ...   2. ...   3. ...   4. ...   5. ...

55. Forms of the Present Perfect Subjunctive

You will hear the following sentences. During the first pause, change the verb in the sentence to the subjunctive and combine it with the phrase **temo que** to create a new sentence. During the second pause, repeat the correct answer.

MODELO: No han traído aspirina. → Temo que no hayan traído aspirina.

1. ...   2. ...   3. ...   4. ...   5. ...   6. ...

56. Subjunctive with Verbs of Disbelief, Doubt, and Denial

A. You will hear the first part of a sentence. Complete each one with the phrase **que es doctora** or **que sea doctora,** according to what is required by the principal verb. During the second pause, repeat the correct answer.

MODELO: No creo... → No creo que sea doctora.

1. ...   2. ...   3. ...   4. ...   5. ...   6. ...   7. ...

B. You will hear a series of sentences. Contradict what you hear by making the first verb negative and changing the second verb to the appropriate indicative or subjunctive form. During the second pause, repeat the correct answer.

MODELO: Creo que tiene fiebre. → No creo que tenga fiebre.

1. ...   2. ...   3. ...   4. ...   5. ...   6. ...   7. ...   8. ...

57. Subjunctive with Impersonal Expressions

You will hear a series of sentences containing an impersonal expression. During the first pause, repeat the sentence, substituting the impersonal expression given in the manual. During the second pause, repeat the correct answer.

MODELO: Es posible que la paciente tenga un virus. (Es cierto...) →
              Es cierto que la paciente tiene un virus.

1. Es probable...   4. Es mejor...
2. Es cierto...   5. Es seguro...
3. No es posible...   6. Es verdad...

58. Comparatives and Superlatives

A. Use the cues given to form sentences establishing comparisons. Repeat the correct answer after the speaker.

MODELO: la aspirina / ser / tan / buena / esta píldora →
              La aspirina es tan buena como esta píldora.

1. Gustavo / cuidarse / menos / Alberto
2. Alberto / estar / tan / enfermo / Luis
3. pero / Luis / tener / tanta fiebre / él
4. Alberto / necesitar / tantos enfermeros / Carlos
5. Carlos / necesitar / más penicilina / Luis

B. You will hear a series of sentences. During the first pause, change each one to a superlative statement, using the proper form of the adjective. During the second pause, repeat the correct answer.

MODELO: Ella es una buena enfermera. → Ella es la mejor enfermera.

1. ...   2. ...   3. ...   4. ...   5. ...   6. ...

Comunicación

A. *¡Maldito resfriado!* You will hear the **Texto** from page 246 of your textbook. Listen carefully and try to follow the gist of the ideas. Then listen to the **Texto** again, followed by some statements based on it. You will hear each statement twice. Circle the letter C (**Cierto**) if you think the statement is true and F (**Falso**) if you think it's false.

1. C (F)   3. (C) F   5. C (F)
2. C (F)   4. (C) F

B. *Una familia enferma.* Study the drawing and listen to the story of the Castaño family. Then make recommendations using the cues given as to what each one of them should do.

1. Alicia, aconsejo que... (no correr por un mes)

_____

2. Betita, es necesario que... (ponerte una inyección de penicilina)

_____

3. Gonzalo, es preciso que... (beber mucho té con limón)

_____

4. Señor Castaño, es necesario que... (ir a la farmacia con esta receta)

_____

5. Berto, es importante que... (descansar hasta el fin de semana)

_____

6. Señora Castaño, es mejor que... (tomar un calmante ahora mismo)

_____

C. *Dictado.* You will hear a short paragraph about health. During the first pause, write each sentence. During the second pause, check what you wrote.

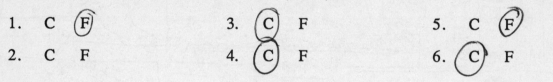

Es necesario tener buena salud. Es preciso que uno se cuide siempre

Es tan importante tener buena salud como tener una buena

~~educación~~ educación.

_____

_____

D. *Sólo tú.* You will hear a series of statements about yourself. Circle C if the statement is true (**Cierto**) or F if the statement is false (**Falso**).

1. C (F)   3. (C) F   5. C (F)
2. C F   4. (C) F   6. (C) F

LECCIÓN TRECE
WORKBOOK

Gráficos

A. *Planes para el futuro.* Complete the following letter from Jorge Luis to Mauro by writing in the names of the articles numbered in the drawing, along with the appropriate definite or indefinite article where needed.

25 de febrero

Mi querido Mauro,

   Espero que recibas esta carta en buena salud y en compañía de tu querida familia. Nunca me olvido de ustedes y de cómo siempre me hacen reír.

   El diez del próximo (*next*) mes pasaré dos semanas de vacaciones en Cartagena. Saldré de aquí el nueve por la noche y llegaré a Cartagena al día siguiente (*following*) por la tarde. ¿Podrás venir al aeropuerto? Iré en el vuelo 911 de AeroCaribe que llega allí a las cinco de la tarde.

   Espero poder ir a Barranquilla y a Bogotá por unos días. Pero sinceramente, lo que más quiero hacer es ver la naturaleza de ese país que tanto extraño (*I miss*). No hay nada como _____(1) tropical y

_____(2) Caribe con sus deliciosas

_____(3) para nadar. Ya verás fotos de mis hijos aquí en

_____(4) construyendo _____(5) con

_____(6). El pasado octubre nos pasamos una semana entera

con _____(7) en mano recogiendo

_____(8) secas.

¿Crees que pasarás unos días de vacaciones conmigo (*with me*) visitando el interior del

país? Sin duda veré el famoso _____(9) Nevado del Ruiz.

También quiero visitar _____(10) Magdalena y

_____(11) de Tota y, ¡claro!, ver

_____(12), _____(13),

_____(14)... en fin, todo.

Bueno, no quiero ponerme demasiado sentimental. Sueño con mi llegada a Colombia.
Nancy les manda saludos a tí, a Cecilia y a los niños. Te veré pronto.

Recibe un abrazo de tu hermano,

Jorge Luis

B. *La llegada de Jorge Luis.* Study the drawing again, read the following dialogue
between Mauro and Cecilia, and answer the questions that follow.

Cecilia: ¿Podrás ir a recogerlo al aeropuerto?
Mauro: Claro que sí. ¿No irás conmigo?
Cecilia: No podré ir ese día. Ya tengo planes. Los niños y yo vamos a navegar en el
          bote de vela del tío Pancho.
Mauro: Ya verás qué bien lo van a pasar.
Cecilia: Eso crees tú. También van los niños de los Gutiérrez y los García.
Mauro: ¡Tanta gente en un bote tan pequeño! ¡Qué lata! Pasarás la tarde entera
          gritando.

1.   ¿Podrá Mauro ir al aeropuerto a buscar a su hermano?

_____

2. ¿Por qué no podrá ir Cecilia?

_____

3. ¿Quiénes irán con Cecilia a navegar en el bote de vela?

_____

4. ¿Cómo piensa Mauro que pasará la tarde Cecilia?

_____

Gramática esencial

59. Future Tense of Regular Verbs

A. Change the following sentences to the future tense.

1. Hoy voy a la playa.

_____

2. Primero entramos en el café Botín.

_____

3. No lo abren hasta las once.

_____

4. ¿Nadas en el mar?

_____

5. La temperatura del agua te sorprende.

_____

6. ¿A qué hora llegáis vosotras?

_____

7. Los niños se pierden en la playa.

_____

8. Rodolfo duerme en la arena.

_____

9. Leo el periódico, tomo un café y después me baño en las olas.

_____

B. Rewrite the following questions by changing the verbs to the future tense. Then answer each one, using the subject given in parentheses.

MODELO: ¿Quién va al campo? (yo) → ¿Quién irá al campo?
Yo iré al campo.

1. ¿Quién los recoge en el aeropuerto? (Paco y Luisa)

_____

2. ¿Quién anuncia el huracán? (el gobernador)

_____

3. ¿Quién nos protege de la inundación? (yo)

_____

4. ¿Quién me trae las noticias sobre el terremoto? (nosotros)

_____

5. ¿Quién ve los relámpagos? (tú)

_____

6. ¿Quién reza por las víctimas del tornado? (mamá y yo)

_____

7. ¿Quién escribe de la tormenta? (tú)

_____

8. ¿Quién nos espera con el bote? (Ud. y Carmen)

_____

60. Future Tense of Irregular Verbs

Complete the following sentences with the future form of the verbs given in parentheses.

1. (poder) ¿_____ ir tú a Iquitos también?

2. (querer) No, ellos no _____ ir ahí.

3. (haber) ¿_____ algún (some) problema con el vuelo?

4. (saber) Bueno, nosotros no _____ nada hasta las cinco.

5. (hacer) Pues, ¿qué _____ ustedes si viene un huracán?

6. (poner) Ellos _____ a todos los turistas en un hotel.

7. (decir) Tú me _____ si no llega el avión.

8. (venir) Claro, yo _____ a buscarte.

9. (tener) ¿Nosotros _____ que ir al refugio (*shelter*)?

10. (salir, decir) _____ un anuncio por la tele y nos

    _____ adónde ir.

11. (haber) ¿Crees que ella ya _____ llegado?

61. Affirmatives and Negatives

A. Rewrite these affirmative sentences as negative sentences.

1. Cecilia nos trajo algo de la playa.

   _____

2. Pues alguien perdió el traje de baño.

   _____

3. Encontrarán algún bote hoy.

   _____

4. ¿No habrá alguna playa linda aquí?

   _____

5. Siempre toman café antes de ir a nadar.

   _____

6. También llevan sándwiches y cerveza al lago.

   _____

B. Answer the following questions affirmatively or negatively, according to the cue given in parentheses.

1. ¿Siempre salía ella en bote de vela? (no)

   _____

2. ¿También recogerán a los niños? (no)

   _____

3. ¿Pero no hay nadie en el mar? (sí)

   _____

4. ¿No hay alguna playa bonita en el río? (no)

   _____

5. ¿Jamás han ido al lago por el caminito? (sí)

   _____

6. ¿Brilla algo interesante en el cielo esta noche? (no)

   _____

62. Uses of **pero**, **sino**, and **sino que**

Complete the following sentences with **pero, sino,** or **sino que.**

1. No sentí el terremoto _____ la tormenta.

2. No nadará _____ montará el bote.

3. No estamos alegres _____ no estamos tristes tampoco.

4. No viajaremos por el mar _____ por el río.

5. El cielo no está azul _____ negro.

6. No irán por el camino _____ volverán por la carretera 101.

7. Quiero ir _____ no tienen un vuelo hoy.

8. No recogieron a Jorge Luis _____ a Mauro.

9. No trajo regalos _____ fotos.

10. Tengo ganas de nadar _____ no entraré en el mar.

Para repasar

Un guía turístico. Complete the following paragraph with the correct indicative or subjunctive form of the verb in parentheses.

Es una lástima que el camino (estar) _____(1) cerrado. Pero no

dudo que nosotros (poder) _____(2) tomar la otra carretera

que pasa por las colinas. Es necesario que nosotros (ser)

_____ (3) los primeros en llegar al hotel para pedir que nos

(dar) _____(4) habitaciones para todos. Recomiendo que todos

(ir) _____(5) en un sólo autobús y que (salir)

_____(6) inmediatamente después de ver el volcán. Estoy

seguro de que todos ustedes (saber) _____(7) la historia del

Nevado del Ruiz y prefiero que uno de ustedes se la (explicar)

_____(8) al resto del grupo. ¿O es mejor que yo se la (contar)

_____(9)? ¿Es posible que alguno de ustedes no (saber)

_____(10) lo qué pasó allí?

Comunicación

A. *Un viaje a Colombia.* You and a fellow traveler are planning a trip through the interior of Colombia and are talking about things you will do. Express in Spanish the following sentences from your conversation.

1. I will fly to Bogotá first, and I will meet you in Calarca.

   _____

2. They will ask for my visa, my passport (**pasaporte**), and my driver's license. What a nuisance!

   _____

3. Then we will go to Leticia.

   _____

4. I'll never return to that part of the country.

   _____

5. Will you spend a few days on the beach?

_____

6. I have never liked the sand, and I never will!

_____

7. Do you think there will be hurricanes on the coast?

_____

B. *Pensando en el futuro*. Answer the following questions and share your answers with the class.

1. Si Ud. se pierde en un bote en el mar, ¿qué es lo primero que hará?

_____

2. ¿Qué hará usted en caso de (*in case of*) un desastre natural?

_____

3. Si Ud. gana un millón de dólares, ¿qué hará con el dinero?

_____

4. ¿A qué país de la América Latina viajará primero?

_____

5. ¿Qué hará Ud. durante este fin de semana?

_____

6. ¿Dónde pasará Ud. sus próximas (*next*) vacaciones?

_____

C. *Proverbios*. Here are a few Spanish proverbs. Express them in English.

1. No serás amado (*loved*), si de ti sólo tienes cuidado.

_____

2. Si bien estás, no te mudarás (*move*).

_____

3. Haz la noche, noche y el día, día y vivirás con alegría.

_____

4. Nadie diga: De esta agua no beberé.

_____

5. Dime con quién andas y te diré quién eres.

_____

LECCIÓN TRECL
LABORATORY MANUAL

Gráficos

A. You will hear a series of phrases with infinitives. Repeat each one, changing the infinitive to the **yo** form of the future tense. Repeat the correct answer during the second pause.

1. ...   2. ...   3. ...   4. ...   5. ...   6. ...   7. ...

B. You will hear a series of statements. You will hear each statement twice. Circle the letter of the rejoinder that you associate most closely with each one.

1. a. Saldré a caminar esta noche.

   b. Podré nadar en el océano mañana.

   c. Saldrás a recoger las hojas secas.

2. a. Las hojas caerán en octubre.

   b. Los oirás cantar.

   c. Plantarás flores.

3. a. Podré hacer un muñeco de nieve.

   b. Disfrutaré de las lluvias y las tormentas.

   c. Veré mariposas y pájaros en las ramas de los árboles.

C. You will hear a set of sentences twice. During the first pause, write in the missing words. During the second pause, check what you wrote.

1. En el mar _____ unos botes de vela.

2. ¿A qué hora _____ para el lago?

3. _____ por el camino frente a tu casa.

4. ¿No _____ traer nada para los niños?

5. _____ al tío Pancho.

Pronunciación

Review of the Hard **g** Sound

A. The hard **g** sound occurs in Spanish before **a, o,** and **u.** Listen and repeat.

| alguno | Gómez | llegada | relámpago |

B. In the combinations **gue** and **gui,** the **u** is not pronounced unless there is a diaeresis (¨) on top of the **u.** Listen and repeat.

| guerra | seguido | vergüenza | lingüístico |

C. Repeat these sentences after the speaker.

1. Guillermo toca la guitarra.
2. Tengo un gato.
3. Alguien necesita gasolina.
4. Olga no pagó nada.
5. Los González no tienen agua hoy.

Gramática esencial

59. Future Tense of Regular Verbs

A. First repeat the model sentence, then substitute the cue words that are given on the tape and repeat the entire sentence. Repeat the correct answer during the second pause.

MODELO: Él volverá a Colombia. (yo) → Yo volveré a Colombia.

1. ...   2. ...   3. ...

Repeat the same steps with this model sentence.

MODELO: Ella llegará mañana. (yo) → Yo llegaré mañana.

4. ...   5. ...   6. ...

Repeat the same steps with this model sentence.

MODELO: Primero iré al mar. (tú) → Primero irás al mar.

7. ...   8. ...   9. ...

B. You will hear a series of sentences. During the first pause, repeat the sentence, changing the verb in the second clause to the future form. During the second pause, repeat the entire sentence.

MODELO: Dice que recoge a Jorge Luis. → Dice que recogerá a Jorge Luis.

1. ...   2. ...   3. ...   4. ...   5. ...   6. ...

60. Future Tense of Irregular Verbs

A. You will hear a series of sentences. During the first pause, change the verb in each one to the future tense. During the second pause, repeat the correct answer.

MODELO: Laura puede ir. → Laura podrá ir.

1. ...   2. ...   3. ...   4. ...   5. ...   6. ...   7. ...   8. ...   9. ...   10. ...

B. You will hear a set of questions. During the first pause, answer the question with a singular or plural verb, as appropriate. During the second pause, repeat the correct answer.

MODELOS: ¿Vendrás? → Sí, vendré.
           ¿Vendrán? → Sí, vendremos.

1. ...   2. ...   3. ...   4. ...   5. ...   6. ...   7. ...   8. ...

61. Affirmatives and Negatives

A. You will hear a series of sentences. During the first pause, rephrase the sentence by placing **no** before the verb and changing the word order. During the second pause, repeat the correct answer.

MODELO: Nunca me recoge. → No me recoge nunca.

1. ...   2. ...   3. ...   4. ...   5. ...

B. You will hear a set of questions. During the first pause, answer the sentence negatively. During the second pause, repeat the correct answer.

MODELO: ¿Hay alguien en el mar? → No, no hay nadie en el mar.

1. ...   2. ...   3. ...   4. ...   5. ...   6. ...

62. Uses of **pero, sino,** and **sino que**

You will hear the following pairs of sentences and phrases. During the first pause, combine each pair, using **pero, sino,** or **sino que.** During the second pause, repeat the correct answer.

MODELO: Me encanta el mar. Prefiero el lago. →
          Me encanta el mar, pero prefiero el lago.

1. ...   2. ...   3. ...   4. ...   5. ...   6. ...   7. ...   8. ...

Comunicación

A. *Pan y poesía.* You will hear the **Texto** from page 269 of your textbook. Listen carefully and try to follow the gist of the ideas. Then listen to the **Texto** again, followed by some incomplete statements based on it. You will hear each statement twice. Circle the letter of the phrase that best completes each statement.

1. a. venderá una mitad del pan.

    b. comprará más pan.

    c. venderá rosas y violetas para comprar más pan.

2. a. pájaros que cantarán.

    b. una luna que brillará.

    c. rosas y violetas.

3. a. los ríos y los mares.

    b. los árboles.

    c. los valles con sus colores.

4. a. comer pan y mantecado.

    b. admirar las flores y los árboles.

    c. caminar por las colinas y los desiertos.

B. *Dictado.* You will hear a fragment from **"El viaje definitivo"** by Juan Ramón Jiménez. During the first pause, write each sentence down in the space provided. During the second pause, check what you wrote.

_____

_____

_____

_____

_____

_____

C. *Sólo tú*. You will hear five incomplete statements. You will hear each statement twice. Write suitable completions according to your own experiences and feelings in the spaces provided below.

1. _____

2. _____

3. _____

4. _____

5. _____

LECCIÓN CATORZE
WORKBOOK

Gráficos

A. *En la recepción.* Study the drawing, read the following dialogues, and complete them with the appropriate nouns.

La madrina: Será una luna de miel maravillosa.

La suegra de la novia: París parece lindo en este _____ (1).

La madre del novio: ¿No desean una copita de _____ (2)?

El suegro del novio: Bueno, Roberto, discúlpame por el mal humor.

Roberto: No hay problema, don Joaquín. Déme un fuerte

_____ (3).

La novia: ¡Qué niña más inteligente! ¿Dónde encontraste

_____ (4)?

La hermanita: Gabi, dame _____ (5) de despedida

(*farewell*).

El padrino: ¡Adelante! (*Come in!*) Ya están casados los enamorados.

El padre de la novia: Pasen. Están servidos _____ (6).

B. *Una boda cómica*. Read the following composition about Roberto and Gabriela's wedding, then answer the questions that follow.

Todo estaba arreglado. Hoy se casaban Roberto y Gabriela. ¡Pero lo más cómico de la ceremonia fue que en el momento de ponerle el anillo en el dedo a la novia, a Roberto se le cayó el anillo! Todos, la novia, el novio, el padrino, la madrina, los suegros—y el cura (*priest*) también—se pusieron de rodillas (*knelt down*) a buscar el anillo. El suegro de Roberto se puso de mal humor. La madre de Gabriela comenzó a reír. Por suerte, la hermanita de la novia encontró el anillo y la boda pudo continuar.

1. ¿Quiénes se casaban hoy?

_____

2. ¿Qué buscaban todos en el suelo (*floor*)?

_____

3. ¿Por quién fue encontrado el anillo?

_____

4. ¿Se puso de mal humor el papá de Gabriela?

_____

5. ¿Qué hizo la madre de Gabriela?

_____

Gramática esencial

63.–64. Passive Constructions and Impersonal **se**

A. Rephrase each model sentence first using the true passive voice, then using the **se** construction.

MODELO: Celebran la boda en la iglesia. →
Celebran la boda en la iglesia. →
La boda es celebrada en la iglesia.
Se celebra la boda en la iglesia.

1. Compran el anillo en los Almacenes Molina.

_____

_____

2. Preparan los canapés en casa.

_____

_____

3. Sirven el vino en copas.

_____

_____

4. Arreglaron la luna de miel en junio.

_____

_____

B. Express in Spanish.

1. Champagne is not served at the reception.

_____

2. The expenses aren't paid in one day!

_____

3. Honeymoons are always arranged early.

_____

4. How do you prepare hors d'oeuvres?

_____

5. How do you explain the ceremony?

_____

65. Resultant State

Write sentences in the present tense that express the resultant state, using the cues given.

MODELO: La iglesia fue decorada por los padrinos. →
         La iglesia está decorada.

1. Los amigos fueron invitados por los suegros.

_____

2. Se sirvieron los canapés a las cinco.

_____

3. Fueron casados por la iglesia.

_____

4. El viaje fue pagado por un amigo del novio.

_____

5. La habitación fue reservada en junio.

_____

6. Fueron divorciados hace un mes.

_____

66. Interrogatives ¿qué? and ¿cuál(es)?

Complete the following sentences with ¿qué?, ¿cuál?, or ¿cuáles?

1. ¿_____ día es la boda?

2. ¿_____ dijo el padrino?

3. ¿_____ es la novia?

4. ¿_____ es su hermanita?

---

5. ¿_____ es el novio, cubano o americano?

6. ¿_____ sirven, champán o vino tinto?

7. ¿_____ es una ceremonia por lo civil?

8. ¿_____ es la diferencia entre una ceremonia por lo civil y una ceremonia por la iglesia?

9. ¿De _____ son los canapés?

10. ¿_____ prefieres, las tapas o los sándwiches de jamón?

67. Relative Pronouns **que** and **lo que**

Complete the following conversation with **que** or **lo que**.

Elena: ¿Qué es _____ (1) trajeron los suegros?

Rita: Dice la hermanita _____ (2) traen los boletos para el viaje de la luna de miel.

Elena: Pero los boletos _____ (3) yo vi no son para Francia. Son para el Japón.

Rita: Pues, no saben _____ (4) hacen porque los novios les dijeron _____ (5) no querían ir al Japón.

Elena: Tú sabes _____ (6) los padres de ella nunca hacen caso a _____ (7) los hijos les dicen.

Rita: Pero se supone _____ (8) los padres les dan _____ (9) ellos quieren. ¡Es una ocasión muy importante!

Elena: Ellos no le hacen caso a nadie.

Para repasar

Complete the following dialogue using the future tense of the verbs given in parentheses.

—Dicen los Morales que no (poder) _____ (1) venir a la

ceremonia mañana. Ellos no (venir) _____ (2) porque siempre

les han tenido odio a las bodas. Dicen que nos (ver) _____ (3)

en la recepción. Yo los (saludar) _____ (4), pero me molesta

que no vayan a la iglesia.

—Pues yo no (tener) _____ (5) tiempo de ir a la recepción,

pero tú me (encontrar) _____ (6) en la ceremonia. (Comprar)

_____ (7) un regalo para los novios y te lo (dar)

_____ (8). ¿Lo (llevar) _____ (9) tú a

la recepción?

—Claro que sí. Yo lo (hacer) _____ (10) con todo gusto.

Comunicación

A. You and a friend are having a conversation about some friends who are rather
   unconventional. Express your conversation in Spanish.

   1. What I don't understand is that they live together (*juntos*) even though (*aunque*)
      they are divorced.

      _____

   2. Well, that's done more and more these days.

      _____

   3. Were they married in church (*por la iglesia*) or in a civil ceremony (*por lo civil*)?

      _____

   4. I don't know. But they were mistaken to (*al*) fall in love.

      _____

   5. One shouldn't say bad things (*hablar mal*) about friends.

      _____

6. Excuse me, but I can't put up with people who don't know what they're doing!

   _____

B. *¿Está Ud. de acuerdo?* Explain why you agree or disagree with the following statements.

   1. Si me equivoco, creo que debo disculparme.

   _____

   2. Las promesas se hacen para no romperse.

   _____

   3. Es necesario soportar los problemas de la familia.

   _____

   4. Si la gente se ama, todo se resuelve.

   _____

C. *Sólo tú.* Tell about yourself using the following phrases.

   1. hace un mes / enamorarse

   _____

   2. la semana pasada / casarse

   _____

   3. ayer / prometer

   _____

   4. esta mañana / tratar de

   _____

   5. cuando / ponerse de mal humor

   _____

   6. los gastos / soportar

   _____

LECCIÓN CATORZE
LABORATORY MANUAL

Gráficos

A. You will hear a series of infinitives. Repeat each one, then state the corresponding noun. Repeat the correct answer during the second pause.

MODELO: abrazar → el abrazo

1. ...   2. ...   3. ...   4. ...   5. ...   6. ...   7. ...

B. You will hear a series of questions twice. Circle the letter of the best response to each one.

1. a. El champán ya está comprado.

   b. Los canapés ya están servidos.

2. a. Se celebró en la iglesia San Martín.

   b. Los novios fueron presentados por un tío.

3. a. Sí, el padrino lo compró.

   b. Sí, el anillo está perdido.

4. a. Sí, está en la recepción.

   b. Sí, está disgustado.

C. You will hear a series of statements. Circle the letter of the word or phrase that you associate most closely with each one.

1. a. el padrino   b. el anillo   c. el divorcio

2. a. los anillos   b. los gastos   c. los suegros

3. a. el vino tinto   b. el beso   c. el folleto

4. a. la paciencia   b. la recepción   c. la boda

Pronunciación

Review of Spanish **r**

A. You will hear and pronounce Spanish **r** in various positions. First you will practice the **r** between vowels. Listen and repeat, pronouncing the **r** with a single tap of the tongue similar to the *t* in English *butter*.

pero	dinero	cuchara
para	periódico	espere Ud.
barato	dólares	paraguas

B. The final **r** in Spanish is a little less audible, since it is not supported by a following vowel. Listen and repeat.

tenedor	odiar	saludar
amar	comedor	suponer
ayer	humor	ver

C. Before most consonants, Spanish **r** is pronounced distinctly. Imagine that there is a brief **e** sound after the **r**. Listen and repeat.

parte	soporta	deportes
tormenta	¿por qué?	aparcar
sorprender	almuerzo	divorcio

D. When **r** follows a consonant, the two are never blended. Again, imagine that there is a brief **e** sound between the two consonants. Listen and repeat.

piedra	estrella	resfriado
promesa	brillar	abrigo
madrina	creer	presumido

E. Spanish **r** before **b, v, d,** and **g** is not easy to pronounce because the supporting consonant is soft. Listen and repeat.

Eduardo	servir	garganta
árbol	alergia	perdió
recordar	cerdo	acuerdo

Gramática esencial

63.–64. Passive Constructions and Impersonal **se**

A. You will hear a series of sentences. Rephrase each one using the passive construction with **se**. Repeat the correct answer after the speaker.

MODELO:　Orlando y Eva celebran la boda hoy. →
　　　　　Se celebra la boda hoy.

1. ...　　2. ...　　3. ...　　4. ...　　5. ...

B. You will hear a series of sentences. During the first pause, change each sentence to the true passive construction. During the second pause, repeat the correct answer.

MODELO:　Se sirvió el vino. → El vino fue servido.

1. ...　　2. ...　　3. ...　　4. ...　　5. ...

C. You will hear a set of questions. Answer them negatively, using the impersonal **se** and the correct form of the verb given in parentheses. During the second pause, repeat the correct answer.

MODELO:　¿Se celebra la recepción aquí? (preparar los canapés) →
　　　　　No, pero se preparan los canapés.

1. ...　　2. ...　　3. ...　　4. ...

65. Resultant State

You will hear a series of sentences. Rephrase each one to express the resultant state, according to the model. Repeat the correct answer after the speaker.

MODELO:　Se sirve la comida. → La comida está servida.

1. ...　　2. ...　　3. ...　　4. ...　　5. ...

66. Interrogatives **¿qué?** and **¿cuál(es)?**

You will hear a series of answers. You will hear each answer twice. Circle the letter of the question that best corresponds to each answer.

1. a. ¿Qué haces tú?　　　　　b. ¿Qué es usted?

2. a. ¿Qué es su padre?　　　　b. ¿Cuál es su padre?

3. a. ¿Cuál es su madre?　　　　b. ¿Qué es su madre?

4. a. ¿Qué es esta calle?　　　　b. ¿Cuál es su dirección?

5. a. ¿Cuál es el anillo que quieres?   b. ¿Qué es un anillo?

67. Relative Pronouns **que** and **lo que**

You will hear a series of sentences twice. During the first pause, substitute **lo que** for the object of the verb. During the second pause, repeat the correct answer.

MODELO: Los regalos que han comprado son estupendos. →
          Lo que han comprado es estupendo.

1. ...   2. ...   3. ...   4. ...   5. ...

Comunicación

A. *Una boda en grande*. You will hear the **Texto** from page 285 of your textbook. First, listen carefully and try to follow the gist of the ideas. Then listen to the **Texto** again, followed by some incomplete statements based on it. You will hear each statement twice. Circle the letter of the word or phrase that best completes each statement.

1. a. le queda muy estrecho.   b. se lo compró su padre.   c. es precioso.

2. a. se perdió.   b. es muy bonito.   c. costó mucho dinero.

3. a. estudiante.   b. trabajador.   c. guitarrista.

4. a. un almacén.   b. un banco.   c. la biblioteca.

5. a. vino tinto.   b. champán.   c. café.

6. a. los ojos.   b. las manos.   c. los pies.

B. *¡Felicidades a los novios!* Your friends Roberto and Gabriela are getting married next week. Listen as the speaker reads the wedding announcement that appears in the paper. It will be read twice. Then answer the questions based on what you hear and on the drawing below. Repeat the correct answer after the speaker.

1. ...   5. ...

2. ...   6. ...

3. ...   7. ...

4. ...

C. *Dictado*. You will hear a short paragraph about Gabriela and Roberto's wedding. During the first pause, write each sentence. During the second pause, check what you wrote.

_____

_____

_____

_____

_____

_____

D. *Sólo tú*. You will hear a series of statements. Circle **Sí** if you agree, or **No** if you disagree. Be prepared to discuss in class your reasons for agreeing or disagreeing.

1. Sí   No   3. Sí   No   5. Sí   No

2. Sí   No   4. Sí   No   6. Sí   No

LECCIÓN QUINCE
WORKBOOK

Gráficos

A. *Un vuelo atrasado* (delayed). Study the drawing and read the following statements. Then match the statement with the number of the person that could have said it.

1. Hija, ¿podrías prestarme un poco de pasta de dientes? _____

2. Me gustaría tener mi maleta y no sólo este maletín. _____

3. Yo diría que el vuelo llegará dentro de dos horas, señorita. _____

4. Querría estar en la cancha ahora mismo y no en este aeropuerto. _____

5. Pero señor, ¿no sería posible tomar otro vuelo? _____

6. ¡Preferiría un cepillo y no este peine! _____

7. ¡Me gustaría tener mi máquina de afeitar! _____

B. *¿Qué harías?* Read the following dialogue between Margarita and Teresa at the airport and answer the questions that follow.

Margarita:	¡Tendría que llegar tarde nuestro vuelo!
Teresa:	Te dije que yo preferiría ir a Barcelona más que a Málaga.
Margarita:	Allí no sería tan fácil jugar al tenis y nadar en el mar como en Málaga.
Teresa:	Sí, pero yo podría comprar ropa de moda y perfumes... en fin, artículos de lujo.
Margarita:	No seas tonta Teresa. En Málaga hay de todo.
Teresa:	¿Discotecas? ¿Hoteles de lujo?
Margarita:	¡Cómo no! ¿Trajiste el bañador? Hay unas playas fantásticas.
Teresa:	¡Ay, no!
Margarita:	No te preocupes. Yo te presto uno de los míos.
Teresa:	¿Qué haría yo sin una buena amiga como tú?

1. ¿Adónde preferiría ir Teresa?

   _____

2. ¿Sería más fácil jugar al tenis en Málaga o en Barcelona, según Margarita?

   _____

3. ¿Qué piensa Teresa que podría comprar en Barcelona?

   _____

4. ¿Podría ir Teresa a una discoteca en Málaga?

   _____

5. ¿Qué no podría hacer Teresa sin la ayuda de Margarita?

   _____

6. ¿Qué harías tú si fueras (*if you were*) un pasajero en este vuelo?

   _____

Gramática esencial

68. Conditional of Regular Verbs

A. Complete these sentences with the conditional form of the verbs in parentheses.

1. Teresa pensó que...

   a. ella (llegar) _____ a Málaga hoy.

   b. (ser) _____ un viaje corto de Madrid a Málaga.

   c. ella (preferir) _____ ir a Málaga.

2. Margarita le dijo a Teresa que en Málaga ellas...

   a. (nadar) _____ en el mar.

   b. (ir) _____ a jugar al tenis.

   c. (comer) _____ parrilladas de mariscos.

3. Antes de ir de viaje, nosotros...

   a. (comprar) _____ los boletos a precio de venta.

   b. (poner) _____ bastante loción bronceadora en la maleta.

   c. (vestirse) _____ con ropa turística.

4. ¿Para ti...

   a. (ser) _____ más interesante hacer un viaje a España o a

   Latinoamérica?

   b. (reservar) _____ una habitación de lujo en un hotel?

   c. (pedir) _____ merluza o biftec en un restaurante en

   Barcelona?

B. Rewrite the following paragraph by expressing all the verbs in the conditional form.

Yo llegué _____ (1) a Barcelona el viernes por la mañana.

Primero, dejé _____ (2) las maletas en el hotel y bajé

_____ (3) a la playa. Después, entré

_____ (4) en un restaurante, me comí

_____ (5) una parrillada de mariscos y me tomé

_____ (6) un buen tinto. Por la tarde, dormí

_____ (7) la siesta en el cuarto del hotel. Por la noche, me

senté _____ (8) en un café y pedí

_____ (9) un vaso de sangría. Después de cenar, di

_____ (10) un paseo por las calles, volví

_____ (11) al hotel y descansé _____ (12).

¡Que agradable es _____ (13) la vida en Barcelona!

69. Conditional of Irregular Verbs

A. Change the meaning of these sentences by changing the verbs to the conditional.

1. ¿No quiere Margarita un hotel con piscina?

   _____

2. No puedo viajar sin mi cepillo de dientes.

   _____

3. No ponemos las maletas en manos de ese botones.

   _____

4. Salieron de Madrid hoy a las cuatro.

   _____

5. ¿No sabes el nombre de un hotel de lujo en Málaga?

   _____

6. ¿Ustedes hicieron el viaje por tren?

   _____

7. Me ha gustado mucho ver el partido de tenis.

   _____

8. ¿No tenías ganas de conocer a los jugadores?

_____

B. Now express in English the new sentences you have created.

1. _____

2. _____

3. _____

4. _____

5. _____

6. _____

7. _____

8. _____

70. Ordinal Numbers

Express in Spanish.

1. The first day, I would sleep until noon.

_____

2. The third day, we would get a suntan at the beach.

_____

3. The fifth day, Teresa would play tennis, and I would go shopping.

_____

4. The sixth day, I would need to buy sunglasses and more suntan lotion.

_____

5. The seventh day, we would dine at that good restaurant that specializes in shellfish.

_____

71. Stressed Possessive Adjectives and Pronouns

A. Change according to the model.

MODELO: Mi perfume es francés. →
El perfume mío es francés. → El mío es francés.

1. Tu agua de colonia es de París.

_____

_____

2. ¿Podrías buscar mi raqueta?

_____

_____

3. ¿Se habrían perdido vuestros aretes de plata?

_____

_____

4. Nuestro fin de semana en Málaga estuvo fantástico.

_____

_____

5. ¿Dónde compraría Teresa su collar de perlas?

_____

_____

Para repasar

Express in Spanish.

1. I don't believe she's as young as Teresa.

_____

2. The agent denies that the plane may arrive late.

_____

3. We're sure that this hotel costs as much as that one.

_____

4. It's necessary that we ask for the cheapest room in the hotel.

_____

5. What you promised me is marvelous!

_____

Comunicación

A. *Un viaje por España.* You are making travel plans for a trip through Spain. Complete the following conversation with your travel agent, using the correct conditional forms of the verbs in parentheses.

A: Me (gustar) _____ (1) pasar los primeros dos días en

Madrid y después (tomar) _____ (2) un tren a Barcelona.

B: ¿No (preferir) _____ (3) ir a Barcelona por avión?

Nosotros le (poder) _____ (4) ofrecer un precio muy

barato.

A: Bueno, a mí me (gustar) _____ (5) ir por avión, pero me

encontraré con mi prima en Madrid y ella (querer) _____ (6)

ir por tren.

B: Pues, señorita, yo no (saber) _____ (7) qué decirle. Ese día

no hay trenes a Barcelona. ¿(Ser) _____ (8) posible salir

otro día?

A: ¡Cómo no! ¿(Poder) _____ (9) usted decirme a qué hora

(salir) _____ (10) el tren el tres de julio?

B: Me (haber) _____ (11) gustado decírselo, pero la

computadora no funciona hoy.

B. *Sólo tú*. Answer the following questions and share your responses with the class.

1. Imagina que te invitan a hacer un viaje. ¿Adónde irías?

   _____

2. ¿Qué ciudad de España te gustaría visitar?

   _____

3. ¿Qué regalo de España le traerías al mejor amigo tuyo?

   _____

4. ¿Cuántas maletas llevarías y qué pondrías en tu maletín?

   _____

5. ¿Qué ropa te pondrías para viajar?

   _____

6. ¿Viajarías por tren, por avión, o tomarías el coche tuyo?

   _____

LECCIÓN QUINCE
LABORATORY MANUAL

Gráficos

A. You will hear a series of phrases with infinitives. Repeat each one, changing the infinitive to the **yo** form of the conditional. Repeat the correct answer during the second pause.

1. ...   2. ...   3. ...   4. ...   5. ...   6. ...   7. ...   8. ...

B. You will hear a series of statements. You will hear each statement twice. Circle the letter of the word or phrase that you associate most closely with each situation.

1. a. el colorete   b. el collar   c. el agua de colonia

2. a. la máquina de afeitar   b. la sombra para los ojos   c. la pulsera

3. a. el estuche de maquillaje b. el golf   c. la cancha

4. a. el jugador   b. las gafas de sol   c. la recepción

C. You will hear a series of sentences twice. Write in the missing words. Check your answers in the answer key in the back.

1. Me _____ reservar una habitación de lujo.

2. ¡Cómo no! ¿_____ una con vista al mar?

3. Yo _____ el lenguado o la merluza.

4. ¿_____ darme la loción bronceadora, por favor?

Pronunciación

<u>Review of Spanish **r, rr**</u>

A. The Spanish double **r** sound is represented in writing in three ways: as an initial **r** (**rosa, Ramón**), as double **r** in the middle of a word (**cerrado, perro**), and as a single **r** after the letter **l** or **n** (**alrededor, Enrique**). Repeat these words containing an initial **r**.

Roberto	radio	río
ropa	rico	rápidamente
regalo	repetir	
rueda	responsabilidad	

B. Now repeat these words that contain the double **r** sound in the middle.

honrado	carroza	pizarra
corren	terremoto	aburrido
borracho	guitarra	
alrededor	arreglado	

C. Next, compare the single **r** and double **r** sounds. Listen and repeat.

pero/perro	cero/cerro	choro/chorro
para/parra	caro/carro	moro/morro
coro/corro	pera/perra	
mira/mirra	ahora/ahorra	

Gramática esencial

68. Conditional of Regular Verbs

A. First repeat the model sentence, then substitute the cue words that are given on the tape and repeat the entire sentence. Repeat the correct answer during the second pause.

MODELO: Yo no iría a Málaga. (tú) → Tú no irías a Málaga.

1. ...   2. ...   3. ...

Repeat the same steps with this model sentence.

MODELO: Reservaríamos un cuarto hoy. (yo) → Yo reservaría un cuarto hoy.

4. ...   5. ...   6. ...

Repeat the same steps with this model sentence.

MODELO: ¿Sería ella jugadora de tenis? (él) → ¿Sería él jugador de tenis?

7. ...   8. ...   9. ...

B. You will hear six sentences. Change their meaning by changing the first verb to the preterite and the second to the conditional. During the second pause, repeat the correct answer.

MODELO: Ileana dice que va a la playa. → Ileana dijo que iría a la playa.

1. ...   2. ...   3. ...   4. ...   5. ...   6. ...

69. Conditional of Irregular Verbs

A. You will hear a series of sentences. During the first pause, change the verb in each one to the conditional. During the second pause, repeat the correct answer.

MODELO: ¿Sabes ir? → ¿Sabrías ir?

1. ...   2. ...   3. ...   4. ...   5. ...   6. ...   7. ...   8. ...   9. ...   10. ...

B. Respond to the following negative statements by using **Pues, yo sí...** or **Pues, nosotros sí...** and the conditional form of the verb. Follow the model. Repeat the correct answer after the second pause.

MODELO: No salgo con ese traje de baño. →
          Pues yo sí saldría con ese traje de baño.

1. ...   2. ...   3. ...   4. ...   5. ...

70. Ordinal Numbers

You will hear a series of sentences. Repeat each one, changing the adjective to the ordinal number indicated. During the second pause, repeat the correct answer.

MODELO: Es el único vuelo a Málaga. (único → 8) → Es el octavo vuelo a Málaga.

1. gran → 2   3. única → 4   5. peor → 1

2. este → 9   4. mejor → 3

71. Stressed Possessive Adjectives and Pronouns

You will hear a series of brief statements containing unstressed possessive adjectives. Substitute the stressed possessive pronoun and repeat the entire sentence. Follow the model. Repeat the correct answer during the second pause.

MODELO: Son mis gafas de sol. → Son las mías.

1. ...   2. ...   3. ...   4. ...   5. ...   6. ...

Comunicación

A. *Excursiones por España.* You will hear the **Texto** from page 304 of your textbook. First, listen carefully and try to follow the gist of the ideas. Then listen to the **Texto** again, followed by some incomplete statements based on it. You will hear each statement twice. Circle the letter of the phrase that best completes each statement.

1. a. más de 140 millones de alemanes e ingleses visitan España.

    b. los españoles se divertirán hablando alemán.

    c. más de 40 millones de turistas hacen viajes a España.

2. a. podría comer merluza.

    b. esquiaría en los lagos.

    c. debería practicar el piragüismo.

3. a. visitando las grandes ciudades.

    b. bronceándose en las playas.

    c. dando paseos por la Mancha.

4. a. podría ver dónde vivió el Greco.

    b. encontraría las islas Canarias.

    c. descubriría la montaña más alta de España.

B. *¡Visite España!* You will hear a short radio ad about travelling to Spain followed by some questions. During the first pause, answer the question. During the second pause, repeat the correct answer.

1. ...   2. ...   3. ...   4. ...   5. ...   6. ...

C. *Dictado.* You will hear a short conversation about the geography of Spain. During the first pause, write each sentence. During the second pause, check what you wrote.

_____

_____

_____

_____

_____

D. *Sólo tú.* You will hear a series of statements about yourself. Circle C if the statement is true (**Cierto**) or F if the statement is false (**Falso**).

1. C F   3. C F   5. C F

2. C F   4. C F

LECCIÓN DIECISÉIS
WORKBOOK

Gráficos

A. *Un viaje a la Argentina*. Complete the following dialogue about Edmundo and Graciela's trip by writing the names of the articles numbered in the drawing, along with the appropriate definite or indefinite article where needed.

Edmundo: ¡Si supieras cuántas _____ (1) he enviado a

nuestros amigos!

Graciela: ¿Necesitas más _____ (2)?

Jorge: Buenas tardes. Soy su _____ (3). Me parece que

estarían más a gusto con una copa de champán, ¿no?

Graciela: Sí, muchas gracias.

Edmundo: ¿Sería posible que usted nos confirmara nuestro vuelo de Buenos Aires a

Iguazú?

Jorge: Señor, sería mucho más fácil si usted lo confirmara en

_____ (4) de Buenos Aires.

Graciela: ¿Pero sería posible que perdiéramos nuestras reservaciones?

Jorge: No, señorita. Si perdieran _____ (5), sí sería un

gran problema. Las reservaciones pueden confirmarlas por teléfono.

Edmundo: Muchas gracias.

B. *En Buenos Aires*. Read the following dialogue and fill in the missing words, according to the items numbered in the drawing.

Edmundo: Estaríamos más cómodos con _____ (6) para ella

y _____ (7) para mí.

El agente: Lo siento mucho, señor. En la sección de no fumar sólo hay asientos de

pasillo. Hoy tenemos muchos _____ (8).

Edmundo: Imagínate, Graciela, si fumáramos (*we smoked*), podríamos tener los

asientos que pedimos.

Graciela: Señor, era imposible que nosotros supiéramos que nuestro

_____ (9) llegaría tarde.

El agente: Lo siento, señorita. Era necesario que ustedes confirmaran sus

reservaciones antes de la una.

Edmundo: Graciela, no tenemos más remedio—o juntos (*together*) con humo o

separados y sin fumadores.

Graciela: ¿Y si estuviéramos en primera clase? ¿Tendríamos los asientos que

queremos?

El agente: Tengo una idea. No es justo que Uds. perdieran sus asientos porque el

vuelo llegó tarde. Yo los voy a poner en primera clase.

_____ (10) ya está en el avión.

Graciela: Muchas gracias.

Edmundo: ¡Fenomenal!

C. *Preguntas*. Answer the following questions on the basis of the preceding dialogue.

1. Si Graciela y Edmundo fumaran, ¿podrían tener los asientos que pidieron?

   _____

2. ¿Era necesario que Graciela y Edmundo confirmaran sus reservaciones?

   _____

3. ¿Qué no es justo?

   _____

4. ¿Es justo que el agente decidiera ponerlos en primera clase?

   _____

5. ¿Era posible que Graciela supiera que el avión llegaría tarde?

   _____

Grámatica esencial

72. Regular Endings of the Imperfect Subjunctive

Complete the second sentence with the imperfect subjunctive form of the verb in the first phrase.

1. Ellas trabajaron mucho antes de las vacaciones.

   Pidió que ellas _____ mucho antes de las vacaciones.

2. Comimos durante el vuelo.

   Dudaban que nosotros _____ durante el vuelo.

3. La pasajera olvidó comprar el boleto.

   Fue probable que la pasajera _____ comprar el boleto.

4. Hablaste con el agente.

   ¿No te dije que tú _____ con el agente?

5. Reservé dos asientos.

   Me aconsejaron que yo _____ dos asientos.

6. Recogió el equipaje.

Le pedí a Edmundo que él _____ el equipaje.

7. Discutió con el auxiliar de vuelo.

No fue posible que Graciela _____ con el auxiliar de vuelo.

8. Se levantaron a tiempo para el vuelo.

No creí que ellos _____ a tiempo para el vuelo.

73. Imperfect Subjunctive of Irregular and Stem-changing Verbs

A. Complete these sentences with the imperfect subjunctive form of the verbs given in parentheses.

1. (ir) La aeromoza nos pidió que _____ a la sección

   delantera.

2. (decir) El agente no creyó que yo le _____ la verdad.

3. (traer) Nos pidieron que sólo _____ una maleta.

4. (poner) No nos gustó que él me _____ en la sección de

   fumar.

5. (querer) ¿Es posible que tú _____ cancelar las

   reservaciones?

6. (poder) Yo dudaba que el tren _____ llegar a tiempo.

7. (saber) Era imposible que nosotros _____ eso.

8. (tener) Les dije a ustedes que _____ mucho cuidado con

   esa línea aerea.

9. (estar) Esperaba que tú _____ lista temprano.

10. (venir) Me pidieron que yo _____ lo más pronto posible.

11. (hacer) ¿Crees tú que ellos _____ un viaje a Iguazú?

12. (dar) Yo no pensé que él me _____ un asiento de

    ventanilla.

B. Form new sentences according to the model.

MODELO: Ella no quería. / Yo me dormí. →
            Ella no quería que yo me durmiera.

1. Me recomendó. / Nosotros pedimos un taxi.

    _____

2. Dudaba. / Se divirtieron en el barco.

    _____

3. Pedimos. / La azafata nos sirvió café en el vuelo.

    _____

4. No era cierto. / Te sentías mal en Iguazú.

    _____

5. ¿Es posible... ? / Casi se murieron de hambre.

    _____

74. Sequence of Tenses with the Subjunctive

A. *Problemas de un fumador*. Complete the following story with the correct past tense form of the verbs in parentheses.

Pedí que el agente me (dar) _____ (1) un asiento en la sección

de fumadores, pero no me lo (poder) _____ (2) dar porque

había muchos pasajeros. Yo le (explicar) _____ (3) que estaba

tratando de dejar de fumar y que (querer) _____ (4) fumar mi

último cigarrillo hoy en el vuelo a Iguazú. Me explicó el agente que trataría de

cambiarme de asiento a la hora de salir. Yo estaba esperando en la sala de espera

cuando (ver) _____ (5) que mi avión había despegado (*taken

off*). Yo le pregunté al agente cómo fue posible que el avión (salir)

_____ (6) sin mí. Él no sabía qué decir; me recomendó que

(buscar) _____ (7) un hotel para esa noche y que (tratar)

_____ (8) de salir el próximo día. Inmediatamente yo me

(comprar) _____ (9) una cajetilla de cigarrillos y (empezar)

_____ (10) a fumar. ¿Cómo (ser) _____ (11)

posible que yo (dejar) _____ (12) de fumar en una situación

como ésta?

B. Change to the present tense according to the model.

MODELO: Dijo que no podría ir a Iguazú. →
          Dice que no puede ir a Iguazú.

1. No estaba segura de que pudiéramos comprar un boleto de ida y vuelta.

    _____

2. Me prometieron que habría espacio en el avión.

    _____

3. ¿Era importante que confirmáramos nuestras reservaciones?

    _____

4. Pedí que anunciaran la hora del vuelo otra vez.

    _____

5. Esperaban que el equipaje llegara en buenas condiciones.

    _____

Comunicación

A. *«El gaucho loco»*. Complete the following account of what happened to Edmundo and
    Graciela in a restaurant in Buenos Aires. Give the appropriate imperfect subjunctive
    form of the verbs in parentheses.

    Un señor que conocimos en el vuelo de Santiago nos recomendó que (comer)

    _____ (1) en un restaurante que se llamaba «El gaucho loco».

    Nos dijo que (hacer) _____ (2) reservaciones antes de ir

    porque era un lugar muy popular.

        Pedimos un taxi para que nos (llevar) _____ (3) al

    restaurante. Allí nos pidieron que (sentarse) _____ (4) en el bar primero y que (esperar) _____ (5) unos minutos por nuestra

mesa.

Después de dos o tres copas de vino chileno nos llevaron a una pequeña mesa.

Graciela pidió que nos (dar) _____ (6) un menú, pero el

camarero se rió. —Señorita, aquí no tenemos menú. Sólo servimos comida típica de los

gauchos. Estoy seguro que les va a gustar.

Cuando nos trajo el primer plato, nos pusimos muy contentos. Era una deliciosa

ensalada de berros (*watercress*). Pero cuando nos trajeron el plato principal casi nos

quedamos muertos de sorpresa. No creíamos que nos (poder)

_____ (7) traer un plato tan enorme de carne. ¡Qué lástima que

Graciela y yo (ser) _____ (8) vegetarianos!

¿Pero qué íbamos a hacer? La cena estaba en la mesa y los dos teníamos hambre. Le

pedí a Graciela que me (perdonar) _____ (9). No quería que

(enojarse) _____ (10) conmigo. Ella me miró muy seriamente

(*seriously*) y me dijo:—Edmundo, mi tía peruana siempre me decía, «En la ciudad en

que estuvieras, haz lo que vieras».

Nunca creímos que (disfrutar) _____ (11) tanto una cena.

¡No dejamos ni un pedacito (*piece*) de carne en el plato!

B. *¡Viajar es difícil!* Respond to the following situations by forming sentences, using the words in parentheses. Be sure that the verb in the dependent clause is in the imperfect subjunctive.

MODELO: Este vuelo va vacío. →
          (yo / pedir / darme / un asiento de pasillo)
          Yo pedí que me dieran un asiento de pasillo.

1. No hay otro vuelo a Iguazú hoy.

   (nosotros / recomendarte / ir a la semana próxima)

   _____

2. No hay taxis después de las ocho.

(yo / querer / ellos / pedirme / uno / en seguida)

_____

3. No llegamos a tiempo al aeropuerto.

(el agente / nos / aconsejar / tomar / un autobús)

_____

4. Graciela trajo una cantidad enorme de equipaje.

(nosotros / decir / a ella / no traer tanto)

_____

5. Olvidé los boletos, las tarjetas y los sellos.

(te / mandar / llevarlos / en / el maletín)

_____

C. *Sólo tú*. Answer the following questions about yourself.

1. ¿Adónde les gustaría a tus padres que fueras para tus próximas vacaciones?

_____

2. ¿Te gustaría que te invitaran a hacer un viaje por la América Latina?

_____

3. ¿Adónde irías primero en la América Latina?

_____

4. ¿Les aconsejarías a tus amigos que fueran a la América Latina?

_____

5. ¿Por qué sí o por qué no?

_____

6. Si no, ¿qué lugar les recomendarías que visitaran?

_____

LECCIÓN DIECISÉIS
LABORATORY MANUAL

Gráficos

A. You will hear a series of statements. You will hear each statement twice. Repeat each one and circle the letter that corresponds to the person who would be most likely to have made the statement.

1. a. el chófer de taxi b. el empleado del hotel c. el pasajero

2. a. el agente de la línea aérea b. la azafata c. el pasajero

3. a. el agente de la línea aérea b. el chófer de taxi c. el pasajero

4. a. el botones b. el empleado del hotel c. el pasajero

5. a. el empleado del hotel b. el pasajero c. el chófer de taxi

B. You will hear the following sentences twice. During the first pause, write in the missing words. During the second pause, check what you wrote.

1. Le recomendaron que _____ las reservaciones.

2. Sería terrible que _____ los boletos.

3. ¡Qué lástima que no _____ a Iguazú!

4. Quería que _____ la hora de mi llegada.

C. You will hear a series of statements. You will hear each statement twice. Circle the letter of the word or phrase that you associate most closely with each situation.

1. a. las estampillas b. el horario c. la postal

2. a. los viajeros b. los boletos c. los fumadores

3. a. la azafata b. el horario c. el agente

4. a. el correo b. el contratiempo c. el auxiliar de vuelo

Pronunciación

Review of Spanish **b** and **v**

Remember that in Spanish the letters **b** and **v** are pronounced exactly alike. Both **b** and **v** have two different pronunciations, however: a hard sound and a soft sound.

A. The hard sound of **b** or **v** is pronounced after a pause and after the letters **m** and **n**. Keep in mind that the letter combinations **nb** and **nv** are pronounced as if they were **mb** and **mv**. Listen and repeat.

¡Vaya!	¡Venga!	en vacaciones	un boleto
un viajero	en bicicleta	un vino tinto	Víctor

B. The soft sound of **b** or **v** is pronounced at all other times. Be particularly careful in pronouncing **b** or **v** between vowels. To pronounce the soft sound, draw your lips close together, but without letting them touch; then let the air pass through to produce a slight friction. Listen: **joven**. Never give Spanish **b** or **v** the sound of *v* in the English word *visit:* this kind of *v* does not exist in Spanish. Repeat these sentences after the speaker.

Sé las palabras nuevas.

Yo vivo en Puerto Vallarta.

Él viaja con Verónica.

¿Cuándo vuelve Vicente?

¿Adónde van los viajeros?

Bárbara vendió noventa billetes.

Bailamos varias veces.

Llevo veinte días en Venezuela.

Gramática esencial

72. Regular Endings of the Imperfect Subjunctive

A. You will hear a series of sentences in the present subjunctive. Rephrase each sentence by changing the second verb to the imperfect subjunctive. During the second pause, repeat the correct answer.

MODELO: Es posible que hable con la azafata. →
          Es posible que hablara con la azafata.

1. ...   2. ...   3. ...   4. ...   5. ...

B. Follow the same steps with this model sentence. This time change the first verb to the imperfect tense and the second verb to the imperfect subjunctive.

MODELO: Queremos que viajes con ella. →
Queríamos que viajaras con ella.

1. ...   2. ...   3. ...   4. ...   5. ...

73. Imperfect Subjunctive of Irregular and Stem-changing Verbs

You will hear a series of statements. First, repeat each one. Then you will hear a pair of sentences. Circle the letter of the one that you most closely associate with the original statement.

1. a b   3. a b   5. a b

2. a b   4. a b   6. a b

74. Sequence of Tenses with the Subjunctive

A. You will hear a series of sentences with verbs in the present tense. During the first pause, rephrase each one with the corresponding imperfect indicative and imperfect subjunctive forms of the verbs. During the second pause, repeat the correct answer.

MODELO: Ella recomienda que compres los boletos. →
Ella recomendaba que compraras los boletos.

1. ...   2. ...   3. ...

B. Repeat the same steps with this model sentence. This time change the first verb to the preterite.

MODELO: Aconsejo que vayas por avión. →
Aconsejé que fueras por avión.

1. ...   2. ...   3. ...

C. Repeat the same steps with this model sentence. This time change the first verb to the conditional.

MODELO: Siento que no vengas a Buenos Aires. →
Sentiría que no vinieras a Buenos Aires.

1. ...   2. ...   3. ...

Comunicación

A. *El diario de Elena.* You will hear the **Texto** from page 325 of your textbook. Listen carefully and try to follow the gist of the ideas. Then listen to the **Texto** again, followed by some incomplete statements based on it. You will hear each statement twice. Circle the letter of the phrase that best completes each statement.

1. a. encontrarías conquistadores españoles.

    b. verías muchas piedras preciosas.

    c. comprarías montañas de sal.

2. a. encontrarías una ciudad vieja y fea.

    b. estarías muy cerca de San Juan.

    c. visitarías un lugar moderno y con sabor antiguo.

3. a. se rompería el cable del funicular.

    b. verías la ciudad de Bogotá.

    c. tendrías que subir a pie.

4. a. tallarías estatuas de sal.

    b. tendrías que comer mucha sal.

    c. estarías a cuarenta minutos de la capital.

B. *Un viaje exótico.* Study the map while you listen to a short account of Graciela and Edmundo's trip from Santiago de Chile to Buenos Aires and Iguazú. Then you will hear some questions. Listen to the passage again, and this time answer the questions. Repeat the correct answer after the speaker.

1. ...   2. ...   3. ...   4. ...   5. ...

C. *Sólo tú*. You will hear a series of statements about yourself. Circle C if the statement is true (**Cierto**) or F if the statement is false (**Falso**).

1. C F   3. C F   5. C F

2. C F   4. C F

LECCIÓN DIECISIETE
WORKBOOK

Gráficos

A. *¿Quién lo diría?* Write in the person who would most likely say each of the following statements.

1. —Con las monedas que tienes en la alcancía puedes abrir una cuenta de ahorros que

    te pague ocho por ciento de interés. _____

2. —La compañía necesita un empleado bancario que hable español y que sepa utilizar

    una computadora. _____

3. —No puedo encontrar la carpeta que tiene la circular sobre los sueldos.

    _____

4. —Si Ud. tuviera su tarjeta de identificación, le podría cambiar el cheque.

    _____

5. —No se preocupe, señor. Si encontráramos su chequera, lo llamaríamos en

   seguida._____

6. —Si yo no tuviera que hacer cola, robaría el banco. _____

B. *Si tuviéramos...* Study the drawing again, read the following dialogue, and answer the questions that follow.

Eugenio:	No hay nada que resulte tan inútil como una computadora que no funciona.
Sara:	Si tuviera papel con membrete, podría escribir las cartas.
Eugenio:	Y claro, tampoco funciona la copiadora.
Sara:	Si hubiera un banco donde pagaran más, cambiaría de trabajo mañana mismo.
Eugenio:	¿Sabes que a la máquina de escribir le hace falta una cinta (*ribbon*) desde la semana pasada?
Sara:	Si llegaran los sobres de la imprenta (*printer*), podría enviarles los estados de cuentas (*statements*) a los clientes.
Eugenio:	Y necesitamos un intercomunicador que funcione.
El jefe:	(Por el intercomunicador) ¡Si tuviéramos empleados que trabajaran en vez de quejarse (*complain*), tendríamos más dinero con que pagarles!

1. ¿Quién tiene una computadora que no funciona?

   _____

2. Si Sara tuviera papel con membrete, ¿qué haría?

   _____

3. ¿Qué necesita Sara para enviar los estados de cuentas?

   _____

4. ¿Quiénes tienen intercomunicadores?

   _____

5. ¿Hay cola en todas las ventanillas?

   _____

6. ¿Cómo podría el banco tener más dinero?

   _____

Grámatica esencial

75.–76. Subjunctive in Adjective Clauses and Clauses Modifying Indefinite Persons or Things

A. Complete the following story with the appropriate form of the verbs in parentheses.

Tengo una cuenta que (pagar) _____ (1) buen interés, pero

necesito invertir (*invest*) el resto de mis ahorros en alguna compañía que (tener)

_____ (2) la posibilidad de hacerme rico en algunos años. Me

gustaría poner el dinero en una compañía que (vender) _____ (3)

computadoras. ¿Sabes de alguna persona que (conocer) _____ (4)

esa industria? Mi amigo Héctor dice que él tiene unas acciones (*stocks*) que le (dar)

_____ (5) un cincuenta por ciento anual. Yo no conozco

ninguna persona rica que no (tener) _____ (6) buen juicio

(*good judgment*).

B. Complete the following sentences with the appropriate form of the verbs in parentheses.

1. Necesito una empleada que (saber) _____ hablar español.

2. Tenemos un cajero que (ser) _____ bilingüe.

3. Prefiero un banco donde (poder) _____ hablar mi idioma.

4. ¿Por qué no buscas un banco que te (pagar) _____ mejor

   interés?

5. ¿Sabes de algún banco donde no (haber) _____ colas?

6. Sólo quieren empleados que (escribir) _____ a máquina.

77. Subjunctive in Clauses Modifying Negative Antecedents

A. Restate the following sentences negatively.

1. Conozco un banco donde pagan el diez por ciento de interés.

   _____

2. Tenemos muchas empleadas que hablan español.

   _____

3. Hay problemas que son fáciles de resolver.

   _____

4. Había un cajero que no sabía usar la computadora.

   _____

5. Sabíamos que había una cuenta que pagaba más interés.

   _____

B. Answer the following questions negatively.

   1. ¿Hay alguna computadora que funcione sin contratiempos?

      _____

   2. ¿Hay alguien en el banco que nos pueda ayudar?

      _____

   3. ¿Tienen un empleado que sepa usar una copiadora?

      _____

   4. ¿Sabes de alguna inversión que sea segura?

      _____

   5. ¿Hay alguien que haya visto al cómplice?

      _____

78. If-Clauses

Express in Spanish.

   1. If I were you, I'd buy a new computer.

      _____

   2. If the check would arrive tomorrow, we would open an account.

      _____

3. If they were to give you 10 percent interest, would you deposit your savings in that
   bank?

   _____

4. We'd help her learn English if she asked us.

   _____

5. Of course if I had a phone I wouldn't need an intercom.

   _____

Para repasar

Change to the subjunctive.

MODELO: Me cambian los cheques sin tener identificación./(Yo esperaba que...) →
          Yo esperaba que me cambiaran los cheques sin tener identificación.

1. Coopero con el empleado bancario./(El jefe quería que...)

   _____

2. Vieron al cómplice con la pistola./(Yo dudé que...)

   _____

3. Esteban firmó el cheque./(Sara no pensó que...)

   _____

4. El niño abrió una cuenta de ahorros./(Era mejor que...)

   _____

5. Después de los problemas de Wall Street perdieron todo el dinero./

   (Fue una lástima que...)

   _____

6. Al llegar al banco le mostraron la pistola al cajero./(Era imposible creer que...)

   _____

Comunicación

A. *Abriendo una cuenta.* You have just moved to Mexico City and are in the process of opening a checking account. Express the following conversation in Spanish between you and the bank officer.

1. Don't you have a checking account that pays interest?

_____

2. In Mexico we only have savings accounts that pay interest.

_____

3. In order to open an account, do I need an identification card that has my photo **(foto)**?

_____

4. If you have a letter from your company that says that you are their employee, there is no problem.

_____

5. Do you want me to bring you bills or a check?

_____

6. If you were to bring us a check, you couldn't use your account for a month.

_____

B. *¿Qué hacer con mi dinero?* Complete the following paragraph with the correct indicative or subjunctive form of the verb in parentheses.

Cuando llevaba una semana en Puerto Ponce busqué un banco que me (pagar)

_____ (1) un diez por ciento en una cuenta de ahorros. Era

imposible porque la economía del país no era muy estable. Decidí buscar un banco

donde no (tener) _____ (2) que hacer cola. Pues eso también

era imposible. Le pregunté a un amigo si él conocía un banco donde

(haber)_____ (3) servicios especiales para extranjeros. Él se rió

y me dijo que si yo le (dar) _____ (4) mi cheque todos los

meses, él me daría dinero para mis gastos e invertiría el resto. Al preguntarle en qué invertiría mi dinero, me explicó que sólo lo pondría en acciones que (ganar)

_____ (5) el veinte por ciento. Yo le dije que si yo

(estar)_____ (6) loco, le daría mi cheque. No creía que

(existir)_____ (7) inversiones que

(pagar)_____ (8) tanto.

C. *Sólo tú.* Answer the following questions about yourself.

1. Si tuvieras un millón de dólares, ¿qué harías?

   _____

2. Si te ofrecieran (*offer*) un trabajo en un banco, ¿lo aceptarías?

   _____

3. Si fueras a abrir una cuenta de ahorros, ¿en qué banco la abrirías?

   _____

4. Si trataran de robarte el dinero del bolsillo, ¿qué es lo primero que harías?

   _____

5. Si encontraras una alcancía llena de monedas, ¿qué harías?

   _____

LECCIÓN DIECISIETE
LABORATORY MANUAL

Gráficos

A. You will hear a series of verb phrases. During the first pause, give the imperfect subjunctive form of the verb. Repeat the correct answer during the second pause.

1. ...   2. ...   3. ...   4. ...   5. ...

B. You will hear a series of statements on the tape. You will hear each statement twice. Circle the letter of the word or phrase that you associate most closely with each situation.

1. a. el membrete   b. la cajera   c. el asaltante

2. a. la cuenta de ahorros b. la calculadora   c. la alcancía

3. a. la computadora   b. la secretaria   c. la nota

4. a. la hoja de depósito b. la empleada bancaria c. la computadora

C. You will hear a series of statements. You will hear each statement twice. Circle C if the statement is true (**Cierto**) of F if the statement is false (**Falso**).

1. C F   2. C F   3. C F   4. C F

Pronunciación

Review of Spanish d

The Spanish **d** is a hard sound at the beginning of a breath group and after **n** and **l**. In all other positions it is a soft, fricative sound. A fricative **d** in Spanish is like the *th* sound in the English word *then*, but less harsh. Be particularly careful to pronounce the fricative **d** between vowels. Listen and repeat.

Soft **d**	Hard **d**
autoridad	el día
partido	¿dónde?
moneda	fin de semana
los dedos	don Daniel
marcado	sueldo
cepillo de dientes	andar

Gramática esencial

75.–76. Subjunctive in Adjective Clauses and Clauses Modifying Indefinite Persons or Things

A. You will hear a series of sentences. During the first pause, rephrase the sentence by changing the first verb to **necesito** and changing the second verb to the subjunctive. During the second pause, repeat the correct answer.

MODELO: Hay un empleado que habla inglés. (Necesito...) →
Necesito un empleado que hable inglés.

1. Necesito...   4. Necesito...

2. Necesito...   5. Necesito...

3. Necesito...

B. You will hear a series of questions. During the first pause, answer each one affirmatively. During the second pause, repeat the correct answer.

MODELO: ¿Conoces algún banco que pague buen interés? →
Sí, conozco un banco que paga buen interés.

1. ...   2. ...   3. ...   4. ...   5. ...

77. Subjunctive in Clauses Modifying Negative Antecedents

A. You will hear a series of sentences. During the first pause, make the sentence negative, changing the second verb to the subjunctive. During the second pause, repeat the correct answer.

MODELO: Conocía a alguien que trabajaba en el banco. →
            No conocía a nadie que trabajara en el banco.

1. ...   2. ...   3. ...   4. ...   5. ...

B. You will hear a series of questions. During the first pause, answer each question negatively, changing the second verb to the subjunctive. During the second pause, repeat the correct answer.

MODELO: Tú tienes una computadora que deseas vender, ¿no? →
            No, no tengo una computadora que desee vender.

1. ...   2. ...   3. ...   4. ...   5. ...

78. If-Clauses

A. You will hear a series of short sentences in pairs. During the first pause, combine sentences of each pair beginning with **si** and using the conditional in the result clause. During the second pause, repeat the correct answer.

MODELO: Soy rico. / Ahorro dinero. → Si fuera rico, ahorraría dinero.

1. ...   2. ...   3. ...   4. ...   5. ...

B. You will hear a sentence containing a present tense verb in the **si** clause and a future tense verb in the result clause. During the first pause, change the sentence to express an improbable future action. During the second pause, repeat the correct answer.

MODELO: Si llama, le diré que no voy. → Si llamara, le diría que no voy.

1. ...   2. ...   3. ...   4. ...   5. ...

Comunicación

A. *En el banco.* You will hear the **Texto** from page 342 of your textbook. Listen carefully and try to follow the gist of the ideas. Then you will hear the **Texto** again, followed by some incomplete statements based on it. You will hear each statement twice. Circle the letter of the phrase that best completes each one.

1. a. que valieran más.

   b. que valieran menos.

   c. y pesos.

2. a. ningún banco que pague menos.

   b. ningún banco que cambie dólares.

   c. ningún banco que pague más.

3. a. la cajera le daría más pesos.

   b. la cajera no le podría cambiar los cheques.

   c. la cajera le abriría una cuenta de ahorros.

4. a. tendría que usar un revólver.

   b. la cajera llamaría al policía.

   c. recibiría más pesos por dólar.

5. a. si el jefe le daría más pesos.

   b. si la cajera le ofreciera pesos a veinte y siete por dólar.

   c. si cambiara los cheques en el mercado negro.

LECCIÓN DIECIOCHO
WORKBOOK

Gráficos

SINDICATO DE TRABAJADORES FEDERALES

Arquitectura   Ingeniería   Pedagogía
Comercio   Medicina   Química
Farmacia   Obreros   Socio-Economía

¡Gastos bajos, ¡sí!
Sueldos bajos, ¡no!

El gobierno quiere rebajar los sueldos de todos los trabajadores federales.

A. *En la reunión del sindicato* (union) *de trabajadores federales*. Study the drawing and then indicate who would most likely say each of the following statements. Each statement may have more than one correct answer.

1. No puedo diseñar (*design*) otro edificio hasta que sepa cuánto me van a pagar.

   _____

2. A menos que me ofrezcan otros beneficios (*benefits*), no podré seguir enseñando a

   mis alumnos. _____

3. Para que yo siga tratando a mis pacientes, me tendrán que dar un aumento (*raise*).

   _____

4. Con tal de que no suba el precio de las medicinas, podremos seguir sirviendo al

   público. _____

5. Antes de que se instale la tubería en el nuevo edificio federal, me tendrán que

   explicar cómo va a vivir mi familia con menos dinero.

   _____

6. Aunque bajen los sueldos y reduzcan los gastos federales, necesitarán personas que

   resuelvan los problemas sociales del pueblo. _____

B. *A menos que...* Study the drawing again, read the dialogue, and answer the questions
   that follow.

   El plomero: Antes de que pasen esta nueva ley (*law*), nos tienen que convencer que
                       será un beneficio para el país.

   El psiquiatra: Después de que nos matamos trabajando por tantos años no es justo
                       que nos pidan que trabajemos por menos.

   El plomero: Con tal de que la economía del país no se caiga por completo, no me
                       importa hacer un sacrificio.

   El psiquiatra: Sí, Martín, tienes razón. Pero a menos que cambien la política
                       extranjera del país, no vale la pena hacer estos cambios.

   El plomero: Es verdad. Hay que tener en cuenta que a menos que vendamos más
                       productos a los países extranjeros, nuestra economía sólo va a
                       empeorar (*get worse*).

   El psiquiatra: Es muy difícil ganarse la vida sin la ayuda del sindicato.

   1. Antes de que el gobierno pase una ley que reduzca los sueldos, ¿qué tiene que

      hacer?

      _____

   2. ¿Es justo que después de que uno trabaja mucho por tantos años le pidan que

      trabaje por menos?

      _____

   3. ¿No le importa al plomero hacer un sacrificio?

      _____

   4. ¿Qué es necesario que haga el gobierno con la política extranjera?

      _____

   5. ¿Qué dice el plomero que hay que tener en cuenta?

      _____

Grámatica esencial

79.–80. Subjunctive in Adverbial Clauses of Purpose and Proviso

Complete these sentences with the appropriate form of the verb in parentheses.

1. (matarse) A menos que uno _____ trabajando, es imposible ganarse la vida.

2. (comer) Con tal de que _____ bien los miembros de mi familia, no me importa hacer un sacrificio.

3. (pedir) En caso de que el gerente me _____ que acepte la reducción, cambiaré de empresa.

4. (valer) Para que _____ la pena seguir cuidando a los enfermos, tienen que ajustar el presupuesto (*budget*).

5. (poder) Trabajo para que tú _____ continuar tu educación.

6. (ganar) No me importan los cambios con tal de que un carpintero no _____ menos que un electricista.

7. (haber) A menos que _____ verdaderos cambios en la política actual, no vamos a resolver nada.

8. (estar) Para que todos nosotros _____ de acuerdo, el gobierno tendrá que hacer muchísimos cambios.

81. Subjunctive in Adverbial Clauses of Time

Combine the adverbial clause in parentheses with the sentence to create a new statement. Be sure to change the first verb to the future tense.

MODELO: Le pago. (cuando el camarero traiga la cuenta) →
Le pagaré cuando el camarero traiga la cuenta.

1. Le compro otro martillo. (cuando llegue el carpintero)

_____

2. El electricista me cobra una fortuna. (después de que pinten la casa)

_____

3. No nos podemos bañar. (hasta que ponga la tubería)

_____

4. Lavamos la ropa. (tan pronto como repares la secadora)

_____

5. ¿No podrás encender las luces? (hasta que venga el ingeniero)

_____

6. Decido si vale la pena trabajar para esa empresa. (cuando me llame el gerente)

_____

82. Subjunctive After **aunque**

A. Use **aunque** to combine each of these pairs of sentences to express a statement of possibility. Make the necessary verb changes.

MODELO: Elisa será una buena psiquiatra. / No tiene mucha experiencia. →
          Elisa será una buena psiquiatra aunque no tenga mucha experiencia.

1. Rolando cobrará mucho por hora. / No es un buen carpintero.

_____

2. El arquitecto cambiará los planes. / No se lo pedimos.

_____

3. Juan defenderá bien a sus clientes. / Él no cree que es un buen abogado.

_____

4. María llegará a ser millonaria. / Ella no ahorra ni un centavo.

_____

5. Aquel economista sacará su título. / Le toma ocho años.

_____

B. Change the following sentences to factual statements by changing the appropriate verb to the indicative.

1. Juan no será nunca un gran pintor, aunque pinte todos los días.

_____

2. Ese señor jamás será un buen carpintero, aunque tenga todas las herramientas.

   _____

3. Aunque cambien la política extranjera, el pueblo no estará contento.

   _____

4. Aunque vea a mil pacientes al año, la doctora Ruiz siempre tiene tiempo para otro.

   _____

5. Aunque no necesite hacerlo, el gobierno ajustará los sueldos.

   _____

Para repasar

Un problema psicológico. Complete the following paragraph with the correct form of the verbs in parentheses.

¿Conoce usted algún psiquiatra que (tener) _____ (1) buena

reputación? Creo que no hay nadie en esta clínica que me (poder)

_____ (2) ayudar. Claro que me va a preguntar «¿Por qué necesitas

que te (ayudar) _____ (3) un psiquiatra?» Pues, la verdad es que

tengo un hermano que (poner) _____ (4) todos sus ahorros en

unas inversiones malísimas. Cada semana dice que sabe de una inversión que (pagar)

_____ (5) tremendas ganancias. En realidad no conoce el mercado

financiero. Soy muy conservador, pero no veo cómo es posible que él (haber)

_____ (6) perdido 20 millones de pesos en dos meses. Por eso

busco un psiquiatra que (saber) _____ (7) curarlo.

Comunicación

A. *Un voto de apoyo* (support). You are the leader of the **Sindicato de Trabajadores Federales** and you are giving a presentation. Use the correct form of the verbs in parentheses to complete your speech.

Señores y señoras, antes de que yo (comenzar) _____ (1) este

discurso (*speech*), quiero que ustedes (saber) _____ (2) que

estoy muy agradecido (*grateful*) de que todos ustedes (encontrarse)

_____ (3) aquí. Aunque todos nosotros (ser)

_____ (4) miembros de distintas profesiones, tenemos que

trabajar en solidaridad para que (tener) _____ (5) éxito.

Tenemos que encontrar a alguien que nos (poder) _____ (6)

representar para que el gobierno (darse) _____ (7) cuenta de

que es necesario solicitar nuestra opinión. En caso de que los líderes de nuestro país

(decidir) _____ (8) que no les importa nuestra opinión,

tendremos que buscar otros métodos de que nos (oír) _____ (9).

Yo estoy dispuesto (*ready*) a hablar con nuestros líderes tan pronto como ustedes

(darme) _____ (10) su voto de apoyo. Aunque ellos (haber)

_____ (11) manejado la economía tan mal, no es justo que

nosotros (tener) _____ (12) que sufrir de esta manera.

B. *Preguntas*. Form questions that could be answered by the following statements.

1. No trabajaremos a menos que nos den un aumento.

   _____

2. Tan pronto como llegue el gerente, te llamaré.

   _____

3. ¡Para que tú seas química, tendrás que estudiar mil años!

   _____

4. No creo que valga la pena terminar las paredes antes de poner el aislamiento.

   _____

5. Aunque practique el piano todos los días, nunca podré tocar esa pieza.

_____

C. *Sólo tú.* Use the following cues to express your professional plans for the future.

1. a menos que / recibir ayuda financiera

_____

2. tan pronto como / recibir mi título

_____

3. para que / ser gerente de una empresa

_____

4. aunque / estudiar todos los días

_____

5. con tal de que / ganar mucho dinero

_____

LECCIÓN DIECIOCHO
LABORATORY MANUAL

Gráficos

A. You will hear a series of statements about different occupations. You will hear each statement twice. Circle the letter of the profession that you associate most closely with each.

1. a. la dentista   b. la psiquiatra   c. la veterinaria

2. a. el abogado   b. el maestro   c. el trabajador social

3. a. el ingeniero   b. la contadora   c. la electricista

4. a. el químico   b. el sociólogo   c. el enfermero

5. a. la abogada   b. el farmacéutico   c. el fontanero

6. a. la trabajadora social   b. el albañil   c. el carpintero

7. a. la ingeniera   b. el técnico   c. el economista

B. You will hear a series of sentences twice. During the first pause, write in the missing words. During the second pause, check what you wrote.

1. _____ la pena, no instalaremos aislamiento.

2. _____ tanto, tendrán que pintar la casa de oro.

3. _____ quisiera repasar la cuenta.

4. _____, es necesario que tomen en cuenta el costo de los

materiales.

Pronunciación

Intonation

When the answer to a question is partially or totally known to the speaker, the intonation pattern is as follows:

¿Francisco viene mañana?

```
                                        ña
        cis   co   vie   ne   ma
                                           na?
  ¿Fran
```

The differentiating feature of this type of question is that the intonation level *goes up* on the last accented syllable (**ña**) and then falls (**na**). There is a comparable pattern in English.

He is coming tomorrow, isn't he?

```
                                        isn't
        com   ing   to   mor   row
    is                                       he?
  He
```

Think of the final syllable in the Spanish question as being similar to English *won't he, don't you, will you,* and so on.

Repeat these questions after the speaker.

¿Tú me has enten*di*do?

¿Ellos vendrán el *mar*tes?

¿Tú vas a comprar *fru*ta?

¿Eso no es poca *co*sa?

¿Esa familia es *ri*ca?

¿Tú comes pes*ca*do?

Gramática esencial

79.–80. Subjunctive in Adverbial Clauses of Purpose and Proviso

A. First repeat the model sentence, then substitute the cue words that are given on the tape and repeat the entire sentence. Repeat the correct answer during the second pause.

MODELO: Lo llamaré hoy para que pague. (a menos que) →
Lo llamaré hoy a menos que pague.

1. ...   2. ...

B. Repeat the same steps with this model sentence.

MODELO: En caso de que me llamen, les escribiré una carta. (para que) →
Para que me llamen, les escribiré una carta.

1. ...   2. ...

81. Subjunctive in Adverbial Clauses of Time

A. First repeat the model sentence, then substitute the cue words that are given on the tape and repeat the entire sentence. Repeat the correct answer during the second pause.

MODELO: No lo pagaremos cuando lo cobren. (tan pronto como) →
No lo pagaremos tan pronto como lo cobren.

1. ...   2. ...   3. ...   4. ...

82. Subjunctive After aunque

You will hear several statements of possibility. During the first pause, change each one to a statement of fact by changing the appropriate verb to the indicative. During the second pause, repeat the correct answer.

MODELO: Aunque gane mucho dinero, no ahorrará un peso en el banco. →
Aunque gana mucho dinero, no ahorrará un peso en el banco.

1. ...   2. ...   3. ...   4. ...

Comunicación

A. *Sobre gustos no hay nada escrito.* You will hear the **Texto** from page 357 of your textbook. Listen carefully and try to follow the gist of the ideas. Then listen to the **Texto** again, followed by some incomplete statements based on it. You will hear each statement twice. Circle the letter of the phrase that best completes each one.

1. a. Nicolás estudie física nuclear.

   b. Nicolás quiera ser médico.

   c. Nicolás tenga afición a las ciencias.

2. a. sus padres prefieren que él haga la elección final.

   b. sus padres quieren que él sea arquitecto.

   c. sus padres le comprarán una tele.

3. a. a menos que a él le guste escribir guiones.

   b. tan pronto como se especialice en computadoras.

   c. después de que él la haya escogido.

4. a. ajustará la tele.

   b. estudiará inglés.

   c. estudiará ingeniería.

B. *Dictado.* You will hear a short paragraph about professions. During the first pause, write each sentence in the space provided. During the second pause, check what you wrote.

_____

_____

_____

_____

_____

C. *Sólo tú.* You will hear a series of incomplete statements. Complete each one according to your own experience and wishes. No answers will be given on the tape.

1. ...   2. ...   3. ...   4. ...   5. ...

Answer Key

PRELIMINARES 1

WORKBOOK

NOMBRES Y PERSONAS **A.** 1. Se llama Sara. 2. Es de Miami. 3. Se llama Patricia Valdés. 4. No, la profesora es de Nueva York. 5. El amigo de Pablo (también) es de Nueva York. **B.** 1. Charles 2. Anne 3. John 4. Richard 5. Peter 6. Alice 7. Joan
EL ALFABETO Y LOS COGNADOS **A.** 1. z 2. b 3. ch 4. q 5. j 6. s 7. y 8. h 9. ll 10. m 11. r 12. rr 13. ñ 14. g 15. t 16. x 17. w 18. l **B.** 1. la democracia 2. la clase 3. la persona 4. el comunismo 5. el socialismo
ASKING QUESTIONS 1. ¿Es de México María Luisa? 2. ¿Cómo se llama el estudiante americano? 3. ¿Es inteligente la profesora colombiana? 4. ¿Es importante la educación? 5. ¿Es famoso el senador de California?

PRELIMINARES 2

WORKBOOK

ME GUSTA/TE GUSTA/LE GUSTA **A.** 1. (No) Me gusta el tenis. 2. (No) Me gusta el vólibol. 3. (No) Me gusta el fútbol. 4. (No) Me gusta el béisbol. **B.** 1. ¿Te gustan las matemáticas? 2. ¿Te gusta la universidad? 3. ¿Te gusta la clase de español? 4. ¿Te gusta la filosofía? **C.** 1. (No) Le gusta la música moderna. 2. (No) Le gustan las discotecas. 3. (No) Le gustan las comedias de la televisión. 4. (No) Le gusta el teatro.
EL CALENDARIO **B.** 1. invierno 2. otoño 3. verano 4. primavera
LAS MATEMÁTICAS **A.** 1. nueve 2. dos 3. veinte y nueve 4. uno 5. veinte y cinco **B.** 1. veinte y nueve 2. diez 3. veinte y siete; veinte y tres 4. treinta y uno 5. diez; veinte; treinta 6. quince; diez y siete; diez y nueve
COMUNICACIÓN **A.** 1. Hola, ¿qué hay? 2. Nada de nuevo. ¿Y tú? 3. Así así. Hasta mañana. 4. Hasta luego. **B.** 1. ¿De dónde es? 2. ¿Son muy inteligentes las dos profesoras de Chile? 3. ¿Quién es? 4. ¿Cómo es el profesor? 5. ¿Cómo se llama usted? *or* ¿Cómo te llamas? **C.** 1. (No) Me gusta el invierno. 2. (No) Me gustan las tragedias. 3. (No) Me gusta la televisión en español. 4. (No) Me gusta la ópera. 5. (No) Me gustan los deportes.

LABORATORY MANUAL

COMUNICACIÓN **B.** 1. No me gusta la universidad. 2. Me gustan mucho los deportes. 3. Me gustan el teatro y la televisión. 4. No me gustan las matemáticas. 5. Me gusta el verano.

LECCIÓN UNO
WORKBOOK

GRÁFICOS **A.** 1. La profesora 2. el alumno 3. la alumna 4. la tiza 5. la pizarra 6. el mapa 7. el bolígrafo 8. el cuaderno 9. el lápiz 10. El libro 11. la mesa 12. el papel 13. la silla **B.** 1. La profesora Tolón enseña la clase de español hoy. 2. Luis estudia en la biblioteca. 3. Luis pronuncia el español bien. 4. Sí, Luis estudia el libro todos los días. 5. Sí, le gusta mucho. 6. Luis contesta en español.

GRAMÁTICA ESENCIAL 1.–3. **A.** 1. el, un 2. la, una 3. la, una 4. el, un 5. la, una 6. el, un 7. la, una 8. el, un **B.** 1. La... la/una 2. El/un... el/un, la/una 3. la/una... la/una 4. El (un)/la(una)... el/un... la/una 5. El... un **C.** 1. unos dibujos en las paredes 2. las profesoras de la Argentina 3. los lápices de Tomás 4. las sillas de las compañeras de clase 5. unas lecciones en los cuadernos 6. unas universidades en las ciudades *4.* **A.** 1. un... español 2. una... francesa 3. un... colombiano 4. una... italiana 5. un... mexicano **B.** 1. La... interesante 2. la... generosa 3. La... importante 4. sentimental la 5. el... famoso *5.–6.* **A.** 1. Él 2. Uds. *or* vosotros/as 3. ellos 4. Ellas 5. Ella 6. Nosotros/as **B.** 1. Yo no estudio, practico... 2. ¿No entra, enseña...? 3. Ellas no conversan, hablan... 4. Julia, mamá y yo preparamos, estudiamos... 5. En la clase nosotros preguntamos, contestamos. **C.** 1. Ellos hablan por la mañana y por la noche. 2. Tú y yo no contestamos en inglés. 3. Nosotros también pronunciamos las palabras nuevas. 4. ¿Cuándo conversas tú con el profesor de matemáticas? 5. Ella no usa la palabra «no». 6. Vosotros practicáis el francés mucho por la mañana. 7. Ustedes sólo contestan en español.

PARA REPASAR G: estás P: nada P: gracias G: dónde P: de G: se P: llama G: soy *or* me llamo G: Te *or* Le R: gusta

COMUNICACIÓN **A.** 1. Hola, Alicia. ¿Cómo estás? 2. Buenas tardes, Ricardo. Bien, gracias. ¿Y tú? 3. Muy bien, gracias. ¿Cuándo es el primer día de la nueva clase de español? 4. Mañana. ¿No practicas para la clase? 5. ¿Mañana? ¡Imposible! Trabajo mañana. 6. ¿Dónde trabajas? ¿Aquí? 7. Sí. Enseño inglés por la tarde. 8. ¿Verdad? ¿Por qué no hablas con el profesor de español? 9. ¡Buena idea! Gracias, Alicia. **B.** 1. ¿Usas lápiz y papel en el trabajo? 2. ¿Qué lenguas hablan ustedes *or* habláis vosotros? 3. ¿Hablan *or* habláis alemán (también)? 4. ¿Conversan ellos en francés? 5. ¿Quién contesta el teléfono? 6. ¿Pronuncian ellos muy bien el español?

LABORATORY MANUAL

PRONUNCIACIÓN **A.** 1. famoso 2. Honduras 3. José 4. contestan 5. Isabel 6. profesor 7. Portugal 8. francés 9. Chile 10. Francia **B.** 1. -- 2. -- 3. Panamá 4. explosión 5. -- 6. América 7. -- 8. Hernández 9. difícil **C.** 1. -- 2. autor 3. diurno 4. -- 5. fraile 6. treinta 7. -- 8. -- **D.** 1. Rodolfo no es generoso. 2. Cecilia es amiga de Enrique. 3. Mateo es un nombre masculino. 4. Antonio es de Buenos Aires. 5. El comercio es importante.

COMUNICACIÓN **C.** La profesora Tolón entra en la clase de español. Conversa con los estudiantes de la clase. Ellos preguntan si le gusta enseñar español. Es una lengua muy importante en los Estados Unidos.

LECCIÓN DOS

WORKBOOK

GRÁFICOS **A.** 1. el Café 2. el Cine 3. la tienda de flores 4. el Almacén 5. el restaurante 6. el Banco 7. el metro 8. el autobús 9. un sándwich 10. vino 11. el periódico 12. el reloj **B.** 1. Necesita visitar a unos clientes. 2. Su amigo Alejandro tiene el automóvil nuevo. 3. No, es muy caro usar el metro. 4. No, sólo hay autobús por la tarde. 5. Hay taxis buenos y baratos en la calle Florida. 6. No, Eugenio no viene. 7. El viejo Molina quiere vender su almacén.

GRAMÁTICA ESENCIAL 7. **A.** 1. del 2. de las 3. del 4. de la 5. a la 6. a los **B.** 1. la... las 2. El 3. las... del 4. Los... los 5. El... la... los 6. El *8.* **A.** 1. mi automóvil/coche/carro 2. sus clientes/clientas 3. sus cartas 4. sus noticias 5. nuestra cámara 6. tu barrio 7. mis periódicos 8. sus dependientes/dependientas **B.** 1. su... el reloj de él 2. su... la casa de ellos/ellas 3. sus... los clientes de ella 4. sus... los vinos de Uds. 5. su... el apartamento de ella *9.* **A.** 1. como... bebo 2. leen... discuten 3. vivimos... vives 4. vendéis 5. escribes **B.** 1. -ís 2. -e 3. -es 4. -emos 5. -o 6. -en 7. -e *10.* **A.** 1. tienen 2. hacéis 3. vienen 4. dicen 5. dicen **B.** 1. digo 2. venís 3. hacemos 4. tiene 5. vienes 6. dicen 7. vengo...vienes *11.* 1. veinte y dos 2. ochenta mil 3. mil setecientos setenta y seis 4. cien 5. ciento cinco 6. un millón

PARA REPASAR **A.** 1. El alemán y la francesa conversan en español. 2. Le gusta trabajar en la biblioteca de la universidad. 3. Hoy es lunes, el catorce de marzo. 4. No me gusta el invierno en Nueva York. 5. ¿Cuándo estudian los alumnos de la profesora Valle? **B.** 1. los bolígrafos caros 2. los españoles románticos 3. los mapas interesantes 4. las sillas nuevas 5. los almacenes baratos 6. las noticias importantes **C.** 1. Vienen del almacén caro. 2. Tomo el autobús en la plaza central. 3. Preguntan al dependiente nuevo. 4. Contestan a la clienta japonesa. 5. Hablan de las noticias de hoy.

COMUNICACIÓN **A.** 1. Necesito un mapa de la ciudad. 2. A veces le gusta tomar/beber café por la tarde. 3. Vienen al hotel mañana. 4. ¿Hay/Tienen Uds. un bar en el hotel? 5. No tengo mi automóvil hoy. Tomo el metro. 6. No, no me gusta discutir con mis clientes. 7. A ver si hay un periódico allí. 8. ¿Vive(s) en una casa o en un apartamento? 9. ¿Hay un restaurante bueno aquí? 10. Hay muchos cuadros bonitos en la tienda. **B.** 1. ¿Dónde desea Ud. comer? 2. ¿Le gusta el centro? 3. ¿Tienen Uds. un regalo para la dependienta? 4. ¿Cuándo hace(s) el café? 5. ¿Necesitan/Necesitáis un reloj bueno? 6. ¿Dónde hay muchos taxis?

LABORATORY MANUAL

PRONUNCIACIÓN **C.** 1. sabemos 2. también 3. barbero 4. vivir 5. buenos días 6. perdón 7. tengo 8. amigo 9. luego 10. Gloria 11. Diego 12. Guillermo **D.** 1. hard G 2. B sound 3. J and G same sound 4. first D hard, second soft 5. soft D
COMUNICACIÓN **B.** 1. Tienen buenos hoteles aquí. 2. No vienen autobuses del barrio de Salamanca. 3. Por la tarde no abren las tiendas. 4. No me gusta vivir en el centro.

LECCIÓN TRES
WORKBOOK

GRÁFICOS **A.** 1. el traje 2. la camisa 3. los jeans nuevos 4. la chaqueta 5. las botas 6. pantalones cortos 7. mi camiseta 8. mis tenis 9. vestido 10. tu bolso 11. tu abrigo 12. tu sombrero 13. las sandalias 14. los zapatos 15. la corbata **B.** 1. Sí, gasta poco dinero. 2. No le gusta pagar interés. 3. No, no le gusta llevar ropa incómoda y manchada. 4. Compra cuando los precios están rebajados. 5. Le pregunta: —¿Cuál es el precio rebajado? 6. No, Benicio es bajo y gordo. 7. Hoy lleva pantalones cortos y una camiseta. 8. Lleva jeans nuevos y una chaqueta a la fiesta.
GRAMÁTICA ESENCIAL 12. **A.** 1. da 2. está 3. voy 4. es 5. vamos... estamos 6. son... soy 7. dan 8. dan 9. vas 10. voy... está *13.–14.* 1. es 2. son 3. es... es 4. están 5. es 6. somos 7. sois... son 8. son 9. Eres... soy 10. estoy *15.* **A.** 1. es... es 2. están... está 3. estoy 4. está... están 5. es... está 6. Es 7. estamos 8. estás 9. eres 10. soy **B.** 1. es 2. estás 3. somos 4. es 5. son 6. está 7. es 8. están 9. sois 10. son... soy 11. están 12. es **C.** 1. Es una clienta muy difícil. 2. Son jeans cómodos, pero no están rebajados de precio. 3. La blusa está rebajada, pero no es de seda. 4. Es fácil usar una tarjeta de crédito. 5. Las botas son del Canadá y están en el nuevo almacén en el centro. 6. Estoy feliz cuando compro ropa nueva. 7. Está joven en sus pantalones cortos. 8. No soy rico, alto o delgado. *16.* **A.** 1. está comprando 2. está ganando 3. estamos buscando 4. estoy dando 5. estás pagando 6. están gastando 7. estás discutiendo **B.** 1. No, Lisa no está trabajando en el Almacén Marroquí. 2. No, la señorita González no está escribiendo una carta. 3. No, Uds. no están vendiendo regalos elegantes. 4. No, no estamos mirando los nuevos vestidos de Europa. 5. No, no estoy bebiendo un vaso de leche en la cafetería. 6. No, Elena no está leyendo los precios de la ropa. 7. No, vosotros no habláis/Uds. no hablan de las nuevas modas.
COMUNICACIÓN **A.** 1. Estoy buscando algo rosado o blanco para mi amiga. 2. ¿No usa/lleva azul or verde? 3. Pues, está muy triste hoy. El rosado y el blanco son colores alegres, ¿verdad? 4. Sí, pero la cosa importante es el sentimiento y, claro, el precio. 5. De acuerdo. Pero no soy rica/o. ¿Cuánto es la blusa blanca de seda? 6. Está rebajada de doscientos dólares a ciento cincuenta. Es bonita, ¿no? 7. Sí, ¿Me presta Ud. cien dólares? 8. Señorita/Señor, Patina es un almacén grande y yo estoy muy ocupada. Vendemos ropa pero no prestamos dinero. **B.** 1. ¿Están/Estáis pagando con una tarjeta de crédito? 2. ¿Cómo son las sandalias? 3. ¿Llevas una camiseta al concierto? 4. ¿Cómo está ella? 5. ¿Cuándo dan Uds. la fiesta? 6. ¿Qué estás/está buscando? 7. ¿Por qué no llevas/lleva la camisa roja?

LABORATORY MANUAL

PRONUNCIACIÓN **B.** 1. rr 2. r 3. r 4. rr 5. r 6. r 7. r 8. r
COMUNICACIÓN **D.** Luis va de compras hoy. Primero va a la Tienda Chévere. Allí está comprando dos camisas de verano. Usa su tarjeta de crédito. Hoy está pobre y es más fácil pagar mañana. ¡No le gusta gastar dinero, pero le gusta la ropa cara!

LECCIÓN CUATRO

WORKBOOK

GRÁFICOS **A.** 1. manzanas 2. plátanos 3. la frutería 4. pan 5. muñeca 6. sombrero de vaquero 7. avión 8. el escaparate/la vidriera 9. platos 10. vasos 11. cubiertos 12. botella 13. mantel 14. flores **B.** 1. La tía Rosa trae el regalo. 2. La tía Rosa tiene que ir al aeropuerto. 3. La tía Rosa oye el avión. 4. La abuela Tina sabe que la tía Rosa tiene prisa. 5. El mantel está manchado. 6. La tía Rosa tiene que salir. 7. La abuela Tina va a poner el mantel nuevo.

GRAMÁTICA ESENCIAL 17. **A.** 1. conoces 2. sé 3. trae 4. sabe 5. veo... oigo 6. salen 7. conocemos **B.** 1. pone... ponemos... ponen; ponéis... pone 2. sale; salimos; salís/salen 3. traigo; traéis; traes 4. ves; ven; vemos 5. oyen; oye; oímos *18.* 1. -- 2. a 3. -- 4. al 5. a... a 6. a 7. a... a 8. a 9. -- *19.* **A.** 1. Hace frío en los Andes. 2. Sí, hace calor en Tejas en el verano. 3. Cuando hay una tormenta, hace mucho viento. 4. Sí, hace sol en el verano en Acapulco. 5. ... **B.** 1. tiene frío 2. tiene 82 años 3. tienes que 4. tienen sed 5. no tienes razón 6. tenemos que... tenemos hambre 7. tiene ganas 8. Tengo prisa *20.* 1. ¡Bebe el vino, tía Rosa! 2. ¡Escribe una carta, abuela Tina! 3. ¡Siempre di la verdad! 4. ¡Haz ejercicio todos los días, abuela! 5. ¡Ve al aeropuerto ahora, tía Rosa! 6. ¡Pon el mantel, Elena! 7. ¡Trae los platos, Lorena! 8. ¡Ven por la tarde, Luis! 9. ¡Ten paciencia, mamá! 10. ¡Lava los vasos, Lorena!

PARA REPASAR 1. es 2. es 3. está 4. Es 5. está 6. está 7. está 8. estamos 9. Es 10. está 11. está 12. están 13. está 14. es 15. somos

COMUNICACIÓN **A.** 1. ¿Por qué tienes que ir al la frutería? 2. Necesito comprar flores para la casa. Mis padres salen de Medellín hoy. 3. ¿Traen a tus hermanos? 4. Traen a mi hermano mayor y a mi hermana menor. 5. ¿Cuántos años tiene ella? 6. Tiene nueve meses y está aprendiendo a caminar ahora. 7. ¿Es su visita una sorpresa? 8. Sí, es una sorpresa. ¡No saben que estoy casado! **B.** 1. escribe... 2. ve... 3. pon... 4. sal... 5. ven... 6. ...

LABORATORY MANUAL

PRONUNCIACIÓN **A.** 1. que 2. ca 3. z 4. x 5. que 6. ch 7. rr 8. que **B.** 1. sounds like "k" 2. sounds like "ss" 3. sounds like "ss" 4. sounds like "k" 5. sounds like **jota** 6. sounds like "ss"

COMUNICACIÓN **D.** La familia latina es diferente de la familia de los Estados Unidos. En una familia latina hay padres, hijos, abuelos, nietos, sobrinos, tíos y amigos. ¡A veces es una sorpresa conocer a una familia latina!

LECCIÓN CINCO

WORKBOOK

GRÁFICOS **A.** 1. la aspiradora 2. sala 3. alfombra 4. un sofá 5. un sillón/unos sillones 6. una mesa 7. refrigerador 8. un fregadero 9. una cocina eléctrica 10. lavaplatos 11. el comedor 12. el dormitorio 13. una cama 14. un ropero 15. una cómoda 16. un estante 17. un escritorio 18. una lámpara 19. cuartos de baño 20. el teléfono **B.** 1. Es muy exigente. 2. Llama a sus clientes por teléfono. 3. Usa la máquina para hacer su reporte de ventas. 4. No, no le gusta limpiar la casa. 5. Para descansar mira la televisión. 6. No, es muy barato tener una sirvienta.

GRAMÁTICA ESENCIAL 21. **A.** 1. ¡Coma Ud. en la cocina! 2. ¡Abra Ud. el periódico! 3. ¡Digan Uds. que el apartamento no está sucio! 4. ¡Haga Ud. la cama todos los días! 5. ¡Ponga Ud. un sofá en el dormitorio! 6. ¡Salga Ud. sin pasar la aspiradora! 7. ¡Compren Uds. una lámpara nueva! 8. ¡Vengan Uds. a ver el apartamento! 9. ¡Vea Ud. su nueva casa! 10. ¡Llame Ud. a sus clientes! 11. ¡Busque Ud. un escritorio práctico! **B.** 1. ¡No oigan Uds. las noticias por la mañana! 2. ¡No cruce Ud. la calle sin mirar! 3. ¡No apague Ud. la lámpara! 4. ¡No den Uds. mil pesos por el sillón! 5. ¡No traiga una cómoda muy moderna! 6. ¡No vayan Uds. a otra tienda mañana! **C.** 1. laves 2. salgas 3. digas 4. leas 5. busques *22.* **A.** 1. Ese... éste 2. Esta... aquélla 3. Esas... estas 4. este... Ése 5. estas... aquellas 6. ese... aquél **B.** 1. Deseo comprar éste, pero deseo ver ése también. 2. Me gusta ésta, si ésa no está rebajada. 3. ¡No laves éste, lava aquél! 4. Esas alfombras son caras, pero ésta es barata y muy bonita. 5. ¡Por favor, no use Ud. éste; use aquél! *23.* **A.** 1. Sale a las siete de la mañana. 2. Llega a las ocho y cuarto de la mañana. 3. Llama a los clientes por teléfono a las once de la mañana. 4. Come su sándwich a la una menos diez de la tarde. 5. Llega a las siete menos cuarto de la tarde. 6. Ponen su programa favorito a las nueve y media de la noche. 7. Terminan a las doce menos cuarto.

PARA REPASAR 1. hace 2. tengo 3. Tengo 4. tengo 5. tengo 6. tengo 7. tienen 8. tengo 9. hace 10. tengo

COMUNICACIÓN A. 1. ¿Qué hora es, Lupe? 2. Casi son las cinco, señorita. ¿Algo más? 3. ¿Las cinco de la tarde? ¡Mis amigos llegan a las seis! 4. ¡Por favor, no grite Ud., señorita! Tengo que pasar la aspiradora y eso es todo. 5. No, Lupe, no pases la aspiradora. Lava estos platos y limpia la cocina. 6. La cocina no está sucia. ¡Mire Ud.! 7. Tienes razón. Bueno, ve a la tienda ahora mismo y compra más flores como éstas. 8. Lo siento, pero tengo que descansar. ¡Por favor, no sea Ud. tan exigente! B. 1. ¿Tiene cuatro dormitorios el apartamento? 2. ¿Vamos al apartamento a las seis de la tarde? 3. ¿Tiene comedor? 4. ¿Tiene lavaplatos y cocina eléctrica? 5. ¿Llamo por teléfono o voy en persona? 6. ¿Sabe Ud. dónde hay apartamentos buenos? 7. ¿A qué hora viene el cliente?

LABORATORY MANUAL

PRONUNCIACIÓN D. 1. I 2. D 3. I 4. D 5. D

COMUNICACIÓN C. Este apartamento tiene una sala grande. También tiene dos dormitorios y un cuarto de baño. Y viene con radio, televisión y lavaplatos. Esto es muy importante.

LECCIÓN SEIS

WORKBOOK

GRÁFICOS A. 1. lechuga 2. tomates 3. papas 4. bistec 5. pescado 6. camarones 7. uvas 8. piña 9. sandía 10. ensalada 11. sopa 12. panecillos 13. mantequilla 14. frijoles 15. pollo 16. té 17. azucar B. 1. Hizo ensalada de frutas. 2. Hizo la ensalada con piña, sandía y uvas. 3. Usó un cuchillo. 4. Hay cucharas, tenedores y cucharitas. 5. Hizo sopa de mariscos. 6. Comió panecillos con mantequilla. 7. Subió a la Cafetería Tin-Tin. 8. Comió papas fritas. 9. No, no compró helado.

GRAMÁTICA ESENCIAL 24. 1. corrí... compré 2. subimos... bebimos 3. gastó... gasté 4. llegaron... decidieron 5. busqué... llegué 6. comimos... terminamos 7. creyeron 8. salieron *25.* A. 1. dimos 2. vinieron 3. vino 4. hizo 5. hicimos 6. dio 7. fueron 8. compró 9. vinieron/vinisteis 10. fue B. 1. Hiciste 2. fueron 3. vine 4. dio 5. vinisteis 6. fuimos *26.* 1. buen 2. mal 3. primer 4. primeras 5. malo... gran 6. gran... grande 7. buenas 8. buenos *27.* 1. por... para 2. por... para 3. Para... por 4. para... por 5. Por 6. por 7. Por 8. para 9. por 10. por

PARA REPASAR A. 1. Son las nueve de la mañana. 2. Son las tres y cuarto de la tarde. 3. Son las seis menos veinte y ocho de la tarde. 4. Son las seis y media de la mañana. 5. Son las once y veinte de la noche. 6. Son las doce (en punto) de la noche. B. 1. las ocho y media 2. las tres menos cuarto 3. las cinco y dos 4. las seis (en punto) 5. las once menos diez 6. las once y media de la noche

COMUNICACIÓN A. 1. No comí esas chuletas. Soy vegetariano/a. 2. Pero en España comiste y bebiste de todo. 3. Bueno, eso fue en el verano de mil novecientos ochenta y cinco. Ahora no como carne de vaca, carne de puerco, carne de cordero o pollo. 4. ¿Diste tus libros de cocina a Alberto por eso? 5. Sí. Él y Rafaela fueron a París a estudiar con un gran cocinero. Aprendieron a cocinar muy bien. 6. ¡Qué bueno! No me gusta cocinar. ¡Solamento me gusta comer! B. 1. ¿Fuiste tú al supermercado o fue Alberto? 2. ¿Qué hizo la tía Rosa? 3. ¿Qué hiciste ayer para la comida? 4. ¿Por qué vinieron/vinisteis temprano? 5. ¿Fueron/Fuisteis buenos amigos por muchos años?

LABORATORY MANUAL

COMUNICACIÓN D. Ayer cociné me plato favorito. Busqué varias legumbres frescas. Preparé una sopa de pollo con maíz. Le serví todo eso a mi familia. Después fui a la Cafetería Flores. Allí comí pollo y papas fritas y un gran helado de piña.

LECCIÓN SIETE

WORKBOOK

GRÁFICOS A. 1. un vídeo 2. la cantante 3. la guitarra 4. la batería 5. un casete 6. la grabadora 7. un disco 8. el tocadiscos 9. los audífonos 10. boletos 11. el radio B. 1. Sintió mucha sorpresa porque le gustan Los Caníbales. 2. Paulina soñó con Micaelo. 3. Bailó con Silvia. 4. Cantaron «Loco de amor». 5. Tocan guitarra y batería.

GRAMÁTICA ESENCIAL 28. **A.** 1. quiero 2. Prefieres 3. pido 4. vuelven... podemos 5. piden 6. entiendes... pedimos... duermo 7. almuerzas... pienso **B.** 1. Si llueve o nieva, los niños juegan en el salón de recreo. 2. ¿No prefieren mirar vídeos en el televisor? 3. Pues, la película comienza en media hora, y no puedo encontrar los boletos/billetes. 4. Vuelvo en un minuto. Pienso que están en el comedor. 5. No, aquí están. Podemos salir ahora. *29.* 1. Sí, piensen... 2. Sí, vuelva... 3. Sí, jueguen... 4. Sí, pidan... 5. Sí, sirva... *30.* 1. están pidiendo 2. no estamos sirviendo 3. está muriendo 4. estoy durmiendo 5. está repitiendo *31.* 1. murió 2. pidieron 3. sirvió 4. durmió 5. prefirió 6. sirvieron 7. volvió *32.–33.* **A.** 1. Los vendiste. 2. No lo pidieron. 3. La tocaste muy bien. 4. No las encuentro. 5. La alquilé. 6. Las vimos en el concierto. 7. La vendimos a mitad de precio. 8. ¿No lo encontraron? 9. La prefirieron. 10. Lo enciendo a las 9:00. **B.** 1. La oímos ayer. 2. ¡Pídela tú! 3. ¿Por qué no la llamamos hoy? 4. Los vamos a ver en la tienda. *or* Vamos a verlos en la tienda. 5. Los estoy pidiendo por carta. *or* Estoy pidiéndolos por carta. 6. Me gusta tocarlas. 7. Uds. me pueden encontrar en el café. *or* Uds. pueden encontrarme en el café. 8. Yo no la encuentro muy interesante. 9. ¿No los van a dar aquí? *or* ¿No van a darlos aquí? 10. ¡Cómprenlo en esa tienda!
PARA REPASAR 1. aplaudieron 2. salió 3. vino 4. para 5. fue 6. por 7. para 8. dio 9. hizo 10. fue 11. para
COMUNICACIÓN **A.** 1. ¿Cuándo comienza tu día con Patricia? 2. Comienza a las tres en punto. No puedo esperar. 3. ¿Entiende español? 4. Sí, lo entiende. Pero, ¿qué hago con ella? 5. Pregunta si prefiere una gran comida o si juega a las cartas o si... 6. ¿Si juega a las cartas? ¡No puedo creer eso! ¿Cuánto cuesta ir al Club Paraíso? 7. Es caro, pero pienso que es bueno. 8. ¿De qué podemos hablar? Yo quiero preguntar si tiene un novio. 9. No seas tonto. Es mejor si solamente hablan del tiempo. **B.** 1. ¿Por cuánto lo pediste/pidió? 2. ¿Sirven Uds. vino aquí? 3. ¿Dónde lo encontraste/encontró? 4. ¿Cuándo volvemos?

LABORATORY MANUAL

COMUNICACIÓN **D.** Los Caníbales dieron un concierto musical fantástico. Tocaron la canción «Adiós, mi vida». Fue en ese momento que los fanáticos comenzaron a aplaudir. Este fanático aplaudió y gritó mucho. Celia Salvaje los enciende a todos con sus canciones.

LECCIÓN OCHO

WORKBOOK

GRÁFICOS **A.** 1. pelo 2. el pie 3. la boca 4. la cabeza 5. el brazo 6. las piernas 7. las manos 8. la cintura 9. la espalda 10. los ojos **B.** 1. Corre al gimnasio. 2. Hace sus ejercicios y sale para el trabajo. 3. Se baña con jabón importado. 4. Se peina delante del espejo. 5. Se enojó porque Héctor pasó dos horas delante del espejo.
GRAMÁTICA ESENCIAL 34. **A.** 1. Eduardo afeita a Cándido hoy. 2. Mamá baña a Lolita por la mañana. 3. Mamá acuesta a Joaquín por la noche. 4. Roberto despierta a Elena temprano. 5. Antes de ir al trabajo Pablo peina a Luisita. 6. A la hora de cenar la tía Rosa sienta a Tina. 7. César viste a Rodolfo para la escuela. 8. Martina levanta a Felipe para desayunar. **B.** 1. me afeité 2. se bañaron 3. se acostó 4. se despertaron/os despertasteis 5. nos peinamos 6. os sentasteis 7. me vestí 8. te levantaste *35.* 1. ¿Por qué no quieren sentarse aquí? *or* ¿Por qué no se quieren sentar aquí? 2. Dicen que ella se siente bien. 3. No se lavan las manos sin jabón. 4. Paco y Alfredo se están sentando a ver el vídeo ahora. *or* Pedro y Alfredo están sentándose a ver el vídeo ahora. 5. Se levantó con un gran dolor de cabeza. 6. Nos sentimos débiles por el calor. 7. Lávese Ud. con esa toalla, por favor. 8. Me canso cuando trabajo mucho. *36.* **A.** 1. dijo... trajo 2. trajimos... pudiste 3. estuvo... puso 4. quisimos 5. tuve 6. quiso 7. estuvimos 8. dijeron 9. tuvimos **B.** 1. estuvimos 2. supisteis 3. quisisteis 4. pudimos 5. pudieron 6. tuvieron 7. trajeron 8. estuvieron *37.– 38.* 1. le 2. nos 3. te 4. Me 5. Les 6. le 7. te 8. le
COMUNICACIÓN **A.** 1. Me siento débil si no me duermo temprano. 2. Me canso fácilmente si me levanto temprano. 3. Puedo hacerlo si me siento. 4. Me despierto por la noche sólo si me llaman por teléfono. 5. Puedo pagarle la cuenta si no me enojo primero. **B.** 1. ¿En qué hotel estuvieron/estuvisteis? 2. ¿Quisiste ir a Cancún? 3. ¿Te pudiste/se pudo bañar en el mar? 4. ¿Qué trajeron para la cena? 5. ¿Qué trajiste/trajo para leer? 6. ¿Dónde están las novelas?

LABORATORY MANUAL

COMUNICACIÓN **D.** Primero él estuvo de vacaciones en el Sol. Después pudo visitar nuestra ciudad por una semana. Pero no tuvo tiempo para ir de compras. No trajo a sus hijos porque ellos no quisieron venir. Por cierto, no trajo mucho dinero.

LECCIÓN NUEVE

WORKBOOK

GRÁFICOS **A.** 1. la playa 2. la costa 3. las montañas 4. la nieve 5. las ruinas 6. el templo 7. la pirámide 8. serpiente **B.** 1. Mateo y su mamá no querían hacer el viaje. 2. Mateo no quería pasar dos semanas en el calor. 3. No, era un centro maya. 4. Los espíritus de los mayas vivían en los templos. 5. Isabel era la que más quería ir. 6. Isabel se sintió mal porque no le gustó el calor.
GRAMÁTICA ESENCIAL 39.– 41. **A.** 1. viajaba 2. creíamos 3. ibas 4. soñábamos 5. ponían 6. describía 7. gustaba 8. pasaba 9. charlábamos 10. almorzabas **B.** 1. éramos 2. era 3. iba 4. iba 5. iban 6. veía 7. iba 8. veía 9. prefería 10. contestaba 11. eran 12. decía 13. veía 14. había *42.* **A.** 1. Viajábamos a Bariloche cada invierno. 2. Mis padres y yo esquiábamos, pero Lili leía libros sobre arqueología. 3. Una noche Lili pensó que estábamos enojados con ella. 4. Se levantó y salió llorando. 5. Yo sabía que le gustaba el chocolate caliente. 6. Le compré una taza grande de chocolate caliente a las diez. 7. Cuando se durmió, yo estaba pensando *or* pensaba que ella era una niña triste. **B.** 1. fui 2. vi 3. tenía 4. miraban 5. pregunté 6. hacían 7. dijeron 8. querían 9. tenían 10. pregunté 11. tenían 12. contestaron 13. comencé 14. conté 15. tenía 16. venía *43.* Me encanta la arqueología y no me gustan los deportes. Esos campeonatos de fútbol no me interesan. Me parecen tan ordinarios. La cosa que me encanta es viajar y ver las ruinas de una antigua civilización. Allí parece que puedo sentir el espíritu de los habitantes. Me interesa aprender cómo vivían. Adoro soñar con las antiguas civilizaciones.
RECUERDOS DEL PASADO **A.** 1. encantó... fuimos 2. viajé... pareció 3. soñaba 4. fui... hacía(n) falta 5. era... interesaba(n) **B.** 1. Me interesaba saber cómo vivía la gente en Cuba. 2. El Brasil parecía un país de precios exorbitantes. 3. Me encantaba la sangría de España. 4. Me hacía falta conocer a los habitantes de Nicaragua. 5. No me gustaron las noticias del periódico en Chile.

LECCIÓN DIEZ

WORKBOOK

GRÁFICOS **A.** 1. la carretera 2. chófer 3. el motor 4. las ruedas 5. las llantas 6. los pedales del freno 7. del acelerador 8. los faros 9. el volante 10. el asiento 11. la llave **B.** 1. Ha venido de la colonia Rosas. 2. Llama de la gasolinera. 3. Tiene que doblar en la segunda glorieta. 4. Sí, los ha visto. 5. Tiene que doblar a la derecha. 6. Sí, las ha comprendido. 7. No viene en coche porque ayer salió a manejar y le pusieron dos multas.
GRAMÁTICA ESENCIAL 44.– 45. **A.** 1. ¿Ha examinado usted las llantas? 2. María Luisa no ha entendido las direcciones. 3. ¿Has recibido una multa tú? 4. ¿De dónde han salido tantos peatones? 5. Ustedes han traído la camioneta. 6. Tú y yo no hemos chocado con la señal. 7. ¿Por qué habéis dejado el carro en la autopista? **B.** 1. El otro chófer no había puesto los frenos. 2. No le habíamos dicho nada al policía. 3. Habían muerto tres peatones en el accidente. 4. No habías abierto la lata de gasolina. 5. Habéis vuelto por la carretera del norte. 6. Laura había hecho un viaje en la camioneta. 7. Me habían escrito una carta con las direcciones. **C.** 1. Había preparado la señal. 2. No había visto el accidente. 3. En la esquina habían puesto un semáforo. 4. El chófer del autobús había bebido demasiado vino. 5. Quince personas habían muerto en la carretera. *46.– 47.* **A.** 1. Él se lo puso. 2. Tú nos los compraste. 3. Pablo y Maritsa me lo trajeron. 4. Ellas no te las dieron. 5. Por favor, enséñenoslas. 6. El peatón me las puede explicar *or* puede explicármelas. **B.** 1. Felipe se la trajo. 2. Ellas se la vendieron. 3. ¿No se las compraste? 4. No, se las di. 5. No las quisimos aceptar *or* no quisimos aceptarlas. 6. Se las compro. **C.** 1. El policía desea dárnosla *or* nos la desea dar. 2. El conductor no se lo quería vender *or* no quería vendérselo. 3. Por cierto, Elena dijo: te la compro. 4. El policía dijo: no te/se lo puedo traer *or* no puedo traérte/selo. 5. Por favor, no me lo explique.

PARA REPASAR **A.** 1. Lo había visto en el bulevar. 2. Pero no la vi. 3. La cruzamos con cuidado. 4. Lo tuvimos que comprar *or* tuvimos que comprarlo. 5. Los venden a precio rebajado. **B.** 1. Por favor, no me invite(n). No tengo el carro ese día. Se lo prestamos a Luis. 2. Me dijo que no doblaron a la izquierda. La verdad es que no leyeron los letreros con cuidado. 3. Tal vez no me explicaron la verdad y no se la dijeron a ella.
COMUNICACIÓN **A.** 1. Ha(s) cruzado tres calles. 2. Ha(s) cruzado la calle Venus, la calle del Cangrejo, la calle Arena y la vía de La Marina. 3. No, no ha(s) tenido que cruzar la calle Venus. 4. Han puesto la zona turística entre la calle Venus y la vía de La Marina. 5. Ha(s) encontrado el parque entre la vía Honda y la vía de La Marina. 6. He doblado a la derecha en la avenida Venus. **B.** 1. ¿Adónde habían/habías ido ese año? 2. ¿Había(s) estado en Manaus antes? 3. ¿A quién le diste (dio) el mapa y los boletos? 4. ¿Dónde habían dejado ellos las llaves? 5. ¿Le había escrito la carta de Río Ana María? 6. ¿Ya han visto Uds. São Paulo?

LABORATORY MANUAL

COMUNICACIÓN **C.** 1. Claro que le he puesto una multa al señor Mendoza. 2. Él ha bebido demasiado y ha manejado su coche. 3. Por cierto que casi ha chocado. 4. He pedido un taxi y lo han llevado para la casa. 5. Ha dejado el carro aquí hasta mañana.

LECCIÓN ONCE

WORKBOOK

GRÁFICOS **A.** 1. la muchedumbre 2. la Reina 3. una banda 4. caballo 5. traje regional 6. banderas 7. carteles **B.** 1. la ruta a la India 2. entre en una nueva época de riqueza 3. Colón pueda viajar con tres carabelas 4. la reina venda sus joyas 5. celebre este viaje con el pueblo
GRAMÁTICA ESENCIAL 48. 1. Pues que salude al locutor. 2. Pues que conozcan al gobernador. 3. Pues que no llegue hasta la una. 4. Pues que no miren el desfile. 5. Pues que invite a Mario a la fiesta. 6. Pues que no ponga tantas velas en el pastel. *49.–51.* **A.** 1. deseo... hables 2. quieren... comamos 3. desea... viva 4. quiere... invite 5. desea... traigan 6. quiero... conozcan **B.** 1. busquen... comience 2. llegues... dirijas 3. piensen... vuelvan 4. pida... almuerces 5. duerman *52.* **A.** 1. Yo deseo que sólo hablen en español. 2. Ud. prefiere que compremos carne aquí. 3. Ella manda que no conversemos en inglés. 4. Ellos no permiten que Alejandro fume en el café. 5. Papá no deja que entre en la heladería con Ana. 6. Yo recomiendo que no tomes más sangría. 7. ¿Ella aconseja que habléis con el locutor? 8. Ellos piden que describamos el desfile. **B.** 1. Nosotros queremos que la reina venga al desfile. 2. El pueblo pide que la banda toque más música. 3. La reina desea que el pueblo ya no celebre su cumpleaños. 4. Las autoridades aconsejan que el alcalde no gaste el dinero así. 5. Los refugiados prefieren que todos vivan en una cultura bilingüe. 6. Sin embargo, el gobernador manda que todo el mundo hable un solo idioma. *53.* 1. traigas 2. guste 3. tengan 4. moleste 5. permitan... fumen 6. sirva 7. conozcan
PARA REPASAR 1. ¿El pastel? Se lo había dado. 2. Pero se lo había prometido a Julia y su hermano. 3. Se lo habíamos explicado. Habíamos hecho el pastel para la fiesta. 4. No habían entendido eso. 5. Pero ya le he comprado las velitas. 6. Volví a la pastelería pero ya la habían cerrado. 7. Por suerte, Ramón había comprado mucho mantecado.
COMUNICACIÓN 1. sientan 2. tengamos 3. comprendan 4. aconsejen 5. sorprendan 6. pidamos 7. permitan 8. podamos **B.** 1. gaste 2. pida 3. mande 4. aprendan 5. enseñen

LABORATORY MANUAL

COMUNICACIÓN **C.** 1. Muchas personas piensan que todos los hispanos somos iguales. 2. En realidad hay una gran variedad de culturas hispánicas. 3. A los hispanos les molesta que la gente piense así.

LECCIÓN DOCE

WORKBOOK

GRÁFICOS **A.** 1. Quiere que sea bueno. 2. No, no cree que tenga nada serio. 3. La madre tiene que darle unas píldoras. 4. Es probable que no haya penicilina. 5. Quiere que sepa que esto les pasa a muchos niños. 6. Quiere que le compre un mantecado. 7. Sí, es un niño mimado. **B.** a. 4 b. 1 c. 6 d. 2 e. 5 f. 3

GRAMÁTICA ESENCIAL **54. A.** 1. Quiero que tú seas doctor. 2. Queremos que haya varios dentistas en el consultorio. 3. Quieren que el paciente esté tranquilo. 4. La doctora quiere que sepan que tienen pulmonía. 5. Quiere que des sangre hoy. 6. La enfermera quiere que vayamos a comprar pastillas para la tos. **B.** 1. Aconseja que yo esté en el hospital una semana. 2. No creemos que sea gripe. 3. Les pido que no me den esas horribles gotas para la nariz. 4. Prefieren que sepas la verdad sobre tu enfermedad. 5. La doctora Valdés manda que yo vaya a un especialista. 6. No creo que haya una cura contra ese virus. **55.** 1. Sí, sentimos que hayan visto la herida. 2. Sí, temo que haya sufrido un ataque al corazón. 3. Sí, me alegro de que haya salido. 4. Sí, nos sorprende que haya tenido cáncer antes. 5. Sí, espero que le hayan puesto una inyección. **56.** 1. seamos 2. sepas 3. van 4. den (_if doubtful_); dan (_if sure_) 5. pide 6. vaya 7. sea 8. vayan 9. esté 10. haya 11. eres 12. haya **57.** 1. Es preciso que la paciente se cuide mucho. 2. Pero es probable que ella no lo haga. 3. Pues, es lástima que ellos la dejen sola. 4. Es mejor que ella acepte responsabilidad por su salud. 5. Es cierto que ella tiene que cuidarse. 6. Es verdad que todos quieren ayudarla. 7. ¿Es posible que le visitemos? **58. A.** 1. tan profunda como 2. tantas horas como 3. menos caras que 4. la más importante 5. más que 6. el más inteligente 7. tan nuevas como 8. la más barata 9. menos problemas que... menos que **B.** 1. Estos pacientes tienen tanto dolor como aquéllas. 2. Ese médico tiene tantas enfermeras en su consultorio como tú. 3. Nosotras tenemos tantas píldoras como la farmacia. 4. Ud. tiene tantas jaquecas como yo. **C.** 1. el más grande 2. el mejor 3. el más viejo 4. mayor 5. más pequeño 6. el peor 7. buena 8. grande... malos 9. más pequeño... mejor 10. la mejor... grande

PARA REPASAR 1. Alberto pide que le compre píldoras para su alergia cada semana. 2. Nadie cree que tenga un problema serio. 3. Su médico le aconseja que no las tome. 4. Pero Alberto manda que le traigamos esas píldoras. 5. Quiero que deje de tomarlas.

COMUNICACIÓN **A.** 1. puede 2. vuelva 3. se cuide 4. comience 5. encuentre 6. guste 7. practique 8. duerma 9. coma 10. beba 11. tome 12. se sienta 13. se moleste 14. lleve 15. pida(n) 16. llame 17. tenga 18. pierda

LABORATORY MANUAL

COMUNICACIÓN **C.** Es necesario tener buena salud. Es preciso que uno se cuide siempre. Es tan importante tener buena salud como tener una buena educación.

LECCIÓN TRECE

WORKBOOK

GRÁFICOS **A.** 1. el sol 2. el mar 3. olas 4. la nieve 5. muñecos de nieve 6. la pala 7. el rastrillo 8. hojas secas 9. volcán 10. el río 11. el lago 12. los árboles 13. los pájaros 14. las lomas **B.** 1. Sí, podrá ir a buscarlo. 2. Celia ya tiene planes. 3. Los niños van con ella. 4. Cree que lo va a pasar bien.

GRAMÁTICA ESENCIAL **59. A.** 1. Hoy iré a la playa. 2. Primero entraremos en el Café Botín. 3. No lo abrirán hasta las once. 4. ¿Nadarás en el mar? 5. La temperatura del agua te sorprenderá. 6. ¿A qué hora llegaréis? 7. Los niños se perderán en la playa. 8. Rodolfo dormirá en la arena. 9. Leeré el periódico, tomaré un café y después me bañaré en las olas. **B.** 1. recogerá... recogerán 2. anunciará... anunciará 3. nos protegerá... nos protegeré 4. me traerá... te traeremos 5. verá... verás 6. rezará... rezaremos 7. escribirá... escribirás 8. nos esperará... nos esperarán **60.** 1. Podrás 2. querrán 3. Habrá 4. sabremos 5. harán 6. pondrán 7. dirás 8. vendré 9. tendremos 10. saldrá... dirá 11. habrá **61. A.** 1. Cecelia no nos trajo nada de la playa. 2. Pues nadie perdió el traje de baño. 3. No encontrarán ningún bote hoy. 4. ¿No habrá ninguna playa linda aquí? 5. Nunca toman café antes de ir a nadar. 6. Tampoco llevan sándwiches y cerveza al lago. **B.** 1. No, nunca salía en bote de vela. 2. No, tampoco los recogerán. 3. Sí, hay alguien en el mar. 4. No, no hay ninguna playa bonita. 5. Sí, han ido al lago alguna vez. 6. No, no brilla nada interesante en el cielo. **62.** 1. sino 2. sino que 3. pero 4. sino 5. sino 6. sino que 7. pero 8. sino 9. sino 10. pero

PARA REPASAR 1. esté 2. podemos 3. seamos 4. den 5. vayamos 6. salgamos 7. saben 8. explique 9. cuente 10. sepa

COMUNICACIÓN **A.** 1. Primero volaré a Bogotá y te encontraré en Calarca. 2. ¡Qué lata! Me pedirán la visa, el pasaporte y el carnet de manejar. 3. Luego iremos a Leticia. 4. Nunca volveré a aquella parte del país. 5. ¿Pasarás unos días en la playa? 6. Nunca me ha gustado la arena y nunca me gustará. 7. ¿Crees que habrá (haya, _if doubt_) huracanes por la costa? **C.** 1. No one will love you if you only think of yourself. 2. If you're happy here, you won't move. (If it's not broken, don't fix it). 3. Let it be, and you'll be happy. 4. Never say never. 5. You can tell who people are by the company they keep.

LABORATORY MANUAL

COMUNICACIÓN **B.** Y yo me iré; y estaré solo, sin hogar, sin árbol verde, sin pozo blanco, sin cielo azul y plácido... Y se quedarán los pájaros cantando.

LECCIÓN CATORCE

WORKBOOK

GRÁFICOS **A.** 1. folleto 2. vino tinto 3. abrazo 4. el anillo 5. un beso 6. los canapés **B.** 1. Se casaban Roberto y Gabriela. 2. Todos buscaban el anillo. 3. Fue encontrado por la hermanita de la novia. 4. Sí, se puso de mal humor. 5. Comenzó a reír.

GRAMÁTICA ESENCIAL 63.– 64. **A.** 1. El anillo es comprado... /Se compra el anillo... 2. Los canapés son preparados... /Se preparan los canapés... 3. El vino es servido... /Se sirve el vino... 4. La luna de miel fue arreglada... /Se arregló la luna de miel... **B.** 1. No se sirve (*or* no es servido) champán en la recepción. 2. ¡No se pagan los gastos en un día! 3. Siempre se arreglan (*or* siempre son arregladas) las lunas de miel temprano. 4. ¿Cómo se preparan los canapés? 5. ¿Cómo se explica la ceremonia? *65.* 1. Los amigos están invitados. 2. Los canapés están servidos. 3. Están casados. 4. El viaje está pagada. 5. La habitación está reservada. 6. Están divorciados. *66.* 1. qué 2. qué 3. cuál 4. cuál 5. qué 6. qué/cuál 7. qué 8. cuál 9. qué 10. cuál *67.* 1. lo que 2. que 3. que 4. lo que 5. que 6. que 7. lo que 8. que 9. lo que

PARA REPASAR 1. podrán 2. vendrán 3. verán 4. saludaré 5. tendré 6. encontrarás 7. compraré 8. daré 9. llevarás 10. haré

COMUNICACIÓN **A.** 1. Lo que no entiendo es que viven juntos aunque están divorciados. 2. Pues, esto se hace más y más en estos días. 3. ¿Se casaron por la iglesia o por lo civil? 4. No lo sé. Pero se equivocaron al enamorarse. 5. No se debe hablar mal de los amigos. 6. Discúlpame, ¡pero no puedo soportar a la gente que no sabe lo que hace!

LABORATORY MANUAL

COMUNICACIÓN **C.** La recepción no se acabó hasta la una de la mañana. Se sirvieron doscientas botellas de champán. Lo que nadie sabía es que el novio odia las bodas. Pero le prometió al padre de la novia que la boda se podía celebrar en una iglesia.

LECCIÓN QUINCE

WORKBOOK

GRÁFICOS **A.** 1. 4 2. 1 3. 6 4. 2 5. 7 6. 3 7. 5 **B.** 1. Preferiría ir a Barcelona. 2. Sería más fácil en Málaga. 3. Piensa que podría comprar ropa de moda y perfumes. 4. Sí, podría ir a una discoteca. 5. No podría ir a la playa. 6. ¿?

GRAMÁTICA ESENCIAL 68. **A.** 1. llegaría... sería... preferiría 2. nadarían... irían... comerían 3. compraríamos... pondríamos... vestiríamos 4. sería... reservarías... pedirías **B.** 1. llegaría 2. dejaría 3. bajaría 4. entraría 5. comería 6. tomaría 7. dormiría 8. sentaría 9. pediría 10. daría 11. volvería 12. descansaría 13. sería *69.* **A.** 1. ¿No querría Margarita... ? 2. No podría viajar... 3. No pondríamos las maletas... 4. Saldrían de Madrid... 5. ¿No sabrías el nombre...? 6. ¿Uds. harían el viaje...? 7. Me habría gustado... 8. ¿No tendrías ganas de conocer...? **B.** 1. Wouldn't Margarita like a hotel with a pool? 2. I couldn't travel without my toothbrush. 3. We wouldn't put the suitcases (luggage) in the hands of that bellboy (i.e., we wouldn't trust him with the luggage). 4. They would leave Madrid today at 4:00. 5. Would you (happen to) know the name of a deluxe hotel in Malaga? 6. Would you travel by train? 7. I would really have enjoyed seeing the tennis match. 8. Wouldn't you like to meet the players? *70.* 1. El primer día, dormiría hasta mediodía. 2. El tercer día, nos broncearíamos en la playa. 3. El quinto día, Teresa jugaría al tenis y yo iría de compras. 4. El sexto día, necesitaría comprar gafas de sol y más loción bronceadora. 5. El séptimo día, cenaríamos en ese restaurante bueno que se especializa en mariscos. *71.* **A.** 1. El agua de colonia tuya es de París. La tuya es de París. 2. ¿Podrías buscar la raqueta mía? ¿Podrías buscar la mía? 3. ¿Se habrían perdido los aretes de plata vuestros? ¿Se habrían perdido los vuestros? 4. El fin de semana nuestro en Málaga estuvo fantástico. El nuestro estuvo fantástico. 5. ¿Dónde compraría Teresa el collar de perlas suyo? ¿Dónde compraría el suyo?

PARA REPASAR 1. No creo que sea tan joven como Teresa. 2. El agente niega que el avión llegue tarde. 3. Estamos seguros que este hotel cuesta tanto (dinero) como ése. 4. Es necesario que pidamos la habitación más barata del hotel. 5. Lo que me prometiste es maravilloso.
COMUNICACIÓN **A.** 1. gustaría 2. tomaría 3. preferiría Ud. 4. podríamos 5. gustaría 6. querría 7. sabría 8. Sería 9. Podría 10. saldría 11. habría

LABORATORY MANUAL

COMUNICACIÓN **C.** 1. ¿Dónde encontraría usted la montaña más alta de España? 2. Podría buscarla en el mapa pero sería difícil. 3. Debería de buscarla en una isla. ¿Cuál de ellas?

LECCIÓN DIECISÉIS

WORKBOOK

GRÁFICOS **A.** 1. postales 2. estampillas 3. El auxiliar de vuelo 4. el aeropuerto 5. los boletos **B.** 1. un asiento de ventanilla 2. uno de pasillo 3. pasajeros 4. avión 5. el equipaje **C.** 1. Sí, podrían tenerlos. 2. Sí, era necesario que las confirmaran. 3. No es justo que perdieran sus asientos. 4. Sí, es justo que decidiera ponerlos en primera clase. 5. No, era imposible que supiera que llegaría tarde.
GRAMÁTICA ESENCIAL **72.** **A.** 1. trabajaran 2. comiéramos 3. olvidara 4. hablaras 5. reservara 6. recogiera 7. discutiera 8. se levantaran **73.** **A.** 1. fuéramos 2. dijera 3. trajéramos 4. pusiera 5. quisieras 6. pudiera 7. supiéramos 8. tuvieran 9. estuvieras 10. viniera 11. hicieran 12. diera **B.** 1. Me recomendó que pidiéramos un taxi. 2. Dudaba que se divirtieran en el barco. 3. Pedimos que la azafata nos sirviera café en el vuelo. 4. No era cierto que te sintieras mal en Iguazú. 5. ¿Es posible que casi se murieran de hambre? **74.** **A.** 1. diera 2. pudo 3. expliqué 4. quería 5. vi 6. saliera 7. buscara 8. tratara 9. compré 10. empecé 11. era 12. dejara **B.** 1. No está segura de que podamos comprar un boleto de ida y vuelta. 2. Me promete que habrá espacio en el avión. 3. ¿Es importante que confirmemos nuestras reservaciones? 4. Pido que anuncien la hora del vuelo otra vez. 5. Esperan que el equipaje llegue en buenas condiciones.
COMUNICACIÓN **A.** 1. comiéramos 2. hiciéramos 3. llevara 4. nos sentáramos 5. esperáramos 6. dieran 7. pudieran 8. fuéramos 9. perdonara 10. se enojara 11. disfrutáramos **B.** 1. (Te) Recomendamos que fueras la semana próxima. 2. Quería que me pidieran uno en seguida. 3. El agente nos aconsejó que tomáramos un autobús. 4. Le dijimos que no trajera tanto. 5. Te mandé que los llevaras en el maletín.

LECCIÓN DIECISIETE

WORKBOOK

GRÁFICOS **A.** 1. el cajero 2. el jefe 3. la secretaria 4. la cajera 5. empleado bancario 6. el asaltante **B.** 1. Eugenio tiene una computadora que no funciona. 2. Si tuviera papel con membrete, podría escribir las cartas. 3. Necesita los sobres de la imprenta. 4. Eugenio y el jefe los tienen. 5. Sí, hay cola en todas. 6. Si los empleados trabajaran en vez de quejarse, el banco tendría más dinero.
GRAMÁTICA ESENCIAL **75.–76.** **A.** 1. paga 2. tenga 3. venda 4. conozca 5. dan 6. tenga **B.** 1. sepa 2. es 3. pueda 4. pague 5. haya 6. escriban **77.** **A.** 1. No conozco ningún banco donde paguen el diez por ciento de interés. 2. No tenemos ninguna empleada que hable español. 3. No hay problemas que sean fáciles de resolver. 4. No había un cajero que supiera usar la computadora. 5. No sabíamos que había una cuenta que pagara más interés. **B.** 1. No, no hay ninguna que funcione sin contratiempos. 2. No, no hay nadie que nos pueda ayudar. 3. No, no tienen un/ningún empleado que sepa usar una copiadora. 4. No, no sé de ninguna inversión que sea segura. 5. No, no hay nadie que lo haya visto. **78.** 1. Si yo fuera tú/Ud., compraría una computadora nueva. 2. Si llegara el cheque mañana, abriríamos una cuenta. 3. ¿Si le/te dieran el diez por ciento de interés, depositaría(s) sus/tus ahorros en ese banco? 4. La ayudaríamos a aprender inglés si nos pidiera. 5. Claro, si tuviera un teléfono no necesitaría un intercomunicador.
PARA REPASAR 1. cooperara... 2. vieran... 3. firmara... 4. abriera... 5. perdieran... 6. le mostraran...
COMUNICACIÓN **A.** 1. ¿No tienen una cuenta corriente que pague interés? 2. En México solamente tenemos cuentas que pagan interés. 3. Para abrir una cuenta, ¿necesito una tarjeta de identificación que tenga mi foto? 4. Si Ud. tiene una carta de su compañía que diga que Ud. es su empleado, no hay problema. 5. ¿Quiere Ud. que le traiga billetes o un cheque? 6. Si nos trajera un cheque, no podría usar la

cuenta por un mes. **B.** 1. pagara 2. tuviera 3. hubiera 4. diera 5. ganara 6. estuviera 7. existieran 8. pagaran

LABORATORY MANUAL

COMUNICACIÓN **C.** El asaltante mandó que le dieran cinco mil pesos. Pidió billetes que no estuvieran marcados. La cajera temía que él usara el revólver.

LECCIÓN DIECIOCHO

WORKBOOK

GRÁFICOS **A.** 1. arquitecto/a 2. maestro/a 3. doctor(a), enfermero/a, dentista, psiquiatra 4. farmacéutico/a 5. plomero/a 6. sociólogo/a, trabajador(a) social **B.** 1. Tienen que convencerles a los trabajadores que la ley será un beneficio para el país. 2. No, no es justo que le pidan que trabaje por menos. 3. No le importa con tal de que no se caiga por completo la economía del país. 4. Es necesario que cambien la política extranjera. 5. Hay que tener en cuenta que a menos que vendan más productos, la economía va a empeorar.
GRAMÁTICA ESENCIAL 79.–80. 1. se mate 2. coman 3. pida 4. valga 5. puedas 6. gane 7. haya 8. estemos *81.* 1. Le compraré otro martillo cuando llegue el carpintero. 2. El electricista me cobrará una fortuna después de que pinten la casa. 3. No nos podremos bañar hasta que ponga la tubería. 4. Lavaremos la ropa tan pronto como repares la secadora. 5. ¿No podrás encender las luces hasta que venga el ingeniero? 6. Decidiré si vale la pena trabajar para esa empresa cuando me llame el gerente. *82.* **A.** 1. Rolando cobra mucho por hora aunque no sea buen carpintero. 2. El arquitecto cambiará los planes aunque no se lo pidamos. 3. Juan defenderá bien a sus clientes aunque no crean que sea un buen abogado. 4. María llegará a ser millonaria aunque ella no ahorre ni un centavo. 5. Aquel economista sacará su título aunque le tome ocho años. **B.** 1. ...aunque pinta... 2. ...aunque tiene... 3. Aunque cambian... 4. Aunque ve... 5. Aunque no necesita...
PARA REPASAR 1. tenga 2. pueda 3. ayude 4. pone 5. paga/pagará 6. haya 7. sepa
COMUNICACIÓN **A.** 1. comience 2. sepan 3. se encuentren 4. somos 5. tengamos 6. pueda 7. se dé 8. decidan 9. oigan 10. me den 11. han 12. tengamos

LABORATORY MANUAL

COMUNICACIÓN **B.** Aunque uno decida estudiar una profesión, no siempre será la que practique. Después de que uno trabaje varios años, puede decidir cambiar de carrera. Con tal de que uno se gane la vida haciendo lo que le guste, uno puede hacer lo que quiera.

940.076 CRA 2017
Cracking the AP. European
history exam.
Carver County Library

The Princeton Review®

Cracking the

AP®

EUROPEAN
HISTORY EXAM

2017 Edition

The Staff of The Princeton Review

PrincetonReview.com

Penguin
Random
House

The Princeton Review
24 Prime Parkway, Suite 201
Natick, MA 01760
E-mail: editorialsupport@review.com

Copyright © 2016 by TPR Education IP Holdings, LLC.
All rights reserved.

Published in the United States by Penguin Random House
LLC, New York, and in Canada by Random House of Canada,
a division of Penguin Random House Ltd., Toronto.

Terms of Service: The Princeton Review Online Companion
Tools ("Student Tools") for retail books are available for only
the two most recent editions of that book. Student Tools may
be activated only twice per eligible book purchased for two
consecutive 12-month periods, for a total of 24 months of
access. Activation of Student Tools more than twice per book
is in direct violation of these Terms of Service and may result
in discontinuation of access to Student Tools Services.

ISBN: 978-1-101-91993-4
eBook ISBN: 978-1-101-92019-0
ISSN: 1522-6409

AP and Advanced Placement Program are registered
trademarks of the College Board, which is not affiliated with
The Princeton Review.

The Princeton Review is not affiliated with Princeton University.

Editor: Colleen Day
Production Editor: Jim Melloan
Production Artist: Deborah A. Silvestrini

Printed in the United States of America on partially
recycled paper.

10   9   8   7   6   5   4   3   2   1

2017 Edition

Editorial

Rob Franek, Senior VP, Publisher
Casey Cornelius, VP Content Development
Mary Beth Garrick, Director of Production
Selena Coppock, Managing Editor
Meave Shelton, Senior Editor
Colleen Day, Editor
Sarah Litt, Editor
Aaron Riccio, Editor
Orion McBean, Editorial Assistant

Random House Publishing Team

Tom Russell, Publisher
Alison Stoltzfus, Publishing Manager
Jake Eldred, Associate Managing Editor
Ellen Reed, Production Manager
Andrea Lau, Designer

Acknowledgments

A very special thanks to Kevin Kelly for his thorough review of this title and fantastic updates to the 2017 Edition.

Contents

Register Your

1 Go to **PrincetonReview.com/cracking**

2 You'll see a welcome page where you can register your book using the following ISBN: 9781101919934

3 After placing this free order, you'll either be asked to log in or to answer a few simple questions in order to set up a new Princeton Review account.

4 Finally, click on the "Student Tools" tab located at the top of the screen. It may take an hour or two for your registration to go through, but after that, you're good to go.

If you are experiencing book problems (potential content errors), please contact EditorialSupport@review.com with the full title of the book, its ISBN number (located above), and the page number of the error. Experiencing technical issues? Please e-mail TPRStudentTech@review.com with the following information:

- your full name
- e-mail address used to register the book
- full book title and ISBN
- your computer OS (Mac or PC) and Internet browser (Firefox, Safari, Chrome, etc.)
- description of technical issue

Book Online!

Once you've registered, you can...

- Find any late-breaking information released about the AP European History Exam

- Take a full-length practice PSAT, SAT, and ACT

- Get valuable advice about the college application process, including tips for writing a great essay and where to apply for financial aid

- Sort colleges by whatever you're looking for (such as Best Theater or Dorm), learn more about your top choices, and see how they all rank according to *The Best 380 Colleges*

- Access comprehensive study guides and a variety of printable resources, including bubble sheets for the practice tests in the book and timelines of key events in European history

- Check to see if there have been any corrections or updates to this edition

Look For These Icons Throughout The Book

Online Articles

Applied Strategies

Proven Techniques

More Great Books

The **Princeton** Review®

Part I
Using This
Book to Improve
Your AP Score

PREVIEW: YOUR KNOWLEDGE, YOUR EXPECTATIONS

Your route to a high score on the AP European History Exam depends a lot on how you plan to use this book. Start thinking about your plan by responding to the following questions.

1. What is your level of confidence about your knowledge of the content tested by the AP European History Exam?

   A. Very confident—I know it all
   B. I'm pretty confident, but there are topics for which I could use help
   C. Not confident—I need quite a bit of support
   D. I'm not sure

2. If you have a goal score in mind, circle your goal score for the AP European History Exam:

   5   4   3   2   1   I'm not sure yet

3. What do you expect to learn from this book? Circle all that apply to you.

   A. A general overview of the test and what to expect
   B. Strategies for how to approach the test
   C. The content tested by this exam
   D. I'm not sure yet

YOUR GUIDE TO USING THIS BOOK

This book is organized to provide as much—or as little—support as you need, so you can use this book in whatever way will be most helpful to improving your score on the AP European History Exam.

- The remainder of **Part I** will provide guidance on how to use this book and help you determine your strengths and weaknesses.

- **Part II** of this book contains Practice Test 1 and its answers and explanations. (Bubble sheets can be found in the very back of the book for easy tear-out.) We strongly recommend that you take this test before going any further in order to realistically determine:

  ○ your starting point right now
  ○ which question types you're ready for and which you might need to practice
  ○ which content topics you are familiar with and which you will want to carefully review

Once you have nailed down your strengths and weaknesses with regard to this exam, you can focus your test preparation, build a study plan, and be efficient with your time.

- **Part III** of this book will:
  - provide information about the structure, scoring, and content of the AP European History Exam
  - help you to make a study plan
  - point you towards additional resources

- **Part IV** of this book will explore various strategies:
  - how to attack multiple-choice questions
  - how to write effective essays: document-based questions (DBQs) and thematic essay questions
  - how to manage your time to maximize the number of points available to you

- **Part V** of this book covers the content you need for the AP European History Exam.

- **Part VI** of this book contains Practice Test 2 and its answers and explanations. (Bubble sheets can be found in the very back of the book for easy tear-out.) If you skipped Practice Test 1, we recommend that you do both (with at least a day or two between them) so that you can compare your progress between the two. Additionally, this will help to identify any external issues: If you get a certain type of question wrong both times, you probably need to review it. If you only got it wrong once, you may have run out of time or been distracted by something. In either case, this will allow you to focus on the factors that caused the discrepancy in scores and to be as prepared as possible on the day of the test.

You may choose to use some parts of this book over others, or you may work through the entire book. Your approach will depend on your needs and how much time you have. Let's now look how to make this determination.

HOW TO BEGIN

1. **Take Practice Test 1**

    Before you can decide how to use this book, you need to take a practice test. Doing so will give you insight into your strengths and weaknesses, and the test will also help you make an effective study plan. If you're feeling test-phobic, remind yourself that a practice test is a tool for diagnosing yourself—it's not how well you do that matters but how you use information gleaned from your performance to guide your preparation.

    So, before you read further, take Practice Test 1 starting at page 7 of this book. Be sure to do so in one sitting, following the instructions that appear before the test.

2. **Check Your Answers**

    Using the answers/explanations that start on page 37, count the number of questions you got right and how many you missed. Don't worry about the explanations for now, and don't worry about why you missed questions. We'll get to that soon.

3. **Reflect on the Test**

    After you take your first test, respond to the following questions:

    *   How much time did you spend on the multiple-choice questions?

    *   How much time did you spend on each essay?

    *   How many multiple-choice questions did you miss?

    *   Do you feel you had the knowledge to address the subject matter of the short-answer questions and essays?

    *   Do you feel you wrote well-organized, thoughtful short-answer responses and essays?

4. **Read Part III of this Book and Complete the Self-Evaluation**

    Part III will provide information on how the test is structured and scored. It will also set out areas of content that are tested.

    As you read Part III, re-evaluate your answers to the questions above. At the end of Part III, you will revisit and refine the questions you answer above. You will then be able to make a study plan, based on your needs and time available, that will allow you to use this book most effectively.

5. **Engage with Parts IV and V as Needed**

   Notice the word *engage*. You'll get more out of this book if you use it intentionally than if you read it passively, hoping for an improved score through osmosis.

   Strategy chapters will help you think about your approach to the question types on this exam. Part IV will open with a reminder to think about how you approach questions now and then close with a reflection section asking you to think about how/whether you will change your approach in the future.

   Content chapters are designed to provide a review of the content tested on the AP European History Exam, including the level of detail you need to know and how the content is tested. You will have the opportunity to assess your mastery of the content of each chapter through test-appropriate questions and a reflection section.

6. **Take Practice Test 2 and Assess Your Performance**

   Once you feel you have developed the strategies you need and gained the knowledge you lacked, you should take Practice Test 2, which starts at page 365 of this book. You should do so in one sitting, following the instructions at the beginning of the test.

   When you are done, check your answers to the multiple-choice sections. See if a teacher will read your essays and provide feedback.

   Once you have taken the test, reflect on what areas you still need to work on, and revisit the chapters in this book that address those deficiencies. Through this type of reflection and engagement, you will continue to improve.

7. **Keep Working**

   As we'll discuss in Part III, there are other resources available to you, including a wealth of information at AP Students, which is the AP section of the College Board's website. (The College Board is the non-profit organization that administers the AP and SAT programs.) You can continue to explore areas that can stand to improve and engage in those areas right up to the day of the test. For updates and information on the AP European History Exam, as well as free practice, check out its home page: **http://apstudent.collegeboard.org/apcourse/ap-european-history**.

Part II
Practice Test 1

- Practice Test 1
- Practice Test 1: Answers and Explanations

Practice Test 1

AP® European History Exam

DO NOT OPEN THIS BOOKLET UNTIL YOU ARE TOLD TO DO SO.

At a Glance
Time
55 minutes
Number of Questions
55
Percent of Total Score
40%
Writing Instrument
Pencil required

Instructions

Section I, Part A, of this exam contains 55 multiple-choice questions. Fill in only the ovals for numbers 1 through 55 on your answer sheet. Because this section offers only four answer options for each question, do not mark the (E) answer circle for any question.

Indicate all of your answers to the multiple-choice questions on the answer sheet. No credit will be given for anything written in this exam booklet, but you may use the booklet for notes or scratch work. After you have decided which of the suggested answers is best, completely fill in the corresponding oval on the answer sheet. Give only one answer to each question. If you change an answer, be sure that the previous mark is erased completely. Here is a sample question and answer.

Sample Question   Sample Answer

Chicago is a   (A) ● (C) (D)
(A) state
(B) city
(C) country
(D) continent

Use your time effectively, working as quickly as you can without losing accuracy. Do not spend too much time on any one question. Go on to other questions and come back to the ones you have not answered if you have time. It is not expected that everyone will know the answers to all the multiple-choice questions.

Your total score on the multiple-choice section is based only on the number of questions answered correctly. Points are not deducted for incorrect answers or unanswered questions.

At a Glance
Time
50 minutes
Number of Questions
4
Percent of Total Score
20%
Writing Instrument
Pen with black or dark blue ink

Instructions

Section I, Part B of this exam consists of 4 short-answer questions. Write your responses on a separate sheet of paper.

This page intentionally left blank.

GO ON TO THE NEXT PAGE.

EUROPEAN HISTORY

SECTION I, Part A

Time—55 minutes

55 Questions

Directions: Each of the questions or incomplete statements below is followed by either four suggested answers or completions. Select the one that is best in each case and then fill in the appropriate letter in the corresponding space on the answer sheet.

Questions 1–3 refer to the passage below.

"A specter is haunting Europe—the specter of Communism. All the powers of old Europe have entered into a holy alliance to exorcise this specter; Pope and Czar, Metternich and Guizot, French radicals and German police spies.

Two things result from this fact.

I. Communism is already acknowledged by all European powers to be in itself a power.

II. It is high time that Communists should openly, in the face of the whole world, publish their views, their aims, their tendencies, and meet this nursery tale of the Specter of Communism with a Manifesto of the party itself."

Karl Marx and Friedrich Engels, *The Communist Manifesto,* 1848

1. In this passage, Marx and Engels seem to be chiefly preoccupied with

   (A) provoking fear to drive their readers to action
   (B) attacking the extreme communists who threatened to sink the entire movement
   (C) demonstrating the understanding of the others in point of fact
   (D) explaining the reasons for debunking opponents of communism

2. To modern historians, the publication of this pamphlet is remembered for coinciding with which of the following events?

   (A) A series of revolutions that gripped Europe in the same year
   (B) The Ottoman Empire's increasing pressure upon the Greek Peninsula
   (C) A new system of underground pamphlet distribution
   (D) The re-emergence of anti-Semitism as a potent European force

3. By 1917, which idea in this pamphlet had become a reality in Russia?

   (A) The avoidance of entangling foreign alliances
   (B) The violent overthrow of the bourgeois by the proletariat
   (C) The establishment of a powerful Russian Parliament
   (D) The adoption of free education for all children in public schools

GO ON TO THE NEXT PAGE.

Questions 4–6 refer to the painting below.

4. The clothing and general feeling of the painting reflect the influence of which important Northern European movement?

   (A) The multiple alliances of the Thirty Years' War
   (B) The Reformation and its insistence upon sobriety and seriousness
   (C) The Counter-Reformation and its insistence upon strict codes of moral conduct
   (D) The end of the manorial system and the rise of cottage industry

5. The typical presence of a single person in the Golden Age of Dutch portraiture such as the one above indicates which of the following?

   (A) A societal preference for landscapes over people
   (B) A renewed interest in the human individual following the Renaissance
   (C) The artist's lack of appropriate subjects for painting
   (D) A preoccupation with the latest trends in painting

6. The artist's choice of depicting a seamstress at work would seem to suggest what about the values of Dutch society in the nineteenth century?

   (A) Mundane but practical work was a necessary part of life.
   (B) The growing middle class was nostalgic for its working-class roots.
   (C) Clothing had recently become an even more essential part of Dutch life.
   (D) Dutch society longed for simpler times in which manual labor was its own reward.

GO ON TO THE NEXT PAGE.

Questions 7–11 refer to the following passage regarding a series of photographs of mentally ill individuals.

"Figures 34 & 23. An exceedingly tragic expression, apparently produced by the powerful contraction of the muscles of the eyebrows, with some elevation of the skin of the forehead & transverse folds. This expression if perfect would produce the so-called 'horse-shoe' on the forehead about which Sir Walter Scott speaks in 'Redgauntlet'. Mrs. Scott Siddons the actress has the power of producing these lines on the forehead with singular precision. She tells me that all her family have been remarkable for this power. The lines referred are if I remember rightly well seen in Sir Joshua Reynolds' portrait of the great Mrs. Siddons as the Tragic Muse. My brother Mr. Balfour Browne informs me that the last descendent of the Griersons of Largg (the Redgauntlets of Sir Walter Scott) prides herself on possessing the family peculiarity, the power of producing in a striking manner, the horse-shoe on the forehead.

Figures 16. 17. 18. The action of the *pyramidalis nasi* does not convey to my mind any idea of an expressive expression. It suggests rather *painful attention*. In cases of profound melancholia I have frequently seen it combined in persistent action with the *corrugatorses superciliorum*, notwithstanding Duchenne's statement that they are antagonistic."

James Crichton-Browne, a British psychiatrist, in a letter to Charles Darwin, 1870

7. Based on the letter, it can be inferred that Crichton-Browne was a supporter of

(A) Romantic thought
(B) natural selection
(C) eugenics
(D) euthanasia

8. The underlying idea of this letter was most challenging to

(A) the classical concept of humans as occupying a special, exalted status in the natural world
(B) the insistence that classic portraiture and science were unrelated
(C) the desire of British upper-class society to colonize portions of Africa, India, and Asia
(D) the belief that medical students who robbed corpses from graves for autopsies were not contributing to modern society

9. This passage suggests what about the state of European scientific society by 1870?

(A) That it had atrophied beyond any hope of repair
(B) That it was beginning to assemble itself into organized groups through underground letters
(C) That it viewed Darwin as an outsider to be shunned
(D) That it had applied the theory of natural selection to humans as well as to animals

10. It can be presumed that one of the changes that prompted Crichton-Browne and Darwin to begin this course of study was

(A) the invention of photography
(B) the recent English adoption of the scientific method
(C) Gregor Mendel's celebrated discovery of what would become the modern field of genetics
(D) a rising middle class that hungered for scientific knowledge

11. The subject matter and tone of this letter directly influenced which subsequent literary movement?

(A) Classicism
(B) Naturalism
(C) Realism
(D) Postmodernism

GO ON TO THE NEXT PAGE.

Questions 12–14 refer to the passage below.

"His Majesty the Emperor of China agrees, that British subjects, with their families and establishments, shall be allowed to reside, for the purposes of carrying on their mercantile pursuits, without molestation or restraint, at the cities and towns of Canton, Amoy, Foochowfoo, Ningpo, and Shanghai; and Her Majesty the Queen of Great Britain, &c., will appoint Superintendents, or Consular officers, to reside at each of the above-named cities or towns, to be the medium of communication between the Chinese authorities and the said merchants, and to see that the just duties and other dues of the Chinese Government, as hereafter provided for, are duly discharged by Her Britannic Majesty's subjects."

Treaty of Nanjing, 1839

12. This treaty was the conclusion of a series of events that began with

    (A) the Boxer Rebellion
    (B) a treaty between China and colonial India
    (C) the elimination of British Corn Laws
    (D) the British forcing the Chinese to participate in the opium trade

13. The concessions offered in this treaty most directly created British

    (A) colonies
    (B) spheres of influence
    (C) protectorates
    (D) businesses

14. How did the Boxers of the early twentieth century react to the legacy of this treaty?

    (A) They initiated an armed resistance against Western interests in Northern China.
    (B) They formed an alliance with Japan to stop Western businesses from operating in China.
    (C) They ran for local political offices on a platform to expand the treaty.
    (D) They defended the treaty from the opposition of Chinese rebels.

GO ON TO THE NEXT PAGE.

Questions 15–18 refer to the passage below.

"The Italian nation has been at last united in our own days, and we all rejoiced in its union. Yet we may be allowed to doubt whether the union was not a little too speedy and a little too thorough. It is surely carrying unity too far to wipe out all traces of the independent being, for most purposes to wipe out the very name, of such a land as Sicily. It jars on our feelings to find that, while Ireland at least forms part of the royal style of its sovereign, Sicily is no longer even a geographical expression. The island realm of Roger has sunk to be seven provinces of the kingdom on the mainland. And there is another result of Italian unity, a result in which we may rejoice without drawbacks, but which still has somewhat of sadness about it as finally ending that great phase of the history of Europe with which we have throughout been dealing. Never were ties with the past so fully snapped as when the army of Italy entered liberated Rome. Of all novelties in European history the greatest was when Rome became the centre of a dominion with acknowledged metes and bounds, the head in short of a local Italian kingdom. "Rome the capital of Italy" was a formula which might well gladden our hearts; but it was a formula which formally swept away the œcumenical position, the œcumenical traditions, of Rome....

But the kingdom of Italy is not an appendage to Rome; Rome is the head of the kingdom. The whole is greater than its part; Rome, by her own free will and by the free will of Italy, has become less than Italy. By becoming the willing head of an Italian kingdom she has formally cast aside her Imperial traditions as they were not cast aside when brute force made her the head of a French department."

Edward A. Freeman, British historian and politician, from *The Chief Periods of European History,* 1885

15. The author expresses bittersweet feelings about the results of what major European political movement of the nineteenth century?

(A) Romanticism
(B) Socialism
(C) Conservatism
(D) Nationalism

16. The author would likely take exception to the methods of which leader during this time period in Italy?

(A) Napoleon III
(B) Giuseppe Garibaldi
(C) Victor Emmanuel
(D) Count Cavour

17. According to the author, Italy's connections to its history and traditions were most "fully snapped" when

(A) Sicily ceased to be an independent kingdom.
(B) Italians liberated Rome.
(C) Rome became the head of a French Department.
(D) French troops abandoned Rome to fight in the Franco-Prussian War.

18. The author laments the loss of which Roman traditions?

(A) Lingual
(B) Religious
(C) Economic
(D) Artistic

GO ON TO THE NEXT PAGE.

Questions 19–22 refer to the following political cartoon created by German cartoonist Ferdinand Schröder in 1849.

19. Which of the following ideologies was NOT a catalyst for the events depicted in this cartoon?

    (A) Liberalism
    (B) Conservatism
    (C) Socialism
    (D) Nationalism

20. The artist conveys that the revolutions of 1848

    (A) largely brought about significant changes to most nations in Europe
    (B) were fairly limited in terms of success due to the power of the authorities they came up against
    (C) inspired widespread popular revolts outside of the European continent
    (D) were more successful on the European mainland than on the British Isles

21. As suggested by the cartoon, why was Russia unique during the revolutions of 1848?

    (A) The success of the Chartist movement rendered such an uprising unnecessary.
    (B) Its revolution was led by a workers' revolt.
    (C) The presence of Austrian forces inside its borders severely limited the ability of the people to revolt.
    (D) Nicholas I held down any popular protest with his repressive regime.

22. The events depicted in this cartoon influenced all of the following events EXCEPT

    (A) the Decembrist Revolt
    (B) the unification of Germany
    (C) the unification of Italy
    (D) the adoption of the Charters by the British House of Commons

GO ON TO THE NEXT PAGE.

Questions 23–25 refer to the passage below.

"I am in some pain lest this custom [of gambling] should get among the ladies. They are, at present, very deep in cards and dice; and while my lord is gaining abroad, her ladyship has her rout at home. I am inclined to suspect that our women of fashion will, also, learn to divert themselves with this polite practice of laying wagers. A birthday suit, the age of a beauty, who invented a particular fashion, or who were supposed to be together at the last masquerade, would, frequently give occasion for bets. This would, also, afford them a new method for the ready propagation of scandal, as the truth of several stories which are continually flitting about the town, would, naturally, be brought to the same test. Should they proceed further, to stake the lives of their acquaintances against each other, they would, doubtless, bet with the same fearless spirit, as they are known to do at brag; one husband would, perhaps, be pitted against another, or a woman of the town against a maid of honour. In a word, if this once becomes fashionable among the ladies, we shall soon see the time, when an allowance for bet money will be stipulated in the marriage articles.

As the vices and follies of persons of distinction are very apt to spread, I am much afraid lest this branch of gaming should descend to the common people. Indeed, it seems already to have got among them. We have frequent accounts of tradesmen riding, walking, eating and drinking for a wager. The contested election in the City has occasioned several extraordinary bets. I know a butcher in Leadenhall Market, who laid an ox to a shin of beef on the success of Sir John Barnard against the field; and have been told of a publican in Thames Street, who ventured a hogshead of entire beer on the candidate who serves him with beer."

John Ashton, *The History of Gambling in England,* 1898

23. Through his description of "persons of distinction" and "common people," the author reveals his worldview as essentially

(A) socialist, given the view of society as an interlocking whole
(B) conservative, given the hierarchical nature of his outlook
(C) egalitarian, given his concern over society's inequalities
(D) progressive, given his need for improved civil rights for gamblers

24. The Victorian tone of the passage can be seen most prominently in which of the following characteristics?

(A) The paternalistic concern that women should avoid gambling, as the pursuit would sully the institution of marriage
(B) The warm-hearted embrace of working-class gamblers
(C) The lack of any mention of children
(D) The absence of distinction between private and public spheres

25. The author displays an attitude toward gambling that most clearly has its roots in

(A) the medieval tradition of *noblesse oblige*
(B) the Restoration era and its witty courtliness
(C) the Industrial Revolution and its emphasis on productivity
(D) the long Puritan tradition of valuing thrift and hard work

GO ON TO THE NEXT PAGE.

Questions 26–28 refer to the painting below.

Leonardo da Vinci, *Mona Lisa*, 1503

26. At the time of this painting, most Italian artists such as da Vinci earned their living through

    (A) the support of a patron
    (B) commercial sales of their paintings
    (C) offerings collected at daily Mass
    (D) taxes levied by the local government

27. As with many Renaissance paintings, the defining characteristic in the portrait depicted above is

    (A) divinity
    (B) religious iconography
    (C) naturalism
    (D) human centrism

28. The single-point perspective used in this painting attempts to pay homage to the

    (A) art present in medieval churches
    (B) Northern Renaissance style
    (C) realism of the Classical period
    (D) imagery of the late Roman Empire

GO ON TO THE NEXT PAGE.

Questions 29–31 refer to the poem excerpt below.

The sea is calm tonight.
The tide is full, the moon lies fair
Upon the straits; on the French coast the light
Gleams and is gone; the cliffs of England stand,
Glimmering and vast, out in the tranquil bay…

The Sea of Faith
Was once, too, at the full, and round earth's shore
Lay like the folds of a bright girdle furled.
But now I only hear

Its melancholy, long, withdrawing roar,
Retreating, to the breath
Of the night-wind, down the vast edges drear
And naked shingles of the world.

Matthew Arnold, English poet and critic, "Dover Beach," 1851

29. The loss that Arnold refers to in the second stanza most likely illustrates which of the following European feelings in the middle of the nineteenth century?

   (A) The awareness that science was losing ground against a new wave of skeptics
   (B) The belief that intellectual revolution was inevitable
   (C) The sense that the old religious traditions were being lost in a wave of technological and cultural transformation
   (D) The idea that excellent artistic expression was being drowned in a tidal wave of mediocrity

30. Based on the poem, it can be inferred that Matthew Arnold was most influenced by which of the following?

   (A) Scholasticism
   (B) Conservatism
   (C) Nationalism
   (D) Postmodernism

31. By the 1920s, the ideas reflected in the poem had undergone which of the following changes?

   (A) Scientific research failed to change European society in any significant way, prompting a return to a culture of faith.
   (B) Europeans rediscovered religion following the terrifying massacres of the Bolsheviks.
   (C) There was greater political stability, as the English and the French had finally made a peace across the English Channel.
   (D) The discoveries of the 1900s and 1910s, including the destabilization of the entire continent during World War I, prompted an even deeper sense of loss and confusion.

GO ON TO THE NEXT PAGE.

Questions 32–36 refer to the passage below.

"The Government of the German Reich and The Government of the Union of Soviet Socialist Republics desirous of strengthening the cause of peace between Germany and the U.S.S.R., and proceeding from the fundamental provisions of the Neutrality Agreement concluded in April, 1926 between Germany and the U.S.S.R., have reached the following Agreement:

Article I. Both High Contracting Parties obligate themselves to desist from any act of violence, any aggressive action, and any attack on each other, either individually or jointly with other Powers.

Article II. Should one of the High Contracting Parties become the object of belligerent action by a third Power, the other High Contracting Party shall in no manner lend its support to this third Power.

Article III. The Governments of the two High Contracting Parties shall in the future maintain continual contact with one another for the purpose of consultation in order to exchange information on problems affecting their common interests.

Article IV. Should disputes or conflicts arise between the High Contracting Parties shall participate in any grouping of Powers whatsoever that is directly or indirectly aimed at the other party.

Article V. Should disputes or conflicts arise between the High Contracting Parties over problems of one kind or another, both parties shall settle these disputes or conflicts exclusively through friendly exchange of opinion or, if necessary, through the establishment of arbitration commissions."

Molotov-Ribbentrop Pact, 1939

32. This agreement allowed both nations involved to freely invade which country?

(A) Denmark
(B) Finland
(C) France
(D) Poland

33. The Soviets were most strongly motivated to create this agreement because

(A) Germany promised to help regain Soviet land lost in the First World War
(B) the attempt by the Soviets to form an alliance with Britain and France had failed
(C) they wanted to assist the Germans in seizing land from Czechoslovakia
(D) they held debt to Germany stemming from the First World War

34. It can be inferred from the text that Germany and the Soviet Union

(A) had some degree of a nonaggression agreement since at least 1926
(B) created their first peace agreement in 1926
(C) had technically been in a state of war since 1926
(D) previously held a peace agreement that expired in 1926

35. The article listed above that was violated by Operation Barbarossa was

(A) Article I
(B) Article II
(C) Article III
(D) Article IV

36. The agreement described in the text is most similar to the

(A) Triple Entente (1907)
(B) Sykes-Picot Agreement (1916)
(C) Lateran Treaty (1929)
(D) Munich Agreement (1938)

GO ON TO THE NEXT PAGE.

Questions 37–41 refer to the passage below.

"But you, my dear Pangloss," said Candide, "how can it be that I behold you again?"

"It is true," said Pangloss, "that you saw me hanged. …A surgeon purchased my body, carried home, and dissected me. He began with making a crucial incision on me from the navel to the clavicula. One could not have been worse hanged than I was. The executioner of the Holy Inquisition was a sub-deacon, and knew how to burn people marvellously well, but he was not accustomed to hanging. The cord was wet and did not slip properly, and besides it was badly tied; in short, I still drew my breath, when the crucial incision made me give such a frightful scream that my surgeon fell flat upon his back … [At length he] sewed up my wounds; his wife even nursed me. I was upon my legs at the end of fifteen days….

One day I took it into my head to step into a mosque, where I saw an old Iman and a very pretty young devotee who was saying her paternosters….She dropped her bouquet; I picked it up, and presented it to her with a profound reverence. I was so long in delivering it that the Iman began to get angry, and seeing that I was a Christian he called out for help. They carried me before the cadi, who ordered me a hundred lashes on the soles of the feet and sent me to the galleys. I was chained to the very same galley and the same bench as the young Baron. On board this galley there were four young men from Marseilles, five Neapolitan priests, and two monks from Corfu, who told us similar adventures happened daily. The Baron maintained that he had suffered greater injustice than I…. We were continually disputing, and received twenty lashes with a bull's pizzle when the concatenation of universal events brought you to our galley, and you were good enough to ransom us."

"Well, my dear Pangloss," said Candide to him, "when you had been hanged, dissected, whipped, and were tugging at the oar, did you always think that everything happens for the best?"

"I am still of my first opinion," answered Pangloss, "for I am a philosopher and I cannot retract, especially as Leibnitz could never be wrong; and besides, the pre-established harmony is the finest thing in the world, and so is his plenum and materia subtilis."

Voltaire, French Enlightenment writer, *Candide*, 1759

37. The themes of the passage and the mode in which Pangloss tells them show the influence of

(A) Medievalism
(B) Empiricism
(C) Rationalism
(D) Romanticism

38. The mockery of the Inquisition executioner who failed to hang Pangloss reflects the era's

(A) personal experience at the hands of Torquemada
(B) embrace of the Islamic way of life
(C) general rejection of Catholic dogma
(D) insistence on even stricter forms of religious discipline

39. The "concatenation of universal events" that brought the men together on the ship illustrates the eighteenth-century fondness of

(A) demonstrating high social status through large vocabulary
(B) exploiting naval power to European nation-states
(C) drawing universal conclusions from a wide range of concrete data
(D) using cause-and-effect to systematize the understanding of human behavior

40. Candide's statement that "everything always happens for the best" can be seen as a reflection of the Enlightenment belief that

(A) society can be perfected if you apply the scientific method to it
(B) a people without a strong central authority are doomed to live in a state of nature
(C) the only purpose of a government is to secure the rights of life, liberty, and property
(D) only free markets can lead nations to wealth and happiness

41. The critiques offered by Voltaire through *Candide* are most closely shared by what other philosopher?

(A) Cesare Baccaria
(B) Jean-Jacques Rousseau
(C) Adam Smith
(D) David Hume

GO ON TO THE NEXT PAGE.

Questions 42–46 refer to the following map showing European gross domestic product in 2005.

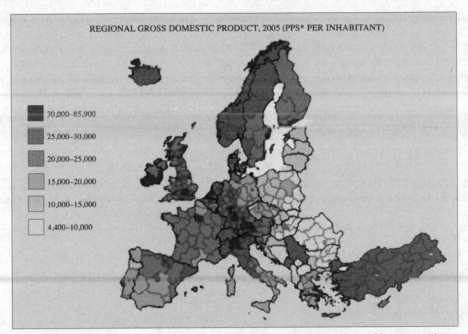

REGIONAL GROSS DOMESTIC PRODUCT, 2005 (PPS* PER INHABITANT)

30,000–85,900

25,000–30,000

20,000–25,000

15,000–20,000

10,000–15,000

4,400–10,000

* PPS, or purchasing power standards, is a standardized unit used to measure the wealth or economic capacity of one country against another.

42. The lower gross domestic product of Eastern European countries is most attributable to

 (A) the tricky definition of what constitutes a domestic product
 (B) their lack of access to marine ports
 (C) their fifty years spent within the centrally planned totalitarian system of the Soviet Union
 (D) the small amount of natural resources that are found in that region

43. All of the following nations exhibited strong economic power in 2005 EXCEPT

 (A) Ireland
 (B) the Netherlands
 (C) England
 (D) Greece

44. The map suggests which of the following about northern and southern Italy?

 (A) The Democratic Party had its base in the skilled northern urban workers.
 (B) Mussolini's Battle For Wheat initiative had finally sprouted some success.
 (C) The rapid changes of parliaments and prime ministers in the post-World War II era had a major effect upon the country.
 (D) The historic gap in economic production between the two regions had yet to be closed.

45. Which of the following generalities about European economics is NOT justified by the map?

 (A) Regions containing major cities tend to have stronger economies than regions without major cities.
 (B) The warmer southern Mediterranean regions of Europe are generally less economically productive than the colder northern regions.
 (C) Turkey's inclusion in the European Union would be advantageous to the entire continent.
 (D) The countries that joined the European Coal and Steel Community first have generally advanced the furthest.

46. According to the map, which of the following countries had the most consistent GDP across its regions?

 (A) Norway
 (B) Poland
 (C) Spain
 (D) Sweden

GO ON TO THE NEXT PAGE.

Questions 47–50 refer to the following account of the Paris Exposition of 1889.

"The opportunities to study the natural history of man in Paris during the Exposition, and especially in August, when the great Congresses and the French Association held their sessions, were unparalleled in the history of anthropology. At any time the French capital affords rare advantages to the anthropologist. The Musée and Laboratoire Broca, the anthropometric operations of Bertillon in the Palais de Justice, the courses of lectures in the École d'Anthropologie, the collections in the Jardin de Plantes, the facilities for original work in the Écoles de Medicine, and the hospitals give to the comparative anatomist and biologist abundant employment."

Otis T. Mason, American ethnologist and curator, 1889

47. It can be inferred from the text that at the time of the Paris Exposition, the scientific community was changing due to

(A) the inclusion of women
(B) an increase in funding from officials in the French capital
(C) the development of universal public education in many European countries
(D) the development of new, specialized fields

48. The field primarily described in this passage was born when

(A) scientific societies needed new ways of attracting members who were less interested in the study of the natural world
(B) there arose a sudden interest in expanding human rights throughout the French colonies
(C) scientific principles were applied to other cultures as a result of the sudden expansion of European dominance across large parts of the globe
(D) a large influx of immigrants from Africa and Asia arrived in Europe

49. The scientists described in the account of the Paris Exposition would have been most influenced by the work of which scientific pioneer?

(A) Einstein
(B) Planck
(C) Nobel
(D) Darwin

50. The opportunities described in the text can be attributed to

(A) the stability brought to France by the Third Republic
(B) France's preparation for the upcoming Franco-Prussian War during the Second Empire
(C) the labor friendly policies of the Second Republic
(D) financial power of the bourgeoisie during the Bourbon Restoration

GO ON TO THE NEXT PAGE.

Questions 51–55 refer to the passage below.

"When a stream is brimful, a slight rise suffices to cause an overflow. So was it with the extreme distress of the eighteenth century. A poor man, who finds it difficult to live when bread is cheap, sees death staring him in the face when it is dear….In 1788, a year of severe drought, the crops had been poor. In addition to this, on the eve of the harvest, a terrible hail-storm burst over the region around Paris, from Normandy to Champagne, devastating sixty leagues of the most fertile territory, and causing damage to the amount of one hundred millions of francs. Winter came on, the severest that had been since 1709….In Vivarais, and in the Cevennes, whole forests of chestnuts had perished, along with all the grain and grass crops on the uplands.

After the spring of 1789 the famine spread everywhere, and it increased from month to month like a rising flood. In vain did the Government order the farmers, proprietors, and corn-dealers to keep the markets supplied. In vain did it double the bounty on imports, resort to all sorts of expedients, involve itself in debt, and expend over forty millions of francs to furnish France with wheat….Neither public measures nor private charity could meet the overwhelming need….In many parishes one-fourth of the population are beggars….In Lorraine, according to the testimony of all observers, 'the people are half dead with hunger.'

In Paris, the number of paupers has been trebled; there are thirty thousand in Faubourg Saint-Antoine alone. Around Paris there is a short supply of grain, or it is spoilt. Paris thus, in a perfect sense of tranquility, appears like a famished city put on rations at the end of a long siege…"

Hippolyte A. Taine, French critic and historian, *The Origins of Contemporary France, Vol. 2*, 1870

51. In the passage, Taine stresses the fact that the roots of the French Revolution were largely agricultural. What evidence would best support this argument?

    (A) A well-preserved stalk of wheat from the era submitted to modern scientific analysis
    (B) Several years' of tax records of various local French food markets
    (C) Sketches of the subsequent mob scenes
    (D) A recipe list compiled by the private chef to a nobleman

52. Which of the following is a factor that contributed to France becoming "brimful," according to Taine's terminology?

    (A) The accumulation of war debt
    (B) The passage of the Stamp Act
    (C) The Tennis Court Oath
    (D) The Commune of Paris

53. The events referred to in the text led most directly to which other event?

    (A) The swift Napoleonic conquest of Europe
    (B) A large-scale uprising launched by the Third Estate
    (C) The assemblage of the Concert of Europe
    (D) The June Rebellion

54. Which of the following periods was most similar to the situation described in the passage?

    (A) 1610s Netherlands
    (B) 1840s Ireland
    (C) 1870s Germany
    (D) 1890s England

55. It can be inferred from the passage that Taine most strongly felt that

    (A) King Louis XIV was primarily responsible for the economic conditions experienced by the French people
    (B) the impact of famine on French history has been surprisingly minimal
    (C) government-led economic interventions usually fail to succeed
    (D) the French Revolution was inevitable, due to particular social and economic circumstances

GO ON TO THE NEXT PAGE.

EUROPEAN HISTORY

SECTION I, Part B

Time—50 minutes

4 Questions

Directions: Read each question carefully and write your responses on a separate sheet of paper.

Use complete sentences; an outline or bulleted list alone is not acceptable. On test day, you will be able to plan your answers in the exam booklet, but only your responses in the corresponding boxes on the free-response answer sheet will be scored.

1. Use the passage below and your knowledge of European history to answer all parts of the question that follows.

    "I can easily conceive, most Holy Father, that as soon as some people learn that in this book which I have written concerning the revolutions of the heavenly bodies, I ascribe certain motions to the Earth, they will cry out at once that I and my theory should be rejected....Accordingly, when I considered in my own mind how absurd a performance it must seem to those who know that the judgment of many centuries has approved the view that the Earth remains fixed as center in the midst of the heavens, if I should, on the contrary, assert that the Earth moves; I was for a long time at a loss to know whether I should publish the commentaries which I have written in proof of its motion... Therefore, when I considered this carefully, the contempt which I had to fear because of the novelty and apparent absurdity of my view, nearly induced me to abandon utterly the work I had begun."

    Nicolaus Copernicus, Dedication of the Revolutions of the Heavenly Bodies to Pope Paul III, 1543

    a)   Describe TWO factors that <u>facilitated</u> the growth of the Scientific Revolution.
    b)   Describe ONE factor that <u>inhibited</u> the growth of the Scientific Revolution.

GO ON TO THE NEXT PAGE.

2. Use your knowledge of European history to answer all parts of the question that follows.

Historians have proposed various causes for the defeat of the Nazi menace at the end of World War II. These include:

- Hitler's relationship with his generals
- the Russian winters
- fighting a war on two fronts
- the German allies
- Nazi ideology

a) Briefly explain why ONE of the above reasons represents the <u>most</u> important factor in the German defeat.
b) Briefly explain why ONE of the above reasons represents the <u>least</u> important factor in the German defeat.

GO ON TO THE NEXT PAGE.

3. Use the following chart and your knowledge of European history to answer the question that follows.

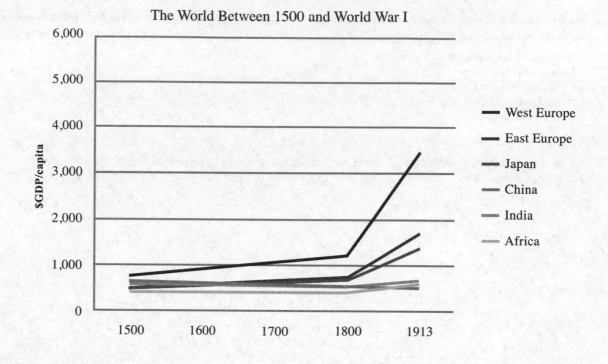

The World Between 1500 and World War I

The chart above measures GDP (gross domestic product), which measures the economic output of a nation or region. Explain TWO reasons for Western Europe's success.

GO ON TO THE NEXT PAGE.

4. Use the passage and your knowledge of European history to answer the question that follows.

"I sometimes think of the time, a year ago, when I came here to The Hague. I had imagined that the painters formed a kind of circle or society in which warmth and cordiality and a certain kind of harmony reigned. This seemed to me quite natural, and I didn't suppose it could be different.

Nor should I want to lose the ideas I had about it then, though I must modify them and distinguish between what is and what might be. I cannot believe so much coolness and disharmony is natural.

What's the reason??? I don't know and it's not my business to find out, but it's a matter of principle with me that I personally must avoid two things. First, one must not quarrel but, instead of that, try to promote peace—for others as well as for oneself. And second, my opinion is that if one is a painter, one must not try to be something other than a painter in society; as a painter, one must avoid other social ambitions and not try to keep up with the people who live in the Voorhout, Willemspark, etc. For in the old dark, smoky studios there was a good fellowship and genuineness which was infinitely better than what threatens to replace it."

Vincent van Gogh, in a letter to his brother Theo, 1882

As described in the letter, van Gogh felt a change in the way art was being created. Explain TWO factors that account for this historical shift.

STOP
END OF SECTION 1
IF YOU FINISH BEFORE TIME IS CALLED, YOU MAY CHECK YOUR WORK ON THIS SECTION.
DO NOT GO ON TO SECTION II UNTIL YOU ARE TOLD TO DO SO.

AP® European History Exam

DO NOT OPEN THIS BOOKLET UNTIL YOU ARE TOLD TO DO SO.

At a Glance

Total Time
1 hour, 30 minutes
Number of Questions
2
Percent of Total Score
40%
Writing Instrument
Pen with black or dark blue ink

Reading Period

Time
15 minutes (suggested). Use this time to read the questions and plan your answer to Question 1, the document-based question.

Writing Period

Time
1 hour, 15 minutes

Question 1 (DBQ): Mandatory

Question 1 (DBQ)
Suggested Time
40 minutes
Percent of Total Score
25%

Question 2 or 3: Choose One Question

Answer either Question 2 or 3
Suggested Time
35 minutes
Percent of Total Score
15%

Instructions

The questions for Section II are printed in the Questions and Documents booklet. You may use that booklet to organize your answers and for scratch work, but you must write your answers in this Section II: Free Response booklet. No credit will be given for any work written in the Questions and Documents booklet.

The proctor will announce the beginning and end of the reading period. You are advised to spend the 15-minute period reading the question and planning your answer to Question 1, the document-based question. If you have time, you may also read Questions 2 and 3.

Section II of this exam requires answers in essay form. Write clearly and legibly. Circle the number of the question you are answering at the top of each page in this booklet. Begin each answer on a new page. Do not skip lines. Cross out any errors you make; crossed-out work will not be scored.

Manage your time carefully. The proctor will announce the suggested time for each part, but you may proceed freely from one part to the next. Go on to Question 2 or 3 if you finish Question 1 early. You may review your responses if you finish before the end of the exam is announced.

After the exam, you must apply the label that corresponds to the long-essay question you answered—Question 2 or 3. For example, if you answered Question 2, apply the label [2]. Failure to do so may delay your score.

This page intentionally left blank.

GO ON TO THE NEXT PAGE.

EUROPEAN HISTORY

SECTION II

Total Time—1 hour, 30 minutes

Question 1 (Document-Based Question)

Suggested reading and writing time: 55 minutes

It is suggested that you spend 15 minutes reading the documents and 40 minutes writing your response.

Note: You may begin writing your response before the reading period is over.

Directions: Question 1 is based on the accompanying Documents 1–7. The documents have been edited for the purpose of this exercise.

In your response you should do the following.

- **Thesis:** Present a thesis that makes a historically defensible claim and responds to all parts of the question. The thesis must consist of one or more sentences located in one place, either in the introduction or the conclusion.

- **Argument Development:** Develop and support a cohesive argument that recognizes and accounts for historical complexity by explicitly illustrating relationships among historical evidence such as contradiction, corroboration, and/or qualification.

- **Use of the Documents:** Utilize the content of at least six of the documents to support the thesis or a relevant argument.

- **Sourcing the Documents:** Explain the significance of the author's point of view, author's purpose, historical context, and/or audience for at least four of the documents.

- **Contextualization:** Situate the argument by explaining the broader historical events, developments, or processes immediately relevant to the question.

- **Outside Evidence:** Provide an example or additional piece of specific evidence beyond those found in the documents to support or qualify the argument.

- **Synthesis:** Extend the argument by explaining the connections between the argument and ONE of the following.

  - A development in a different historical period, situation, era, or geographical area.

  - A course theme and/or approach to history that is not the focus of the essay (such as political, economic, social, cultural, or intellectual history).

  - A different discipline or field of inquiry (such as economics, government and politics, art history, or anthropology).

GO ON TO THE NEXT PAGE.

Question 1: Using the documents and your knowledge of European history, describe and analyze the responses to the issue of human rights in France during the French Revolution.

Document 1

Source: Denis Diderot, excerpt from *Encyclopédie*, 1755.

It is to the general will that the individual must address himself to learn how to be a man, citizen, subject, father, child, and when it is suitable to live or to die. It fixes the limits on all duties. You have the most sacred *natural right* to everything that is not disputed by the rest of the species. The general will enlightens you on the nature of your thoughts and your desires. Everything that you conceive, everything that you meditate upon will be good, grand, elevated, sublime, if it is in the general and common interest . . . Tell yourself often: I am a man, and I have no other true, inalienable *natural right* than those of humanity.

Document 2

Source: Royal Edict of Toleration, granting Calvinists certain rights within France, 1787.

. . . The Catholic religion that we have the good fortune to profess will alone enjoy in our kingdom the rights and honors of public worship, while our other, non-Catholic subjects, deprived of all influence on the established order in our state…will only get from the law what natural right does not permit us to refuse them, to register their births, their marriages, and their deaths, in order to enjoy, like all our other subjects, the civil effects that result from this.

Document 3

Source: Abbé Siéyès, leading writer during the French Revolution, *What Is the Third Estate?*, 1789.

Who therefore dares to say that the Third Estate does not contain within itself all that is needed to form a complete Nation? The Third Estate is like a strong and robust man with one arm still in chains. If we remove the privileged order, the Nation will not be something less but something more. Thus, what is the Third Estate? All but all that is shackled and oppressed. What would it be without the privileged order? All, but an all that is free and flourishing. Nothing can be done without it; everything would be infinitely better without the other two orders.

Document 4

Source: *Declaration of the Rights of Man and Citizen*, 1789.

1. Men are born and remain free and equal in rights. Social distinctions may be founded only upon the general good.

2. The aim of all political association is the preservation of the natural and imprescriptible rights of man. These rights are liberty, property, security, and resistance to oppression.

4. Liberty consists in the freedom to do everything which injures no one else; hence the exercise of the natural rights of each man has no limits except those which assure to the other members of the society the enjoyment of the same rights. These limits can only be determined by law.

GO ON TO THE NEXT PAGE.

Document 5

Source: Report presented to the National Assembly dealing with the question as to who should be allowed to vote, 1789.

The Committee proposes that the necessary qualifications for the title of active citizen in the primary assembly of the canton be: 1) to be French or to have become French; 2) to have reached the age of one's majority; 3) to have resided in the canton for at least one year; 4) to pay direct taxes at a rate equal to the local value of three days of work . . . ; 5) to not be at the moment a servant.

Document 6

Source: La Fare, Bishop of Nancy, *Opinion on the Admissibility of Jews to Full Civil and Political Rights*, 1790.

Thus, Sirs, assure each Jewish individual his liberty, security, and the enjoyment of his property. You owe it to this individual who has strayed into our midst; you owe him nothing more. He is a foreigner to whom, during the time of this passage and his stay, France owes hospitality, protection, and security. But it cannot and should not admit to public posts, to the administration, to the prerogative of the family a tribe that, regarding itself everywhere as foreign, never exclusively embraces any region.

Document 7

Source: Olympe de Gouges, a self-educated woman who wrote pamphlets and plays on various political topics, *The Declaration of the Rights of Woman*, 1791.

1. Woman is born free and remains equal to man in rights. Social distinctions may be based only on common utility.

2. The purpose of all political association is the preservation of the natural and imprescriptible rights of women and men. These rights are liberty, property, security, and especially resistance to oppression.

13. For maintenance of public authority and for expenses of administration, taxation of women and men is equal; she takes part in all forced labor service, in all painful tasks; she must therefore have the same proportion in the distribution of places, employments, offices, dignities, and in industry.

END OF PART A

GO ON TO THE NEXT PAGE.

EUROPEAN HISTORY

Question 2 or Question 3

Suggested writing time: 35 minutes

Directions: Choose EITHER Question 2 or Question 3.

In your response you should do the following.

- **Thesis:** Present a thesis that makes a historically defensible claim and responds to the question. The thesis must consist of one or more sentences located in one place, either in the introduction or the conclusion.

- **Application of Historical Thinking Skills:** Develop and support an argument that applies the historical thinking skill of continuity/change over time.

- **Supporting the Argument with Evidence:** Utilize specific examples of evidence to fully and effectively substantiate the stated thesis or relevant argument.

- **Synthesis:** Extend the argument by explaining the connections between the argument and ONE of the following.

  - A development in a different historical period, situation, era, or geographical area.

  - A course theme and/or approach to history that is not the focus of the essay (such as political, economic, social, cultural, or intellectual history).

  - A different discipline or field of inquiry (such as economics, government and politics, art history, or anthropology).

Question 2: Evaluate the extent to which the English Revolution of 1642 can be considered a pivotal point in the history of England, as well as Western Europe in general. In the development of your argument, consider what changed and what stayed the same after the English Revolution of 1642.

Question 3: Evaluate the extent to which the revolutionary sentiment in Europe between 1815 and 1830 can be considered a pivotal moment in the history of Europe. In the development of your argument, consider what changed and what stayed the same after this period, as well as how the great powers of Europe attempted to address revolutionary sentiment.

END OF EXAMINATION

Practice Test 1:
Answers and Explanations

PRACTICE TEST 1 ANSWER KEY

1.	D	29.	C
2.	A	30.	B
3.	B	31.	D
4.	B	32.	D
5.	B	33.	B
6.	A	34.	A
7.	B	35.	A
8.	A	36.	A
9.	D	37.	C
10.	A	38.	C
11.	B	39.	D
12.	D	40.	A
13.	B	41.	D
14.	A	42.	C
15.	D	43.	D
16.	B	44.	D
17.	D	45.	C
18.	B	46.	A
19.	B	47.	D
20.	B	48.	C
21.	D	49.	D
22.	A	50.	A
23.	B	51.	B
24.	A	52.	A
25.	D	53.	B
26.	A	54.	B
27.	D	55.	D
28.	D		

PRACTICE TEST 1: ANSWERS AND EXPLANATIONS

Section I, Part A: Multiple Choice

1. **D** Read the final sentence of the excerpt, and you'll see that the authors are trying to explain that the world is misinformed about what communism really is. Therefore, they explain, they have been forced to create the book that this is excerpted from, *The Communist Manifesto*, which is one of the most famous political tracts of all time.

2. **A** The Revolutions of 1848 occurred in the same year as the publication of *The Communist Manifesto*, but the two events were actually unrelated. In fact, the revolutions of the minorities against the multiethnic empires were largely unsuccessful, leading to a decade of stagnation.

3. **B** This is the lynchpin of the Marxist cultural view: the proletariat rising up against the bourgeoisie to take control of the reins of capitalism. This was also the deep impetus behind the Bolshevik revolution of 1917, which also included dismantling the three-hundred-year-long Romanov tsarist reign.

4. **B** Though created centuries after the Reformation, this painting nonetheless exhibits classic Dutch traits of seriousness, sobriety, and simple work. These are Protestant traits too, which is fitting since the Reformation was a northern European phenomenon.

5. **B** During the medieval era, it was rare for artists to paint much else besides the ubiquitous Madonna and Child. Portraits were almost unheard of. The rising middle class of the Italian Renaissance changed all that, and their innovations were eventually exported to northern Europe, including the Netherlands.

6. **A** Don't read too much into a painting. When asked to draw conclusions, choose the safest one possible—and in this case, it's to say that simple manual work was valued, since it was the subject of a portrait. Choosing vast pronouncements about huge trends in history is going to be dangerous, particularly from a single canvas.

7. **B** Even if you've never studied natural selection, using Process of Elimination (a strategy we will discuss in Chapter 1) will bring you to the correct answer. There is nothing Romantic—a theory of life as dynamic, spiritual, and intensely emotional—in the empirical study of photos of mentally ill humans, so eliminate (A). Eugenics aims to improve the genetic quality of the human population, but these were not the author's stated goals, so (C) is also incorrect. Euthanasia is mercy-killing and is stated neither explicitly nor implicitly, which means (D) can be eliminated as well.

8. **A** The history of natural selection is paralleled by the history of angry reactions to this idea. Most angry were the Christian religious community, which held that God created man especially in God's image, separate from all the animals. They were enraged by the implication that humans were subject to the same evolutionary processes as insects.

9. **D**   Going unspoken in the letter is the idea, promoted by Darwin himself, that heritable biological traits become either more or less common in a population as a function of the effect of inherited traits on the differential reproductive success of organisms interacting with their environment. This is *natural selection*, and Darwin was one of many scientists of that era who promoted the idea, including Alfred Russel Wallace and several others.

10. **A**   By the time this letter had been written, plate photography and daguerreotypes had been in existence for several decades, and Europeans were beginning to realize the various ways that they were superior to oil portraits, particularly in the accuracy of representation. While Mendel's work did create the modern field of genetics, he was only noted for his contribution posthumously. The scientific method had been in use for two centuries, and the public rarely hungered for scientific knowledge at any time.

11. **B**   Naturalism was a literary movement of the late nineteenth century, in both Europe and America. It was characterized by a bleak, deterministic view of human life, which was strongly influenced by the theory of natural selection. Writers such as Émile Zola designed their novels to exhibit the dismal truths of social existence, to teach the prosperous middle class how the working class truly lived, and to disgust the sensitive with the squalid animalistic facts of human life.

12. **D**   The key to this question is the phrase that calls for British citizens "to reside, for the purposes of carrying on their mercantile pursuits, without molestation or restraint." This was the purpose of the Opium Wars. The British wanted to trade with China, but China refused. Having brought the opium trade into China, the British were able to easily defeat a weakened Chinese army and demand an open border for the purposes of mercantilism.

13. **B**   The term *spheres of influence* refers to lands in which the trade ports are monopolized by an outside country. Britain never fully colonized China, as it was interested in China only for economic purposes, so eliminate (A). Nor did it provide the country with protection, which eliminates (C). Choice (B) is the answer.

14. **A**   The Boxer Rebellion was a reaction to foreign countries setting up spheres of influence in China. By the end of the nineteenth century, the Boxers, a group of citizens who opposed outside nations being present in China, rebelled against the Western culture present in Beijing, which included businesses and Christian missionaries.

15. **D**   The nationalistic movement began in the nineteenth century and culminated in the unification of Italy and Germany. Conservatism would've been opposed to such sweeping new changes, and socialists weren't necessarily opposed to or supportive of them.

16. **B**   The author finds the unification of Rome with the rest of the Italian states to be a disservice to the legacy of Rome. While Garibaldi ultimately did not seize Rome, he intended to do so and was stopped only by Cavour's much stronger forces. Therefore, the answer here is (B), Garibaldi.

17. **D** The author writes, "Never were ties with the past so fully snapped as when the army of Italy entered liberated Rome." This could not happen until the French army, which was occupying Rome, left its post. Only during the 1870 Franco-Prussian War did the French leave the city, and the Italian armies could finally declare Rome the capital of the newly unified nation.

18. **B** In the final sentence of the first paragraph, the author states that "it was a formula which formally swept away the ecumenical position, the ecumenical traditions, of Rome." The term ecumenical refers to the church, and so the author is lamenting that the city would no longer be viewed primarily in terms of its importance to the Church, making (B) the correct answer.

19. **B** Conservatism, as outlined by Edmund Burke, advocated for slow change rather than reactionary movements, which were common during the 1848 wave of revolutions. Liberalism, the fight for individual rights, was a catalyst for many of the 1848 revolutions, as was nationalism. Some movements, especially in France, were motivated by workers' rights and socialist tendencies. Therefore, (B) is the correct answer.

20. **B** The cartoon depicts leaders from around Europe sweeping away revolutionary activists, as well as using violence. This suggests that the rebellions were not very successful when they came up against the powerful leaders of Europe, so (B) is correct.

21. **D** In the cartoon, the czar of Russia is using a sword to presumably punish a commoner. Unlike other European countries, Russia did not experience a revolution in 1848 due to the oppressive regime of Nicholas I, who squashed popular protest. The answer is (D).

22. **A** The nationalist feeling at work during the 1848 revolutions did not go away. Nationalist fervor persisted and led to the unification movements in Italy and Germany. The Chartist movement, which prevented a revolution in Great Britain at the time, gained steam, and the British parliament slowly adopted the Charter over the coming decades. The Decembrist Revolt occurred some 20 years prior to this cartoon and, therefore, could not be influenced by the events.

23. **B** The conservative outlook viewed European society in an essentially feudal manner, meaning that there were only three groups—the peasants, the landlords, and the clergy. This author clearly delineates the "persons of distinction" from everybody else. This is the opposite of (C), egalitarian, and (A) and (D) are off topic.

24. **A** If there's one thing that Victorian era was known for, it was the pedestalization of women into "glorious motherhood," and the elevation of the family unit into something nearly worth worshipping. Children, (C), and the distinction between public and private spheres, (D), were very much a part of Victorian life. The middle class didn't embrace working-class life, since most of them had just pulled themselves out of that existence.

25. **D** For centuries, English society hosted a group of people, the Puritans, who placed incredible emphasis upon plainness, thrift, and hard work. Gambling exhibits none of these characteristics; often gamblers lose their money, and when a gambler wins, it isn't through hard work.

26. **A** While occasionally the Catholic Church hired artists directly—think of the blockbuster works such as Michelangelo's Sistine Chapel—don't let that fool you. Typically it was wealthy merchants who hired artists for specific tasks. There was great competition among artists to land the most lucrative commissions.

27. **D** Artists of the southern Renaissance veered away from the religiosity of their medieval predecessors and instead began to focus on humans and human potential. Da Vinci's Mona Lisa is an example of this human focus. Choice (D) is correct.

28. **D** Italian artists of the Renaissance such as Da Vinci looked to their ancient heritage—in this case, the art of ancient Rome—for inspiration. Ancient Roman works featured a focus on human potential and, as such, was borrowed by the Italian artists of the Renaissance.

29. **C** The key here is the word "religious" in the answer choice. It reflects the "melancholy, long, withdrawing roar" of "the sea of faith" that is described in the second stanza. This is likely referring to the decline of the Catholic Church (and Protestant sects) as the organizing power behind European life. It was replaced by patriotism and nationalism as the organizing principles of European life.

30. **B** Expressing a profound sadness for what society is leaving behind may be the very definition of conservative. Think of the etymology; a conservative seeks to "conserve" what is already possessed, not to admit new ideas. Arnold had grown up in the era of Metternich and had likely read Edmund Burke as well.

31. **D** Einstein's 1905 theory of relativity was the last nail in the coffin of absolutism. Other nails included electrified streets that literally turned night to day, new knowledge of human disease, the invention of physics, radios in every living room, airplanes, machine guns, mustard gas, and millions dead in a massive war. There was no going back to the old traditional Catholic ways. The stability that such a worldview promoted had been blown apart—literally.

32. **D** In 1939, Germany signed a nonaggression pact with the Soviet Union. Germany was free to invade Poland without intervention from the Soviets, who, interestingly enough, also invaded Poland from the east.

33. **B**   Germany was actually not the Soviet Union's first choice. The Soviets wished to create a non-aggression pact with Great Britain and France, neither of which trusted Stalin. Ultimately, Stalin was unable to forge such a pact with the Western European nations and turned to Hitler for an allegiance.

34. **A**   The key phrase in the text is "proceeding from the fundamental provisions of the Neutrality Agreement concluded in April, 1926 between Germany and the U.S.S.R." It would appear that this current pact follows (proceeds from) one that was penned in 1926. Do not confuse the term "concluded" with "expired." "Concluded" refers to negotiations, which concluded in 1926, as the deal was signed by both sides.

35. **A**   Article I states that Germany and the Soviet Union (the "contracting parties") "obligate themselves to desist from any act of violence, any aggressive action, and any attack on each other." Operation Barbarossa, in which the Germans invaded the Soviet Union, was a pretty clear violation of this article.

36. **A**   This pact is a nonaggression agreement. Similar agreements led to the alliance system that was at the heart of World War I. One such alliance system was the Triple Entente, which is (A).

37. **C**   Rationalism, or reason, is the hallmark of European intellectual history of the eighteenth century. It was a natural outgrowth of the scientific revolution, and its proponents included Hume, Rousseau, Locke, Hobbes, Diderot, and a hundred other famous names of the era. In France, aristocratic women hosted salons to discuss the matters of the day in a reasoned manner.

38. **C**   Voltaire had spent three years in England, where he saw how a less intrusive government could help promote its citizens' better interests. Most importantly, he saw how a society thrived economically minus the choking weight of religious institutions, and upon his return to France became an impassioned critic of the Catholic Church.

39. **D**   Cause and effect is an extension of the belief in reason as the guiding principle to human life. If $a = b$, and $b = c$, then $a = c$. This is a syllogism, and the *philosophes* used it to understand human laws in the same way that the scientists were using it to understand natural laws.

40. **A**   Choices (B), (C), and (D) are the central tenets of Thomas Hobbes, John Locke, and Adam Smith, respectively. While it's true that all of them were Enlightenment figures, none of these particular beliefs were shared by any of the others. Furthermore, none of the three statements are very applicable to the principle of optimism that so pervaded the upper classes during this century.

41. **D** Voltaire was highly critical of religion, which he did not consider to be in line with rationalism. The excerpt of *Candide* provides examples of this. Similarly, David Hume viewed religion as an institution that lacked empirical proof. Therefore, (D) is the answer.

42. **C** Having a history of private entrepreneurship is vital to the success of any capitalistic society. That, unfortunately, is exactly what Eastern Europe is lacking. After spending fifty years under a rigid communistic system, the people in this region were still learning how to run private businesses in 2005. It's a challenge that persists.

43. **D** This question tests your knowledge of geography, but you can also determine the correct answer by using your knowledge of recent history and current events. Over the past several years, Greece has been in the news for having the highest per capita debt of any country in Europe. So if you were aware of this fact, you might have guessed the right answer.

44. **D** Choices (A), (B), and (C) are totally unsupported by the map. But the map does clearly show that the northern half of the boot is very dynamic, while the southern half is less so. This is an old dichotomy. The northern Italian city-states hosted the Renaissance, built educational systems, traded with the Arabs, and eventually welcomed the technological advances of the Industrial Revolution. Southern Italy, on the other hand, hasn't changed in centuries—it is almost totally agricultural.

45. **C** There are too many variables in play on this map to be able to prove that the inclusion of Turkey in the European Union would benefit all of Europe. (This is a broad, bold statement, and you should avoid choosing answers that contain any kind of "extreme" language, as they are almost always incorrect.) Therefore, you should have chosen (C). You could also have answered this question correctly in a different way—if you'd remembered the strong feelings created by the question of the inclusion of Turkey in the EU. Quick summary: Capitalistic Europe did not want want its lower classes to lose jobs to Turkish workers who would undercut their hourly wages.

46. **A** As you can see on the map, Norway appears to be in only one shade, indicating that its GDP stays consistent, no matter where one travels in the country. Therefore, the best answer is (A). Norway, by the way, is the Scandinavian country on the left.

47. **D** The scientific developments contemporary with the Second Industrial Revolution influenced other fields, which began to apply scientific methodology. These social sciences, which included anthropology (as described in the text), were brand-new fields at the time of the Paris Exposition.

48. **C** It should come as no surprise that anthropology, the study of humans, came about in Europe during a time in which Europeans were beginning to experience, often through violent imperialism, an array of cultures throughout the world. Scholars aimed to identify which characteristics are common to all humans and which factors account for the variances in human societies.

49. **D**   The passage states that the facilities of the Paris Exposition "give to the comparative anatomist and biologist abundant employment." Anatomy and biology are fields that are more closely related to Darwin than to the other answer choices.

50. **A**   The Paris Exposition took place under the Third French Republic (1870–1940). Despite challenges such as the Boulanger Affair, which took place the same year as the Paris Exposition, the relative stability of the government allowed for innovation and economic prosperity in late-nineteenth-century France.

51. **B**   Because the passage lists the various ways in which the people were starving, and how the grain was getting spoiled, it would stand to reason that records showing less food being sold would support the author's contention. Choice (A) may be tempting, but scientific analysis of a stalk of wheat wouldn't tell the modern historian the amount of food being sold.

52. **A**   The use of "brimful" in the first sentence metaphorically refers to a political situation in which people are on the verge of rebellion, much like a stream on the verge of overflowing. The factors that created such a condition were largely economic, as the author states that poverty was prevalent throughout the nation. Perhaps the largest economic stressor on France during the eighteenth century was the wars it carried out against Great Britain, particularly in the Americas. The burden to pay off these war debts ultimately fell on the Third Estate via taxation. As described in the passage, the Third Estate was largely made up of people in poverty.

53. **B**   The economic stress placed on the Third Estate was enough to push this segment of the French people to demand equal participation in government. When this demand was denied, members of the Third Estate incited an uprising, (B).

54. **B**   The famine described in the passage should call to mind the famous potato famine that struck Ireland in 1848. Choice (B) is the correct answer.

55. **D**   Think again about the "brimful" stream in the first sentence of the passage: "When a stream is brimful, a slight ride suffices to cause an overflow." This sentence serves as evidence that the author saw the impending revolution as an unsurprising consequence of famine and poverty. Choice (D) is therefore correct.

Section I, Part B: Short Answer

Question 1

- Factors that *facilitated* the growth of the Scientific Revolution include (1) advances in technology, (2) more wealth to support scientific societies, (3) new ideas gleaned during the age of expansion, (4) the declining power of the Catholic Church due to the Reformation, (5) more correspondence between intellectuals in various countries, and (6) the printing press, which moved ideas efficiently.

- As seen in the passage, scientists felt enormous pressure to not confront the Catholic Church on areas of disagreement. For this part of the question, you can point to factors that *restricted* growth of the Scientific Revolution, such as the still-considerable power of the Church. For instance, you can reference its Index of banned books. Galileo's battle with the Church over his discovery of astronomical truth is a good example, as is the case of Copernicus, which was referenced in the passage.

Question 2

Students can pick and choose at their discretion, but the discussion of each factor should include the following points.

- **Hitler's relationship with his generals:** Hitler did not have a good relationship with his generals. Following the failure of Operation Barbarossa, he didn't trust them, even naming himself Commander-in-Chief of the military. He ignored all their advice.

- **The Russian winters:** The Russian winters were equally bad. Following a six-week delay in attacking the Soviets, the German army didn't even arrive in Russia until the autumn, and the devastating Battle of Stalingrad cemented their loss.

- **Fighting a war on two fronts:** Nazis unwisely chose to engage with English, French, and U.S. forces in the West and with the Soviets in the East. They might have been able to achieve victory on one front, but not both.

- **The German allies:** Germany allied with Italy, Hungary, and Romania, none of whom were remotely able to help with the war effort. It ignored Japan, which actually would have been able to assist.

- **Nazi ideology:** Empires that last tend to promote democracy, cooperation, and empowerment. (The British Empire is a good example.) Empires that tend to collapse are built upon racial hatred, ethnic "purification," and subjugation. Guess which one the Nazis represented.

Question 3

Reasons for the increased GDP of Western Europe is essentially asking for the reasons for the birth of the Industrial Revolution. Those include any of the following:

- the birthplace of the Second Industrial Revolution, particularly England

- natural resources such as coal, necessary for steam engines, that are absent from other portions of Europe

- a national system of banks with plenty of capital to invest in startup companies

- mobility of the serfs (peasants) who were emancipated from the land and thus able to move into the cities quickly to work in factories

- less centralized government to regulate or inhibit private industry

Question 4

There many reasons for the shift in how art was created. A good answer would include any **two** of the following:

- The final destruction of the guild system occurred in the nineteenth century. The loneliness that van Gogh describes would have been avoided by working with a group of like-minded apprentices, journeymen, and masters.

- The Romantic viewpoint of artists was that of tortured, solitary geniuses.

- Financial support for artists shifted from wealthy, aristocratic patrons to art galleries. This is otherwise known as the shift to a market economy, and it affected every level of society, including artists.

- The Second Industrial Revolution eliminated "the human touch" out of production of goods. Contrast that with the putting-out system.

Section II, Part A: Document-Based Question (DBQ)

The Document-Based Question (DBQ) section begins with a suggested 15-minute reading period. During these 15 minutes, you'll want to (1) come up with some information not included in the given documents (your outside knowledge) to include in your essay, (2) get an overview of what each document means and the point of view of each author, (3) decide what opinion you are going to argue, and (4) write an outline of your essay.

The DBQ in Practice Test 1 concerns the issue of human rights during the French Revolution. You should be prepared to discuss how the French Revolution advanced the cause of human rights and also explain the ways that some individuals wanted a more narrow definition of who should be eligible to enjoy these rights. You will need to know something about human rights in France prior to the outbreak of the Revolution in 1789 and also know how the concept of human rights changed over the course of the Revolution.

The first thing you want to do, BEFORE YOU LOOK AT THE DOCUMENTS, is to brainstorm for a minute or two. Try to list everything you know (from class or leisure reading or informational television programs) about the issue of human rights in France both prior to the French Revolution and after. This list will serve as your reference to the outside information you must provide to earn a top grade.

Next, read over the documents. As you read them, take notes in the margins and underline those passages that you are certain you are going to use in your essay. Make note of the opinions and position of the document's author. If a document helps you remember a piece of outside information, add that information to your brainstorming list. If you cannot make sense of a document or it argues strongly against your position, relax! You do not need to mention every document to score well on the DBQ.

Here is what you might assess in the time you have to look over the documents.

The Documents

Document 1

This excerpt comes from an article on Natural Law written by Diderot, which appeared in his *Encyclopedia*. You should note the date of the passage, 1755, which means it was written several decades prior to the French Revolution.

The passage refers to the term "natural rights," which it defines as those inalienable rights you enjoy as a human being, so long as the enjoyment of those rights does not impose on the rights of others. There is also the notion that these rights, because they are natural rights, are enjoyed by all of humanity without distinction as to time or place. Diderot's point of view is that those individuals who focus on the common interest will achieve greatness.

Document 2

This document also dates prior to the French Revolution and should be duly noted; you will need to address the question of rights prior to the French Revolution in your essay. The passage is an excerpt from a Royal Edict of Toleration granting certain, very basic rights rights to Calvinists within France.

The document makes it clear, however, that the right of public worship would remain the sole preserve of Catholics. Calvinists are to be granted only those things that "natural right" no longer allows the French government to deny them: the right to publicly register their births, marriages, and deaths.

Document 3

Document 3 comes from *What Is the Third Estate?*, a pamphlet written by the Abbé Siéyès, who is identified as a leading writer during the French Revolution.

The passage refers to the role of the Third Estate (the commoners) and contends that the Third Estate is essentially the French nation. Should the privileged order (the nobility) be removed from France, the Third Estate would not decline but would rise up "free and flourishing." The passage also contains the rather sharp line "everything would be infinitely better without the other two orders," an attack on the privileges of both the clergy and the nobility.

Again, the date of the passage should be duly noted. In this case it is 1789, the year of the French Revolution.

Document 4

Of all the documents in this DBQ, this should be the one with which you are most familiar. This is the *Declaration of the Rights of Man and Citizen* and therefore one of the documents that certainly was discussed in class while you were studying the French Revolution.

You'll notice that the document begins with the idea "Men are born and remain free and equal in rights." Think about how this idea is linked to the issues raised in Document 1. Article 4 in Document 4 is also linked to Document 1 in that it says, "each man has no limits except those which assure to the other members of the society the enjoyment of the same rights." What specific rights is the author discussing here? Article 2 tells us these rights are "liberty, property, security, and resistance to oppression." So Document 4 seems to echo the sentiments of Document 1.

Document 5

This passage comes from a committee report prepared in 1789 by members of the National Assembly who submitted the report to the entire National Assembly during the debate over who should be allowed to vote. The committee decided that there had to be some restrictions on voter eligibility. They had to be French citizens, meet certain residency requirements, and have reached the age of maturity (the exact age is not spelled out in the document and the assumption throughout the document is that voters will be exclusively male). The committee also decided that the vote should be restricted to those who had enough income that they paid taxes that were equal to the wages paid to the average worker for three days of work. In addition, servants were excluded from the vote.

Document 6

Document 6 comes from a pamphlet written by the Bishop of Nancy that was about whether Jews should be granted the full rights of citizens. The Bishop is clearly unsympathetic to Jews, who he claims had "strayed into our midst" and therefore should still be considered foreigners, not French. He does allow that Jews should be provided with their personal liberty and enjoy certain property rights. Political rights, however, were out of the question.

Document 7

Document 7 comes from the pen of Olympe De Gouges, who is identified as a self-educated woman who wrote pamphlets and plays that dealt with political topics. Notice that the title of her work is *The Declaration of the Rights of Woman*, an obvious play on the title *Declaration of the Rights of Man* (Document 4). Keep this in mind for your essay because there are some obvious comparisons that can be made between the two documents.

In this passage by De Gouges, she has obviously taken the natural rights language found in the *Declaration of the Rights of Man* and modified it to argue for the rights of women. Women, according to De Gouges, were like men, born free and equal in rights. This also meant that women, as seen in Article 13, also shared in the same public responsibilities as men, such as the payment of taxes, eligibility for forced public labor in times of emergency, and "all painful tasks" (yikes!). These responsibilities, however, also bring with them certain rights, and therefore women should have equal access to government offices and employment.

Outside Information

We have already discussed much more than you could possibly include in a 40-minute essay. Do not worry. You will not be expected to mention everything or even most of what we have covered in the section above. You will, however, be expected to include some outside information, that is, information not mentioned directly in the documents. Here is some outside information you might incorporate in your essay.

- During the Enlightenment (the intellectual movement that dominated eighteenth-century thought) the idea of natural rights, or what we might call today human rights, became highly significant. There was a question, however, as to what exactly was meant by natural rights. For the seventeenth-century English philosopher John Locke, natural rights were life, liberty, and property; however, his definition of who should enjoy such rights was narrow and did not extend to women, slaves, and those without property. In France, the question of natural rights was also debated. The philosopher Rousseau took perhaps the most radical position when he suggested that natural rights extend to all men, regardless of class. Rousseau, however, did not consider that natural rights extended to women.

- In France, prior to 1789, the Bourbon monarchy gave certain rights that were not considered natural rights, but rather special privileges extended by the monarchy to specific groups or individuals. For example, the nobility was exempt from the payment of most taxes. This was a right that was extended to them as a special caste within France and was certainly not a privilege held by all. Because such grants of rights or privileges were not grounded on the notion of being natural rights, they had the distinct problem that they could be revoked. For example, in 1685 Louis XIV revoked the Edict of Nantes, a list of privileges that Calvinists had received from an earlier French monarch.

- In 1763, the philosopher Voltaire wrote *Treatise on Toleration*, a work inspired by the execution of Jean Calas, a Calvinist who was wrongfully accused of murdering his son because of the son's supposed desire to convert to Catholicism. Voltaire argued that religious toleration was necessary because it was a natural right that should not be impinged on by government. Calvinists were not the only religious minority in France that lacked a legal standing. After Louis XIV's seventeenth-century conquest of Alsace and Lorraine, lands that were formerly part of the Holy Roman Empire, France suddenly had a significant Jewish population. These individuals were banned from most occupations and were restricted in terms of where they could live.

- The question of human rights was front and center at the start of the French Revolution. In 1789, the Third Estate refused to meet as a separate legislative body because they were frustrated that commoners (of which the Third Estate was comprised) were excluded from special privileges enjoyed by the other two estates. For the remainder of the revolutionary period (1789–1799), the question of how far human rights should be extended was a hotly debated issue. For every argument made in favor of extending rights to some previously denied group, counter-arguments could be made as to reasons why legal restrictions should remain in place.

- A primary issue throughout the revolutionary period was defining who was a citizen and, therefore, entitled to enjoy the rights and privileges that came with citizenship. From 1789 to 1792, France was a constitutional monarchy, while the constitution drawn up in 1791 limited full political participation to men who owned property. When France became a republic in 1792, full political rights were extended to all men regardless of whether they owned property. During the revolutionary period, a backlash against this sentiment erupted, and once again only men who possessed property were granted the right to full political participation.

- *The Declaration of the Rights of Man* said that no one should be disturbed for holding contrary opinions including, the document specifically noted, religious opinions. Whether religious minorities should be granted full political rights was another question, however, and heated opposition existed in some quarters about granting such rights to Calvinists and Jews. By 1791, the question had been resolved by making it clear that political rights were not to be denied to anyone on the basis of one's religious beliefs.

- The struggle for human rights for slaves was in many ways a more difficult issue to resolve than the question of human rights for religious minorities. This was in part because money was at stake, as so much of the economy of the French colonies was connected to slave labor. Initially, the National Assembly eliminated slavery in France (where it had already died out as an institution) but gave in to a heavy lobbying effort by white plantation owners in their Caribbean colony of Hispaniola and allowed slavery to remain there. This instigated Toussaint L'Ouverture to lead a slave revolt on the island. By 1794, the National Convention did away with slavery in all French colonies, though L'Ouverture's rebellion resulted in France losing the eastern half of the island of Hispaniola, which became the independent nation of Haiti.

- Although wealthy French women played an important role as sponsors of Enlightenment authors, the question of rights for women was not central to Enlightenment thought. At no point following the French Revolution did the National Assembly pay any notice to the idea of extending political rights to women, and by 1793 women were banned from even participating in political clubs. Women did receive some rights in some non-political areas, such as the right to initiate divorce proceedings and to inherit property.

Choosing a Thesis Statement

This DBQ is not asking you to take a side in a debate. Instead, you can stick with a central theme such as discussing how the question of human rights was fundamental to the entire history of the French Revolution. You might try to show how these rights were defined in different ways at various points during the Revolutionary period, or you might attempt to show that the initial debate over the question of political rights was never fully resolved. Another way to approach the question is by comparing human rights prior to the French Revolution to how it was redefined during the course of the French Revolution.

Planning Your Essay

Unless you read extremely quickly, you probably will not have time to write a detailed outline for your essay during the 15-minute reading period. However, it is worth taking several minutes to jot down a loose structure of your essay because it will actually save you time when you write. First, decide on your thesis and write it down in the test booklet. (There is usually some blank space below the documents.) Then, take a minute or two to brainstorm all the points you might put in your essay. Choose the strongest points and number them in the order you plan to present them. Lastly, note which documents and outside information you plan to use in conjunction with each point. If you organize your essay before you start writing, the actual writing process will go much more smoothly. More importantly, you will not write yourself into a corner, suddenly finding yourself making a point you cannot support or heading toward a weak conclusion (or worse still, no conclusion at all).

For example, if you wanted to discuss how the question of human rights was defined in increasingly broad terms as the Revolution progressed, you could brainstorm a list of ideas and issues that you want to raise in your essay such as the following:

> *Rights before the French Revolution*
> *Enlightenment and natural rights*
> *Royal absolutism*
> *Calling of the Estates General*
> *Special privileges for specific estates*
> *Property and political rights*
> *Political rights for religious minorities*
> *Abolishment of slavery*
> *Limited rights granted to women*

Next, you would want to figure out which of your brainstorm ideas could be the main idea of your first paragraph, which could be used as evidence to support a point, and which should be eliminated. You should probably begin your first paragraph with your thesis, and then discuss what was meant by rights prior to the French Revolution. Since the first two items on your brainstorming list can be used in conjunction with a discussion of rights prior to 1789, you'll want to mark all three with "1" to show that it's your first paragraph, then get more specific with a note if it's evidence. Your list might look this way:

> *Rights before the French Revolution*   *1*
> *Enlightenment and natural rights*   *1-evidence*
> *Royal absolutism*   *1-evidence*
> *Calling of the Estates General*
> *Special privileges for specific estates*
> *Property and political rights*
> *Political rights for religious minorities*
> *Abolishment of slavery*
> *Limited rights granted to women*

What else would you want to mention in this paragraph? You should certainly refer to Documents 1 and 2. Document 1 reveals the way in which the writers of the Enlightenment addressed the issue of natural rights, and Document 2 is a nice example of how privileges could be extended to specific groups in France, though only through royal grant.

Your second paragraph could deal with the issue of political rights at the very onset of the French Revolution, when the Estates General was called in 1789. Your list could now look like this:

> *Rights before the French Revolution*   *1*
> *Enlightenment and natural rights*   *1-evidence*
> *Royal absolutism*   *1-evidence*
> *Calling of the Estates General*   *2*
> *Special privileges for specific estates*   *2-evidence*
> *Property and political rights*
> *Political rights for religious minorities*
> *Abolishment of slavery*
> *Limited rights granted to women*

In this paragraph, you should certainly incorporate Document 3, which challenges the entire concept of specific rights being granted to the first two estates to the complete exclusion of the third. You can also reference Document 4, the *Declaration of the Rights of Man*, which reveals that after the calling of the Estates General in May 1789, by July of that same year special rights based on social caste were eliminated from French political life.

Keep numbering the topics and brainstorming useful documents and information until you have finished planning your strategy entirely. Try to fit as many of the documents into your argument as you can, but do not stretch too far to fit one in. An obvious, desperate stretch will only hurt your grade. Also, remember that history is often intricate and that the readers of your exam want to see that you respect the intrinsic complexity behind many historical events.

Section II, Part B: Long Essay

Because you only have 35 minutes to plan and write this essay, you will not have time to work out an elaborate argument. That's okay; nobody is expecting you to read two questions, choose one, remember all the pertinent facts about the subject, formulate a brilliant thesis, and then write a perfect essay. Here is what you should do. First, choose your question; brainstorm for two or three minutes, and edit your brainstorm ideas. Then, number those points you are going to include in your essay in the order you plan to present them, just as we did for the DBQ. Last, think of a simple thesis statement that allows you to discuss the points your essay will make.

Question 2—English Revolution (Option 1)

Question 2: Evaluate the extent to which the English Revolution of 1642 can be considered a pivotal point in the history of England, as well as Western Europe in general. In the development of your argument, consider what changed and what stayed the same after the English Revolution of 1642.

About the Structure of Your Essay

The causes of the English Revolution are rather involved since they straddle a number of different areas. One can find political, social, economic, and religious issues behind the outbreak of revolution in 1642. You would certainly be very hard pressed in a 35-minute essay to fully discuss all of these issues, but here are some points that you can mention in your essay (and relate to the idea of the English Revolution being a pivotal moment in European history). Be sure to address how these issues connect to other historical events (and not just in England).

- Financial problems were a critical issue for the English monarchy. The cost of governing had increased dramatically over the course of the sixteenth century, although many Members of Parliament could not accept the idea that the King could need almost annual grants of money from Parliament. They assumed that the crown must be wasteful, so to keep the government functioning, James I (r. 1603–1625) was forced to sell noble titles and monopolies to individuals who then had the sole right in England to sell items like coal. King James had stated early in his reign his goal of reforming the system of royal finance, but Parliament grew concerned that such a plan would mean additional taxes and scuttled any discussion of the issue.

- The question of prerogative rights was central to the English Revolution. What political rights were inherently the King's and what political rights were inherently Parliament's? The English Constitution, that blending of written law and unwritten tradition, lacked a precise answer to this question. Both King and Parliament grappled with this issue. Members of the House of Commons began to support the idea during the reign of James I that the King's ministers should be acceptable to Parliament. During the reign of James's son Charles I (r. 1625–1649), Parliament began to argue that the King's ministers should be responsible to Parliament by allowing both houses to select and remove royal ministers.

- Parliament was concerned over its lack of input in foreign affairs. During the Elizabeth's reign, her parliaments began to press her on certain foreign policy issues, though Elizabeth insisted they had no right to speak on such questions. Increasingly, James and his parliaments saw themselves at odds over foreign affairs. Parliament wanted English involvement in the Thirty Years' War; James wisely knew that this was a conflict that England should not enter.

- The early seventeenth century was a period of economic difficulty in England and throughout much of Europe; high inflation and a series of poor harvests were among the most significant problems faced by the early Stuart monarchs and the people of England. Although not perhaps a direct cause of the English Revolution, this economic downturn played a role in undermining the social stability that had been so critical for the success of the Tudors.

- Religious issues were critical for the outbreak of revolution in 1642. In fact, the English Revolution was more commonly referred to as the Puritan Revolution. The Puritans, a faction within the Church of England, wanted to see their Church move more in the direction of Calvinism. They disliked the fact that the Church of England had a religious hierarchy that included bishops and archbishops. They wanted to see religious authority in the hands of local synods, or councils, as was the case in Geneva and other centers of Calvinism. Additionally, Puritans wanted to see the Church of England purged of anything that (to them) was reminiscent of Catholicism, which they hated intensely. Although a minority within England, the Puritans were a very important minority, as many of their adherents were wealthy, and had a large representation in the House of Commons.
  The problem was that neither James I nor Charles I had any interest in the Puritan agenda. James had been raised in the Calvinist Church of Scotland, but when he became king of England, he immediately began to prefer the practices of the Church of England because he believed that its ornate ceremonial and hierarchical structure were important buttresses of the English monarchy. His son was even more hostile to the Puritans. During his reign, Charles I increasingly began to support another faction within the Church of England: the Arminians. The Arminians rejected such Calvinist doctrines as predestination and the lack of human free will, but supported church services that emphasized ornate ceremony and the importance of the clerical hierarchy. Charles eventually selected William Laud, a leading Arminian, as his Archbishop of Canterbury, thus enraging Puritans.

- When Charles came to the throne in 1625, the problems that his father had had with Parliament grew significantly worse, and by 1629, Charles decided to rule without a parliament. This "personal rule" (also known as Eleven Years Tyranny) lasted eleven years (hence the name), until Charles was forced to call a parliament in 1640 to raise money to calm a rebellion in Scotland, which broke out when Charles wanted to introduce the Church of England's prayer book into the Calvinist Church of Scotland. By 1641, Parliament had passed what was known as the "Grand Remonstrance," a document of 204 clauses that listed all parliamentary grievances over the past decade. It demanded that the King appoint ministers that Parliament could trust and called for a bill to totally reform the Church of England along more Puritan lines. In response, Charles tried to seize five of the leaders of Parliament. This attempt failed and he left London in January of 1642 to raise his royal standard at Nottingham and to show he was ready to go to war.

Parliament responded to this action by passing its most radical plan, which demanded that supreme authority in the government should be in the hands of Parliament. Royal advisors were to be subject to parliamentary approval and all military and ecclesiastical appointments were to be approved by Parliament. Clearly the King could never accept such demands, and by the end of the summer of 1642, the nation was locked in a civil war between King and Parliament.

Question 3—Containment of Revolution (Option 2)

Question 3: Evaluate the extent to which the revolutionary sentiment in Europe between 1815 and 1830 can be considered a pivotal moment in the history of Europe. In the development of your argument, consider what changed and what stayed the same after this period, as well as how the great powers of Europe attempted to address revolutionary sentiment.

About the Structure of Your Essay

This essay is essentially asking you to deal with the political backlash that swept through Europe following the final defeat of Napoleon in 1815. The ensuing fifteen years witnessed an attempt by the major European powers to place the revolutionary genie back in the bottle with varying degrees of success. You should begin your essay with a discussion of the Congress of Vienna (1814–1815) and how the nations of Europe attempted to turn back the clock to a time before everything was disrupted by the events of the French Revolution of 1789. From there you should discuss the repressive steps taken in many European capitals to ensure that revolutionary sentiments were kept under control. Finally, in the last part of your essay, you should write about some of the revolutions that broke out in places like Spain, Italy, France, and Russia, despite, or perhaps because of, the concerted effort to contain all revolutionary ideas.

Your essay should mention at least some of the following signs of political backlash against revolutionary sentiment:

- At the Congress of Vienna there was an attempt by the five major powers in attendance (Prussia, Austria, Great Britain, Russia, and France) to ensure that the ideas of the French Revolution would remain contained so that they would not contaminate the rest of Europe. To that end it was agreed (with the sole dissent of Great Britain), that the great powers had the right to interfere in the internal affairs of other nations to contain the possibility of revolution. The Congress of Vienna refused to address such issues as nationalism and political reform, two issues that had been stirred up by the French Revolution and were now deemed too dangerous to even contemplate.

- A new, conservative political ideology began to emerge in the years following the defeat of Napoleon. Rather than the more nuanced conservatism found in the writing of Edmund Burke, who believed that gradual, evolutionary change could be beneficial for the state, this new breed of conservatism was completely reactionary. One prominent writer of this tradition was Joseph de Maistre, a Frenchman who had fled France during the Revolution. De Maistre believed that all political sovereignty came from God, while also writing that "the first servant of the king should be the executioner."

- Monarchs across Europe established secret police forces (modeled on Napoleon's) in order to deal with suspected revolutionaries. They also committed resources to create government agencies that would censor books and newspapers. Workers were banned from forming unions and political meetings were made illegal.

- Across Europe there was a tremendous religious revival in the years after 1815. Religious institutions had gone into decline as a result of the Enlightenment and the French Revolution. After 1815, there was a concerted effort by the European states to bring about a revival of religion, since it was believed that organized religion was an important bulwark of the conservative state.

Your essay should also deal with the various revolutionary movements that emerged in the period from 1815 to 1830, despite the attempt to contain all signs of revolution.

- Ferdinand VII, the King of Spain, was restored to his throne in 1814 following the withdrawal of French troops from his country. During his years in exile, he promised that should he regain the throne of Spain, he would abide by a constitution that had been written by a group of Spanish liberals. By 1820, seeing that the King was not going to honor his promise, a group of army officers and liberals revolted and forced the King to accept the constitution. Two years later a French army, with the tacit support of Prussia, Austria, and Russia, swept into Spain and restored Ferdinand to absolute rule.

- In 1822, a revolt broke out in Naples when the members of a secret society called the *Carbonari* (which had initially formed to fight against Napoleon) decided to overthrow King Ferdinand I, the Neapolitan King, after the King refused to implement liberal reforms such as the granting of a constitution. The Austrians rushed troops to the south of the Italian peninsula to put down the revolt, as they were fearful that the revolt in Naples could spread to their own territories.

- In Greece, a revolt broke out against the rule of the Ottoman Turks in 1821. This revolt captured the attention and imagination of liberals across Europe, since Ancient Greece was the birthplace of democracy. Britain, France, and Russia came to the aid of the Greek rebels, not because they were inspired by liberal sentiment or even by the idea of Greek nationalism, but because they all saw it as being in their best interest to weaken the Ottoman Turks. By 1832, the Greeks had won their independence, though the newly created Greek state became a monarchy and was certainly not a bastion of liberal values.

- In December 1825, a group of liberal army officers attempted to establish a republic in Russia. The rebels failed to inspire more soldiers to join them, and the "**Decembrists**," as they came to be known, were caught and executed.

- In France, Louis XVIII (the brother of the executed Louis XVI) was restored to the throne for a second time in 1815, following the final defeat and exile of Napoleon. Upon his return, he granted the French people a charter, which established France as a constitutional monarchy. After his death in 1824, power moved to the hands of his reactionary younger brother, Charles X, who did his best to undermine the constitutional guarantees that Louis XVIII had established. By 1830, liberal dissatisfaction with the King's contempt for the constitution led to a rebellion that resulted in the exile of Charles X and the crowning of Louis-Philippe, a cousin of Charles X and a man who had a reputation for liberal views.

Part III
About the
AP European
History Exam

THE STRUCTURE OF THE AP EUROPEAN HISTORY EXAM

The AP European History Exam, which was redesigned for the May 2016 administration of the test, is 3 hours and 15 minutes long and broken up into two sections, each of which consists of two parts. Your performance on these four parts, outlined in the table below, is compiled and weighted to find your overall exam score.

	Question Type (#)	Time
Section I	Part A: Multiple Choice (55 questions)	55 minutes
	Part B: Short Answer (4 questions)	50 minutes
Section II	Part A: Document-Based Question (1 question)	55 minutes (includes a reading period with a suggested time of 15 minutes)
	Part B: Long Essay (1 question, chosen from a pair)	35 minutes

Here's what to expect in each of these parts:

- **Multiple Choice:** Questions will be grouped into sets of two to five and based on a primary or secondary source, including excerpts from historical documents or writings, images, graphs, maps, and so on. Each set of questions will be based on a different piece of source material. You'll have 55 minutes to answer 55 multiple-choice questions. This section will test your ability to analyze and engage with the source materials while recalling what you already know about European History.

- **Short Answer:** This section consists of four questions that will be based on a primary or secondary source. All questions will ask you to identify and analyze historical evidence. The time allotted for this section is 50 minutes, which means you'll have a little over 12 minutes for each question.

- **Document-Based Question (DBQ):** Here you'll be presented with a variety of historical documents that are intended to show the complexity of a particular historical issue. You will need to develop a thesis that responds to the question prompt and support that thesis with evidence from both the documents and your knowledge of European history. To earn the best score, you should incorporate outside knowledge and be able to relate the issues discussed in the documents to a larger theme, issue, or time period. The 55-minute timeframe for this section includes a suggested 15-minute reading period so that you can familiarize yourself with the question and documents.

- **Long Essay:** You'll be given a choice of two essay options, and you must choose one. The long essay is similar to the DBQ in that you must develop a thesis and use historical evidence to support your thesis, but there will be not be any documents on which you must base your response. Instead, you will need to draw upon your own knowledge of topics you learned in your AP European History class. You'll have 35 minutes to write this essay.

HOW THE AP EUROPEAN HISTORY EXAM IS SCORED

Each of the four parts is weighted differently to determine your overall score.

Test Section	Percentage of Overall Score
Multiple Choice	40%
Short Answer	20%
DBQ	25%
Long Essay	15%

As you can see, the writing portions of the exam count a little more heavily toward your total score (a combined total of 60 percent) than the multiple-choice section (40 percent). The DBQ and long essay are scored according to separate rubrics. You can earn a maximum of 7 points on the DBQ, and 6 points on the long essay.

Here's how those points are earned:

DBQ Scoring Rubric		
(Note: Numbers marked with an asterisk [*] are based on a document-based question that contains 7 documents.)		
Task	**Points Possible**	**Description**
Thesis and Argument Development	2	1. Presents a thesis that can be backed by historical evidence and responds to all parts of the question. The thesis must be at least one sentence, located in either the introduction or conclusion. **(1 point)** 2. Develops and supports a cohesive argument that addresses historical complexities and shows the relationships among historical evidence. **(1 point)**
Document Analysis	2	1. Uses at least 6* of the documents to support the thesis or a relevant argument. **(1 point)** 2. Explains the significance of the author's point of view or purpose, audience, and/or historical context for at least 4* documents. **(1 point)**
Using Evidence Beyond the Documents	2	1. *Contextualization*: Places the argument within the broader historical context—events, developments, processes, etc.—relevant to the question. Note that this requires an explanation (consisting of several sentences or a full paragraph), not just a brief mention. **(1 point)** 2. *Evidence Beyond the Documents*: Gives an example or additional piece of evidence beyond what is found in the documents to support an argument. Note that the example must be different from the evidence used to earn other points on the rubric, and include an explanation of how that evidence supports or qualifies the argument. **(1 point)**
Synthesis	1	Extends the argument by explaining the connections between the argument and ONE of the following: a. A development in a historical period, era, or geographical area that is different from the one in the question b. An AP European History course theme and/or approach to history (e.g., political, economic, cultural) that is not the focus of the essay c. A different discipline or field (e.g., economics, art history, anthropology)
		Maximum Points: 7

Long Essay Scoring Rubric		
Task	**Points Possible**	**Description**
Thesis	1	Presents a thesis that can be backed up by historical evidence and that responds to all parts of the question. The thesis must be at least one sentence, located in either the introduction or conclusion.
Using Targeted Historical Thinking Skills	2	*Skill #1—Comparison*: Develops and supports an argument that: a. Describes the similarities <u>and</u> differences among historical figures, developments, processes, or events. (**1 point**) b. Explains the reasons for the similarities <u>and</u> differences among historical figures, developments, processes, or events. OR (depending on the essay prompt) Evaluates the significance of historical figures, developments, processes, or events. (**1 point**) *Skill #2—Causation*: Develops and supports an argument that a. Describes causes <u>and/or</u> effects of a historical event, development, or process. (**1 point**) b. Explains the reasons for the causes <u>and/or</u> effects of a historical event, development, or process. (**1 point**) *[Note: If the question asks about both causes and effects, you must discuss both in order to earn the full 2 points.]* *Skill #3—Continuity/Change over Time*: Develops and supports an argument that a. Describes historical continuity <u>and</u> change over time. (**1 point**) b. Explains the reasons for historical continuity <u>and</u> change over time. (**1 point**) *Skill #4—Periodization*: Develops and supports an argument that a. Describes how the historical development from the essay prompt is different from and similar to developments that preceded and/or followed it. (**1 point**) b. Explains the extent to which the historical development from the essay prompt is different from and similar to developments that preceded <u>and/or</u> followed it. (**1 point**)

(Rubric continues on the next page.)

Long Essay Rubric (continued)		
Task	Points Possible	Description
Using Evidence	2	1. Addresses the essay topic with specific examples and a broad range of evidence. (**1 point**) 2. Uses specific examples and a broad range of evidence to completely and effectively support or justify the stated thesis or a relevant argument. (**1 point**)

Synthesis	1	Extends the argument by explaining the connections between the argument and ONE of the following:
		  a. A development in a historical period, era, or geographical area that is different from the one in the question
		  b. An AP European History course theme and/or approach to history (e.g., political, economic, cultural) that is not the focus of the essay
		  c. A different discipline or field (e.g., economics, art history, anthropology)

Maximum Points: 6

OVERVIEW OF CONTENT TOPICS

The AP European History course is broken down into four key time periods:

> Period 1: c. 1450 to c. 1648
>
> Period 2: c. 1648 to c. 1815
>
> Period 3: c. 1815 to c. 1914
>
> Period 4: c. 1914 to Present

We've organized the chapters in this book to reflect this periodization.

In addition, the course focuses on five major themes: (1) interaction of Europe and the world, (2) poverty and prosperity, (3) objective knowledge and subjective visions, (4) states and other institutions of power, and (5) the individual and society. The goal of the course is to get you to think conceptually about European history and understand how these themes are manifested throughout history. The questions on the exam will also be rooted in these five themes, which, like the time periods listed above, will receive about equal coverage on the test. While there is no rigid set of topics that fall into each of these theme categories, the following table highlights some topics that will likely be addressed. (Please keep in mind that this list is *not* in chronological order, nor is it a comprehensive list. This is just a small sampling of the kinds of topics that fall under these thematic umbrellas. There are many, many more topics!)

Theme	Relevant Course Topics
1. Interaction of Europe and the World	• commercial and religious motivations to interact with the world • competition for trade • commercial rivalries • Christianity • social Darwinism • mercantilism; slave-labor system; expansion of slave trade • slave revolt and Haitian independence • national self-determination • extreme nationalist political parties • increased immigration into Europe, anti-immigrant policies • Woodrow Wilson's political/diplomatic idealism • causes of World War I • Columbian exchange • Marshall Plan • 1929 stock market crash • Cold War outside Europe • responses to imperialism • diplomacy and colonial wars
2. Poverty and Prosperity	• industrialization; Second Industrial Revolution • French Revolution • Russian reform and modernization • world monetary and trade systems • European economic and political integration • baby boom • the putting-out system • Agricultural Revolution and population growth • mechanization; the factory system • migration from rural to urban areas • critiques of capitalism • evolution of socialist ideology • Russian Revolution • Lenin's New Economic Policy; Stalin's economic modernization • fascism • the Great Depression • green parties; revolts of 1968 • labor laws and reform programs

3. Objective Knowledge and Subjective Visions	• revival of classical texts • invention of the printing press • Renaissance art • scientific method • rational thought • theories of Locke and Rousseau • humanism • romanticism • fascist nationalism
4. States and Other Institutions of Power	• English Civil War • French Revolution • wars of Napoleon • Enlightenment principles • Congress of Vienna • social contract • post-1815 revolutions • nation-building • industrialization • Russian Revolution • constitutionalism • rise of the Nazis • mass media and propaganda • total war • post-1945 nationalist/separatist movements • genocide • imperialism • colonial independence movements • League of Nations • collapse of communism
5. Individual and Society	• gender roles and marriage patterns • hierarchy and social status • urban expansion; rise of commercial and professional groups • family economy • Napoleon and meritocracy • industrialization and class • destructive effects of technology • religious minorities • social Darwinism

Additionally, the AP European History course emphasizes key historical thinking skills, which will also be tested on the exam in how you grasp the source material presented throughout the test, as well as how demonstrate your ability to make historical connections in writing for the DBQ and long essay. The historical thinking skills you will develop in the course and be tested on are grouped into four main areas: (1) analyzing historical sources and evidence; (2) making historical connections; (3) chronological reasoning; and (4) creating and supporting a historical argument.

HOW AP EXAMS ARE USED

Different colleges use AP Exams in different ways, so it is important that you go to a particular college's web site to determine how it uses AP Exams. The three items below represent the main ways in which AP Exam scores can be used:

- **College Credit.** Some colleges will give you college credit if you score well on an AP Exam. These credits count towards your graduation requirements, meaning that you can take fewer courses while in college. For those who pay for college per credit or course, rather than per semester or year, this could be quite a benefit, indeed.

- **Satisfy Requirements.** Some colleges will allow you to "place out" of certain requirements if you do well on an AP Exam, even if they do not give you actual college credits. For example, you might not need to take an introductory-level course, or perhaps you might not need to take a class in a certain discipline at all.

- **Admissions Plus.** Even if your AP Exam will not result in college credit or even allow you to place out of certain courses, most colleges will respect your decision to push yourself by taking an AP course or even an AP Exam outside of a course. A high score on an AP Exam shows mastery of more difficult content than is taught in many high school courses, and colleges may take that into account during the admissions process.

OTHER RESOURCES

There are many resources available to help you improve your score on the AP European History Exam, not the least of which are your **teachers**. If you are taking an AP class, you may be able to get extra attention from your teacher, such as obtaining feedback on your essays. If you are not in an AP course, reach out to a teacher who teaches European History, and ask if the teacher will review your essays or otherwise help you with content.

Another wonderful resource is **AP Students**, the official site of the AP Exams. The scope of the information at this site is quite broad and includes the following items:

Go Online!
Head over to the AP European History AP Students home page for information on the exam, including sample questions, scoring details, and any late-breaking updates.

- course description, which includes details on what content is covered and sample questions
- essay prompts from previous years
- AP European History Exam tips

The AP Students home page for the AP European History Exam can be found here: https://apstudent.collegeboard.org/apcourse/ap-european-history.

Finally, The Princeton Review offers tutoring for the AP European History Exam. Our expert instructors can help you refine your strategic approach and add to your content knowledge. For more information, call 1-800-2REVIEW.

DESIGNING YOUR STUDY PLAN

As part of the Introduction, you identified some areas of potential improvement. Let's now delve further into your performance on Practice Test 1, with the goal of developing a study plan appropriate to your needs and time commitment.

Read the answers and explanations associated with the multiple-choice questions (starting at page 37). After you have done so, think about the following items:

Prep Like a Pro
Need some help devising a plan of action for your studying? Check out our free AP European History Exam study guide on AP Connect. See the "Register Your Book Online!" page for details about accessing your online tools.

- Review the Overview of Content Topics and decide which areas you feel confident about and which you need to further review.

- How many days/weeks/months away is your AP European History Exam?

- What time of day is your best, most focused study time?

- How much time per day/week/month will you devote to preparing for your AP European History Exam?

- When will you do this preparation? (Be as specific as possible: Mondays and Wednesdays from 3:00 to 4:00 P.M., for example.)

- Based on the answers above, will you focus on strategy (Part IV), content (Part V), or both?

- What are your overall goals in using this book?

Part IV
Test-Taking Strategies for the AP European History Exam

PREVIEW

Review your responses to the first three questions on page 2 of Part I and then respond to the following questions:

- How many multiple-choice questions did you miss even though you knew the answer?

- On how many multiple-choice questions did you guess blindly?

- How many multiple-choice questions did you miss after eliminating some answers and guessing based on the remaining answers?

- Did you create an outline before you wrote each essay?

- Did you find any of the essays easier/harder than the others—and, if so, why?

HOW TO USE THE CHAPTERS IN THIS PART

For the following Strategy chapters, think about what you are doing now before you read the chapters. As you read and engage in the directed practice, be sure to appreciate the ways you can change your approach. At the end of Part IV, you will have the opportunity to reflect on how you will change your approach.

Chapter 1
How to Approach
Multiple-Choice
Questions

THE BASICS

The multiple-choice portion of this exam is organized in sets of two to five questions, each set centering upon a primary or secondary source. Expect to see primary texts in translation, texts by contemporary historians, cartoons, paintings, charts, graphs, and tables.

The good news: You'll be tested primarily on that source material, along with a certain amount of outside knowledge. The bad news: You'll be responsible for understanding the grand sweep of European history—causes and effects, continuity and change, comparing and contextualizing.

Unlike several other AP exams, there are only four answer choices for each multiple-choice question. The exam seeks to achieve a measure of balance between the period from the High Renaissance to Napoleon and the period after 1815. Also, note that equal emphasis is placed on political and diplomatic history, cultural and intellectual questions, and social and economic themes. Remember this as you study.

TYPES OF QUESTIONS

The majority of questions on the multiple-choice section of the test are similar to this:

3. As described in the passage, the Dreyfus Affair had political repercussions that lasted well into the twentieth century because

   (A) it helped deepen the religious and political conflicts that plagued the Third Republic
   (B) it created a consensus in French politics which eventually led to a strengthening of the Third Republic
   (C) it reminded people of the German threat
   (D) it ultimately helped the French army get ready for the First World War

(Answers to the sample questions are on page 81.)

Sometimes, the College Board makes the questions a little trickier. One way it does this is by phrasing a question so that you are actually looking for the answer choice that is *incorrect*. We call these questions "NOT/EXCEPT" questions because they usually contain one of those words (in capital letters, so they're harder to miss). Look at the following example:

6. The author indicates that all of the following led to the Russian Revolution of 1917 EXCEPT

   (A) the outbreak of World War I
   (B) the failure of autocratic government
   (C) growing disenchantment of the intellectual class
   (D) a decline in the rate of industrialization in the decade leading up to 1917

The answer choices will occasionally rely upon the source material, but at other times will bring in outside information that may not even be from the period discussed in the question. When that happens, understand that the College Board is testing you on your knowledge of themes that recur throughout European history—rise of the middle class, end of religion as an organizing force, and so on. It doesn't necessarily mean that the answer choice is wrong.

Here is an example:

Source: Daily Mail

45. The political cartoon above implies that

    (A) Hitler broke his promise not to destroy the German Communist Party

    (B) Hitler betrayed his 1939 nonaggression pact with Stalin

    (C) Stalin was warned by the Western Allies that Hitler was dangerous

    (D) a nonaggression pact with Germany was fraught with problems

Other types of primary source materials will be statistical in nature. Be sure to read the chart carefully. If there are easily observed trends, mark these trends in the margin using up-arrows, down-arrows, bell curves, and so on.

Here's an example:

Rate of Industrial Production in Great Britain
(percentage increase per decade)

1800 to 1810	22.9
1810 to 1820	38.6
1830 to 1840	47.2
1840 to 1850	37.4
1850 to 1860	39.3
1860 to 1870	27.8
1870 to 1880	33.2
1880 to 1890	17.4
1890 to 1900	17.9

13. Which of the following conclusions can be drawn from the information presented in the chart above?

(A) The rate of increase of industrial production in the 1860s was due to the American Civil War.

(B) The rate of industrial production remained steady throughout the century.

(C) By the last decades of the century, the increase in industrial production was in an irreversible decline.

(D) The period between 1830 and 1860 witnessed the greatest increase in industrial production.

No Military History and No Trivial Pursuit

Here's some good news. The AP European History Exam doesn't ask specifically about military history. You will *never* see a question on the AP exam like the one below:

16. During the First World War, the Battle of Passchendaele

(A) was a British defeat due to the weakening of their right flank at a critical time

(B) ended with a German counterattack and breakthrough of the British lines

(C) was a British defeat due to insufficient artillery support

(D) witnessed the last attempt by the British to blast their way through the German lines without the element of surprise

Although the British assault on German positions at the Battle of Passchendaele serves as an important example of the foolhardiness of Britain's military leadership, you won't be asked about it on the test. The AP European History Exam does not ask about military strategy per se. When it asks about war, the questions concern the political or social implications of a war or the introduction of new technology rather than strategic questions. The correct answer, by the way, is (D).

The Big Picture

The questions and answers are designed to illustrate **basic principles** of European history. Multiple-choice questions will NOT ask about exceptions to historical trends; the test ignores these, because the test writers are trying to determine whether you have mastered the important generalizations that can be drawn from history. They do not want to know whether you have memorized your textbook (they already know that you haven't).

Therefore, you should always keep the **big picture** in mind as you take this exam. Even if you cannot remember the specific event or concept being tested, you should be able to answer the question by remembering the general social and political trends of the era.

Let's look at this illustrative example, which would be accompanied by a passage on the actual exam:

---

68. As evidenced by the last paragraph of the excerpt, John Calvin argued that from the beginning of time, God

    (A) allowed humans to select their own path to salvation, provided that it included some degree of faith
    (B) knew few would be granted salvation unless they performed charitable works
    (C) selected those who would be saved and those who would be condemned, and that human actions play no role in this
    (D) operated as the divine creator but played no real role in the daily workings of this world

Here's How to Crack It

Using general knowledge of the Protestant Reformation can potentially help you as much as, or sometimes even more than, analyzing the text closely. For example, this question is really asking whether you understand the fundamentals of John Calvin's theology. Calvin believed God selected only a very few individuals to be saved. Nothing these individuals did affected their own ultimate salvation, because to imply they had a role in it would mean that God's authority was not total, something Calvin did not accept. Choices (A) and (B) are thus incorrect, as they both imply some measure of human free will. Choice (D) could not be correct; it represents the Deist point of view dating from the eighteenth-century Enlightenment and bears little resemblance to what a sixteenth-century theologian like Calvin would have believed. The correct answer is (C), which illustrates a "big picture" principle, the primacy for Protestants of faith over works.

Process of Elimination and Guessing

There will be times, however, when you can eliminate one or more clearly wrong answers and still have more than one reasonable answer choice left over. You may not be able to decide which one is right. When this happens, you should guess. Does this advice take you by surprise? Lots of students think that they should never guess on an exam. But even the College Board will tell you that's not true. As we mention in Part II, AP exams do not have any sort of "guessing penalty" for every incorrect answer. Instead, students are assessed only on the total number of correct questions. A lot of AP materials, even those you receive in your AP class, may not include this information. It is really important to remember that if you are running out of time, you need to fill in all the bubbles before the time for the multiple-choice section is up. Even if you don't plan to spend a lot of time on every question, and even if you have no idea what the correct answer is, you need to fill something in. We don't recommend random guessing as an overall strategy, but taking smart guesses at the right time can substantially increase your raw score on the multiple-choice section of the test.

Let's see exactly how guessing can help you. There are four answer choices for each multiple-choice question. If you cannot eliminate any answer choices at all, random odds say that you would get one-fourth of the questions correct. That's about 13 out of 54 questions. If you were able to eliminate just one wrong answer for each question on the entire multiple-choice section, random odds say that you would get one-third of the questions correct. That's about 18 out of 54. And so on. What does that mean for you when you take the test? It means that you should take your best guess, period—no matter how many answer choices you can eliminate. However, you will rarely be faced with a question for which you can't eliminate at least one of the answer choices. In many cases, you will be able to eliminate two or even three incorrect answers. Whenever you get this far but can go no further, you *must* guess from among the remaining answer choices.

If it seems that we are focusing more on eliminating incorrect answers than on finding the correct answers, it's because this is the most efficient way to take a multiple-choice exam. Use **Process of Elimination** to whittle down the answer choices to one on all but the easiest questions (on easy questions, the correct answer will be obvious), because incorrect answers are much easier to identify than the correct one. When you look for the correct answer among the answer choices, you have a tendency to try to justify how each answer *might* be correct. You'll adopt a forgiving attitude in a situation in which tough assertiveness is rewarded. Eliminate incorrect answers. Terminate them with extreme prejudice. If you have done your job well, only the correct answer will be left standing at the end.

This all probably sounds pretty aggressive to you. It is. The fact is, aggressiveness pays on this test. Sift through the answer choices, toss incorrect answers into the bin, guess without remorse, and prowl the test searching for questions you can answer—all with the tenacity and ruthlessness of a shark. Okay, maybe that overstates the case a *little*, but you get the point.

Guess Aggressively
Because you don't lose points for incorrect answers, you should always guess on questions you don't know—no matter how many answer choices you can eliminate. Be aggressive.

Common Sense Can Help

Sometimes, an answer on the multiple-choice section contradicts common sense. Eliminate those answers. Common sense works on the AP European History Exam. Which of the answer choices to the question below don't make sense?

26. During the period when England was a republic (1649–1660), which of the following applied to Ireland?

(A) Ireland became primarily Protestant.
(B) Ireland won its independence.
(C) Ireland obtained extensive military assistance from the French.
(D) An army led by Cromwell invaded Ireland and solidified English control.

Here's How to Crack It

Common sense should allow you to eliminate (A) immediately, since you are probably aware that all of Ireland has never been primarily Protestant. Choice (B) can be eliminated because independence only came for the Republic of Ireland in the early twentieth century. If (C) actually occurred, then perhaps (B) would have taken place, but that was not what happened. Also, while there is a wonderful Irish literary tradition, there was no "renaissance" during the Cromwellian wars. That leaves (D) as the only correct answer.

Context Clues

If the question compares periods or themes in history, there will be context clues or even vocabulary words that will help lead you to the correct answer or eliminate an incorrect answer. Take a look at the following question:

---

60. In his *Economic Consequences of the Peace* (1919), John Maynard Keynes contradicts the author's statement when he

    (A) supported the reparations payments by the Germans as a necessary evil

    (B) argued that the reparations amount was too low to seriously compromise the German economy

    (C) charged that by punishing the Germans with a large reparations bill, the entire European economy was threatened

    (D) urged that the issue of reparations be postponed for a decade so that the postwar economies could adjust to peace

Helpful Hints

Key words in the question and answer choices will often guide you to the correct answer. In this question, the book title contains a helpful hint: "Consequences" suggests that the work is critical, so look for the choice that aligns with this idea.

Here's How to Crack It

Again, you are dealing with a book and an author that you might be less than familiar with, but don't panic—the question itself contains a major clue. The word "consequences" in the title of Keynes's work provides you with the hint that Keynes was possibly critical of the reparations component of the Treaty of Versailles. This bit of information allows you to eliminate (A), (B), and (D), because these answers indicate at least some level of support by Keynes for reparations. The one that stands out from the others is (C); it alone seems to be critical of the very concept of German reparations.

SKILL TYPES

Read the following passage closely. As you work through the four questions that follow it, be sure to read the commentary before and after each question. Each contains a description of a type of multiple-choice question that you're sure to encounter. Because it's good to know thy enemy, it's recommended that you commit these four question types to memory.

Presently two other figures caught our eye: a man in a long cape to the tops of his boots, made of sheepskin, the wool inside, the outside decorated with bright-coloured wools, outlining crude designs. The black fur collar was the skin of a small black lamb, legs and tail showing, as when stripped off the little animal. The man wore a cone-shaped hat of black lamb and his hair reached to his shoulders. He smoked a very long-stemmed pipe with a china bowl, as he strolled along. Behind him a woman walked, bowed by the weight of an immense sack. She wore boots to the knees, many full short skirts, and a yellow and red silk head-kerchief. By her head-covering we knew her to be a married woman. They were a farmer and his wife! Among the Magyars the man is very decidedly the peacock; the woman is the pack-horse. On market days he lounges in the sunshine, wrapped in his long sheepskin cape, and smokes, while she plies the trade. In the farmers' homes of southern Hungary where we passed some time, we, as Americans, sat at table with the men of the house, while wife and daughter served. There was one large dish of food in the centre, into which every one dipped! The women of the peasant class never sit at table with their men; they serve them and eat afterwards, and they always address them in the second person as, "Will your graciousness have a cup of coffee?" Also they always walk behind the men. At country dances we have seen young girls in bright, very full skirts, with many ribbons braided into the hair, cluster shyly at a short distance from the dancing platform in the fair grounds, waiting to be beckoned or whistled to by one of the sturdy youths with skin-tight trousers, tucked into high boots, who by right of might, has stationed himself on the platform. When they have danced, generally a czardas, the girl goes back to the group of women, leaving the man on the platform in command of the situation! Yet already in 1897 women were being admitted to the University of Budapest. There in Hungary one could see woman run the whole gamut of her development, from man's slave to man's equal.

—Emily Burbank, *Woman as Decoration,* 1917

Chronological Reasoning

The first and most common type of question you'll see is about causes and effects, how things have stayed the same or changed over time, and awareness of the various periods of European history. These are habits of mind that historians have when they approach the past in a critical way.

Try this one.

1. In the passage, the author primarily describes

   (A) A pair of Magyars representing all those who had survived the horrors of World War I
   (B) The fundamental injustice shown towards women of the European peasant classes
   (C) The traditional role of women in Europe that the feminist movement had just begun to change
   (D) The dress and carriage of the inhabitants of an unusual corner of Eastern Europe

While (A) places World War I in the correct time period, it incorrectly assumes that this is relevant to the passage, or that the people in the passage actually experienced the war. You can eliminate it. Because this author is describing the habits of only the rural Magyar people, you have to eliminate (B), which is both too broad and too negative. Choice (D) is out because we don't know that this was unusual for this part of Eastern Europe. By Process of Elimination, (C) is correct, and it uses a word ("feminism") that was not present in the text. Your job is to associate that movement with the themes of the passage. Note also the year of the passage's publication, 1917. You should remember that the feminist movement reached its apogee in that decade.

Comparison and Contextualization

In these various types of questions, you'll be asked to compare similar themes across different time periods and societies. For example, recall the attempts at reform in Russia, Prussia, and Austria under the enlightened monarchs of the mid-eighteenth century. Each ruler pursued similar yet different courses of action. Each ruler succeeded and failed to different degrees.

You could also be asked to view the same event from different perspectives, since people have vastly different viewpoints on life depending upon their place of birth, class, education, and so on.

Let's use the Magyar passage again.

2. The author's surprise at the traditional customs of the Magyar community is at least partly attributable to

(A) The more modern behaviors exhibited by women in other parts of the Austro-Hungarian Empire

(B) The nearly uniform adherence to these strict gender roles within the community that she had visited

(C) The expectations that she had developed according to her knowledge of customs in the capital city of Budapest

(D) Her background as an American, where the women were already more liberated from traditional gender roles

Choice (A) is possible but unsupported by any evidence in the passage. Choice (B) also could be true, but it's unclear that the uniform adherence was what caused her surprise. Choice (C) is similarly unsupported; we don't know how much she'd studied about Hungarian traditions. Choice (D) is the default answer, and in this case, it's the only one actually supported by the passage. Recall those two small words "as Americans." This indicates her own background, and it's quite conceivable—given the year of publication, the name of her book, and the final sentence of the passage—that she was a proto-feminist.

Creating and Supporting a Historical Argument

The test makers also want to see that you can support a thesis with evidence. Clearly, this is evident on all of the essays; however, it can also occur on multiple-choice questions, where it will take the form of identifying a piece of evidence that would (or would NOT) support an idea that was present in the text.

Here's an example:

3. In the passage, Emily Burbank argues that women were on a trajectory that led them from "man's slave to man's equal." What evidence would NOT support this idea?

   (A) The passage of various women's suffrage laws in the decade of publication
   (B) Photos of working-class women protesting the violent attacks upon public property that were committed by Emiline Pankhurst in the name of feminism
   (C) A letter from a department store manager describing his new squadron of female employees as cooperative, efficient, and punctual
   (D) A political cartoon mocking the cult of domesticity

Notice that none of these answer choices are actually present in the passage. Of the four answer choices, three of them demonstrate that the old view of women was rapidly receding, to be replaced by the more modern equalist view. The correct answer, (B), describes the public reaction against violent tactics used by the more extreme wing of the feminist movement.

Historical Interpretation and Synthesis

The data-based question (DBQ) is the undisputed king of this type of question. However, multiple-choice questions can also, in a general way, test your ability to synthesize information from various parts of your studies.

Here's an example:

> 4. By the 1990s, the idea of women leading lives independent of men, as implied in the passage, had undergone what type of change?
>
>   (A) The idea gradually grew more accepted, though slightly dampened by the economic fallout from World War II.
>   (B) The idea was gradually weakened by a renewed interest in conservative lifestyles.
>   (C) The idea came to be regarded with suspicion by many of the new Third-World immigrants to Europe.
>   (D) The idea was entirely supplanted by new ways of looking at gender relations.

Choice (A) is correct here, as evidenced by present-day daily life of millions of European women, as well as the large number of female heads of state in Europe. However, it depends almost entirely upon your knowledge of everything you've learned about women's history—in your classwork, reading, exams, conversation, even personal experience of Europe (if you've visited).

———————○———————

Finally, here are the answers to the questions that appear in the first part of this chapter: 3: (A); 6: (D); 45: (B); 13: (D); 16: (D).

Summary

○ Familiarize yourself with the different types of questions that will appear on the multiple-choice section. Be aware that you will see almost an even split between questions on political and diplomatic history, cultural and intellectual trends, and social and economic themes. Tailor your studies accordingly.

○ Look for "big picture" answers. Correct answers on the multiple-choice section confirm important trends in European history. The test will not ask you about weird exceptions that contradict those trends. It also will not ask you about military history. You will not be required to perform miraculous feats of memorization; however, you must be thoroughly familiar with all the basics of European history. There are a lot of them! See our history review in Part V.

○ Understand how the College Board divides European history into four periods. Memorize these four periods, and practice saying or writing the major themes found within each one.

○ The multiple-choice questions accompanying a passage do not necessarily have to be about the same time period of the passage. Given the College Board's desire to emphasize general trend rather than specific factoids, there is a lot of "weaving" between eras.

○ Practice. Practice a lot.

Chapter 2
How to Approach
Short Answers
and Essays

THE BASICS

There are three types of essay questions on the AP European History Exam. The first are the Short-Answer Questions. There are four of these, and they require students to use historical-thinking skills to respond to a primary source, a historian's argument, secondary sources such as data or maps, or general propositions about European history. No thesis is necessary. You have 50 minutes to complete them, and they count for 20 percent of your score.

The second type of essay question is the Document-Based Question (DBQ), which requires you to answer a question based on approximately seven source documents and whatever outside knowledge you have about the subject. There are no choices for this section, besides selecting which documents you will address in your essay. You have 55 minutes, which includes a suggested 15-minute reading period. It counts for 25 percent of your score.

The third type is the Long-Essay Question. This is more like a typical essay on a history exam in your class. For this essay, you are given two choices, usually from different time periods but often related by theme. You are required to pick one and are given 35 minutes to write it. This counts for 15 percent of your score.

We will discuss each of these question types in greater detail in the rest of this chapter. First, let's talk about the basics of writing a successful long AP essay.

WHAT ARE THE AP ESSAY GRADERS LOOKING FOR?

In conversations with those who grade AP European History Exams, it is clear that what they want above all else is for you to address the question. In some of your classes, you may have gotten into the habit of throwing everything but the kitchen sink into an essay without truly addressing the question at hand. Do not try to fudge your way through the essay. The graders are all experts in history, and you will not be able to fool them into thinking you know more than you actually do.

Essay Rule #1
Answer the question! Writing down every fact you know won't help you unless they address what the question is asking.

It is also very important to focus on the phrasing of the question. Some students are so anxious to get going that they start writing as soon as they know the general subject of the question, and many of these students lose points because their essays do not answer the question being asked. Take, for example, an essay question that asks you to discuss the effects of fascism on the daily life of the average German in the 1930s. If you are an overanxious test taker, you might start rattling off everything you know about German fascism—the reasons for its electoral success in the years leading up to 1933, the personality cult around Adolf Hitler, the Holocaust, and so on. No matter how well this essay is written, you will lose points for one simple reason—not answering the question!

Second, a good essay does more than rattle off facts. Just as the multiple-choice questions seek to draw out certain general principles or the "big picture" of European history, the essay questions seek to do the same. The readers are looking to see that you understand some of the fundamental issues in European history and that you can successfully discuss this material in a coherent manner.

If all this sounds intimidating, read on! There are a few simple things you can do to improve your grade on the AP essays.

REASONS TO BE CHEERFUL

AP graders know that you are given very little time to write the DBQ and the long essay question. They also know that is not enough time to cover the subject matter tested by the question. The fact is, many very long books have been written about any one subject that you might be asked about on the DBQ and the free-response question.

The College Board's *AP European History Course and Exam Description* (which can be downloaded from AP Students) advises students to write an essay that has a well-developed thesis, provides support for the thesis with specific examples, addresses all parts of the question, and is generally well organized. Therefore, expressing good ideas and presenting valid evidence in support of those ideas are important. Making sure you mention every single relevant piece of historical information is not so important.

Also, you should remember that graders are not given a lot of time to read your essays. When they gather to read the exams, they each go through more than one hundred per day. No one could possibly give detailed attention to all points in your essay when he or she is reading at such a fast clip. What he or she can see in such a brief reading is whether you have something intelligent to say and whether you have the ability to say it well. As many teachers and professors will tell you, when you read several bad essays (and there will be quite a few even among AP students), you tend to give those that are not completely awful more credit than they possibly deserve. Just hope that the essay being read before your own was written by someone who didn't buy this book and was therefore completely unprepared.

Essay Rule #2
Don't just rattle off facts—show that you understand and can effectively analyze historical developments in a clear, cohesive way.

Download It
Visit the AP Students home page for AP European History to download a course description that covers everything from course learning objectives to scoring rubrics for the essay questions on the exam.

THINGS THAT MAKE ANY ESSAY BETTER

There are two essential components to writing a successful timed essay. First, plan what you are going to write before you start writing! Second, use a number of tried-and-true writing techniques that will make your essay appear well-organized, well-thought-out, and well-written. This section is about those techniques.

Before You Start Writing

Read the question carefully. Underline key words and circle dates. Then, brainstorm for one or two minutes. Write down everything that comes to mind in your test booklet. (There is room in the margins and at the top and bottom of the pages.) Look at your notes and consider the results of your brainstorming session as you decide what point you will argue in your essay; that argument is going to be your thesis. Tailor your argument to your information, but by no means choose an argument that you know is wrong or with which you disagree. If you do either of these things, your essay will be awful. Finally, sort the results of your brainstorm. Some of what you wrote down will be "big picture" conclusions, some will be historical facts that can be used as evidence to support your conclusions, and some will be garbage.

Next, make an outline. You should plan to write five paragraphs for each of the two essay questions, and plan to go into special detail in each of the paragraphs on the DBQ. (Remember: You will have the documents and your outside knowledge to discuss on the DBQ. Plus, you will have more time.) Your first paragraph should contain your thesis statement, in which you directly answer the question in just a few sentences. Your second, third, and fourth paragraphs should each contain one argument (for a total of three) that supports that statement, along with historical evidence to support those arguments. The fifth paragraph should contain your conclusion and reiterate your answer to the question.

Before you start to write your outline, you will have to decide what type of argument you are going to make. Here are some of the classics.

1. Make Three Good Points

This is the simplest strategy. Look at the results of your brainstorming session, and pick the three best points supporting your position. Make each of these points the subject of one paragraph. Make the weakest of the three points the subject of the second paragraph, and save the strongest point for the fourth paragraph. If your three points are interrelated and there is a natural sequence to arguing them, then by all means use that sequence, but otherwise, try to save your strongest point for last. Begin each paragraph by stating one of your three points, and then spend the rest of the paragraph supporting it. Use specific, supporting examples whenever possible. Your first paragraph should state what you intend to argue. Your final paragraph should explain why you have proven what you set out to prove.

2. Make a Chronological Argument

Many questions lend themselves to a chronological treatment. Questions about the development of a political, social, or economic trend can hardly be answered any other way. When you make a chronological argument, look for important transitions and use them to start new paragraphs. A five-paragraph essay about the events leading up to the French Revolution, for example, might start with an introductory discussion of France and the role of royal absolutism. This is also where you should state your thesis. The second paragraph might then discuss the economic crisis that led to the calling of the Estates-General. The third paragraph could deal with concern among members of the third estate that their interests might not be represented at Versailles, despite the vital economic role they played in eighteenth-century France. The fourth paragraph could be concerned with the events leading up to and including the King's agreement to meet the three estates as a National Assembly. Your conclusion in this type of essay should restate the essay question and answer it. For example, if the question asks whether the French Revolution was inevitable, you should answer "yes" or "no" in this paragraph.

3. Identify Similarities and Differences

Some questions, particularly on the long essay question, ask you to compare events, issues, and/or policies. Very often, the way the question is phrased will suggest the best organization for your essay. Take, for example, a question asking you to compare the impact of three events and issues on the decision to execute the English monarch Charles I in 1649. This question pretty much requires you to start by setting the historical scene prior to the three events/issues you are about to discuss. Continue by devoting one paragraph to each of the three, and conclude by comparing and contrasting the relative importance of each. Again, be sure to answer the question in your final paragraph.

Other questions will provide options. If you are asked to compare Italian and Northern humanism during the Renaissance, you might open with a thesis stating the essential similarity or difference between the two. Then, you could devote one paragraph each to a summary of certain trends and authors, while in the fourth paragraph you could point out the major similarities and differences between Italian and Northern humanism. In the final paragraph, you could draw your conclusion (for example, "their similarities were more significant than their differences," or vice versa).

Or, using another angle altogether, you might start with a thesis, then discuss in the body of your essay three pertinent philosophical, religious, or political issues, then discuss how Italian humanists dealt with such questions, then move on to the Northern humanists, and wrap up with an overview of your argument for your conclusion.

4. Use the Straw Dog Argument

In this essay-writing technique, choose a couple of arguments that someone taking the position opposite yours would take. State their arguments, and then tear them down. Remember that proving your opposition wrong does not mean that you have proved you are correct; that is why you should choose only a few opposing arguments to refute. Summarize your opponent's arguments in paragraph two, dismiss them in paragraph three, and use paragraph four to make the argument for your side. Or, use one paragraph each to summarize and dismiss each of your opponent's arguments, and then make the case for your side in your concluding paragraph. Acknowledging both sides of an argument, even when you choose one over the other, is a good indicator that you understand that historical issues are complex and can be interpreted in more than one way, something teachers and graders like to see.

Conclusion

No matter which format you choose, remember to organize your essay so that the first paragraph addresses the question and states how you are going to answer it. (That is your thesis.) The second, third, and fourth paragraphs should each be organized around a single argument that supports your thesis, and each of these arguments must be supported by historical evidence. Your final paragraph ties the essay up into a nice, neat package. Your concluding paragraph should also answer the question. And remember, stay positive!

As you are writing, observe the following guidelines:

- **Keep sentences as simple as possible.** Long sentences get convoluted very quickly and will give your graders a headache, putting them in a bad mood.

- **Throw in a few big words.** But don't overdo it, because it will look like you are showing off. Remember that good writing does not have to be complicated; some great ideas can be stated simply. NEVER use a word if you are unsure of its meaning or proper usage. A malapropism (misuse of a word) might give your graders a good laugh, but it will not earn you any points, and it will probably cost you.

- **Write clearly and neatly.** As long as we are discussing your graders' moods, here is an easy way to put them in good ones. Graders look at a lot of chicken scratch; it strains their eyes and makes them grumpy. Neatly written essays make them happy. When you cross out, do it neatly. If you are making any major edits—if you want to insert a paragraph in the middle of your essay, for example—make sure you indicate these changes clearly.

- **Define your terms.** Most questions require you to use terms that mean different things to different people. One person's "liberal" is another person's "conservative," and yet another person's "extremist."

Writing Wins
If you follow the guidelines and strategies highlighted in this chapter, you'll be on your way to a high-scoring essay!

What one person considers "expansionism," another might call "colonialism" or "imperialism." The folks who grade the test want to know what you think these terms mean. When you use them, define them. Take particular care to define any such terms that appear in the question. Almost all official College Board materials emphasize this point, so do not forget it. Be sure to define any term that you suspect can be defined in more than one way.

- **Use transition words to show where you are going.** When continuing an idea, use words such as *furthermore*, *also*, and *in addition*. When changing the flow of thought, use words such as *however* and *yet*. Transition words make your essay easier to understand by clarifying your intentions. Better yet, they indicate to the graders that you know how to make a coherent, persuasive argument.

- **Use structural indicators to organize your paragraphs.** Another way to clarify your intentions is to organize your essay around structural indicators. For example, if you are making a number of related points, number them ("First…Second…And last…"). If you are writing a compare/contrast essay, use the indicators "on the one hand" and "on the other hand."

- **Stick to your outline.** Unless you get an absolutely brilliant idea while you are writing, do not deviate from your outline. If you do, you will risk winding up with an incoherent essay.

- **Try to prove one "big picture" idea per paragraph.** Keep it simple. Each paragraph should make one point and then substantiate that point with historical evidence.

- **Back up your ideas with examples.** Yes, we have said it already, but it bears repeating: Do not just throw ideas out there and hope that you are right (unless you are absolutely desperate). You will score big points if you substantiate your claims with facts.

- **Try to fill the essay form.** An overly short essay will hurt you more than one that is overly long.

- **Make sure your first and last paragraphs directly address the question.** Nothing will cost you points faster than if the graders decide you did not answer the question. It is always a safe move to start your final paragraph by answering the question. If you have written a good essay, that answer will serve as a legitimate conclusion.

- **Always place every essay into a historical context.** For example, if you are given an essay asking you to compare and contrast Newton's and Einstein's ideas on the universe, don't make it an essay on science. Instead, show how each of these men was a product of his respective time period, and show how their ideas influenced their contemporaries as well as future generations.

Key Words

Using transition words (such as "however" and "furthermore") and structural indicators (such as "first," "second," and "finally," for example) in your essay is a great way to organize your writing and give the reader a sense of where your essay is headed. This will also make your writing seem more coherent and persuasive.

Summary

- Read questions carefully. Be sure you are answering the question that is asked. You must answer the question in order to get full credit.

- Do not start writing until you have brainstormed, chosen a thesis, and written an outline.

- Follow your outline. Stick to one important idea per paragraph. Support your ideas with historical evidence.

- Write clearly and neatly. Do not write in long, overly complex sentences. Toss in a couple of "big" words you know you will not misuse. When in doubt, stick to simple syntax and vocabulary.

- Use transition words to indicate continuity of thought and changes in the direction of your argument.

- Provide a strong historical context. You may be faced with questions focusing on science, economics, philosophy, literature and art, religion, and other disciplines. Always remember this is a history exam.

- Remember also that this is a European history exam (not an American history exam). So, for example, if you get a question on technological changes in the nineteenth century, you should focus on Marconi, Siemens, or Bessemer, not on Edison or Bell. Similarly, on Cold War questions, don't avoid the United States, but have your answer reflect Europe's situation as much as possible.

- Study the question. Make sure you understand what it is asking you to write about. Address all parts of the questions. If it asks for "social, political, and economic changes," make sure you discuss all three. If you cannot address the whole question, either choose another question or fake it. If you don't know anything about the social impact, then try to use logic—how would something like this affect society?

- Try for at least two or three concrete facts to support each of your themes or assertions.

CRACKING THE SHORT ANSWERS

The short-answer section is the second part of Section I of the exam, immediately following the multiple-choice questions. There is no break between the multiple-choice and short-answer portions. There are four short-answer questions, which you'll have 50 minutes to complete.

This is supposed to be a fairly straightforward section designed to test your recall of historical material. Each question will be accompanied by some piece of source material (whether a graph, passage, or map) or a historian's argument. The questions ask you to analyze the source and incorporate it into your response. Responses should not be lengthy; they are not meant to be long essays. Instead, write a few sentences or a full paragraph to concisely answer the question.

A short-answer question might look something like this:

2. Use the passage below and your knowledge of European history to answer all parts of the question that follows.

"In England the legal method of executing a witch was by hanging; after death the body was burnt and the ashes scattered. In Scotland, as a rule, the witch was strangled at the stake and the body burned, but there are several records of the culprit being sentenced to burning alive. In France burning alive was the invariable punishment. In cases where popular fury, unrestrained by the law, worked its own vengeance on individuals, horrible scenes occurred; but these were the exception, and, examining only the legal aspect of the subject, it will be found that witches had a fair trial according to the methods of the period, and that their punishment was according to the law."

Margaret Alice Murray, *The Witch-Cult in Western Europe,* 1921

a) Briefly explain TWO factors that led to a change in the way suspected witches were punished.
b) Briefly explain ONE thinker who may have opposed the burning of witches on intellectual grounds.

This is deceptively difficult, since witchcraft isn't exactly covered in most AP European curriculums. You need to connect this subject with something that you learned in your course. The words traditional European would tell you that this occurred prior to the disruptions of modern European life. You should also sense that witchcraft might've been a major issue during the religious period of European history, which was prior to the Scientific Revolution.

A high-scoring response to this question might look like this:

> One factor included a change in intellectual thought. As Europe moved from a system of law based religious tradition (that had been popular since the medieval period) and towards a system of law based on reason, the idea of burning suspected witches became harder to justify. Another factor might include a more political change: with the rise of representative democracy, the whim of a single mayor, governor, noble, or king no longer carried as much weight, and suspected witches probably couldn't be condemned as quickly. John Locke, the great Enlightenment thinker, most likely considered witchcraft irrelevant, if he even believed in it at all, since his organizing principles of life included liberty and personal property.

Part (b) of the question was the tipoff that the test makers want you to connect witchcraft with the rise of Enlightenment thought. Notice also the conjecture that was present; if you get a question like this, feel free to speculate based on your studies.

Summary

○ The AP European History Exam features a short-answer section, which is found in Section I after the multiple-choice section. There are four short-answer questions that you will have 50 minutes to complete.

○ The short-answer questions will be based on a primary or secondary source, which may be a chart, map, or excerpt from a historical document, for example. These questions will require you to analyze the source and connect it to your knowledge of European history.

○ Do not go overboard in composing your responses! Short-answer questions are meant to be just that—short. Although length may vary, a paragraph will usually suffice.

CRACKING THE DOCUMENT-BASED QUESTION (DBQ)

What Is the DBQ?

DBQ stands for "Document-Based Question." The DBQ is an essay question that requires you to interpret primary source documents. (There are typically no more than seven documents in a DBQ.) These documents might come from newspaper articles and editorials, letters, diaries, speeches, excerpts from legislation, political cartoons, charts, or graphs. The documents will *not* include excerpts from current textbooks. Occasionally, one or two of the documents will be taken from something "classic" that you may have seen previously, but generally, the documents will be new to you. However, they will discuss events and ideas with which you should be familiar. All of the documents will pertain to a single subject. The average document is about six lines long, although occasionally you will see something longer.

The 55-minute DBQ is the first part of Section II of the exam. At the beginning of the DBQ, you will be handed a green booklet in which the essay question and documents are printed, as well as a separate form on which to write your essay. The DBQ session begins with a suggested 15-minute reading period, during which you are allowed to read the documents and take notes in the DBQ booklet. It is suggested that you spend 15 minutes reading the documents and 40 minutes writing your response. You may begin writing your response before the reading period is over.

To give you an idea of what you can expect on your DBQ, let's look at what appeared on a previous test. The question asked students to discuss and evaluate problems in the relationship between the English and Irish in the period from 1800 to 1916. The documents included excerpts from the following:

- A quote from English Prime Minister William Pitt, the creator of the Act of Union of 1801, in which he states that "Ireland must be governed in the English interest"

- A parliamentary speech by a Protestant Irish leader dating from 1805 demanding the continuation of exclusive Protestant political rights within the United Kingdom

- A poem written in 1842 by an Irish Nationalist that speaks of the commonality of interests between Irish Protestants and Catholics

- An article in the English Conservative Party newspaper from 1848 that claims that anything good in Ireland is due to the influence of England, while the Irish have only themselves to blame for all their problems

- A declaration of principles from 1879 by the National Land League that states that the "land of Ireland belongs to the people of Ireland."

- A piece of writing from 1900 by Maud Gonne, founder of the Daughters of Ireland, in which she declares that her organization wants to help establish Irish independence in part through a revival of indigenous Irish culture

- A map showing the distribution in 1901 of Protestants and Roman Catholics in the Irish population

Although you may not know much about the authors of these documents, the tensions between England and Ireland might be familiar to you. In other words, you will not be starting from square one, even when the documents are new to you.

Is There a "Right" Answer to Each DBQ?

No. DBQs are worded in such a way that you can argue any number of positions. In the previous example, the documents provide evidence for various issues that stand at the heart of the Irish-English conflict, such as religious bigotry and questions concerning Home Rule. As long as you support your argument with evidence, you can argue whatever thesis you want.

Graders are supposed to take into account the strength of your argument and the evidence you offer in support of it. In other words, if you forget to mention a good, illustrative historical event but manage to back your point up in some other way, you will not be penalized.

However, the best DBQ responses will contain relevant *outside information*. As you can see from the rubric on the next page, you cannot get the maximum number of points for this essay unless you incorporate outside evidence and knowledge.

Using the Documents AND Your Knowledge of the Subject...

"Your knowledge of the subject" is the outside information. It includes historical facts and ideas that are relevant to the question but that are not mentioned in the DBQ documents. For example, in the England and Ireland DBQ described earlier, any information offered about the writers' backgrounds would count as outside information, as would information concerning, for example, Charles Stuart Parnell and the Land League. Some students make the mistake of throwing everything they know about a subject into their essays, whether or not it pertains to the question. That type of information receives partial credit at best.

HOW IS THE DBQ SCORED?

You can earn up to 7 points on the DBQ. For a breakdown of those points, here's the rubric that we showed you on page 60:

DBQ Scoring Rubric		
(Note: Numbers marked with an asterisk [*] are based on a document-based question that contains 7 documents.)		
Task	**Points Possible**	**Description**
Thesis and Argument Development	2	1. Presents a thesis that can be backed by historical evidence and responds to all parts of the question. The thesis must be at least one sentence, located in either the introduction or conclusion. (**1 point**) 2. Develops and supports a cohesive argument that addresses historical complexities and shows the relationships among historical evidence. (**1 point**)
Document Analysis	2	1. Uses at least 6* of the documents to support the thesis or a relevant argument. (**1 point**) 2. Explains the significance of the author's point of view or purpose, audience, and/or historical context for at least 4* documents. (**1 point**)
Using Evidence Beyond the Documents	2	1. *Contextualization*: Places the argument within the broader historical context—events, developments, processes, etc.—relevant to the question. Note that this requires an explanation (consisting of several sentences or a full paragraph), not just a brief mention. (**1 point**) 2. *Evidence Beyond the Documents*: Gives an example or additional piece of evidence beyond what is found in the documents to support an argument. Note that the example must be different from the evidence used to earn other points on the rubric, and include an explanation of how that evidence supports or qualifies the argument. (**1 point**)
Synthesis	1	Extends the argument by explaining the connections between the argument and ONE of the following: a. A development in a historical period, era, or geographical area that is different from the one in the question b. An AP European History course theme and/or approach to history (e.g., political, economic, cultural) that is not the focus of the essay c. A different discipline or field (e.g., economics, art history, anthropology)
		Maximum Points: 7

Getting the Points

Here are concrete ways to earn the points for each of the DBQ tasks.

- Study the question carefully; make sure you are writing about what the question is actually asking. Misinterpreting the question is the most common mistake students make and results in a zero on the essay. Also, be careful to provide a thesis that is not a regurgitation of the exam question. Failure to come up with your own thesis will also result in a zero.

- Try to use every document. For a DBQ that contains seven documents, you need to explicitly use six of them to support your argument in order to earn those points on the rubric.

- Show your reader that you understand the basic meaning of the documents. This doesn't mean that there won't possibly be a number of ways of interpreting the document, but make it clear that you understand the connection of your document to the topic at hand.

Tone

Don't forget about the importance of tone when analyzing the documents, particularly in regard to point of view. Tone can also present a point of view: for example, outrage, contempt, or concern.

- Try to organize your documents into groups, and then write each of your body paragraphs about one of your document groups. Start off with a topic sentence, and write an analysis of the information drawn from the documents in that group. Use quotes or examples to support your analysis. Just quoting for the sake of quoting is a common error among students. Do not assume that quotations can simply stand on their own without any elaboration. Be sure to show the graders that you understand what the quotation means and use the quote in a manner that furthers your argument.

- The documents may not be fact; they may be opinions. Write the essay in such a way that this is made clear to the reader.

  ○ Make a big effort to find point of view. Before you read the document, look at who the author is and when he or she made this statement. Why did the author have this particular point of view? What about the author's background or the time, place, or historical circumstance shaped the writer's outlook on life? Is there an ulterior motive behind the statements made? Do not hesitate to use logic. For example: If the DBQ is about the various views on German unification in the 1860s, why would a German poet, the Italian Foreign Minister, and Otto von Bismarck support unification, while an ethnically French citizen of Alsace-Lorraine, a French socialist politician, and Napoleon III all oppose it?

  ○ Demonstrate that you are aware that certain documents are more credible than others. A document giving statistics from a government census, for example, is considered more credible than claims made by an editorialist for a party newspaper.

- Have three or more groupings. A group cannot contain just one document, and it's safest to use more than two (in case one is used incorrectly). It is fine to use a document more than once.

- The thesis is not simply restating the question. It must also answer the question and indicate the various groupings into which the essay is divided.

- Use attribution as much as possible. Attribution means that you give credit to the authors of the statements used. It is also useful to cite the document you are quoting. For example, you might write "British Prime Minister William Gladstone stated in his address to Parliament 'blah-blah-blah' (Document 7)." (Citing the document is not mandatory, but it makes it easier for the reader to see which documents you used.) Never write an essay that says, "In Document 7, such-and-such is said, which is contradicted by Document 5." Your essay is not about the documents; it is about the opinions of the people quoted in the documents.

- To earn the maximum number of points on the DBQ, you now need to bring in outside examples into your essay. This shows a greater historical understanding, so be sure to spend some time during the 15-minute reading period brainstorming a couple examples that go beyond the scope of the documents.

How to Group Documents

How to group will vary according to the question. Some DBQs, for example, may ask you to show how various segments of society view a particular issue; some will ask how views on a particular issue have changed over time. Find the documents that have similar points of view and write about those views; in other words, pro versus con, German versus French, liberal versus conservative, nineteenth century versus twentieth century.

You may group according to the reasons and motives behind the arguments. Your groups might be, for example, individuals influenced by nationalist idealism, individuals representing the power politics of the era, and groups representing the internationalism promoted by Karl Marx.

GETTING STARTED ON THE DBQ: READ THE QUESTION

Start by reading the question. This direction may seem obvious, but it really is not, given how many students write essays on subjects that are only marginally related to the question being asked. Students miss the question because they get anxious during the exam. They panic. They think they are going too slowly. In an effort to speed up, they read half the question, say to themselves, "A-ha! I know what they're going to ask!" and stop reading. Do NOT make this mistake! The question is probably the shortest thing you have to read on the DBQ. Take your time; savor it. Explore its nuances. Essays that address the question fully earn huge bonuses; those essays that ignore parts of the question are doomed to get lower scores.

Here's a sample question:

> **Question 1:** Using the documents and your knowledge of European history, evaluate the reasons why the year 1848 brought about an explosion of revolutionary activity throughout Europe.

As you look over the question, you should ask yourself two questions.

- Do I have an opinion about this subject?
- What must I discuss in order to write a successful essay?

Of the two questions, the second is much more important. You can construct a position later, after you have gathered the information you want to include in your essay. First, you need to figure out what issues you must address and what data you will use in your discussion.

To begin, you might want to break down the question in a variety of ways. Perhaps focus first on economic issues, such as the economic downturn of the 1840s, a decade that some referred to as the "hungry forties." Then move on to critical political issues such as a backlash against the repressive nature of politics in the decades after 1848 or the role of nationalism in the revolutions of 1848. Others might find it more useful to discuss events in 1848 on a nation-by-nation basis, beginning with the collapse of the Orleans monarchy in France and moving on to the revolutionary movements in places such as the German states, the Austrian Empire, Italy, and so on. Finally, you must include a discussion of the given documents and your outside knowledge in the essay.

However you decide to approach the question, it is essential that you take your time. Read carefully to make sure that you understand what issues must be addressed in your essay. Then, determine how to organize the information you plan to collect from the documents and from memory for inclusion in the essay.

Organizing Your Essay: Use Grids and Columns

Many DBQs ask you to draw comparisons. For those questions, you can always organize your thoughts about a DBQ in a grid. Drawing a grid helps in seeing all sides of an argument, which is important because DBQ graders will reward you for acknowledging arguments other than your own.

For the DBQ on the revolutions of 1848, you may find it useful to create a grid like the one shown on the next page. Such a grid will allow you to see the complexity of the events of 1848 and how economics, domestic politics, and nationalism all played a role in fanning the flames of revolution across Europe.

	Economics	Politics	Nationalism
France			
Prussia			
Austria			
Italian States			

Set Up a Grid
As you remember appropriate outside information and as you read the documents, take notes in the appropriate boxes. When it comes time to write your essay, you will find it easier to compare and contrast because your information will already be organized in a way that makes similarities and differences more obvious.

If you cannot draw a grid for a question, you can instead set up column headings. Because every DBQ can be argued from at least two different positions, you can always set up two (or more) columns, designating one for each position. Consider the DBQ about Ireland, which we discussed at the beginning of the chapter. You could create one column, entitled "England," where you can provide examples of English justification for holding onto Ireland. A second column, labeled "Unionist," will give the Unionist argument for remaining part of the United Kingdom, and a third, labeled "Nationalist," can provide their argument for creating an independent Irish state, free from British domination. You might even want a fourth column, for information that you know belongs in your essay but that you cannot yet classify (give that the title "To be classified").

Good essays do not just flow out of your pen by accident. They happen when you know what you are going to say *before you start writing*. Although it is difficult (if not impossible) to prepare your entire DBQ essay before you begin writing, given the time constraints, pre-organization and a good outline will get you much closer to that goal.

A Sample Question

Let's take a look at another possible DBQ.

> **Question 1:** Using the documents and your knowledge of European history, discuss whether Napoleon was a supporter of the ideas espoused in the eighteenth-century Enlightenment or whether he was an enemy of individual liberty.

Your essay will have to show whether you understand certain basic tenets of the Enlightenment and also show your knowledge of the period of Napoleon's domination over France (1799–1815). You will, of course, have to include both analysis of the documents and outside information. Since the question is asking for a basic comparison, you might want to make a simple three-column grid like the one below:

Ideals of Enlightenment	Napoleon pro	Napoleon con

Once you have created your grid, begin organizing information for your essay. At this point, you are probably anxious to start reading the documents. Resist the temptation. You have one more important job to do before you start reading.

Gather Outside Evidence

Most students read the DBQ documents first and *then* try to think of outside evidence and examples to supplement their essays. This is a mistake. The reason? *The power of suggestion.* Once you have read the documents—a chore that can take from six to eight minutes—those documents will be on your mind. If you read the provided passages and *then* brainstorm outside information, you will invariably think of things you *just* read about, rather than things you *have not* read about.

Plus, reading and processing the documents is a big task. Once you have accomplished that, you will want to get started right away on organizing and writing your essay while the documents are fresh in your mind. So, brainstorm outside evidence *before* you read the documents.

Here's what you should do. Look at your grid or columns and brainstorm. In a separate blank space in your green booklet (*not* in your grid/columns), write down everything you can think of that relates to the question. Spend just two or three minutes on this task, and then look at what you have written. Enter the useful information into your grid/columns in the appropriate spaces.

Chances are that some of the outside evidence you think of will be mentioned in the documents, which means that it will not be outside information any more. That is no big deal. In fact, you should think of it as something good. If some of what you remembered shows up in the documents, that means you are on the right track toward answering the question!

This is what a brainstorming grid for the Napoleon question might look like.

Ideals of Enlightenment	Napoleon pro	Napoleon con
religious tolerance	• extended religious freedom throughout the empire • concordat	
rational government	• Napoleonic Code • increased centralization of government	
equality of individuals	• favored meritocracy	• created imperial title and a new aristocracy • placed relatives on foreign thrones
freedom from repression		• created secret police censorship • jailed and executed political opponents

Brainstorming Grid
Before you even read the documents, spend 2–3 minutes writing down everything you can think of relating to the question. This mini-brainstorming session will help you organize your thoughts before you begin writing, as well as provide you with some relevant outside information to use in your response.

Read the Documents

After you have gathered outside evidence and examples to include in your essay, you are ready to read the documents. As you read, keep the following things in mind:

- **The order in which documents appears may be helpful.** The documents in the DBQ may appear in chronological order, which could indicate that you are expected to trace the historical development of the DBQ subject. On such questions, you do not have to write an essay that adheres strictly to chronological order, but chronology should play an important part in the development of your thesis. When the documents appear in an order other than chronological, they are usually organized so that you can easily compare and contrast different viewpoints on a particular event or issue. On these questions, one of your main goals should be to draw those same comparisons.

- **Watch for inconsistencies within and among the documents.** The documents will not necessarily agree with one another. In fact, they are almost certain to present different viewpoints on issues and almost as certain to present conflicting accounts of a historical event. Some documents might even contradict themselves! This is intentional. The exam is testing your ability to recognize these contradictions. You are expected to resolve these conflicts in your essay. To do so, you will have to identify the sources of the documents. (See below.)

- **Identify the sources of the documents.** Why do two accounts of the same event contradict each other? Why do two historians, looking at the same data, come up with dissimilar interpretations of their significance? Is it because the people giving these accounts—the sources of the documents—have different perspectives? Identify the sources and explain why their opinions differ. As you explain these differences, look for the following differences among sources:

  - political ideology
  - class
  - race
  - religion
  - gender

Consider the question on Napoleon. A supporter of the exiled Bourbons would offer a very different point of view on this question than a member of Napoleon's inner circle. The graders will be looking specifically to see if you have tried to explain those differences.

- **Look for evidence that could refute your argument.** Once you have decided what your thesis will be, you will be looking through the documents for evidence to support your argument. Not all the documents will necessarily back you up. Some may appear to contradict your argument. Do not simply ignore those documents! As you read them, try to figure out how you might incorporate them into your argument.

As you read the documents, be aware that each one holds a few morsels of information for your essay. Do not fixate on any one document, but at the same time, do not ignore any. Also, as you read the documents, take note of any outside information that the document reminds you of and enter it into your grid/columns.

Don't Discount Counter-Evidence

Let's consider the Napoleon DBQ. Suppose you argue that Napoleon was a supporter of the ideals of the Enlightenment. Now suppose that one of the documents presents evidence that Napoleon kidnapped a Bourbon prince living in exile in one of the German states and then had him killed. You might be tempted to pretend that the document does not exist. However, you will be better off if you incorporate the document into your essay. By doing this you are acknowledging that this historical issue, like all historical issues, is complex. This acknowledgment is good. AP essay graders are instructed to look for evidence that you understand that history has no simple answers and to reward you for it.

DRILL

Below is a "mini-DBQ" (it has only four documents, which is fewer than you will see on the actual exam). Read through the documents, taking notes in the margins and blank spaces.

Question 1: Using the documents and your knowledge of European history, evaluate the roles of women in the religious conflicts of the sixteenth century.

Document 1

Source: A printed pamphlet addressed to Katharina von Bora, the wife of Martin Luther.

Woe to you, poor fallen woman, not only because you have passed from light to darkness, from the cloistered holy religion into a damnable shameful life, but also that you have gone from the grace to the disfavor of God, in that you have left the cloister in lay clothes and have gone to Wittenberg like a chorus girl. You are said to have lived with Luther in sin.

Document 2

Source: Letter written in 1523 by Argula von Grumbach, the daughter of a Bavarian noble, to the faculty of the University of Ingolstadt after they had forced a young member of the teaching staff to recant his belief in Luther's theology.

What have Luther and Melanchthon taught save the Word of God? You have condemned them. You have not refuted them. Where do you read in the Bible that Christ, the apostles, and the prophets imprisoned, banished, burned, or murdered anyone? You tell us that we must obey the magistrates. Correct. But neither the pope, nor the Kaiser, nor the princes have any authority over the Word of God.

Document 3

Source: Examination of Elizabeth Dirks before a Catholic court in 1549 on the charge of being an Anabaptist.

Examiner: We understand that you are a teacher and have led many astray. We want to know who your friends are.

Elizabeth: I am commanded to love the Lord my God and honor my parents. Therefore I will not tell you who my parents are. That I suffer for Christ is damaging to my friends.

Examiner: What do you believe about the baptism of children, seeing that you have had yourself baptized again?

Elizabeth: No my Lords, I have not had myself baptized again. I have been baptized once on my faith, because it is written, "Baptism belongs to believers."

Document 4

Source: *The Way of Perfection* by St. Teresa of Avila (1515-1582), a prominent Catholic reformer and author of spiritual books.

At about this time there came to my notice the harm and havoc that were being wrought in France by these Lutherans and the way in which their unhappy sect was increasing. I felt that I would have laid down a thousand lives to save a single one of all the souls that were being lost there. And, seeing that I was a woman, and a sinner, I determined to do the little that was in me—namely, to follow the evangelical counsels as perfectly as I could, and to see that these few nuns who are here should do the same.

Here's How to Crack It

Here you are provided with four different examples of the ways in which women participated in the religious disputes of the sixteenth century.

Document 1 may initially look somewhat confusing until you take a moment to think about the source: It is a pamphlet addressed to the wife of Martin Luther. If you forgot about the story of Katharina von Bora and her marriage to Luther, you're in luck, since the document provides you with some background. You should be aware, however, that the position taken in the pamphlet is entirely hostile to both Katharina and Martin Luther. Therefore, it does not take much of a leap of faith to conclude that the document was written by a Catholic who was horrified by Katharina's leaving the cloistered life and by her marriage to Luther.

Document 2 reveals another side of the participation of women in the religious debates of the Reformation. It is from a woman who actively participated in such questions by championing a young Lutheran teacher. The author, Argula von Grumbach, will not be a familiar name to you, but you can see from the document that she was fully aware of the major issues of the conflict, such as Luther's emphasis on the Bible as the sole source of faith and his rejection of papal authority. Challenging the authorities on behalf of this young man is an interesting example of open defiance, something not usually expected from women in the sixteenth century.

Document 3 is part of a transcript of a trial of a woman who was accused of being an Anabaptist. Don't panic if you have forgotten what the Anabaptists believed in, since the document explains that Anabaptists believed in adult baptism. As the accused woman Elizabeth Dirks says, "Baptism belongs to believers," implying that it's not appropriate for unaware infants. There are other things that you can pull from this document. One of the accusations that the Catholic authorities mentioned is that she was a teacher, albeit one who was leading people astray. Considering that women were rarely literate in this age, her profession is something to be noted, as should her intense loyalty to her friends, whom she refuses to betray by revealing their presence at her rebaptism. She must have been aware that such a refusal would bring her additional torture, the typical means of extracting a confession.

Document 4 can be compared with Document 2, since, once again, a woman actively threw herself into the religious debates of the period. This time, however, our author, St. Teresa of Avila, used her pen not to challenge the Catholic Church but to defend it. She revealed that she found herself as a defender of the Church in response to Lutheranism taking root in France. She also grappled with the question as to how, as a woman, she could best serve her church. She would have liked, if the opportunity arose, to "have laid down a thousand lives to save a single one of all the souls that were being lost there," but since that cheery prospect was not open to her, she had to find some other outlet for her anger. So she organized the nuns who still remained in the monastery and recommitted them to the Catholic Church.

That's it for the documents. Now, formulate a thesis, figure out how and where to fit all your information into your argument, and write an essay. Relax. It is easier than it sounds.

Develop a Thesis

Before you decide on your thesis, GO BACK AND READ THE QUESTION ONE MORE TIME! Make sure that your thesis addresses all the pertinent aspects of the question. Your thesis should not simply restate the prompt; it also needs to answer the question and pose an argument or position.

For this sample question, your thesis might read as follows:

> Women played an active role in the religious debates of the six-teenth century, both as supporters of a break with Rome and as defenders of the Catholic Church.

You can then bring in the variety of experiences revealed in the four sources to buttress this thesis.

Create an Outline

At this point, you should still have time left in the suggested 15-minute reading period. Create an outline with one Roman numeral for each paragraph. Decide on the subject of each paragraph and on what information you will include in each paragraph. Do not rely on your grid/columns if you do not have to. The grid/columns are good for organizing your information but are less efficient for structuring an essay.

Write Your Essay

The most important advice when writing your exam is to stay confident. Everyone else taking the test, all across the country, is at least as nervous about it as you are.

Summary

○ The DBQ consists of an essay question and approximately seven historical documents. Most likely, you will not have seen most of the documents before, but they will all relate to major historical events and ideas you should be familar with. You'll have 55 minutes to prepare and write your essay. It is suggested that you spend 15 minutes reading the documents and 40 minutes writing your response.

○ There is no single "correct" answer to the DBQ. DBQs are framed so that they can be successfully argued from many different viewpoints.

○ Read the essay question carefully. Circle and/or underline important words and phrases. Once you understand the question, create a grid or columns in which to organize your notes on the essay.

○ Before you start reading the documents, brainstorm about the question. This way you will gather additional evidence before you submerge yourself in the documents.

○ Read the documents. Pay attention to contradictions and connections within and among the documents and also to who is speaking and what sociopolitical tradition he or she represents. If you have decided on a thesis, keep an eye out for information that might refute your thesis, and be prepared to address it in your essay.

○ Decide on a thesis; then write an outline for your essay.

○ Use the provided historical background sparingly in your essay.

o   Your introductory paragraph should set the historical scene and include a thesis that takes a position on the issue posed by the question.

o   Try to include as many of the documents as you can in your essay.

o   When you write the essay, do not be concerned with literary merit. Be sure your essay is logically organized, easy to understand, and always focused on the thesis.

o   Stay positive. Do not panic. Everyone else is as nervous as you are.

CRACKING THE LONG ESSAY QUESTION

What Is the Long Essay?

The long essay section consists of two questions, and you must choose ONE to answer.

The long essay question is found in Section II, immediately following the DBQ. It's the final portion of the exam, and you do not get a break before it begins. You'll have 35 minutes to write this essay.

The long essay question, like the DBQ, has no single "correct" answer. Unlike the DBQ, though, the long essay questions are not accompanied by documents; *everything* you include in your essay response will be outside information. Also, because you have less time to plan and write the long essay, it will likely be shorter than your DBQ response. A clear, relevant thesis, accompanied by an organized essay laying out supporting evidence and solid examples, should earn a good score. Here are two examples of the types of questions you might see on this section.

> **Question 2:** Evaluate the extent to which the growth of industrialization in Great Britain in the first half of the nineteenth century C.E. can be considered a pivotal point in European history. In the development of your argument, consider what changed and what changed the same after the growth of industrialization in Great Britain after the first half of the nineteenth century C.E.

> **Question 3:** Evaluate the extent to which Renaissance humanism and its effects on the concept of the individual can be considered a pivotal point in European history. In the development of your argument, consider what changed and what stayed the same after the revival of humanistic thought during the European Renaissance.

As you can see, the long essay allows you to expound upon the themes and topics you learned in the course to craft a historical argument.

The maximum number of points you can earn on the long essay is 6. Here's how that total score breaks down:

Long Essay Scoring Rubric		
Task	**Points Possible**	**Description**
Thesis	1	Presents a thesis that can be backed up by historical evidence and that responds to all parts of the question. The thesis must be at least one sentence, located in either the introduction or conclusion.
Using Targeted Historical Thinking Skills	2	*Skill #1—Comparison*: Develops and supports an argument that: a. Describes the similarities <u>and</u> differences among historical figures, developments, processes, or events. (**1 point**) b. Explains the reasons for the similarities <u>and</u> differences among historical figures, developments, processes, or events. OR (depending on the essay prompt) Evaluates the significance of historical figures, developments, processes, or events. (**1 point**) *Skill #2—Causation*: Develops and supports an argument that a. Describes causes <u>and/or</u> effects of a historical event, development, or process. (**1 point**) b. Explains the reasons for the causes <u>and/or</u> effects of a historical event, development, or process. (**1 point**) *[Note: If the question asks about both causes and effects, you must discuss both in order to earn the full 2 points.]* *Skill #3—Continuity/Change over Time*: Develops and supports an argument that a. Describes historical continuity <u>and</u> change over time. (**1 point**) b. Explains the reasons for historical continuity <u>and</u> change over time. (**1 point**) *Skill #4—Periodization*: Develops and supports an argument that a. Describes how the historical development from the essay prompt is different from and similar to developments that preceded <u>and/or</u> followed it. (**1 point**) b. Explains the extent to which the historical development from the essay prompt is different from and similar to developments that preceded <u>and/or</u> followed it. (**1 point**)

Using Evidence	2	1. Addresses the essay topic with specific examples and a broad range of evidence. (**1 point**) 2. Uses specific examples and a broad range of evidence to completely and effectively support or justify the stated thesis or a relevant argument. (**1 point**)

Synthesis	1	Extends the argument by explaining the connections between the argument and ONE of the following:
		  a. A development in a historical period, era, or geographical area that is different from the one in the question
		  b. An AP European History course theme and/or approach to history (e.g., political, economic, cultural) that is not the focus of the essay
		  c. A different discipline or field (e.g., economics, art history, anthropology)

Maximum Points: 6

Which Question to Choose

Choose the question about which you know the most specific details, NOT the one that looks easiest at first glance. The more you know about the subject, the better your final grade will be.

How to Write the Essay

Since we have covered this information already in the previous two chapters, here are brief directions for how to structure your essay.

- Read the question and analyze it.
- Assess your information and devise a thesis.
- If you have time, write a quick outline.
- Write your essay.

A Final Note

This section is short, not because the the long essay question is unimportant, but because we have already discussed in previous chapters what you need to know to write successful AP essays. Many students are tempted to ease up when they finish the DBQ because 1) it's so challenging, 2) they're tired, and 3) the test is three-fourths of the way over. Do not make that mistake. Reach down for that last bit of energy like a long-distance runner coming into the home stretch. After all, this is where you can truly shine—with no stimulus material whatsoever, the more you recall, the more you will shine. You can take it easy *after* you finish this final essay.

Summary

o The long-essay portion of the exam consists of two prompts. You must answer one of them.

o Choose the question about which you know the most specific details, not the one that looks easiest.

o Study each question carefully. Make sure you are answering the question exactly. If you misinterpret a question and write about something other than what the prompt asks, you will receive a 0 for that question.

o Circle all key words. Consider the dates given; they are clues to what you are to write about. If, for example, a question asks, "How did the nature of the Soviet regime change after 1924?", the question is in fact asking you to show the differences between the leadership and policies of Lenin and Stalin.

o Do not ignore any part of the question. If a question asks you to "Compare and contrast the different personalities and leadership styles of Charles V, Holy Roman Emperor, and his son Philip II, King of Spain, and how these influenced the methods they used to counter the Protestant movement," be sure to address *personalities*, *leadership styles*, and *the ways these influenced policy toward the Reformation*. If you find yourself in a situation in which you do not know enough to answer a part of the question, do not ignore that part. Use the historical knowledge you have, combined with logic, to guess at the answer.

- Decide on a thesis, and then write an outline for your essay.

- Follow your outline. Stick to one important idea per paragraph. Provide concrete examples to support the point you are making. We recommend at least two examples per issue.

- Stay focused on the question, and don't go off on tangents. Write only about what the question asks, and carefully choose the evidence to support it. You have very little time to throw together these essays. Do not spend time including information that isn't directly relevant.

- Your introductory paragraph is more than just your thesis statement. It should also set the historical scene (time, place, historical situation) so that the reader can more clearly understand what your essay is about. In your thesis, do not simply restate the question; be sure to also *answer* the question. The thesis tells the reader what the main points of the essay are.

- Remember: This is a European history exam. If you write about the Cold War, for example, put as much focus as possible on what the Europeans are doing. If your essay deals with literature, art, philosophy, science, economics, social issues, and so on, place the discussion in the correct historical context.

- Do not be concerned with literary merit. Be sure your essay is logically organized, easy to understand, and **always focused on the thesis.** Each paragraph should have a topic sentence, and the essay should close with a concluding paragraph.

o   Write clearly and neatly. Do not write in overly complex sentences. Toss in a couple of "big" words that you know you will not misuse. When in doubt, stick to simple syntax and vocabulary.

o   Use transition words to indicate continuity of thought and changes in the direction of your argument.

o   Keep a close watch on the time. Remember that 35 minutes for an essay is less time than you may think. Be sure to pace yourself by taking no more than five minutes to brainstorm and outline, and by working steadily through the essay. Remember that the style of the sentences is less important than the quality of the ideas.

o   Stay positive. Do not panic. Everyone else is at least as nervous as you are.

Chapter 3
Using Time
Effectively to
Maximize Points

BECOMING A BETTER TEST TAKER

Very few students stop to think about how to improve their test-taking skills. Most assume that if they study hard, they will test well, and if they do not study, they will do poorly. Most students continue to believe this even after experience teaches them otherwise. Have you ever studied really hard for an exam, then blown it on test day? Have you ever aced an exam for which you thought you weren't well prepared? Most students have had one, if not both, of these experiences. The lesson should be clear: Factors other than your level of preparation influence your final test score. This chapter provides some insights that will help you perform better on the AP European History Exam as well as other tests.

PACING AND TIMING

A big part of scoring well on an exam is working at a consistent pace. The worst mistake made by inexperienced or unsavvy test takers is that they come to a question that stumps them, and rather than just skip it, they panic and stall. Time stands still when you're working on a question you cannot answer, and it is not unusual for students to waste five minutes on a single question (especially a question involving a graph or the word EXCEPT) because they are too stubborn to cut their losses. It is important to be aware of how much time you have spent on a given question and on the section you are working. There are several ways to improve your pacing and timing for the test:

- **Know your average pace.** While you prepare for your test, try to gauge how long you take on 5, 10, or 20 questions. Knowing how long you spend on average per question will help you identify how many questions you can answer effectively and how best to pace yourself for the test.

- **Have a watch or clock nearby.** You are permitted to have a watch or clock nearby to help you keep track of time. It is important to remember, however, that constantly checking the clock is in itself a waste of time and can be distracting. Devise a plan. Try checking the clock after every 15 or 30 questions to see if you are keeping the correct pace or whether you need to speed up; this will ensure that you're cognizant of the time but will not permit you to fall into the trap of dwelling on it.

- **Know when to move on.** Since all questions are scored equally, investing appreciable amounts of time on a single question is inefficient and can potentially deprive you of the chance to answer easier questions later on. If you are able to eliminate answer choices, do so; but don't worry about picking a random answer, and move on if you cannot find the correct answer. Remember: Tests are like marathons; you do best when you work through them at a steady pace. You can always come back to a question you don't know. When you do, very often you will find that your previous mental block is gone, and you will wonder why the question perplexed you the first time around (as you gleefully move on to the next question). Even if you still don't know the answer, you will not have wasted valuable time you could have spent on questions that you found easier.

- **Be selective.** You don't have to do any of the questions in a given section in order. If you are stumped by an essay or multiple-choice question, skip it or choose a different one. In the section below, you will see that you may not have to answer every question correctly to achieve your desired score. Select the questions or essays that you can answer and work on them first. This will make you more efficient and give you the greatest chance of getting the most questions correct.

- **Use Process of Elimination on multiple-choice questions.** Many times, one or more answer choices can be eliminated. Every answer choice that can be eliminated increases the odds that you will answer the question correctly. The section on multiple-choice questions will go through strategies to find these incorrect answer choices and increase your odds of getting the question correct.

Remember: When all the questions on a test are of equal value, no one question is that important; your overall goal for pacing is to answer the most questions correctly. Finally, you should set a realistic goal for your final score. In the next section, we will break down how to achieve your desired score as well as how to pace yourself.

GETTING THE SCORE YOU WANT

Depending on the score you need, it may be in your best interest not to try to work through every question. Check with the schools to which you are applying to see what score you need to earn credit.

AP exams in all subjects no longer include a "guessing penalty" of a quarter of a point for every incorrect answer. Instead, students are assessed only on the total number of correct answers. It is really important to remember that if you are running out of time, you should fill in all the bubbles before the time for the multiple-choice section is up. Even if you don't plan to spend a lot of time on every question and even if you have no idea what the correct answer is, you need to fill something in.

TEST ANXIETY

Everybody experiences anxiety before and during an exam. To a certain extent, test anxiety *can* be helpful. Some people find that they perform more quickly and efficiently under stress. If you have ever pulled an all-nighter to write a paper and ended up doing good work, you know the feeling.

However, *too much stress* is definitely a bad thing. Hyperventilating during the test, for example, almost always leads to a lower score. If you find that you stress out during exams, here are a few preemptive actions you can take.

- **Take a reality check.** Evaluate your situation before the test begins. If you have studied hard, remind yourself that you are well prepared. Remember that many others taking the test are not as well prepared, and (in your classes, at least) you are being graded against them, so you have an advantage. If you didn't study, accept the fact that you will probably not ace the test. Make sure you get to every question you know something about. Don't stress out or fixate on how much you don't know. Your job is to score as high as you can by maximizing the benefits of what you do know. In either scenario, it is best to think of a test as if it were a game. How can you get the most points in the time allotted to you? Always answer questions you can answer easily and quickly before you answer those that will take more time.

- **Try to relax.** Slow, deep breathing works for almost everyone. Close your eyes, take a few slow, deep breaths, and concentrate on nothing but your inhalation and exhalation for a few seconds. This is a basic form of meditation, and it should help you to clear your mind of stress and, as a result, concentrate better on the test. If you have ever taken yoga classes, you probably know some other good relaxation techniques. Use them when you can (obviously, anything that requires leaving your seat and, say, assuming a handstand position won't be allowed by any but the most free-spirited proctors).

- **Eliminate as many surprises as you can.** Make sure you know where the test will be given, when it starts, what type of questions are going to be asked, and how long the test will take. You don't want to be worrying about any of these things on test day or, even worse, after the test has already begun.

The best way to avoid stress is to study both the test material and the test itself. Congratulations! By buying or reading this book, you are taking a major step toward a stress-free AP European History Exam.

REFLECT

Respond to the following questions:

- How long will you spend on multiple-choice questions?

- How will you change your approach to multiple-choice questions?

- What is your multiple-choice guessing strategy?

- How much time will you spend on the DBQ? The long essay? The short-answer questions?

- What will you do before you begin writing an essay?

- How will you change your approach to the essays?

- Will you seek further help outside of this book (such as a teacher, tutor, or AP Students) on how to approach multiple-choice questions, the essays, or a pacing strategy?

Part V
Content Review for the AP European History Exam

HOW TO USE THE CHAPTERS IN THIS PART

For the following content chapters, you may need to come back to them more than once. Your goal is to obtain mastery of the content you are missing, and a single read of a chapter may not be sufficient. At the end of each chapter, you will have an opportunity to reflect on whether you truly have mastered the content of that chapter.

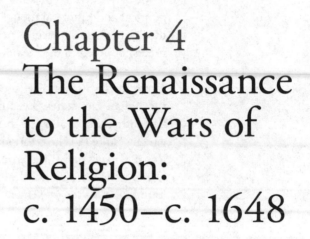

Chapter 4
The Renaissance
to the Wars of
Religion:
c. 1450–c. 1648

THE RENAISSANCE: AN OVERVIEW

Fifteenth- and sixteenth-century intellectuals and artists believed that they were part of a new golden age. **Georgio Vasari**, a sixteenth-century painter, architect, and writer, used the Italian word *rinascità*, meaning **"rebirth,"** to describe the era in which he lived. Vasari and other artists and intellectuals believed that their achievements owed nothing to the backwardness of the Middle Ages and instead were directly linked to the glories of the Greek and Roman world. History tells us that they were kidding themselves. The **Renaissance** artisans owed far more to the cultural and intellectual achievements of the medieval world than they cared to acknowledge. Nevertheless, the Renaissance was a time in which significant contributions were made to Western civilization, with particular gains in literature, art, philosophy, and political and historical thought. Our modern notion of **individualism** was also born during the Renaissance, as people sought to receive personal credit for their achievements, opposed to the medieval ideal of all glory going to God.

These intellectual and artistic developments first took place in the vibrant world of the Italian **city-states**. Eventually, the invention of the **printing press** in the mid-fifteenth century allowed these cultural trends to spread to other parts of Europe, which resulted in the creation of the **Northern Renaissance** movement. The Italian Renaissance writers were primarily interested in secular concerns, but in the north of Europe, the Renaissance dealt with religious concerns and ultimately helped lay the foundation for the movement known as the **Protestant Reformation**.

THE ITALIAN CITY-STATES

THE ITALIAN STATE SYSTEM DURING THE RENAISSANCE

The Italian States During the Renaissance

The city-states of Renaissance Italy were at the center of Europe's economic, political, and cultural life throughout the fourteenth and fifteenth centuries. During the Middle Ages, the towns of northern Italy were nominally under the control of the **Holy Roman Empire**; residents, however, were basically free to decide their own fate, which resulted in a tremendously vibrant—and at times violent—political existence. The old nobility, whose wealth was based on land ownership, often conflicted with a new class of merchant families who had become wealthy in the economic boom times of the twelfth and thirteenth centuries. Both groups had to contend with an urban underclass, known as the *popolo*, or "the people," who wanted their own share of the wealth and political power.

In Florence in 1378, the *popolo* expressed their dissatisfaction with the political and economic order by staging a violent struggle against the government that became known as the **Ciompi Revolt**. The revolt shook Florence to its very core and resulted in a brief period in which the poor established a tenuous control over the government.

This struggle reverberated in the other city-states throughout Italy. In Milan, the resulting social tensions led to the rise of a tyrant, or *signor*, and the city eventually came to be dominated by the family of a mercenary *(condottiero)* named Sforza. Florence and Venice remained republics after the revolt, but a few wealthy families dominated them. The most noteworthy of these families, the **Medici**, used the wealth gained from banking to establish themselves first as the behind-the-scenes rulers of the Florentine republic and later as hereditary dukes of the city.

The internal tensions within the city-states were matched by external rivalries as the assorted city-states were engaged in long-term warfare among themselves. By the mid-fifteenth century, these external wars had effectively narrowed the numerous city-states of the medieval age to just a few dominant states—Florence, Milan, and Venice in the north, the **papal states** in central Italy, and the Kingdom of Naples in southern Italy.

In addition to every city-state's internal and external tensions that may have helped stir the creative energy that was so important to the Renaissance, economic factors were also a significant energy-creating agent. The Italian city-states were generally more economically vibrant than the rest of western Europe, with merchants carrying Italian wool and silk to every part of the continent, and with Italian bankers providing loans for money-hungry European monarchs. Wealthy Italian merchants became important **patrons** of the arts and insisted on the development of secular art forms, such as portraiture, that would represent them and their accumulated wealth to the greatest effect.

Geography also played a role in the vibrant cultural life of the Italian Renaissance. Italy's central location in the Mediterranean was ideal for creating links between the Greek culture of the east and the Latin culture of the west. Additionally, southern Italy had been home to many Greek colonies and later served as the center for the Roman Empire. In essence, classical civilization had never totally disappeared from the Italian mainland, even following the collapse of the western half of the Roman Empire in the fifth century.

HUMANISM

Humanism is a highly debated term among historians. Most would characterize it not as representing a particular philosophical viewpoint but rather as a program of study, including rhetoric and literature, based on what students in the classical world (c. 500 B.C.E. to 500 C.E.) would have studied. **Francesco Petrarch** (1304–1374) is often considered the father of humanism. Petrarch became dissatisfied with his career as a lawyer and set about to study literary classics. It was Petrarch who coined the phrase "**Dark Ages**" (c. 400–900) to denote what he thought was the cultural decline that took place following the collapse of the Roman world in the fifth century.

While literate in *medieval* Latin from his study of law, Petrarch learned *classical* Latin as preparation to study these important literary works. In a task that was to become exceedingly important during the Renaissance, Petrarch sought classical texts that had been largely unknown during the Middle Ages. It was common in the Middle Ages to become familiar with classical works not by directly reading the original manuscripts but rather by reading secondary commentaries about the works. Petrarch set out to read the originals and quickly found himself engaged with such works as the letters of **Cicero**, an important politician and philosopher whose writings provide an account of the collapse of the Roman Republic. Cicero was a brilliant Latin stylist. To write in the Ciceronian style became the stated goal of Petrarch and those humanists who followed in his path.

Although his contemporaries accused him of turning to the pagan culture of ancient Greece and Rome, Petrarch—despite his fascination with classical culture—did not reject Christianity. Instead, he argued for the universality of the ideas of the classical age. Petrarch contended that classical works, although clearly written by pagans, still contained lessons that were applicable to his own Christian age.

Petrarch's work served as inspiration to a group of wealthy young Florentines known as the "**civic humanists.**" They viewed Cicero's involvement in political causes as justification to use their own classical education for the public good. They did this by serving Florence as diplomats or working in the chancellery office, where official documents were written. They also went beyond Petrarch's achievements by studying a language that had almost been completely lost in western Europe—classical Greek.

Renaissance humanist scholarship branched out in a number of different directions. Some writers strove to describe the ideal man of the age. In **Castiglione's** *The Courtier* (1528), such a person would be a man who knew several languages, was familiar with classical literature, and was also skilled in the arts—what we might label today as a "Renaissance Man" (or *l'uomo universale*). Other contributions were made in the new field of critical textual analysis. **Lorenzo Valla** was one of the critical figures in this area. Working in the Vatican libraries, he realized that languages can tell a history all their own. In 1440, he proved that the *Donation of Constantine*, a document in which Constantine, the first Christian Emperor, turned control of the western half of his empire over to the papacy, could not have been written by Constantine. Valla noticed that the word *fief* was used by Constantine in describing the transfer of authority to the pope, a word that Valla knew was not in use until the eighth century, around four hundred years after Constantine's death. In another work that influenced the humanists in northern

The Italian Renaissance and the Greek Revival

The revival of Greek is one of the most important aspects of the Italian Renaissance. It allowed Westerners to become acquainted with that part of the classical heritage that had been lost during the Middle Ages—most significantly the writings of the ancient Greek philosopher **Plato** (427–348 B.C.E.). In particular, these writers were fascinated by Plato's belief that ideals such as beauty or truth exist beyond the ability of our senses to recognize them, and that we can train our minds to make use of our ability to reason and thus get beyond the limits imposed by our senses. This positive Platonic view of human potential is found in one of the most famous passages from the Renaissance, **Pico della Mirandola's** *Oration on the Dignity of Man*. In addition, the **Florentine Platonic Academy**, sponsored by Cosimo d'Medici, merged platonic philosophy with Christianity to create **Neoplatonism**. A closely-related school of thought was hermeticism, a pantheistic philosophy stating that God is in everything and that humans were created divine but chose to live in a material world. It was associated with astrology, alchemy, and the kabbalah—all important parts of Italian Renaissance intellectual life.

Europe, Valla took his critical techniques to the Vulgate Bible, the standard Latin Bible of the Middle Ages, and showed that its author, Jerome, had mistranslated a number of critical passages from the Greek sources.

Women were also affected by the new humanist teachings. Throughout the Middle Ages, there were women, very often attached to nunneries, who learned to read and write. During the Renaissance, an increasing number of wealthy, secular women picked up these skills. The humanist scholar **Leonardo Bruni** even went so far as to create an educational program for women, but tellingly left out of his curriculum the study of rhetoric or public speech, critical parts of the male education, since women had no outlet to make use of these skills. **Christine de Pisan**, an Italian who was the daughter of the physician to the French King Charles V, received a fine humanist education through the encouragement of first her father and later her husband. She wrote *The City of Ladies* (1405) to counter the popular notion that women were inferior to men and incapable of making moral choices. Pisan wrote that women have to carve out their own space or move to a "City of Ladies" in order for their abilities to be allowed to flourish. (Virginia Woolf would later espouse this idea in her early twentieth-century work, *A Room of One's Own*.)

RENAISSANCE ART

It is arguably in the area of fine arts that the Renaissance made its most notable contribution to Western culture. A number of different factors drove Renaissance art. In a reflection of the shift toward individualism, Renaissance artists were now considered to be important individuals in their own right, whereas in the Middle Ages they toiled as anonymous craftsmen. These artists sought prestige and money by competing for the patronage of secular individuals such as merchants and bankers, who wanted to sponsor art that would glorify their achievements rather than tout the spiritual message that was at the heart of medieval art.

These patrons demanded a more naturalistic style, which was aided by the development of new artistic techniques, including the rejection of the old practice of hierarchical sealing, in which figures in a composition were sized in proportion to their spiritual significance. In the Middle Ages, painting consisted of **fresco** on wet plaster or tempera on wood. In the fifteenth century, oil painting, which developed in the north of Europe, became the dominant method in Italy. Artists also began to make use of *chiaroscuro*, the use of contrasts between light and dark, to create three-dimensional images. Perhaps the most important development was in the 1420s with the discovery of **single-point perspective,** a style in which all elements within a painting converge at a single point in the distance, allowing artists to create more realistic settings for their work.

Classical Motifs in Renaissance Art

In architecture, one can see the increasing influence of classical motifs, such as the use of simple symmetrical decorations and classical columns. Perhaps the most noteworthy architectural achievement of the Early Renaissance period was the building of a dome over the Cathedral of Florence by **Filippo Brunelleschi**, the first dome to be completed in western Europe since the collapse of the Roman Empire.

The end of the fifteenth century marked the beginning of the movement known as the **High Renaissance.** During the High Renaissance, the center of the Renaissance moved from Florence to Rome. Florence had experienced a religious backlash against the new style of art, while in Rome, a series of popes (most notably **Michelangelo**'s great patron **Julius II**) were very interested in the arts and sought to beautify their city and their palaces. The High Renaissance lasted until around the 1520s, when art began to move in a different direction. We sometimes label this art as Late Renaissance, or **Mannerism,** an art that showed distorted figures and confusing themes and may have reflected the growing sense of crisis in the Italian world due to both religious and political problems.

There are three major High Renaissance artists with whom you should be familiar: Leonardo da Vinci, Raphael, and Michelangelo.

Leonardo da Vinci

While it is a bit of a cliché to label **Leonardo da Vinci** (1452–1519) as a Renaissance man, the label is accurate. Leonardo was a military engineer, an architect, a sculptor, a scientist, and an inventor whose sketchbooks reveal a remarkable mind that came up with workable designs for submarines and helicopters. Recent reconstructions of his sketches show that he even designed a handbag. Oh yes, he was also a painter, as the hordes of tourists snaking their way through the Louvre to see the *Mona Lisa* will attest to.

Fun Fact
Leonardo da Vinci's famous sketchbooks are now owned by none other than Bill Gates.

Raphael

In an age of artistic prima donnas, **Raphael** (1483–1520), a kindly individual, stands out for not being despised by his contemporaries. He came from the beautiful Renaissance city of Urbino and died at the early age of 37, but in his brief life, he was given some very important commissions in the Vatican palaces. Besides his wonderfully gentle images of Jesus and Mary, Raphael links his own times and the classical past in *The School of Athens*, which shows Plato and Aristotle standing together (in a crowd that also features the images of Leonardo and Michelangelo) in a fanciful classical structure and uses the deep, single-point perspective characteristic of High Renaissance style.

Michelangelo

Like Leonardo, **Michelangelo** (1475–1564) was skilled in numerous areas. His sculptural masterpiece *David* was commissioned by Michelangelo's native city, Florence, as a propaganda work to inspire the citizens in their long struggle against the overwhelming might of Milan. Four different popes commissioned works from him, most notably the warlike Julius II, who gave Michelangelo the task of creating his tomb. Julius II also employed Michelangelo to work on the **Sistine Chapel** in the Vatican, a work that Julius II began to have doubts about as he rushed to have the revealing anatomy of some of the figures covered up with fig leaves, much to the anger of its creator. Michelangelo, who enjoyed a very long life, lived to see the style of art in Italy change from the harmony and grace of the High Renaissance to the more tormented style of the Late Renaissance, as viewed in his final work in the Sistine Chapel, the brilliant yet disturbing *Final Judgment*.

THE NORTHERN RENAISSANCE

By the late fifteenth century, Italian Renaissance humanism began to affect the rest of Europe. Although the writers of the Italian Renaissance were Christian, they thought less about religious questions than their northern counterparts. In the north, questions concerning religion were paramount. Christianity had arrived in the north later than in the south, and northerners at this time were still seeking ways to deepen their Christian beliefs and understanding and display what good humanists they were. They believed they could achieve this higher level by studying early Christian authors. In this sense, the Northern Renaissance was a more religious movement than the Renaissances in Italy. Eventually, northern writers such as Erasmus and More, often referred to as **Christian Humanists**, criticized their mother church, only to find to their horror that more extreme voices of dissent—for example, that of Martin Luther—had not used their methodology to find ways to better the Catholic Church, but to show why the Church had strayed from the will of God.

Erasmus and Sir Thomas More

The greatest of the northern humanists was **Desiderius Erasmus** (1466?–1536). You can thank Erasmus the next time you use such tired clichés as "Where there's smoke, there's fire," since he collected this and many other ancient and contemporary proverbs in his *Adages*. Erasmus's *In Praise of Folly* used satire as a means of criticizing what he thought were the problems of the Church. His *Handbook of the Christian Knight* emphasized the idea of inner faith as opposed to the outer forms of worship, such as partaking of the sacraments. Erasmus's Latin translation of the New Testament also played a major role in the sixteenth-century movement to better understand the life of the early Christians through its close textual analysis of the *Acts of the Apostles*. Erasmus was at first impressed with Luther's attacks on the Church and even initiated a correspondence with him. Eventually, however, the two men found that they had significant disagreements. Unlike Luther, Erasmus wanted to reform the Church, not abandon it, and he could never accept Luther's belief that man does not have free will.

More Facts
Sir Thomas More coined the term *utopia*, which literally means "nowhere."

Another important northern humanist was the Englishman **Sir Thomas More** (1478–1535). A friend of Erasmus, he wrote the classic work *Utopia* (1516). More was critical of many aspects of contemporary society and sought to depict a civilization in which political and economic injustices were limited by having all property held in common. More, like Erasmus, was highly critical of certain practices of his church, but in the end he gave his life for his beliefs. In 1534, Henry VIII had More, who was serving the King as his chancellor, executed for refusing to take an oath recognizing Henry as Head of the Church of England.

Northern Renaissance Culture

The Northern Renaissance also represented more than simply the Christian humanism of individuals such as More and Erasmus. Talented painters from the north, while clearly influenced by the artists of the Italian Renaissance with whom they often came into contact on visits to the Italian peninsula, also created their own unique style. This is seen, for example, in the work of **Albrecht Durer**, a brilliant draftsman, whose woodcuts powerfully lent support to the doctrinal revolution brought about by his fellow German Martin Luther: The illiterate peasants were moved more by Durer's art than by Luther's texts.

The greatest achievement in the arts in northern Europe in the sixteenth and early seventeenth centuries took place in England, a land that had, up until then, been a bit of a cultural backwater, with the notable exception of **Geoffrey Chaucer**, whose *Canterbury Tales* were based on *The Decameron* by **Boccaccio** (both works written during the fourteenth century). There is perhaps no way to explain the emergence of the sheer number of men possessing exceptional talent during the reign of Queen Elizabeth, since providing her with much credit for this cultural awakening seems to be unwarranted. In fact, much of what we refer to as the **Elizabethan Renaissance** occurred during the reign of her cousin and heir, James I.

Although **Christopher Marlowe** and **Ben Jonson** are both writers of significant repute, the age produced an unrivaled genius in **William Shakespeare** (1564–1616). Though little is known of Shakespeare's life and the question of the provenance of his plays will never be answered to the satisfaction of all, this man, who received little more than a primary school education, apparently was able to author plays such as *Hamlet* and *King Lear*, works that reveal an unsurpassed understanding of the human psyche as well as a genius for dramatic intensity.

The Printing Press

The search for new ways to produce text became important in the late medieval period, when the number of literate individuals rose considerably as the number of European universities increased. The traditional method of producing books, via a monk working dutifully in a monastic scriptorium, was clearly unable to meet this heightened demand. **Johannes Gutenberg**, from the German city of Mainz, introduced movable type to western Europe. Between 1452 and 1453, Gutenberg printed approximately 200 Bibles and spent a great deal of money making his Bibles as ornate as any handwritten version. He eventually went broke. The significant increase in literacy in the sixteenth century supports the theory that few inventions in human history have had as great an impact as the printing press. It is hard to imagine the Reformation spreading so rapidly without the books that informed people of the nature of the religious debate.

Power of the Printing Press

Historians consider the printing press to be one of the most culturally significant inventions in all of human history. The ability to rapidly disseminate printed material almost certainly led to the spread of the Reformation, among other historical events.

THE PROTESTANT REFORMATION

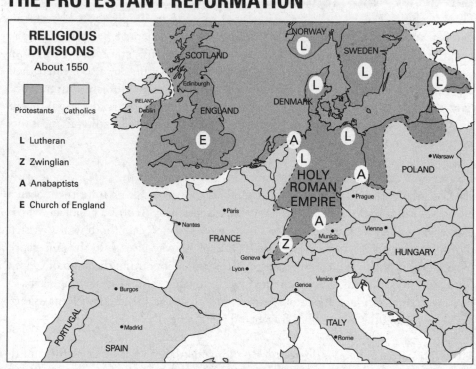

Religious Divisions Around 1550

In western Europe in the year 1500, the simple declarative sentence, "I went to church on Sunday," could mean only one thing, as only one church existed in the West. At the top of this hierarchical church sat the pope in Rome, to whom all of Europe looked for religious guidance. Several decades later, the **Protestant Reformation** movement resulted in the great split in Western Christendom, which dethroned the pope as the single religious authority in Europe. Although it took several decades, eventually there was a Catholic response to this challenge known as the **Catholic Reformation**.

In part, the Reformation of the sixteenth century was a reflection of the ways in which Europe was changing. The humanism of the Renaissance, particularly in the north of Europe, had led individuals to question certain practices such as the efficacy of religious relics and the value to one's salvation of living the life of a monk. In addition, the printing press had made it possible to produce Bibles in ever greater number, which made the Church's exclusive right to interpret the Scriptures seem particularly vexing to those who could now read the text themselves. The rise of powerful monarchical states also created a situation in which some rulers began to question why they needed to listen to a distant authority in Rome or Vienna.

> One important thing to keep in mind is that on the AP European History Exam, you are not looking for absolute religious truths. So, when dealing with religious questions, leave your personal beliefs at the door and think as a historian.

Problems Facing the Church on the Eve of the Reformation

It is important for the student of the sixteenth-century Reformation to remember that the Reformation is far more than just the story of **Martin Luther** (1483–1546). While Luther is a central figure in the story, to reduce it simply to his own struggles against the Catholic Church oversimplifies what is actually a complex and compelling story.

The Church was facing significant problems on the eve of the Reformation. Some of these problems resulted from the crisis of the fourteenth century, when the **Black Death**, a ferocious outbreak of plague, struck the population of Europe. These problems included a growing **anticlericalism**—a measure of disrespect toward the clergy, stemming in part from what many perceived to be the poor performance of individual clergymen during the crisis years of the plague. Geoffrey Chaucer's *The Canterbury Tales* and Boccaccio's *The Decameron* reveal some of the satirical edge with which literate society now greeted clergymen. Additionally, this period witnessed a rise in **pietism**, or the notion of a direct relationship between the individual and God, thereby reducing the importance of the hierarchical Church based in Rome. The fourteenth century was undoubtedly a disaster for the Church, with the papacy under French dominance in the city of Avignon for almost 70 years. It was further damaged by the **Great Schism**, which for a time resulted in three competing popes excommunicating each other.

Other problems on the eve of the Reformation included a poorly educated lower clergy. Peasant priests, who in many cases knew just a bit of Latin, proved to be unable to put forward a learned response to Luther's challenge to their Church. **Simony**, the selling of church offices, was another considerable problem, as was the fact that some clergy held multiple positions, thus making them less than effective in terms of ministering to their flocks.

In response to some of these problems, a number of movements arose in the late Middle Ages that would be declared heretical by the Church. In England, **John Wycliffe** (1329–1384) questioned the worldly wealth of the Church, the miracle of transubstantiation, the teachings of penance, and, in a foretaste of the ideas of Luther, the selling of indulgences. Wycliffe urged his followers (known for unclear reasons as the **Lollards**) to read the Bible and to interpret it themselves. To aid in this task, Wycliffe translated the Bible into English.

In Bohemia (the modern-day Czech Republic), **Jan Hus** (1369–1415) led a revolt that combined religious and nationalistic elements. Hus, the rector of the University of Prague, argued that it was the authority of the Bible and not the institutional church that ultimately mattered. Like Wycliffe, he was horrified by what he saw as the immoral behavior of the clergy. This antagonism toward the clergy and its special role in administering the sacraments led Hus to argue that the congregation should be given the cup during the mass as well as the wafer, something that only clergymen were allowed. Hus was called before the **Council of Constance** in 1415 by **Pope Martin V**, and although he was promised safe passage, he was condemned as a heretic and burnt at the stake. In response, his followers in Bohemia staged a rebellion, which took many years to put down.

Luther and Indulgences
One of Martin Luther's main criticisms of the Catholic Church was the selling of indulgences, which the papacy claimed released the buyer from purgatory into heaven. Luther pointed to this practice as a sign of the Church's corruption. The term "preaching an indulgence" refers to a practice of ministers by which they would peddle the sale of indulgences in their sermons.

Martin Luther

The initial issue that first brought attention to Martin Luther (1483–1546) was the debate over indulgences. The **selling of indulgences** was a practice that began during the time of the Crusades. To convince knights to go on crusades and to raise money, the papacy sold indulgences, which released the buyer from **purgatory**. Eventually, long after the crusading movement had ended, the Church began to grant indulgences as a means of filling its treasury. In 1517, **Albert of Hohenzollern**, who already held two bishoprics, was offered the Archbishopric of Mainz. He had to raise 10,000 ducats, so he borrowed the money from the great banking family of the age—the **Fuggers**. To pay off his debt, the papacy granted him permission to raise money from the preaching of an indulgence, with half of the money going directly to Rome, where the papacy was in the midst of a program to finally complete St. Peter's Basilica. **Johann Tetzel**, a Dominican friar, was sent to preach the indulgence throughout Germany with the famous phrase "As soon as gold in the basin rings, right then the soul to heaven springs."

Luther was horrified by the behavior of Tetzel and tacked up his *95 Theses* on the Castle Church at **Wittenberg**, which was the medieval way of indicating that an issue should be debated. Part of Luther's complaints dealt with German money going to Rome. Another major point involved control over purgatory. If the pope had control over it, Luther wondered, why didn't he allow everyone out? Luther believed that a pope could only remit penalties that he himself had placed on someone. Therefore, the pope had no right to sell misleading indulgences.

In a reflection of the power of the printing press, the *95 Theses* were quickly printed all over Germany. At first, the papacy was not concerned. **Pope Leo X** reportedly said he was not interested in a squabble between monks. The Dominicans wanted to charge Luther with heresy, but Luther soon found himself with a large number of supporters.

Luther began to move in a more radical direction. In part, a great deal of his attack on the Church was based on his own fears that he was unworthy of salvation. Back in 1505, he was caught in a thunderstorm and a bolt of lightning struck near him. He cried out, "St. Anne help me; I will become a monk." Luther kept his promise and joined the Augustinian order. However, Luther was dissatisfied leading the life of a monk. In later years, he claimed that if any monk could have been saved by what he termed "monkery," it was he:

> Though I lived as a monk without reproach, I felt that I was a sinner before God with an extremely disturbed conscience. I could not believe that He was placated by my satisfaction. I did not love, yes, I hated the righteous God who punishes sinners, and I was angry with God.

Still troubled, Luther went on to be appointed Professor of Scriptures in Wittenburg in Electoral Saxony (northern Germany).

Following the publication of his *95 Theses*, Luther engaged in a public debate on these issues in Leipzig, where **John Eck**, a prominent theologian, challenged him.

Eck then called Luther a Hussite, while Luther claimed that Hus had been unjustly condemned at the Council of Constance. After this debate, Luther spent the year 1520 writing three of his most important political tracts.

1) In his *Address to the Christian Nobility*, he urged that secular government had the right to reform the Church.
2) In *On the Babylonian Captivity of the Church*, Luther attacked other teachings of the Church, such as the sacraments.
3) Finally, in *Liberty of a Christian Man*, he hit on what would become the basic elements of Lutheran belief: Grace is the sole gift of God; therefore, one is saved by faith alone, and the Bible is the sole source of this faith.

In response to these works, Pope Leo X finally decided he had to act. He issued a papal bull (an official decree) that demanded that Luther recant the ideas found in his writings or be burnt as a heretic. In a highly symbolic gesture, Luther publicly burned the bull to show that he no longer accepted papal authority. In turn, the pope excommunicated Luther.

Luther was fortunate in that, unlike Hus, he had some important patrons. Some North German princes, such as **Frederick the Elector of Saxony**, were either sympathetic to Luther's ideas or at least wanted him to be given a public hearing. To that end, in 1521 Luther appeared before the **Diet of Worms**, a meeting of the German nobility. In one of the most famous scenes in history, Luther was asked by **Charles V, the Holy Roman Emperor**, "Do you or do you not repudiate your books and the errors they contain?" Luther began to answer with a quivering voice but then gathered his courage and said:

> Unless I am convicted by Scripture and plain reason—I do not accept the authority of popes and councils, for they have contradicted each other—my conscience is captive to the Word of God. I cannot and I will not recant anything, for to go against conscience is neither right nor safe. God help me. Amen.

In response, Luther was placed under the ban of the Empire but was safely hidden over the next year in Wartburg Castle by the Elector of Saxony. In the castle, Luther continued to write prolifically and finished some of his most important works, including a translation of the Bible into German.

Since he now considered papal authority to be a human invention, Luther and his friend Philip Melanchthon decided to form a new church based on his revolutionary ideas free from papal control. Instead of the seven **sacraments** of the Catholic Church (Marriage, Ordination, Extreme Unction, Confirmation, Penance, Communion, Baptism), he reduced them to two—baptism and communion. Luther changed the meaning of the latter (also called the Holy Eucharist) by rejecting the Catholic idea of **transubstantiation**, the miraculous transformation of the bread and wine into the flesh and blood of Christ, an act that could be performed only by an ordained priest. Instead, Luther claimed that Christ was already present in the sacrament. Luther also did away with the practice of monasticism and the insistence on the celibacy of the clergy. He himself went on to have a happy marriage with a former nun with whom he had several children.

Why Did the Reformation Succeed?

The Origins of the Term *Protestantism*

The term today is used very broadly and means any non-Catholic or non-Eastern Orthodox Christian. Initially, it referred to a group of Lutherans who in 1529 attended the Diet of Speyer in an attempt to work out a compromise with the Catholic Church and ended up "protesting" the final document that was drawn up at its conclusion.

Within three decades after Luther posted his *95 Theses*, **Protestantism** had spread to many of the states of northern Germany, Scandinavia, England, Scotland, and parts of the Netherlands, France, and Switzerland. There are a number of possible explanations for its phenomenal success.

Luther and the church that he founded were socially conservative and therefore not a threat to the existing social order. Luther's conservatism can be seen clearly in the **German Peasants' Revolt** of 1525. The revolt was the result of the German peasants' worsening economic conditions and their belief, articulated in the **Twelve Articles**, that Luther's call for a **"priesthood of all believers"** was a message of social egalitarianism. It certainly was not. The revolt and the distortion of his ideas horrified Luther. He published a violently angry tract entitled "Against the Robbing and Murderous Hordes of Peasants," in which he urged that no mercy be shown to the revolutionaries.

Another reason Luther's movement was allowed to grow was that Luther was willing to subordinate his church to the authority of the German princes. As his response to the Peasants' Revolt shows, political questions were not of great importance to Luther, who felt that what occurred on this Earth was secondary to what truly mattered—the Kingdom of Heaven. He was not critical of the German princes who created state churches under their direct control. Luther also encouraged German princes to confiscate the lands of the Catholic Church, and many rulers did not have to be asked twice, in part because one-quarter of all land in the Holy Roman Empire was under Church control.

Political issues within the Holy Roman Empire produced turmoil. When the **Emperor Maximilian** died in 1519, his grandson and heir **Charles V** was caught in a struggle with the French King **Francis I** to see who would sit on the imperial throne. Although Charles V was able to muster enough bribe money, borrowed from the Fuggers, to convince the rulers of the electoral states to select him, he was ultimately unable to effectively control his empire. Also, as ruler of a vast multinational empire that included Spain and its possessions in the New World, the Netherlands, southern Italy, and the Habsburg possessions in Austria, Charles had huge commitments. He was unable to deal with the revolt in Germany for several critical decades because he was involved in extended wars with France as well as with the powerful **Ottoman Empire** to the east.

In the 1540s, the **Schmalkaldic War** was fought between Charles and some of the Protestant princes. While for a time Charles had the upper hand, by 1555 he was forced to sign the **Peace of Augsburg**. This treaty granted legal recognition of Lutheranism in those territories ruled by a Lutheran ruler, while a Catholic ruler ensured that the territory remained Catholic.

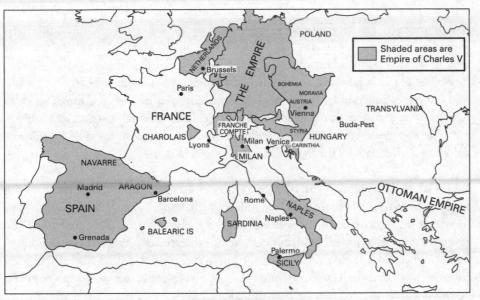

The Empire of Charles V

Radical Reformation

Historians sometimes use the term **"Radical Reformation"** to describe a variety of religious sects that developed during the sixteenth century, inspired in part by Luther's challenge to the established Church. Many felt that Luther's Reformation did not go far enough in bringing about a moral transformation of society.

One such group was the **Anabaptists**, who upon reading the Bible, began to deny the idea of infant baptism. Instead they believed that baptism works only when it is practiced by adults who are fully aware of the decision they are making. Eventually, rebaptism, as the practice became known, was declared a capital offense throughout the Holy Roman Empire, something on which both the pope and Luther heartily agreed. Attacks against Anabaptists became even worse following the Anabaptist takeover of the city of Munster in 1534, during which time they attempted to create an Old Testament theocracy in which men were allowed to have multiple wives. Following the capture of Munster by combined Catholic and Protestant armies, Anabaptism moved in the direction of pacifism under the leadership of Menno Simons.

Besides Anabaptists, other groups such as the **Antitrinitarians**, who denied the scriptural validity of the Trinity, were part of the Radical Reformation. Both Catholics and Lutherans hunted down those who held such beliefs.

Zwingli and Calvin

Shortly after the appearance of Luther's *95 Theses*, **Ulrich Zwingli's** (1484–1531) teachings began to make an impact on the residents of the Swiss city of Zurich. Like Luther, Zwingli accused monks of indolence and high living. In 1519, Zwingli specifically rejected the veneration of saints and called for the need to distinguish between their true and fictional accounts. He announced that unbaptized children were not, in fact, damned to eternal hellfire. He questioned the power of excommunication. His most powerful statement, however, was his attack on the claim that tithing was a divine institution. Unlike Luther, however, Zwingli was a strict sacramentarian in that he denied all the sacraments. To him, the Last Supper was a memorial of Christ's death and did not entail, as it did for Luther, the actual presence of Christ. Zwingli was also a Swiss patriot in ways that Luther could not be called a German patriot. Zwingli was far more concerned with this world and called for social reform. He died leading the troops of Zurich against the Swiss Catholic cantons in battle.

John Calvin (1509–1564) was born in France, although he eventually settled in Geneva, Switzerland. His main ideas are found in his *Institutes of the Christian Religion*, in which he argued that grace was bestowed on relatively few individuals, and the rest were consigned to hell. This philosophy of predestination was the cornerstone of his thought, and one that does not make any room for free will. This was contrary to everything that the Catholic Church taught about death. Although many of the Catholic Church's practices, such as the sale of indulgences, were extremely corrupt, the Church also taught that people have the ability to save their souls following death. Calvin preferred for his followers to focus on correct living in earthly matters. He was a strict disciplinarian who did his best to make Geneva the new Jerusalem. He closed all the taverns and inflicted penalties for such crimes as having a gypsy read your fortune.

Calvinism began to spread rapidly in the 1540s and 1550s, becoming the established church in Scotland, while in France—where the Calvinists were known as **Huguenots**—only a significant minority joined. In many ways, it can be said that Calvinism saved the Protestant Reformation, since in the mid-sixteenth century, it was a dynamic Calvinism—rather than the increasingly moribund Lutheranism—that stood in opposition to a newly aggressive Catholic Church during the Catholic Counter-Reformation. It's also worth noting that it was a group of English Calvinists (who were called Puritans) who grew tired of religious harassment from the mainstream Anglican church and fled England to Holland. In the shipbuilding capital of Europe, they saved enough money to build a pair of ships, which they used to sail across the Atlantic Ocean, where they established a new colony in Massachusetts based on religious freedom. Yes, these were the Pilgrims.

THE ENGLISH REFORMATION

The English Reformation was of a different nature—a political act rather than a religious act as in other parts of Europe. **Henry VIII** (reign 1509–1546), the powerful English monarch, was supportive of the Catholic Church. He even criticized Martin Luther in a pamphlet that he wrote, *The Defence of the Seven Sacraments*. Henry was never comfortable with Protestant theology. He did not believe in salvation by faith and saw no need to limit the role of the priest. The story of the English Reformation begins with what became known as the **"King's Great Matter,"** which involved King Henry VIII's attempt to end his marriage to his Spanish wife, **Catherine of Aragon.** Henry had grown concerned that he did not have a male heir, and he began to question whether Catherine's failure to produce sons (a man of his times, he blamed his wife) was a sign of God's displeasure at his marriage to Catherine, who had earlier been married to Henry's deceased older brother. Because the Catholic Church did not recognize divorce, Henry would have to go through the process of getting an annulment. During this time, Henry fell in love with a young woman at his court, **Anne Boleyn,** who virtuously refused to sleep with him unless he made her his queen.

When the papacy showed no signs of granting the annulment, primarily because Catherine was the aunt of the powerful Charles V, Henry decided to take authority into his own hands. Starting in November 1529 and continuing for seven years, he began what became known as the **Reformation Parliament,** which Henry used as a tool to give him ultimate authority on religious matters. This parliament would come to be very useful, since by 1533, Henry was on a short timetable. He had bribed Anne Boleyn into joining him in bed. Three months later she was pregnant and had secretly married Henry, although Henry was still married to Catherine as well. If Henry was to be saved from bigamy, and if his child was to be legitimate, he had only eight months to end his marriage to Catherine. Henry decided the only way to do this was by cutting off the constitutional links that existed between England and the papacy. In April 1533, Parliament enacted a statute known as the **Act in Restraint of Appeals,** which declared that all spiritual cases within the Kingdom were within the King's jurisdiction and authority and not the pope's. A month later, Henry appeared before an English church tribunal headed by the man he selected to be Archbishop of Canterbury. The tribunal declared that his marriage to Catherine was null and void and that Anne Boleyn was his lawfully wedded wife. That September, a child was born, but it was a baby girl, **Elizabeth Tudor,** instead of the boy Henry so desperately wanted. Eventually, Henry would marry a total of six times; his third wife, **Jane Seymour,** provided him with a son, Edward. In 1534, the English Reformation was capped off by the **Act of Supremacy,** which acknowledged the King of England as the Supreme Head of what became known as the Church of England.

While Henry may have been merely interested in creating what we might call Catholicism without the pope—in that he wanted to keep all the aspects of Catholic worship without acknowledging the primacy of the pope—it proved to be difficult to stem the tide of change. Henry himself played a role in this by closing all English monasteries and confiscating their lands. The brief reign of his son **Edward VI** (r. 1547–1553) saw an attempt to institute genuine Protestant theology into the church that Henry had created.

During the similarly short reign of his half-sister **Mary Tudor** (r. 1553–1558), the daughter of Catherine of Aragon and wife of the fanatically Catholic Philip II of Spain, there was an attempt to bring England back into the orbit of the Catholic Church. While succeeding in restoring the formal links between England and the papacy, Mary found that many still held to their Protestant beliefs. To end this heresy, she allowed for several hundred Englishmen to be burnt at the stake, thus earning her the sobriquet "**Bloody Mary**." It was only during the long, successful reign of her half-sister Elizabeth (r. 1558–1603), the daughter of Anne Boleyn, that a final religious settlement was worked out, one in which the Church of England followed a middle-of-the-road Protestant course.

THE COUNTER-REFORMATION

Although it took several decades to be effective, eventually there was a Catholic response to the Protestant Reformation. Initially, historians referred to this movement as the **Counter-Reformation**, although today it is more commonly known as the **Catholic Reformation**. To a certain extent, both labels are appropriate. It was Counter-Reformation in the sense that the Catholic Church was taking steps to counteract some of the successes of the Protestant side. Among these steps was the creation of the notorious **Index of Prohibited Books**, including works by writers such as **Erasmus** and **Galileo**. Also, the medieval institution of the **papal Inquisition** was revived, and individuals who were deemed to be heretics were put to death for their religious beliefs. The term Catholic Reformation is also apt in that the Catholic Church has a long tradition of adjusting to changed conditions, whether it was the papal Reform Movement of the eleventh century or, more recently, the Second Vatican Council of the 1960s.

The centerpiece of the Catholic Reformation was the **Council of Trent** (1545–1563). Unlike the medieval conciliar movement, which sought to place the papacy under the control of a church council or parliament, the Council of Trent was dominated by the papacy and, in turn, enhanced its power. The council took steps to address some of the issues that had sparked the Reformation, including placing limits on simony, the **selling of church offices**. Recognizing that the poorly educated clergy were a major problem, the council mandated that a seminary for the education of clergy should be established in every diocese. The Council of Trent refused to concede any point of theology to the Protestants. Instead they emphatically endorsed their traditional teachings on such matters as the sacraments, the role of priests, and the belief that salvation comes from faith as well as works, and that the source for this faith was the Bible and the traditions of the Church. Although it is incorrect to say that the council created the idea of the **baroque** style of art, the council was critical of what it deemed to be the religious failings of the mannerist style and urged that a more intensely religious art be created, something that did play a role in the development of the early baroque.

Perhaps the greatest reason for the success of the Catholic Reformation was the founding of the **Society of Jesus (Jesuits)** organized by **Ignatius Loyola (1491–1556)**, a Spanish noble who was wounded in battle and spent his recuperation time reading various Catholic tracts. After undergoing a religious conversion, he attempted, not unlike Luther, to reconcile himself to God through austere behavior. He became a hermit but still felt that something was amiss. While Luther, in his search for spiritual contentment, decided that the Bible was the sole source of faith, Loyola believed that even if the Bible did not exist, there was still the spirit.

Loyola's ideas are laid out in his *Spiritual Exercises*; one passage in particular states his belief in total obedience to the Church:

> To arrive at complete certainty, this is the attitude that we should maintain: I will believe that the white object I see is black if that should be the desire of the hierarchical church, for I believe that linking Christ our Lord the Bridegroom and His Bride the church, there is one and the same Spirit, ruling and guiding us for our souls' good. For our Holy Mother the church is guided and ruled by the same Spirit, the Lord who gave the Ten Commandments.

This total and complete loyalty is why the Jesuit order, although at first under suspicion by a cautious papacy uncomfortable with Loyola's mysticism, would be accepted as an official order of the Church in a papal bull in 1540. The Jesuits began to distinguish themselves as a teaching order and also worked as Catholic missionaries in places where Lutheranism had made large inroads. Poland served as a strong example of where Catholicism was re-prosthelitized.

THE PORTUGUESE AND SPANISH EMPIRES

If geography is destiny, then it is not surprising that the Portuguese would look to the sea. Living in a land that was not well suited to farming, the Portuguese had always looked to distant lands for sources of wealth. In 1415, **Prince Henry the Navigator**, a younger son of the King of Portugal, participated in the capture of the North African port of Ceuta from the Muslims. This conquest spurred his interest in Africa. It also inspired him to sponsor a navigational school in Lisbon and a series of expeditions, manned mainly by Italians, which aimed not only to develop trade with Africa but also to find a route to India and the Far East around Africa and thereby cut out the Italian middlemen.

In 1487, a Portuguese captain, **Bartholomew Dias**, sailed around the **Cape of Good Hope** at the tip of Africa. A decade later, in 1498, **Vasco da Gama** reached the coast of India. The Portuguese defeated the Arab fleets that patrolled the Indian Ocean by being the first to successfully mount cannons on their ships and also by deploying their ships in squadrons rather than individually, which gave them a huge tactical advantage. The Portuguese established themselves on the western coast of India and for a while controlled the lucrative spice trade.

With the Portuguese having a head start on the African route to the Indian Ocean, the Spanish decided to try an Atlantic route to the East. **Christopher Columbus**, a Genoese sailor, set sail on August 2, 1492, certain that he would find this eastern route. Although Columbus was not unique in insisting that the world was round, he did believe he would fulfill medieval religious prophesies that spoke of converting the whole world to Christianity. After a thirty-three-day voyage from the Canary Islands, Columbus landed in the eastern Bahamas, which he insisted was an undeveloped part of Asia. He called the territory the "Indies" and the indigenous population "Indians" and noted ominously in his diary that they were friendly and gentle and therefore easy to enslave.

Although Columbus's failure to locate either gold or spices during his voyages was a disappointment, within a generation, others built on Columbus's discoveries. The most important of the journeys was undertaken by **Ferdinand Magellan** in 1519, who set out to circumnavigate the globe. Although Magellan did not live to see the end of his voyage (he died in the Philippines), he did prove that the territory where Columbus landed was not part of the Far East but rather an entirely unknown continent, a continent that the Spanish planned to conquer.

In 1519, **Hernán Cortés** landed on the coast of Mexico with a small force of 600 men. He had arrived at the heart of the **Aztec Empire**, a militaristic state, which through conquest had carved out a large state with a large central capital, **Tenochtitlán** (modern-day Mexico City). The Aztecs were less than popular with the people they conquered, primarily because they practiced human sacrifice to appease their gods. These conquered people felt no loyalty to the Aztec state and were willing to cooperate with the Spanish.

The Aztecs viewed the light-skinned Spaniards, who were riding on horses (unknown at this time in North and South America), wearing armor, and carrying guns, as gods. At first, Montezuma, the Aztec ruler, tried to appease them with gifts of gold. Unfortunately for the Aztecs, this just further whetted the appetite of the Spanish, who seized the capital city and took Montezuma hostage. He died mysteriously while in Spanish captivity. While rebellions against Spanish rule continued, the Aztec ability to fight was sapped by smallpox and other European diseases foreign to the indigenous peoples. By 1521, Cortés declared the former Aztec Empire to be New Spain.

The Spanish also succeeded in destroying another great civilization, the **Inca Empire of Peru**. Like the Aztecs, the Incas had carved out a large empire by conquering and instigating harsh rule over many other tribes. In 1531, **Francisco Pizarro**, a Spanish soldier, set out for Peru with a tiny force of approximately 200 men. Pizarro, following Cortés's brutal example, treacherously captured the Inca Emperor Atahualpa, who then had his subjects raise vast amounts of gold for ransom. By 1533, Pizarro had grown tired of ruling through Atahualpa, and he had him killed. Once again, Western technology and diseases sapped the indigenous population's ability to fight back, and while it took longer for the Spanish to secure their hold over the Inca territories, by the 1560s, they had stamped out the last bit of resistance.

The impact of this age of exploration and conquest was immense, not just for Europe but for the entire globe. The Spanish set out to create *haciendas*, or plantations, to exploit both the agricultural and mineral riches of the land. The indigenous population, compelled to work under a system of forced labor called *encomienda*, continued to die at an incredible pace from both disease and overwork. So to provide labor for their estates, the Spanish and Portuguese began to take captured Africans from their homeland to serve on the farms and in the mines of the **New World**. It has been estimated that by the time the slave trade ended in the early nineteenth century, almost 10 million Africans were abducted from Africa, with countless numbers dying as a result of the inhumane conditions on the difficult overseas passage.

Another consequence of the Spanish and Portuguese empires in the New World was what became known as the Columbian Exchange—the transatlantic transfer of animals, plants, diseases, people, technology, and ideas among Europe, the Americas, and Africa. (See the map on the next page.) As Europeans and Africans crisscrossed the Atlantic, they brought the Old World to the New and back again. From the European and African side of the Atlantic, horses, pigs, goats, chili peppers, and sugarcane (and more) flowed to the Americas. From the American side, squash, beans, corn, potatoes, and cacao (and more) made their way back east. Settlers from the Old World carried bubonic plague, smallpox, typhoid, influenza, and the common cold into the New, then carried Chagas and syphilis back to the Old. Guns, Catholicism, and slaves also crossed the Atlantic. Never before had so much been moved across the oceans, as ship after ship carried the contents of one continent to another.

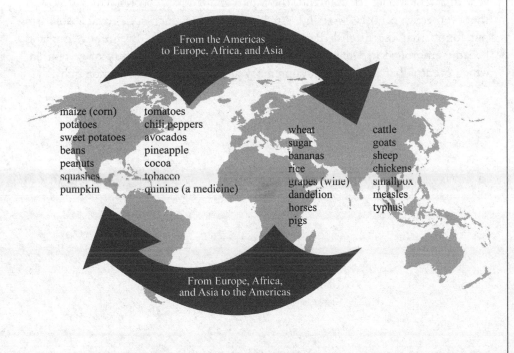

From the Americas to Europe, Africa, and Asia

maize (corn)   tomatoes
potatoes   chili peppers
sweet potatoes   avocados
beans   pineapple
peanuts   cocoa
squashes   tobacco
pumpkin   quinine (a medicine)

wheat   cattle
sugar   goats
bananas   sheep
rice   chickens
grapes (wine) smallpox
dandelion measles
horses   typhus
pigs

From Europe, Africa, and Asia to the Americas

THE DEVELOPMENT OF MONARCHICAL STATES

Tools of statecraft, such as permanent embassies in foreign lands, were first developed in the city-states of Renaissance Italy. Large, unified nation-states began to develop in northern Europe during the early modern period. These city-states ultimately came to dominate the Italian peninsula and contributed to the transition away from the medieval notion of feudal kingship. Prior to the sixteenth century, the king was not an absolute ruler; instead he had to rule with the consent of his great vassals. In the age of the new monarchical state, it was deemed that monarchical power was God-given and therefore by its very nature absolute. Although in the Middle Ages, parliamentary institutions developed throughout Europe as a means of placing limits on kings, in the early modern period, thought shifted. The sixteenth-century French philosopher Jean Bodin wrote of this new style of monarchy:

> It is the distinguishing mark of the sovereign that he cannot in any way
> be subject to the commands of another, for it is he who makes law for
> the subject, abrogates laws already made, and amends absolute law.

The French monarchy is the most important example of how this power shift came about. It was not an easy victory for the French monarchy, which had to deal with assorted aristocratic and religious conflicts that threatened to destroy the state. Eventually, under Louis XIV, France created a centralized monarchy in which the power of the king was absolute, although it came at a high price as it helped pave the way for the late eighteenth-century French Revolution. England serves as a very different model. In England, the Stuart monarchs, who reigned for most of the seventeenth century, were interested in adopting French-style royal absolutism but found that the English Parliament stood in their way. Eventually, England became embroiled in what one historian has labeled as a "century of revolution," which eventually resulted in the supremacy of Parliament over the monarchy.

Be aware of these important characteristics of the new nation-states:

1. Growing Bureaucratization

Across Europe, salaried officials began to depend on the monarchy for their livelihood. In France, the monarchy established the new office of intendant, which employed individuals to collect taxes on behalf of the monarch. Corruption was still a part of this system, as was the practice of buying and selling royal offices to satisfy the short-term financial needs of the monarch. England was the exception to this trend. In England, the older system of cooperation between the crown and its leading subjects continued.

2. Existence of a Permanent Mercenary Army

In the late medieval/early modern periods, a revolution in warfare came about. In the fourteenth century, Swiss mercenary infantrymen lined up in a phalanx of 6,000 men and used their pikes to kill aristocratic horsemen, but by the end of the century, gunpowder further eroded the dominance of the mounted knight and made feudal castles far easier to conquer. The rising cost of warfare, most particularly the need to provide for an army on an annual (as opposed to occasional) basis, played into the hands of the developing monarchical state, which alone could tap into the necessary resources. Again, England was the exception, since it did not establish a permanent army until the end of the seventeenth century when it was firmly under parliamentary control.

3. Growing Need to Tax

This is an instance where 1 + 2 = 3. Countries like France basically faced a vicious circle: Monarchs were in constant need of taxes to pay for their permanent armies, while it was the army that the monarchy needed to ensure control over a rebellious peasantry who resented the high rate of taxation. Traditionally, medieval monarchs were supposed to live off their own incomes, although in the early modern period this was becoming impossible due to the Price Revolution and the increased costs of managing a centralized state.

ITALY

Not every part of Europe followed this process of national consolidation under a centralizing monarchy. The Italian peninsula remained divided throughout this period, and thus it became an easy target for ambitious monarchs of centralized states such as France and Spain.

The **Treaty of Lodi** (1454) had provided for a balance of power among the major Italian city-states. It created an alliance between long-term enemies Milan and Naples and also included the support of Florence. Their combined strength was enough to ensure that outside powers would stay out of Italian affairs. This system came to an end in 1490, when **Ludovico il Moro**, upon becoming despot of Milan, initiated hostilities with Naples and then four years later invited the French into Italy to allow them to satisfy their long-standing claims to Naples. **Charles VIII**, the King of France, didn't have to be asked twice; he immediately ordered his troops across the Italian Alps.

Charles and his forces crossed into Florence, where a radical Dominican preacher, **Savonarola** (1452–1498), had just led the Florentine population in expelling the **Medici** rulers and then had established a puritanical state. This complete religious and political transformation of the city marked the end of Florence's leading role in Renaissance scholarship and art. Eventually, by 1498, Ludovico il Moro recognized the folly of what he had wrought and joined an anti-French Italian alliance that ultimately succeeded not only in expelling the French but also in restoring the Medici in Florence. The Medici promptly burnt Savonarola at the stake with the support of the papacy, which hated the Dominican friar because of his pre-Lutheran call for a complete overhaul of the Church, including the institution of the papacy.

The damage to the independence of the Italian city-states had already been done. Throughout the sixteenth century, Italy became the battlefield in which Spain and France fought for dominance. The collapse of Italian independence was the historical context in which **Niccolò Machiavelli** wrote what is generally seen as the first work of modern political thought, *The Prince* (1513). Machiavelli had happily served his beloved Florentine Republic as a diplomat and official in the chancellery. When the Republic was overthrown by the Medici, Machiavelli was forced into exile to his country estate. *The Prince* is a résumé of sorts in which Machiavelli tried to convince the Medici to partake of his services. Although some scholars have debated whether he was serious about his ideas, it does appear that Machiavelli was genuinely horrified by the increasing foreign domination of the Italian peninsula and believed that only a strong leader using potentially ruthless means could unify Italy and expel the foreigners.

ENGLAND

The Tudors

England had achieved a measure of unity under a centralized monarchy in the medieval period, well before its continental counterparts. The fifteenth-century **Wars of the Roses** (commonly known to us, although a bit inaccurately, through the plays of Shakespeare) were not aristocratic attempts to break the power of the monarchy but rather a series of civil wars to determine which aristocratic faction, York or Lancaster, would dominate the monarchy. In the end, it was a junior member of the Lancastrian family, **Henry Tudor (Henry VII)**, who won central authority in England when he established the Tudor dynasty following his defeat of Richard III in 1485 at the battle of Bosworth Field.

Following the death of his autocratic father in 1509, **Henry VIII** became king and maintained his father's policies to strengthen the crown. The near total decimation of aristocratic opponents during the Wars of the Roses and an expanding economy, which benefited the Tudor dynasty throughout the sixteenth century, helped the King to restore royal authority. Henry created a small but efficient bureaucracy that made the King's intentions known throughout the land. Henry, however, believed that his sovereignty would not be manifest so long as England was under the religious leadership of the papacy. In 1534, he made a political—not a religious—decision when he broke with Rome and created the Church of England. Although their tenures on the throne were short and full of religious tension, Henry VIII's children, Edward VI and Mary Tudor, enjoyed the benefits of the restored prestige of the monarchy, which resulted from the efforts of Henry VII and Henry VIII.

The greatest of all the Tudors was **Queen Elizabeth** (r. 1558–1603), Henry VIII's daughter with **Anne Boleyn**. Elizabeth was an intelligent woman who had been educated in the Italian humanist program of classical studies. She was a diligent worker and had excellent political instincts like her father. Also like her father, Elizabeth knew how to select able ministers who would serve the crown with distinction—men such as William Cecil (Lord Burghley)—but she always kept herself as the ultimate decision maker in the land. Elizabeth used the prospect of marriage as a diplomatic tool and allowed almost every single ruler in Europe to imagine that he could possibly marry her—a powerful way to build alliances whenever the need arose. Whether she truly was the **"Virgin Queen"** is a question that no one—not even the wise folks who write the questions for the AP exam—could ever answer. She did seem to regard marriage as incompatible with her sovereignty. Yet by staying single, she exposed England to the risk of religious war, since as long as she remained single, the Catholic **Mary Stuart**, the ruler of Scotland, was her legal heir.

The relationship between England and Scotland was a complex affair that continued to plague both lands throughout the sixteenth and seventeenth centuries. For years, Mary lived as Elizabeth's prisoner, following a rebellion by Scottish nobles that forced her from the throne. Elizabeth treated Mary as the rightful ruler of Scotland and the probable heir to the English crown, though she kept her under house arrest because she feared that Mary was plotting against her. Only after Mary conspired with Philip II of Spain did Elizabeth decide to settle relations with the Scots and distance herself from Mary. In the Treaty of Berwick in 1586, she entered into a defensive alliance with Scotland; she recognized James, Mary's son who was being raised as a Protestant, as the lawful king; gave him an English pension; and while she never specifically said so, let it be known that James was the heir to her throne. In 1587, Elizabeth finally took a step that she had been reluctant to take: She ordered the execution of **Mary, Queen of Scots**.

In 1588 came the greatest moment in Elizabeth's reign—the defeat of Philip II's **Spanish Armada**, which ensured that England would remain Protestant and free from foreign dominance. Although at least part of Elizabeth's authority gradually eroded as she grew older and people began to look beyond her reign to the future, the decades that followed the Armada conquest were also a period of an incredible cultural flourishing. This was the age of **Shakespeare**, **Christopher Marlowe**, **Ben Jonson**, and **Edmund Spenser**; and while Elizabeth may not have been a significant direct patron of this **English Renaissance**, the stability that she provided England during her reign allowed it to take place.

SPAIN

Prior to the fifteenth century, Spain was divided into several Christian kingdoms in the north, while the south had been under Islamic control since the eighth century. The 1469 marriage of **Ferdinand, King of Aragon**, and **Isabella, Queen of Castile**, laid the groundwork for the eventual consolidation of the peninsula, with the final stage of the *Reconquista* taking place in 1492, when their armies conquered the last independent Islamic outpost in Spain—the southern city of Grenada. The same year also marks the beginning of a new wave of religious bigotry, as the ardently Catholic Ferdinand and Isabella began to demand religious uniformity in their lands and formally expelled the Jewish population that had been established in Spain since the time of the Roman Empire. Those Jews and Moors who converted so they could remain in Spain were later hounded by the **Spanish Inquisition**, an effective method that the Spanish monarchy would later use to root out suspected Protestants.

Through a series of well-planned marriages, Ferdinand and Isabella's grandson, **Charles V,** eventually controlled a vast empire that dominated Europe in the first half of the sixteenth century. His Spanish possessions were the primary source of his wealth and also supplied him with the tough Castilian foot soldiers who were the best in Europe. When Charles V—exhausted from his struggles to destroy Protestantism in the Holy Roman Empire—abdicated in 1556, he gave his brother **Ferdinand** (whom he disliked intensely) the troublesome eastern Habsburg lands of Austria, Bohemia, and Hungary as well as his title of Holy Roman Emperor, while Charles's son **Philip** (r. 1556–1598) received the more valuable part of the empire—Spain and its vast holdings in the New World, along with southern Italy and the Netherlands.

Philip gained a vast wealth from the New World's silver mines. Yet surprisingly, Philip spent most of his reign in debt as he used his riches to maintain Spanish influence. In the Mediterranean, the Spanish fought for supremacy against the Ottoman Empire and won a notable success against that eastern power at the **Battle of Lepanto** in 1571. In northern Europe, however, Philip was caught in a quagmire when he attempted to put down a revolt in the Netherlands. This revolt combined religious and nationalistic ideas, as did the whole Reformation, and began in 1568 following an attempt by Philip to impose the doctrines of the Council of Trent and the Inquisition in a land where Calvinism had made significant inroads, particularly among key members of the aristocracy. For the next several decades, Philip expended huge amounts of money to try to restore Spanish control. Inquisition-based efforts such as the **Duke of Alva's Council of Troubles** (aka the "Council of Blood") failed, as did the effort of military hero **Don Juan**. It was for this reason that Philip launched the great **Spanish Armada** in 1588 as an attempt to conquer England, which, under Queen Elizabeth's rule, was aiding the Dutch rebels. By 1609, an exhausted Spain conceded virtual independence to the northern provinces of the Netherlands (while still maintaining control over the southern part of the country) and in 1648 formally acknowledged their independence.

THE HOLY ROMAN EMPIRE

The Holy Roman Empire, a large "state" that straddled central Europe, can be said to date back to 962, when the Saxon King Otto I was crowned emperor in Rome by the pope. In the late-tenth and eleventh centuries, the Empire was the most powerful state in Europe, but it was eventually weakened as a result of a series of conflicts with the papacy. While lacking the soldiers to stem the ambitions of the Holy Roman emperors, successive popes were able to find support among the German nobility, who chafed under strong imperial leadership. By 1356, the practice of electing the emperor was formally defined in the **Golden Bull** of **Emperor Charles IV**. This document, which granted to seven German princes the right to elect an emperor, made it clear that the emperor held office by election rather than hereditary right. The electors usually chose weak rulers who would not stand in the way of their own political ambitions.

In the ensuing centuries, the empire continued to splinter into numerous semi-autonomous territorial states so that by 1500 it consisted of more than 300 semi-autonomous entities over which the emperor ruled but had very little actual authority. Charles V, the powerful Habsburg (also spelled Hapsburg) ruler who was elected emperor in 1519, attempted to establish genuine imperial control over the state. He soon found that the Lutheran Reformation provided a new weapon for those German princes and cities that wanted to avoid losing their independence.

Golden Age in Spain

The sixteenth and early seventeenth centuries were a cultural golden age that featured the writings of **Cervantes** (1547–1616), possibly Spain's greatest writer, whose masterpiece, *Don Quixote*, bemoans the passing of the traditional values of chivalry in Spain. It was also a period of remarkable Spanish painters such as the Greek-born **El Greco** (1541–1614), whose magnificent yet somber works reveal much about a Spain that appeared to have it all, only to find it could not maintain its preeminent European position. In fact, the golden age of Spain did prove to be short-lived. The constant wars, the effects of the **Price Revolution**, and the economic collapse of the Castilian economy led to a decline in Spain's power by the end of the seventeenth century.

The **Peace of Augsburg** (1555) signified the end of the religious wars in the time of Charles V, who now agreed to adhere to the basic principle that the prince decides the religion of the territory. The treaty, however, did not grant recognition to Calvinists, thus creating a problem when **Frederick III**, the ruler of the Palatinate, (a region in southwest Germany) converted to Calvinism in 1559. What further complicated the situation was that as the ruler of the Palatinate, Frederick was one of the seven electors of the Holy Roman Emperor.

Within the next two decades, several other German princes followed Frederick's lead and aggressively challenged the religious status quo achieved by the Peace of Augsburg. The tremendous success of the Catholic Counter-Reformation in Southern Germany further stoked religious tensions in Germany.

In areas such as Bavaria, all traces of Protestantism were stamped out as Jesuits were invited to take charge of Bavarian schools and universities. Although Charles V failed in his attempt to create a unified German state, the dream would continue. The **Thirty Years' War (1618–1648)**, a struggle that combined political and religious issues, marked one final attempt within the Holy Roman Empire to make that dream a reality.

The Thirty Years' War (1618–1648)

The Thirty Years' War began in **Bohemia** (the modern-day Czech Republic), where in 1617 Ferdinand of Styria, an avid Catholic, was crowned King of Bohemia. The majority of Bohemians were Protestant, and they were angered with their new King Ferdinand's intolerance toward their religious beliefs. In May of 1618, a large group of Bohemian Protestant nobles surrounded two of Ferdinand's Catholic advisors and threw them out of a window (the second Defenestration of Prague). They survived by landing in a dung heap. The next year, Matthias, the Holy Roman Emperor, passed away, and his cousin Ferdinand, the King of Bohemia, was elected Emperor in his stead. A few hours after being elected, Ferdinand learned to his horror that rebels in Bohemia had deposed him and elected **Frederick**, the **Calvinist Elector of the Palatinate**, as their king. Since he did not have an army, Ferdinand had to turn to the Duke of Bavaria, who agreed to lend his support in exchange for the electoral right enjoyed by the Palatinate. At the **Battle of White Mountain**, the Bavarian forces won a major victory, and Frederick became known as the Winter King since he held onto the Bohemian throne for only that season. By 1622, he had lost not only Bohemia but also the Palatinate.

The question now arises as to why the Thirty Years' War didn't end in 1622 (and force historians to give it a different name). Part of the problem was that there were still private armies throughout the Empire that wanted to fight to keep earning a living. The perceived threat to Protestants in Germany drew outsiders, such as the King of Denmark, into the fight. Additionally, both Catholic and Protestant rulers were concerned that the traditional constitution of the Holy Roman Empire had been dramatically altered when the Palatinate's electoral vote was given to Bavaria. Taking away this vote from the Palatinate was deemed an attack on what contemporaries called "German liberties," by which they meant the independence and political rights enjoyed by territories within the Holy Roman Empire.

This issue of liberties also came to the foreground when Emperor Ferdinand confiscated defeated Protestant princes' land in the north and created the genuine opportunity to forge a unified state under Habsburg control. Given this opportunity, Ferdinand first had to find a new army, since he could no longer rely on the Duke of Bavaria, who began to fear Habsburg domination. He turned to a Bohemian noble by the name of **Albrecht von Wallenstein** for this second phase of the war, who promised to create a vast mercenary army. By 1628, Wallenstein controlled an army of 125,000 and had won a series of major victories in the north.

The high-water mark for Habsburg success in the Thirty Years' War came with the **Edict of Restitution** of 1629. The edict outlawed Calvinism in the empire and required Lutherans to turn over all property seized since 1552—16 bishoprics, 28 cities and towns, and 155 monasteries and convents. This led the King of Sweden, **Gustavus Adolphus,** to enter the war, triggering a third phase. Although he claimed that he became involved to defend Protestant rights in Germany, Adolphus was also interested in German territory along the Baltic. To make matters even more confusing, the French government financially supported the Swedish army, because France's chief minister, **Cardinal Richelieu,** was concerned about the increase of Habsburg strength in Germany. Clearly this skirmish had ignited far beyond a religious war.

The Swedes rolled back the Habsburgs until 1632, when Adolphus died in battle. The next year, Wallenstein was murdered on orders of the emperor, since Ferdinand began to fear that his general was negotiating with his opponents. The final phase of the war consisted of the French and Swedes fighting against the Austrian Habsburgs and their Spanish allies. This was the most destructive phase of the war; German towns were decimated, and a general agricultural collapse and famine ensued. By the end of the war in 1648, the Empire had eight million fewer inhabitants than it had in 1618.

The **Peace of Westphalia** (1648) marked the end of the struggle. Thirty years of war had brought about very little. The Holy Roman Empire maintained its numerous political divisions, and the treaty ensured that the Emperor would remain an ineffectual force within German politics. The treaty also reaffirmed the Augsburg formula of each prince deciding the religion of his own territory, although the new formula now fully recognized Calvinism.

The Cost of War
By the end of the Thirty Years' War in 1648, the Empire's population had decreased by about eight million.

FRANCE

By the end of the reign of the powerful **Francis I**, it appeared as if the struggle between the feudal aristocracy and the monarchy had been settled in favor of the newly powerful centralized monarchy. However, the **French Wars of Religion** (1562–1598) revealed that the struggle was not quite over. Although ostensibly concerned with religious ideas, this series of civil wars was part of a long tradition, dating back to the very roots of French history, in which the aristocracy and monarchy battled one another for supremacy.

French Calvinists
In France, Calvinists were known as Huguenots.

In part because Calvin himself was French, Calvinism had made early inroads in France. Religious conflicts rose to the surface following the French monarch Henry II's 1559 death when his eye was pierced with a lance in a jousting accident while celebrating the end of the wars between the Habsburgs and the French Valois monarchs. On Henry's death, his sickly fifteen-year-old son Francis II came to the throne, only to be replaced the next year by his brother, who reigned as Charles IX (r. 1560–1574) and then fourteen years later by a second brother, the last of the Valois kings, Henry III (r. 1574–1589). All three boys would be dominated by their mother, one of the most remarkable women of the age, **Catherine de' Medici**.

Behind the scenes of the French monarchy, a power struggle began to emerge among three prominent families. The rise of the nation-state in France had contributed to a decline in the power of the old aristocratic families. These three families hoped that with a weak monarch on the throne they could reverse this trend. The **Guises**, the most powerful of the three, turned toward a militant, reactionary form of Catholicism. Meanwhile, partly through religious convictions and partly out of political opportunism, **Admiral Coligny**, the leader of the Montmorency family, and the **Prince of Conde**, the leading Bourbon, both converted to Calvinism.

The Wars of Religion began in 1562 when the Duke of Guise was infuriated to see a group of Huguenots worshipping in a barn and had them killed. After ten years of combat, in which both the Duke of Guise and the Prince of Conde were killed, the Huguenots had the upper hand. As a sign of this Calvinist ascendancy, **Henry of Navarre**, a young Bourbon prince, married King Charles IX's sister. The political eclipse of the Valois family greatly concerned Catherine de' Medici, who, although not the religious bigot of legend, constantly sought to balance out the power of the aristocratic families to protect the interest of her sons. When the cream of the Huguenot aristocracy gathered in Paris in 1572 to celebrate the wedding, Catherine encouraged her son the king to set in motion the **St. Bartholomew's Day Massacre,** in which an estimated 3,000 died in Paris. Possibly 20,000 Huguenots in total were killed in organized attacks throughout France. Admiral Coligny was killed, but Henry of Navarre's life was spared when he promised to return to Catholicism.

In 1574, Henry III, the last of the Valois kings, turned to the Huguenots to defeat the powerful Catholic League that the Guise family had formed to serve their interests. He eventually made Henry of Navarre his heir and in 1589, following the assassination of Henry III, Henry became **King Henry IV**, thus beginning the **Bourbon** dynasty that would rule France up to the time of the French Revolution. Above all else, the new King wanted peace in his kingdom. Faced with a struggle with Spain, a nation that sought to keep France both politically weak and Catholic, and because most Parisians remained fiercely Catholic, Henry IV—having switched numerous times for political reasons between Calvinism and Catholicism—in 1593 converted permanently to Catholicism. He marked this occasion with the noteworthy words: "Paris is worth a Mass."

In many ways, Henry's actions instigated a new way of thinking in France, the idea of the *Politique*, putting the interests of France before the goal of religious unity. Although his Calvinist allies and the Anglican Queen Elizabeth were horrified by Henry's final religious conversion, he did not forget them. In 1598, he issued the **Edict of Nantes**, granting the Huguenots freedom of worship and assembly as well as the right to maintain fortified towns for their protection.

CHAPTER 4 TIMELINE

Just before the Review Questions at the end of each chapter, you'll find a time-line of events for the relevant period. The timeline below includes events not only mentioned in this chapter, but also events discussed in the next chapter. This is due to the overlap in time frames between chapters. Use the timelines as quick reviews of key events; don't obsess over memorizing every date.

Year(s)	Event
1341	Petrarch crowned Poet Laureate in Rome
1378	Ciompi Revolt
1378	Black Death hits Europe
1387	Chaucer starts *The Canterbury Tales*
1397	Establishment of the Medici Bank
1403	Alberti begins work on the doors of the baptistery in Florence
1405	Christine de Pisan's *City of Ladies*
1406	Florence conquers Pisa
1415	Burning at the stake of Jan Hus at the Council of Constance
1415	Prince Henry the Navigator participates in capture of Ceuta in northwestern Africa
1417	Great Schism comes to an end
1420s	Development of single-point perspective
1440	Lorenzo Valla's *On the Donation of Constantine*
1440s	Donatello's *David*
1452	Gutenberg prints Bible
1453	End of the Hundred Years War
1453	Fall of Constantinople
1454	Treaty of Lodi
1469	Marriage of Ferdinand of Aragon to Isabella of Castile

1485	Henry VII begins Tudor dynasty following Battle of Bosworth
1486	Pico's *Oration on the Dignity of Man*
1487	Bartholomew Dias sails around Cape of Good Hope
1490	Ludovico il Moro becomes despot of Milan
1492	Columbus leaves Spain for what he believes will be Asia
1492	Expulsion of the Jews from Spain
1492	*Reconquista* of Spain completed
1492	Lorenzo de Medici dies
1494	King Charles VIII of France invades Italy
1494	The Treaty of Tordesillas divides the discoveries in the New World between Spain and Portugal
1498	Vasco da Gama reaches the coast of India
1498	Burning of Savonarola
1501	Michelangelo's *David*
1503	Leonardo's *Mona Lisa*
1509	Raphael's *School of Athens*
1513	Machiavelli writes *The Prince*
1515	Erasmus' *In Praise of Folly*
1516	More's *Utopia*
1517	Luther's *95 Theses*
1519	Charles V becomes Holy Roman Emperor
1519	Ferdinand Magellan sets out to circumnavigate the globe
1519	Hernán Cortés lands on the coast of Mexico
1521	Luther called before the Diet of Worms
1522	Ignatius Loyola begins *The Spiritual Exercises*

1525	German Peasant Revolt
1528	Castiglione's *The Courtier*
1529	Diet of Speyer
1529	Henry VIII summons the "Reformation Parliament"
1531	Zwingli dies in battle
1531	Francisco Pizarro sets out for Peru
1534	Henry VIII's Act of Supremacy
1534	Anabaptists seize Munster
1535	Sir Thomas More executed by Henry VIII
1536	Calvin publishes first edition of his *Institutes*
1540	Jesuits receive official papal sanction as religious order
1540	Henry VIII marries Anne Boleyn
1540s	Schmalkaldic War
1543	Copernicus publishes his *Concerning the Revolutions of the Celestial Spheres*
1543	Andreas Vesalius writes *De humani corporis fabrica* with its critique of the anatomical work of Galen
1545	Council of Trent convenes
1553	End of reign of Edward VI of England
1553	Michael Servetus burnt at the stake in Geneva
1555	Peace of Augsburg
1556	Philip II becomes King of Spain after Charles V abdicates
1558	Death of Queen Mary of England
1558	Beginning of reign of Elizabeth Tudor
1559	Frederick III of the Palatinate converts to Calvinism

1559	Death of King Henry II of France
1559	Elizabethan religious settlement
1562	Beginning of the French Wars of Religion
1571	Battle of Lepanto
1572	St. Bartholomew's Day Massacre during the French Wars of Religion
1587	Execution of Mary, Queen of Scots
1588	Failure of the Spanish Armada to invade England
1589	Henry Bourbon becomes King Henry IV
1593	Henry IV converts to Catholicism
1598	Edict of Nantes
1600	Giordano Bruno burned at the stake
1602	First known performance of Shakespeare's *Hamlet*
1602	Dutch East India Company established
1603	James I becomes king following death of Elizabeth
1603	Michael Romanov begins new dynasty in Russia
1605	Cervantes publishes first part of *Don Quixote*
1607	Founding colony at Jamestown
1610	Assassination of Henry IV
1610	Galileo begins astronomical observations with his telescope
1613	Galileo publishes *Letters on Sunspots*
1616	William Harvey announces his discovery of the circulatory system
1618	Johannes Kepler reveals his third and final law of planetary motion
1618	Beginning of the Thirty Years' War
1620	Battle of White Mountain
1620	Founding of Plymouth Colony

1620	Francis Bacon publishes *Novum Organum*
1624	Cardinal Richelieu becomes Louis XIII's chief minister
1625	Charles I becomes king upon death of James I
1628	Petition of Right
1628	Murder of the Duke at Buckingham
1629	Edict of Restitution
1629	Personal Rule of Charles I begins and will last eleven years
1632	Gustavus Adolphus dies at the Battle of Lutzen
1632	Galileo's *Dialogue on the Two Chief Systems of the World*
1633	Trial of Galileo
1633	Murder of Albrecht von Wallenstein
1637	Charles introduces the Book of Common Prayer into Scotland
1637	René Descartes publishes *Discourse on the Mind*
1640	Beginning of the reign of Frederick William (Great Elector)
1640	Charles forced to summon Parliament to deal with Scottish revolt
1641	Rebellion in Ireland
1642	Execution of the Earl of Strafford
1642	Issuing of Grand Remonstrance
1642	Beginning of English Revolution
1643	Five-year-old Louis XIV becomes King of France
1645	Execution of Archbishop Laud
1648	Peace of Westphalia

CHAPTER 4 REVIEW QUESTIONS

Try these questions to assess how well you understood and retained the information covered in the chapter. Answers and explanations are in Chapter 8.

1. Humanist scholars broke with the medieval scholarly tradition

   (A) in declaring that all knowledge was relative
   (B) by insisting on reading original manuscripts and not second-hand commentaries
   (C) by challenging the existence of God
   (D) by supporting the idea of scientific experimentation

2. All of the following are characteristics of Renaissance art EXCEPT

   (A) the emphasis on naturalism
   (B) artists' desire to create three-dimensional images
   (C) secular portraiture
   (D) hierarchical scaling

3. What was the initial reaction of Pope Leo X to the posting of Luther's *95 Theses*?

   (A) He immediately summoned Luther to Rome.
   (B) He recalled Tetzel from Germany in order to have him stop selling indulgences.
   (C) He declared that Luther's action was a significant threat to the unity of the Church.
   (D) He claimed he was not interested in a squabble among monks.

4. Which of the following best describes Luther's position on the social questions of his day?

   (A) He wanted to see marked improvements in the lives of the peasantry.
   (B) He was deeply concerned about these questions but feared antagonizing his aristocratic supporters.
   (C) He was a deeply conservative man who did not want to upset the traditional social order.
   (D) He feared that his religious reforms would fail unless they were combined with a program to address social concerns.

5. Following the death of her half-sister Mary, Queen Elizabeth of England pursued which of the following religious policies?

   (A) She followed her father's example and refused to embrace either Protestantism or Catholicism.
   (B) She followed Mary's policy by keeping England within the Catholic Church.
   (C) She began a massive persecution of Catholics on the charge of heresy.
   (D) She broke with Rome and established a moderate Protestant church.

6. Expectations for the sixteenth-century Protestant family were influenced by

   (A) the doctrine of salvation by grace alone
   (B) changes in land-holding patterns by German peasants
   (C) Protestant emphasis on primogeniture
   (D) Martin Luther's decision to marry and start a family

7. For most Florentines, work was tied to

   (A) banking
   (B) the production of wool cloth
   (C) mercenary activities
   (D) the Church

8. Which of the following European states was the first to send sailors into the Indian Ocean?

   (A) France
   (B) Great Britain
   (C) Portugal
   (D) Spain

9. The Spanish term *Reconquista* refers to which of the following?

   (A) Spain's victory over the French in northern Italy
   (B) The defeat of the Islamic states on the Spanish peninsula
   (C) The long sought rapprochement with Portugal
   (D) The beginnings of Hapsburg rule in Spain

10. King Gustavus Adolphus of Sweden entered the Thirty Years' War in 1629 in order to

   (A) forestall the entry of France into the conflict
   (B) aid the Hapsburg cause
   (C) neutralize the potential threat from England
   (D) defend Protestant interests in the Holy Roman Empire

REFLECT

- For which content topics discussed in this chapter do you feel you have achieved sufficient mastery to answer multiple-choice questions correctly?

- For which content topics discussed in this chapter do you feel you have achieved sufficient mastery to discuss effectively in an essay or short answer?

- For which content topics discussed in this chapter do you feel you need more work before you can answer multiple-choice questions correctly?

- For which content topics discussed in this chapter do you feel you need more work before you can discuss effectively in an essay or short answer?

- What parts of this chapter are you going to re-review?

- Will you seek further help outside of this book (such as a teacher, tutor, or AP Students) on any of the content in this chapter—and, if so, on what content?

Chapter 5
Monarchical States
to Napoleon:
c. 1648–c. 1815

FRANCE

Royal Absolutism

Until his assassination in 1610, Henry IV worked to revitalize his kingdom. With his finance minister, the **Duke of Sully**, Henry established government monopolies over a number of key commodities (such as salt) to restore the finances of the monarchy. He also limited the power of the French nobility by reining in its influence over regional parliaments. Despite this strengthening of monarchical power, Henry's assassination in 1610 and the ensuing ascension of his nine-year-old son, Louis XIII, made France once again vulnerable to aristocratic rebellion and the potential of religious wars. Louis needed a strong minister, and he found one in **Cardinal Richelieu**. Richelieu defeated the Huguenots and took away many of the military and political privileges granted them by the Edict of Nantes. He brought France into the Thirty Years' War, not as the defender of Catholic interests, but on the side of the Protestants in order to counter the traditional French enemy, the Spanish Habsburgs.

The death of Louis XIII in 1643 once again left France with a minor on the throne; the five-year-old **Louis XIV** was unable to benefit from Richelieu's guidance because the great minister had predeceased Louis XIII by one year. Louis XIV's mother, Ann of Austria, selected **Cardinal Mazarin** to be the regent during the King's childhood. Mazarin had a less sure political hand than Richelieu, and once again, France had to grapple with a series of rebellions known as the *Fronde* in the period between 1649 and 1652. These events scarred the young Louis XIV, who at one point during the rebellion had to flee from Paris. Following the death of Mazarin in 1661, Louis decided to rule without a chief minister and to finally grapple with the central issue that had dominated France for more than a hundred years—how to deal with an aristocracy that resented the ever-increasing powers of the French monarchy.

One way that Louis achieved this goal was to advocate a political philosophy that had been developing in France since the sixteenth century—the notion that the monarch enjoyed certain **divine rights**. Using Old Testament examples of divinely appointed monarchs, Louis's chief political philosopher, **Bishop Bossuet**, wrote that since the king was chosen by God, only God was fit to judge the behavior of the king, not parliamentary bodies or angry nobles.

Louis built the palace of **Versailles** twelve miles outside of Paris as another way to dominate the French nobility and the Parisian mob. Although his grandfather had converted to Catholicism to appease the people of Paris, Louis felt he could safely ignore the people from the confines of his palace. Eventually, 10,000 noblemen and officials lived at Versailles, a palace so immense that its facade was a third of a mile long, with grounds boasting 1,400 fountains. While it cost a huge amount of money to maintain Versailles, Louis thought it was worth it. Instead of plotting against the King, the aristocrats were distracted by court intrigue and gossip and by ceremonial issues such as who got to hold the King's sleeve as he got dressed. Those members of the aristocracy who did not live at Versailles were pleased with their tax exemptions as well as their high social standing.

"I Am the State"
Although it is unclear whether Louis ever said the famous line *"L'état, c'est moi"* ("I am the state"), the statement does assert Louis's belief that no political or religious authority existed, either within or beyond the borders of France, that had any right to encroach on his sovereignty.

To administer his monarchy, Louis made use of the upper bourgeoisie. No member of the high aristocracy attended the daily council sessions at Versailles. Instead, his most important minister was **Jean-Baptiste Colbert**, the son of a draper. Colbert centralized the French economy by instituting a system known as **mercantilism**. The central goal of mercantilism was to build up the nation's supply of gold by exporting goods to other lands and earning gold from their sale. To do this, Colbert organized factories to produce porcelains and other luxury items. He also tried to abolish internal tariffs, ultimately creating the **Five Great Farms**, which were large, custom-free regions.

Part of mercantilism was a reliance on foreign colonies to buy the mother country's exports. To that end, Colbert succeeded in helping to create France's vast overseas empire. By the 1680s, Louis controlled trading posts in India, slave-trading centers on the west coast of Africa, and several islands in the Caribbean, while the largest colonial possession was New France, the territory we know today as Quebec. Colbert particularly wanted to strike at the rich commercial empire of the Dutch, so he organized the **French East India Company** to compete with the Dutch. It enjoyed only limited success as a result in part of excessive government control and a lack of interest in such ventures by the French elite.

Louis XIV touted religious unity in France as a means of enhancing royal absolutism. While during the reign of his father the rights of Huguenots had declined due to the hostility of Richelieu, the Edict of Nantes was still in effect. Louis decided that the time had come to eradicate Calvinism in France. In 1685, he **revoked the Edict of Nantes**, a fateful decision that would greatly weaken the French state. He demolished Huguenot churches and schools and took away their civil rights. Some remained underground, but as many as 200,000 were exiled to England and the Netherlands. The Huguenots were an important part of the French economy; by fleeing to enemy lands, they aided the two countries that were at war with Louis. For Louis, however, such economic considerations meant little in comparison to what he thought was the more important goal and the one most pleasing to God—the elimination of religious heresy from France.

During the reign of Louis XIV, France was involved in a series of wars as a means to satiate Louis's desire for territorial expansion. In the early part of his reign, this policy was quite successful, as France conquered territories in Germany and Flanders. This success lasted until 1688, when the English—in a move that marked the Glorious Revolution—replaced James II, the king who had received subsidies from the French, with a new monarch, **William of Orange**, who as leader of the Netherlands was committed to waging total war against Louis. After 1688, another series of wars erupted that lasted for twenty-five years, including the **War of Spanish Succession** between the French and the English and Dutch allies, which lasted from 1702 to 1713 and concluded with the **Treaty of Utrecht**, which left a Bourbon (Louis's grandson) on the throne of Spain but forbade the same monarch from ruling both Spain and France. These wars ultimately resulted in the containment of Louis XIV's France but left the French peasantry hard pressed to pay the taxes to support Louis's constant desire for glory.

ENGLAND

The Stuarts

When Elizabeth died childless in 1603, as promised, her cousin **King James VI of Scotland** inherited the throne. To a certain extent, James was ill suited for the role of English king. The Scottish Parliament was a weak institution that did not inhibit the power of the monarch. James's interest lay in asserting his divine notion of kingship, which he had been exposed to by reading French writings on the subject. He told the English Parliament the following during the first session with them:

> The state of monarchy is the supremest thing upon Earth: for Kings are not only God's lieutenants upon Earth and sit upon God's throne, but even by God Himself they are called gods. As to dispute what God may do is blasphemy, so it is sedition in subjects to dispute what a King may do in height of his power. I will not be content that my power be disputed on.

Such words could not have pleased his audience. In the relationship between the king and Parliament at the start of the seventeenth century, the monarch held the upper hand—only the king could summon a parliament, and he could dismiss it at will. James did, however, have to consult the two-house English Parliament, the **House of Commons** and the **House of Lords**, when he needed to raise additional revenue beyond his ordinary expenses. This parliamentary control over the financial purse strings in an age when the cost of governing was dramatically increasing played a crucial role in Parliament's eventual triumph over royal absolutism.

Religious issues further complicated James's reign (he was always suspected of being a closet Catholic). The religious settlement worked out by Elizabeth in 1559 was no longer adequate in an age in which English religious passions grew increasingly intense. It failed to satisfy the radical Calvinist Protestants, known as **Puritans**, who emerged during the **Stuart period**. In 1603, most Puritans still belonged to the Church of England, although they were a minority within the Church. For the most part, what distinguished the Puritans was that they wanted to see the Church "purified" of all traces of Catholicism. Although raised in Calvinist Scotland, James, on his arrival in England, found the Church of England with its hierarchical clergy and ornate rituals more to his taste. He believed its Episcopal structure was particularly well suited to his idea of the divine right of kings. In 1604, when a group of Puritans petitioned the new king to reform the Church of England, James met them with the declaration: "I will have one doctrine, one discipline, one religion, both in substance and in ceremony." He added words that would prove to be rather prophetic for his son: "**No Bishop, No King,**" meaning that by weakening the Church, the monarchy in turn weakens. James's opposition to the Puritan proposal drove the more moderate of the Puritans—individuals who just wanted to rid the Church of England of its last traces of Catholic ritual—onto a more extreme track. Some Puritans even decided to leave England; one such group founded the colony of Plymouth, Massachusetts, in 1620.

James's three-part program—to unite England with Scotland, to create a continental-style standing army, and to set up a new system of royal finance—met with little support from Parliament. James's son, **Charles I** (r. 1625–1641), did not possess even the somewhat limited political acumen of his father. Like his father, Charles felt that the Anglican Church provided the greatest stability for his state, and he further enflamed passions by lending his support to the so-called **Arminian** wing of the Anglican Church. **Arminius** was a Dutch theologian of the early seventeenth century who argued in favor of free will as opposed to the Calvinist doctrine of **predestination**. In 1633, Charles named **William Laud**, a follower of this doctrine, his Archbishop of Canterbury. The Arminians, although certainly not pro-Catholic, refused to deny that Catholics were Christians; this philosophy greatly angered the Puritans. The Arminians further antagonized Puritan sentiment by advocating a more ornate church service.

The relationship between Charles and Parliament got off to a bad start when Parliament granted him **Tonnage and Poundage** (custom duties) for a one-year period rather than for the life of the monarch, as had been the custom since the fifteenth century. Charles, however, was committed to the war against Spain, so he cashed in his wife's dowry and sent an expedition to the Spanish port of Cadiz; the mission was a complete failure. To pay for these military disasters, Charles requested a forced loan from his wealthier subjects. Several Members of Parliament refused to pay this loan and were thrown in jail. Parliament was called in again in 1628, at which time it put forward a **Petition of Rights**, which Charles felt forced to sign. It included provisions that the king could not demand a loan without the consent of Parliament and that Parliament must be called frequently. The petition also prohibited individuals from being imprisoned without published cause and the government from housing soldiers and sailors in private homes without the owner's permission. Finally, it outlawed using martial law against civilians, which Charles had used to collect his forced loan.

In August 1628, Charles's chief minister, the dashing but incompetent **Duke of Buckingham**, was murdered by an embittered sailor who blamed him for England's recent military disasters. Charles, on the other hand, blamed the leaders of the House of Commons, most notably John Eliot, for inflaming passions against Buckingham. When Parliament was again called in January 1629, both sides felt that the issue of exclusive rights would lead to a conflict between Parliament and the King. In March 1629, the issue came to the foreground when Eliot proposed three resolutions.

1. High churchmen and anyone suspected of popery (practicing Catholicism) should be branded as capital enemies of the state.

2. Any of the King's advisors who recommended that he raise funds without Parliament's approval should be tried as capital enemies of the state.

3. Anyone who paid tonnage and poundage, which the King was still illegally collecting, would be betraying the "liberties of England."

After hearing these demands, which he thought outrageous, the King summoned the Speaker of the House of Commons and ordered him to dissolve Parliament. Two Members of Parliament held the Speaker in his chair, a treasonable act because it disputes the right of the king to dissolve Parliament. Once Eliot's resolutions were passed, the King's messengers announced that he had dissolved Parliament.

For the next eleven years, what is known as the **Personal Rule of Charles** was the law of the land. Charles decided to govern England without calling a Parliament. Charles could have carried this off successfully and brought about the end of Parliament, as occurred in France during the same period of time. The major problem of how to raise enough revenue was solved by extending the collection of ship money throughout the kingdom, a politically explosive decision. Traditionally, certain coastal cities were responsible for raising funds for naval defense during times of national emergency. In 1634, Charles declared an emergency (although England was at peace), and two years later he extended this tax to inland cities and counties, areas that had never before paid ship money. This was such a substantial source of income that it could possibly have freed the King from ever having to call a Parliament.

The Case of John Hampden

The collection of ship money led to a famous legal case involving John Hampden, a Puritan Member of Parliament, who, having already challenged the legality of the forced loan, now questioned Charles's raising of ship money. While the judges found against Hampden by a vote of seven to five, he was viewed as having achieved a moral victory.

By 1637, Charles was at the height of his power. He had a balanced budget, and his government policies and restructuring appeared to be effective. Yet within four years of this peak, the country would be embroiled in a civil war. Charles ultimately ruined his powerful position by insisting that Calvinist Scotland adopt not only the Episcopal structure of the Church of England, but also follow a prayer book based on the *English Book of Common Prayer*. The Scots rioted and signed **a national covenant** that pledged their allegiance to the King but also vowed to resist all changes to their Church.

In 1640, Charles called an English Parliament for the first time in eleven years, because he believed it would be willing to grant money to put down the Scottish rebellion. This became known as the **Short Parliament** because it met for only three weeks and was dissolved after it refused to grant funds prior to Charles addressing their own grievances. Charles was still determined to punish the Scots; after he dissolved Parliament, he patched together an army with the resources he could muster. The Scots were the victors on the battlefield and invaded northern England. They refused to leave England until Charles signed a settlement and, in the meantime, forced him to pay £850 per day for their support.

To pay this large sum, Charles was forced to call another Parliament. This became known as the **Long Parliament**, since it met for an unprecedented 20 years. The House of Commons launched the Long Parliament by impeaching Charles's two chief ministers, the Earl of Strafford and Archbishop Laud (Strafford was executed in 1641 and Laud in 1645). Parliament abolished the king's **prerogative courts**, like Henry VIII's Court of Star Chamber, which had become tools of royal absolutism. Tensions grew even higher when a rebellion broke out in Ireland, which had been ruled with a strong hand since the time of the Tudors.

Parliament took the momentous step of limiting some of the king's prerogative rights. They supported what was known as the **Grand Remonstrance**, a list of 204 parliamentary grievances from the past decade. They also made two additional demands: that the king name ministers whom Parliament could trust and that a synod of the Church of England be called to reform the Church of England. In response Charles tried to seize five of the leaders of the House of Commons, an attempt that failed, resulting in Charles leaving London in January 1642, to raise his royal standard at Nottingham. This marked the beginning of the **English Revolution**.

The English Revolution

During the initial stage of the English Revolution, things went poorly for Parliament. Their military commander, the Earl of Manchester, pointed out the dilemma when he noted: "If we beat the King 99 times, he is still the King, but if the King defeats us, we shall be hanged and our property confiscated." Individuals, such as **Oliver Cromwell**, who were far more dedicated to creating a winning war policy, soon replaced the early aristocratic leaders. It was Cromwell who created what became known as the **New Model Army**, a regularly paid, disciplined force with extremely dedicated Puritan soldiers. By 1648, the King was defeated, and in the following year, Cromwell made the momentous decision to execute the King, a move that horrified most of the nation.

From 1649 to 1660 England was officially a republic, known as **The Commonwealth**, but essentially it was a military dictatorship governed by Cromwell. Cromwell had to deal with conflicts among his own supporters, such as the clash between the **Independents** and the **Presbyterians**. The Independents, who counted Cromwell among their ranks, wanted a state church, but were also willing to grant a measure of religious freedom for others (although Catholics were to be excluded from this tolerant policy). On the other side of the divide were the Presbyterians, who wanted a state church that would not allow dissent. Cromwell also had to deal with the rise of radical factions within his army, groups like the **Levellers and Diggers**, who combined their radical religious beliefs with a call for a complete overhaul of English society. They touted a philosophy that included such radical ideas as allowing all men, not just those who owned land, to vote for members of the House of Commons.

Cromwell destroyed the Leveller elements in his army in 1649 after several regiments with large Leveller contingents revolted against his rule. In the following year, Cromwell led an army to Ireland, where he displayed incredible brutality in putting down resistance by supporters of the Stuarts.

Cromwell would find, as Charles I had earlier, that Parliament was a difficult institution to control. In 1652, he brought his army into London to disperse a Parliament that dared to challenge him only to replace them with hand-selected individuals who still earned his displeasure within a matter of months. Over the next year, a group of army officers wrote the "Instrument of Government," the only written constitution in English history and a document that provided for republican government (the Protectorate) with a head of state holding the title

Lord Protector and a parliament based on a fairly wide male suffrage. Cromwell stepped into the position of Lord Protector, but still found Parliament difficult to control. Finally in 1655, Cromwell gave up all hope of ruling in conjunction with a legislature, and divided England into 12 military districts, each to be governed by a major general.

By the time Cromwell died, an exhausted England wanted to bring back the Stuart dynasty. In 1660, the eldest son of the executed monarch became **Charles II**. The return of the Stuarts turned back the clock to 1642 as the same issues that had led to the revolution against Charles's father remained unresolved: What is the proper relationship between king and Parliament? What should be the religious direction of the Church of England? These issues were not fully addressed during Charles's reign although they came to the forefront during the reign of his younger brother, **James II**, who succeeded Charles on the throne in 1685.

Suspected of being a Catholic like all previous Stuarts, James immediately antagonized Parliament by demanding the repeal of the **Test Act**, an act passed during Charles II's reign that effectively barred Catholics from serving as royal officials or in the military (there was no law at this time barring Catholics from the monarchy). James also issued a **Declaration of Indulgence**, which suspended all religious tests for office holders and allowed for freedom of worship. On the surface, James appeared to have been a champion of religious freedom; this was deceptive. What James really wished to achieve in England was royal absolutism; however, the steps that he took to achieve this goal were illegal. The final stages of this conflict took place in 1688. Early in the year, James imprisoned seven Anglican bishops for refusing to read James's suspension of the laws against Catholics from their church pulpits, the usual way of informing the community of royal edicts in an age before modern communications. James also unexpectedly fathered a child in June 1688 and now had a male heir who would be raised as a Catholic, in contrast to his previous heir, his daughter Mary, who was a Protestant. These moves to create a Catholic England created unity among previously contentious Protestant factions within England. One faction of this political and religious elite invited **William, the Stadholder** of the Netherlands and the husband of Mary, to invade England. When his troops landed, James's forces collapsed in what was basically a bloodless struggle (except for in Ireland, where there was tremendous violence over the next several years), known as the "**Glorious Revolution**." James was overthrown, and William and Mary jointly took the throne.

What followed was a constitutional settlement that finally attempted to address the pervasive issues of this century of revolution.

What's a Stadholder?
In case you've never heard this term used before, a *stadholder* is a Dutch word referring to an office that primarily served a military function between the 15th and 18th centuries in the Netherlands.

The settlement consisted of the following acts:

- **The Bill of Rights** (1689) forbade the use of royal prerogative rights as Charles and James had exercised in the past. The power to suspend and dispense with laws was declared illegal. Armies could not be raised without parliamentary consent. Elections to Parliament were to be free of royal interference. The monarchs also had to swear to uphold the Protestant faith, and it was declared that the monarchy could not pass into the hands of a Catholic. Most importantly, Parliament's approval was now officially required for all taxation.

- **The Act of Toleration** (1689) was in many ways a compromise bill. To get nonconformists' (Protestants who were not members of the Church of England) support in the crucial months of 1688, Whigs and Tories (Whigs being the more liberal parliamentary faction than the Tories) had promised them that an act of toleration would be granted when William became king. The nonconformists could have achieved liberty of worship from James II's act of toleration, but an act from a popular Protestant monarch would prove to be a better safeguard to their liberties. The Act of Toleration granted the right of public worship to Protestant nonconformists but did not extend it to Unitarians or to Catholics (those two groups were also left alone, although legally they had no right to assemble to pray). The Test Act remained, which meant nonconformists, Jews, and Catholics could not sit in Parliament, until the law was changed in the nineteenth century.

- **The Mutiny Act** (1689) authorized the use of civil law to govern the army, which previously had been governed only by royal decree. It also made desertion and mutiny civil crimes, for which soliders could be punished during peacetime. But the act was only in effect on a year-by-year basis, which meant that a Parliament had to be summoned annually if for no other reason than to pass this act. Along with the Bill of Rights' provision against standing armies in peacetime, the Mutiny Act brought the army under effective parliamentary control.

- **The Act of Settlement** (1701) was passed to prevent the Catholic Stuart line from occupying the English throne. In 1714, when Queen Anne, the second Protestant daughter of James II, died childless, the throne passed to George I, the Elector of Hanover, a Protestant prince and a distant kinsman of the Stuarts.

- **The Act of Union** (1707) marked the political reunification of England and Scotland, forming the entity known as Great Britain. This union was by no means a love match and, in fact, primarily occurred because relations between the two previously independent states were so bad that on his deathbed, William III urged that union take place to forestall Scotland from going to war with England as an ally of France. As part of the agreement, Scotland gave up its parliament but was allowed to maintain the state-sponsored Presbyterian Church and its Roman-based legal system.

THE NETHERLANDS

A Center of Commerce and Trade

The relative decline of Spain as an economic power was in part due to the growing competition from the Netherlands. The Netherlands had already achieved a central role in inter-European trade due to its geographic position and large merchant marine fleet. For example, it was the Netherlands that provided a connection between the raw material producers in the Baltic region and the rest of Europe. Beyond Europe, control over the lucrative spice trade in Asia was wrested out of the hands of the Portuguese, a situation which was made worse when Spain took control over Portugal in 1580 and found itself without the resources to rival the Dutch in Asia.

Increasingly, it was the city of Amsterdam (the capital of the Netherlands), rather than the Spanish-controlled city of Antwerp, that became the center of commerce in northern Europe. The sacking of the city of Antwerp in 1576 during the **Dutch War for Independence** and the permanent closing of the Scheldt River that led to its harbor, as part of the Peace of Westphalia, also aided in the decline of Antwerp and its replacement as an economic center by Amsterdam.

Dutch dominance in part came from technological achievements such as the development of less expensive but ocean-worthy cargo ships, but the Dutch also proved to be creative in their establishment of financial and commercial institutions. The **Bank of Amsterdam**, founded in the early part of the seventeenth century, issued its own currency and increased the amount of available capital, while also making Amsterdam the banking center of Europe. In 1602, the **Dutch East India Company** was established. The company operated under quasi-governmental control and was funded by both public and private investment. This kind of investment, used in the past but most successfully in the Netherlands, gave rise to the popularity of **joint-stock companies**. Such companies allowed risks and profits to be shared among many individuals. The large capitalization behind the Dutch East India Company allowed for the purchasing of more ships and warehouses. The Dutch also proved to be very nimble businessmen, so that when the prices of spices decreased due to oversupply, they quickly turned to other commodities such as coffee, tea, and fabrics, although by the beginning of the eighteenth century, Dutch commercial power, although continuing down to this day, would lose its preeminent place in Europe to the English.

This **"Golden Age"** in the Netherlands produced a high standard of living, with wealth being more equally distributed than any other place in Europe. The Netherlands also stood out from the rest of Europe for its **tolerant attitude toward religious minorities**, with Jews fleeing from the Spanish Inquisition and Anabaptists as well as Catholics finding a place among the majority Calvinist population.

Political Decentralization

Dutch exceptionalism also extended to the political realm because politically, the Netherlands didn't look like any other state in Europe. For most of the seventeenth century, it was politically decentralized, with each of the seven provinces retaining extensive autonomy. Wealthy merchants dominated the provincial Estates, which retained powers far more extensive than those of national Estates General, particularly in the area of taxation. Executive power, such as it was, came from the noble **House of Orange**, whose family members had achieved prominence for leading the revolt against Spain. The male head of this family held the title of *stadholder*, an office with primarily a military function, no mere formality as the Netherlands switched from fighting for its independence from Spain to economic wars against the English and a long-term struggle for survival against France. During the struggle with Louis XIV's France, the power of the provincial Estates went into decline, while the authority of **William of Nassau**, the head of the House of Orange, increased tremendously, particularly when William became King of England after the Revolution of 1688.

Dutch Autonomy
Unlike other countries in Europe during the same period, the Netherlands did not have a centralized government. Rather, each of the seven provinces was politically autonomous.

A Golden Age of Art

Culturally, the seventeenth century proved to be a golden age as well. Dutch artists, reflecting the fact that the majority of the population was Calvinist, didn't receive large commissions to be placed in churches, although the Baroque style of painting penetrated the Netherlands through Catholic Flanders. Instead, Dutch artists painted for private collectors, who supported an incredibly large number of painters and a wide range of styles, including the production of a large number of landscapes. Like so much else in the Netherlands, pictures were treated as commodities, with prices at times reaching speculative rates.

The art market didn't just flourish in Amsterdam, as shown by the thriving career of **Franz Hals** (c. 1580–1666), the great portrait painter from Haarlem. Another gifted Dutch painter, **Jan Vermeer** (1632–1675), had initially thought of being a painter of historical scenes, but when he received no commissions, he turned to the carefully composed genre scenes of everyday Dutch life, for which he has become justifiably famous. The greatest genius of the Dutch golden age was **Rembrandt Van Rijn** (1606–1669), whose paintings, which were initially influenced by the High Baroque style and were later in his career more subtly painted, are fraught with a deep emotional complexity. One of his masterpieces, *The Night Watch* (1642), transforms a standard group portrait of a military company into a revealing psychological study.

ECONOMIC AND SOCIAL LIFE IN EARLY MODERN EUROPE

It's a little difficult to generalize about life in early modern Europe because conditions varied from region to region, but general trends do emerge for the period.

Economic Expansion and Population Growth

By the end of the fifteenth century, Europe was ushering in an age of economic expansion that sharply contrasted with the decline that had taken root in the fourteenth century with its disastrous famines and plagues. The key development in the period was the **growth in population**. To use France as a typical example, the population doubled from 10 million to 20 million from 1450 to 1550. This significant population expansion was very important for economic productivity, in an age in which manpower was still far more important than labor-saving technology. The expansion of Europe's population also provided for additional consumers, which meant that there was greater incentive to bring more food and other essentials to market.

The growth of population also had an impact on another important development: the significant increase in prices in the early modern period, which has become known as the **Price Revolution**. Initially, historians thought that this increase came from the influx of precious metals from the New World and the debasement of their coinage by money-hungry monarchs, but it is now apparent that it was population growth that put pressure on the prices of basic commodities such as wheat. This inflation did not increase at a rate that would impress a modern consumer, with grain prices increasing 500 percent—which sounds much more impressive until you take into account that this increase took place in the 150-year period from 1500 to 1650. Nevertheless, for a society that was accustomed to stable prices, a price increase of this magnitude came as a shock. Historians have even tried to find ways of connecting the Price Revolution to the political and religious struggles of the age, based on the theory that periods of high inflation can be an important factor behind the development of social tensions.

Rural Life and the Emergence of Economic Classes

One way in which rural life was transformed in this period, in part due to the Price Revolution, was the emergence of a class of wealthy individuals, located socially below the aristocracy, who began to buy significant amounts of newly valuable landholdings. In England, this class of individuals, who often had their economic roots in fortunes made in towns and cities, were known as the **gentry**, and would play a major role in the political struggles that the English Parliament would wage against the monarchy in the seventeenth century. The land-buying habits of the gentry forced up the price of land. In addition, the gentry were able to use their social connections to get local authorities to accept the **enclosure** of lands for their own personal use, land that had previously been available for the grazing of animals by the entire community.

More Sheep
In Book 1 of *Utopia*, Sir Thomas More refers to the notion of sheep devouring men, a criticism of the displacement of the small farmer by valuable herds of sheep.

The problem of rural poverty became significantly worse in the early modern period, with many small farmers reduced to the role of beggars, spending their days tramping from one locale to another. Increasingly, the problem of poverty weighed on the political elite; in Catholic lands, the Church remained the major provider of social services, while in Protestant countries it became the task of the state to provide for the destitute, such as the first **English Poor Law** during the reign of Queen Elizabeth. Although rural overpopulation was a problem throughout most of western Europe, in eastern Europe, low population density was a much more serious problem, leading wealthy landowners to solve their labor shortages by binding the formerly free peasantry to the land in a process of enserfment.

Farm Life

For the majority of individuals in Europe, who lived in rural areas as small-scale farmers, life was fairly dismal and revolved around a constant struggle to find the resources to survive. Life centered on the small village, often with fewer than fifty households, with most people never traveling a few miles beyond the location of their birth. Housing in rural villages offered little protection from the cold and wet winters. Homes were generally made of wood, with packed mud on the walls and straw on the floor, lacking windows and adequate ventilation. For the most part, they consisted of one main room that possessed a stone hearth that provided heat. The possessions that went into these houses were as simple as their surroundings. The worldly possessions of most rural households could fit in a single chest, which could double as a table and could be carried away by the family in case they had to flee during an emergency, such as the arrival of mercenaries looking for plunder.

The workdays were long during the summer harvests, and shorter in the winter, with late winter offering the rural household the terrifying prospect of not having enough resources to tide them over until the coming of spring. Although farming began to change by the end of the seventeenth century in the Netherlands and in England with the beginnings of what we may refer to as scientific methods, for the most part, Europeans were farming in 1800 the same way they had farmed going back to the High Middle Ages (c. 1001–1300). The **three-field system** (where crops were rotated across three pieces of land) was used in the north of Europe, while the two-field system (crops rotated on two pieces of land) predominated in the Mediterranean region. Farmland in most rural areas was set out in long strips, with individual peasant families owning a portion of land in each of the strips. Because animals such as cows or sheep needed copious amounts of food, common lands in each village were shared, although the wealthy rural elite was increasingly coveting this common land. Most of what was grown was used by the farmers for their own households, leaving very little to be brought to market. The diet of the average European peasant farmer was incredibly monotonous, with most calories coming from grain in various forms, ranging from dark bread to gruels and beer.

Life in the Cities and Towns

Although towns and cities held scarcely more than 10 percent of the overall population, they provided for some variation from what Karl Marx would call "the idiocy of rural life." Townspeople in general lived better than their rural counterparts, with better housing and a more varied diet, although urban poverty was also increasing in this period.

There was also a much greater variety of occupations, with a much greater emphasis on specialization, with specific tasks such as baking or brewing taking place in specific quarters of the town. **Guilds**, which began to dominate the urban economy during the High Middle Ages, continued to play a role in the production of commodities down to the time of the French Revolution.

However, the guild method of production was being supplanted by a new means of production that was in part directed by the expansion of population and the growth of markets. Cloth was now produced on a much larger scale by a new group of **capitalist entrepreneurs** and required a large outlay of money to get started. These individuals would provide the money and the organizational skills, which they used to direct every stage of the production of broadcloth, beginning with the cleaning of the wool and ending with the weaving. This work provided a benefit in some rural households (where the various stages of production would now take place), adding an important source of revenue particularly during the long winter months.

For guild members, however, this new competition created great hardships. Also, for apprentices and journeymen the dream of becoming a full-fledged guild master was becoming an increasingly rare occurence. These men essentially became wage earners with little hope of rising up the economic and social ranks. Dissatisfied journeymen and apprentices would play an important role in the urban revolts of the period.

Family Life and Structure

Although we tend to assume that some notion of the extended family existed in the past, with several generations living under one roof, the family in the Early Modern period would not look significantly different from today's nuclear family. Family size was smaller than what one might have imagined for the period, with the average family consisting of no more than three or four children. The relatively small number of children was partly the result of fewer childbearing years resulting from later marriages, with women on average marrying around age 25 and men two years later. Traditionally, marriages were either arranged by the parents or at least formally approved, in part because even in the poorest of rural communities, marriage involved some transfer of property. Weddings were important community events, because the married husband and wife were now considered to be full-fledged members of society, and in general, single adults were looked on as potential thieves or troublemakers if they were male and as prostitutes if they were female.

The Role of Men in the Family

In many ways, the family with the father as the patriarchal head served as a reflection in miniature of the larger hierarchical ordering of early modern society. In wealthier families, the father had to ensure that the family's wealth remained intact, which meant that the oldest male child inherited most of the estate (**primogeniture**), with younger sons being guided toward careers in the Church, military, or in the increased opportunities offered by the burgeoning administration of the early modern state.

The Role of Women

The only claim that daughters would have on the parental estate would come with the **dowry** that they would receive upon marriage. Wives could usually determine who should receive their dowry upon their death, although during their own lifetimes their husbands would manage the dowry. Among the poor, arrangements would be different, with boys apprenticed off to a trade or as servants at the age of seven, and domestic service being the only opportunities for girls, who in the poorest of families were left with the difficult task of trying to raise their own dowries.

The Family as Economic Unit

Early modern families, whether rich or poor, can be seen as economic units. Before the late Industrial Revolution, child labor was accepted and commonplace. To some extent, jobs were gendered: Men played a larger role in the "public" sphere, such as plowing, planting, and commerce, while women had responsibility over the home. However, in agricultural communities, everyone was expected to work in the fields; and among merchant classes, the "private" sphere might include bookkeeping and other administration of the family business while the men went on purchasing tours. In some cases, the main difference between women's work and men's work was that women's work included all the men's work, plus taking care of the house and the cooking. The strongest division between men's and women's roles was in the upper classes and the nobility. Only these very wealthy people could afford the luxury of an idle woman. This, combined with better diet, wet-nursing, and more sanitary conditions, was why wealthier families might see annual pregnancies (as opposed to every two or three years for poorer women), as well as why the wealthy had a much lower childhood mortality rate.

How the Protestant Reformation Changed Family Life

Although one can scarcely talk about a revolution taking place in family life in this period, the Protestant Reformation did usher in some changes. In Protestant lands, the household became the center of Christian life, rather than the church or monastery. Arguably, paternalism increased, as the father now assumed a spiritual role as the chief intermediary between the family and God, while also more strictly enforcing moral standards and the value of hard work. For women who wanted to avoid marriage and constant childrearing, the option of convent life came to an end, and frugal fathers lost the opportunity to save dowry money. In some places, divorce was allowed, something that was anathema to the Catholic Church.

Women in Protestant lands were conceivably freer in the sense that they were able, like any man, to directly communicate with God without relying on a male priest as an intermediary. However, those women who wanted to take a more active role by leading congregations and preaching—as seen in some of the more radical Protestant sects such as the Anabaptists—were brutally persecuted.

EVENTS LEADING TO THE SCIENTIFIC REVOLUTION

In 1611, the English poet John Donne wrote *The Anatomy of the World*, in which he reflected on the multitude of ways that his world had changed as a result of the new discoveries in science.

> New philosophy calls all in doubt
> The element of fire is quite put out;
> The sun is lost, and th' Earth, and no man's wit
> Can well direct him where to looke for it.
> And freely men confess that this world's spent,
> When in the Planets, and the new firmament
> They seeke so many new; then see that this
> Is crumbled out againe to his Atomies
> 'Tis all in peeces, all coherance gone;
> All just supply, and all Relation.

As Donne understood, the scientific discoveries of the sixteenth and seventeenth centuries brought about a fundamental change in the way Europeans viewed the natural world. To call this change a revolution may be misleading in light of the length of time over which it occurred, but the implications from these discoveries were truly revolutionary. Not only did it change the way Europeans viewed the world around them, but it also had significant implications in such areas as religion, political thought, and how they fought wars.

Why was it that seventeenth-century thinkers challenged the medieval view of the natural world? What possibly occurred in that age that led them to question ideas that previously had been readily accepted? The following are some possibilities.

Discovery of the New World

The period of exploration and conquest led to the discovery of new plant and animal life and possibly encouraged greater interest in the natural sciences. Also, the traditional link between navigation and astronomy and the great advances made by Portuguese navigators in the fifteenth century helped fuel an interest in learning more about the stars.

Invention of the Printing Press

Scientific knowledge could spread much more rapidly because of the printing press. By the second half of the seventeenth century, there were numerous books and newsletters keeping people informed about the most recent scientific discoveries. It is because of the printing press that Thomas Hobbes, sitting in England, was cognizant of scientific discoveries coming out of Italy.

Rivalry Among Nation-States

The constant warfare between the various nation-states may have pushed scientific development by placing an increasing importance on technology, or applied science. Further, Europe was a region with many powerful leaders who could fund scientific development. Columbus, an Italian, could find funding for his voyages from Ferdinand and Isabella of Spain after being turned down by John of Portugal. Compare this to the situation in China; with few technological competitors and a single ruler capable of canceling major projects, Chinese technological development slowed relative to that of Europe.

Reformation

The historian Robert K. Merton suggested a number of years ago that the English who professed Calvinist beliefs were somehow linked to those who were active in the new science. Even earlier than Merton, one of the fathers of sociology, Max Weber, argued that the worldly asceticism found in Protestantism helped create capitalism, which in turn helped propel the Scientific Revolution. These theories, however, ignore the fact that much of the Scientific Revolution came from Catholic Italy. The telescope and microscope, for example, were Italian in origin, as was the new botany. Nevertheless, the Protestant Reformation, by encouraging people to read the Bible, did help create a larger reading public. And although Luther, Calvin, and the like were not interested in challenging the traditional scientific worldview, their opposition to the religious hegemony of Rome did provide a powerful example of challenging established authority.

Renaissance Humanism

Humanist interest in the writings of the classical world also extended to the scientific texts of the ancient Greeks. Certain texts, such as Archimedes's writings on mathematics and Galen's anatomical studies, were rediscovered in the Renaissance. Although the Scientific Revolution ultimately rejected the ideas contained in such works, this basic familiarity with the past was a necessary stage in order for modern scientific thought to mature.

PRE-SCIENTIFIC WORLDVIEW

The medieval worldview was based on **scholasticism**, a synthesis of Christian theology with the scientific beliefs of the ancient authors. The great architect of this synthesis was **Thomas Aquinas** (1225–1274), who took the works of **Aristotle** and harmonized them with the teachings of the church. Knowledge of God remained the supreme act of learning and was to be attained through both reason and revelation. The value of science, for those living in the Middle Ages, was that it offered the possibility of a better understanding of the mysterious workings of God. To view science without this religious framework was simply inconceivable in the Middle Ages.

Medieval "Science"
In the Middle Ages, people believed the world was made up of exactly four elements—earth, fire, air, and water— which in the human body were combined to make the four humours: yellow bile, black bile, blood, and phlegm. Mmm.

Influenced by the work of Aristotle, medieval people thought that the material world was made up of four elements: earth, air, fire, and water. Earth was the heaviest and the basest of the elements and therefore tended toward the center of the universe. Water was also heavy but lighter than Earth, so its natural place was covering the Earth. Air was above water, with fire as the lightest element of all. It was this notion of the four elements that gave rise to the idea of **alchemy**, or the perfect compound of the four elements in their perfect proportions. Less perfect metals such as lead might be transformed by changing the proportion of their elements. The four-element approach also dominated the practice of medicine. The four elements combined in the human body to create what were known as the four humours: blood, phlegm, yellow bile, and black bile. An excess of any one of the humours produced one's essential personal characteristics.

People in the Middle Ages did not have a great interest in astronomy; the popular work of the Greek astronomer **Ptolemy** (c. 85–165 A.D.) was not questioned. The Ptolemaic, or Geocentric, system placed the Earth as a stationary object around which heavenly bodies moved, while the stars were fixed in their orbits. One problem with this system was addressed rather early: How does one explain the unusual motion of the planets in relation to the fixed stars? At times planets even appeared to be moving backward. To cope with these problems, epicycles—planetary orbits within an orbit—were added to the system.

After Copernicus

The Earth-centered system would not go away that quickly. The Danish astronomer **Tycho Brahe** (1546–1601) tried to come up with a different Earth-centered system rather than just relying on the Ptolemaic system. Brahe had plenty of time on his hands to construct the best astronomical tables of the age, as his social life was nonexistent after he lost part of his nose in a duel and rebuilt it with a prosthetic made of silver and gold alloy. Brahe proposed a system in which the moon and the sun revolved around the Earth, while the other planets revolved around the sun.

Brahe's student, **Johannes Kepler** (1571–1630), disagreed with his teacher concerning Copernicus's findings. Kepler ended up using Brahe's own data to search for ways to support Copernicus and eventually dropped Copernicus's "planets move in a circular motion" theory, instead proposing that their orbits were elliptical. However, it would take the greatest mind of the next age, **Isaac Newton**, to explain why this elliptical motion was in fact possible.

THE COPERNICAN REVOLUTION

In 1543, **Nicholas Copernicus** (1473–1543), a Polish mathematician and astronomer, wrote *Concerning the Revolutions of the Celestial Spheres*. Copernicus was a cleric, and because he was afraid of the implications of the ideas contained in the work, he waited many years before he finally decided to publish. When he finally took that step, Copernicus cautiously dedicated the book to **Pope Paul III** and included a preface that claimed that the ideas contained in it were just mathematical hypotheses. Even the language of the work was moderate as Copernicus merely suggested that should the Earth revolve around the sun, it would solve at least some of the problematic epicycles of the Ptolemaic system. However, since the Copernican, or **Heliocentric**, system explains that the planets move in a circular motion around the sun, it did not completely eliminate all the epicycles. Despite his book's famous reputation, Copernicus's ideas did not stir a revolution in the way in which people viewed the planets and the stars.

Galileo

The first scientist to build on the work of Copernicus was a Florentine by the name of **Galileo Galilei** (1564–1642). In 1609, he heard about a Dutchman who had invented a spyglass that allowed distant objects to be seen as if close up. Galileo then designed his own telescope that magnified far-away objects thirty times the naked eye's capacity. Using this instrument, he noticed that the moon had a mountainous surface very much like the Earth. For Galileo, this provided evidence that it was composed of material similar to that on Earth and not some purer substance as Aristotle had argued. Galileo also realized that the stars were much farther away than the planets. He saw that Jupiter had four moons of her own. This challenged the traditional notion of the unique relationship between Earth and her moon. Sunspots and rings around Saturn also put the whole Ptolemaic construct into doubt.

Galileo was also interested in the question of motion. He may not have really thrown a ten-pound weight and a one-pound weight from the top of the Leaning Tower of Pisa, but he did notice that heavier weights do not fall any faster than lighter ones. He also noticed that under ideal conditions a body in motion would tend to stay in motion. It was therefore relatively easy for him to deduce from this the possibility that Earth is in perpetual motion.

Following the publication of his *Dialogues on the Two Chief Systems of the World* (1632), the Catholic Church began to condemn Galileo's work. The Church authorities warned Galileo not to publish any more writings on astronomy. Throwing caution to the wind, he wrote a book that compared the new science with the old; an ignorant clown Simplicio represented the old science. Pope Urban VIII thought the book was making fun of him, and he put Galileo under house arrest for the remainder of his life. This did not stop Galileo from writing, although he was forced to send his manuscripts to Holland where the mood was more tolerant.

Sir Isaac Newton

The greatest figure of the Scientific Revolution was **Isaac Newton** (1642–1727). Newton wanted to solve the problem posed by the work of Copernicus, Kepler, and Galileo: How do you explain the orderly manner in which the planets revolve around the sun? Newton worked for almost two decades on the problem before he published his masterpiece, *Principia*, in 1687. Galileo's work on motion influenced Newton, a sign of the intellectual link between southern and northern scientists. Newton wondered what force kept the planets in an elliptical orbit around the sun, when theoretically they should be moving in a straight line. Supposedly Newton saw an apple drop from a tree and deduced that the same force that drew the apple to the ground may explain planetary motion. Newton finally posited that all planets and objects in the universe operated under the effects of gravity.

It is important to remember that Newton was an extremely religious man and often wondered why, when he delivered public talks, his audiences were more interested in his scientific discoveries than in theology. He spent a great deal of time making silly calculations of biblical dates and practicing alchemy.

Giordano Bruno

Galileo proved to be far more fortunate than his fellow Italian, **Giordano Bruno** (1548–1600), a Dominican friar who was executed by the **papal Inquisition** in 1600 for arguing that there may be a plurality of worlds in the universe. The Church took this as an implication that there might be a multiplicity of redeeming Christs—an intolerable heresy.

More importantly, he began to experiment with optics, thus making the study of light a new scientific endeavor. It was Newton who showed that white light was a heterogeneous mixture of colors rather than the pure light many believed it to be. Newton is also the father of differential **calculus** (much to the regret of those of you who have to take it in high school). Finally, Newton also eventually became head of the British Royal Society, an organization committed to spreading the new spirit of experimentation.

THE IMPACT OF THE SCIENTIFIC REVOLUTION ON PHILOSOPHY

Among the philosophers affected by the new science was **Francis Bacon** (1561–1626). Bacon led an extraordinarily varied life. He was a lawyer, an official in the government of James I, a historian, and an essayist. The one thing he did not do in his life, it seems, was perform scientific experiments. What he did contribute to science was the experimental methodology. In his three major works, *The Advancement of Learning* (1605), *Novum Organum* (1620), and *New Atlantis* (1627), Bacon attacked medieval scholasticism with its belief that the body of knowledge was basically complete and that the only task left to scholars was to elaborate on existing knowledge. Instead, Bacon argued that rather than rely on tradition, it was necessary to examine evidence from nature. Bacon's system became known as **inductive reasoning**, or **empiricism**. In France, this debate over the new learning became known as the conflict between the ancients and the moderns, while in England it was known as the "Battle of the Books."

René Descartes

The French philosopher **Descartes** (1596–1650) can in some ways be seen as the anti-Bacon. For Descartes, **deductive thought** (also referred to as **Rationalism**)—using reason to go from a general principle to the specific principle—provided for a better understanding of the universe than did relying on the experimental method. However, like Bacon, Descartes believed that the ideas of the past were so suffocating that they all must be doubted. In his famous quote, **"I think, therefore I am,"** Descartes stripped away his belief in everything except his own existence. Another way that Descartes broke with the past was by writing in French rather than Latin, which had been the language of intellectual discourse in the Middle Ages. Descartes was also a highly gifted mathematician who invented analytical mathematics.

Descartes's system can be found in his *Discourse on Method* (1637). In the work, he reduced nature to two distinct elements: mind and matter. The world of the mind involved the soul and the spirit, and Descartes left that world to the theologians. The world of matter, however, was made up of an infinite number of particles. He viewed this world as operating in a mechanistic manner, as if in a constant whirlpool that provided contact among the various particles.

Blaise Pascal

Pascal (1623–1662) saw his life as a balancing act. He wanted to balance what he saw as the dogmatic thinking of the Jesuits with those who were complete religious skeptics. His life's attempt to achieve this balance is found in his *Pensées*, particularly in the idea that became known as **Pascal's Wager**, in which Pascal concluded that it was better to wager on the existence of God than on the obverse, since the expected value that comes from believing is always greater than the expected value of not believing. Pascal became involved with the **Jansenists**, a Catholic faction that saw truth in St. Augustine's idea of the total sinfulness of mankind and the need for salvation to be achieved through faith because we are predestined—ideas that were also followed by the Calvinists.

Thomas Hobbes

Thomas Hobbes (1588–1679) personally knew Galileo, Bacon, and Descartes and was also friends with **William Harvey** (1578–1657), who, rather than relying on the writings of the Ancient Greeks, used dissections to show the role the heart plays in the circulation of blood through the body. His contact with the leading figures in the world of science influenced Hobbes to apply the experimental methods they used in the study of nature to the study of politics. Hobbes was horrified by the turmoil of the English Revolution and was convinced of the depravity of human nature; man was like an animal in that he was stimulated by appetites rather than by noble ideas. Hobbes wrote in his classic work, *Leviathan*, that life without government was "nasty, brutish, and short."

Hobbes's view of the depravity of human nature led him to propose the necessity for **absolutism**. Man formed states, or what Hobbes called the great Leviathan, because they were necessary constructs that worked to restrain the human urges to destroy one another. Out of necessity, the sovereign has complete and total power over his subjects. The subjects are obliged never to rebel, and the sovereign must put down rebellion by any means possible. When the parliamentary side won the civil war, Hobbes went back to England and quietly went on with his life. He readily accepted any established power, and could therefore live under Cromwell's firm rule. His theories did not please traditional English royalists, since his brand of absolutism was not based on the divine right theory of kingship.

Science and Hobbes
Hobbes' willingness to think scientifically shows the way in which the world had changed from the time of Machiavelli, whose work reflects the world as it was before the Scientific Revolution.

John Locke

Like Hobbes, **John Locke** (1632–1704) was interested in the world of science. His *Two Treatises on Government*, written before the Revolution of 1688, was published after William and Mary came to the throne and served as a defense of the revolution as well as a basis for the English Bill of Rights. It also proved critical for the intellectual development of the founders of the United States. Locke argued that man is born free in nature, although as society gets more advanced, government is needed to organize this society. Because man is a free and rational entity, when he enters into a **social contract** with the state, he does not give up his inalienable rights to life, liberty, and property. Should an oppressive government challenge those rights, man has a right to rebel.

Locke was an opponent of religious enthusiasm. In his *Letter Concerning Toleration*, Locke attacked the idea that Christianity could be spread by force. His influential *Essay on Human Understanding* contained the idea that children enter the world with no set ideas. At birth, the mind is a blank slate or *tabula rasa,* and infants do not possess the Christian concept of predestination or original sin. Instead, Locke subscribed to the theory that all knowledge was empirical in that it comes from experience.

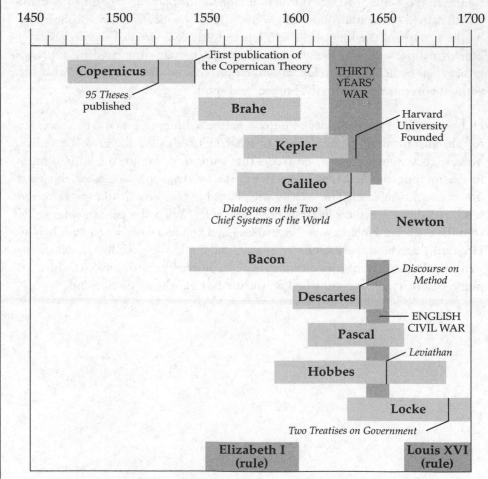

Scientists and Philosophers of the Scientific Revolution, 1450–1700

THE EIGHTEENTH-CENTURY ENLIGHTENMENT

Although his response has become a bit of a cliché, there is no better answer to the question "What is the Enlightenment?" than that offered by the German philosopher **Immanuel Kant** (1724–1804). For Kant, the answer was clear: "Dare to know." By this, he meant that it was necessary for individuals to cast off those ideas of the past that had been accepted simply because of tradition or intellectual laziness and instead use one's reason to probe for answers to questions on the nature of mankind. The ultimate reward, stated Kant, would be something that all previous generations had so woefully lacked—freedom. This freedom would extend to the political and religious realms and would also lead the writers of the Enlightenment to cast doubt on such ancient human practices as slavery.

Traditionally, the Enlightenment has been associated with France, where they use the term *philosophes* to describe the thinkers of the age. These *philosophes* were not organized in any formal group, although many of the most prominent displayed their erudition at salons, which were informal discussion groups organized by wealthy women. Others would hang around the print shop putting the final touches on their pamphlets. No matter where their ideas were produced, French thinkers helped produce the so-called **"Republic of Letters,"** an international community of writers who communicated in French. This Republic of Letters extended throughout much of western Europe and, of course, to the American colonies, where the ideas of the Enlightenment would play a significant role in the founding of the United States.

The direction of the Enlightenment changed over the course of the eighteenth century. The early Enlightenment was deeply rooted in the Scientific Revolution and was profoundly influenced by Great Britain, which appeared to continental writers as a bastion of freedom and economic expansion, while also providing the world with such inestimable thinkers as John Locke. Locke's idea, expressed in his *Essay Concerning Human Understanding*, that the individual is a blank slate at birth, provided a powerful argument for the potential impact of education as well as for the inherent equality among all people. Locke also greatly influenced eighteenth-century thought through his contention that every person has the right to life, liberty, and property, and that there is a contractual relationship between the ruler and the subjects.

As the age of Enlightenment continued, it moved beyond the influence of Locke, who had refused to see how freedom could be granted to slaves in the Americas. Writers such as **Voltaire** and **David Hume** would offer a powerful challenge to established religion. By the end of the century, people such as **Adam Smith** had veered into other areas such as economic thought. **Jean-Jacques Rousseau** inspired people of the age to seek to find truth not through the cold application of reason, but rather through a thorough examination of their inner emotions. Meanwhile, in places such as Russia, Prussia, and Austria, rulers sought to find ways to blend their royal absolutism with some of the ideas of the Enlightenment, although little would come out of this attempt except perhaps a further enhancement of their absolute authority.

Overseas Enlightenment
Enlightenment principles extended all the way to the American colonies and provided the philosophical and political foundation of the United States. Because the U.S. Constitution has since been a model for so many others across the globe, it's safe to say that Enlightenment thinkers changed the world.

Voltaire's Famous *Candide*

Voltaire's most famous work is *Candide* (1759), which he was inspired to write following an earthquake that completely leveled the city of Lisbon in 1755. Voltaire was particularly struck by the story of a group of parishioners who, following the earthquake, went back into their church to give thanks to God for sparing their lives, only to have the weakened foundations of the church collapse on them. One of the false stereotypes concerning the Enlightenment is that it was fundamentally optimistic. *Candide* is a deeply pessimistic work, as young Candide and his traveling companions meet with one disaster after another. The book basically touts the idea that humans cannot expect to find contentment by connecting themselves with a specific philosophical system. Instead, the best one can hope for is a sort of private, inner solace, or as Voltaire put it, "one must cultivate one's own garden."

Voltaire

Perhaps the greatest of the *philosophes* was **Voltaire** (1694–1778). After writing a number of rather forgettable volumes of poetry and drama, Voltaire went to England, a trip that would forever change his life. He was struck by the relative religious tolerance practiced there as well as the freedom to express one's ideas in print—far greater than that which existed in France. Voltaire was also struck by the honor the English showed Newton when the scientist was buried with great pomp at a state funeral. To Voltaire, England seemed to offer those things that allowed for the happiness of the individual, which seemed so desperately lacking in his own land of France.

Although educated by the Jesuits, Voltaire hated the Catholic Church and despised what he thought was the narrowness and bigotry that was at the heart of all religious traditions. Voltaire, like many of his contemporaries, was a **deist**, one who believes that God created the universe and then stepped back from creation to allow it to operate under the laws of science. Voltaire felt that religion crushed the human spirit and that to be free, man needed to *Écrasez l'infame!* (Crush the horrible thing!)—his famous anti-religious slogan.

Voltaire became an intellectual celebrity across Europe following his involvement in the case of Jean Calas, a French Protestant who was falsely accused of murdering his son after learning that the son was planning to convert to Catholicism. In 1762, the Parlement of Toulouse ordered Calas's execution, and he was brutally tortured to death. In the following year, Voltaire published his *Treatise on Toleration* and pushed for a reexamination of the evidence. By 1765, the authorities reversed their decision, and while it was obviously too late to aid the unfortunate Calas, Voltaire was able to use the case as a lynchpin in his fight against religious dogmatism and intolerance, one of the greatest legacies of the Enlightenment.

Montesquieu

Montesquieu's View

Like Voltaire, Montesquieu believed that societies and their political institutions could be studied in a scientific manner.

Charles Louis de Secondat, **Baron de Montesquieu** (1689–1755), wrote what was perhaps the most influential work of the Enlightenment, *Spirit of the Laws* (1748). Montesquieu, who became president of the Parlement of Bordeaux, a body of nobles that functioned as the province's law court, was, like Voltaire, inspired by the political system found in Great Britain. He incorrectly interpreted the British constitution, and in the *Spirit of the Laws*, Montesquieu wrote of the English **separation of powers** among the various branches of government providing for the possibility of **checks and balances**, something that did not exist in the British system. In many ways Montesquieu was a political conservative who did not believe in a republic—which he associated with anarchy—but rather wanted France to reestablish aristocratic authority as a means of placing limits on royal absolutism.

In an earlier work, *Persian Letters* (1721), Montesquieu critiques his native France through a series of letters between two Persians traveling in Europe. To avoid royal and church censorship, Montesquieu executed a deeply satirical work that attacked religious zealotry, while also implying that despite the differences between the Islamic East and the Christian West, a universal system of justice was necessary. Another aspect of Montesquieu's universal ideals was his anti-slavery sentiment; he deplored slavery as being against natural law.

Diderot and the *Encyclopedia*

The *Encyclopedia*, the brainchild of **Denis Diderot** (1713–1784), was one of the greatest collaborative achievements of the Enlightenment and was executed by the community of scholars known as the Republic of Letters. The *Encylopedia* exemplifies the eighteenth-century belief that all knowledge could be organized and presented in a scientific manner. The first of 28 volumes appeared in 1751, with such luminaries as Voltaire, Montesquieu, and Rousseau contributing articles. Diderot, the son of an artisan, also had a great deal of respect for those who worked with their hands, and included articles on various tools and the ways in which they made people more productive.

The *Encyclopedia* was also important for spreading Enlightenment ideas beyond the borders of France; copies were sent to places as far away as Russia and Scandinavia, and on the American shores, Thomas Jefferson and Benjamin Franklin purchased their own sets. In various parts of Europe, the work was attacked by the censors, particularly in places like Italy where the Catholic Church was highly critical of what it viewed as thinly veiled attacks on its religious practices. In France, the work was at various times placed under the censor's ban, since it was highly critical of monarchical authority. Ironically, Diderot had to turn to the throne for protection of his copyright when printers published pirated copies.

Jean-Jacques Rousseau

Enlightenment thought did not consist of a single intellectual strand. The work of **Rousseau** (1712–1778) provides one of the best examples of this fact. He lived a deeply troubled and solitary existence, and at one point or another antagonized many of the other leading *philosophes*, including Voltaire, who hated Rousseau's championing of emotion over reason. Rousseau was perhaps the most radical of the *philosophes*. Unlike many of the *philosophes* who believed in a constitutional monarchy as the best form of government, Rousseau believed in the creation of a direct democracy. Although during his lifetime his works were not widely read, following Rousseau's death, his ideas became far more influential, and many of the leading participants in the more radical stages of the **French Revolution** studied his work.

Rousseau and Romanticism
Rousseau helped set the stage for the **Romantic Movement** of the late eighteenth and nineteenth centuries. His pedagogical novel *Émile* (1762) deals with a young man who receives an education that places higher regard on developing his emotions over his reason. To achieve this, the character Émile is encouraged to explore nature as a means of heightening his emotional sensitivity. Rousseau was also important for emphasizing the differences between children and adults. He argued that there were stages of development during which the child needed to be allowed to grow freely without undue influence from the adult world.

His greatest achievement, *The Social Contract* (1762), begins with the classic line: "All men are born free, but everywhere they are in chains." He once again differed from many of the other *philosophes*, however, in that he had little faith in the individual's potential to use reason as a means of leading a more satisfactory life. Instead, Rousseau explained that the focus needed to be placed on reforming the overall community, since only through the individual's attachment to a larger society could the powerless people hope to achieve much of anything. Sovereignty would be expressed in this ideal society not through the will of the king but rather via the **general will** of the populace; only by surrendering to this general will could the individual hope to find genuine freedom.

THE SPREAD OF ENLIGHTENMENT THOUGHT

Although originally rooted in France, over the course of the eighteenth century, the Enlightenment spread to other parts of Europe.

Germany

The greatest figure of the German Enlightenment, **Immanuel Kant** (1724–1804), argued in his *Critique of Pure Reason* (1781) against the idea that all knowledge was empirical, since the mind shapes the world through its unique experiences. Like Rousseau, Kant's emphasis that other, possibly hidden, layers of knowledge exist beyond the knowledge that could be achieved through the use of reason served to inspire a generation of Romantic artists, who felt stifled by the application of pure reason.

Italy

In Italy, **Cesare Beccaria** (1738–1794), in his work *On Crimes and Punishment* (1764), called for a complete overhaul in the area of **jurisprudence**. For Beccaria, it was clear that those who were accused of perpetrating crimes should also be allowed certain basic rights, and he argued against such common practices of the day as the use of torture to gain admissions of guilt as well as the application of capital punishment. Beccaria's work can be seen as part of the overall theme of humanitarianism found in the Enlightenment, which extended from such areas as the push to end flogging in the British navy to the call for better treatment of animals.

Scotland

One of the most vibrant intellectual centers of the eighteenth century was Scotland, a place that hitherto had not been at the center of European intellectual life. The philosopher **David Hume** (1711–1776) pushed his thinking further than French deists and delved directly into the world of atheism. In *Inquiry into Human Nature*, Hume cast complete doubt on revealed religion, arguing that no empirical evidence supported the existence of those miracles that stood at the heart of Christian tradition.

Another Scottish author, **Edward Gibbon** (1737–1794), reflected the growing interest in history that was first seen during the Enlightenment with his monumental *Decline and Fall of the Roman Empire*. His work criticized Christianity in that he viewed its rise within the Roman Empire as a social phenomenon rather than a divine interference. He also asserted that Christianity weakened the vibrancy of the Empire and contributed to its fall.

The Scottish Enlightenment also made a huge impact on economic thought through the work of **Adam Smith** (1723–1790), a professor at the University of Glasgow. In 1776, Smith published *Inquiry into the Nature and Causes of the Wealth of Nations*, in which he argued against mercantilism, a term that refers to the system of navigation acts, tariffs, and monopolies that stood as the economic underpinnings for most of the nations of Europe. Smith became associated with the concept of *laissez-faire*, literally to "leave alone," since he argued that individuals should be free to pursue economic gain without being restricted by the state. Rather than producing economic anarchy, such a system would be self regulating, as if controlled by an **invisible hand,** which would lead to the meeting of supply and demand. Smith's thinking proved influential for both the **Manchester School** of economists in England and the **Physiocrats** in France.

WOMEN AND THE ENLIGHTENMENT

Women figured prominently in the Enlightenment; most of the Parisian **salons** were organized by women. At times, these wealthy and aristocratic individuals would use their social and political connections to help the *philosophes* avoid trouble with the authorities or perhaps aid them in receiving some sort of government sinecure to allow them greater freedom to work. Perhaps surprisingly, given the great help that women proffered to the *philosophes*, these male thinkers for the most part were not tremendous advocates of the rights and abilities of women. The *Encyclopedia* barely bothered to address the condition of women, although the work may never have reached the reading public without the aid of the **Marquise de Pompadour**, Louis XV's mistress, who played a critical role in helping Diderot avoid censorship.

Some writers were more sympathetic to women's issues than others. Montesquieu, in his *Persian Letters*, included a discussion of the restrictive nature of the Eastern harem, which by implication, was a criticism of the treatment of women in western Europe. Rousseau, on the other hand, while a radical on many issues, was an advocate of the idea that men and women occupied separate spheres and that women should not be granted an equal education to men. By the end of the century, inspired partially by the French Revolution and partially by the Enlightenment, the Englishwoman **Mary Wollstonecraft** (1759–1797) wrote in her *Vindication of the Rights of Women* that women should enjoy the right to vote as well as to hold political office, the first openly published statement of such ideas.

THAT'S A LOT OF NAMES, HUH?

Many AP European History students struggle with the sheer volume of ideas and thinkers during the Age of Enlightenment. Check out this handy graphic to help you review who said what and hailed from where.

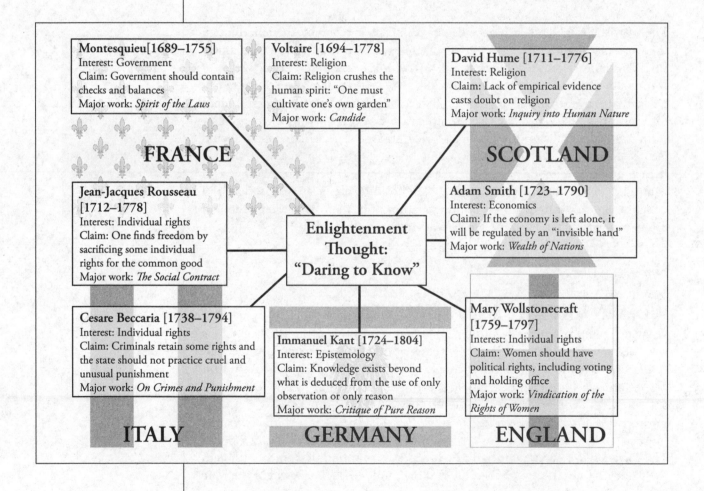

Montesquieu[1689–1755]
Interest: Government
Claim: Government should contain checks and balances
Major work: *Spirit of the Laws*

Voltaire [1694–1778]
Interest: Religion
Claim: Religion crushes the human spirit: "One must cultivate one's own garden"
Major work: *Candide*

David Hume [1711–1776]
Interest: Religion
Claim: Lack of empirical evidence casts doubt on religion
Major work: *Inquiry into Human Nature*

FRANCE

SCOTLAND

Jean-Jacques Rousseau [1712–1778]
Interest: Individual rights
Claim: One finds freedom by sacrificing some individual rights for the common good
Major work: *The Social Contract*

Adam Smith [1723–1790]
Interest: Economics
Claim: If the economy is left alone, it will be regulated by an "invisible hand"
Major work: *Wealth of Nations*

Enlightenment Thought: "Daring to Know"

Cesare Beccaria [1738–1794]
Interest: Individual rights
Claim: Criminals retain some rights and the state should not practice cruel and unusual punishment
Major work: *On Crimes and Punishment*

Immanuel Kant [1724–1804]
Interest: Epistemology
Claim: Knowledge exists beyond what is deduced from the use of only observation or only reason
Major work: *Critique of Pure Reason*

Mary Wollstonecraft [1759–1797]
Interest: Individual rights
Claim: Women should have political rights, including voting and holding office
Major work: *Vindication of the Rights of Women*

ITALY

GERMANY

ENGLAND

EUROPEAN POWERS IN THE AGE OF ENLIGHTENMENT

The eighteenth century witnessed a number of significant developments for the European nation-states. Two major powers, Prussia and Russia, emerged over the course of the century, while Austria, France, and Great Britain adjusted to changing political, economic, and social circumstances.

The century would also be noteworthy for the monarchs who sought to govern using ideas taken from the writings of the French *philosophes*. Rulers such as **Catherine the Great** of Russia, **Joseph II** of Austria, and **Frederick II** of Prussia are generally referred to as "**Enlightened Absolutists.**" They could safely toy with the ideas of the *philosophes* without threatening their own power because most of the *philosophes* were not republicans but were believers in monarchical authority (although they felt that the power of the monarchy should be wielded in a more rational manner). These monarchs found that the writings of the *philosophes* on economics and education could mesh with their own desires to enhance the power of their states within the community of European nations and their personal authority within the state. What made this even more appealing for these Enlightened Absolutists was that this would be achieved at the expense of those elements in society, such as the nobility or the Church, that had previously stood in the way of this centralizing tendency.

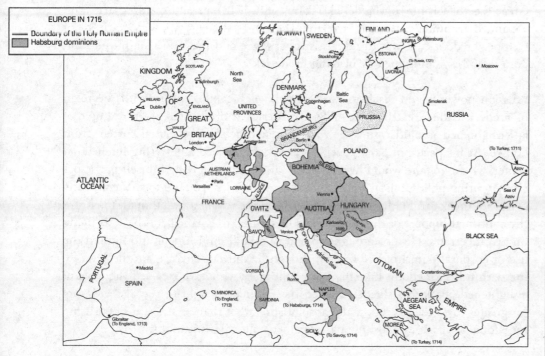

Europe in 1715

Prussia and Austria

It is perhaps rather surprising that Prussia would emerge in the eighteenth century as one of the dominant European powers and a rival to Austria for hegemony in Germany. In the seventeenth century, Prussia was a poor German state that was devastated by various marauding armies during the **Thirty Years' War**, although in the **Peace of Westphalia**, marking the end of the conflict, Prussia did receive some minor territorial gains. Relatively poor agricultural land and labor shortages led to the establishment of serfdom by the sixteenth century. This led to the state receiving some badly needed support from the Prussian nobility, the **Junkers**, who looked to the ruler to ensure control over their serfs.

The first ruler to tap into whatever potential the Prussian state possessed was **Frederick William** (r. 1640–1688), often referred to as the **"Great Elector"** since in his capacity as ruler of Brandenburg he served as one of the electors of the Holy Roman Emperor. Because his state consisted of three noncontiguous chunks of land without natural borders, Frederick William wanted to build an army. As he was without significant resources of his own, he worked out an agreement with the Junkers, according to which they would provide him with revenue in exchange for his acceptance of their control over the serfs. This was the beginning of a long and mutually beneficial relationship between the Prussian monarchy and the Junkers, who found that Frederick's expanded army offered them the opportunity to leave their poor agricultural lands and engage in more appealing careers as officers. The Great Elector left his son Frederick III (r. 1688–1713) a well-organized army, an expanded territorial base, and arguably the most efficient civil service in all of Europe. Frederick III was to take this inheritance and make Prussia into a kingdom in 1701, gaining the title of **King Frederick I**.

Prussian power would reach its zenith in the eighteenth century with the reign of **Frederick the Great** (r. 1740–1786). Frederick is often cited as an example of an enlightened absolutist, since he was fascinated by the intellectual current from France. At his palace of Sans Souci, Frederick established a glittering intellectual center, where Voltaire would live for a time and where the King himself participated by writing philosophical tracts, which may have led Voltaire to make an early exit from the court. Frederick freed the serfs on the royal estates, though to ensure the continual support of the Junker class he refused to emancipate the serfs living on private estates. He also brought an end to capital punishment and limited the use of corporal punishment on serfs, though he did not emancipate the Jews living within his kingdom. Like his royal colleagues who have received the label of enlightened absolutists, Frederick used the rational thought of the age as a tool for greater royal centralization and absolutism, rather than as a means of ensuring individual rights or establishing participatory political institutions.

A more thoroughgoing series of reforms inspired by the Enlightenment took place in Austria, where the Empress **Maria Theresa** pushed a series of reforms that removed some of the hardships that had been placed on the serf population. Her son **Joseph II** (r. 1765–1790) was impressed with the idea of religious toleration, mainly because he wished to reduce the power of the Catholic Church within his own domains. He viewed the Church as hostile to his plan for greater centralized authority. In 1781, he issued the first of a series of Edicts of Toleration granting Jews, Lutherans, and Calvinists freedom of worship. Civil liabilities were still left in place for Jews—while Protestants could enter into the Habsburg civil service, Jews were still barred and were forced to pay special taxes for the right to worship. Joseph antagonized his aristocracy by making them responsible for taxes and by abolishing serfdom. Following his death in 1790, his brother and heir, **Leopold II** (r. 1790–1792), was forced to back away from some of Joseph's enlightened policies in order to put an end to a series of aristocratic and peasant revolts.

Unfortunately, when they were not perusing the writings of the *philosophes*, the rulers of Prussia and Austria were often engaged in violent conflict. The roots of the **War of the Austrian Succession** (1740–1748) began during the reign of the Holy Roman Emperor **Charles VI** (r. 1711–1740), who, because he lacked a male heir, pushed the other European states to accept what was known as the **Pragmatic Sanction**, allowing for the assorted Habsburg lands under his control to remain intact under one ruler and granting the right of a female to succeed to the throne of Austria if there was no direct male heir.

When Charles died without leaving a son, his daughter Maria Theresa came to the throne. While both France and Prussia had promised to respect the Pragmatic Sanction, both nations viewed the death of Charles as an opportunity to gain territory at the expense of the Austrians. Frederick immediately launched an attack to seize **Silesia**, the richest part of the Austrian empire at the northeastern border of Bohemia. Regaining Silesia was to prove impossible for Maria Theresa, but with the help of Hungarian nobility, which had agreed to the Pragmatic Sanction in exchange for recognition of Hungary as an independent kingdom, she was able to put down a dangerous revolt in Bohemia and remain on the throne.

The conflict became a general European war with Austria gaining support from Russia, Sweden, Denmark, and eventually Great Britain, which feared French territorial gains in the Austrian Netherlands. Opposing them was an alliance made up of Prussia, France, and Spain. By the time the war came to a close in 1748 with the signing of the **Treaty of Aix-la-Chapelle**, the Austrian throne was ultimately saved for the Habsburgs. (Because women remained ineligible to head the Holy Roman Empire, Maria Theresa's husband was to hold that position as Emperor Francis I.)

One result of the war was that Prussia emerged as a German state and a major rival to Austria. Understanding that Prussia, under its aggressive King Frederick, would continue to be a threat, in 1756, Maria Theresa's able foreign minister, Count Kaunitz, brought about what became known as the **Diplomatic Revolution** (or reversal of alliances) by working out an alliance with France, the traditional enemy of the Austrian Habsburgs and a state that was increasingly wary of growing Prussian power. France also demanded the Austrian Netherlands as their price for this alliance. Sweden and Russia signed on as part of an alliance that increasingly looked as if it would result in significant territorial gains at the expense of the Prussians.

The other side of this Diplomatic Revolution was that Great Britain broke off its ties with Austria and became allies with Prussia, and while the British did not contribute men to the war on the continent, their financial subsidies were vital in enabling Frederick to continue fighting. The Diplomatic Revolution led directly to the **Seven Years War** (1756–1763), which started when Frederick launched an attack in 1756 in order to quickly put down his enemies before they had an opportunity to form a cohesive military plan to defeat Prussia. Initially, the bold Prussian plan paid off as Frederick first defeated a French and then an Austrian army, but disaster struck when a massive Russian army arrived from the east and took Frederick's capital of Berlin. Only the crowning of a new Russian tsar, **Peter III**, in 1762 staved off the complete destruction of the Prussian state, since Peter, an admirer of Frederick, wanted no part in the conflict and brought his army home. So Frederick, by preserving the Prussian state, was the clear winner on the continent, while his British allies had won a series of tremendous victories overseas against the French, particularly in the **French and Indian War**, resulting in the confiscation of French colonies in India and Canada.

Russia

Until the eighteenth century, Russia remained largely closed off to western Europe as a result of the Mongol invasion of the thirteenth century. Some trade did exist; for instance, Elizabethan England imported Russian timber for the building of ships, but for the most part Russia was not affected by developments in the West, most notably missing out on the humanistic culture of the Italian Renaissance.

By the sixteenth century, the Duchy of Muscovy would emerge as the dominant state within the Russian steppe, an area that had absorbed a number of other rival states while pushing the Mongols back to the east. During the reign of the appropriately named **Ivan the Terrible** (r. 1533–1584), there was a significant expansion of the territory under the control of Muscovy, while Ivan also sought, often through staggeringly violent means, to gain control over a recalcitrant nobility. Following his death in 1584, Russia entered into the period known as the **"Time of Troubles,"** which lasted until the selection of a tsar from the **Romanov family** in 1603, the dynasty that would continue to rule Russia until the Revolution of 1917.

The individual who did the most to transform the Russian state into a major European power was **Peter the Great** (r. 1682–1725). As a young man, Peter traveled to the West where he became fascinated by the work done in Dutch shipyards and other examples of Western technology. Upon his return to Russia, Peter was determined to Westernize his backward state. Peter expanded the revenue available to the monarchy by imposing head taxes on Russian serfs while also establishing monopolies on essential commodities such as salt. Peter used this expanded revenue to follow the lead of the absolutist states in Europe and establish a centralized bureaucracy. In order to ensure the loyalty of his nobility as well as use them for governance, Peter established a Table of Ranks, in which all positions in the state had graduated rankings, which also provided an opportunity for commoners to rise up the ranks and reach a coveted position as a noble. Just as in Prussia, the nobility were to be used as an essential tool of royal absolutism. In keeping with his desire to keep a **"window to the West,"** Peter

Off with Their Beards!
Peter famously forced his nobles to shave their beards, as was the style in the West, as his first step in Westernizing his state.

established the eponymous city of **St. Petersburg** in 1703. The city was built on what seemed to be unpromising marsh land, and thousands of serf laborers would lose their lives in the building of a grand city with architecture that mimicked the newest styles from France.

At the start of World War I, many of the Russian officers had German names, the descendents of the Western military experts that Peter invited to Russia to help him establish a standing army. To ensure that he had enough soldiers, Peter conscripted serfs to serve in his force for the interminable period of twenty years. Peter also built the first Russian navy. Peter used his army to greatly expand Russian territory, and in achieving this goal, he was fortunate that his state was becoming more powerful at the same time that the major states on his borders, the Ottoman Empire and the Kingdom of Poland-Lithuania, were in relative decline. Most notably, he defeated the Swedes in the **Great Northern War** (1700–1721), which marked the end of the brief period going back to the age of Gustavus Adolphus in the seventeenth century when Sweden was a great European power.

Love and Politics
Catherine didn't hesitate to mix love and politics. Her affair with Stanislaw August Poniatowski resulted in not only the birth of Catherine's second child, Anna, but also the election of Poniatowski as King of Poland-Lithuania.

The westward outlook of Russia during the reign of Peter would continue under his successors. Western thought, particularly the writings of the French *philosophes*, would play a role in inspiring the reign of **Catherine the Great** (r. 1762–1796). While the story of Catherine and the horse is most likely the stuff of legend, she was a robust, sexually active woman who read Montesquieu and Voltaire and toyed with ways to apply their ideas to her still semi-barbaric state. Catherine began the process of revising and codifying Russian law, but for the most part, she only dabbled with bringing about actual reform. Once she became convinced later on in her reign that enlightened thought could pose a challenge to her monarchy, she dropped the idea entirely. While few practical results stemmed from Catherine's infatuation with Enlightenment thought, it did help establish the primacy of French culture and ideas among the Russian aristocracy.

Spain

Before he ascended to the throne of Spain, Charles III (r. 1759-1788) was the well-regarded King of Naples. Having studied the essays of Benito Feijóo, Spain's foremost Enlightenment thinker, Charles embarked to bring about reforms that echoed Feijóo's challenges to the more orthodox teachings of the Catholic Church. One of Charles' first standoffs with the Church came in 1735 when Pope Clement XII refused to recognize Charles' legitimacy as King of Naples. Naples was seen by the Church as just another region under control of the Papal States; accordingly, the Church considered the pope the one and only authority in this kingdom.

Prosperity Under Charles
The prosperity of Charles' reign had much to do with Spain finally being viewed as a unified nation.

When Pope Clement died and was replaced by Pope Benedict XIV in 1740, Charles seized the opportunity to assert his firm belief that the Church should hold no special authority in his kingdom. Benito Feijóo's writings that rejected the harsh orthodoxy of the Church came into practice as Charles negotiated a concordat with Pope Benedict to tax church officials and hold them equal under the law.

In 1759, Charles III ascended to the Spanish throne following the death of his brother. Charles was determined to continue his Enlightenment-inspired reforms, which included laws from banning bullfighting to protecting free trade to developing roads and canals. In Spain, Charles continued his goal of limiting the Church's power in his sovereign state. He was able to decrease the number of clergy, who many Spanish felt were not contributing adequately to society. At the same time, due to the respect garnered by the Spanish Enlightenment philosophers, the Inquisition was increasingly viewed largely as an antiquated mission.

Russia: Catherine the Great (1762-1796)
Enlightened influence: Montesquieu and Voltaire
Enlightened actions: systemized laws, brought ideas of French philosophy to Russian aristocracy

Prussia: Frederick II (the Great) (1740-1786)
Enlightened influence: Voltaire
Enlightened actions: freed the serfs, supported academia, ended capital punishment

Austria: Joseph II (1769-1790)
Enlightened influence: Voltaire
Enlightened actions: issued the Edicts of Tolerance, weakened the Church

Spain: Charles III (1759-1788)
Enlightened influence: Benito Feijóo
Enlightened actions: weakened the Church, funded science and academia, kept peace

0   200   400 Miles
0   200   400 Kilometers

N
W — E
S

Poland

The story of Poland in the eighteenth century consists of the complete eradication of a nation that had previously played a critical role in the affairs of central Europe. The traditional starting date for the history of Poland is 966, when Prince Mieszko, who was to be the founder of a dynasty (Piast) that would rule Poland for four centuries, accepted Roman Catholicism, firmly tying Poland to the culture of western Europe. Vulnerable to attacks due to a lack of natural borders, the Poles in the Middle Ages had to deal with threats from the Mongols from the East as well as the Teutonic Knights from the West. In order to deal with the threat from the crusading order, a new dynasty was established in 1385 (Jagiellon) through uniting Poland with Lithuania, when the Lithuanian Grand Duke Jagiello, the ruler of the last pagan state in Europe, married the Polish Queen Jadwiga. This newly created **Polish-Lithuanian Commonwealth** met its initial goal of defeating the Teutonic Knights by securing an important victory at the Battle of Grunwald (Germans refer to it as the Battle of Tannenberg).

The fatal flaw for the Polish-Lithuanian state was the failure to create a strong, centralized government in the face of a recalcitrant nobility that feared the loss of authority. By the end of the sixteenth century, the nobles had greatly weakened the crown by making it an elective position and often selecting foreign princes to further ensure it would remain a weak title. This policy became increasingly dangerous in the seventeenth century, as new threats appeared from the Swedes and the Russians. The Polish-Lithuanian state still remained a significant player in Europe up until the end of the century, when King Jan Sobieski played a critical role in driving the Turks from the gates of Vienna in 1683, but by the middle of the eighteenth century, Poland was so weak that it maintained its independence only by the good graces of Russia. Poland's luck ran out, however, eventually resulting in the loss of a great deal of land.

When Poniatowski became king in 1764, he displayed an independent streak that Catherine the Great did not expect from her former lover. This did not bode well for Poniatowski's attempt to move the nation's political system in a more centralized direction, an attempt that was met with displeasure by all of Poland's neighbors. In 1772, Russia, Prussia, and Austria forced Poland to accept a **partition** that cost Poland 30 percent of its territory. In some ways, this first partition provided the nudge for Poland to finally get its political house in order. Influenced by the ideas of the Enlightenment, in 1791, the Polish-Lithuanian parliament (*Sejm*) produced Europe's first written **constitution**. The constitution, which was never fully implemented (although it remained a beacon for later generations of Polish reformers), angered many nobles who saw their influence reduced as well as Poland's neighbors who feared a national revival. The anti-Poniatowski nobles applied to the Russians for assistance, and Catherine, with the aid of Prussia, was more than willing to intercede.

Russia and Prussia insisted on the removal of the constitution and also carried out the **Second** Partition in 1793. This led to the loss of vast lands in the eastern part of the nation and reduced Poland to a rump state. In a heroic, last ditch effort to retain statehood, a Polish revolt broke out in 1794 under the military leadership of

Tadeusz Kosciuszko, who had fought with distinction in the American Revolution. Overwhelmed by more powerful enemies, Poniatowski was forced to abdicate, and a **third and final partition** took place in 1795, wiping Poland off the map. Despite the best hopes of Polish nationalists throughout the nineteenth century, an independent Polish state would only be revived in the aftermath of World War I.

Great Britain

After the turmoil of the seventeenth century, Great Britain became the most stable nation in Europe in the eighteenth century. The triumph of Parliament in its struggle against Stuart absolutism put Great Britain in a position of political stability that would provide one of the critical foundations for the establishment of a vast overseas empire, as well as the industrial transformation that would begin by the middle of the century.

With the death of Queen Anne in 1714, the throne passed to **George I** (r. 1714–1721), the ruler of the German state of Hanover, whose sole qualification was that he was a Protestant cousin of the late queen. Like his son **George II** (r. 1727–1760), he was far happier spending time in Hanover, where he could reign as an unquestioned absolutist, rather than having to deal with the independent-minded British Parliament. While there is a historical debate over the strength of support within Great Britain for the Stuart cause, the eighteenth century did experience two pro-Stuart revolts, in 1715 and 1745, the latter one famous for the involvement of "Bonnie Prince Charles," who saw his dream of being restored to the throne dashed at the Battle of Culloden in 1746.

While it was clear that after 1688 the Houses of Parliament would dominate political life within the country, how that power was to be utilized in an efficient manner remained one of the significant questions in the early part of the eighteenth century. The most significant development in this regard was the evolution of the office of prime minister, which, while not officially recognized until 1905, became a political reality in all but name during **Robert Walpole's** tenure as Chancellor of the Exchequer from 1721 to 1741. The fact that both George I and George II were less than attentive to British domestic politics meant that Walpole had a free hand to mold the political system to his advantage. Walpole used a complex system of political patronage to maintain his control over the House of Commons. This support in the lower house became the vital component for ministerial power, and when Walpole lost that support in 1741 over a conflict over the direction of British foreign policy, he resigned his post as Chancellor of the Exchequer even though he still enjoyed the support of George II.

Another development that shaped British politics in the eighteenth century was the formation of two parliamentary blocks: **Tories** and **Whigs**. While Tories stood for the prerogative rights of the monarch and support of the Church of England, the Whigs were more closely allied to the spirit of the Revolution of 1688 and the idea of religious tolerance. When George III (r. 1760–1820) came to the throne, he claimed that he wanted the throne to rise above party strife, though **Edmund Burke** in his *Thoughts on the Cause of the Present Discontent* (1770) argued that parties were essential to parliamentary government and were a fundamental component for political stability. George III's desire to choose his own chief minister during the first ten years of his reign remained problematic until Lord North assumed the mantle of chief minister in 1770 and held the position for the next twelve years.

The problems stemming from the first ten years of George III's rule were to have important consequences as the colonists in the thirteen American colonies became increasingly restless, laying the groundwork for the **American Revolution**. The British government ended the Seven Years War with a tremendous victory over the French but also with an enormous deficit. In order to pay for the increasing costs of administering their far-flung empire, the British government looked for new sources of revenue. The passage of the **Stamp Act** in 1765, during the ministry of George Grenville, was probably a mistake, since it ticked off the two groups in society you don't want to anger: publishers and lawyers. While the British government continued to assert its right to tax the colonists as it pleased, the colonists responded that without parliamentary representation, no taxes could ever be acceptable. By 1774, American anger at what was viewed as high-handed British policies led to the establishment of the **First Continental Congress**, with open hostilities breaking out the following year at Lexington and Concord in Massachusetts. Eighteenth-century wars seemingly always brought about curious alliances, and the Americans were eventually to win their independence by 1783 with the help of France and Spain, with both states seeking to deliver a major blow to the British as payback for the Seven Years War.

The struggle for independence by the American colonists also helped to inspire a movement for parliamentary reform in Great Britain. Voting in eighteenth-century Britain was primarily the prerogative of the landed classes, but there were plenty of anomalies in the system, including a fairly wide franchise in London, while in other areas there were "rotten" boroughs such as Old Sarum, where no one had lived since the Middle Ages but which still duly provided two members to the House of Commons. The parliamentary reform movement was to emerge as a significant factor in British political life in the 1780s, but the advent of the French Revolution and, more specifically, its increasing violence and radicalism, by 1792, brought about a backlash against political reform in Great Britain, so that any expansion of suffrage would have to wait until the **Great Reform Bill** of 1832.

The Road to American Independence...

...is a topic we discuss in much greater detail in *Cracking the AP U.S. History Exam*! If you're taking AP U.S. History, check out our book for a thorough content review and lots of practice questions.

Wilkes and Liberty

In 1763, John Wilkes, a member of the House of Commons and part-time pornographer, was arrested for publishing a satirical attack on George III in his paper *The North Briton*. This event provided an outlet for those Englishmen, who, by shouting "Wilkes and Liberty" in the streets, saw the possibility of bringing about what they viewed to be much needed reforms in the political system, including greater freedom of the press and an expansion of suffrage.

France

Perhaps not surprising given the increased power of the throne during the reign of Louis XIV, a backlash against royal absolutism set in during the following century. Compared to its fellow absolutist states in central and eastern Europe, French absolutism seemed to hardly deserve the term at times, but for some Frenchmen, particularly those influenced by Enlightenment thought, the powers of the crown were seen as increasingly despotic.

An opportunity to challenge the throne came about at mid-century, when a papal decree attacked the **Jansenists**, a Catholic sect that held beliefs on predestination that were similar to the Calvinist point of view. **Louis XV** (r. 1714–1774) wished to support the papal decree and ban the group, but found himself blocked by the various provincial *parlements*, law courts primarily made up of nobles who had the prerogative right of registering royal edicts before they could be enforced. Many of those who sat in these parlements, while opposed to Jansenist teachings, also opposed registering the edicts since they felt it was emblematic of royal despotism.

During the long reign of Louis XV, the financial troubles of the monarchy increased, particularly as a result of the disastrous Seven Years War, but once again, the parlements stood in the way of any significant reform in the revenue system. Finally, in frustration, Louis XV abolished the parlements, but Louis XVI (r. 1774–1792) felt forced to bring them back in an attempt to curry favor with the nobility. The recalcitrance of the parlements in allowing the establishment of a more rational revenue system was to play a significant role in bringing France to the point of revolution by 1789.

THE FRENCH REVOLUTION

Before 1789	Pre-revolutionary period (Ancien Régime)
1789–1792	Liberal phase (Constitutional Monarchy)
1792–1793	Moderate Republic (Girondins)
1793–1794	Radical Republic (Jacobins)
1795–1799	Directory (Moderate Republic)
1799–1804	Consulate
1804–1815	Napoleonic Empire

Background to the Revolution: The Ancient Régime

Unpopularity with the Peasants

We'll never know whether Marie Antoinette truly said, "Let them eat cake," when told that the people were starving, but the fact that she and her ladies-in-waiting enjoyed pretending to be peasants (for fun) at a specially created peasant village situated at Versailles points to her general insensitivity.

Under different circumstances, Louis XVI might have made a decent constitutional monarch. He possessed the two main qualities needed for success in that job—he was rather kind and quite stupid. Unfortunately, France at this time was an absolute monarchy, and Louis's personal limitations were significant. Louis was not helped by the tremendous unpopularity of his wife, Marie Antoinette, an Austrian princess who was extremely unhappy with her marriage to the sexually impotent Louis; theirs was an arranged marriage meant to aid relations between France and Austria. Rumors regarding acts of infidelity on her part continued to plague the monarchy and helped to widen the gap between the court and the rest of the country.

The major problem facing the monarchy was financial. France was not bankrupt in 1789, although the same could not be said for the French monarchy. Throughout the eighteenth century, the country had been at war, mostly with Great Britain, a conflict that dated back to the Glorious Revolution of 1688. The ignoble defeat of French forces in the Seven Years War and the more successful involvement of French forces in the American Revolution helped exacerbate the financial difficulties facing the monarchy. The debt grew so large that interest and payments on the debt absorbed slightly more than half the annual budget. While all European nations in the eighteenth century had racked up large debts, and by comparison the French debt was not particularly onerous given the great wealth of France, the problem was that the French monarchy was unable to tap into the wealth of the nation.

In the seventeenth century, the French monarchy, in an attempt to pacify a potentially rebellious nobility, had basically granted the nobility freedom from most taxation. It would be the task of Louis XVI (r. 1774–1792) to try to convince the nobility to give up their cherished tax-free status. This meant that Louis, a weak man, would have to break the back of the Paris and regional *parlements*, royal law courts that claimed the right of judicial review of all royal edicts, therefore empowering them to veto any attempt to tax the nobility. These parlements had gained influence throughout the eighteenth century and were a bastion of aristocratic intransigence on the taxation question.

The Calling of the Estates-General and the Demand for a National Assembly

By 1787, the financial situation grew so bad that Louis XVI called an **Assembly of Notables** made up of leading aristocrats and churchmen to see if they would willingly pay a new land tax that would apply to all, regardless of social status. The notables at the meeting refused to consider the tax and instead demanded that they be granted a greater share in governing the nation. This refusal by the nobility marks the start of the process by which France would be enveloped by the Revolution. Ironically, it is the nobles who set the stage for their own downfall with their demand for the **Estates-General**, an institution from medieval times that consisted of a three-house body made up of clergy (the first estate), nobility (the second estate), and commons (the third estate). "Commons" referred to everyone from bourgeoisie to peasants who were neither clergy nor nobility. Traditionally, each house received one vote, so the clergy and nobility dominated the proceedings. The notables assumed that calling the Estates-General, which had last met in 1614, would be an effective means of ensuring that the monarchy would not implement any economic reform that would place limits on their privileges. It also ensured that the bourgeoisie would not be able to limit the rights of the nobility.

By 1788, Louis XVI decided that in the following year he would call the Estates-General. To the chagrin of the conservative nobles, the question of the assembly's voting structure immediately arose. Increasingly, writers began to declare that the **Third Estate,** consisting of all nonclergy and nonaristocracy (the majority of Frenchmen), was the true embodiment of the political will of the nation. Though the clergy were officially the **First Estate,** many simple parish priests felt more aligned with the Third Estate. Indeed, the most famous pamphlet from this period was written by the **Abbé Siéyès** (1748–1836), an obscure lower clergyman, who wrote:

What is the Third Estate? Everything.

What has it been in the political order up to the present? Nothing.

What does it ask? To become something.

By the end of 1788, the King agreed to double the number of representatives to the Third Estate, which meant little since voting would still be cast by each estate as a unit and not as individuals. Since no one has ever followed Shakespeare's sage advice on what to do with lawyers, a large portion of the 600 members of the Third Estate were from that profession. No peasants attended the sessions, which would be held in the very home of royal absolutism—Versailles.

This sense of wanting change but ultimately not knowing what direction this change should take can be seen in the thousands of *cahiers de doléances*, or lists of grievances, that were presented to the King by the various electoral assemblies at the start of the meeting of the Estates-General. Many of these documents survive, and they reveal an assortment of grievances, such as the demand for a tax system that would be more equitable and the call for regular meetings of the Estates-General, along with some more practical notions, such as the need to limit the size of sheep herds, since their bad breath was destroying French pastures. While many of the *cahiers de doléances* demanded a lessening of royal absolutism, all were loyal to the idea of monarchy and to the concept that the monarchy would continue to lead the French state. Many believed that abuses would be promptly rectified if only the King knew of them.

May 5, 1789, marked the first day of the meeting of the Estates-General. Immediately, Louis XVI angered the members of the Third Estate by keeping them waiting for several hours as he formally received the credentials of members of the first two estates. Since it was clear that the King would not compromise on voting as individuals, the members of the Third Estate delayed formally submitting their credentials for several weeks. On June 17, in a momentous decision, the Third Estate declared that it would not meet as a medieval estate based on social status but instead would only assemble before the King as a national assembly representing the political will of the entire French nation, including representatives from all three estates.

From this point on, things moved rapidly. The First Estate, although it included great clerics like the Bishop of Paris who were a part of the nobility, also included those simple parish priests who saw themselves as having more in common with the members of the Third Estate. These parish priests voted to join the Third Estate and to meet as a national assembly. Rumors began to swirl that the King was preparing to take action against leading members of the Third Estate, and they also found that their meeting hall was closed off. In one of the famous scenes from the Revolution, members of the Third Estate gathered at a tennis court on the grounds of Versailles and, in what became known as the **Tennis Court Oath**, promised to continue to meet "until the constitution of the kingdom is established and consolidated upon solid foundations." In response, the King granted a number of concessions, such as promising to periodically call the Estates-General and to drop some of the more onerous taxes on the Third Estate. Just one year earlier, such acts would have been greatly welcomed, but by this point, the King's small concessions were "too little, too late." Finally, on June 27, a desperate Louis XVI formally agreed to the consolidation of all three estates into a new national assembly.

The Storming of the Bastille and the Great Fear

The implications from these momentous events would extend far beyond the confines of Versailles. Indeed, the Revolution was about to see the first incident of violence. In Paris, panic began to set in as people continued to try to cope with a shortage of food that many blamed on the rapacious nobility and the acts of hoarders. The populace believed the rumors that the King was not interested in meeting with the National Assembly and was instead organizing troops that would be used to scatter the National Assembly and to reestablish royal absolutism. This created a panic in Paris as people searched for weaponry to defend themselves against the royal troops.

There is an ongoing debate among historians as to whether the crowds that gathered around the **Bastille**, a fortress prison in Paris famous as a symbol of royal despotism since it had held critics of the monarchy, were there spontaneously or whether they were organized by bourgeois (or middle class) elements. Regardless, the crowd of around 80,000 demanded the surrender of the fortress so they could confiscate the arms they believed were inside. Although the rebels promised safe passage to the small garrison inside, the crowd eventually surrounded them, cut off the head of the commander of the troops, and marched around the city with his head on a pike. When Louis heard about the storming of his fortress he asked, "Is this a revolt?" In response he was told, "No sire, it is a revolution."

Once again, Louis quickly made concessions. He sent away some of the troops that he had possibly planned to use to disperse the National Assembly. He formally recognized the **Commune of Paris**, the new municipal government that would come to play a pivotal role in the later stages of the Revolution. He also agreed to the formation of a National Guard under the leadership of the **Marquis de Lafayette** (1757–1834), who was already known as a champion of liberty because of his involvement in the American Revolution.

In the countryside, things also began to spiral out of control. Just as rumors had spurred on events in Paris, rumors in the countryside brought about further changes in the direction of the Revolution. For the peasants, the decade of the 1780s had been a period of poor harvests. This, combined with a crushing tax burden, had resulted in a resentful and fearful peasantry. A general panic set in known as the **Great Fear**, which consisted of rumors that the nobility were using the increasingly anarchical situation both at Versailles and in Paris to organize groups of thugs to steal from the peasants. In response, peasants began to attack some of the great noble estates, carefully burning documents that verified some of their old manorial obligations.

The Great Fear contributed to one of the most remarkable moments in the Revolution. On August 4, 1789, aristocrats in the National Assembly decided that the only way to halt the violence in the countryside was by renouncing their feudal rights. In a highly emotional scene, aristocrat after aristocrat stood up—some sincerely, others out of peer pressure—to renounce those rights that had made them a separate caste in French society. Peasants were no longer obligated to work on the local lord's land, nor were they barred from fishing in common streams or hunting in the forests, restrictions that the hungry peasantry found particularly onerous. As a result of the events of August 4, all the people of France were subject to the same laws and obligations to society.

The Constitutional Monarchy

Because there was no time to write a constitution, the National Assembly decided to put forward a document that would declare the rights of the new French citizen. Lafayette, aided by Thomas Jefferson, wrote the *Declaration of the Rights of Man and Citizen*, one of the most influential documents in European history. Using the language of the Enlightenment, the work declared that political sovereignty did not rest in the hands of a monarch but rather in the nation at large. It also stated that all citizens were equal before the law and in their enjoyment of all rights and responsibilities of the society. Because all men were "born and remain free and equal in rights," they were entitled to enjoy freedom of religion, freedom of the press, and the freedom to engage in the economic activity of their choice. Befitting the bourgeois audience for whom this document was primarily intended, it also offered that property was inviolable and sacred.

The Language of Liberty
De Gouges's book would be the inspiration for Mary Wollstonecraft's *Vindication of the Rights of Women*.

Lafayette was being quite literal when he referred to the "Rights of Man." He, like most other males, believed that women were clearly not entitled to the same rights as men because their domestic role precluded the possibility of a life beyond the household. Nevertheless, the language of liberty tugged at women's sense of independence and by 1791, **Olympe de Gouges** wrote *The Rights of Women*, in which she argued that women should enjoy such fundamental rights as the right to be educated, to control their own property, and to initiate divorce. She did not, however, go so far as to demand full political rights for women. During this stage of the Revolution, women did gain certain rights over their property and the right to divorce, although these rights would be rolled back in the backlash that took place during the rule of the Directory and the reign of Napoleon. De Gouges herself would be executed during the Reign of Terror.

The events of the summer of 1789 had left Louis XVI unsure as to how to respond. He hesitated to accept the dramatic changes posed by the renunciation of aristocratic privileges on August 4. Although Louis vacillated, events would once again overtake him. On October 5, a large crowd of women, angry over the shortage of bread in Paris, decided to go to Versailles to meet with "the baker, the baker's wife, and the baker's little boy" (or as they were previously known, the royal family). At first, unsure of how to proceed, the crowd decided the surest way to hold the King to his promise to respect the decrees of the National Assembly was to escort him back to Paris where they could watch him more closely. This proved to be a pivotal decision; the King was now under the control of the people of Paris, whose revolutionary zeal far outstripped that of the rest of the country.

Another reason for the increasingly radical moves of the French revolutionaries was the steps taken by the National Assembly to control the Catholic Church in France. Part of the incentive for taking control of the Church was that the assembly now had to address the financial crisis that was initially the monarchy's undoing and was now their responsibility. To pay for the financing of the French debt, the assembly took the very risky step of confiscating and selling the property of the Church. The assembly decided to issue *assignats*, government bonds that were backed by the sale of Church lands.

Along with the confiscation of the Church's property, it was decided that the entire constitutional status of the Catholic Church needed to be altered. In July 1790, the King was forced, to his horror, to accept the passage of the **Civil Constitution of the Church**, legislation that basically made the Church a department of state. Bishops were to be chosen by assemblies of parish priests, who themselves were to be elected by their parishioners. Clergy were now civil servants with salaries to be paid by the state. In addition, clergy had to swear an oath of loyalty to the French state and to uphold the Civil Constitution of the Church. While these measures might have seemed appealing to earlier monarchs seeking to consolidate their power at the expense of Rome, Louis would not be choosing them himself as a divine-right prerogative, making the idea much less palatable.

In response, **Pope Pius VI** denounced the Civil Constitution and the *Declaration of the Rights of Man*. This set in motion a major nineteenth century conflict, the dispute between church and state. In France, these attacks on the privileges of the Church instigated a counter-revolutionary movement comprised of people who were committed to undoing what they thought was the sacrilegious treatment of their church. Counter-revolutionary reaction, royalism, and Catholicism became associated in the public mind. With the King and the National Assembly safely ensconced in Paris, steps were taken by the National Assembly to establish a workable system of government. In 1791, a constitution for France was promulgated, creating a constitutional monarchy. The King had the right to delay legislation passed by the unicameral, or single house, legislature, for at most four years, although the monarch retained significant powers including control over foreign policy and command of the army. Because the framers of the constitution feared how popular influence would affect the political process, a complex system of indirect elections was set up. The men of France were split into two different categories: active and passive citizens. Only those men who paid taxes that equaled three days of a laborer's wages were allowed to vote for electors. Electors had to meet higher property requirements to qualify to vote for members of the assembly. Women were not given any sort of franchise, so out of a population of roughly 25 million, only 50,000 qualified as electors.

The National Assembly brought about other significant changes. The old French system of provinces was abandoned and replaced by 83 departments, which, making use of the rational spirit of the Enlightenment, were each roughly equal in size and still in use today. In a stunning development for the cause of religious liberty, Jews and Protestants were granted full political rights. Slavery, although still practiced in the colonies, was abolished in France. This led to a slave rebellion led by Toussaint L'Ouverture, a former slave, on the Caribbean island of Hispaniola. By 1794, slavery was abolished throughout the empire, although by that time, Haiti, the eastern half of the island of Hispaniola, had broken free from France and was the first independent black state in the Caribbean.

Revolution in Haiti
The spirit of liberty in France extended to their colonies, including Haiti. The Haitian Revolution is the only slave uprising in history to have resulted in the formation of an independent state.

The End of the Monarchy

By 1791, not only was there a growing counter-revolutionary movement within France, but on the borders of France resided thousands of nobles who had fled their country and were actively working to restore the *ancien régime* and their feudal privileges. The leader of these *émigrés* was the **Count of Artois**, the youngest brother of Louis XVI, and it was he who made the fatal decision to encourage his brother to flee France. On June 20, 1791, the royal family reached the French town of Varennes, on the border with the Netherlands, where the King was recognized and escorted back to Paris. Because the leaders of the National Assembly were still interested in maintaining the constitutional monarchy, they lied and said that the King had not fled Paris but instead had been abducted. Despite this attempt to keep Louis on the throne, the stage was set for the eventual collapse of the constitutional monarchy.

Although the new legislative assembly that was created out of the Constitution of 1791 stayed in existence for only one year, it was crucial for changing the course of the Revolution. The contentious debate within the assembly was matched by the factious debates that took place within the hundreds of political clubs that emerged throughout France. The most famous and popular of these clubs was the **Jacobins**, so named because they met in the Jacobin monastery in Paris. The Jacobins were represented in the National Assembly, although at this time, the **Girondins** faction primarily filled the leadership role in the assembly. The Girondins, named for the Gironde department in southwestern France where many in the faction came from, favored starting a revolutionary war to free from tyranny those people living in absolutist states, such as Austria and Prussia, the two nations on which France declared war in April 1792. This declaration of war ultimately sealed the fate of the royal family and helped further radicalize the Revolution.

Despite Girondin assurances that victory would be easy, the early stages of the war did not go well for France, which was forced to cope with an officer corps that was depleted by aristocratic defections. The war brought about an increasingly radical situation in Paris where the *sans-culottes* tried to deal with the scarce supply of bread and feelings of chagrin at being labeled passive citizens without the right to vote. They were also fearful following a manifesto issued by the Prussian commander, the **Duke of Brunswick**, which promised that he would destroy Paris if the royal family was harmed. In Paris, this helped create a political transformation that led to a demand for wider political participation and the establishment of a radical government, the Commune, in the city.

On August 10, a large mob of *sans-culottes* stormed the Tuileries palace, where the King and the Queen were living, and slaughtered 600 of the King's Swiss guards. This was followed by another act of horrendous violence. In September, following a series of defeats by French armies, around 1,200 individuals who had been arrested as potential counter-revolutionaries were slaughtered by a frenzied mob that was reacting to rumors that the prisoners were about to escape and attack French armies from behind. The Paris Commune then forced the National Assembly to call for elections for a new legislative body using universal male suffrage. This body, known as the Convention, was given the task of drawing up a new constitution ending the constitutional monarchy. Meanwhile, the military acts that

Cu-Whats?
Culottes were the fancy breeches worn by the aristocracy, so *sans-culottes* literally referred to those who did not wear them.

had spurred on these developments began to change. The threat to Paris, which had spurred on the September massacres, ended quickly when a French army, inflamed by revolutionary passion, stopped the combined Austrian and Prussian advance at the battle of Valmy. With the Revolution apparently saved from the combined threat of foreign armies and counter-revolution, France officially became a republic on September 21, 1792, and the royal family was placed under arrest. Following the discovery of a cache of letters that Louis XVI had exchanged with his brother-in-law, the Austrian Emperor, Louis was tried and in early 1793 guillotined before a large crowd yelling for his blood.

European Reactions to the French Revolution

The French Revolution had a huge impact on the rest of Europe. For those on the continent who had been influenced by the ideas of the Enlightenment, the events in France seemed like a breath of fresh air, and they eagerly created radical political associations of their own in places like the Italian states and the German states. At first, Austria and Prussia thought that the Revolution would be useful for bringing about the eclipse of France as the major power on the continent. They soon came to regret their initial complacency and began to see the Revolution for its potential to spread to other areas and possibly to threaten their own thrones.

In Great Britain, the immediate reaction to the fall of the Bastille and the abolition of French feudalism, along with the establishment of a constitutional monarchy, was quite friendly. For many, it appeared as if the violent rivalry between the two nations would finally come to a peaceful conclusion. **William Pitt the Younger**, the British Prime Minister, stated, "The present convulsions in France must sooner or later culminate in general harmony and regular order and thus circumstanced, France will stand forth as one of the most brilliant powers of Europe. She will enjoy just that kind of liberty which I venerate." His chief political opponent, Charles Fox, was even more enthusiastic. He called the revolt "the greatest event that ever happened in the history of the world."

Britain was eventually brought into the Europe-wide war sparked by the Revolution. By the fall of 1792, French armies, following initial setbacks, were pushing the enemy back and began to occupy territories, such as the Austrian Netherlands. They also captured much of the Rhineland and the important city of Frankfurt. Wherever French armies went they brought with them the ideas of the Revolution. Although the National Convention promised "fraternity and assistance to peoples who want to recover their liberties," the French armies soon became more of an occupying force than liberators.

Burke's Conservatism

Only **Edmund Burke**, a leading British politician attached to the Whig faction, was cautious. In 1790, he wrote *Reflections on the French Revolution*, which expressed his opposition to the Revolution. Burke was not against reform; he himself had been interested in the reform of certain aspects of English political life. He feared, however, that once the traditional system of deference was removed, it would dramatically alter the role of such institutions as the monarchy and the Church, and eventually force would rule. To that end, he predicted that the Revolution would take a more violent direction, something that was rather prescient considering he was writing in only 1790. Burke believed that reform could take place only by keeping the present political structure and seeking to achieve evolutionary rather than revolutionary change. His work serves as the foundation piece for modern political conservatism.

THE REIGN OF TERROR

In the Convention, the Girondins and Jacobins continued to disagree over the direction of the Revolution. The radical Jacobins sat on the left side of the hall where the Convention met on a raised platform; this seating arrangement earned them the label **"the Mountain."** On the right sat the more conservative Girondins. This configuration was the origin of our modern political designations of left and right. In the middle of the hall sat those who were not directly tied to either faction; this section became known as **"the Plain."** It was this group that held the key to the Revolution, since whichever side they aligned with would ultimately triumph.

While both the Girondins and the Jacobins were both considered republican, they had diverging opinions regarding some of the most pressing issues of the day. The Girondins wished to make a clean break from the absolutist government of the previous decades, while still maintaining the democratic spirit of the revolution. Towards this end, they favored exile for the King (rather than execution). When creating policies for the new French government, the Girondins pushed to maintain a degree of local autonomy instead of allowing all authority to be centralized in Paris. They were also fearful of the political influence of the *sans-culottes* and hoped to stem their influence by maintaining a policy of voting rights based on property ownership. With regard to the economy, the Girondins favored *laissez-faire*, the idea that the government should not play an active role in regulating the economy.

In contrast, the Jacobins took a more radical stance. They believed that the king was a traitor and should therefore be executed. They also felt that the only way to maintain the spirit of the revolution was through a powerful centralized government in Paris. Economically, the Jacobins argued for selective regulation of industries like the wheat trade in order to fight against wild inflation. Their policies were not specifically antagonistic towards the common people of Paris. Therefore, they garnered the increasing support of the *sans-culottes,* a group that would be critical to Jacobin success in the next phase of the revolution.

The spring of 1793 marked the beginning of what became known as the **"Reign of Terror."** In part, it was inspired by the counter-revolutionary revolt that began in March in a western region of France known as the **Vendée**, a counter-revolution that was largely inspired by anger toward the restrictions placed on the Church. French armies met a major defeat that same month in the Austrian Netherlands, followed by the betrayal of their commanding officer, General Dumouriez, who fled to join the Austrians. In response to these provocations, the Convention created two committees, the Committee of General Security and the **Committee of Public Safety**; the latter assumed virtually dictatorial power over France throughout the following year. The leaders of the security committee included **Danton**, **Carnot**, and **Robespierre**, a lawyer. These men were associated with the Jacobin faction, which was becoming more influential at the expense of the Girondins. The Girondins were tainted by having made the traitor Dumouriez commander of French forces in the Netherlands and by their perceived lack of sympathy toward the Parisian masses.

The King and I
Robespierre's anti-monarchical sentiments may have started at the age of eleven, when a coach carrying the royal family splashed him with mud just as he was about to read some Latin verses he had written in their honor.

The *sans-culottes* continued to be a useful tool for the Jacobins, and it was a mob of the former who stormed the hall where the Convention met and successfully demanded the expulsion of Girondin members. This allowed the Mountain to further consolidate its control, which had already been enhanced following the uproar in July, when Charlotte Corday, a Girondin sympathizer, stabbed to death the radical journalist **Marat**, a hero of the *sans-culottes*, while he lay in his bath. To appease the *sans-culottes*' sensibilities, the Mountain-led Convention established a law of maximum prices, which placed limits on the price of bread and taxed the wealthy to pay for the war effort.

In August 1793, **Lazare Carnot**, the head of the military, issued his famous proclamation calling for a *levée en masse*, drafting the entire population for military service. This marks the first time that all citizens of a nation were called on to serve their country. According to the proclamation, men were expected to go into battle; women should "make tents and clothing and…serve in the hospitals." Children were to "turn old linen into lint," and the old folks were to go to public places and "arouse the courage of the warriors and preach the hatred of kings and the unity of the Republic." The armies created out of this *levée en masse* proved to be surprisingly successful against the well-trained but unmotivated soldiers of Austria and Prussia, and the war once again began to turn in the French favor.

Once in power, the Jacobins worked to create what they considered to be a **Republic of Virtue**. To achieve this ideal, they felt that they had to obliterate all traces of the old monarchical regime. To that end they came up with a new calendar based on weeks made up of ten days. The months were renamed to reflect the seasons, and 1792, the first year of the Republic, was labeled as year one. There was also an attack on Christianity and churches, and those in power forced the removal of religious symbols from public buildings. To move people away from what he thought was the corrupting influence of the Church, Robespierre established a **Cult of the Supreme Being**, turning the cathedral of Notre Dame into a Temple of Reason. Most of these steps proved to be quite unpopular and eventually led to a political backlash against the Committee of Public Safety.

From the summer of 1793 to the following summer, France was embroiled by the workings of the Reign of Terror. Because the Revolution was believed to be threatened by both internal and external enemies, courtesies such as the rule of law—or fair trials—were thrown out the window. The Committee of Public Safety first began by banning political clubs and popular societies of women. Next, they executed leading Girondin politicians who were accused of being traitors, and the **guillotine** became a symbol of the age. In the end, around 20,000 individuals were executed. Approximately 15 percent of these were nobles and clergy; the majority were peasants who had been involved in counter-revolutionary activities.

Eventually, the Terror began to turn on those who had first set it in motion. By March 1794, under the leadership of Robespierre, it had an extreme radical faction known as the **Hébertists**, who were violently anti-Christian and wanted to see the government implement further economic controls. Soon afterward, Danton, one of the Jacobin committee leaders, and his followers were brought to the guillotine for arguing that it was time to bring the Terror to a close. The surviving followers of

Hébert and Danton were joined by members of the National Convention who feared that they were next in line for the guillotine. The end was fairly anticlimactic: On 8 *Thermidor* (July 26, 1794), Robespierre spoke before the Convention about the need for one more major purge. Someone in the assembly shouted "Down with the tyrant," and for once, Robespierre seemed at a loss for words and left the building. The next day, he and his leading supporters were arrested by the **Thermidorians**, the label for those who were opposed to Robespierre, and after a quick trial that very same day, one hundred leading Jacobins were escorted to the guillotine.

THE DIRECTORY (1795–1799)

Following the execution of the leading members of the Convention and the Committee of Public Safety, the Thermidorians abolished the Paris Commune, a hotbed of radical sentiment, along with the Committee of Public Safety. They produced a government known as the **Directory** because it was led by an executive council of five men who possessed the title of director. The new constitution provided for a two-house legislature, made up of a **Council of the Ancients**, which discussed and voted on legislation proposed by the second house, the **Council of Five Hundred**.

As part of the backlash against the radical republic established by Robespierre, the franchise was limited to those men who possessed property, and only those who possessed significant property were allowed to hold public office. In general, the Directory witnessed the triumph of men of property over the *sans-culottes*. One sign of this was the revival of ornate dress, which members of the *sans-culottes* had been proud to not possess, along with the removal of all price ceilings on staples such as bread. Another part of this backlash against the radical phase of the Revolution was the attack on Jacobin club meetings by wealthy young men whose families had grown rich by providing French troops with supplies or through the confiscation of church property.

The Directory also had to be concerned with the possibility of a royalist reaction, and on 13 *Vendémiaire* (October 5, 1795), a royalist rebellion did break out in parts of Paris. A young general named **Napoleon Bonaparte** was told to put down the rebellion, and with a "whiff of grapeshot," his cannon dispersed the rebels. The Directory had been saved, but soon it was to be destroyed by its savior.

NAPOLEON

Domestically, the Directory did little to solve the economic problems still facing the French nation, nor did it solve the ongoing conflict with the Catholic Church. Its armies, however, did meet with tremendous success on the battlefield. Among the rising generation of new French generals, the most important was Napoleon Bonaparte. Napoleon was born in 1769 to a family of minor nobles on the island of Corsica, which had been annexed by France the year prior to his birth. He attended a French military academy, and in 1785 he was commissioned as an artillery officer.

Had it not been for the French Revolution, Napoleon would have remained a junior officer for the remainder of his military career owing to his relatively humble birth and Corsican background. However, the Revolution offered tremendous opportunities to young men of ability, and Napoleon became a strong supporter of the Revolution and was aligned with the Jacobin faction. In 1793, after playing a major role in the campaign to retake the French port of Toulon from the British, he was made a general. Napoleon was nothing if not lucky during his career, and while other Jacobins were dragged off to the guillotine during the Thermidor reaction, Napoleon was left unscathed.

Desperate for military victories that might take the people's minds off the dismal conditions at home, the Directory sent Napoleon to Italy. In a series of stunningly quick victories, Napoleon destroyed the combined Austrian and Sardinian armies, and before long, France controlled northern and central Italy. With the Austrians and the Prussians now out of the war, the only enemy was Great Britain. Instead of trying to cross the English Channel with an invasion force, a battle that Napoleon knew would have limited chance of success due to the powerful British navy, he decided to invade Egypt in order to cut Britain's ties with its colony of India. Napoleon succeeded in conquering Egypt (and ushered in a new age of appreciation for Ancient Egyptian civilization, in part inspired by the discovery of the Rosetta Stone). He was unable to do much with his victories on land because a British fleet under the command of **Admiral Horatio Nelson** defeated a French fleet at the Battle of Abukir on August 1, 1798.

Seeing that the situation in Egypt was doomed, Napoleon abandoned his army and rushed back to France where he had received word that the Directory was increasingly unstable. On 19 *Brumaire* (November 10, 1799), Napoleon joined the Abbé Siéyès, who at the time was one of the five Directors, staged a *coup d'état*, and overturned the Directory. Siéyès, who thought Napoleon could be controlled, established a new constitution with a powerful executive made up of three consuls, which included one of the sitting directors, Roger-Ducos, and Siéyès and Napoleon as the other two. One month after the coup, the politically ambitious Napoleon set up a new constitution with himself as **First Consul**. This structure granted universal male suffrage to satisfy republican sentiment but left Napoleon firmly in control over the real workings of the state. Using a technique that he would find increasingly useful, Napoleon staged a **plebiscite** (a vote by the people) for his new constitution to show popular support, and they passed it overwhelmingly.

Napoleon attempted to end some of the bitterness that had arisen out of the Revolution. A general amnesty was issued, and *émigrés* began to stream back to France. Since Napoleon only required that public servants be loyal to him, he was able use the talents of those Jacobins and monarchists who were willing to accept his dominance over the French state. Napoleon treated those who were not willing with brutal cruelty. He established a secret police force to root out his opponents. Following a plot on his life, Napoleon purged the Jacobins, and he kidnapped and executed the Bourbon Duke of Enghien after falsely accusing the Duke of plotting against him.

Napoleon recognized that a major problem during the course of the Revolution was the ongoing hostility of French Catholics. He himself was not religious, but he recognized that religion could be a useful tool for maintaining political stability and that the Church would continue to be important for many French people. In 1801, Napoleon created a **concordat** with Pope Pius VII. Basically, the settlement worked to the benefit of Napoleon. The concordat declared that "Catholicism was the religion of the great majority of the French"; it did not, however, reestablish the Catholic Church as the official state religion, and it remained tolerant toward Protestants and Jews. The papacy would select bishops, but only on the recommendation of the First Consul. The state would pay clerical salaries, and all clergy had to swear an oath supporting the state. In addition, the Church gave up its claims to those lands confiscated during the Revolution. The Church was able to get Napoleon to do away with the calendar that had been established during the period of Jacobin dominance, which the Church particularly hated since it did away with Sundays and religious holidays.

Napoleon's Legacy
The Napoleonic Code provides the framework for the French legal system to this day.

Following a plebiscite in 1802 that made him Consul for Life, Napoleon set about to reform the French legal system. **The Civil Code of 1804**, commonly known as the **Napoleonic Code**, provided for a single unitary legal system for all of France, rather than the hundreds of localized codes that had been in existence under the monarchy. The code enshrined the equality of all people before the law and safeguarded the rights of property holders. Reversing the advances made by women during the Revolution, the code reaffirmed the paternalistic nature of French society. Women and children were legally dependent on their husbands and fathers. A woman could not sell or buy property without the approval of her father or husband, and divorce, while still legal, became much harder for women to obtain.

In 1804, Napoleon decided to make himself emperor. Once again, he held a plebiscite as a means of trying to show popular support, and again his wishes were overwhelmingly affirmed by vote. He invited the pope to take part in the ceremony, which took place in Notre Dame, rather than in Rheims Cathedral, the traditional place where French kings had been crowned. During the point in the ceremony at which the pope was about to place the crown on the Emperor's head, Napoleon yanked it out of the pope's hands and placed it on his own head and then took a second crown and placed it on the head of his wife, Josephine. Napoleon wanted to make it clear that he was Emperor of the French not based on the will of God or through accident of birth, but rather as a result of the weight of his own achievements. Napoleon also created a new aristocracy that was based on service to the state rather than birth. Members of the new aristocracy did not enjoy any special privileges before the law, nor could their titles be passed on to their children.

FRANCE AT WAR WITH EUROPE

Constant warfare was a hallmark of the reign of Napoleon. Although he is considered to be one of the geniuses in the history of warfare, in many ways his greatest skill was in taking advantage of certain developments that were taking place in eighteenth-century warfare. In 1792, with the *levée en masse*, French armies became larger than their opponents' forces, and Napoleon became masterful at moving these large armies to outmaneuver his opponents. In part, he could do this because he could trust his highly motivated citizen-soldiers, unlike his opponents, who employed unreliable mercenaries who were given little independence on the battlefield for fear of desertion. Napoleon certainly did not invent the new lighter artillery found in the eighteenth century, but he skillfully recognized that this new artillery could be fully integrated with the infantry and cavalry as a very effective fighting tool. Although Napoleon supposedly said that an army "moves on its stomach," he did little to feed those stomachs. He encouraged his men to live off the land, rather than using costly time to provide adequate provisions through the maintenance of a supply line, something that added to the great unpopularity of French occupying armies.

Although France was officially at peace with Great Britain as a result of the **Treaty of Amiens** (1802), Napoleon saw it only as a temporary measure as he sought for means to limit British influence. To antagonize the British, who had colonies in the Caribbean, he sent troops to Haiti, where a slave rebellion had created an independent republic. After most of the French troops died from disease, Napoleon turned his interest away from the colonies and even sold the **Louisiana Territory** to the United States for the paltry sum of around $15 million. Napoleon refocused on Europe and readied plans to invade England, but first the powerful Royal Navy would have to be defeated. At the **Battle of Trafalgar** on October 21, 1805, Admiral Nelson died in the struggle that ultimately destroyed the French fleet and with it any hope of the French landing in England.

On land, however, Napoleon was in his element. Following the formation of the **Third Coalition**, in which Austria and Russia joined Great Britain, Napoleon set out to first destroy the Austrians, a goal which he achieved at the **Battle of Ulm** in October 1805, and then he won his greatest victory over a Russian force at **Austerlitz**. Following these battles, Napoleon decided to abolish the Holy Roman Empire and created the **Confederacy of the Rhine**, a loose grouping of sixteen German states that were placed under the influence of France. Ironically, just as in Italy, Napoleon's victories in Germany resulted in the redrawing of the map, although with long-term consequences not favorable to the French nation. When the Prussians, who had previously worked out a treaty with France, saw the extent of French control over German territories, they hastily joined the Third Coalition. To punish them, Napoleon quickly gathered his forces, and at the **Battle of Jena** he obliterated the Prussian army and occupied their capital city of Berlin.

Following the complete collapse of the Prussian army, the Russian Tsar **Alexander I** (r. 1801–1825) decided that it was necessary to make peace with France. He met with Napoleon on a raft on the Nieman River, and on July 7, 1807, the two monarchs signed the **Treaty of Tilsit**, with the Prussian monarch eagerly waiting on the shore to see what Alexander and Napoleon cast as the fate of his defeated kingdom.

Because of the insistence of Alexander, Prussia was saved from extinction, but it was reduced to half its previous size and was forced to become an ally of France in its ongoing struggle against Great Britain. Seeing that he could not defeat the British navy, Napoleon decided to wage economic war. He established the **Continental System**, an attempt to ban British goods from arriving on the continent. Rather than damaging Great Britain, however, the Continental System weakened the economies of those states that Napoleon had conquered and achieved little to advance French economic interests.

The Continental System and the resentment it caused throughout Europe helped galvanize support against French rule. Initially, wherever French troops went, they brought with them the ideals of the Enlightenment and the French Revolution. French troops arriving in Venice broke down the walls of the ghetto where Jews had been forced to live since the High Middle Ages and established full religious toleration. They also brought about the end of social distinctions wherever they went and imposed the Civil Code as the basic rule of law. Despite this, the French were still occupiers, and as time went on, increasingly harsh ones. Napoleon placed his generally worthless family on the various thrones of Europe, essentially as figureheads, because all authority came from Paris.

THE DEFEAT OF NAPOLEON

Napoleon's eventual defeat came about for three reasons: the peninsula war in Spain, growing nationalism in French-occupied Europe, and the fateful 1812 invasion of Russia.

The War in Spain

In 1807, a French army passed through Spain on its way to conquer Portugal, an ally of Great Britain. When a revolt broke out against the incompetent Spanish King Charles IV the next year, bringing his son, the almost-as-incompetent Ferdinand VII (r. 1808–1833) to its throne, Napoleon decided to take the opportunity to occupy Spain and place his brother Joseph on its throne. Almost immediately, the Spanish nation rose up in a nationalistic fervor to expel the French, who in turn used tremendous brutality against the Spanish people. Napoleon was eventually forced to leave 350,000 troops in Spain where they were tied down in a costly struggle against Spanish patriots who fought with guerilla tactics against the more static French troops.

Growing Nationalism in Europe

While Napoleon continued to struggle with what he called his "Spanish ulcer," stirrings of nationalism also began to churn in other parts of Europe. In the German states, intellectuals began to see that a struggle against the French might be just the tool to create that unified German state for which they longed. These writers looked to Prussia for leadership, while within Prussia, there were stirrings of reform as the nation began to grasp the magnitude of its defeat at Jena. Fortunately for Prussia, it was blessed with two administrators who possessed immense abilities: **Baron von Stein** (1757–1831) and **Count von Hardenberg** (1750–1822). These men were hardly democratic reformers; they wanted to see the continuation of monarchical power and aristocratic privilege. They did, however, bring about much-needed reforms, such as ending the Junker (Prussian noble) monopoly over the ownership of land and the abolition of serfdom. To create an army of motivated soldiers led by competent leaders like the French model, Stein appointed some bourgeois officers and removed some of the more incompetent Junker officers. He also established a professional ministry of war. Stein eliminated some of the harsher elements of military discipline to encourage the peasant soldiers to fight loyally for the state, and he established a large reserve army made up of part-time soldiers.

The 1812 Invasion of Russia

Some of Napoleon's advisors warned him that the constant wars came at a high cost to the French nation. Napoleon, however, still looked for new lands to conquer. Russia seemed a suitable target, particularly because after the defeat of Prussia and Austria, only Russia was still standing as a strong continental rival. In June 1812, Napoleon took his **"Grand Army"** of 600,000 men into Russia, where he fully expected to defeat the Russians in open battle. To his great annoyance, the Russians merely retreated within their vast landscape. When Napoleon took Moscow in September, he found the city a smoking ruin, with fires set by the retreating army of the tsar. Since there was no enemy to fight and few supplies left in the part of Russia occupied by French troops, Napoleon decided to withdraw his army in one of the most famous retreats in military history. The combination of Russian attacks and the brutal winter made the withdrawal a disaster; only 40,000 of the original Grand Army finally returned to France.

The Russian retreat marked the beginning of the end. In 1813, Russia, Prussia, Austria, and Great Britain formed a coalition to fight together until all of Europe was freed from French forces. While British forces under the **Duke of Wellington** pushed forward toward France through Spain, a combined Russian, Prussian, and Austrian force entered eastern France. By March of 1814, they were in Paris, and in the following month, after learning that the allies would not accept his young son on the French throne, Napoleon abdicated.

THE CONGRESS OF VIENNA, THE BOURBON RESTORATION, AND THE HUNDRED DAYS

In victory, the allies demanded the restoration of the **Bourbon monarchs** as outlined in the Treaty of Chaumont, which brought the Count of Provence, a brother of the executed Louis XVI, to the French throne as Louis XVIII. Meanwhile, Napoleon was exiled to the Mediterranean island of Elba, although the allies generously (and fearfully) paid off his debts and allowed him to maintain the title of Emperor and keep a small army on his tiny island state.

To create a lasting peace and to try to put the revolutionary genie back in the bottle, the allies met at the **Congress of Vienna** beginning in September 1814. The four great powers, Great Britain, Austria, Prussia, and Russia, dominated the proceedings, although the great architect of the Congress settlement was the Austrian Chancellor, **Prince Metternich** (1773–1859). Metternich was aware that the social and political changes brought about by the French Revolution had been detrimental to his own state and that it was necessary to turn back the clock. Metternich and the other representatives wanted to make sure that such ideas emanating out of the French Revolution, such as **nationalism** and **liberalism**, would have no place in a redrawn Europe. To that end, they made sure that Polish demands for a free and independent Poland went unanswered and gave the territory to the Tsar of Russia as the Duchy of Poland.

The great powers also wanted to ensure that no nation, least of all France, should ever dominate Europe again. To keep order in France, and to ensure that the Bourbons' subjects would not greatly resent them, France walked away with rather generous peace terms, including the right to hold onto all territorial gains made prior to November 1, 1792. The great powers also erected a series of states that would serve as a barrier to future French expansion. They created the Kingdom of the Netherlands by incorporating the Dutch territory with the Austrian Netherlands to the south, gave Prussia important territories along the Rhine River to block future French expansion to the east, and gave Piedmont the territory of Genoa.

While the victors debated the future course of Europe, the past came back to haunt them. On March 15, 1815, Napoleon returned to France having escaped from Elba. He found many in the army and in the country at large willing to support him, particularly since the return of the Bourbons had led to an unleashing of a violent **white terror** (white signifying the royalist flag and those loyal to the monarchy) against Jacobins and Bonaparte supporters. Louis XVIII was once again forced to flee his homeland as Napoleon was rapidly reinstalled as Emperor. Although he promised France a liberal constitution and the end to foreign aggression, he knew that the other great powers would not allow him to maintain the throne, so once again he raised an army. At the **Battle of Waterloo** (June 18, 1815), Wellington, the British commander, aided by Marshal Blucher, the leader of the Prussian forces, defeated Napoleon. Following the **Hundred Days**, the name given to Napoleon's remarkable return, he was exiled once again, although this time to the distant island of St. Helena, in the middle of the Atlantic, where he died in 1821.

CHAPTER 5 TIMELINE

Year(s)	Event
1610	Assassination of Henry IV
1610	Galileo begins astronomical observations with his telescope
1613	Galileo publishes *Letters on Sunspots*
1616	William Henry announces his discovery of the circulatory system
1618	Johannes Kepler reveals his third and final law of planetary motion
1618	Beginning of the Thirty Years' War
1620	Battle of White Mountain
1620	Founding of Plymouth Colony
1620	Francis Bacon publishes *Novum Organum*
1624	Cardinal Richelieu becomes Louis XIII's chief minister
1625	Charles I becomes king upon death of James I
1628	Petition of Right
1628	Murder of Duke of Buckingham
1629	Edict of Restitution
1629	Personal Rule of Charles I begins and will last eleven years
1632	Gustavus Adolphus dies at the Battle of Lutzen
1632	Galileo's *Dialogue on the Two Chief Systems of the World*
1633	Trial of Galileo
1633	Murder of Albrecht von Wallenstein
1633	France enters the Thirty Years' War
1637	Charles introduces the Book of Common Prayer into Scotland
1637	René Descartes publishes *Discourse on Method*
1640	Beginning of reign of Frederick William (Great Elector)

1640	Charles forced to summon Parliament to deal with Scottish revolt
1641	Rebellion in Ireland
1642	Execution of Archbishop Laud
1648	Peace of Westphalia
1649	Beginning of the Fronde
1649	Execution of Charles I and establishment of English republic
1653	Oliver Cromwell becomes Lord Protector
1659	Death of Cromwell
1660	Restoration of Charles II
1660	Thomas Hobbes publishes *Leviathan*
1661	Death of Cardinal Mazarin; Louis XIV becomes own chief minister
1662	Royal Society established by Charles II
1664	Chartering of the French East India Company
1669	Louis XIV begins construction of the Palace of Versailles
1669	Posthumous publication of Pascal's *Pensées*
1682	Beginning of the reign of Peter the Great
1682	Rembrandt paints *The Night Watch*
1685	Revocation of the Edict of Nantes
1685	James II, a Catholic, becomes King of England
1687	Newton publishes his *Principia*
1688	John Locke's *Two Treatises on Government*
1688	Glorious Revolution
1689	Art of Toleration
1690	John Locke's *Essay on Human Understanding*
1701	Prussia becomes a kingdom

1701	Act of Settlement passed to bypass potential Catholic kings
1703	Cornerstone laid for the new city of St. Petersburg
1707	Act of Union brings about political unification of England and Scotland
1713	Treaty of Utrecht marks the end of the War of the Spanish Succession
1714	George I becomes first Hanoverian King of England
1721	End of the Great Northern War between Russia and Sweden
1721	Start of Robert Walpole's tenure as prime minister
1739	Hume's *Inquiry into Human Nature*
1740	Frederick the Great becomes King of Prussia
1740	Start of the War of the Austrian Succession
1746	Battle of Culloden
1748	Montesquieu's *Spirit of Laws*
1748	Treaty of Aix-la-Chapelle marks end of War of the Austrian Succession
1751	The first volume of Diderot's *Encyclopedia* appears
1755	Lisbon earthquake
1756	Maria Theresa carries out the "Diplomatic Revolution"
1756	Beginning of the Seven Years War
1759	Voltaire's *Candide*
1762	Rousseau's *The Social Contract*
1762	Rousseau's *Émile* is published
1762	Start of the reign of Catherine the Great
1763	Voltaire pushes for reexamination in the trial of Jean Calas
1763	Peace of Paris marks end of Seven Years War
1764	Beccaria's *On Crime and Punishment*
1765	Stamp Act

1770	Burke writes *Thoughts on the Cause of the Present Discontent*
1770	Marriage of the future Louis XVI to Marie Antoinette
1774	Louis XVI becomes King of France
1774	First Continental Congress
1775	Fighting begins between American colonists and British
1776	Jefferson writes the Declaration of Independence
1776	The first volume of Edward Gibbon's *The History of the Decline and Fall of the Roman Empire* is published
1776	Adam Smith's *Wealth of Nations*
1778	France goes to war against Britain in support of the American colonies
1781	Kant's *Critique of Pure Reason*
1781	Joseph II of Austria issues Edicts of Toleration
1786	Calonne, finance minister to Louis XVI, informs him that the crown is bankrupt
1787	Assembly of Notables meets
1788	Louis XVI decides to call the Estates-General
1788	Abbé Siéyès writes *What Is the Third Estate?*
1789	Estates-General meets for the first time (May 5)
1789	Third Estate declares that they will only meet as a National Assembly (June 17)
1789	Tennis Court Oath (June 20)
1789	Storming of the Bastille (July 14)
1789	Lafayette selected as commander of the National Guard
1789	Great Fear (July–August)
1789	Renunciation of aristocratic privileges (August 24)
1789	*Declaration of the Rights of Man* is adopted by the Constituent Assembly (August 26)

1789	Women's march on Versailles (October 5)
1789	Jeremy Bentham's *Introduction to the Principles of Morals and Legislation*
1790	Civil Constitution of the Clergy
1790	Edmund Burke's *Reflections on the Revolution in France*
1791	Constitution adopted
1791	Revolt breaks out in French colony of St. Domingue
1791	Louis XVI attempts to flee Paris (June 20)
1792	Mary Wollstonecraft's *Vindication of the Rights of Women*
1792	France declares war on Austria (April 20)
1792	Mob of *sans-culottes* storms the Tuileries Palace (August 10)
1792	September Massacres
1792	Battle of Valmy (September 20)
1792	France becomes a republic (September 21)
1793	Execution of Louis XVI (January 21)
1793	Universal conscription for the French armies begins (February 24)
1793	Execution of Marie Antoinette (October 16)
1793	Britain enters the war against France
1793	Counter-revolution breaks out in the Vendee (March)
1793	Establishment of the Committee of Public Safety (April)
1793	Expulsion of Girondins from the Convention (June 2)
1793	Ratification of new republican constitution (June 24)
1793	*Murder of Marat* by Charlotte Corday (July 13)
1793	Napoleon retakes Toulon from counter-revolutionaries
1794	Execution of Danton (April 6)
1794	Festival of the Supreme Being (June 8)

1794	Fall of Robespierre and the Jacobins (July 27)
1795	Establishment of the Directory
1795	Napoleon puts down royalist revolt (October 5)
1796	Napoleon launches invasion of northern Italy
1798	Napoleon begins invasion of Egypt
1798	French fleet defeated at the Battle of the Nile (August)
1798	Thomas Malthus' *Essay on Population*
1799	Napoleon involved in coup overthrowing Directory
1799	Napoleon becomes First Consul
1800	Eli Whitney's cotton gin
1801	Napoleon and Pope Pius VII sign concordat
1802	Plebiscite establishes Napoleon as Consul for Life
1802	Treaty of Amiens between Britain and France
1803	Napoleon sells Louisiana territory to the United States
1804	Napoleon crowned Emperor
1804	Murder of the Duke of Enghien
1804	Promulgation of the Civil Code
1805	British victory over French-Spanish fleet at Trafalgar
1805	Defeat of the Prussians at the Battle of Jena
1805	Formation of the Third Coalition
1805	Defeat of the Austrians and Russians at Austerlitz
1806	Abolition of the Holy Roman Empire
1807	Napoleon and Alexander I sign Treaty of Tilsit
1807	Continental System implemented
1807	Invasion of Spain by French forces

1807	British Parliament votes for the end of the slave trade
1807	First passenger train line
1812	Napoleon's invasion of Russia
1812	Occupation of Moscow (September)
1813	Retreat from Russia
1813	Battle of Leipzig (October)
1814	Napoleon forced to abdicate and the reign of Louis XVIII begins
1814	Congress of Vienna convenes (September)
1815	Napoleon escapes from Elba (March 15)
1815	Battle of Waterloo marks end of the Hundred Days (June 18)
1815	Napoleon sent into exile on St. Helena
1821	Death of Napoleon

CHAPTER 5 REVIEW QUESTIONS

Try these questions to assess how well you understood and retained the information covered in the chapter. Answers and explanations are in Chapter 8.

1. Which of the following individuals said "Paris is worth a Mass"?

    (A) Cardinal Richelieu
    (B) Henry IV
    (C) Louis XIII
    (D) Catherine de Medici

2. King Charles I of England was forced to call a Parliament in 1640 following

    (A) the outbreak of a rebellion in Scotland
    (B) the declaration of war between France and England
    (C) the demands of Parliament to be called into session
    (D) a mass public outcry demanding that a new parliamentary session be called

3. In the early modern era, urban disturbances among journeymen and apprentices were most often related to

    (A) the banning of guilds by increasingly centralized monarchies
    (B) a decline in population leading to falling prices
    (C) growing tensions between various guilds
    (D) social tensions stemming from the inability to enter the rank of masters

4. Which of the following best describes the early modern family as an economic unit?

    (A) Males were in the public sphere while females were in the domestic sphere.
    (B) Male and female roles were largely interchangeable among the peasantry but not among the bourgeoisie.
    (C) The family as an economic unit was collapsing following the introduction of capitalist production methods.
    (D) Larger immediate families meant that extended families were no longer part of the same economic unit.

5. Medieval science was primarily based on

    (A) close observations of nature
    (B) pure superstition
    (C) the experimental method
    (D) a blending of Christian theology and the writings of classical authors

6. Which of the following individuals was responsible for first describing the elliptical motion of the planets around the sun?

    (A) Newton
    (B) Galileo
    (C) Copernicus
    (D) Kepler

7. In *Leviathan*, Thomas Hobbes became an advocate for which of the following types of government?

    (A) Absolute monarchy
    (B) Parliamentary government
    (C) Divine-right monarchy
    (D) Constitutional monarchy

8. Women played their most prominent role during the Enlightenment by

    (A) serving as a major topic for the *philosophes*
    (B) writing books and political tracts
    (C) declining to participate in any social events
    (D) sponsoring salons

9. Deists such as Voltaire believe that

    (A) God reveals himself through miracles
    (B) there is no God
    (C) God created the universe but then played no additional role in shaping the course of events
    (D) a state church is necessary

10. Rousseau's *Émile* influenced the way people viewed childhood

    (A) by emphasizing the need to teach emotional restraint
    (B) by suggesting it as the time in which to instill the benefits of a rational education
    (C) by emphasizing that children were not merely small adults
    (D) by positioning it as the critical focus for the family dynamic

11. Mary Wollstonecraft's *Vindication of the Rights of Women*

   (A) focused primarily on economic issues such as property rights
   (B) served as the inspiration for a small group of eighteenth-century women who formed the first female suffrage organization
   (C) was the first work in English to openly advocate for full political equality for women
   (D) failed to find a publisher during her lifetime

12. At the start of the Estates-General, members of the Third Estate refused to have their credentials officially recognized because

   (A) they resented that the three estates met and voted separately
   (B) they doubted that decisions would be made by fully democratic means
   (C) the aristocracy also refused to show credentials
   (D) they resented the attempt to include peasants within the Third Estate

13. The Bastille was a symbol of royal power because

   (A) the King used it as his residence in Paris
   (B) it had housed political prisoners
   (C) wheat for bread was stored there
   (D) it was located at Versailles

14. The significance of the women's march on Versailles on October 5, 1789, was that

   (A) it led to cheaper bread prices
   (B) it resulted in the King being brought back to Paris
   (C) the leaders of the march were immediately arrested
   (D) it was used by the Jacobins as justification for the elimination of the Girondins

15. The Continental System represented Napoleon's attempt to

   (A) lead the continent in a potential struggle with the United States
   (B) close off the continent to British trade
   (C) create a continent-wide parliament
   (D) issue a new code of law

16. Napoleon's Civil Code allowed for

   (A) the elimination of private property
   (B) full property rights for women
   (C) special rights for those holding aristocratic titles
   (D) taxation of all social classes

17. The *sans-culottes*

   (A) recoiled from the use of violence
   (B) failed to recognize the legitimacy of the National Guard
   (C) were primarily peasants
   (D) consisted of the working-class people of Paris

18. Baron von Stein challenged the traditional social structure in Prussia by

   (A) allowing the bourgeoisie to enter the officer corps
   (B) advocating for a constitutional monarchy
   (C) pushing for a bourgeois-led government
   (D) ending agricultural subsidies for the Junkers

REFLECT

- For which content topics discussed in this chapter do you feel you have achieved sufficient mastery to answer multiple-choice questions correctly?

- For which content topics discussed in this chapter do you feel you have achieved sufficient mastery to discuss effectively in an essay or short answer?

- For which content topics discussed in this chapter do you feel you need more work before you can answer multiple-choice questions correctly?

- For which content topics discussed in this chapter do you feel you need more work before you can discuss effectively in an essay or short answer?

- What parts of this chapter are you going to re-review?

- Will you seek further help outside of this book (such as a teacher, tutor, or AP Students) on any of the content in this chapter—and, if so, on what content?

Chapter 6
Age of
Revolutions to
World War I:
c. 1815–c. 1914

RESTORATION AND REVOLUTION

Following the final fall of Napoleon in 1815 and the restoration of the Bourbons to the throne of France, the rulers of Europe were faced with a daunting task—restoring stability to the relationships between the nations of Europe while also ensuring that the specter of revolution did not reappear within their domains. To aid in this task, one aspect of Napoleon's reign was widely copied throughout Europe—France's efficiency in controlling its population. In the period following the Napoleonic wars, states created larger and more efficient bureaucracies, secret police forces, and more efficient censorship offices. In an undeveloped nation such as Russia these oppressive institutions were the only well-functioning part of the state.

States used another strategy to try to turn back the clock—attacking the legacy of the Enlightenment. No institution had suffered as much from the Enlightenment and the French Revolution as the Church. The German Romantic poet Novalis wrote in 1799, "Catholicism is almost played out. The old papacy is laid in the tomb, and Rome for the second time has become a ruin." Despite this prediction, the churches of Europe, both Catholic and Protestant, witnessed a remarkable recovery in the Restoration period (1815–1830). States viewed religion as a useful tool to aid in repression. In England, the Anglican clergy worked in the House of Lords to block parliamentary measures such as the bill in favor of Catholic emancipation and the Great Reform Bill. In Russia, the Orthodox clergy remained a bulwark of the reactionary policies of the state. The same was true in Catholic lands such as Spain, where the Inquisition was once again allowed to operate following its disappearance during the Napoleonic domination of Spain.

AN AGE OF COMPETING IDEOLOGIES

The Restoration period was a highly ideological period in which ideas inspired either from support or approbation of the French Revolution played a role in whether one was committed to the restored order that emerged after 1815 or wanted to see its demise.

Conservatism

Modern conservatism is rooted in the writings of **Edmund Burke** whose *Reflections on the Revolution in France* (1790) was widely read throughout Europe. Two components of Burke's work were extremely popular in the Restoration period: his attack on the principle of the rights of man and natural law as fundamentally dangerous to the social order, and his emphasis on the role of tradition as the basic underpinning for the rights of those in positions of authority. Burke, a member of the English House of Commons, proposed a conservatism that was not reactionary in nature. He believed in the possibility of slow political change over the passage of time.

On the continent, however, a more extreme form of reactionary conservatism appeared in the writings of such men as **Joseph de Maistre** (1753–1821), an *émigré* during the French Revolution. The Church, argued de Maistre, should stand as the very foundation of society because all political authority stemmed from God. De Maistre advocated that monarchs should be extremely stern with those who advocated even the slightest degree of political reform and that the "first servant of the crown should be the executioner."

Nationalism

Nationalism is based on the idea that all peoples' identities are defined by their connection with a nation and that it is to this nation that they owe their primary loyalty as opposed to their king or local lord. The roots of nationalism date back to the early modern period; however, nationalism emerged as an important ideology during the French Revolution. At this time, developments like national conscription, the calling of all young men for military service, helped create the idea of a citizen whose primary loyalty lies not to a village or province but to the nation instead.

Nationalism became important in other parts of Europe in reaction to the expansion in France. In the German and Italian states, the desire to rid their lands of French soldiers created a unifying purpose that helped establish a national identity. This growing national identity also had a literary component. Writers such as the Grimm brothers recorded old German folk tales to reveal a traditional German national spirit that was part of a common past, whether one lived in Bavaria, Saxony, or any of the other German states. Early nineteenth-century nationalism was often, though not exclusively, tied to liberalism because many nationalists, like the liberals, wanted political equality and human freedom to serve as the bedrock for the new state.

Liberalism

The foundations for nineteenth-century liberalism can be found in the writings of the philosophers of the Enlightenment, with their emphasis on the **individual's natural rights** and support for limits on political authorities through the writing of **constitutions** and the formation of **parliamentary bodies**. Liberalism was also connected to the events of the early stages of the French Revolution with the establishment of the constitutional monarchy and with Lafayette's *Declaration of the Rights of Man* serving as a basic foundational document. Liberals hoped to protect the rights of individuals by limiting the power of the state and by emphasizing the individual's right to enjoy religious freedom, freedom of the press, and equality under the law.

Besides being a political theory, liberalism was also a school of economic thought. The most important of the early liberal economists—individuals who collectively formed what became known as the **classical school**—was **Adam Smith** (1723–1790), who published his most important work, *An Inquiry into the Nature and Causes of the Wealth of Nations*, in 1776. **Mercantilism** held that nations' wealth could be measured only in gold reserves and that foreign trade would necessarily hurt one side or the other. However, Smith realized a nation's true wealth was the goods produced by the labor of its citizens. Smith introduced two revolutionary ideas. First, specialists (whether individuals or countries) have natural skills and can produce their specialties better and faster than others. Trade could thus enrich everyone: France and Scotland would both be richer if they traded wine and coal, rather than the French mining in the vineyards and the Scots growing grapes in the highlands. Second, government price-fixing was unnecessary and counterproductive. Instead, governments should follow a *laissez-faire* policy and let individual businesses set their own prices and production levels; individual decisions, as though guided by an "invisible hand," would provide a balance between supply and demand, while also providing businesses an incentive to find cheaper ways to produce more goods, lower prices, and increase sales.

Smith's *Laissez-Faire*
The concept of laissez-faire, originated by Adam Smith, is the basis of free-market capitalism.

Economics is sometimes referred to as "the dismal science," because the classical economists—men such as **Thomas Malthus** (1766–1834) and **David Ricardo** (1772–1823)—reached conclusions that can only be viewed as deeply depressing. Malthus, a country parson, argued in his *Essay on Population* that the population was growing at a rate that would eventually outstrip the food supply. Factory owners were pleased to read in Malthus a justification for the payment of miserable wages to their workers because according to Malthus, if they were better compensated, they would be more likely to produce more children, ultimately leading to only more misery as increasing numbers of workers competed for fewer jobs and less food. According to Ricardo, the only way factory owners could find an advantage over their competitors was by offering lower wages, resulting in a steady downward spiral in their earnings. This **"Iron Law of Wages"** must also have pleased factory owners because once again their parsimony could be presented as if it were actually essential for the public good. Ironically, Malthus and Ricardo were both writing at a time when the dramatic expansion of production brought on by the Industrial Revolution was making their negative predictions obsolete.

Some writers, although we still apply to them the label of "liberal," began to question certain classical, liberal orthodoxies on the workings of the economy as well as the role of the state. **John Stuart Mill** (1806–1873) began as a disciple of **Jeremy Bentham** (1748–1832), who had provided a justification for an expanded role for government by suggesting that governments should seek to provide "the greatest happiness for the greatest number." Bentham's views, which are given the label of **utilitarianism**, were taken further by Mill, who wrote in his *Principles of Political Economy* that it may be necessary for the state to intervene and help workers achieve economic justice.

In some of Mill's later works, he began to move into a direction that brought him ever closer to socialism, with his questioning of the absolute right to hold private property while also suggesting that there needed to be a more equitable way for societies to distribute their wealth. Mill's most famous work, *On Liberty*, was a clarion call for personal freedom. Although in the past the struggle for liberty involved placing constraints on monarchs, in Mill's day the danger was that in democratic governments, the majority could deny liberty to the minority, thus squashing the personal liberty that Mill cherished in the name of majority rule.

Unlike other male liberals who saw political liberty solely as a male domain, Mill was greatly influenced by the feminist thought of his wife, **Harriet Taylor** (1807–1856). Inspired by her, *On the Subjugation of Women* consists of arguments in favor of granting full equality to women.

Socialism

Socialism, like the other ideologies discussed above, was also partly rooted in the French Revolution, with a number of radical Jacobins taking the idea of political equality for all and moving it to the next step: economic equality for all through the common ownership of all property. The early socialist writers are sometimes given the label "**Utopian Socialists**," a phrase coined by **Karl Marx**, who viewed these early writers with contempt because he felt they offered non-scientific, unrealistic solutions to the problems of modern society. Utopian Socialists believed that expansive possibilities were available to mankind and that poor environments corrupted human nature. The Utopians also believed that capitalism over-emphasized production, under-emphasized distribution, and possessed other serious flaws such as unemployment and the suffering brought about by low wages.

Early Socialists

These early Socialists provided no single answer to society's problems. **Henri de Saint-Simon** (1760–1825) argued that society needed to be organized on a scientific basis. He argued for the creation of a hierarchical society led by an intellectual class that improved society and, most important, the lot of those on the bottom of the social ladder. Contemporary events in Europe are currently heading in a direction that Saint-Simon imagined: He hoped to witness the rise of a community of European nations that would have a common currency, transportation, and a parliament, among other things.

Another Utopian Socialist was **Charles Fourier** (1772–1837) who created a blueprint for a cooperative community. The blueprint consisted of a self-contained group of precisely 1,620 people living on 5,000 acres of land. Fourier hoped to make the workday more satisfying by rotating tasks so that everyone would do the boring tasks but not exclusively—Fourier thought that because children liked to play with dirt, they should take care of the community's garbage.

Another individual who designed a planned community—and unlike Fourier he actually built it—was **Robert Owen** (1771–1858), a self-made manufacturer. Like Fourier, he blamed environment for man's corruption and in response built New Lanark, a mill town in Scotland, where workers were housed decently and children received an education. These early Socialists had relatively little impact in comparison with Karl Marx's proletarian socialism which came later.

POLITICAL RESTORATION AND REFORM

France

The term *restoration* literally refers to the events in France where the Bourbons were restored to the throne following the final defeat of Napoleon at Waterloo. The throne that **Louis XVIII** returned to was different from the one his older brother had enjoyed up until 1789. The Charter of 1814—a hastily written constitution—contained many of the freedoms from the revolutionary period, such as freedom of religion, even though it was presented to the French people by the King and contained no notion of popular sovereignty. The charter angered many royalists by confirming land purchases made from nationalized Church property. Politically, it allowed for a constitutional monarchy with a chamber of peers and a chamber of deputies made up of a very restricted franchise. The King held the firm reins of power, however, because only he could introduce legislation, and ministers were responsible to him instead of to the assembly.

In 1820, the son of the younger brother of Louis, Duke de Berry, was assassinated. The ultra-royalists, individuals who wanted to see the revival of absolute monarchy, used the assassination to pressure the King to clamp down on the press and to give more rights to the aristocracy, including compensation for nobles who had lost land during the Revolution.

Political repression increased after the death of Louis XVIII in 1824. At that time, Louis's younger brother **Charles X** came to the throne. Charles felt more bitter about the Revolution than his brother Louis had. A year after taking the throne, he introduced a Law of Sacrilege, which ruled death as the penalty for any attack on the Church. In 1829, Charles appointed the Prince of Polignac as his chief minister, a man disliked throughout the country for being a leading ultra-royalist. In the following year, Polignac issued what became known as the **July Ordinances**, which dissolved the newly elected assembly, took away the right to vote from the upper bourgeoisie, and imposed rigid censorship.

That same month, revolution broke out in Paris. Leading liberals were afraid of the Parisian mob and wanted to avoid the creation of a republic because they associated republics with the violence of the first French republic dating back to 1792. Instead, they turned to Louis Phillipe, the Duke of Orleans, a liberal who had stayed in France during the Revolution. The **July Revolution** of 1830, which sparked revolutions throughout Europe, ended with the crowning of Louis Phillipe and the creation of what became known as the bourgeois, or **July monarchy**.

Revolutionary Movements

By the third decade of the century, people across Europe showed signs that it would be impossible to stem their desire for change.

Spain

In Spain, King Ferdinand VII had been restored to the throne following the collapse of French control in 1814. Ferdinand was restored on the condition that he honor the liberal constitution of 1812 drawn up by the Cortes, the Spanish parliament, which had met in Cadiz (in Andalucia, the southwestern coast of Spain)—the one part of Spain that was not conquered by Napoleon. Once restored to his throne, Ferdinand dissolved the Cortes and persecuted those liberals who had drawn up the constitution.

In 1820, a rebellion began among army divisions that were about to be sent to South America to put down the rebellions against the Spanish Empire. The small Spanish middle class soon joined the army divisions in the rebellion. Although the King agreed to rule under the laws of the constitution to end the rebellion, Austria, France, Prussia, and Russia wanted to intervene to stem the tide of the revolt. The British, however, refused to directly intervene; they did not want the five great powers of Europe to be involved in putting down internal rebellions in other nations. Two years later, a French army acted unilaterally—although with the tacit support of Russia, Prussia, and Austria—and restored Ferdinand to absolute power.

Italy

A more serious revolt broke out in Naples, a revolt that the Austrian statesman Metternich labeled as the "greatest crisis" of his career. Similar to the situation in Spain, King Ferdinand of Naples had made promises while in exile to rule as a constitutional monarch, although once restored to the throne, he refused to give up any of his absolute powers. Neapolitan army officers, perhaps inspired by French ideas, joined with members of the bourgeoisie and began, with the assistance of secret nationalistic societies such as the **Carbonari**, to oppose the monarch. The revolt led to nationalistic stirrings throughout Italy and to another revolt in the Kingdom of Sardinia, which ultimately came to nothing.

Metternich wanted to put down the revolt in Naples, but once again, the British refused to participate in a joint attack. Metternich wanted the support of the other great powers, so he called the rulers of Austria, Prussia, and Russia to the Austrian town of Troppau to create what became the **Troppau Protocol**, which stated that the great European powers had the right to intervene in revolutionary situations. The following year, the rebellion in Naples was put down with the help of Austrian troops.

Greece

With the forces of repression everywhere triumphant, Western European liberals looked to the Greek revolt of 1821 to free the "birthplace of democracy" from "Eastern despotism"—though this was also part of a thousand-year prejudice that claimed

Portuguese Power Play
A similar revolt took place in Portugal, where a group of army officers wanted to draw up a constitutional monarchy under John VI who had fled to Brazil during the Napoleonic Wars.

Turkish citizens lived and died at the whims of a tyrannical Emperor (an especially ironic claim in a time of resurgent absolutism in France, Prussia, Italy, and elsewhere). Some leading liberals even went to Greece to aid the rebels; the British Romantic poet **Lord Byron** (1788–1824), for instance, sent his own money to refit the Greek fleet, and died amidst the struggle in Greece (not on the battlefield, but from a fever). By 1827, Britain, France, and Russia organized a combined naval force to intervene on the side of the Greek revolutionaries, and in the following year, the Russians attacked the Ottomans on land. By 1832, Greece declared its independence from the Ottoman Empire—and became a monarchy with an imported Bavarian prince.

The Greek revolt was also tied to what became known as the **"Eastern Question"**—what should be done about the increasingly weak Ottoman Empire, appropriately nicknamed **"the Sick Man of Europe."** Like other multi-ethnic empires, the Ottoman Empire was breaking down after a series of rulers who could not keep the groups united. Europeans were also uncomfortably reminded of the threat the Ottomans had posed—the Ottoman Empire had most recently besieged Vienna less than 150 years earlier. As the Greeks were breaking away from the Ottoman Empire, so were the **Serbians**, who had established effective independence by 1830. The new Serbia was a small kingdom about the size of South Carolina, located north of Greece on the southern border of the Austro-Hungarian Empire. Ironically, this tiny kingdom would be a much greater threat to Austrian, and thus European, stability than the mighty Ottoman Empire ever was: The independent Serbian state strongly promoted nationalism in the Balkan regions of Austria, which ultimately led to the ethnic conflicts and revolutionary movements that started World War I.

Russia

Russia had emerged as a great European power as a result of the Napoleonic Wars, although in many ways, Russia was a much more backward nation than the other European countries. **Alexander I** (r. 1801–1825) had ruled Russia and at various times had toyed with the idea of political reform, although in the latter part of his reign he grew increasingly reactionary.

Alexander's death in 1825 produced confusion as to the succession; Constantine, the older of his two surviving brothers, turned down the throne, so **Nicholas I** (r. 1825–1855) stepped up. In the confusion, a small group of military officers decided to stage a revolt in support of Constantine, who they wrongly thought was in favor of a constitutional monarchy and had been unfairly removed from the succession. This **"Decembrist" revolt** was put down rapidly and with great brutality. In the following years, Nicholas ruled with an iron fist, making sure to stamp out any additional movements for reform within his vast empire.

Great Britain

The French Revolution and the wars against Napoleon had created a backlash against the idea of political reform in Great Britain. The governing elite were also wary of possible social unrest owing to the economic downturn that occurred following the end of the Napoleonic Wars. Such fears were realized in a catastrophe in 1819 when a large crowd of 60,000 people gathered in St. Peter's field in

Manchester to demand fundamental political changes, including universal male suffrage and annual parliaments. Although those who attended the meeting were for the most part peaceful, the soldiers on hand shot eleven members of the crowd. This became known as the **Peterloo Massacre**, an obvious play on the Battle of Waterloo. Soon after this disgraceful event, Parliament passed the repressive **Six Acts**, which banned demonstrations and imposed censorship.

The mood in Great Britain became more conducive to reform beginning in 1824 with the repeal of the **Combination Acts**, which had banned union activity. In 1829, restrictions dating back to the seventeenth century on the rights of Catholics to hold political office and government posts were lifted. In 1832, the **Great Reform Bill** was passed. The bill was hardly radical. Although it expanded the electorate to include those who had become wealthy as a result of industrialization, only one in five males in Great Britain could vote. It reduced but did not completely eliminate the number of so-called rotten boroughs, which were sparsely populated electoral districts. The bill succeeded in showing that political reform was possible in Great Britain without having to resort to the barricades as in continental Europe.

The new electorate created out of the Great Reform Bill undertook additional reforms. Although inspired by the middle-class Members of Parliament, they showed a new harshness toward the poor. The **Poor Law of 1834** forced the destitute to enter into workhouses where conditions were purposefully miserable to discourage people from seeking assistance.

On a more humanitarian level, in 1833, slavery was banned in the British Empire, and the **Factory Act of 1833** reduced the number of hours that children could work in factories and established government inspectors to ensure adequate working conditions. One sign that the new political order in Great Britain was now dominated by manufacturing interests as opposed to the old landed class was the 1846 elimination of the **Corn Laws**, which had imposed high tariffs on imported grain to support domestic growers. Manufacturers had long supported the end of the Corn Laws, believing that lower food prices would allow them to pay lower wages to their factory workers.

THE REVOLUTIONS OF 1848

On January 12, 1848, there was a rebellion in the Kingdom of the Two Sicilies against King Ferdinand II. This rebellion was to be the first of approximately fifty revolts that convulsed Europe in the first four months of that year. The rebellions were disjointed with very little cooperation or coordination between nations. However, there were a few key themes that ran through most of these contemporaneous upheavals. Primarily, widespread dissatisfaction with political leadership and an upsurge in nationalism motivated citizen demands for democratic government as well other liberal reforms. Following the revolutions of 1848, the Austrian Empire, now under the rule of **Emperor Francis Joseph** (r. 1848–1916), relied heavily on military force to subdue all forms of liberalism and nationalism. Magyars, Slavs, Italians, and

Germans would have to wait to see nationalist reforms realized. The 1840s were a terrible decade for agriculture and have accordingly been labeled the **"hungry forties."** The Irish experienced the most terrible conditions, with the Irish **potato famine** of 1846 leading to the death of one million individuals and the emigration of an additional million out of Ireland.

France

There is an old saying that when France coughs, the rest of Europe catches a cold. In 1848, a rebellion in France created the spark for revolution throughout Europe. In France, the revolution of 1830 brought about only slight changes. The wealthy bourgeoisie dominated the July Monarchy, while the workers who had played such a pivotal role in the revolution of 1830 felt that they had received little for their efforts. Louis Phillipe's chief minister, Francoise Guizot (1787–1874), believed that France had evolved politically as far as it should and that everyone who resented their lack of political rights should simply "get rich." With the rise of censorship and the banning of openly political meetings, opponents of the regime turned to the practice of holding banquets that were thinly disguised political meetings. Over the winter, there had been more than seventy of these banquets with the largest one scheduled for February 22, 1848, to honor George Washington, a great hero to continental liberals. On the day of the banquet, Guizot issued an order banning it, which resulted in four days of revolution in the streets of Paris. After the first day, Louis Phillipe forced the resignation of Guizot, which may have been enough to placate the liberals; however, the workers on the barricades were not satisfied until they forced Louis Philippe to flee to England.

Political disagreements between the liberals and the radicals plagued this revolution in France from the start, with the liberals focusing on political issues such as an expansion of suffrage. The radicals, led by socialist journalist **Louis Blanc** (1811–1882), spoke of the need for fundamental social and economic change. Blanc's supporters successfully pressured the provisional government to set up **national workshops** to provide jobs for the unemployed.

Outside of Paris, however, the nation was more conservative, as seen by the national assembly election held on April 23, which elected an assembly made up primarily of moderate republicans. The election, which had employed universal male suffrage, created a government run by a five-man executive committee comprised of moderates. In May, anger over the election results led to a **workers' revolt** in Paris that was quickly put down. In the following month, the government believed itself in a strong enough position to do away with the national workshops, which they had felt pressured to support.

The surprising outcome of this year of revolution came in December when the first election for president was held and the victor was **Louis Napoleon** (1808–1873), a nephew of the Emperor. Louis

June Days and the French Second Republic

The termination of the workshops led to what became known as the **"June Days,"** essentially a violent class struggle in the streets of Paris in which 10,000 people died. The June Days further strengthened the hands of the moderate republicans, and in November, they felt confident enough to create the French **Second Republic**, headed by a president who would be elected by a universal adult-male body of voters and who would not be responsible to the legislature.

Napoleon was able to capitalize on the appeal of his name and made vague promises to aid the embittered workers.

After being elected, he created a rather conservative government, and by 1851, during a constitutional crisis, he assumed dictatorial powers. In 1852, seeking to emulate his famous relative, he made himself **Emperor Napoleon III**.

The German States

Events in France had huge repercussions in the German states. In Prussia, **Frederick William IV** (r. 1840–1861) had promised to promote moderate reform for many years, but he never implemented any changes. In March 1848, disturbances erupted in the streets of Berlin. Frighteningly, two shots rang out and struck two people. Horrified by the bloodshed, Frederick ordered his army to leave the city, which left him with no defense. The King then allowed for an election for a constituent assembly, which would have the task of drawing up a new constitution for Prussia. Several months later, the King was confident enough to call back the troops, and the constituent assembly was dissolved. Nevertheless, in December 1848, the King did draw up his own constitution, which was rather close to what the assembly had planned. It allowed for personal rights such as freedom of the press and created a two-house legislature with adult-male universal suffrage for the lower house, although in the end, this provision was watered down by giving weighted votes to those who paid more taxes.

In Austria, news of the revolution in France inspired assorted nationalists to break free from the control of the Austrian monarchy. In Hungary, **Lajos Kossuth** (1802–1894) demanded a constitution that would provide for responsible government for Hungary. In Prague, a similar revolt called for the creation of a semi-autonomous Czech homeland. From May to October, Vienna was under the control of students and workers who demanded freedom of the press, an end to censorship, and also the removal from office of the hated Metternich. As in Prussia, at first the emperor did not want bloodshed and called off his troops. By June, however, the revolt in Prague was put down by military force, and in November, the emperor was firmly in control in Vienna, although he needed Russian help to put down the Hungarian rebellion.

A paralyzing dispute also emerged over the question of where to draw the borders of the new Germany. Those who favored the **Grossedeutsch** plan wanted to see all German lands, including German sections of Austria and Bohemia, united under German rule. **Kleindeutsch** supporters felt that the more realistic solution would be to include only Prussia and the smaller German states. Eventually, the delegates settled on the Kleindeutsch, and they offered the German Imperial throne to William IV, the King of Prussia. He responded that he did not want a "crown picked up from the gutter" and declined the offer.

The Frankfurt Parliament

Another notable event in 1848 was a concerted effort to establish a unified German state. On May 18, elected representatives from all the German states gathered in Frankfurt to participate in what they thought was going to be the birth of a nation. From the start, the **Frankfurt Parliament** was hampered by the political inexperience of its participants and by conflicting aims; while all wanted to see a unified German nation, major disagreements arose over whether it should be a monarchy or a republic.

This was a lost opportunity to build a German nation under a liberal parliament rather than by a militaristic Prussian state, as would be the case in 1871. Perhaps the future course of German history would have been very different had Germany united under a liberal parliament. The German liberals at Frankfurt, however, had proven to be quite militaristic when they helped put down a revolt in some of Prussia's Polish territories and had also been completely unconcerned with the rights of those Czechs who had no desire to see their lands included in the new Germany.

The Italian States

In the Italian states, the revolt that first broke out in Sicily led Ferdinand II to grant a liberal constitution. Eventually, similar revolts broke out and terrified monarchs granted charters in Tuscany and Sardinia. Even the pope granted a liberal constitution: The Papal States, at the time still a substantial territory in central Italy under papal rule, also saw revolts. After the revolt, the territory was governed by a short-lived Roman Republic. In the north of Italy, revolts broke out in the Austrian-dominated provinces of Lombardy and Venetia. This led to a call by Italian liberals for a war of unification, with **Charles Albert**, the ruler of the Kingdom of Sardinia, reluctantly taking up the banner of Italian nationalists and attacking Lombardy, only to be easily defeated by the Austrians.

For Italy, the lesson for the future was that unification would not take place under the auspices of the papacy, as some Italian liberals prior to 1848 had assumed. On the other hand, the possibility of the Kingdom of Sardinia serving as the foundation for a unified state improved, because in the group of Italian states that were granted constitutions in 1848, only Sardinia governed via the constitutional monarchical course in the following years. A final important lesson that had future ramifications: The Italians could not eject Austria from its possessions within Italy without the aid of another European power.

Russia and Great Britain

Two nations avoided the turmoil of revolution in 1848: Russia and Great Britain. Repression in Russia was so complete under the reign of Nicholas I that the nation passed the year with hardly a yawn. In Great Britain, the story was quite different, since 1848 marked the peak year for a movement known as **Chartism**, which dated back to the previous decade. Chartism centered on the belief that the problems of the working class could be corrected by changes in the political organization of the country. The **People's Charter of 1838**, from which the movement received its name, contained six points.

- universal adult-male suffrage (some Chartists did favor female suffrage as well)
- the secret ballot
- abolition of property requirements for Members of Parliament
- payment to Members of Parliament
- equal electoral districts
- annual parliaments with yearly elections

In many ways, working-class dissatisfaction with the House of Commons after the passage of the Great Reform Bill was a motivating factor behind the Chartist movement, because working-class citizens believed (correctly) that the reformed Parliament was completely unresponsive to their demands.

In April 1848, a mass meeting was scheduled in London for the presentation of the Charter to the House of Commons. If the petition were once again rejected by Parliament, the Chartist Convention planned to transform itself into a National Assembly that would take over the government of the country. The mood in the capital was apprehensive. One middle-class man wrote to his wife:

> London is in a state of panic from the contemplated meeting of the Chartists, 200,000 strong on Monday; for myself, nothing that happened would in the least surprise me: I expect a revolution within two years: there may be one within three days. The *Times* is alarmed beyond all measure. I have it from good authority that the Chartists are determined to have their wishes granted.

In London, there were preparations for a violent conflict, and Queen Victoria was sent out of London for safety. On April 10, the day of the mass meeting, the situation was tense as 200,000 individuals gathered to sign the petition. The petition was presented to the House of Commons, and basically, everyone went home peacefully. The House of Commons, however, refused to even debate the clauses contained in the petition. At this point, Great Britain appeared to be on the verge of revolution, but the country emerged far more fortunate than its continental counterparts. Reform did eventually come about in incremental stages; by the early twentieth century, five of the six acts of the Charter (the annual parliaments didn't pass) were established parts of the British Constitution.

THE INDUSTRIAL REVOLUTION (1750–1850)

Historians had formerly placed the beginning of the Industrial Revolution at 1760, when a group of new inventors appeared from nowhere and began to develop factories, bringing an end to the **domestic system** of production that had guided manufacturing since the early modern period. Experts have modified this belief over the last several decades; some historians even avoid the term "Industrial Revolution," which they claim implies far too dramatic a change. We now know that technological progress did not begin in 1760; it had been occurring for centuries. This much is true: The second half of the eighteenth century saw a quickening of an age-old evolutionary process rather than a fresh break from the past. By the middle of the nineteenth century, particularly with the advent of the railroad, industrialization was beginning to reshape the European landscape and to dramatically alter the way in which people lived.

Great Britain's Industrial Lead

Great Britain was the first European nation to begin the process of industrialization. What motivated England to change so dramatically? Although numerous books and articles have dealt with this question, conclusive or definitive answers for queries of this sort are rare. Several possible factors may have contributed to England's role as the leader of the industrialization of Europe:

- In the years following the Glorious Revolution of 1688, Great Britain achieved a degree of **political stability** that created an environment friendly to economic investment.

- Compared to most other European states (the exception being the Netherlands), Great Britain permitted a much greater degree of **religious toleration**. For example, the Quakers, while closed off by law from parliamentary careers, had no such restrictions placed on their economic activities and were able to play a central role in the Industrial Revolution.

- **Expanding population**—which almost doubled in Great Britain over the course of the eighteenth century, due in large part to a lower death rate thanks to better diet and hygiene—is of particular importance to the Industrial Revolution. Britain's increased population size produced not only a large body of potential low-wage workers for the factories but also a steady supply of consumers.

- The **Agricultural Revolution** of the eighteenth century, initiated by men such as Jethro Tull, introduced scientific farming to Great Britain. Their observations led them to realize that continuous rotation of crops, instead of the traditional method of allowing land to lay fallow, allowed for an increase in crop yield while also leading to the growth of turnips and beets that could be used to feed larger quantities of animals during the difficult winter months.

- As a result of the Agricultural Revolution and the rise of cottage industries, England was already involved in **manufacturing industries**. Traditional manufacturing, like spinning and weaving, could be industrialized through labor-saving devices that improved production; it would be at least a hundred years before agriculture was industrialized to the same degree.

- The **Enclosure Acts** of the late eighteenth and early nineteenth centuries forced small-scale farmers into urban areas, both increasing the efficiency of the now larger farms and providing a low-paid workforce for the factories.

- The increased prosperity of English farms led to an **increase in capital** that could be used to invest in the new industries. Great Britain also had a central bank (The Bank of England, chartered in 1694) that encouraged the flow of money in the economy. Interest rates were lower in Great Britain than in any other part of Europe in this period.

- The eighteenth century witnessed a significant increase in Great Britain's **overseas trade**. Besides supplying additional investment capital, it provided the nation with the world's largest merchant marine. It is important to remember, however, that the eighteenth century also witnessed the height of the Atlantic slave trade, although the valiant efforts of individuals such as William Wilberforce finally paid off when Parliament brought the brutal trade to an end in 1807.

- **Transportation** within Great Britain was enhanced by the fact that the entire nation lies within close proximity to the sea. Internally, a network of navigable rivers and the creation of canals made water transport efficient. Turnpike trusts built new roads in Great Britain on a scale not seen since the end of Roman rule.
- Availability of the two critical natural resources of the Early Industrial Revolution: **coal** and **iron**.

The first eighteenth-century technological advances occurred in cotton manufacturing. In 1733, **John Kay** (1704–1764) invented the flying shuttle, which greatly increased the speed at which weavers could make cloth. Kay's invention created a problem: Cloth could be made so rapidly that it outstripped the supply of thread. By 1765, **James Hargreaves** (d. 1778) solved this problem by inventing the **spinning jenny**, a machine that initially spun sixteen spindles of thread at one time, and by the end of the century, improvements allowed it to spin as many as 120 spindles at once. Kay's and Hargreaves's machines were small enough that they could still be used in the traditional location of cloth manufacturing—the home. Note that these labor-saving de-

> ### Arkwright's Water Frame
> If what was truly revolutionary about the Industrial Revolution was the displacement of domestic manufacturing by the factory system, then it was **Richard Arkwright's** invention of the **water frame** that marked the beginning of this development. The water frame was a huge apparatus that combined spindles and rollers to create a spinning machine to spin cloth. By 1770, Arkwright employed 200 individuals under one roof in what is known to be the first modern factory, and in so doing, made a half-million-pound fortune for himself.

vices, including Arkwright's water frame (see inset), were in the field of cloth production. Labor-saving was useful because British cloth manufacturing was constrained by labor supply: thanks to cotton imports (from colonization of India and trade with the American South) and increased wool supply (due to enclosure and the agricultural revolution), labor savings actually resulted in more cloth to sell, giving factory cloth producers a strong price advantage over their competition. However, the cotton industry came at a cost: The cotton imports which fueled the Industrial Revolution were available only because of colonization and slavery.

The first factories were originally located along streams and rivers so that water could provide the energy needed to work the machinery. The invention of the **steam engine** made it possible to build factories in other locations. The ancestor of the steam engine was the steam pump, which was used to remove water from mines. **James Watt** (1736–1819) studied the steam pump and adapted it for use in industry. His invention was the first true steam engine, as opposed to a steam pump, since it worked by pushing steam into each end of a closed cylinder, resulting in the upward and downward movement of the pistons. A decade later, Watt invented an engine that turned a wheel. This made factories independent of waterpower and dramatically increased the pace of industrial change.

Another factor that increased the pace of industrialization was the greater ability to **smelt iron**. Traditionally, iron was smelted in extremely hot ovens fueled by charcoal, but by the eighteenth century, England was devoid of forests, and the resulting lack of charcoal seriously limited the production of iron. **Abraham Darby** (1677–1717) discovered a means of smelting iron using coal. Like the inventions discussed earlier, the economy experienced a multiplying factor as a result of Darby's invention, as more productive machines made of iron replaced those previously made from wood.

Iron and steam were the combination behind perhaps the most important invention of the nineteenth-century Industrial Revolution—the **railroad**. The first passenger railroad traveled between Liverpool and Manchester in 1830, and by the middle of the century, Britain was crisscrossed with railroad tracks that carried passengers and goods throughout the land. The railroads had an immense impact on the economy. Engines, tracks, stations, tunnels, and hotels for travelers were just some of the machines and structures that were connected with the railroads. It is estimated that by 1880, one in ten jobs in Great Britain was in some way connected either directly with the railroads or with services tied to rail transportation.

The British took the lead in manufacturing, but it wasn't long before methods pioneered by the British appeared on the continent. Belgium was the first to industrialize, possibly because, like Great Britain, it had a plentiful supply of coal and iron. Other nations industrialized with varying degrees of rapidity. The German states were hampered by numerous tolls and tariffs, making the transportation of goods extremely expensive. To aid in the spread of trade and manufacturing, Prussia in 1834 took the lead by creating the *Zollverein*, a customs union that abolished tariffs between the German states.

As certain German states, most notably Prussia, achieved significant industrial growth by the middle of the century, France lagged behind by comparison. Historians often make telling comparisons between Great Britain and France. Unlike Great Britain, France was wracked by political instability in the first half of the nineteenth century. France also lacked the centralized banking structure enjoyed by British entrepreneurs. Additionally, French population growth was only half that of the other European nations during this period. French peasants remained relatively content to stay on the land, unlike their British counterparts who had little choice but to go to the cities in search of low-paying factory jobs.

French Contributions to Industrialization
In certain industries, however, such as in the manufacturing of luxury goods, the French took the lead, and while their economic growth was not quite as dramatic as the British and Prussian models, it remained constant throughout most of the nineteenth century.

The Impact of Industrialization

Industrialization dramatically changed life in Europe. Because the location of factories tended to be concentrated in certain areas, cities began to grow and develop rapidly. Industrialization, and the urban movement it spawned, replaced the **putting-out** (or domestic) **system**, in which raw materials were delivered to the homes of peasants and then the finished products were collected and sold by merchants. The change from rural manufacturing to bringing workers to a location significantly affected life in Britain.

By the middle of the century, Great Britain became the first nation to have more people living in the cities than in the countryside, one of the most dramatic transformations in the history of humankind. Unfortunately, the cities that grew from the ground up as a result of industrialization tended to be awful places for the working poor. Poor ventilation and sanitation led to conditions in which the mortality rates were significantly higher for urban dwellers than for those who resided in the countryside. Because people had to use a water supply that came into direct contact with animal and human feces, cholera became part of the early nineteenth century urban landscape, killing tens of thousands of individuals.

Industrialization greatly affected the family structure. The fact that the entire family was working was not new; the earlier domestic system had relied on the family as a cohesive working unit. What was different was that the family no longer worked together under one roof, with women and children now often working under conditions even more deplorable than the men, since factory owners thought they were less likely to complain. Great Britain's **Sadler Committee** exposed that children were being beaten in the factories. As a result, the House of Commons passed the Factory Act (1833), which mandated that children younger than nine could not work in textile mills, that children younger than twelve could work no more than nine hours per day, and that children younger than eighteen couldn't work more than twelve hours each day. But the act provided for only seven inspectors to ensure compliance.

Industrialization and Child Labor

Interestingly, many workers were against placing constraints on child labor. It was not that they were monstrous parents; it was simply that wages were so low that children were providing funds that were an essential part of the family budget. There has been a long-standing—and perhaps tired—historical debate about the wages earned by industrial workers and the type of life such wages provided. The "optimist" school on this standard-of-living debate argues that in the first half of the nineteenth century, wages did rise somewhat for workers while prices remained steady or in fact declined, thus allowing for improved living conditions. The "pessimists," on the other hand, claim that horrible working conditions and miserably low wages provided for an increasingly bleak existence for the working poor.

Working-Class Responses to Industrialization

At first, workers were befuddled as to how to grapple with the economic and social problems caused by industrialization. For some individuals, such as handloom weavers, complete economic dislocation ensued, and their traditional way of life was threatened by machinery. Some laborers tried to destroy the machines, which they blamed for their problems. Their fictional leader was Ned Lud, and the term **Luddite** has stayed in the modern vocabulary in reference to those who refuse to embrace new technologies. Machinery also caused hardship for many laborers on the farms. They created an imaginary character known as Captain Swing, who righted the wrongs imposed on hardworking individuals by the advent of technology. After these rather primitive means of dealing with industrialization proved to be ineffective, workers sought to create **cooperative societies**, small associations within a given trade that provided funeral benefits and other services for their members.

Despite government disapproval, workers in Great Britain in the late eighteenth century organized what first were known as "friendly societies," and these eventually evolved into full-blown unions once the ban on such activities was lifted in 1824. On the continent, it was not until the 1860s that unions were allowed to freely operate in France and in Prussia. Great Britain also took the lead in establishing the first unions that represented more than a single industry. In 1834, Robert Owen helped form the Grand National Consolidated Trades Union, which several decades later evolved into the Trade Union Congress, pulling together workers from disparate industries. Skilled laborers formed the first unions; by the end of the nineteenth century, however, unions were being formed by dockworkers and other non-skilled workers. Unions were a critical reason for the steady improvement in wages and factory conditions that took place in the second half of the nineteenth century.

Socialism and Karl Marx

Some workers—particularly on the continent—found that although the unions' emphasis on gradual improvements in wages and hours worked, it was at best only a partial solution to the problems caused by industrialization. Many turned to **socialism**, believing that it offered a complete overhaul to an oppressive society. Socialism had early roots in the writings of such individuals as Saint-Simon, Robert Owen, and Charles Fourier; the most significant strand in socialist thought, however, was the so-called **scientific socialism** offered by **Karl Marx** (1818–1883).

Marx was born in the German city of Trier and eventually received a university education at Jena. As a young man, he became the editor of a Cologne newspaper, the *Rheinische Zeitung*, but he soon found that his political views were considered too radical by the authorities, who banned the newspaper, leading Marx to seek the freer intellectual climate of Paris. The French, however, quickly grew tired of Marx, so he left Paris for London where he spent the remainder of his life.

Marx and his colleague **Friedrich Engels** (1820–1895) organized a **Communist League** to link the far-flung German Socialists, many of whom, like Marx, were living in exile. In 1848, they teamed up to write a pamphlet that was to serve as a basic statement of principles for the organization. This document was *The Communist Manifesto*, one of the most influential political tracts in history. The very first line contains Marx and Engels's view that all history from the beginnings of time consists of the struggle between social classes, an idea that was labeled as historical materialism, or the material dialectic. The origin of this idea can be found in the writings of the German philosopher Georg Wilhelm Friedrich Hegel, whose dialectic differed from Marx's in that it saw economic conditions emanating from ideas rather than the reverse. Hegel's thinking influenced Marx and many others, as it seemed to suggest a means toward analyzing historical events.

Marx posited that the feudal age was supplanted by the triumph of the bourgeois class in the nineteenth century. The development of capitalism led to the creation of a new class, the **proletariat** (the working class), who would one day arise and supplant those capitalists who had exploited them. In the beginning of this supplantation, the state would dominate in what Marx admitted would be a violent, though triumphant, struggle by the workers; eventually, the state would wither away when it was no longer needed as a result of the elimination of all other classes besides the proletariat. Marx is also known for *Das Kapital*, an enormous treatise on capitalism that explains the mechanics by which capitalists extract profit from labor.

Marx brought a revolutionary dynamism to the class struggle, since he believed that the working class had to constantly prepare itself by organizing socialist parties. In 1864, he organized the **First International**, which Marx said was created to "afford a central medium of communication and cooperation" for those organizations whose aim was the "protection, advancement, and complete emancipation of the working classes." This First International was not a completely Marxist organization—Trade Unionists, Mazzini Republicans, Marxists, and Anarchists were all members. Internal conflicts eventually led the First International to dissolve in 1876. After Marx's death, Engels helped organize the **Second International**, a loose federation of the world's socialist parties heavily influenced by Marxism that met for the first time on July 14, 1889. It was, of course, no accident that this meeting took place on the hundredth anniversary of the storming of the Bastille—Marxists were consciously referencing the beginning of the French Revolution and calling for one of their own.

THE AGE OF NATIONAL UNIFICATION (1854–1871)

Metternich once remarked that Italy was "a mere geographical expression." He could have said the same for Germany, because up until the second half of the nineteenth century, both lands consisted of a number of independent territories, a disunity that dated back to the Middle Ages. In the late Middle Ages (c. 1100–1500) and the early modern period (c. 1500–1789), the rulers of France, Spain, and Great Britain successfully expanded their authority. In France, this expansion resulted in the monarchy destroying the independence of the rulers of Normandy, Brittany, and Aquitaine and incorporating them into the domains of the French king. This process was not predestined: We could just as easily imagine a Europe where modern Spain is divided between a large nation of Portugal and a small Aragon; and as it happened, the process of consolidation did not take place in either the northern German territories or on the Italian peninsula. However, by the early nineteenth century, individuals in both the German and Italian states sought to create a nation-state that would unite all Italians or all Germans under one political banner because they shared either a common culture, or language, or a fear of foreign domination. This process of national unification would have a tremendous impact on the future course of European history.

The Crimean War (1854–1856)

The Crimean War was critical to the formation of centralized states in both Italy and Germany, though initially it was impossible to foresee such a result when the war began in 1854. Several factors led to the outbreak of hostilities, including a controversy over which nation would control access to the religious sites sacred to Christians in Jerusalem. The main issue, however, was the fear among British and French statesmen that Ottoman weakness was encouraging Russian adventurism in the Balkans and the possibility that the Russians might gain access to the Mediterranean by occupying the port city of Istanbul.

War in Poetry
Alfred Lord Tennyson's famous poem, "The Charge of the Light Brigade," captures just one instance of battlefield stupidity during the Crimean War.

Following a naval defeat by the Ottomans, who had declared war on the Russians in 1853 with British encouragement, France and Great Britain declared war on the Russians. Most of the fighting took place in the Crimean region and was notable for the incredible incompetence of all participants. Most of the half-million casualties did not die in battle but perished due to disease in filthy field hospitals, something that inspired **Florence Nightingale** (1820–1910) to revolutionize the nursing profession.

The war came to an ignominious end after the fall of the Russian fortress of **Sevastopol**, Russia's chief port in the northern Black Sea, and the closest Russia had to access to the Mediterranean. Though reluctant to quit, the Russians were forced to reconsider when the Austrians threatened to enter the war on the side of the British and the French unless Russia accepted the offered peace terms. Russia was forced to cede some territories on the Danube River and to accept a ban on warships in the Black Sea region. This was a major blow to Russian ambitions of involvement in European politics. Since the time of Peter the Great, Russia had sought a warm-water port in the south which could provide access to the Mediterranean Sea through the Bosporus and the Aegean. Without power in the Black Sea or along the Danube, the Russian navy was trapped in ports along the Baltic, subject to Swedish and Danish tolls.

Breakdown of European Unity
Following the Crimean War, European efforts toward cooperation broke down, and Great Britain became more isolationist.

The real cost of the war, however, was that the **Concert of Europe**, the idea that the great powers (France, Prussia, Austria, Russia, and Great Britain) should work together—a concept that emerged from the Congress of Vienna—was finally shattered. This conflict was the first European war since the Napoleonic era. Previously, Russia and Austria had worked together to resist the trend toward nation-building. After all, both were large, multi-ethnic empires with much to fear from nationalist movements among ethnic minorities. During the Crimean War, the Germans and other Europeans had no sense of unity on such questions. Additionally, the British public was horrified by the course of events in the Crimean region; as a result, Great Britain became more isolationist regarding European affairs. This meant that when Austria stood in opposition to the building of states in Germany and Italy, it received no support from an embittered Russia, and when France found itself confronting Prussia in 1870, it would find little sympathy across the English Channel.

The Unification of Italy

The Unification of Italy

In 1848, Italian liberals made an aborted attempt to create an Italian state. Although the attempt failed, the dream for a state never disappeared. Following the collapse of the short-lived Roman Republic, **Pope Pius IX**—when his authority in Rome was restored—inspired increasingly reactionary policies. Liberals no longer saw any potential for the realization of a federation of Italian states headed by the pope. Although some liberals wanted nothing less than the creation of an Italian republic, an increasing number looked with hope to the Kingdom of Piedmont-Sardinia, the one Italian state that had preserved its liberal constitution since the year of revolutions.

The true architect of Italian unification, or what is referred to in Italian as the ***Risorgimento***, was not the King of Piedmont-Sardinia, Victor Emmanuel (r. 1849–1878), but **Count Camillo di Cavour** (1810–1861), his chief minister. Cavour was quite different from earlier Italian nationalists like **Giuseppe Mazzini** (1805–1872), who saw state-building in romanticized terms. Cavour was a far more practical individual who primarily sought ways to enhance the power of the Sardinian state.

Cavour realized that creating an Italian state would require the expulsion of Austria from the Italian peninsula. Events in 1848 foreshadowed the impossibility of succeeding in this expulsion without the aid of some other European state,

What's the Kingdom of Piedmont-Sardinia?
This kingdom consisted of the island of Sardinia and Piedmont, a northern Italian territory that borders France and Switzerland. In some history textbooks you may see this kingdom labeled as the Kingdom of Sardinia, or sometimes simply as Piedmont, though all these labels refer to the same state.

so Cavour entered into a secret alliance with France. Cavour had set the groundwork for this relationship by cleverly entering the Kingdom of Piedmont-Sardinia in the Crimean War on the side of France and Great Britain, and although its participation was minimal, it earned Napoleon III's gratitude. Napoleon III was additionally interested in aiding the Sardinians because Austria was a traditional enemy of the French state. Napoleon III also periodically looked for foreign military adventures, so that he could live up to his famous namesake, something that would eventually lead to his downfall.

The war began in April 1859. The combined French and Sardinian forces won a series of battles against the Austrians, but Napoleon decided to bring the conflict to a close before expelling the Austrians from all Italian lands. He was horrified by the high number of casualties from the conflict (something that never seemed to bother his uncle) and was threatened by Prussia who was massing troops on the Rhine to come to the aid of the Austrians. Cavour was so angered over Napoleon's abortion of the war and his betrayal of the treaty with Sardinia that he resigned as prime minister, though a year later he resumed the office.

Both Cavour and Napoleon sought to create a state that would unite northern Italy. Napoleon did not want to see the entire Italian peninsula unified for fear that a large Italian state could be a threat to France. But to Cavour's and Napoleon's surprise and to the latter's great displeasure, the war against Austria helped inspire popular rebellions throughout the Italian peninsula. In the Austrian-dominated regions of Tuscany, Parma, and Modena, revolts led plebiscites to join with Sardinia.

Meanwhile, in the south of Italy, one of the most intriguing characters in Italian history, **Giuseppe Garibaldi** (1807–1882), emerged. Garibaldi was a link to the old romantic tradition of Italian nationalism; he had at one time been a member of Mazzini's **Young Italy** movement. Horrified by the terms of the treaty between Sardinia and France, which required Italy to hand over Savoy and Nice to the French, Garibaldi at first threatened to attack France over the loss of what he considered to be Italian territories. Cavour instead encouraged Garibaldi to invade the Kingdom of the Two Sicilies, thinking that it would be a suicide mission. To everyone's surprise, Garibaldi led his famous army of 1,000 **"red shirts"** and conquered this southern Italian kingdom, which had been ruled with great incompetence by the Bourbons. Garibaldi wanted to march on Rome and make it the new capital of a unified Italy, but this threat to papal control of the city would have greatly antagonized Napoleon III, who found it useful for his popularity among the French to portray himself as a defender of the Church.

Cavour was horrified by the idea that the vastly popular Garibaldi might seek to unify Italy under his own charismatic leadership rather than under the Piedmont's control. To curtail this possibility, Cavour rushed troops to Naples to block Garibaldi from his march. Cavour was interested in the papal lands, however, and he shrewdly waited for a popular revolt in the papal states to commence, and only then, under the pretext of restoring order, moved Sardinian troops into all of the lands controlled by the pope except for the city of Rome. This was followed by the declaration of **Victor Emmanuel** as the first king of Italy on March 17, 1861. After the successful invasion of papal lands, only Venetia and Rome were not under the unified Italian flag. In 1866, after Prussia's victory over Austria, the Italians used the opportunity of Austria's vulnerability to seize Venetia. Rome was added to Italy in 1870 and named as its new capital following the withdrawal of French troops from the city as a result of the **Franco-Prussian War**.

The new Italian nation was beset with problems and plagued by corruption and bribery. For more romantically oriented nationalists like Garibaldi, the new Italy was a cold bureaucratic state led by petty officials from Sardinia, inspiring little of the passion that they had felt for the cause of statehood. To this day, there is an economic divide between the north of Italy, which is highly industrialized, and the far more economically backward south. A major problem for the new state was the continuing hostility of the Catholic Church, which banned Catholics from participating in national elections, even though Catholics widely ignored this order. In fact, the Church would not fully reconcile with the Italian state until 1929 when Mussolini agreed to restore the sovereignty of Vatican City to the papacy.

German Unification

Although Italian unification had important implications for the rest of Europe, the rise of a unified German state in 1871 totally altered the balance of power in Europe owing to the great military and economic strength of this new state. The story of German unification is rooted in the Napoleonic era. Napoleon's domination of large parts of Germany not only increased the demand among German patriots for the creation of a unified nation but also reduced the sheer number of independent German states, which eventually aided in the actual process of unification.

Following the fall of Napoleon, Austria and Prussia were the two dominant states within the German Confederation. In 1848, it appeared as if German unification would be achieved when the Frankfurt Parliament offered the crown to the Prussian King, but Frederick William's refusal delayed the process until it was achieved through means that the Prussians found more conducive to their interests.

Although it was not a foregone conclusion that it was to be Prussia rather than Austria that would take the lead in creating a unified Germany, Prussia did enjoy a number of significant advantages. Prussia, through its creation of the *Zollverein*, had achieved an economic preeminence over the other member states, while Austria was specifically excluded by Prussia for membership in the *Zollverein* customs union. By mid-century, Prussia had achieved a significant measure of industrialization while Austria remained a primarily agricultural state. In addition, the Austrian Empire was a polyglot state made up of numerous nationalities while Prussia was primarily a German state. Perhaps most important to its dominance, Prussia enjoyed the services of one of the most remarkable statesmen of the nineteenth century, **Otto von Bismarck** (1815–1898).

On taking the throne of Prussia, **William I** (r. 1861–1888) made the most important decision of his reign when he selected Bismarck as his prime minister. William was engaged at the time in a fight with his parliament over military reforms that he wanted in order to challenge Austrian supremacy in the German Confederation. To break the impasse, William turned to Bismarck, a Junker (Prussian noble), who was known for his arch-conservative views. Standing before the parliamentary budget commission, Bismarck delivered his **"Blood and Iron"** speech in which he said, "Germany is not looking to Prussia's liberalism but to her power… it is not by speeches and majority resolutions that the great questions of the time will be decided—that was the mistake of 1848 and 1849—but by iron and blood." Despite the colorful speech, the parliament still refused to vote in favor of the military budget. Never one to bother with constitutional niceties, Bismarck simply ignored parliament and proceeded to collect the taxes and implement the reforms. To their great discredit, the Prussian liberals did nothing to oppose this blatant disregard for their authority.

The key to his plan to create a unified German state was to modernize the Prussian army by giving it the latest weapons. The first stage in this plan took place in 1864 and involved an alliance with Austria against Denmark over the disputed territories of Schleswig and Holstein. After easily defeating the Danes (the **Danish War**, also known as the German-Danish War or Danish-Prussian War), Schleswig came under Prussian control while Holstein was run by the Austrians. Bismarck cunningly set up this system, since he wanted the Danish dispute to help achieve his next goal—war with Austria.

In 1866, after securing an alliance with Italy (who wanted to see the final removal of Austria from Italian lands) and securing a promise of non-participation from the French, Prussia, under Bismarck's orders, declared war on Austria, citing the petty dispute over the governance of Holstein as the reason for the attack. The modernization program undertaken by the Prussian army proved to be astonishingly successful, as Prussian forces brought about the defeat of Austria in a matter of seven weeks (the **Seven Weeks War**, or Austro-Prussian War). Ignoring the advice of both his King and the generals who wanted to stage a victory parade through the streets of Vienna and to annex large pieces of the Austrian Empire, Bismarck wisely treated Austria with courtesy to keep her out of the next stage of his plan—a war with France.

After the defeat of the Austrians, Bismarck annexed those small German states in the north that had supported Austria in the conflict. Other northern German states were convinced to join Prussia in the creation of what became known as the North German Confederation. The states of southern Germany, while remaining independent, concluded a military alliance with Prussia in case of French aggression.

In 1870, the final stage of Bismarck's plan was set in motion when he provoked a war with the French (the **Franco-Prussian War**). Bismarck, with great cunning, made France the outward aggressor in a conflict that began when a prince, who was a kinsman of the Prussian King (a Hohenzollern), was invited to take the vacant throne of Spain. To Napoleon III, the thought of Hohenzollern rulers on two fronts was too much to contemplate. Napoleon III initially won a diplomatic victory when

William I agreed to withdraw his cousin's name. However, Bismarck, who desperately wanted war, rewrote the so-called "**Ems dispatch,**" a telegram sent by the Prussian King to Bismarck informing him of what had transpired in the conversation between the King and the French ambassador, to make it appear as though the King had insulted France. Bowing to the demands of an outraged French public, Napoleon III declared war on Prussia. Following the decisive battle of Sedan, France, who many believed had the finest army in the world, was soundly defeated by Prussia. Using Prussia's new found prestige earned by achieving this victory, Bismarck was able to either convince or bribe the rulers of the other German states to accept the creation of a Germany under Prussian leadership. On January 18, 1871, William I was proclaimed in the palace of Versailles as German Emperor.

The creation of a German Empire completely changed the direction of European history. The following are some examples:

- The new German state created a bitter enemy of France, who lost the territories of Alsace and Lorraine and was forced to pay a huge indemnity to Germany for having started the war.
- The economic power of this new German state created rising tensions with Great Britain and helped set into motion the rush to build colonial empires in the last quarter of the nineteenth century. The mad scramble began when Bismarck encouraged the French to build an empire in Africa to distract from the loss of Alsace-Lorraine.
- Eventually, all the nations of Europe sought to create overseas empires as a means to further their political and economic interests within a Europe that was trying to adjust to the tensions that arose from the development of a powerful German state.

This new Germany was also not necessarily a very stable entity. Created by military might, its military commanders had a great influence over the nation at large, particularly following the forced retirement of Bismarck in 1890. Prior to being put out to pasture, Bismarck had worried about the internal dangers facing the new nation and therefore attacked two groups he deemed to be a threat to the internal cohesion of the Reich—the Catholics and the Socialists.

Fearful that Catholics owed an allegiance to a church that extended beyond nationalism to Germany, Bismarck responded with an attack on the Catholic Church in a conflict known as the "**Kulturkampf,**" in which he insisted on controlling all church appointments and on gaining complete supervision over Catholic education. Eventually, because of Catholic resentment toward such policies, Bismarck backed away from this struggle.

He turned to another perceived enemy—the **Socialists**—and in 1878, Bismarck called for the passage in the Reichstag of a ban on Socialists' right to assemble and to publish materials. Bismarck also attempted to limit the political appeal of the

Socialists by establishing old-age pensions and other social benefits for all Germans. However, as in the case of the Catholics, Bismarck found that oppressing the German Social Democratic Party merely increased its appeal.

Despite his seemingly hostile nature, Bismarck was seen as having helped establish the glory of Germany and its peoples. His efforts to co-opt the appeal of socialism increased his prestige in his later years. However, he ultimately rose to power (and remained in power for over twenty-five years) thanks to his careful manipulation of the press and the monarchs of Germany. Prussia (and later, Germany) was a conservative, aristocratic state. Bismarck ruled at the pleasure of the King, not the people; and his poor relations with Wilhelm II led to less able statesmen taking his place, jeopardizing his fragile peace with Russia, and ultimately sacrificing German stability for the sake of German glory.

France

France seemed to have a tortured existence throughout the nineteenth century as it continued to grapple with the legacy of the French Revolution. A measure of stability finally emerged with the rise of the **Third French Republic** (1870–1940), though it too had to deal with a past that still divided segments of the French public.

Following his victory in the December 1848 election, **Louis Napoleon** became the first and only president of the short-lived Second Republic. He used a tool developed by his uncle, Napoleon. Following a constitutional dispute with the legislature, he staged a plebiscite in 1851 that polled the people about whether to grant him dictatorial powers for a ten-year period. After winning this vote, Napoleon moved on in the following year to stage another plebiscite, this time on the question of whether to create a second French empire. Although there were numerous electoral irregularities, apparently large numbers of Frenchmen were perfectly content to see the revival of the empire in the hope of once again seeing France take the dominant position in Europe.

France prospered greatly during the first ten years of the reign of **Napoleon III**. Cheap credit provided by the government allowed for a significant economic expansion during this period. The city of Paris underwent a remarkable transformation from a medieval city to a modern one under the guidance of **Georges Haussmann** (1809–1891), who cleared many of the slums of the city and in their place built the wide avenues that have become a hallmark of Paris. Besides making the city more attractive visually, this new Paris was a much cleaner place, with aqueducts to bring fresh water into the city and sewers to remove waste, resulting in the elimination of one of the great scourges of the earlier part of the century—cholera.

The New Paris
It's said that one British visitor told the Emperor with a bit of sarcasm, "May it be said of you that you found Paris stinking and left it sweet."

Despite the economic improvements during the first decade of his reign, politically Napoleon III led an authoritarian regime. Beginning in 1860, Napoleon began to make a number of concessions, such as the easing of censorship, in part because of the unpopularity of his wars in the Crimean region and the Italian states. However, this liberalization had the opposite effect of what he intended; it led the people to openly display their disenchantment with his reign. Napoleon was, nevertheless, an effective politician, and he took a bold gamble in 1859 when he declared the creation of a "**liberal empire**," making his state a constitutional monarchy. This intriguing experiment never had the opportunity to succeed. Napoleon blundered into the Franco-Prussian War and was captured in battle. Eventually, he was sent into exile in Britain where he soon died.

Following the collapse of the Second Empire, France created what became known as the **Third Republic**. Right away, the Republic had to deal with the daunting task of putting down a revolt in Paris, which resulted in the rise of the **Paris Commune**, a radical government created out of the anarchy brought about by the Franco-Prussian War. The republican government restored order in Paris only after winning an armed struggle that resulted in the massacre of 25,000 Parisians. By 1875, the republic was firmly established and consisted of a two-house parliamentary body, with a chamber of deputies, or lower house, elected by a universal male pool of voters and a senate chosen by indirect elections. The president, or head of government, was a relatively weak office, directly responsible to the chamber of deputies. The Third Republic would face its greatest challenge in 1889, when a *coup d'état* looked probable. What became known as the **Boulanger Affair** severely weakened the monarchist movement. Although it was marked by significant problems, such as tensions between the state and the Catholic Church and significant anti-Semitism, the Third Republic proved to be the most durable of all the French republics.

Great Britain

In contrast to France, Great Britain enjoyed remarkable stability and prosperity in the second half of the nineteenth century. A general sense of self-satisfaction pervaded in Victorian England. Nowhere was this more apparent than in the **Great Exhibition of 1851**, which boasted more than 13,000 exhibitors displaying the variety of British goods that were now available as a result of industrialization. To accommodate the exhibits and the millions of visitors, the architect John Paxton constructed the first prefabricated building, which became known as the **Crystal Palace**. One contemporary wrote that because buildings represent the society that builds them, the Crystal Palace revealed "the aesthetic bloom of its practical character, and of the practical tendency of the English nation."

Politically, the nation was slowly evolving in the direction of increased democracy. The **Great Reform Bill of 1832** was only the first in a number of steps that were taken to expand the franchise. In 1867, under the direction of prime minister **Benjamin Disraeli** (1804–1881), one of the most remarkable men to ever hold that post, the **Second Reform Bill** passed, which extended the vote to urban heads of households. In 1884, during the Prime Ministership of Disraeli's great rival, **William Gladstone** (1809–1898), the vote was further extended to heads of households in the countryside. The rivalry between Disraeli and Gladstone was emblematic of another important aspect of Victorian politics—the evolution of a political system dominated by two political parties, in this case, Disraeli's Tory or Conservative party and Gladstone's Liberal party. The long reign of **Queen Victoria** (r. 1837–1901) saw a continuing deterioration in the political power of the monarchy, resulting in the crown's inability to play a significant role in the selection of a prime minister, which meant that at times Victoria had to live with Gladstone as her chief minister, even though she detested him and adored Disraeli, who knew how to flatter her vanity.

Russia

The stresses of war can show a nation at its best or they can reveal significant problems. For Russia, the poor showing in the Crimean War, fought in her own backyard, revealed the backwardness of her society in comparison to the nations of western Europe. Although Nicholas I was far too reactionary to contemplate reform, his successor **Alexander II** (r. 1855–1881) recognized that the greatest problem facing Russia was serfdom. In 1861, he issued a proclamation freeing the serfs, though the former serfs had to buy their freedom with payments that were to extend over fifty years (a practice that was stopped following the Russian Revolution of 1905). The peasants were also generally given the poorest lands by their former owners, which meant that life remained harsh for many agricultural laborers.

Administratively, to cope with a Russia that faced a burgeoning population throughout its far-flung empire, Alexander introduced *zemstvos*, or district assemblies, that had mandates to deal with local issues such as education and social services. The *zemstvos* were dominated by the local gentry and were hardly bastions of democracy, though some Russian reformers saw their existence as the potential for greater political freedoms. Alexander enacted further reforms, such as a revision of the legal system, although at heart he remained an autocrat and saw no need to implement fundamental changes like the introduction of a written constitution and parliamentary bodies. His intransigence on these points led to a rise in revolutionary organizations such as the **People's Will**, which assassinated Alexander in 1881. The succession to the throne of his reactionary son Alexander III (r. 1881–1894) brought about a new round of repression and an attempt to weaken even the tentative reforms of Alexander II.

Austria

The nineteenth century was not kind to the Austrian Empire, a multinational empire in an age of growing nationalist sentiment. By 1866, the Habsburgs had lost all their territories in Italy, and their shattering defeat by the Prussians at the Battle of Sadowa made Austria no longer a factor in German affairs. In 1867, the government in Vienna found it necessary to sign an agreement with the Magyars in Hungary, creating a dual Austrian-Hungarian empire. Each state was to be independent but united under the mutual leadership of **Francis Joseph**, who became Emperor of Austria and King of Hungary. Perhaps not surprisingly, the Magyars, having achieved a measure of independence, turned around and did their best to ensure that the Croats, Serbs, Romanians, and other nationalities located within Hungary were denied any form of self-rule. As a result of a lessening influence in western Europe, Austria-Hungary attempted to become more influential in the Balkan region, ultimately with disastrous consequences.

The Ottoman Empire

Another multinational empire at the crossroads was the Ottoman Empire. Commonly referred to as "the sick old man of Europe," the Ottoman state attempted in the second half of the nineteenth century to implement a process of modernization. This reform program, which began during the reign of **Sultan Abdul Mejid** (r. 1839–1861) and was known as the *Tanzimat*, was an attempt to adopt Western methods of waging wars, to bring about a much needed overhaul of the Ottoman economy, and to introduce such notions as equality before the law and freedom of religion.

The introduction of Western education played a significant role in forming a group of liberal intellectuals known as the "**Young Turks**." The Young Turks were eventually able to push reform further than the government had ever planned and in 1876 helped establish the Ottoman state as a constitutional monarchy. However, when the brutal **Sultan Abdul Hamid II** (r. 1876–1909) came to the throne, the constitution was scrapped as part of his attempt to subjugate the non-Muslim peoples within his empire. His policies led to the deaths of thousands of Armenians (though they were only a precursor to the full-fledged Armenian Genocide that would take place under the Young Turks during the years following 1915) and general repression throughout the state, although by the end of his reign, the Young Turks once again restored a measure of constitutional rule.

Ottoman weakness, however, continued to plague the empire up until it sided with the Central Powers in the First World War. The Ottomans could do little but sit idly by when, at the **Congress of Berlin** (1878), after another humiliating defeat at the hands of the Russians (the **Russo-Turkish War**), the other European powers recognized the independence of Serbia, Montenegro, Romania, and Bulgaria—all former Ottoman territories in the same Balkan region where the Austro-Hungarian Empire would soon have so much trouble.

THE SECOND INDUSTRIAL REVOLUTION

By the middle of the nineteenth century, Europe had undergone a dramatic process of economic expansion. These economic changes—sometimes referred to as the Second Industrial Revolution—and their impact on human lives may have been even greater than what occurred during the initial stages of industrialization.

Steel

The label "**Age of Steel**" is an apt one for the second half of the century. Previously, steel production was expensive. In 1856, an Englishman, **Henry Bessemer** (1813–1898), introduced a method that became known as the Bessemer Process that produced steel in far greater quantities without increasing costs. A few years later, **William Siemens** (1823–1883), a German, introduced an even better method of making steel that produced a higher quality product at significantly reduced costs.

Because of its strength and durability, steel became the metal of choice for buildings and ships, resulting in a revolution in architecture and shipbuilding.

Electricity

Few developments have affected the way people live their lives as significantly as the invention of the means to harness **electrical power**. In 1879, Thomas Edison invented the incandescent lamp. Two years later, the first electrical power station was built in Great Britain. Soon after that, European cities began to be lit after dark, and populations moved through the streets of the city more effectively with the introduction of electric tramways. Electric lights made cities far safer and even led to the expansion of nighttime activities in London and Paris, where the late nineteenth century saw a tremendous growth in the number of public opera houses and theaters.

Transportation

The second half of the nineteenth century witnessed many significant developments in all forms of transportation.

- Europe's rail network expanded dramatically. By the end of the century, well over 100,000 miles of track had been laid.

- In 1869, the French built the **Suez Canal**, though it was the British who gained control over the canal in 1875, eager to ensure their continued use of a waterway that almost halved the amount of time it took to travel from Great Britain to India.

- Speedy clipper ships began to set records for crossing the Atlantic Ocean, though by the end of the century they were to be replaced by steamships.

- Trains and steamships, using the ice-making machines that were introduced in the 1870s, were able to transport perishables around the world and made the United States, Australia, and Argentina major providers of European provisions.

- In 1885, Karl Benz invented an internal combustion engine powered by gasoline. Automobiles, however, would remain a plaything of the very wealthy until Henry Ford started producing his Model T in 1908.

- Finally, a whole new area of transportation was opened up when Orville and Wilbur Wright, brothers whose background was in the building of bicycles, launched the first successful airplane at Kitty Hawk, North Carolina, in 1903.

Communication and Education Advances

- Britain was the first European nation to establish a national postal system, with users able to send a letter for a penny, affordable to almost all.

- The development of universal public education also meant that more people were inclined to communicate in writing.

- In 1844 the first telegraph line was completed and by the second half of the century, Europe was covered with telegraph lines.

- In 1876, Alexander Graham Bell invented the telephone, and Germans were making 700 million calls per year by 1900.

- Some of those calls might have been to make social arrangements around the new entertainment options of the age, such as attending motion pictures, first shown publicly in the 1890s, while stay-at-home sorts could enjoy the phonograph, invented by the incredibly prolific Thomas Edison in 1877.

Other Scientific Developments

Science began to play an increasingly important role in industrial expansion. In particular, the second half of the nineteenth century produced a series of major developments. While this trend was to continue into the first decades of the twentieth century, in many ways, the optimism that one could sense in the 1880s concerning the world of science was not to be found some forty years later. Even before the First World War delivered a terrible blow to the belief in rational progress, scientists were revealing that nature was incredibly complex and that many questions would remain unanswered while at least some of the basic assumptions concerning the workings of the universe were under attack.

- The introduction of synthetic dyes revolutionized the textile industry.

- The invention of man-made fertilizers led to increased crop yields.

- The invention of dynamite by the Swedish chemist **Alfred Nobel** (1833–1896) made it possible to blast tunnels through rock and to remove those hills that nature had placed in inconvenient spots. Nobel, however, was horrified by the potentially destructive uses of his invention, and in his will he entrusted money for a prize to be given in his name to those who served the cause of peace.

Increasingly, the nineteenth and early-twentieth centuries witnessed greater specialization in the sciences, as scientists provided some of the key foundational work in areas such as physics and chemistry. Some of these developments include the following:

- Michael Faraday produced groundbreaking work on electricity and electromagnetism.

- Amateur scientist James Joule defined many of the laws of thermodynamics.

- In chemistry, Dmitri Mendeleev developed the periodic table, arranging the known elements by atomic weight while leaving empty spaces in his table for those elements then predicted but as yet unknown.

- In 1895, Wilhelm Röntgen made an accidental discovery of X-rays.

- In the following year, in another fortuitous accident, Antoine Henri Becquerel discovered radioactivity, although he did not follow this up with additional work. That task would be undertaken by the Curies—Marie and her husband, Pierre—who would spend their lives studying radioactivity. In 1910, four years after the death of her husband, **Marie Curie** isolated radium.

- In England, **Ernest Rutherford** laid the groundwork for an understanding of atomic structure by showing that atomic particles had a central core called the nucleus. Rutherford had once famously said that a theory in physics wasn't any good unless it could be explained to a barmaid, yet his own work became part of an increasingly complex body of knowledge that left many ordinary people feeling alienated from the world as revealed by science.

- As a young student, **Max Planck** was told that there was nothing further to be discovered in physics, yet his work was to revolutionize the field. In 1901, he devised a theory based on the idea that energy did not flow in a steady stream, but rather was delivered in discrete units, or quanta. His quantum physics spelled an end to the dominance of the mechanistic interpretation of physics that stemmed from the work of Newton.

- Further undermining Newton's concept of the universe was **Albert Einstein's** special theory of relativity, where time, space, and movement are not absolute entities but are understood to be relative in accordance with the position of the observer.

Philosophy

Just as scientific inquiry was revealing ideas and principles that appeared to be less than rational, philosophers such as **Friedrich Nietzsche**, for a time a professor of classical languages at the University of Basel, began to question and even to reject the ideas of the eighteenth-century Enlightenment. In Nietzsche's most influential work, *Thus Spake Zarathustra*, he argued that it was necessary to break free from traditional morality, which is why he famously proclaimed that "God is dead."

It was necessary, according to Nietzsche, to "kill" God, since religion was at the center of a Western model of civilization that he despised. Nietzsche hated the Germany created by Bismarck and instead yearned for the emergence of the artist-warrior superman. Unfortunately, after his death in 1900, his pro-Nazi sister was in charge of his literary estate, and she edited his writings to make them supportive of Hitler's extreme nationalism and anti-Semitism, two modern chauvinisms that he, in fact, despised.

Psychoanalysis

Sigmund Freud, the father of psychoanalysis, took the methods of modern science and proposed to find a way to treat mental disorders by delving into the human subconscious, using what he referred to as the "talking cure." As he spelled out in *The Interpretation of Dreams*, Freud believed that dreams revealed the inner workings of a subconscious world and devised a list of Freudian symbols—items or events that appear in dreams that actually represent other items or events stored in the unconscious. In *Civilization and Its Discontents*, a book written in his more pessimistic later years, Freud questioned the very premise of continuous progress for the human race and instead posited that despite attempts to suppress it, violence lies at the very core of our being.

Advances in Medicine

The beginnings of modern Western medicine took root in the nineteenth century, marking the first time in history that going to the doctor was not such a bad idea.

- Surgery, previously dominated by practitioners who bragged about their ability to remove a leg in under 90 seconds, was transformed in 1846 when American dentist William Morton began to introduce anesthesia in the form of ether, followed by the use of chloroform anesthesia a few years later.
- Overall, the most significant change in medicine in the period was that the experimental method found in the sciences was applied to medicine. Applying the experimental method, **Louis Pasteur** discovered that microbes—small, invisible organisms—caused diseases.
- Pasteur also explained how vaccines, which had been in use since the eighteenth century to fight against smallpox, worked within the body, with the immune system producing antibodies after coming into contact with a weak form of the bacilli.
- The English surgeon Joseph Lister, building on Pasteur's discoveries, initiated the use of carbolic acid as a disinfectant during surgery.
- A Hungarian doctor, Ignaz Semmelweis, made childbirth much safer for women, demonstrating that if doctors and nurses thoroughly washed their hands prior to delivery, it could dramatically reduce the number of women who died from what was known as "childbed fever."

Darwin

Few individuals had a greater impact on the intellectual world of the nineteenth century than **Charles Darwin** (1809–1882), an English naturalist who traveled on the *H.M.S. Beagle* to the Galápagos Islands off the coast of South America. Prior to Darwin, there were some, including his grandfather, who had challenged the biblical account of creation found in Genesis, which states that creation was a one-time event and that species therefore never undergo a process of change (evolution), since God created the world in six days and then stopped. In addition, geologists, like **Charles Lyell** (1797–1875), claimed that geological evidence proved that the Earth was much older than the biblical age of approximately 6,000 years.

Although Darwin was not operating in an intellectual vacuum, he was the first to offer an explanation for the process of change. Darwin argued that certain members of a species inherit traits that over time may make them more successful in the struggle for survival. These traits are then passed down, while those members of the species who lack such characteristics ultimately do not reproduce. Darwin labeled this process **"natural selection"** in his epochal book *The Origin of Species* (1859). It was not until more than a decade after the publication of his first book that Darwin, a cautious man, would take his idea to its natural conclusion. In *The Descent of Man* (1871), Darwin argued that humans were not exempt from this process of evolutionary change and that human beings have therefore evolved from simpler forms of life. The opposition to Darwin was swift and vehement, particularly from religious groups, who saw such ideas as a direct threat to the very basis of their beliefs.

Darwin's Followers and "Survival of the Fittest"

Darwin did attract a number of followers. Although Darwin was always calculating in his own speculative thought, many of his followers pursued his ideas with wild abandon. It was **Herbert Spencer** (1820–1903) who first used the phrase **"survival of the fittest,"** a phrase never in fact uttered by Darwin. For Spencer, such an idea provided justification for governments to abandon the poor; he believed that giving aid on their behalf would upset the natural order of survival. Such ideas, which received the label **"Social Darwinism,"** were used to justify the idea that Europeans were superior to Africans and Asians and therefore should dominate them. Across Europe, ardent nationalists used the concept of survival of the fittest to explain the constant state of tensions between nations and why some states thrived while others didn't. Social Darwinism also played a role in the heightened anti-Semitism found across Europe in the last quarter of the nineteenth century, as some argued that Jews were a lesser race and could never be integrated within the larger fabric of society.

Social Class and the Second Industrial Revolution

Such far-reaching industrial developments played a significant role in changing the social dynamic in western Europe. One group in decline was the traditional aristocracy. The French Revolution created the concept of a meritocracy, thereby eliminating any special privileges based on birth. In Great Britain, the development of refrigerated railcars meant that less expensive agricultural products could be imported from the United States, Argentina, and Australia, which resulted in the propitious decline in the wealth of many of the great noble families, whose wealth was primarily based on land. The implementation of competitive examinations for civil service and military positions served to reduce the aristocracy's role in two of their traditional endeavors: government administration and command of the military.

The second half of the nineteenth century has sometimes been called the "**Age of the Middle Class.**" Middle classes were not new: During the Renaissance, a different "middle class" was largely responsible for the changes that radically transformed society. That middle class consisted of wealthy, city-dwelling merchants, who lay somewhere between the three traditional classes or "estates" of medieval society—the peasants, the priesthood, and the nobility. The money of these merchants, and their secular interests, contributed to the intellectual progress of the Renaissance.

In the late nineteenth century, however, the middle class was growing in size and importance. The merchants were joined by members of newly-created professions (such as industrialists and engineers) and of newly-wealthy ones (lawyers and journalists, doctors and teachers). These people were "middle class" in the sense that they fell outside the earlier class system. On the whole they were not middle-income; they were instead quite wealthy. The late 1800s were significant not because the middle class was new, but because it was larger than ever before.

As a group, the middle class enjoyed new luxuries such as fresh running water and central heating. All families that were considered middle class had at least one servant, while wealthier families had large staffs to attend to their every need. Department stores began to cater to the increasing taste for consumer goods that became a hallmark of middle-class existence. Travel in the eighteenth century had been the preserve of the extremely wealthy, when it was considered an essential part of a young gentleman's education to go on a "Grand Tour" of the capitals of Europe. However, this too changed. **Thomas Cook** (1808–1892) popularized travel among the middle class when he organized day trips to the Great Exhibition in London, thus giving rise to the tourist trade. For those seeking less vigorous relaxation than seeing ten countries in as many days, spas and resorts became common vacation destinations.

For workers, the Second Industrial Revolution brought about some improvements in their standard of living. One example of this is the development of popular entertainment such as dance halls and professional sports leagues, a sign that the working-class income was not entirely consumed by survival necessities, such as food and housing. Yet, for many workers across western Europe, the improvements were slight at best. Many still saw socialism as the best means to change their dreary existence. Socialism itself underwent some significant developments in the latter part of the nineteenth century. **Eduard Bernstein** (1850–1932), a German intellectual, challenged some of Marx's basic ideas in *Evolutionary Socialism* (1898). He and his followers, who were labeled "**revisionists,**" argued that capitalism was not, as Marx claimed, about to collapse.

A "Victorian" Morality

Another sign that the middle class enjoyed preeminence at this time was that its standards of behavior became the societal norms. In some instances, this trend produced positive results; for example, certain barbaric forms of popular entertainment, such as animal fights, ceased. Unfortunately, the middle class often obeyed a rather priggish, or what we today refer to as "Victorian," morality. This sense of propriety also greatly affected middle-class women: Victorian sensibilities seemed to preclude them from living fulfilled lives. Women were excluded from the professions and from enrollment in institutions of higher education. The late Victorian period did witness the development in Great Britain, the United States, and, to a lesser extent, France and Germany, of a women's rights movement that sought to dramatically change the status of women.

The Beginnings of Anarchism

Another political ideology that began to attract some workers by the end of the century was anarchism. **Joseph Proudhon** (1809–1865), a self-educated typesetter, is often considered to be the father of anarchism. In 1840, he wrote *What Is Property?*, and his answer to that question was simply that "property is theft." Proudhon, who was the first to use the term "**anarchist**," believed that the true laws of society had little to do with authority and came from the nature of society itself. Anarchism touted the idea that bringing these laws to the surface should be the ultimate goal of any society. Anarchists like Proudhon wanted workers to organize small groups of independent producers that would govern themselves without interference from the state, an institution that anarchists wanted to see abolished. Anarchism never gained the support of as many workers as socialism, but in certain regions, such as in the Spanish province of Andalusia, the movement had a significant following.

Because capitalism was firmly rooted in society, it was necessary for socialists to work toward the progressive improvement of working-class conditions within a capitalist framework rather than focus on revolutionary upheaval. Their more radical views had been mollified in part due to the development of parliamentary democracy and universal male suffrage in parts of western Europe, which led them to believe that socialism could be achieved through the ballot box.

Radicals such as the German **Karl Kautsky** (1854–1938) held firm to the validity of Marx's "laws" and were harsh toward the revisionists, whom they considered heretics, although Kautsky himself in fact altered some of Marx's ideas. Unlike Marx, he claimed that the proletarian revolution would not be a bloody affair but a civilized process. A socialist movement could be a passive evolution since it was inevitable. Such views were in turn declared heretical by more extreme socialists such as **Lenin** and **Rosa Luxemberg**.

SOCIAL AND CULTURAL DEVELOPMENTS

Religion

Religious beliefs and institutions made a significant recovery in the period after 1815, particularly considering the extent of the challenges posed to organized religion by the Enlightenment, the French Revolution, and the Napoleonic era. Secular rulers saw religion as an important bulwark for the existing social order, with the revolutions of 1848 further spurring this trend toward state support of religion.

Catholicism

Spain, in 1851, declared Catholicism the only religion of the Spanish people, while in Austria, the reforms that Joseph II had imposed on the Catholic Church in the late eighteenth century over areas such as the training of priests were repealed.

Nowhere were the events of 1848 felt more than in Rome, where a revolution forced Pius IX to flee his city. Restored to power with the help of French troops, he issued the encyclical *Syllabus of Errors*, which listed liberalism as one of the errors of modern life. In 1870, Pius put forward the doctrine of "**papal infallibility**," which posits that when making an official statement on matters of faith, the pope could not be in error, a controversial doctrine that alarmed moderate Catholics.

Perhaps inevitably, there was a backlash against religious institutions where they appeared to be standing in the way of change. Such criticism could be clearly expected from liberal circles, but even conservative politicians could be antagonistic toward religious bodies. In the newly unified Germany, Bismarck saw Catholicism as a force that could rip the nation apart, because Catholics were tied to a supranational institution that would be the object of their primary loyalties. To deal with this purported threat, Bismarck, with the support of German liberals, attacked Catholic institutions in what was known as the *Kulturhampf* (cultural war), taking control over Catholic schools and the appointment of bishops. After seeing that this was having little effect, Bismarck stopped this harassment in 1878.

In the last quarter of the nineteenth century, there was a growing sentiment among both Catholic and Protestant clergy that religion needed to address the social issues of the day. In 1891, **Pope Leo XIII** (r. 1878–1903) issued *Rerum Novarum* ("Of New Things"), and although the encyclical reaffirmed the right of private property and bashed socialism, it said that Christians in general and the Church specifically had a responsibility toward the poor. In primarily Catholic countries such as France and Italy, this message led to the establishment of the **Catholic Social Movement**, while in Protestant lands, churches expanded their efforts on behalf of the poor.

The Bible as History

In the German states in the early nineteenth century, a group of theologians began to study the Bible as history in search of the **"historical" Jesus**. A critical step in this effort was the publication in 1835 of *The Life of Jesus Critically Examined* by **David Friedrich Strauss** (1808–1874). For Strauss, the Bible consisted of a series of myths formulated by the early Christians, ultimately providing for a scripture that contained, in his famous phrase, a "Christ of faith, rather than the Jesus of history." The work of these German theologians was brought to England by Samuel Taylor Coleridge as well as by George Eliot, who translated Strauss's *Life* as well as Ludwig Feuerbach's (1804–1872) *Essence of Christianity*, which argued that God was a man-made device that reflected our own inner sense of the divine.

Religion for the Working Class and Peasants

In Great Britain, a religious census taken in 1851 revealed that attendance at church (it assumed everyone was Christian) was much lower than expected and that the working class in particular had very little connection with organized religion. On the other hand, the nineteenth century was not without some interesting examples of the continuing strength of popular religious sentiment. One well-known incident dates back to 1858, when a young French peasant girl named Bernadette saw a vision of the Virgin Mary, an event that was repeated eighteen more times. The waters from the grotto at Lourdes where she saw the vision became an important religious shrine.

The Lourdes Shrine
To this day, the grotto at Lourdes remains a place where those who are ill drink the waters in the hope of being cured.

Judaism, Anti-Semitism, and Zionism

For Jews, the nineteenth century presented new opportunities as well as new pressures. The legal status of Jews improved throughout the century. In 1858, Jews were allowed to enter the House of Commons in Great Britain, and in the following decade, Jews received full political rights in Austria-Hungary and Germany. Despite their newly enhanced legal status, social discrimination remained endemic. Those Jews who wanted to rise in certain professions or in government often found the path blocked to them unless they converted.

The last quarter of the nineteenth century was a period of increasing hardships for Jews. For many, Jews were seen as responsible for new and troubling trends in modern economic life, such as the creation of the department store, which put small shopkeepers out of business. The economic depression of 1873, which lasted for most of the remainder of the decade, led to an increase in prejudice. Economic resentment was combined with a new form of **anti-Semitism** (the word was first used in 1879) based on Social Darwinist notions of Jews as being part of a distinct and foreign race and not just members of a religious denomination.

Hitler's early years in Vienna were spent in a city governed by Karl Lueger (1844–1928), who was elected mayor of the city on an openly anti-Semitic platform. Anti-Semitic political parties formed in Germany, while in France, the **Dreyfus Affair** helped give rise to *Action Française*, a monarchist group that was also virulently anti-Semitic.

In Russia, the monarchy used attacks on Jews, or *pogroms,* as a tool for redirecting popular anger, which might otherwise have been directed toward the throne. Several millions Jews left Russia at the turn of the century to escape the persecution that grew worse after the 1905 Revolution.

For many Jews, the optimism they felt at mid-century that the future would bring ever greater social acceptance was by the end of the century being destroyed by a wave of hatred. For some, this would lead to the conclusion that the only hope to live in peace would be through the establishment of a Jewish homeland. The leading advocate for **Zionism**, as this idea was called, was **Theodore Herzl** (1860–1904), an Austrian journalist who was horrified over the anti-Semitism that bubbled over the surface as a result of the Dreyfus Affair. In *The Jewish State*, he argued that Jews must have a state of their own and began to form a worldwide organization to achieve this goal, with the First Zionist Congress meeting in Switzerland in 1897.

The Rights and Role of Women

The role of the family changed in the nineteenth century, with one of the most significant developments being that families, which at one time operated as a cohesive economic unit, no longer functioned in such a manner. Increasingly, there were now separate spheres for both male and female endeavors, with the male going off to earn the money that provided for the family's support. In the late nineteenth century, the rise of a sizable, wealthy middle class created new gender standards. Middle-class city-dwellers had the money and the energy to record their social views and set standards of taste for their nations. And, among those families who had the money, the new standard was for a man's place to be in the workforce and a woman's to be in the home, which was increasingly seen as a haven in an ever-changing world.

This idealization of the household and the female's place within it led in the Victorian period to the rise of what is known as the **"cult of domesticity."** Among the well-off, women were expected to exhibit certain traits that were to make the home a blissful paradise. Submissiveness was one of the traits that women were expected to exhibit, along with sexual purity and religious piety, because women were expected to be responsible for the religious life of the family. Books were written to provide women with tips on running their households and raising their children. Standards were quite different for the poorer majority of the country. Working-class women worked just as hard as working-class men, whether in factories, or in forms of domestic labor (such as taking in laundry), or as servants. Many worked multiple jobs, and had little time or energy left to raise children, let alone read books on the subject. The working class would, nevertheless, sometimes receive visits from well-meaning but patronizing middle-class women offering to instruct them in the new ways of home economics.

Limits to Women's Education and Work

Keeping women in the home was in part ensured by outside institutions that limited the opportunities that were available to females. Higher education was generally reserved for men, although cracks began to appear, with women being allowed to attend the University of Zurich by 1865 and the University of London in 1878. With the development of professional societies in areas such as medicine and law, women found an additional barrier, as the bylaws of these societies generally excluded women. For those middle-class women who did work outside the home, certain professions such as primary school teacher, nurse, secretary, and librarian became almost completely female, which also ensured that they were poorly paid jobs in comparison to those held by men.

Some women were able to move beyond the bounds of convention. Frances Power Cobbe (1822–1904) was one of the first women to make a living as a journalist and later became an active campaigner against medical vivisection, and Josephine Butler (1828–1906) challenged a basic Victorian prohibition simply by talking about sex publicly. Butler helped found the Ladies National Association in 1869, an all-female organization that fought against the Contagious Diseases Act, which allowed for women, who were deemed to possibly be infected by sexually transmitted diseases, to be dragged off the street for examination while males went unaccosted.

Women's Struggles for Increased Rights

As the century continued, a growing number of women began to criticize the civil disabilities under which they lived, such as the lack of right to divorce or to possess property rights. These women, who adopted the French word **"feminist"** to describe themselves, began to organize organizations to help bring about change. Even in unexpected places, such as in a conservative society like Greece, a feminist newspaper existed that advocated for both professional and civil rights and survived for more than twenty years with a circulation of 20,000.

Cross-national cooperation existed among the various feminist groups, and there were also transatlantic links with feminists in the United States. Although there

Who Is Mary Mayson Beeton?
She wrote the most famous advice book for women during this period. Her *Book of Household Management* was second in sales in Great Britain only to the Bible.

was a general desire for cooperation, these first-generation feminists tended to split over the issue of whether the primary struggle should be for the vote or for the improvement of social conditions.

Some progressive women scorned feminism altogether, as was the case with the German Marxist Clara Zetkin (1857–1933), who saw socialism as offering women the only possibility for ending their oppression. In Great Britain, there was a split among those women who were working to achieve the vote. **Suffragists,** women who worked peacefully for the vote, were at times overshadowed in the public consciousness by the individuals who joined the **Women's Social and Political Union** formed by **Emmeline Pankhurst** (1858–1928). With her daughter Christabel (1880–1958) at her side, Emmeline and her followers (called **Suffragettes**) pursued a militant campaign of heckling political speakers, breaking church windows, and committing arson. These were serious crimes, and there was no sense of mercy on account of their gender or their wealthy backgrounds (poorer women did not usually have the luxury of being involved in politics). On the contrary, suffragettes were punished severely for the significant threat they posed to the established social order: They were arrested for their actions, and frequently beaten. They went on hunger strike in prison, only to be force-fed.

In 1918 women in Great Britain finally achieved the right to vote. There is ongoing historical debate regarding whether it was the suffragettes or the suffragists who ultimately deserve the credit for this momentous achievement. However, there is an additional factor that allowed women across Europe to achieve the vote in the early twentieth century: the significant contribution that women made to the war effort during the First World War.

Culture Changes

Meanwhile, there were cultural changes taking place that provided the foundations for the emergence of the so-called **"new woman." Maria Montessori** (1870–1952) exemplifies this new woman in Europe at the turn of the century. An Italian, Montessori became a famous educator and physician who was renowned for her teaching strategies. Factors such as the increased availability of birth control and greater educational and professional opportunities offered new horizons for women. For some men, this new woman was unsettling, with the British novelist D. H. Lawrence noting in an essay that women, who used to "see themselves as a softly flowing stream of attraction," were now "pointed and they want everything."

Emergence of the Social Sciences

History

In the nineteenth century, there was a new impetus to take the methodology established in the sciences and apply it to the workings of society. One result of this was the emergence of history as a modern academic discipline. One of the pioneers in the new historical methods was **Barthold Niebuhr** (1776–1831), who introduced the close examination of primary source documents into the writing of classical history. His *Roman History* influenced **Leopold von Ranke** (1795–1886) and led von Ranke to challenge the traditional way of looking at history as revealing some grand design, whether that design was the revealed work of God or led to a more secular purpose. Ranke felt that the historical texts of his day were unreliable and instead felt that it was necessary, like Niebuhr, to go to original sources.

Anthropology

Another social science, anthropology, was born out of the sudden expansion of European dominance over large parts of the globe as a result of the new imperialism. Across Europe, national anthropological societies were established, although unfortunately, due to the endemic "scientific" racism of the age, such societies often spent their time exploring the "inferiority" of non-Europeans.

Sociology

Sociology, the study of human social behavior, was in part inspired by the growing tendency of governments to keep statistics on the conditions of their citizenry. Émile Durkheim (1858–1917) held the first chair in sociology at the University of Bordeaux, an appointment that was met with skepticism by the more traditional faculty.

Archaeology

Scientific principles were also used in the field of archaeology, which in the nineteenth century still remained the preserve of dedicated amateurs such as **Heinrich Schliemann**, a German businessman who searched for the ruins of ancient Troy, and the Englishman **Sir Arthur Evans** (1851–1941), who excavated the Minoan culture of Crete.

The Arts

Romanticism began in the second half of the eighteenth century as a rejection of what was viewed as the cold rationalism of eighteenth century Neoclassicism and instead placed a much higher value on the primacy of emotions and feeling.

Romanticism in Literature

Part of the inspiration for Romanticism came from the writer **Jean-Jacques Rousseau**, who in his novel *Émile* proposed an educational program for a young man in which the education was derived from nature and not from rote memorization of facts.

Artists who worked in the Romantic tradition extolled both the beauty and mystery of nature. They also exhibited a great deal of interest in the supernatural, as for example in Goethe's *Faust*, which deals with a man who sells his soul to the devil in order to achieve worldly success.

Wolfgang von Goethe

The most important of the early Romantic writers is arguably **Wolfgang von Goethe** (1749–1832). In his *Sorrows of Young Werthe*, an epistolary novel, young Werthe kills himself when his love for a woman is not returned. The novel proved to be so popular that young men throughout Europe began to dress in clothes similar to Werthe and, in some extreme cases, killed themselves. Goethe was the greatest figure of the *Sturm und Drang* (Storm and Stress) generation of German Romantic writers of the 1770s and 1780s, who were introduced to an interested French public by the author Madame de Staël (1766–1817), who was living in exile in Switzerland after angering Napoleon.

Romantics explored folklore and traditional peasant life, because country people were idealized as living closer to nature. Romantics also found it necessary to break with the traditional styles of the past. In their jointly written *Lyrical Ballads*, the English poets **William Wordsworth** (1770–1850) and **Samuel Taylor Coleridge** (1772–1834) completely ignored the rules of punctuation, revealing their rejection of classical poetic forms.

Many of the artists who worked in the Romantic tradition became fascinated with the Middle Ages. Although their glorification of the medieval past, an age of theocratic kingship, would have seemingly pointed them into a more conservative direction, many of the Romantics were political liberals. **Sir Walter Scott** (1771–1832) and **Victor Hugo** (1802–1885) in many ways invented the popular image of the Middle Ages in novels such as *Ivanhoe* and *The Hunchback of Notre Dame*. Their influence can be felt when you look at almost any church in the United States from the second half of the nineteenth century; the odds are that it's built in the Gothic style.

Many in the Romantic movement not only rejected traditional literary and artistic styles, but also rejected the traditional political order. **Percy Bysshe Shelley** (1792–1827), an English Romantic poet, rebelled against the conservative values found in his country. In *Prometheus Unbound*, a lyrical drama, the mythical protagonist challenges the established order by stealing fire from the gods, and *Mask of Anarchy* was written as a political protest after the Peterloo massacre. George Gordon, **Lord Byron** (1788–1824), challenged the political status quo and ended up dying in Greece fighting in the rebellion against the Ottoman Turks. Amandine-Aurore Dupin (1804–1892), who wrote under the intentionally male-sounding pen name **George Sand**, challenged the endemic oppression that weighed down women. Sand was involved in a famous affair with Frederic Chopin, who initially said about her to his family, "Something about her repels me." In *Indiana,* we have the story of a woman who is desperate for love but finds herself abused by both her husband and a selfish lover. Sand broke with stereotypes not only with her pen name but by smoking cigars, dressing like a man, and engaging in affairs with married men.

Music

In addition to its impact on literature and art, Romanticism influenced the world of nineteenth-century music. **Ludwig von Beethoven** (1770–1827) began to write compositions that broke with earlier classical forms by adjusting their length and doing unheard-of things such as putting a vocal soloist toward the end of the last movement of a composition. Beethoven was able to break with tradition because he was the first composer to earn his living directly with proceeds from compositions and performances, earning enough to not have to rely on either aristocratic or religious patrons.

Other innovative composers include **Franz Schubert** (1797–1828), who invented the *lied*, or art song, which involves a solo voice performing a melody to piano accompaniment. **Hector Berlioz** (1803–1869) wrote pieces in which for the first time there was an attempt to tell a story without the use of singers and a written text, such as when he set Goethe's *Faust* to music. Some composers made use of traditional oral tales or folk songs: **Frederic Chopin** (1810–1849) was influenced by the music of the peasants of his native Poland, and **Franz Liszt** (1811–1886) wrote music based on traditional gypsy music. At the turn of the century, a self-styled avant-garde sought to break with convention, so that when Sergei Diaghilev presented his ballet *The Rite of Spring* in 1913, the odd costumes, peculiar dancing, and jarring music by **Igor Stravinsky** seemed to be an utter rejection of every element of classical ballet. The artists were often well ahead of their skeptical audiences, and the premiere performance of *The Rite of Spring* was famous for the mayhem that ensued among the proper bourgeois crowd.

Art

Romantic artists became fascinated with what they deemed to be "exotic," and leading painters traveled to North Africa and to the Middle East in search of subjects. Also, like their literary counterparts, many artists rejected the political order in their works. For example, **Eugène Delacroix's** (1798–1863) *Liberty Leading the People*, painted one year after the overthrow of Charles X, captures the stirring events of the revolution in the streets of Paris.

By the mid-century mark, **photography** was beginning to have a significant impact on painting while also serving as a new art form in its own right. One of the pioneers was **Louis Daguerre** (1789–1851), who in 1835, accidentally discovered that he could produce an image when he put an exposed plate in a chemical cupboard where mercury vapor was present. It still took him several years to find a way to fix the image, a process that received the name of **daguerreotype**. Photography would enter into the mainstream with the introduction of celluloid film, and in the 1880s, **George Eastman** introduced flexible film and the first box camera, which made photography into something far less expensive that could be enjoyed by the masses.

The development of photography made it increasingly clear to painters that there would be less demand for realistic landscapes and portraits. Some artists began to look to new subjects, such as those we refer to as the **realists**, who sought to paint the world around them without any illusions. In part inspired by the revolutionary upheavals of 1848, **Gustave Courbet** (1819–1877) began to paint works like *The Stone-Breakers* that rejected the romantic traditions of the day and instead focused on showing the world of the peasants in all its grim reality. **Jean-Francois Millet** (1814–1875) is most famous for *The Sowers*, which shows hardscrabble peasants who seem, like the wheat, to be growing out of the earth. Millet was himself from the peasant class and refused to paint them in an idealistic manner, nor did he seek to show that hard labor brought happiness. The artist **Honoré Daumier** (1808–1879) is best known for his cartoons that lifted the curtain on the corrupt politicians and legal system of the July Monarchy. In his later years, he turned to painting and sculpture, with one of his most famous works being *The Third Class Carriage*, focusing on a group of French peasants, their faces creased with the legacy of their difficult lives, sitting in the obviously uncomfortable setting of the railcar.

Realism in Literature

Realism was also an important movement in literature. Just as realist painters wanted to show the world the actual conditions of those on the bottom of the social order, so too did novelists like **Charles Dickens** (1812–1870), who used his brief experience in a blacking factory as the basis for his critique of industrialized society. In *Hard Times*, the noble workingman Stephen Blackpool struggles against forces over which he has no control. He can't divorce his drunken wife and marry his beloved Rachael, because divorce is available only to the wealthy. Meanwhile, he's falsely accused of being a troublemaker at work and finds himself unable to make a living. Such works, although at times a shade maudlin, introduced many middle-class individuals in Great Britain to the hardships of working-class life.

Other realist authors focused on what they perceived to be the barrenness of middle-class domestic life and most notably the institution of marriage. One such writer was Mary Ann Evans (1819–1880), who wrote under the name **George Eliot**. In *Middlemarch*, her most important work, Eliot deals with English provincial life on the eve of the Great Reform Bill. Her main character, Dorothea Brooke, despite her own beauty, marries an unattractive older cleric named Casaubon, in the failed hope that his scholarly ways will broaden her world. Although her second marriage, to Casaubon's young cousin, is a happy one, frustration still remains over her inability to realize her dream of improving the living conditions for their tenant farmers. Emma Bovary, the title character in **Gustave Flaubert's** (1821–1880) *Madame Bovary*, marries a mediocre village doctor only to find that reality is far different from the romantic notions of marriage she received from books. In search of excitement, she engages in a series of affairs, but the emptiness continues, and finally disappointment in love and financial failure lead her to commit suicide by taking arsenic. In **Leo Tolstoy's** (1828–1910) *Anna Karenina*, once again we have a beautiful but bored woman who engages in an affair that also meets with disastrous results.

Tolstoy's fellow Russian, **Fyodor Dostoyevsky** (1821–1881), was almost executed for his participation in an illegal political group, after which he was forced to spend ten years in Siberia. The experience transformed him, pushing in a conservative direction both his politics and his interest in the psychological and moral obligations of man, an interest that was revealed in his classic novels, *Crime and Punishment* and *The Brothers Karamazov*.

Back in France, **Émile Zola** (1840–1902) found himself applying the social sciences to the novel. Using this "naturalistic" technique, he wrote a series of novels dealing with a family over several generations, showing how environment and heredity were the critical factors in explaining their moral and physical degeneration. Zola also defended Alfred Dreyfus from charges of treason in his open letter entitled *"J'accuse,"* which appeared on the front page of the French daily, *L'Aurore*.

History in Literature
Tolstoy's masterpiece, *War and Peace*, takes the grand events of Napoleon's 1812 invasion of Russia and reveals how ordinary people can get caught up in the swirl of events over which they have no control.

Post-Realist Art: The Impressionists and Expressionists

Although some painters, such as **Édouard Manet** (1832–1883), were inspired by the realists, they wished to push their techniques in new directions. Manet's *Luncheon on the Grass* shows a rather peculiar picnic, with two fully clothed males and a nude female. The work was in part startling to contemporaries because nudes were acceptable only if they were figures from classical mythology and not the people who packed the ham sandwiches. But besides the perplexing subject matter, Manet was changing the way we look at art. Dating back to the Renaissance and the introduction of single-point perspective, paintings served to open the window into another world. Now, however, instead of looking through the painting, Manet has us stop at the surface of the canvas, something that was to be pivotal for the development of modern art.

Although Manet was a quiet man who was not looking to be controversial, he and other innovative artists of the day were to find themselves at the center of a controversy when they were not allowed to show their work at the official 1863 *Salon*, an annual public exhibition held in Paris. In response to the public outcry over the hanging committee's refusal to show these paintings, Napoleon III decided that the public should be given an opportunity to see them and make their own judgments, which led to the establishment of the *Salon des Refusés*, or "exhibition of the rejected."

Those artists who took the techniques of Manet are labeled **impressionists**, although the term was initially used as one of derision after a critic first used it in 1874 to blast a work by **Claude Monet** (1840–1926) entitled *Impression: Sunrise*. Instead of shying away from the label, painters embraced it, with the exception of Manet who refused to use it for his own work. Impressionists wanted to capture the shimmering effects of light, and to do this, they were the first to take their easels outdoors. They were aided in this desire to leave their studios by the invention of portable paint tubes. Monet would take the same theme, such as a haystack or the Cathedral of Rouen, and paint it at different times of day or different seasons to show how the impact of light would transform it. Although Monet is most famous for his landscapes, he didn't shy away from scenes of modern life such as railroad stations. Other impressionists, like **Auguste Renoir** (1841–1919), captured everyday scenes such as couples flirting in a dance hall, or in the case of **Edgar Degas** (1834–1917), numerous works showing the behind-the-scenes world of the ballet.

By the end of the 1880s, impressionism, which had once seemed so revolutionary, had become widely accepted. Some artists, while acknowledging their debt to the impressionists, wanted to push things even further. **Paul Cézanne** (1839–1906) challenged traditional perspective, composition, and the use of color. His work had a great influence on twentieth-century artists; he is therefore often referred to as the "father of modern art." Cézanne said that he wanted to make impressionism into "something solid and durable, like the art of the museums." Taking the forms of geometry that he believed were most commonly found in nature—the cylinder, sphere, and cone—he took the somewhat abstract technique used in his landscapes and applied it to numerous still-lifes of fruit.

If Cézanne became the inspiration for artists who would completely challenge the traditional three-dimensional picture frame, artists like Pablo Picasso, who said of Cézanne that he was his "one and only master," then **Vincent Van Gogh** (1853–1890) would influence those twentieth-century Expressionists who sought to put their deepest emotions on canvas. Van Gogh, a native of Holland, had a very brief ten-year career ended by his tragic suicide. Although his dark early paintings, such as *The Potato Eaters*, reveal his deep sensitivity to those who were economically struggling, his style changed following a trip to Paris where he met a number of leading artists through his brother Theo's gallery. In Arles, in the south of France, he painted his most famous works, landscapes of sunflowers or cypress trees, using bright colors and broad brush strokes to provide them with a deep emotional intensity.

The Genius of Picasso

The most revolutionary artist of the twentieth century was **Pablo Picasso**, who, with his nearly abstract *Les Demoiselles d'Avignon* (1907), made an irreparable break with the single-point perspective that had been central to Western art since the time of the Italian Renaissance. Later on, Picasso became famous as the co-founder (with Georges Braque) of cubism.

Painters such as the Norwegian **Edvard Munch** (*The Scream*) also sought to reveal the emotions rather than portray the way things looked on the surface. In Vienna, one of the centers of the avant-garde movement, artists such as **Gustave Klimt** saw themselves as rejecting the values of mass society and proceeded to find ways to shock their viewers through the vibrant use of color or by showing classical images in strange, unfamiliar ways.

The New Imperialism: Colonization of Africa and Asia

In the 1880s, the nations of Europe began an expansion into Africa and Asia that was unprecedented both for its speed and its scale. This period of conquest and the establishment of colonies is referred to as the **"new imperialism."** The term is used in part to separate the period from earlier periods of overseas conquest, such as the Spanish conquest of Central and South America, but also to denote the fundamental ways in which life was transformed in those regions that were now under the sway of Europeans.

The new imperialism was built on a foundation of **technological advances**:

- Breech-loading rifles, which allowed the user to fire from a prone position, offered a significant advantage over the nuzzle loaders still in use by those Africans who had guns. Even greater firepower was provided by the introduction of rapid-fire weapons such as the Gatling gun.

- Steamships allowed for rapid transport across oceans without having to deal with the vagaries of wind power, and smaller steam-driven river boats allowed Europeans to penetrate into the heart of Africa. The construction of the **Suez Canal**, which was finished in 1869, significantly reduced the time it took to go to Asia.

- One of the most important technological developments for imperialism was the telegraph, which allowed for the exchange of messages between India and London over the course of a day—a dramatic decrease over the two years it took at the start of the century.

- The discovery in 1820 of quinine, a drug made from the bark of the cinchona tree, was an effective treatment for the great scourge of the tropics—malaria.

Although technology was vital for the new imperialism, it would have made little difference without the various motivating factors that stirred Europeans to conquer foreign lands. One important factor was the search for profits that were assumed to be had from imperialism. With the establishment of higher tariff barriers in Europe in the last quarter of the century, nations began to look to colonies as potential free trade zones. Raw materials, such as the palm oil that was used as an industrial lubricant, or precious metals such as gold and silver, led individuals to the African heartland.

Yet those imperialists who saw colonies as a source of unimaginable wealth were going to be disappointed, because many colonies lacked any economic value, or if they did, the extensive investments necessary to make them economically viable never arrived from Europe. The exception to this was India, where the British were able to extract enough wealth for it to be justifiably referred to as the "jewel in the crown."

Other motivating factors came from **social imperialists**, who viewed imperialism as a means of relieving certain domestic social problems such as overpopulation. This would also prove to be disappointing because, for example, in the case of Italy, those who left the country much preferred to go to the United States, rather than to an uncertain existence in the Italian colonies in East Africa.

Nationalism also played a major role in empire building. European states believed that the only way they could matter on a global scale would be through the establishment of colonies. For France, building an overseas empire was a way of showing it still mattered, even after its horrific defeat by the Prussians in 1870.

Religion also served as a motivating factor, and Christian missionaries were actually the first Europeans to penetrate central Africa. Some skeptics questioned the actual motivation behind the missionaries, as can be seen in a German political cartoon from the period, which showed an English preacher droning on while behind a curtain, a businessman involves himself in the real business of empire—financially squeezing the Africans.

Social Darwinism and the New Imperialism

Social Darwinism also influenced the new imperialism. There was a genuine belief that the white races were destined to have sovereignty over the inferior peoples of Asia and Africa. Paintings would often show colonists with local children, the implied message being that all Africans were children who would benefit from the guidance of Europeans in the role of parents. Elements of this *noblesse oblige* can be found in Rudyard Kipling's (1865–1936) famous poem "The White Man's Burden," in which he writes that Europeans have a moral obligation to "bind your sons to exile/To serve your captives' need." The so-called moral imperative behind imperialism was also discussed at the **Berlin Conference** (1884–1885), ostensibly called to deal with the control of the Congo, where it was stated that one of the goals for the imperialist nations was "to care for the improvement of the conditions of their [the Africans] moral and material well-being and to help in suppressing slavery, and especially the slave trade."

Balance-of-power politics was perhaps the most significant reason for the acquisition of even unprofitable pieces of land. Nations wanted colonies so that other nations would not get them. Great Britain in particular, led by the adventurer **Cecil Rhodes**, attempted to gain colonial advantage from the Cape of Good Hope to Cairo.

In what has become known as the **"mad scramble"** for colonies, Europeans drew new borders that demonstrated their lack of concern for tribal and cultural differences with imperial territories. The Berlin conference ultimately set up rules for the establishment of colonies. Organized by Bismarck, nations had to prove that they established sufficient authority in a territory to protect existing rights, such as freedom of trade and transit. This set off the mad dash that left every square inch of Africa divided among the European powers, with the exception of **Ethiopia**, which repelled an Italian invasion in 1896, and the small state of **Liberia** on the west coast of Africa, which remained independent as a result of its unique historical link to the United States.

British dominance over **India** began to take shape following the withdrawal of the French from the Indian subcontinent as a result of the Seven Years War (1756–1763). As the nineteenth century continued, additional, formerly independent Indian territories fell under British control, with the last being the Punjab region in 1849. Following what the British refer to as the **"Indian Mutiny"** or **"Sepoy Rebellion"** of 1857, colonial control became more centralized with the establishment of an administrative structure to replace the British East India Company. By 1877, Prime Minister Disraeli went so far as to make Queen Victoria the Empress of India, thus flattering his queen while perhaps more importantly issuing a warning to the other European powers on the significance of India for Great Britain.

In **China**, Great Britain was the first European state to practice what is referred to as **"informal empire,"** where a state has significant influence over another nation's economy without actual territorial or political control. After fighting and losing a series of wars with assorted European powers in the second half of the century, China was forced to grant European states sovereign control over a series of **"treaty ports"** along the coast. In Southeast Asia, although Thailand was able to maintain its independence, the French seized control over **Indochina** with its vital rubber plantations.

Other nations involved in colonialism in Asia included the Dutch, who controlled Indonesia, and the United States, which seized the Philippines in the aftermath of the **Spanish-American War**. **Japan**, which had imitated Britain and Germany in its economic transformation into an industrial power, would also mimic their taste for colonial expansion by seizing control over **Korea** in 1910 after the **Russo-Japanese War**.

Colonialism could also provide certain benefits for the colonized nation. Again, the example of India stands out because here, the British made actual investments in infrastructure. Irrigation systems, railways, and cities were all byproducts of British rule. Concepts such as nationalism and political liberty, which were later to be used by colonial people as a tool for their own liberation, were also European exports. It was those Africans and Asians who had the most contact with the West, often through study abroad in Europe, who were the most committed nationalists.

Colonialist Violence

Violence was often a part of the colonial enterprise. The German explorer Carl Peters (1856–1914), whom Hitler admired, established a German colony in East Africa where he was referred to by the local population as the "man with blood on his hands." The most horrific example of colonial exploitation took place in the Belgian Congo. **King Leopold II** (r. 1876–1909), one of the pioneers in the scramble for Africa, personally established this massive colony many times the size of Belgium and expected the proceeds from this wealthy land to line his own pocket. Millions were enslaved, maimed, or killed in the crazed pursuit of profits. Eventually, there was an international outcry over these atrocities, including the publication of Mark Twain's sarcastic *King Leopold's Soliloquy*, forcing the King to concede control to the Belgian government, which corrected some of the worst abuses.

Views and Consequences of the New Imperialism

In recent years, historians have asked whether imperialism was ever actually popular among the mass of population, and the question has not been fully answered. Newspaper editors, who enjoyed an enlarged readership in this age of growing literacy, apparently saw imperialism as a topic of interest to their readers because they filled their pages with colonial exploits. In Britain, the pro-imperial Primrose League had more than a million members, and in Germany, Italy, and France, similar organizations existed, although with far fewer members. The **Boer War** (1899–1902) possibly helped dim public support in Great Britain for empire, although across Europe, the working class seemed to have little interest in such affairs.

Although some hoped that the building of colonies would lead to a diminishing of tensions on the European continent, the opposite was the case. Rivalries among the European powers led to further imperial expansion, as in the case with British establishment of a protectorate over Egypt and the Suez Canal in 1882 in order to ensure Britain's dominance over India. Both the British and Russians were involved in what was referred to as the **"great game"**—a struggle over the generally worthless territory of Afghanistan—because for the Russians, British control over this region would put Russia's recent expansion into Central Asia in jeopardy, whereas the British were once again concerned for the security of India.

Also, Britain and France almost went to war over **Fashoda** in the Sudan in 1898, and France and Germany twice almost went to war over Morocco in 1905 and 1911. One of the problems that helped bring about the First World War was the sense among leading German political and military figures that their country did not have a colonial empire commensurate with its position in Europe. The problem dated back to Bismarck's lack of interest in colonies, which he once displayed by pointing to a map of Europe and stating, "This is my Africa" to show his true object of fascination. Bismarck's lack of interest was opposed by those Germans who joined the Society for German Colonization (1884). When **Kaiser Wilhelm II** pushed Bismarck into retirement in 1890, one of his reasons for removing the Chancellor was his lack of interest in colonies, something by which the new Kaiser simply couldn't abide.

CHAPTER 6 TIMELINE

Year	Event
1717	Abraham Darby smelts iron using partially burnt coal
1733	John Kay's flying shuttle
1764	James Hargreaves's spinning jenny
1769	Richard Arkwright patents the water frame
1774	James Watt patents the first steam engine
1776	Adam Smith's *An Inquiry into the Nature and Causes of the Wealth of Nations*
1779	First iron bridge completed in Shropshire, England
1785	Power loom invented by Edmund Cartwright
1789	Jeremy Bentham's *Introduction to the Principles of Morals and Legislation*
1790	Burke's *Reflections on the Revolution in France*
1793	Eli Whitney's cotton gin
1798	Thomas Malthus' *Essay on Population*
1807	British Parliament votes for the end of the slave trade
1807	First passenger train line
1815	Napoleon escapes from Elba (March 15)
1815	Battle of Waterloo marks end of the Hundred Days (May 15)
1815	Napoleon sent into exile on St. Helena
1817	David Ricardo's *Principles of Political Economy*
1819	Peterloo Massacre in Great Britain
1819	Combination Acts ban union activity
1820	Troppau Protocol (agreement among Eastern Great Powers to oppose revolutionary states)
1820	Rebellion in Spain put down with French support in 1824

1821	Beginning of Greek revolt
1821	Death of Napoleon
1823	Revolt in Naples
1824	Charles X becomes King of France
1825	Decembrist revolt in Russia
1829	George Stephenson invents the early locomotive, the Rocket
1830	Charles X issues July Ordinances
1830	July Revolution topples the last French Bourbon monarch
1830s	Cholera outbreak in Europe
1831	Charles Darwin leaves on five-year voyage that will take him to the Galapagos Islands
1832	Sadler Committee looks into child labor in Great Britain
1832	Great Reform Bill
1833	Slavery banned within the British empire
1833	Factory Act
1833	English Poor Law
1834	Robert Owen establishes the Grand National Consolidated Union
1835	David Friedrich Strauss's *The Life of Jesus Critically Examined*
1835	Daguerreotype (early form of photograph) invented
1837	Beginning of the reign of Queen Victoria
1838	Beginning of the Chartist movement
1839	First in a series of Opium Wars between Great Britain and China
1840	Napoleon's body brought back to France for reburial
1840	Joseph Proudhon writes the anarchist tract *What Is Property?*
1842	British gain control over Hong Kong

1846	Repeal of the Corn Laws
1846	Irish potato famine
1847	Liberia established as independent African republic
1848	*The Communist Manifesto* by Karl Marx and Friedrich Engels (February)
1848	Overthrow of Louis Philippe (February)
1848	Unrest in various German states (March)
1848	Nationalist revolts break out throughout Austrian Empire (beginning in March)
1848	Charles Albert of Savoy goes to war against Austria (March)
1848	Meeting of the Frankfurt Parliament (May)
1848	"June Days" uprising in Paris
1848	Louis Napoleon elected president of the Second Republic (December)
1851	Louis Napoleon stages coup against the Second Republic Crystal Palace exhibition
1852	Development of the safety elevator
1852	David Livingstone begins exploring the African interior
1852	Commodore Perry arrives in Japan
1852	Establishment of the Second Empire by Napoleon III
1854	Charles Dickens publishes *Hard Times*
1854	Start of the Crimean War
1856	Development of Bessemer process for manufacturing steel
1856	Synthetic dyes developed
1857	Flaubert publishes his masterpiece, *Madame Bovary*
1857	Indian Rebellion
1858	Jews allowed to enter the British Parliament

1859	Darwin's *Origins of Species*
1859	France and Piedmont-Sardinia go to war against Austria
1859	Garibaldi invades the Kingdom of Two Sicilies
1861	Victor Emmanuel II becomes the first King of Italy
1861	Alexander II emancipates the serfs
1863	Opening of the Salon des Refusés (art rejected by the jury of the Official Paris Salon)
1864	Establishment of the First International in London
1864	Prussia and Austria go to war against Denmark
1866	Italians seize Venetia from Austria
1866	Austro-Prussian War
1867	Establishment of the Austro-Hungarian Empire
1867	Alfred Nobel patents dynamite
1869	Suez Canal completed
1869	John Stuart Mill's *On Liberty*
1870	Doctrine of Papal Infallibility
1870	Rome becomes capital of Italy
1870	Franco-Prussian War
1870	French Third Republic created
1871	Establishment of the German Empire
1871	End of the French Second Empire
1871	Paris Commune
1871	Darwin's *The Descent of Man*
1874	Typewriters invented
1874	Claude Monet paints *Impression: Sunrise*

1875	Constitution establishes the French Third Republic
1876	Serbia becomes independent
1876	Alexander Graham Bell's telephone
1877	Thomas Edison's phonograph
1877	Queen Victoria becomes empress of India
1877	Russo-Turkish War
1878	Congress of Berlin
1879	Dual Alliance between Germany and Austria-Hungary
1879	Thomas Edison invents the incandescent lamp
1881	Assassination of Alexander II
1882	Great Britain seizes control over the Egyptian government
1884	Berlin Conference
1885	Introduction of the internal combustion engine
1885	First meeting of the Indian National Congress
1885	Friedrich Nietzsche's *Thus Spake Zarathustra*
1887	Reinsurance Treaty between Germany and Russia
1890	Kaiser Wilhelm II forces Bismarck to retire as Chancellor
1890	Germany fails to renew Reinsurance Treaty
1891	Pope Leo XIII issues Rerum Novarum
1894	Beginning of the Dreyfus Affair
1894	Russo-Japanese War
1894	Russian-French alliance
1896	Italians defeated by the Ethiopians at the Battle of Adowa
1897	First Zionist Congress meets in Switzerland
1898	Eduard Bernstein publishes *Evolutionary Socialism*

1898	Spanish-American War
1898	France and Britain almost go to war over incident at Fashoda
1899	Start of the Boer War
1900	Sigmund Freud's *The Interpretation of Dreams*
1901	Max Planck introduces quantum physics
1902	J. A. Hobson's *Imperialism: A Study*
1903	Emmeline Pankhurst forms the Women's Social and Political Union
1903	First successful airplane flight by the Wright brothers
1904	Herero War
1904	British-French entente (Entente Cordial)
1905	Revolution in Russia leads to granting of a Duma
1905	First Moroccan Crisis
1905	Separation of church and state in France
1906	HMS Dreadnaught launched
1907	British-Russian entente
1908	Henry Ford's Model T
1908	Austria-Hungary annexes Bosnia
1910	Madame Curie isolates radium
1911	Agadir Crisis in Morocco (aka Second Moroccan Crisis)
1913	Sergei Diaghilev revolutionizes ballet with *The Rite of Spring*
1913	Socialists become largest political party in Germany

CHAPTER 6 REVIEW QUESTIONS

Try these questions to assess how well you understood and retained the information covered in the chapter. Answers and explanations are in Chapter 8.

1. The end of the Corn Laws in Great Britain in 1846 was an indication that

    (A) the Industrial Revolution was beginning to slow down
    (B) grain was now available in abundance
    (C) the role of the monarchy was in decline
    (D) the old landed classes no longer fully dominated British politics

2. During the 1848 revolution in France, liberals and radicals differed over

    (A) whether to establish a republic
    (B) allowing Louis Napoleon to return to France
    (C) whether political changes or social and economic changes should take priority
    (D) what to do concerning Louis Philippe and his family

3. All of the goals of the Chartist movement were eventually achieved in Great Britain EXCEPT

    (A) the secret ballot
    (B) annual parliaments
    (C) equal electoral districts
    (D) abolition of property requirements for Members of Parliament

4. The first nation to industrialize on the continent was

    (A) Prussia
    (B) France
    (C) Belgium
    (D) Russia

5. Rome became the capital of the new Italian nation

    (A) immediately upon the creation of Italy in 1861
    (B) after the withdrawal of French troops from the city during the Franco-Prussian War
    (C) as a result of its conquest by Garibaldi
    (D) after Cavour successfully negotiated the surrender of the city to the Italian government

6. The significance of the Sadler Committee of 1832 was that it

    (A) eradicated the practice of child labor
    (B) refused, for political reasons, to come to firm conclusions
    (C) was the first parliamentary commission
    (D) revealed to a larger public the existing conditions of child labor

7. The freeing of Russia's serfs in 1861

    (A) led to an agricultural depression
    (B) required them to pay for their freedom in annual payments over fifty years
    (C) was met with firm opposition by the Tsar
    (D) led to a large emigration of Russian peasants to the United States

8. The development of national postal services in the nineteenth century reveals all of the following EXCEPT

    (A) an increased role for government
    (B) the growth of the rail network
    (C) an increase in privatization of previously public services
    (D) an expansion of public education

9. The latter nineteenth century can be considered the "Age of the Middle Class" mainly because

    (A) this period was the first challenge to the old class system
    (B) the middle class was large and wealthy enough to set tastes and values for society
    (C) traditional nobility lost its prestige at this time
    (D) members of the middle class finally won political rights in the wake of the 1848 revolutions

10. The term "informal empire" best describes the situation in

    (A) the Congo
    (B) Indochina
    (C) India
    (D) China

11. All of the following were invented during the Second Industrial Revolution (1850–1914) EXCEPT

(A) synthetic dyes
(B) dynamite
(C) the power loom
(D) the Bessemer process of steel production

12. The literary works of Charles Dickens, Émile Zola, and Gustave Flaubert are all considered to be part of which movement of literature?

(A) Realism
(B) Gothic
(C) Neoclassicism
(D) Romanticism

13. The Berlin Conference of 1885 was called to address the status of

(A) India
(B) the Congo
(C) the Balkans
(D) South Africa

14. The Thomas Cook Company

(A) developed the idea of the "Grand Tour"
(B) was the first firm to sell rail tickets
(C) received a parliamentary charter in 1887
(D) introduced package tours to Britain's middle class

REFLECT

- For which content topics discussed in this chapter do you feel you have achieved sufficient mastery to answer multiple-choice questions correctly?

- For which content topics discussed in this chapter do you feel you have achieved sufficient mastery to discuss effectively in an essay or short answer?

- For which content topics discussed in this chapter do you feel you need more work before you can answer multiple-choice questions correctly?

- For which content topics discussed in this chapter do you feel you need more work before you can discuss effectively in an essay or short answer?

- What parts of this chapter are you going to re-review?

- Will you seek further help outside of this book (such as a teacher, tutor, or AP Students) on any of the content in this chapter—and, if so, on what content?

Chapter 7
Global Wars to Globalization: c. 1914–Present

THE FIRST WORLD WAR (1914–1918)

Causes of the War

Although the Versailles Treaty, which marked the end of the First World War, stated emphatically that the Germans and their allies were responsible for starting the war, the reality is a bit more complicated. The following are some of the major reasons why Europe exploded in 1914, setting the stage for a conflict that would shatter the very foundations of the continent.

Political and Social Tensions in Europe

The first decade of the twentieth century witnessed a number of political and social crises around Europe that may have led politicians to willingly pursue a foreign war with the hope that it would divert attention from domestic issues.

Great Britain and Ireland

Great Britain faced the contentious issue of Ireland, which threatened to explode as Nationalist forces began to press for independence (a movement called **Home Rule**, with roots dating back to the 1860s), while their political opposites, the Unionists, expressed their increasingly determined desire to remain a part of Great Britain. These parties were associated with religious communities; the Nationalists were overwhelmingly Catholic, and hoped to break away from what they viewed as Protestant rule, while Unionists tended to be Protestant. Leading into World War I, Unionism grew around Protestant areas in the north of Ireland, most significantly in the province of Ulster. Great Britain was also shaken, as was France, by a growing number of labor conflicts that resulted from the overall stagnation of wages during this period.

France

In France, the Third Republic was in crisis over the **Dreyfus Affair,** which began in 1894 and involved a Jewish officer who was falsely accused of telling military secrets to the Germans. The incident revealed the virulence of French **anti-Semitism** while also showing the extent to which many in France despised the very idea of a republican form of government.

The "Affair" was also tied to another contentious issue splitting the French public—the question concerning the proper role of the Catholic Church in a democratic French state. Increasingly, by the end of the century, the individuals who governed France were openly hostile to the Catholic Church which they considered to be anti-republican. These politicians worked to exclude the Church from French life by enacting laws such as one that eliminated the Church from primary and secondary education.

Russia

Russia rang in the twentieth century with the **Russo-Japanese War** in 1904, which, when Russia lost once again, revealed the complete bankruptcy of the Tsarist state. This led to a revolution in the following year. Initially, the goal of the revolution was met—the creation of the **Duma,** or parliament—that would transform Russia into a constitutional monarchy. Tsar **Nicholas II** agreed to rule in conjunction with the Duma. Throughout the following years, the Tsarist regime recovered and once again functioned primarily as an unwieldy autocracy.

Germany and Austria-Hungary

The other imperial regimes, Germany and Austria-Hungary, also saw war as a possible means of escaping from a relatively bleak domestic political situation. In Germany, worker agitation was on the rise, and the Kaiser and his inner circle dreaded the possibility of a Socialist revolution, although the threat did not really exist.

Austria-Hungary had to deal with its constant, seemingly insurmountable nationality problems. In the Hungarian part of the empire, the process of "Magyarization," the mandatory dominance of the Magyar language and culture, created great hostility among the other nationalities, who in fact made up the majority of the Hungarian population. As the Austro-Hungarian Empire lumbered from one crisis to the next, it appeared as though the union's demise was always just around the corner.

Entangling Alliances

In 1879, Bismarck created the **Dual Alliance,** a military treaty with the Austro-Hungarians. However, because Bismarck correctly foresaw that it would be suicidal for Germany to face a war on two fronts, he signed the **Reinsurance Treaty** with Russia in 1887 in order to make it clear that the treaty with Austria-Hungary was purely defensive in nature and not meant to show possible hostile intent toward Russia. Unfortunately, once Kaiser Wilhelm II (r. 1888–1918), an inordinately pigheaded man, pushed Bismarck out of office, the Russians began to view the Germans with increased trepidation, particularly since Wilhelm didn't bother to renew the Reinsurance Treaty in 1890.

While France had remained diplomatically isolated after 1870, Germany's diplomatic missteps led the Russians to join the French in a military treaty that pledged that the two countries would fight together in the event of an attack on either state by the Germans. German fears of being encircled were enhanced when in 1904 Great Britain signed an **Entente Cordiale** with France, resolving certain contentious colonial issues. German fears were further increased when three years later, Great Britain signed another entente with the Russians. This is why during the First World War, Britain, France, and Russia were referred to as the **"Entente" powers.**

Increased Militarization

One of the worst decisions that the Kaiser and his officers made was to build a high seas fleet in 1897. Britain and Germany were not necessarily natural enemies, with the British readily accepting the fact that Germany possessed the most powerful army on the continent. Navies, however, were a completely different matter for the British, because they saw their fleet as their only means to protect their vast colonial empire. The British were particularly horrified given that the Germans took advantage of a revolution in battleship design and built powerful new ships known as Dreadnoughts, thus making the British fleet suddenly obsolete. The rivalry between Great Britain and Germany now became far more openly hostile, as each side scrambled to enhance its fleets. In the end, navies were not particularly significant in the outcome of the First World War; the Battle of Jutland in 1916 was the only major naval battle of the war. Across Europe, the production of vast stores of weapons by the Great Powers dramatically increased tensions and played a critical role in the advent of the war.

Crisis in the Balkans

The immediate crisis that led to the war was the assassination on June 28, 1914, in Sarajevo, the capital of Bosnia, of **Archduke Franz Ferdinand**, heir-presumptive to the Austrian and Hungarian thrones. Ferdinand was murdered by a Bosnian Serb who wanted to see Bosnia become part of an enlarged Serbian state.

The crisis in the Balkans had brought Europe to the brink of war in 1908, following the annexation of Bosnia and Herzegovina, previously Ottoman territories, by Austria-Hungary. The weakness of the Ottoman state allowed Bosnia and Herzegovina to be taken away from it. The Austro-Hungarians annexed these territories, not because they wanted more Serbs within their empire, but because they feared the lands would be taken by the Serbian state, a national state that the Austro-Hungarians saw as the greatest threat to their own survival as a multinational empire. Gavrilo Princip (1895–1914), the Archduke's assassin, had operated with the full cooperation of the **Black Hand**, a secret Serbian nationalist group with strong ties to Serbian officials in both the government and the army. Seeing that Serbian authorities were tied to the bloodshed, the Austrians issued an ultimatum that was clearly designed to provoke a Serbian refusal and achieve what the Austrians truly wanted—war with the Serbian state.

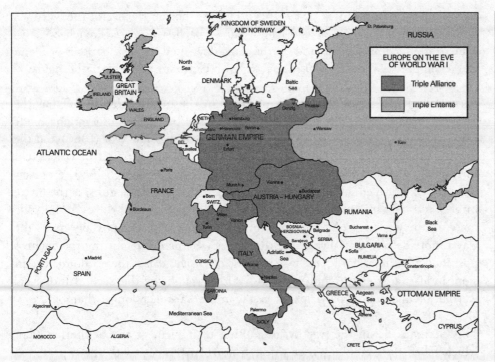

Europe on the Eve of World War I

The Course of the War

On July 28, 1914, Austria-Hungary declared war against Serbia, knowing that it risked setting off a larger European conflict. Russia had promised to protect the Serbs, but despite this pact, the Austria-Hungarians felt that they had to take the risk or their multinational empire would collapse. Additionally, Austria-Hungary had the backing of Germany, the "blank check," which bears significant responsibility for the start of the war because it was the one power that could have possibly restrained the Austria-Hungarians from taking such an aggressive stance.

As a precautionary measure, Russia responded to the Austria-Hungarian declaration on Serbia by beginning the process of mobilization. Germany demanded that Russia stop the process, which the Russians refused to do, in part because they knew that their own mobilization would take much longer than that of the Germans. They also feared that if the war spread beyond just the struggle between Austria-Hungary and Serbia, they could be caught unprepared. The Germans, seeing the continuation of Russian mobilization, decided that they had to declare war on the Russians, which they did on August 1. The whole net of entangling alliances began to fall into place as France started to mobilize on that same day, which led the Germans to respond with a declaration of war on the French.

When the shelling began in August 1914, there was tremendous enthusiasm among the citizens of the combatant nations. To their great discredit, the parties of the Second International, which for years had claimed that they would not support a capitalist European war and spoke glowingly of international brotherhood, voted in each of their respective nations to support the war effort. One of the few Socialists who spoke out against the war was the idealistic leader of the French

Socialist Party, **Jean Jaurès** (1859–1914). He was shot on the eve of the war by a fanatical French nationalist who hated Jaurès's pacifist posture. French Socialist leaders attended his funeral and on the same day voted in the Chamber of Deputies to support the government in the war with Germany and Austria-Hungary.

Part of the enthusiasm for war stemmed from the misbegotten belief that the struggle would be a short one. This premise was based on observations made from such admittedly quick conflicts as the **Austro-Prussian War** (1866) and the **Franco-Prussian War** (1870), both of which lasted only a matter of weeks. Unfortunately, the decades following those conflicts had witnessed the rise of new weapons that favored soldiers on the defensive, such as machine guns, barbed wire, mines, and more powerful artillery shells, all of which created the eventual stalemate on the western front. Even the introduction of airplanes possibly made the war a more defensive affair because the planes were used for spotting the enemy's positions, making it harder to stage surprise offensives. Also, the economic expansion, industrial strength, and national wealth wrought by the Second Industrial Revolution allowed the participants to stay in the war much longer than before.

The Germans began the war by attempting to implement the **Schlieffen Plan**, which relied on a rapid advance through northern France, with the expectation that France would be knocked out of the war in six short weeks, allowing Germany's military might to be transported by rail to the east where it would be used to defeat the Russians. The German plan required the invasion of Belgium, a nation created in 1830 with the promise that its neutrality would be guaranteed by the major European powers. The German sweep through Belgium, which broke this guarantee, brought Great Britain into the war on the side of the French and Russians. The brutal German occupation of the small nation inflamed public opinion in the United States.

The German plan had succeeded in the early weeks of the war, although, with hindsight, the Belgians' spirited defense would prove very costly to the Germans, who were operating on a strict timetable. By the first week of September, German troops had threatened Paris, leading the French government to flee the capital. After the Germans crossed the Marne river, a French army under General Joffre (1852–1931) counterattacked and stopped the Germans at what became known as the **First Battle of the Marne**. For the remainder of the fall season, the various armies to the northern coast of Flanders made a mad scramble to see if either side could be outflanked. By the first winter of the war, both sides settled down to what now looked like a much longer contest. Both sides would hold positions that would remain virtually unchanged for the next three years.

Although everyone expected the war to be a glorious affair, trench warfare proved to be anything but glamorous. At first, the trenches were just rapidly dug ditches, but as the stalemate continued, huge networks of defensive fortifications were built. Life in the trenches was a series of horrors as the men had to deal with rats bloated from chewing on readily available corpses, noise from artillery, and extreme boredom as the war dragged way past the time that soldiers had expected to be heading home. The soldiers were fairly well protected in their trenches, but unfortunately, both sides insisted on periodically sending their soldiers "over the top" into no man's land to stage assaults on enemy trenches. These excursions often became little more than suicide missions, as soldiers got caught on the barbed wire or found that their artillery did little to break the fighting spirit of the opposing side.

The war in the east was rather different from that in the west. At first, the Russians met with success against the Austro-Hungarians, but as the fighting began to stalemate in the west, German forces shifted to the east, where they began to pile up victories against the brave but poorly equipped Russians. The eastern front never became bogged down with trenches like in the west, in part because the huge size of the theater of war made it much easier to maneuver.

> ## The Horrors of Modern Warfare
> In early 1915, poison gas began to be used by both sides. The petrochemical revolution of the Second Industrial Revolution had unleashed a new weapon on the battlefield, and while the introduction of gas masks cut down on the losses from these gases, it was another sign that modern warfare was an increasingly inhumane affair.

Attempting to break the stalemate in the east, the British decided to launch an attack on Turkey, which had entered the war on the side of the central powers. **Winston Churchill** (1874–1965), who at the time was the First Lord of the Admiralty, organized the plan, which was such a disaster that it almost led to the complete obliteration of his political career. Churchill reasoned that knocking the Turks out of the war would allow the British to send supplies to the hard-pressed Russians through the Black Sea. In April 1915, five divisions landed on the beach of **Gallipoli**. Unfortunately for the soldiers, who were for the most part from Australia and New Zealand, the Turks were well dug in and the attack failed. By January, the British withdrew after suffering withering losses.

The British were not the only ones who sought the pivotal breakthrough that would end the stalemate. In 1916, the Germans decided to launch a massive offensive against the French fortress of **Verdun**, a fortress that France would have to defend at all costs or risk creating a disaster in French public opinion. The Germans organized a huge number of artillery pieces, including some "Big Bertha" guns that fired shells weighing more than a ton. While it appeared as though the Germans might take the fortress, the French were able to put up a spirited defense under **General Philippe Pétain** (1856–1951), who unfortunately survived the battle to later become the disgraced leader of the defeated Vichy French state following the German victory in 1940. While the Germans hoped to bleed France dry by attacking Verdun, in the end, both sides together lost 600,000 troops in one of the most costly battles of the war. The French and British, however, learned little from the failure of the German offensive. Each side was convinced that it held the secret to breaking the stalemate, and over the next year, both Entente powers launched wasteful and ineffective offensives, such as the **Battle of the Somme** and the **Battle of Passchendaele**, in an attempt to break the German lines.

THE END OF THE WAR

The year 1917 turned out to be the critical turning point in the war. The war in the eastern front came to a close as Russia became embroiled in revolution, and by December 1917, the leaders of the new Bolshevik state sued Germany for peace. For the Germans, this looked like it could be the turning point, enabling them to focus all their forces on breaking the impasse in the west. This German advantage was never to occur because of the entry of the United States into the war on April 6, 1917, a result of Germany's policy of unrestricted submarine warfare and the ill-considered **Zimmermann Telegram**. In 1915, the Germans declared that the waters around Great Britain were a war zone and warned that they would sink any ship—either British vessels or those from neutral lands—that tried to enter into British ports. Although this policy may appear to have been inhumane, at that time, the British were blockading German ports, but because of their powerful surface fleet, they did not have to rely on using submarines to indiscriminately sink ships. In May 1915, a German U-boat sank the *Lusitania,* a British passenger ship, stirring tremendous anger in the United States, from which 120 of the ship's passengers hailed. As a result of an American warning, the Germans agreed to end their attacks on neutral shipping, but as the war continued to drag on, the Germans decided in early 1917 to resume the practice.

Although it would take roughly a year for the Americans to make an impact in the war, their entry turned out to be a decisive factor. The Germans decided in 1918 that they had to move quickly if they hoped to achieve victory before the Americans could send in large numbers of fresh troops. Beginning in March, the Germans decided to gamble everything on victory. For four months, German troops met with the kind of success they had enjoyed in the first months of the war. Paris was once again evacuated, but Germany lacked the manpower and raw materials to exploit its initial victory, and by the summer, large numbers of Americans played a critical role in blocking any further German advance. By August, the German offensive was turning into a retreat, as Germany increasingly revealed how absolutely exhausted it was from the fighting.

After realizing that there was little it could do to block the Entente powers from marching all the way to Berlin, the German high command informed the Kaiser that Germany had to sue for peace. A new German government, led by **Prince Max von Baden** (1867–1929), a man known for his moderate political views, contacted the American President, **Woodrow Wilson** (1856–1924), and asked for an armistice that would be based on Wilson's **Fourteen Points**—an idealistic document that sought to reduce future tensions between nations by maintaining free trade and an end to secret negotiations. Events in Germany, however, were spiraling out of control, and throughout November, soldiers and workers began to form soviets, or councils, and to demand that these loosely organized political debating societies be given authority to rule the state. Fearing that Germany would follow Russia's example and undergo a Bolshevik Revolution, the Kaiser was convinced to abdicate, leading to the creation of a republic, which was empowered for the signing of the armistice that brought the war to a close on November 11, 1918.

The War on the Home Front

The First World War was the first armed struggle to witness the complete mobilization of society at large. This was total war—something that would be experienced again during the Second World War—in that no segment of the population within any of the participating nations could avoid its impact.

Once people realized that their initial expectation of a quick war was wrong, political leaders began to understand that they would have to mobilize all national resources. The war, therefore, was a major contributing factor to the increased role that government played in the twentieth century. All aspects of the economy became regulated to support the war effort, including price controls, the banning of strikes, rationing, and the planned use of national resources such as coal. In Great Britain, the government regulated pub hours, ensuring that they closed in the afternoon to prevent factory workers from staggering back to work drunk.

Governments also began to play a larger role in trying to manipulate public opinion. Censorship became a basic task for all governments. They read and censored the letters soldiers sent home to shield the public from the full extent of the horrors of trench warfare. The governments believed that if the people realized the true nature of the war, support for it would rapidly diminish. Governments also set up **propaganda** offices to create films and posters to help boost morale. One reason so many Germans were later willing to believe Hitler's claims that Germany had not lost the war on the battlefield but had been "stabbed in the back" by Jews and other so-called enemies of the German people was that they had been told by their government, up until the day that Germany surrendered, that all was going well at the front and that victory was just around the corner.

Total War

World War I was history's first total war, in which all of society was mobilized and affected by the war effort.

War and Civil Rights

War has a way of quickening long-term trends. In the United States, the Second World War helped pave the way for the Civil Rights movement, and the First World War helped bring about the greater emancipation of women. Prior to the war, Great Britain saw an expanding female suffrage movement. The Women's Social and Political Union, better known as the **Suffragettes**, under the leadership of **Emmeline Pankhurst** (1858–1928), organized a militant campaign to win the vote. The Suffragettes disturbed political meetings, destroyed stained-glass windows in historical churches, and set fires to draw attention to their cause. Once the war began, the Suffragettes supported the war effort and encouraged women to do their share for the nation. By the end of the war, more than 5 million British women were employed, many in dangerous jobs such as those in munitions factories. At the end of the war, British women were rewarded for their contribution to victory by being granted the **right to vote** in 1918. At the same time, in Germany, the Weimar Republic granted complete female suffrage as well.

The Versailles Treaty and the Costs of the War

It is impossible to determine a precise count of the human costs of the war. Around 9 million men lost their lives in battle, and approximately 23 million more were wounded. Many men who came home from the front were permanently affected by gas. Germany suffered about 6 million casualties (killed and wounded combined). France's losses were 5.5 million, proportionally much greater than Germany's losses, as France's pre-war population had been less than two-thirds that of Germany's. Very few French families escaped losing a loved one, and today, if you travel to France, you'll find a memorial in every town to those lost in the war. Incredibly, the loss of life from the war was soon dwarfed by an outbreak of **influenza**, which claimed an estimated 30 million lives worldwide.

Besides the loss of lives, the economic costs of the war were unprecedented. Hundreds of towns and villages in France and Belgium were destroyed, and even today, an occasional Belgian farmer is killed while plowing over an unexploded shell dating back to the trench wars in Flanders fields. Economically, both victors and vanquished were shattered. The nations of Europe, which had been the creditors to the rest of the world, were now heavily in debt to the United States, the only participant that still had a fully functioning economy. After the war, the Carnegie Endowment for International Peace attempted to discern the war's actual cost and estimated a figure of $338 billion. The wealth accumulated from the unprecedented economic growth of the Second Industrial Revolution dissipated in a matter of five years.

The terrible human and economic costs of the war must be considered when looking at the negotiations marking the end of the conflict. Five separate settlements were reached at the peace conference that took place in Paris, though the first and most famous of them was the **Treaty of Versailles**, signed on June 28, 1919, in the Hall of Mirrors, the same place that the German Empire had been declared back in 1871. This event witnessed several competing visions on how to reshape the postwar world:

Wilsonian Idealism
Woodrow Wilson is known for his political and diplomatic optimism. Perhaps the best example of this is the League of Nations, which was based on his hope for international cooperation and harmony.

- Wilson wanted to reshape the world on the basis of the principles outlined in his **Fourteen Points**, a peace that would allow for national self-determination and an international body, the **League of Nations**, that would work to settle disputes between nations. Yet it was easy for an American president to be conciliatory, particularly because none of the fighting had taken place on American soil, and the loss of American lives, though significant, paled beside that of France and Great Britain.

- The French Premier, **Georges Clemenceau** (1841–1929), represented a completely different outlook from Wilson's. No nation had suffered during the war more than France, and Clemenceau had to satisfy a French public that wanted to ensure that Germany would never again be a threat.

- The third major participant, the British Prime Minister **David Lloyd-George** (1863–1945), while not as intransigent as Clemenceau, also wanted to see Germany punished. England was, as usual, interested in naval superiority and colonies. In the end, the treaty represented the triumph of Clemenceau's position over Wilson's.

To justify the demand for German payment of reparations, the victorious allies included Article 231 in the final treaty, which forced Germany to accept all responsibility for the outbreak of the war on behalf of herself and her allies. Although Germany may have had an additional measure of blame, all the nations of Europe bore some guilt, so Article 231 was quite unfair. Germany also had to pay a huge reparation sum of 132 billion gold marks to the Entente powers. Other clauses of the treaty included the return of **Alsace-Lorraine** to France and the occupation of French troops in those parts of Germany on the western bank of the Rhine and a strip of land on the right bank. These territories, while still German, were to remain demilitarized. France would maintain economic control over the coal and iron mines of the Saar border region for fifteen years. Additionally, Germany was to have an army of no more than 100,000 men, was banned from having an air force, and could maintain only a tiny navy to protect its coastal waters.

Other treaties signed in Paris in 1919 reordered the map of Europe. With the demise of the Austro-Hungarian Empire and the reduction in size of Germany, new nations were re-created in central Europe.

- Czechoslovakia was born, combining the lands of the Czechs and Slovaks and also including a significant number of Germans.

- Hungary became fully independent, though it was somewhat reduced in size.

- An independent Romania was also created out of former Austro-Hungarian lands.

- Serbia was rewarded with additional territories for being on the victorious side; the resulting enlarged state, Yugoslavia, was what the Serbs had dreamed of. This dream had been one of the root causes of the war.

- For the first time since the eighteenth century, there was an independent Poland.

- The Baltic states of Lithuania, Latvia, Estonia, and Finland were carved out of parts of the former Russian Empire.

- Although most of these states started as democracies, within a short time span, a host of problems, including economic and social issues, led all of them—with the exception of Czechoslovakia—to become dictatorships.

Middle East and Africa Post-World War I

One place where nationalist sentiments were not satisfied was in the Middle East following the collapse of the Ottoman Empire. During the war, the British made numerous promises to both Arabs and Jews to gain their support for the war effort. With the advent of peace, the British ignored these hasty wartime promises, and Great Britain and France divided the area into colonial spheres of influence. Also, despite the contributions that colonial soldiers made to the war effort, the French and British made no move to reward their African colonies with independence.

THE RUSSIAN REVOLUTION

Though it is hard to imagine, some Russian soldiers were thrown into battle during the First World War without guns, having been told to pick up rifles from their fallen comrades. This is just one way in which the First World War revealed the complete incompetence of the tsarist regime. Although it is hard to imagine any autocratic state functioning well during an unprecedented crisis like a world war, the problem was made more severe by the sheer stupidity of Russia's last tsar, **Nicholas II** (1868–1918), who decided during the second year of the conflict that he should emulate the warrior tsars of the past and assume personal command of the army.

In his absence, Nicholas left his wife **Empress Alexandra** in charge of the state. Alexandra turned out to be completely ignorant in matters of statecraft and was personally under the influence of a mystical Russian monk named **Gregory Rasputin** (1872–1916), who, she believed, had the power to control the bleeding of her son Alexis, a hemophiliac. Rasputin took advantage of Nicholas's absence to encourage the empress to place his friends in important state offices despite their obvious incompetence. With the war going badly for the Russians, false rumors began to spread that Alexandra and Rasputin were lovers and that the German-born empress was doing her best to make sure that Russia was defeated. (Similar rumors were spread about the British royal family, who also had German roots, leading them to change their family name from Saxe-Coburg to the more English-sounding Windsor.) Rasputin met his end in 1916 when he was killed by a group of arch-monarchists, who feared he was destroying the prestige of the throne. The problems in Russia, however, extended well beyond what could be solved by removing the monk from his position of influence.

The Provisional Government

Two revolutions occurred in Russia in 1917. The first was in March, when order collapsed in the capital city of Petrograd (formerly and currently St. Petersburg) as the population grappled with a severe shortage of food. Troops were called out to disperse the demonstrations, but instead of following their orders, the solders joined with the strikers. On March 14, the tsar abdicated. What became known as the Provisional Government took over authority. This government was made up of members of the **Duma**—the Russian parliament that arose out of the 1905 revolution—and was provisional because it was supposed to exist only long enough to establish a constituent body which would then write a constitution for the new Russian republic.

One sign of future trouble was that workers and soldiers continued to form soviets, as was the case in the revolution of 1905. These soviets consisted primarily of assorted Russian Socialists, with the majority belonging to the **Menshevik** and **Socialist Revolutionary** wings, while only a minority belonged to the most extreme of the social groups, the **Bolsheviks**. Russian socialism had split into assorted factions back in 1903 when **Vladimir Lenin** (1870–1924) insisted that a small party of professional revolutionaries could seize power on behalf of the working class. His followers became known as the Bolsheviks. The group that insisted that Russia had to proceed through the proven historical stages before it could achieve an ideal socialist society, as Marx had mandated, became known as the **Mensheviks**.

This led the Mensheviks, who dominated the Petrograd Soviet, to initially support the Provisional Government, since it fit their idea that a bourgeois revolution needed to precede a socialist revolution.

Tragically for the history of Russia, this short-lived republic faced problems of the greatest magnitude. One controversial decision was made when the Provisional Government decided to remain in the First World War rather than withdraw from the fighting. This decision stemmed partly from a sense of responsibility to the other Entente powers, but more important to this decision was the presence at that time of German troops on Russian soil. This presence led the Provisional Government to believe that a renewed war effort, led by a democratic regime, would inspire Russian support. The Provisional Government also decided to delay the redistribution of the great estates, which were supposed to be broken up to provide land for the peasantry. Seeing that their demands were not being met, the peasants acted on their own initiative and seized the great estates.

The Triumph of the Bolsheviks

In April, Lenin returned from exile in Switzerland, aided by the Germans who transported him through their territory in a sealed railcar. The Germans did this because they thought that Lenin would undermine the Russian war effort, never expecting that he would be able to seize power. Over the ensuing months, the Bolsheviks continued to build up their strength, particularly among the workers and soldiers in Petrograd. By the fall of 1917, the Bolsheviks were the largest party in the soviets.

As the situation in the city became more desperate and unrest continued, Lenin decided to seize the moment, and on November 9, new Bolshevik figurehead **Leon Trotsky** (1870–1940) rode the momentum of his party's electoral success to take over key positions in the city, including power stations and communication centers. The revolution came off without much violence as the Provisional Government simply collapsed. Much violence would ensue, however, over the next three years, as the Bolsheviks had to cope with a bloody civil war to maintain their power.

Lenin and his party operated under the assumption that the revolution in Russia was only the first in a series of Communist revolutions that would begin in Germany and then move on to the remainder of western Europe. Therefore, the Bolsheviks were willing to accept a draconian peace with Germany, because they believed that Imperial Germany would shortly disappear and the territorial settlements would no longer matter. By the end of 1917, the Germans and the new Bolshevik state had signed the **Treaty of Brest-Litovsk**, thus removing Russia from the war. The treaty was exceedingly harsh and involved German confiscation of huge tracts of Russian land (perhaps more unfair than what the Germans were punished with in the Treaty of Versailles). The Treaty of Brest-Litovsk was never fully implemented because of Germany's defeat in the war and the Allies' refusal to allow Germany to gain territories in the east. Much of the territory became Poland and the Baltics instead.

THE INTERWAR YEARS

The German Weimar Republic

The story of the German Weimar Republic is nothing short of tragic, though its ultimate failure should not be surprising given its problematic birth at the end of a disastrous war. It has sometimes been argued that the death of Weimar came not in 1933 with the triumph of Hitler and his Nazi party, but rather in 1919, in the very early days of the republic, when its leaders were forced to sign the vastly unpopular Versailles Treaty.

Although forces from the extreme political right caused its final demise, in the first years of the republic, the far left was a much greater threat to its stability. The republic was created in November 1918 and was initially led by **Friedrich Ebert** (1871–1925), a moderate Socialist, who served as its first president. To put down a rebellion led by radical Marxists like **Karl Liebknecht** and **Rosa Luxemburg**, and to secure his republican regime, Ebert was forced to rely on the old imperial officer corps. Because the army was in no position to put down the rebellion alone, Ebert gave approval for the formation of "**Free Corps**," voluntary paramilitary groups often with extreme right-wing leanings. In 1920, some of these Free Corps became involved in an attempt to overthrow the democratic state, but a general strike by workers put an end to what became known as the **Kapp Putsch**. However, by 1920, it was clear that although the threat from the left was eradicated, the far right was an even greater danger to the long-term viability of the Weimar state.

By 1924, the republic had achieved some degree of stability, despite the continuing effects of the Versailles Treaty penalties. In the postwar years, Germany suffered from terrible inflation as a result of the government's wild printing of money to pay its reparations debt. This insanely high inflation, which eventually led to an exchange rate of 11 trillion marks to the dollar, shattered the German middle class who saw its life savings disappear overnight. In 1923, the Chancellor of Germany was **Gustav Stresemann** (1878–1929), the leader of the German People's Party, a conservative party that supported the Weimar Republic. Although this hyperinflation may have done more than even the Great Depression to damage the long-term possibility of success for the republic, in the short term, Stresemann was able to get the economy back on its feet. He was even able to work out a new agreement on reparations, making them less damaging to the German economy.

By 1925, Germany was slowly rebuilding its relations with the other nations of Europe. Germany signed the **Lucarno Agreement** with France, by which Germany agreed to accept the current borders between France and Germany (and therefore French control over Alsace-Lorraine). They also resolved other issues, such as initiating the withdrawal of French troops from the Rhineland. In the following year, Stresemann capped off these efforts by entering Germany into the **League of Nations**. By 1929, the republic appeared as though it was taking root within Germany, though the outbreak of the Great Depression would reveal how shallow German support for republican government truly was.

The Soviet Experiment

Following the Bolshevik revolution of November 1917, Lenin and his tiny party ruled over a land that had been completely shattered. An indication of how little support they held within the nation can be seen by the elections for the constituent assembly that were finally held a few weeks after the Bolshevik revolution. Despite attempts to intimidate voters at the polls, the best the Bolsheviks could garner was one-quarter of the seats in the assembly. With such a showing, it was not surprising that armed Red Guards dispersed the assembly at the end of its first and only meeting.

Over the next several years, the **Communists** (the name adopted by the Bolshevik party in 1919), worked to solidify their control over the vast Russian state. For three years they had to fight a life-or-death struggle against the **"White" forces**, a loose term for the various anti-Communist factions, including dedicated monarchists and ardent republicans. The Whites received support from a British and American contingent, who nominally were sent to protect supplies the Allies had sent during the war but were really in Russia to keep an eye on events. The Civil War provided justification for Lenin and Trotsky to launch a **"Red Terror"** against their opponents, some of whom were right-wing extremists who were genuine enemies of the Bolshevik state; others were fellow Socialists, like the members of the Menshevik party, who feared the formation of a Communist dictatorship in Russia. By 1920, the Communists had defeated the various White armies and firmly established Bolshevik rule over Russia.

In the early days of the Soviet Union, there was still an expectation that the revolutionary tide would sweep across western Europe. To that end, in 1919, the Russian Communists founded the **Third (or Communist) International** to aid in the cause of revolution. The rise of this body, often referred to as the **Comintern**, had a major impact on the various Socialist parties of western Europe, as some Marxists turned to the new Soviet state for guidance. The majority of Socialists, however, were horrified by the obviously repressive nature of Lenin's regime. This led to a split across Europe between those who formed Communist parties and those who maintained their ties to the original Socialist parties. In Germany, this split within the ranks of the left played a major role in the eventual rise of the Nazis; the German Communists saw the Social Democratic Party as more of a threat to their eventual success than the Nazis. By 1920, when it was becoming clear that the revolutionary tide across Europe was barely a trickle, the Comintern shifted its focus more toward aiding the success of the one Marxist state, the Soviet Union, which filled all the leadership posts in the organization.

As the leaders of the Soviet Union increasingly turned their attention to internal questions within Russia, a debate ensued within the party concerning economics. During the Civil War, the party imposed "war communism," extremely tight control over all aspects of the economy. In 1921, anger over the harshness of this program led to a rebellion by the sailors of the Kronstadt Naval Base, once one of the primary strongholds of Bolshevik support. While the rebellion was crushed with stunning brutality, it did lead Lenin to replace war communism with the **New Economic Policy (NEP)**. This policy placed the "heights of industry" in government hands but also allowed a significant scope for private enterprise. Under this program, the economy made a quick recovery to pre-war levels.

The question remained, however, as to how to build a socialist state. This debate became closely intertwined with the issue of who would succeed Lenin as the leader of the party after he died in 1924. One possible candidate for the post was Trotsky, who enjoyed immense prestige as the builder of the Red Army that had won the Civil War. Trotsky thought that the NEP was too much of an ideological compromise, and he envisioned the return of an economic structure more akin to war communism. Trotsky, as the leader of the "**Left Opposition**," also argued that it was necessary to focus on the spread of revolution to the industrialized nations of western Europe; he believed that communism could not survive unless it spread to other lands. His major opponent in this debate was **Nikolai Bukharin** (1888–1938), the "**Right Opposition**" leader who advocated continuing the NEP and building communism within the Soviet state.

Stalin

In the end, it was neither Trotsky nor Bukharin who took up the mantle of Lenin but **Joseph Stalin** (1879–1953) instead, a Georgian who had joined the party in 1902 but played a relatively minor role in the seizure of power in November 1917. Stalin was completely uninterested in ideological debates; he wanted to establish his own power within the Soviet system. To achieve this power, Stalin cunningly worked with Bukharin to maneuver Trotsky out of authority. In 1927, Trotsky and his ally Gregory Zinoviev (1883–1936) were expelled from the party. Stalin waited two years before he also ousted Bukharin. Eventually, beginning in 1936, Stalin launched a series of show trials in which his former opponents were tortured until they confessed to all sorts of crimes against the state.

While the complete story of Stalin's brutality will never be fully known, close to 10 million Russians were arrested in the late 1930s; several million were executed immediately or eventually died in the brutal detention camps that Stalin set up in Siberia. Stalin eventually decimated the ranks of the "Old Bolsheviks" who had joined the party prior to 1917; he destroyed the officer corps and anyone else he perceived as disloyal to the state or to him. In 1940, an agent sent by Stalin assassinated Trotsky, who had earlier been sent into exile.

Once in a position of undisputed authority, Stalin adopted the policy of the Left Opposition and its program to rapidly turn Russia into an industrial nation. To achieve this goal, in 1928 Stalin implemented the first **Five-Year Plan**, a comprehensive, centrally controlled plan for industrial expansion. To pay for this unprecedented economic growth, Stalin followed Trotsky's plan to extract the necessary money by squeezing the peasantry through the forced **collectivization** of Russian agriculture. The state waged an open war on the *kulaks*—the wealthy peasants— and sent party cadres to the countryside with the order to kill any peasant who refused to join the collective farm. Millions of *kulaks* were shot or died from starvation, as they destroyed their crops and farm animals rather than turn them over to the hated Communist state. The human cost was staggering; perhaps 10 million people in the countryside died as Stalin moved the available crops to urban areas. The result, however, was that by the end of the 1930s, the Soviet Union emerged as a major industrial power while the western nations were embroiled in a devastating economic depression.

The Great Depression

Traditionally, we think of the Great Depression as beginning in October 1929 with the stock-market crash, which was soon followed by people hurling themselves out of windows (though there is little evidence such suicides took place). It should be understood, however, that the roots of the problem were deeper than just a crash of the financial markets, and the worldwide depression would not begin in earnest until the banking crisis in 1931.

In May 1931, the collapse of Vienna's most powerful bank, the Credit-Anstalt, created a domino effect. Banks throughout Germany and eastern Europe started to fail as citizens began to question banks' solvency. They withdrew their savings rapidly, which depleted available reserves until otherwise-healthy banks could not return depositors' money and were forced to fold. Meanwhile, in the highly uncertain economic environment, banks stopped making loans and individuals started trying to save whatever money they could. This resulted in a major drop in demand for industrial goods. With the decline in demand came a corresponding decline in the number of available jobs, since there was less of a market for goods produced. However, rising unemployment only suppressed demand further, since unemployed workers had no money. Many countries worsened these problems by trying to remain on a **gold standard**, a fixed exchange rate between their currencies and gold. The gold standard prevented countries from using controlled inflation to help get out of the depression. Inflation, by increasing the amount of available money, allows individuals to meet their increased desire for savings while having some money left over to spend; it also discourages people from saving too much, since they realize their money will be worth less in the future than it is today.

> ## The 1920s: Perception vs. Reality
>
> Our image of the 1920s is that of the **"Jazz Age,"** a glittering time chronicled in the novels of **F. Scott Fitzgerald**. The reality was far less festive. The war had been incredibly devastating to the worldwide economy. In places such as Great Britain, the 1920s remained a time of economic stagnation. Much of the postwar economic recovery in Germany was dependent on the availability of American bank loans, monies that the Germans in turn used to lend at higher interest to the newly emerging nations of eastern Europe. This led to what looked like solid financial gains in both the United States and Germany from 1924 to 1929, but in many ways it was a false prosperity. The decline in available credit brought on by the collapse of the American stock market caused the veneer of prosperity to rapidly fade.

The problems of the gold standard were made even worse by the common belief that the way to deal with an economic depression was to further tighten the supply of money, until all the "bad loans" went bust and "failed companies" went out of business (even though many of these were perfectly sound and were essentially innocent bystanders to the total economic collapse). Governments also tried to rein in their spending to balance their budgets, which only further suppressed the overall demand for goods (while also exposing unemployed workers to worse suffering, as social support programs, veterans' benefits, and so on, were cut). The English economist **John Maynard Keynes** (1883–1946) was almost a singular voice of dissent. He argued that since the problem was a lack of demand in the private sector, governments could best fix it through deficit spending, temporarily providing people with jobs and income again to enable a spending recovery, and thereby restore the economy to health. This was known as "priming the pump," as this temporary increase in government spending in areas like public works would unfreeze the economy and get money moving again.

The depression worsened as governments took further misguided measures such as raising tariff barriers to protect domestic manufacturing. The United States was the first to take this step when it raised the tariff wall in 1930. All the other nations of Europe soon followed, including Great Britain, where free trade was a doctrine held with almost religious intensity.

The depths of the depression were truly staggering. By 1932, the economies of Europe were performing at only half the 1929 level. The depression hit hardest in the United States and in Germany, where eventually almost one-third of the available workforce was unemployed. In the United States—a stable democracy—those embroiled in the depression elected **Franklin Roosevelt** as president and subscribed to his **New Deal**. In Germany—a shaky democracy at best—the crisis resulted in the death of republican institutions and the triumph of a political ideology that was anathema to the very spirit of democracy—**fascism**.

Fascism

During the interwar years, as democracy appeared to be faltering, millions of people across Europe looked to fascism as a movement that offered the means to rebuild their shattered lives. Historians actively debate the definition of fascism; some claim that nothing really can be labeled as a fascist ideology outside the regimes of Hitler and Mussolini. Fascist parties emerged across Europe and in other parts of the world, including the United States. They did not all possess the exact same set of beliefs; there are certain ideas, however, they all hold in common, which can be useful in defining the movement.

The word *fascism* comes from the Latin term *fasces*, a reference to a small bundle of sticks the Romans carried as symbols of authority and community. These bound sticks were symbolic of one central goal of fascism—to destroy the notion of the individual and instead push for a common community. In some ways, this sounds similar to what the Communists wanted to achieve—a unified society devoid of class differences. But the fascist concept was not tied to an international identity, as communism was, nor did fascism advocate the end of class distinctions. Instead, fascism pushed for another identity, one that was rooted in both extreme nationalism and often in some mystical racial heritage, such as that found in the Volkish ideology pursued by the German Fascists.

Fascists were deeply antagonistic to the idea of parliamentary democracy, which they viewed as anarchical and effete. Instead, fascism favored the idea of a strong leader; the Italian Fascists had *Il Duce*, the Germans, the *Führer*, men who, in an almost mystical manner, represented all the desires and dreams of the nation. This antagonism toward democracy is interesting, because in the two nations where fascism triumphed, Italy and Germany, Fascist governments were created using the ballot box and not forced by an armed coup. While despising democracy, Fascists also rejected all forms of socialism, a significant factor in why the movement rose to power. Many middle-class individuals were fully aware that the Soviet regime had collectivized all private property and saw fascism as the only barrier to the triumph of the hated communism. While many Fascists, like Hitler, hardly bothered to contemplate a fascist economic program, Mussolini promised that an Italian fascist state would implement what he called **corporatism**— an association of employers and workers within each industry that would iron out all contentious issues regarding production and wages.

To a certain extent, fascism was antagonistic toward much of what is representative of the modern world. Fascists were against the political emancipation of women, they hated modern art, and they despised a religious faction that had become emancipated in modern times—Jews. **Anti-Semitism** was a key component in Fascist movements throughout Europe, except in Italy, in part because Jews were seen as standing outside the arch-nationalistic identity that was so dear to the heart of all Fascists.

Fascism in Italy

The first state to have a Fascist government was Italy, and because the empowerment of fascism occurred prior to the Great Depression of 1929, it was not this financial devastation that caused the movement. In Italy, fascism emerged partly out of a deep national dissatisfaction with its participation in the First World War. In 1915, Italy decided to enter the war on the side of the Entente powers, in part because it was interested in extending Italian control over those areas of Austria-Hungary that were home to a significant number of people who spoke Italian as their mother tongue. Italy's military participation was initially disastrous, leading to the almost total collapse of the Italian front in 1917, but Italy stayed in the war and played a role in the eventual triumph of the Entente powers. It was a costly victory, but many Italians thought it would be justified with the gains they would receive at the peace table. In the event, Italy got most of what it had been promised by the British and French, but with the collapse of the Austro-Hungarian state, many Italians believed that they should have been more generously rewarded for their participation.

Following the war, Italy underwent a marked political transformation. In 1919, the political system adopted proportional representation, whereby parties would be rewarded seats in the legislature on the basis of their percentages in the national vote. This new system favored the creation of mass parties such as Mussolini's Fascist movement. Italian politics were also transformed by events in 1919 and 1920, years that witnessed a series of factory occupations by angry workers who seemed to portend the advent of a Bolshevik state. This led many landowners and businessmen to turn against democratic politics. They began to look for another political solution and thought they had found it in fascism, a political movement that was just emerging in Italy.

The founder and leader of the Italian Fascists was **Benito Mussolini** (1883–1945). His father was a Socialist, who named his son after the Mexican revolutionary Benito Juarez. Mussolini adopted his father's Socialist beliefs and became the editor of the party newspaper. Interestingly, for a man who would eventually become an extreme nationalist, during his years as a Socialist, Mussolini wrote, "The national flag is a rag that should be placed in a dunghill." His views began to shift during the war when Mussolini broke with his fellow Socialists and supported

Italy's entrance into the war, a war in which Mussolini eventually served but without any particular distinction, like Hitler.

Returning to civilian life, Mussolini founded a new party, the **National Fascist Party**. The party quickly formed paramilitary squads (the Blackshirts) to fight leftist organizations, thus earning them the gratitude of factory owners and landowners who filled the party coffers with much-needed cash. By 1921, the party had begun to seat members in the Italian parliament and emerge as a significant presence in Italian political life.

Although his party still only had a few seats in the legislature, by October 1922, Mussolini demanded that **King Victor Emmanuel III** (r. 1900–1946) name him and several other Fascists to cabinet posts. To provide support for his demands, Mussolini organized his black-shirted thugs to march on Rome and possibly attempt to seize power. If the King had declared martial law and brought in the army, there is little doubt that the Fascists would have been easily scattered. The King, however, was a timid man who was not altogether unsympathetic to the Fascist program, so he named Mussolini as Prime Minister. The Fascist march on Rome turned into a celebration instead of a possible coup.

Fortunately for Mussolini, there was very little opposition to his consolidation of political power. He played at being a parliamentary leader for only several months after taking over in 1922. He then implemented a number of constitutional changes to ensure that the niceties of democracy no longer limited his actions. Mussolini's grip on power in the early years was only shaken in 1924 when he and the party were involved in the murder of a Socialist politician. Mussolini, however, was able to take this crisis and turn it to his advantage: He further consolidated his power by basically banning all non-Fascist political activity.

Perhaps because of the nature of the land that he governed, Mussolini found it hard to recast Italy in his Fascist image. Rather than achieving the revolution that many of his followers wanted, he made peace with more established institutions, such as the Catholic Church, when in 1929 he signed the **Lateran Pact** with the papacy; for the first time, the papacy officially recognized the Italian state. In the latter part of the decade, Mussolini tried to implement the corporatist economic program that was supposed to be a hallmark of the new Italy, but in practice it never lived up to the promise. Italy did rebound economically in the late 1920s, but then again, so did the rest of the world economy.

German Fascism

A more thorough Fascist reordering of the state took place in Germany. While the Nazi regime in January 1933 marks the final stage in the collapse of the Weimar Republic, in many ways the failure of the republic dates back to the first years of the **Great Depression**. In March 1930, a government led by Hermann Müller (1876–1931), a Socialist, resigned over a crisis concerning unemployment insurance, which because of the depression was beginning to be an unbearable burden for the German government. This was the last truly democratic government in Germany until the end of the Second World War.

The long-term health of the Weimar Republic was shaky in that the president was **Paul von Hindenburg** (1847–1934). If there had been a genuine reordering of German society following the collapse of the imperial regime and the rise of a republic, then a bombastic general like Hindenburg would have been cast aside with scorn. Unfortunately, Weimar never really escaped its recent past. The republic had as its leader a dedicated monarchist, who in 1925, prior to running for the office of president, contacted his former emperor in exile in Denmark to ask the emperor's approval to run for office.

President Hindenburg took the opportunity of the resignation of the Socialist Chancellor to install a more authoritarian government. Hindenburg selected **Heinrich Brüning** (1885–1970), the leader of a middle-of-the-road Catholic party. Brüning proposed an economic program that would have done little to solve the economic crisis and simply led to increased political opposition by the left and the right. Because Brüning could not achieve a parliamentary majority, he took the terrible step of involving Article 48, an emergency decree within the Weimar Constitution that enabled him to govern under presidential decree.

For the remainder of his long life, Brüning would try to defend his next decision, which was to call for new parliamentary elections in September 1930, just as the economic crisis worsened. Brüning thought the electorate would back him on his austerity measures, while what actually happened was that the two most extreme political parties, the Communists and the **Nazis**, emerged as the big winners. The election transformed the Nazis from a tiny party with only twelve seats in the Reichstag to a major force holding 102 seats.

Why the Nazis?

The rise of the Nazi Party seems bizarre in hindsight, but made more sense to people who had not yet seen the horror of rampant nationalism in the form of the war and the Holocaust. Many Germans were still powerfully angry about the Treaty of Versailles, which the Nazis denounced as an affront to national pride (and a serious drain on resources). Many early Nazi supporters also believed in the *Dolchstosslegenda* (stab-in-the back legend) which was the claim that the German army only lost World War I because it was "stabbed in the back" by various hated groups: Jews, Communists, Weimar-Republicans, big businesses, and so on.

Despite their conservatism, the Nazis were also one of the few groups to provide some coherent social support during the depression. While denouncing "Bolshevism," they championed certain moderate socialist rhetoric (such as increasing workers' wages and improving the common well-being), provided some support in the form of soup kitchens, and served free beer at political meetings. Most importantly, though, the Nazi Party indulged the people's desire for blame: The Nazis combined violent hatred of the Communists and the moderate Socialist party with denunciations of international capitalism as a "Jewish conspiracy" bent on war-profiteering and extorting workers, all while telling Germans that they were superior simply by virtue of being German. These positions were self-contradictory nonsense—but very appealing nonetheless.

With such a hostile Reichstag, Brüning continued to govern under Article 48. For the next two years he attempted to implement his austerity program, which only served to deepen the economic crisis. By the spring of 1932, Hindenburg removed Brüning and put in his place Franz von Papen (1879–1969), a wealthy anti-parliamentary conservative. In the elections held in November, the Nazis became the largest party in the Reichstag with 196 seats, and in January 1933, Hindenburg, despite a certain measure of personal disgust for Hitler, asked him to become chancellor.

It was a remarkable achievement for the Austrian-born **Adolf Hitler** (1889–1945). As a young man, he had gone to Vienna to study at its Academy of Fine Arts, but unfortunately for the history of Europe, Hitler proved to have little talent as an artist and was rejected. It was while living in Vienna that Hitler developed his virulent anti-Semitism, although the roots of his hatred toward Jews are hotly disputed. Because he had little sympathy for the multinational character of the Habsburg Empire when war began in 1914, he volunteered to serve in the German army where he survived a poison gas attack.

In 1919, he joined the **German Workers' Party**, which was renamed the **National Socialist German Workers' Party**, one of the small extremist groups that formed in the early days of the Weimar Republic. By 1923, he thought the party was strong enough to seize power, so he launched the **Beer Hall Putsch** in Munich, falsely believing that it would set the stage for a revolt throughout Germany. Following this failure he was put on trial but used this opportunity to stage a spirited defense before the court and to gain greater attention for himself and his movement. In prison, Hitler wrote *Mein Kampf* (*My Struggle*), outlining his extremist views, along with his desire, shared by Germans of assorted political persuasions, to overturn the Treaty of Versailles.

Following the Beer Hall failure in 1923, Hitler decided that in the future he had to use the existing political structure to achieve power rather than use extraordinary means like a coup. The **Nazis**, however, were not just a simple political party politely trying to convince the German electorate of the reasonableness of its views. Like Mussolini's Fascists, the Nazis enlisted a corps of armed thugs to support their political rallies and to disrupt opposing groups' meetings. This helped lead to an increase in political violence in Weimar, as all political parties had begun to sponsor armed factions; street fighting became endemic in the streets of Berlin and other German cities. Ironically, even though the Nazis often instigated the violence, Hitler had strong appeal as a "law-and-order" candidate who would put an end to the brawls.

When Hitler was named Chancellor in 1933, he rapidly sought to consolidate his power. On February 27, 1933, the Reichstag building in Berlin was set on fire, although to this day it is not entirely clear who set it. The Nazis, who may have set the fire themselves, blamed the Communists for the incident. By claiming that there was a Communist plot against the state, Hitler encouraged the Reichstag to vote to grant him emergency powers, allowing him to eliminate virtually all human rights while granting the executive branch of the government almost total authority. In the last election held in Germany until the end of the Second World War, the Nazis, despite having control over the state, received only 44 percent of the vote. Hitler followed the vote with an **Enabling Act**, which gave the party emergency powers to govern the state and combined the authority of the chancellor and the president into one with a new non-republican sounding title—the führer (or leader). Finally, by the summer of 1933, Hitler banned all political parties except the Nazis and followed with an attack on the independent trade union movement.

Consolidation of power also meant that Hitler had to work out an arrangement with the one institution within the state that was still a threat—the army. The army was highly concerned about the growing size and power of the **S.A.**, the Nazi political army that had played such an important role in the party's rise to power. Once Hitler was in power, the S.A. was expendable. In June 1934, Hitler organized the "**Night of the Long Knives,**" in which he murdered his old ally Ernst Röhm (1887–1934), the leader of the S.A., who had wanted to make it the backbone of a new revolutionary army. Following the attack on the S.A., the members of the German army agreed to give their complete loyalty to the new German state and eventually would swear a personal oath to Hitler.

The Nazification of the German state soon proceeded apace. To create support for such a program, the Nazis put a great deal of effort into creating a Ministry of Propaganda under the leadership of **Joseph Goebbels** (1897–1945). German life had always been chock full of organizations like hiking groups and choral societies. The Nazis did their best to reorganize such groups along lines that the state could control, and huge organizations such as the **Hitler Youth** were established to indoctrinate the young. For those who refused to accept the new state of affairs, the Nazis organized a ruthlessly efficient police apparatus to silence political opposition and to intimidate anyone who even considered dissenting from the party line.

Western Democracies in Crisis

Woodrow Wilson had promised that the First World War was fought "to make the world safe for democracy," and for a time it looked as if his vision was accurate as democracies began to sprout throughout Europe in such places as the newly emerging nations of eastern Europe and in formerly monarchical states like Germany. Sadly, this democratic renaissance was to be short lived. By the 1930s, not only had democracy faltered in almost all the new states that had been born out of the Versailles Treaty (with the exception of Czechoslovakia), but it also appeared to be in crisis in western Europe, as France and Spain struggled with contentious political issues that threatened the very existence of parliamentary sovereignty.

Great Britain

Just as in the nineteenth century, Great Britain remained politically stable, though it certainly did not remain stagnant. One significant change was the emergence of the **Labour Party**, as it supplanted the liberals to become Britain's second-largest political party. The First World War had revealed fundamental problems within the **Liberal Party**, which was much more comfortable with the trappings of the Victorian world, as opposed to the age of total war. Labour had achieved prominence by more effectively voicing the concerns of the working man. British Prime Minister **David Lloyd-George** had encouraged British soldiers and civilians to fight hard for the war effort by promising to make their country after the war a "land fit for heroes." Unfortunately, unless heroes happen to like high unemployment, urban slums, and a growing number of labor disputes, all of which were endemic in the 1920s and 1930s, they may have been rather disappointed, yet accurate, in thinking this new Britain was much like the old.

France

France had won an incredible victory in the First World War and had achieved such long-term goals as the recapture of Alsace-Lorraine and what she thought was the permanent reduction of the threat posed by Germany. However, just as in Great Britain, the war merely diverted attention from, but did not solve, the tremendous economic and social tensions on the eve of the war. Economically, France did grow in the 1920s, but it could hardly offset the tremendous impact of the Great Depression. The economic crisis helped spur the radicalization of French politics, as groups from the far left and far right gathered support. In February 1934, following a right-wing riot that looked like it was going to shake the French Republic to its core, a number of parties on the center and left began to work together to form a "**Popular Front**" to block the possibility of a Fascist victory in France as had occurred the previous year in Germany.

This "Popular Front" proved to be successful in May 1936, when a coalition of Communists, Socialists, and Radicals (the name belies the fact that this was a center-left party) won a majority in the Chamber of Deputies. They selected the leader of the Socialist Party, **Léon Blum** (1872–1950), to be Prime Minister. The new government worked to solve some of the labor issues that had plagued France for decades. In June, they put through the **Matignon Agreement**, allowing workers to collectively bargain with employers, reducing the work week to forty hours, and granting the right to fully paid vacations. Attention to social problems, however, had to be delayed, as France had to now grapple with an issue that challenged the very existence of the Popular Front, the **Spanish Civil War**.

In the past few chapters, you have read a lot about the twists and turns of the French government. Let's review all of that in the following handy chart:

Brief History of French Governments from the Ancien Régime until WWII

Bourbon Monarchy	

Constitutional Monarchy	(1791)
Based off of *Declaration of Rights of Man and Citizen*	

First Republic	(Sept 1792)
Reign of Terror	
Jacobins	
National Convention	(1792–1795)
Directory	(1795–1799)
Oversaw France's first bicameral legislature	
Marked by partisanship stemming from the Revolution	
Consulate	(1799–1804)
Napoleon's coup d'état	

First Empire	(1804–1814)
Think of the painting of Napoleon as Emperor	
Ends with Hundred Days after escape from Elba	

Bourbon Restoration	(1814–1848)
Louis XVIII	(1814–1824)
Charles X	(1824–1830)
Experiences tide of revolutions common in Europe in 1830	
Bourgeoisie tired of his absolutist rule	
Louis-Philippe	(1830–1848)
Takes power in bourgeoisie-led July Revolution	
Reign is called the July Monarchy (bourgeoisie friendly)	
Class tension—Workers call for a Representative Democracy	

Second Republic	(1848–1852)
Workers revolt in June (June Uprising)	
Louis-Napoleon elected leader (calls himself Napoleon III)	

Second Empire	(1852–1870)
Move to empire is approved on referendum	
Otto von Bismarck eventually removes Napoleon III from the throne	
Franco-Prussian War	

Third Republic	(1870–1940)
Strong bicameral parliament, weak president	
Conflict with Catholic Church	
Paris Commune	(1871)
Radical movement arose during the vacuum created by Franco-Prussian War	

The Spanish Civil War

Spain had become a parliamentary democracy only in 1931, following the fall of the Spanish monarchy in that year. The first elections in the Spanish republic brought about a victory for a coalition of liberals and Socialists. Unfortunately, the problems facing Spain were extremely severe, and the new government had trouble finding solutions. Many landless farm laborers waited in vain as the government failed to implement a promised land reform that would break up the vast estates of the rich. Increasingly, the failings of the government created more radical sentiments among the workers, which was matched by equally aggressive action from the parties of the far right.

In February 1936, a Popular Front coalition of the leftist parties—created to avert what they felt was a threat from Spanish Fascists—won a narrow electoral victory. This government attempted to achieve what the earlier socialist government could not, including significant reforms such as land redistribution. They still did not operate quickly enough to satisfy the disaffected masses who seized land and factories. This failure to maintain order was used by the far right to stage a coup to overturn the government.

In the summer of 1936, a group of army officers under the leadership of **General Francisco Franco** (1892–1975) took control of large parts of Spain. Their belief that the republic would simply collapse proved to be false, as republican loyalists bravely organized to defend the state against the nationalist insurgents. Spain was swept into an incredibly brutal civil war, which soon brought about the participation of German and Italian support for the nationalists.

Picasso's *Guernica*
As a reflection of his horror over the attack, the Spanish artist Pablo Picasso painted his masterpiece, Guernica, which he willed to Spain. The painting was to be handed over to the government only when the nation was once again a republic, something that happily occurred in the years following Franco's death in 1975.

The fascist states of Germany and Italy were interested in testing out their new armaments, thus leading to one of the most brutal events in the war. On market day, in the city of **Guernica**, German and Italian planes bombed and strafed the civilian population. Guernica was not a military target in the least; it was targeted simply to instill fear among republican supporters. Although the Fascists willingly offered their support to those on the Spanish right, France and Great Britain refused to come to the aid of their fellow democracy. Instead of assistance, they promoted a nonintervention policy, which meant that the Spanish Loyalists had to make a Mephistophelean pact with the Soviet Union, whereby the Soviets would provide desperately needed arms in exchange for Spanish gold. Because of Soviet support, the Communists, who were initially a small faction on the Spanish left, began to play the preeminent role on the republican side.

Tragically, the Communists, having received their marching orders from Stalin, put as much effort into destroying their allies on the left as they did to defeating the nationalists. George Orwell wrote a fascinating firsthand account of these events in his story *Homage to Catalonia*, which details how the Communists destroyed the anarchist movement in Catalonia in June 1937. After reading Orwell, you will not be surprised to learn that by 1939, the nationalists had captured Madrid and triumphed over the republic.

The Road to the Second World War

From the very beginning of his political career, Hitler had made clear his desire to overturn the Versailles Treaty. Once in power, he set about to keep that promise. In 1935, he openly began the rearmament of Germany, something that was prohibited by Versailles. Seeing that France and Britain did not respond to such an act of provocation, in the following year, the Germans remilitarized the Rhineland. While the French contemplated an aggressive response to this act, they knew that since they lacked British support, they would have to act unilaterally, and so they did nothing. Rather than satisfying Hitler, these steps convinced him of the weakness of the democracies, so he continued with his plans.

Germany Invades Austria

The very first sentence of *Mein Kampf* states Hitler's desire to absorb Austria into the larger **German Reich**. In March 1938, this became a reality as German troops moved into Vienna. Despite postwar claims by the Austrians that they were the first victims of Nazi aggression, the *Anschluss* was welcomed by a majority of Austrians who celebrated by wildly greeting Hitler on his arrival in the city and by attacking their Jewish neighbors.

Germany Invades Czechoslovakia

Hitler next set his sights on Czechoslovakia. Czechoslovakia was the singular success story of eastern Europe; it was a thriving democracy, had a strong industrial base, and a relatively strong army. It was burdened with nationality problems, most particularly the animosity toward the state from the 3.5 million Sudeten Germans who lived in the western part of the nation. France had assured the Czechoslovak state that in the event of German aggression it would come to its aid. Unfortunately, these assurances, which also included guarantees for its security from the Soviet Union, ultimately came to nothing.

Great Britain Tries to Appease Germany

The British eventually settled on a policy known as **Appeasement**. In 1937, **Neville Chamberlain** (1869–1940) became British Prime Minister and head of a conservative government. Chamberlain recognized that events in 1936 had been detrimental to British interests. These events included the German occupation of the Rhineland, the creation of the **Rome-Berlin Axis**, and even the Olympic games that had been held that year in Berlin, which were a propaganda victory for Germany. Chamberlain was not a fool, and he certainly had little sympathy for the brutality of the Nazi state, but he believed that it was impossible for Great Britain to fully rearm against the combined strength of Germany and Italy. As a result, he wanted to work out some sort of understanding with either Mussolini or Hitler.

Appeasement began with British recognition of Italy's annexation of Ethiopia. The British did nothing when Hitler annexed Austria. However, the policy of appeasement would stand a real test over the question of Czechoslovakia, which Germany threatened to invade unless the **Sudetenland**, the western part of the Czechoslovak state that was largely inhabited by ethnic Germans, was turned over to the Reich. In a radio address during this crisis, Chamberlain said it was "fantastic and incredible to be involved in a war because of a quarrel in a faraway country between people of whom we know nothing." In September, with Europe on the verge of war, Chamberlain flew to Munich to attend a four-power summit with France, Italy, and Germany to discuss the future of Czechoslovakia, whose leaders were not even invited to attend. At this summit, the powers signed the **Munich Agreement**, which led to the transfer of all Sudenten territories to Germany. In return, Hitler promised to respect the sovereignty of what remained of Czechoslovakia. Chamberlain returned home to London and was met by a huge crowd that roared with joy as Chamberlain announced that there would be "peace in our time." Rather than peace, his actions led to destruction in Czechoslovakia one year later when the Germans ignored the Munich Agreement and seized most of what remained of the nation.

Before we are too quick to criticize the appeasers, we need to remember several things.

- First, politicians such as Chamberlain saw it as almost a sacred responsibility to remove the specter of war from Europe. The First World War was still vividly remembered by all who had lived through it.

- Also, from the British point of view, the Versailles Treaty was unjust, and part of what Hitler wanted appeared to be self-determination for nationalities, an idea that the respected President Wilson had promoted in his Fourteen Points.

- Finally, with hindsight, it is clear that Hitler never intended to maintain any of his promises. It may be unfair to have expected that the appeasers would have been able to foresee Hitler's intentions. In 1938, few individuals in Great Britain other than Winston Churchill fully understood that Hitler had to be stopped at all costs.

Germany and the Soviet Union Invade Poland

Following the dismemberment of Czechoslovakia, Hitler's attention was now drawn to the next contentious area—Poland. The Polish nation born out of Versailles included land that had once been part of the German Empire. To allow Poles access to the sea, the new nation was given a strip of territory that split East Prussia from the rest of Germany. Now that he realized Hitler's intentions following the complete occupation of Czechoslovakia, Chamberlain was determined to stop further German aggression. He worked out an arrangement with France whereby the two nations would respond in the event that Poland's borders were threatened.

At the same time, the Soviet Union was inquiring as to whether the British and French would consider forming a military alliance directed against the Germans. The British and French rebuffed the Soviets in part because, after Stalin's purge of the officer corps, they questioned the effectiveness of the Soviet military, and they found little evidence that Stalin was any more a man of his word than Hitler. Once Stalin realized that he was getting nowhere with the British and French, he announced on August 22, 1939—to the shock of the rest of the world—that Germany and the Soviet Union had signed a **nonaggression pact**. The way was now open for Germany to invade Poland, while the Soviets were able to seize eastern Poland, Finland, and the Baltic states, all lands that Russia had lost in the First World War.

THE SECOND WORLD WAR (1939–1945)

The war began on September 1, 1939, with an attack on Poland. The Poles fought bravely; however, the Germans had learned critical lessons from the First World War and practiced *blitzkrieg* warfare, swift attacks using tanks and other highly mobile units, supported by warplanes. Within a month, the Polish army was routed and the British and French forces to the west maintained their defensive positions.

Over the winter of 1939–1940 little warfare occurred, earning the time period the nickname the **"Phony War."** This lull came to a shattering end in April 1940 when the Germans attacked Norway and Denmark to secure necessary iron ore supplies for Germany. In May, the Germans followed up these successes with an invasion of Belgium and the Netherlands before launching their ultimate goal, an attack on France. In six short weeks, the French army, considered after the First World War to be the finest in the world, was destroyed.

The Fall of France

Part of the problem for the French was that in 1940, their hearts were just not in the war. The *blitzkrieg* attacks in the east and the quick defeat of the Scandinavian countries bred tremendous pessimism among the French political and military leadership. The French were still following a military strategy that was tied to the way the First World War had been fought. During the interwar period, they built the **Maginot Line**, a series of seemingly impregnable defenses to protect their soldiers during what they automatically assumed would be another war of stagnant positions. The Germans simply bypassed the fortifications, which were not extended to the Belgian frontier, and encircled the French armies. The British, seeing that France was about to fall, staged a heroic retreat from the Belgian beaches at **Dunkirk**, in which every available British ship, no matter the size, was used to take the British army back to Great Britain so that it might fight another day.

Following the military debacle, a new government was formed in France under the elderly **Marshal Pétain**, the hero of the Battle of Verdun. Pétain had been a bit of a defeatist in the First World War, and those pessimistic tendencies rose to the forefront once again as he decided to pull France out of the war and use the opportunity to create a more authoritarian French government. Pétain's **Vichy** regime brought to an end the Third Republic that was blamed for France's defeat.

Although almost the entire officer corps had been defeatists, one charismatic general, **Charles de Gaulle** (1890–1970), arrived in London and from there issued a call for French forces in the colonies to form a new French army to retrieve the national honor. Vichy authorities immediately labeled de Gaulle a traitor and began to happily assist the Germans. Nevertheless, a free French force did flourish under de Gaulle's leadership. On French soil, the *Maquis*, or French resistance, found itself fighting against both the Germans and against the Vichy state.

Germany Against Great Britain

Hitler always believed that the British shared similar traits with the German Aryans. Because of such foolish racial theories, he thought that the British would see the folly of their ways after the fall of France and make peace with Germany. Great Britain, however, was gearing up for what would be the most dangerous moment in its history. Fortunately for the survival of the nation, it had an extraordinary leader in **Winston Churchill**, who had replaced Chamberlain as Prime Minister. Churchill committed the nation, which he inspired through a series of stirring speeches, to continue the war no matter what may come. In the House of Commons, Churchill declared, "I have nothing to offer but blood, toil, tears, and sweat" and that the only goal for Britain was to "wage war against a monstrous tyranny, never surpassed in the dark, lamentable catalogue of human crime." In response to Britain's refusal to sue for peace, Hitler decided to attack.

The **Battle of Britain** was not the one-sided struggle that is often portrayed. It is true that the *Luftwaffe*, the German air force, had many more planes and trained pilots. But the British had radar, which had been developed at Cambridge University and could detect oncoming German attacks. The British Spitfires and Hurricanes were better planes than the German Messerschmits. Unbeknownst to the Germans, the British had also cracked the German secret military code. Furthermore, there was no comparison in terms of military leadership. Hitler was convinced that he was a military genius following the rapid fall of Poland and France, although fortunately for the eventual triumph of the Allies, that was clearly not the case. The German air force was led by the incompetent morphine addict **Hermann Göring** (1893–1946), who, after a token group of British planes dropped bombs on Berlin, decided to end the effective raids that had been staged on British air bases and directed the *Luftwaffe* to attack British cities. This strategy created tremendous suffering in the cities (the Blitz), and it also allowed the **Royal Air Force (RAF)** time to recover. By the end of September 1940, Hitler decided to drop the plan to invade Britain and move on to his ultimate dream, the defeat of the Soviet Union.

The Holocaust

The Holocaust, the slaughter of six million Jews, did not begin suddenly, nor is it clear at what point the Nazis decided to destroy European Jewry. Anti-Semitism had always been at the heart of Nazi ideology. Soon after taking power, the Nazis implemented the **Nuremberg Laws**, depriving Jews of citizenship and forcing them to wear a yellow Star of David on their clothing whenever they left their homes. Marriage and sex between Jews and Gentiles were also forbidden. While some Jews left Germany immediately after these restrictions were implemented, many refused to leave, thinking that things could not get any worse. Nevertheless, the following years would witness only a slow, steady decline for German Jews as they were forced out of all professions and had their stores boycotted and property confiscated. On November 9, 1938, the Nazis launched *Kristallnacht*, the "night of broken glass," so called because of the resonating sound of shattered glass from Jewish stores and homes that rung out throughout that night. The events of that night proved that the Germans were interested in eliminating the Jews, as several hundred people were killed and 30,000 Jews were shipped to concentration camps.

One sign that demonstrates the Nazi obsession with the so-called "**Jewish Question**" is that when the Russians were putting up stiff resistance and Germany had not been able to defeat them, the Nazis still chose to direct resources that could have been used in the war effort to exterminate European Jewry instead. The conquest of Poland had placed the largest concentration of Jews in the world directly under German control. To deal with them, as well as with the large numbers of Jews from the other conquered territories, Hitler had his top lieutenants organize the "**Final Solution**." By the end of 1941, 1 million Jews were slaughtered, most in mobile vans poisoned by carbon monoxide gas or machine-gunned by specially designated S.S. troops. This was not efficient enough for the Germans, however, and so in January 1942, the top leadership met in **Wannsee**, a suburb of Berlin, to plan a more efficient slaughter.

The Nazis organized a camp system throughout Poland, including concentration camps, where Jews from around occupied Europe were gathered, and extermination camps, the most notorious of these being **Auschwitz**. Upon arrival in the camps, the prisoners would be subject to a sorting process, where S.S. doctors, including the notorious **Doctor Mengele**, selected who would be sent to work camps and who would be sent immediately to die in the gas chambers. Besides Jews, the camps also contained "gypsies" (or Roma as they prefer to be called), homosexuals, Jehovah's Witnesses, Russian prisoners of war, Communists, and others considered by the Nazis to be "undesirables." Approximately 7 million such individuals were slaughtered, in addition to 6 million Jews.

The "Final Solution"

Many historians argue that Hitler's fixation on eradicating the Jews ultimately hurt Germany's war effort, as valuable resources that could have been used to defeat the Russians were instead spent on killing the Jewish people.

How Much Did the Allies Know?

There has always been a debate over what the Allies knew about the Holocaust and what they could have done to stop the German death machine. Although the S.S. took every precaution to hide the Final Solution, which was partly why the Nazis chose Poland as the site of the camps, word of the terror reached the West right from the beginning. Such reports were initially doubted: Who could believe such monstrosities were taking place? The sheer bulk of reports, many from eyewitnesses to the slaughter, however, made it clear that an unprecedented event in human history was taking place. The debate on what could have been done will never be resolved. Many believe that attacks on the German rail network used to bring Jews to the camps could have possibly been of help, although Allied military leaders always claimed that the planes that could have been used for such raids were needed for more immediate military targets.

One reason why two-thirds of European Jews were so effectively rounded up for slaughter was that the Nazis never lacked help among the conquered peoples of Europe to assist in this task. Yad Vashem, the Holocaust museum and memorial in Israel, has a special row of trees in honor of those Gentiles who risked their lives to help rescue Jews; however, a forest would be needed to represent the sheer number of people who aided the Germans in implementing the Holocaust. In France, Vichy officials rounded up Jews and turned them over to the Nazis before the Germans even asked for their help. In the Ukraine, Croatia, and in other parts of eastern Europe, the local population set off on their own initiative to exterminate their Jewish neighbors. Anti-Semitic feelings obviously ran deep throughout European society in the early twentieth century.

The Turning of the Tide

The Second World War had three critical turning points. The Battle of Britain was certainly one, as was the eventual entry of the United States into the war. The third turning point may be the most important of all—Operation Barbarossa, the German attack on the Soviet Union on June 22, 1941.

Germany Invades the Soviet Union

Initially, the attack went according to plan, as German forces drove deep into Russian territory, catching the Soviet forces completely unprepared, even though Stalin had been warned by numerous sources, including his own intelligence agency, that such an attack was imminent. By the end of 1942, the Germans had reached the outskirts of Stalingrad and Leningrad, but both cities were held owing to the Russian forces' dogged defense and the extraordinary sacrifices of the citizens of the Soviet Union. Because of their common enemy—Germany—Great Britain, the United States, and the Soviet Union were to form a rather unlikely alliance that would not only destroy the Third Reich but also shape the postwar world.

The War in North Africa

By 1941, the war had become a global conflict. The Italians under Mussolini had entered the war as allies of Germany just as France was about to collapse. The Italians also extended the war to North Africa, as they attempted to push the British out of Egypt. The Italians were hard-pressed to achieve this goal, forcing the Germans to come to their aid. The Germans had one of their best officers, **Erwin Rommel** (1891–1944), the "Desert Fox," positioned in this theater of the war. For a while he met with remarkable success, eventually proceeding within sixty miles of the Egyptian city of Alexandria. However, at the **Battle of El Alamein** in November 1942, a British army under the leadership of General Montgomery (1887–1976) pushed the German and Italian forces back to Tunisia.

U.S. Involvement

Following the Japanese attack on Pearl Harbor and Hitler's declaration of war on the United States in 1941, the United States was involved in the conflict with the Axis powers (Germany, Italy, and Japan). The entry of the United States into the war sparked a new energy to the war in the west, as the United States landed troops in Africa and joined with the British in pushing back the Germans and Italians. By 1943, the **Allies** had pushed the last of the **Axis forces** out of Africa and sent troops to Italy, the "soft underbelly" of the Axis. By 1943, Italy was knocked out of the war, although in many ways, the Italian campaign did not have a huge impact on the eventual course of the war.

Following a meeting between Stalin, Churchill, and Roosevelt in Tehran in November 1943, the decision was made that the British and Americans should stage an invasion of western Europe from Great Britain. On June 6, 1944, the Allies launched the **D-Day** invasion. While another year of brutal fighting was yet to be experienced, the landing of the Allied forces in Europe and the Russian counterattack following the lifting of the siege of Leningrad marked the beginning of the end for Nazi Germany.

On May 8, 1945, a week after the suicide of Hitler, Germany surrendered unconditionally. Japan had entered the Second World War with the goal of creating a vast empire in the Pacific where it would be able to exploit the natural resources of the conquered lands and use these territories as a market for Japanese manufactured goods. Such dreams of hegemony over the Pacific ended violently with the dropping of the first **atomic bomb** on the city of **Hiroshima** on August 6, 1945, which was followed two days later by a second atomic bomb, this time on the city of **Nagasaki**. On August 14, the Japanese surrendered (signing the formal surrender document on September 2), thus bringing to an end the bloodiest conflict in human history.

The Aftermath

The Second World War was even more staggering in its destructiveness than the First World War. Civilian casualties—rather than military deaths—made up the majority of the **50 to 60 million** people who lost their lives during the conflict. For the Soviet Union alone, although the precise numbers remain the subject of debate and will ultimately never be fully known, losses were upwards of 25 million. Cities across the continent were leveled as brutal attacks on civilian targets, initiated when the Germans bombed Warsaw in 1939 and then followed up in places such as Rotterdam and London, were eventually thrown back on the Germans, with 50,000 killed in the **fire bombing of Dresden** and with almost every German target of any military, economic, or administrative value laying in ruin. In Berlin and in other German cities, one found the *Truemmerfrauen*, or "rubble ladies," who in the absence of men and machinery began the slow process of removing the wreckage by hand.

In 1945, it seemed as if all of Europe was on the move. The roads were clogged with displaced persons, including Jews who had survived the death camps and couldn't go back to their homes but also seemingly had no place to go. In many cases, Jews would live for the next several years under difficult conditions in camps the British set up in places such as Cyprus, unable to follow their dream and go to Palestine.

Russian POWs returned to the Soviet Union and immediately faced rearrest under the orders of Stalin, who thought their failure to die in battle might be an indication they were spies or had seen too much of life in the West to be satisfied with conditions in the Soviet Union. This was in spite of the fact that Soviet POWs had been treated with incredible brutality by the Germans, who saw them as subhuman.

Millions of Germans also poured west, fleeing from the forces of the Soviet Union, who were extracting their revenge through mass rape. Other Germans were forced from their homes in Poland and Czechoslovakia, as the civilians in those countries refused to countenance living with ethnic Germans they blamed for the start of the war.

At the end of the First World War, cries of "Hang the Kaiser!" could be heard in the capitals of the victors, but in the end, nothing was done to punish those individuals who were blamed for the war. However, by 1945, with the liberation of the Nazi death camps and the realization of the unspeakable scale of the slaughter, it was agreed by the Allies that Germany would not only have to undergo a process of **denazification,** but that the perpetrators of these crimes would have to be punished as well.

The new legal concept of **"crimes against humanity"** was applied to the defendants who took part in the first **Nuremberg Trial** that began on November 20, 1945, and ended on October 1, 1946. With the suicides of Hitler and Goebbels, the leading Nazi to stand trial was Hermann Göring, who escaped the hangman's noose by swallowing poison that was smuggled into his cell, while eleven others were sentenced to death. Other trials were held for leading industrialists, military commanders, judges, and those involved in the Final Solution. Many Nazis escaped justice by fleeing to the Middle East and South America, such as the infamous **Dr. Josef Mengele,** while some, such as Gestapo officer Adolf Eichmann, were eventually brought to justice. Questions arose over what to do about the rank-and-file Nazi party members, and although millions were investigated, relatively few received punishment. By June 1946, the Americans transferred responsibility for denazification to the German legal authorities, who quietly brought the process to a close.

In the years following the war, West Germans would refer to 1945 as **"Zero Hour,"** marking the darkest point in their national history. Many commentators thought that not only Germany but all of Europe would remain on its back, with minimal economic development and the renewed threat of war. Remarkably, Europe staged a thorough recovery over the next twenty years and in the process transformed the lives of people throughout the region and ushered in an age of political and social stability.

Denazification
Following the end of the war, the Allies implemented the process of *denazification* in Germany, in which all remnants of Nazi ideology were removed from the German culture, and all Nazi Party members were removed from positions in the government. Any organizations associated with Nazism were disbanded.

EUROPEAN STABILITY

The most important factor in European affairs in the period after 1945 was the emergence of political, economic, and social stability. Even while the war was raging, Allied statesmen began to think about ways of rebuilding Europe and creating lasting peace.

In 1941, President Roosevelt put forward the **Atlantic Charter**, advocating the establishment of an international organization to replace the ineffective League of Nations. Four years later, this dream became a reality when delegates from fifty nations met in San Francisco to formally create the **United Nations**. To ensure the participation of the United States, whose nonparticipation in the League of Nations doomed that body to failure, the new organization was to be based in New York. In July 1945, the U.S. Senate ratified the agreement (with others signing onto it in October), indicating that the United States was not going to return to its interwar isolationism and would instead remain committed to European recovery and stability.

Besides the significance of America's commitment to European affairs, other reasons help account for the development of stability in Europe. The level of destruction brought by Germany and Italy in a war they initiated and the extent of their atrocities against civilians led to a discrediting of Fascism as a political movement. *Revanchism*, a French word for revenge and often applied to the desire to regain so-called lost territories, was a major factor in destabilizing European affairs during the interwar period, as many nations—besides the most prominent example of Germany—sought to regain territories lost in the peace treaties following the Great War. In part due to the mass expulsion of ethnic Germans from Poland and Czechoslovakia, *revanchism* became the cry of fringe groups in the postwar period rather than the stated policy of national governments.

Probably the most important factor in explaining postwar European stability was the emergence of **democratic governments** that were able to carry out policies that dramatically improved the economic conditions for their citizenry. Class conflict, which had been a destabilizing factor in the 1920s and 1930s, was replaced by a new **social contract** in which workers, in exchange for giving up their most extreme demands, received promises of full employment, living wages, and social welfare.

THE BEGINNING OF THE COLD WAR

There have been three major schools of thought on the causes of the Cold War.

1. For the **Traditionalists** (a position that emerged in the earliest days of the Cold War), the Soviet Union, under the brutal dictatorship of Joseph Stalin, was fundamentally responsible for the development of hostilities between the East and West.

2. Beginning in the 1960s (in part a reflection of the challenges that were being posed to all forms of established authority and anger over the Vietnam War), a new school of Cold War thought, known as **Revisionism**, began to appear. For the Revisionists, fear of a postwar economic downturn (as was the case after 1918) meant that, in 1945, the United States was not seeking to make the world safe for democracy but was instead seeking to make it safe for American trade.

3. By the 1980s, a third position began to emerge, that of the **Post-Revisionists**, which perhaps not surprisingly took a middle ground. For the Post-Revisionists, even if the Soviet Union bore the brunt of the responsibility, the United States was more active than the Traditionalists might argue.

In many ways, the views of historians have not been altered all that fundamentally by the collapse of the Soviet Union and the opening, if at times tentatively, of their archives. What is often today referred to as the neo-Traditionalist point of view is currently in the ascendancy, although one can easily find in scholarly books and journals writings reflecting the other two traditions.

One can make the argument that the Cold War rivalry was largely inevitable. In an often-quoted passage, Alexis de Tocqueville, in *Democracy in America,* wrote,

> There are now two great nations in the world, which starting from different points, seem to be advancing toward the same goal: the Russians and the Anglo-Americans...Each seems called by some secret design of Providence one day to hold in its hands the destinies of half the world.

When de Tocqueville wrote that passage in 1835, he certainly wasn't thinking about ideological differences, but such differences did emerge dating back to the establishment of the communist state in 1917, which was followed by limited Allied involvement in the Russian Civil War. Even during the war, although cooperation certainly existed, mistrust played a role in the relationship between the Soviet Union and its Western allies, ranging from Soviet anger over the delay in opening a second front to fears that the British and Americans were seeking to negotiate a separate peace with the Germans.

The Yalta Conference on the Future of Germany

Once the war came to an end and cooperation was no longer necessary for victory, mutual antagonism came out, beginning with the debate over the future of Germany. At **Yalta**, the Big Three agreed to the **temporary division of Germany**, and in the aftermath of the war, Germany was divided into four zones (France was given a zone at the insistence of the British), with an **Allied Control Council** to make joint decisions. None of the Allies apparently wanted or expected dismemberment. Nevertheless, Yalta had provided each of the Allies with the opportunity to effect transformation in their own zone, with the end result that the Soviet Union would obviously transform their zone in a far different manner than the Western Allies. Ultimately, Germany would become a Cold War showcase for the rival ideologies.

The method chosen by the Soviet Union to gain control over political life in its zone was the subversion of a democratic structure it pretended to support. The Soviets began in their zone by allowing for the reestablishment of all non-right-wing parties that had existed in the Weimar Republic. **Walter Ulbricht**, the Soviet-selected leader of the German Communist Party (KPD), thought that because most Germans didn't want to go back to the world of Weimar and its capitalist crises, there would be genuine support for the KPD. The problem was that mass rape, dismantling of factories to be sent back to the Soviet Union, and the failure of land reform led to anger at the Soviets and their clients in the KPD. Seeing that no groundswell of electoral support would be forthcoming, Ulbricht brought about the forced merger of the KPD and the more popular Social Democratic Party (SPD) in 1946 and created a one-party state, a technique the Soviets were to find useful as they sought to gain control over other governments in Eastern Europe.

While these political developments were taking place, tensions were increasing over the issue of **reparations**. Neither the Americans nor the British were diametrically opposed to reparations, and an agreement had been reached at Yalta with an amount set at 20 billion dollars. At Potsdam, further negotiations led to the agreement that each occupying power would collect reparations in its own zone, with the hard-pressed Soviets receiving 25 percent from the amount collected by the other three.

The problem was that the Western Allies began to fear that carrying out a reparations program would leave the German economy prostrate, with the British and American public left paying the bill to feed the Germans. Even President Truman had been shaken by what he saw when he traveled to Germany for the Potsdam conference and noted, "Unless we do what we can to help, we may lose next winter what we won at such terrible cost last spring." On his own initiative, in May 1946, General Lucius Clay, the commander of the American zone, ended the collection of reparations, which was soon to be followed by the other two Western Allies, which meant that goods stopped flowing to the Soviet Union.

Increasing Tensions Outside of Europe

Tensions were also increasing between the Americans and Soviets in regions outside of Europe. Back in 1941, the Soviets and British jointly divided and occupied Iran, with an agreement that they would both leave at the end of the war. In 1945, the British promptly left, but the Soviets refused and demanded oil concessions. When Truman heard that Soviet tanks were heading to the capital of Tehran, he sent warships into the Persian Gulf, and Stalin responded by removing his troops.

Stalin also tried to intimidate **Turkey**, which was neutral in the war, into granting the Soviets naval bases along the straits to give the Soviet fleet access to the Mediterranean, something Russia had long desired. To show the Turks he was serious, Stalin massed troops along their common border, and it was only when he understood that the United States would fight to protect Turkey that he backed down and withdrew his forces.

American foreign policy toward the Soviet Union was in a state of flux in the immediate postwar period. In part, this reflected the replacement of Franklin Roosevelt, who felt that his good wartime relationship with Stalin could serve as the basis of postwar ties, with the no-nonsense Harry S. Truman, who saw Stalin in a more wary light.

American policy was also influenced by the writings of **George Kennan**, an official in the State Department. In 1947, Kennan wrote what became known as the **Long Telegram**, in which he indicated that in our relationship with the Soviets, we were dealing with a state that viewed us as an ideological enemy and would never seek to find the means for coexistence. In this and in articles that appeared under the pseudonym "X" in the journal *Foreign Affairs*, Kennan became the architect of the policy of **Containment**, in which our goal needed to be the "long-term, patient but firm and vigilant containment of Russian expansive tendencies."

Containment and the Creation of NATO

Containment as an actual policy was first tested in Greece, where a Communist-led insurgency was fighting against the newly reestablished Greek government. Great Britain, which had assumed a watchdog position in Greece at the end of the war, informed the United States in 1947 that it lacked the economic resources to continue to support the Greek government. Seeing this as a major Soviet attempt to gain control over a strategically important nation (even though Soviet aid to the Greek Communists would later be shown to be quite minimal), Truman went before a joint session of Congress on March 12, 1947, and stated in what is known as the **Truman Doctrine** that, "it must be the policy of the United States to support free peoples who are resisting attempted subjugation by armed minorities or by outside pressures." He then proceeded to ask for money, which eventually reached the amount of $400 million to be given to the Greek and Turkish governments.

Containment was also going to figure into one of the most important decisions made by the United States in the postwar period. Rejecting George Washington's admonition in his farewell address to stay clear of permanent alliances with foreign powers, the United States decided to counter directly the threat posed by the millions of Soviet soldiers based in Eastern Europe by establishing the **North Atlantic Treaty Organization (NATO)** in 1949. Joining the United States as initial members were Great Britain, France, Canada, Denmark, Belgium, Iceland, Italy, the Netherlands, Portugal, and Norway, with Greece and Turkey joining the alliance in 1952.

SOVIET DOMINANCE OVER EASTERN EUROPE

In 1944, seeing that Soviet troops were advancing through Eastern Europe, Winston Churchill traveled to Moscow to meet with Stalin. As Churchill recalled years later, after pushing a piece of paper in front of Stalin, "There was a slight pause. Then he [Stalin] took his blue pen and made a large tick upon it, and passed it back to us. It was all settled in no more time than it takes to set down." This document became known as the **Percentages Agreement**, because it divided the various nations of Eastern Europe into spheres of influence based on percentages, with for example, Soviet influence being at 90 percent in Romania and only 50 percent in Hungary. The agreement was seriously flawed, as Poland was left out of it entirely. The United States refused to accept the agreement.

With the war in Europe winding down, Stalin expected to be able control the future of those areas liberated by the Red Army. With the enormity of Soviet losses in the war in mind and unwilling to see Roosevelt's Atlantic Charter as a source of future peace, Stalin wanted to establish a protective shield to protect the Soviet Union from any future invasion from the west. Meeting in **Yalta**, on the Crimean Sea, the British and Americans were able to get the Soviets to accept a high-minded **Declaration of Liberated Europe**, stating that in those countries that were Axis or liberated, governments were to be formed that were "broadly representative of all democratic elements in the population" and that free elections were to be held at the earliest possible time.

The Iron Curtain
Churchill rushing to get an agreement signed in in 1944 reveals his growing concern that Eastern Europe would become dominated by the Soviet Union and that there was not that much that the Western Allies could do to block this development. Several years later, it was Churchill who delivered his famous speech at Westminster College and used a metaphor that would represent Soviet control over Eastern Europe when he decried the fact that "From Stettin in the Baltic to Trieste in the Adriatic, an **iron curtain** has descended across the Continent."

Poland

On the question of **Poland**, Stalin was going to continue with his plans to establish a government dominated by Polish Communists; the only concession he granted was that an undetermined number of anticommunist Poles based in London would be added to this provisional government. This aspect of the Yalta Conference has proven to be very controversial, with Roosevelt being accused of selling out the Poles. The tragic reality was that the Soviets had troops on the ground in Poland, and there was little that the United States and Great Britain could do about it short of war. There was going to have to be a price for having the Soviet Union for an ally against Germany.

When the promised elections in Poland were finally held under conditions of intimidation in 1947, the Communists received 80 percent and proceeded to bring any sign of a multiparty state to an end. The Soviets understood that they would have to use force to maintain Communist control over Poland because they were hated in that nation—a loathing that grew worse when the role of the Soviets was revealed in the murder of 15,000 Polish officers in the forests of **Katyn** at the start of the war.

Elsewhere in Eastern Europe

Nevertheless, in the rest of Eastern Europe, the Soviets hoped that control could be achieved through less violent means. The Soviet Union seemingly had a number of advantages in this goal, including the economic and social failure of the states of Eastern Europe during the interwar period (with the exception of Czechoslovakia). This meant that few were advocating a return to the politics of the past, although in most of Eastern Europe, the Soviets were viewed as liberators from the horrors of German dominance. With the exception of Poland, the Soviet Union initially tried to establish "**People's Democracies**" in Eastern Europe. For the Communists, this was a go-slow program, with governments that were more proletarian than in the bourgeois West but were still not ready for a full-fledged Communist system as found in the Soviet Union.

In many ways, the push for tighter control over Eastern Europe came about in reaction to the offer of **Marshall Plan** money to all the nations of Europe. Stalin saw the Marshall Plan as a threat to informal Soviet control over countries like Hungary or Czechoslovakia, because by taking the money, those countries would automatically be drawn toward the capitalist West, so Stalin moved to assert more direct control. In Hungary, the Communists practiced "salami" tactics, where intimidation and false plots against non-Communist political leaders sliced them away from the body politic. Using such tactics, the Hungarian Communist Party forced its competitor, the Smallholders' Party, out of existence by 1948 and in the following year won a tainted election with 95 percent of the vote.

Czechoslovakia

In Czechoslovakia, the situation was different, because in the immediate postwar period, the government was dominated by men like President Eduard Benes, who although a non-Communist understood that it would be necessary to maintain a pro-Soviet foreign policy if Czechoslovakia were to retain its national independence. Also, the Czechs were more favorably disposed toward the Soviet Union, whom they gratefully saw as liberators, while feeling they didn't owe anything to the West, which had sold them out at Munich in 1938. This balancing act failed in the wake of Czech desire to accept badly needed Marshall Plan monies. To put pressure on Benes's government, the Czech Communists formed a "People's Militia," which intimidated Benes into forming a new government dominated by Communists.

When the body of Foreign Minister Jan Masaryk, the son of the founder of Czechoslovakia, was found shattered outside his window—either a suicide or a murder victim—it was clear that a multiparty Czechoslovak state was coming to an end. The Social Democrats were forcibly absorbed into the Communist Party, and in controlled elections in May 1948, the Communists won a complete victory and proceeded to set up a Soviet-style state.

Yugoslavia

The major exception to Soviet control over Eastern Europe took place in Yugoslavia. Initially, Yugoslavian resistance was based on a broad alliance against the brutal Croatian puppet government established by the Germans. As the war continued, however, a civil war broke out among the partisan groups with the Communists, led by **Josip Tito**, fighting against the royalist Chetniks. The civil war ended with the triumph of Tito's Communists, but Stalin never trusted Tito, in part because of the assistance he received during the war from the British and Americans, as well as the fact that Stalin never liked indigenous Communist movements that he couldn't directly control. Relations between the two states remained poor in the ensuing years, and by 1948, a formal break took place. Although Tito became the West's favorite Communist due to his independent foreign policy, at home he maintained a brutal, communist-style police state.

THE END OF IMPERIALISM

The British had hoped to maintain their vast empire following the war. The United States, however, was extremely reluctant to allow this, and Great Britain, which was dependent on American loans, was forced to concede the point. The beginning of decolonization took place on August 15, 1947, when India declared independence, initiating a domino effect throughout the rest of the Empire.

Israel

In 1947, the British announced that they were withdrawing from Palestine, leaving the United Nations to determine its fate. Demands for a Jewish homeland had grown louder following the Holocaust, and Arabic nationalist sentiment also had increased. In response, the United Nations agreed to partition Palestine into Jewish and Arab homelands. On May 14, 1948, the Jewish state of Israel was founded, but it was immediately attacked by its Arab neighbors. Surprisingly, the small Jewish state pushed back its enemies and the proposed Arab Palestinian state never left the drawing boards.

Egypt and Africa

Great Britain maintained significant influence in Egypt, even though the latter had been an independent nation since 1922. This began to change when **Abdul Nasser** (1918–1970) became president. In 1956, he announced the nationalization of the Suez Canal, which the British still controlled. In response, Britain, France, and Israel planned a surprise attack on Egypt. The immediate outcry from the American and Soviet governments made it quite clear to Britain and France exactly who were the dominant powers in this postwar world. They bowed to the American and Soviet demands to withdraw.

Soon after, the British saw the writing on the wall, and they began the process of decolonization in sub-Saharan Africa. In 1957, the nation of Ghana declared its independence from Great Britain, and in the ensuing years Nigeria, Sierra Leone, Uganda, and Kenya followed Ghana's lead. Because these territories all contained few British settlers, independence came about without too much trouble. In Rhodesia, on the other hand, in 1965, the large number of British settlers formed their own white-supremacist government and declared their independence from Britain. Not until 1980 would Africans win control over that land, which they renamed Zimbabwe.

Indonesia, Vietnam, and Algeria

For nations such as France and the Netherlands that had a less-than-sterling military record in the Second World War, holding on to their colonies became an important part of restoring national honor. The Dutch maintained a costly and ultimately unwinnable struggle in the East Indies to keep the land they had first occupied in the seventeenth century. By 1949, the Netherlands reluctantly agreed to recognize Indonesian independence.

France almost ripped itself apart in its attempt to hold on to Algeria. This followed a bitter loss in Indochina (Vietnam), where a nationalist movement under the leadership of **Ho Chi Minh** (1890–1969) fought first against the Japanese during the Second World War and then against the French, as the latter attempted to restore its colonial authority. By 1954, France realized it was an impossible task and agreed to divide Vietnam into two states: a northern Communist-led nation and a republic in the south dominated by the United States.

Although the French could accept the loss of Indochina, Algeria was different; it had been a French possession since 1830 and more than a million native French lived in the territory. France almost erupted in civil war over the Algerian question in 1958, until de Gaulle took the helm of the French government and used his immense prestige four years later to grant Algerian independence.

THE CREATION OF A EUROPEAN UNION

In the aftermath of the war, there were several factors that contributed to the goal of establishing greater European cooperation. For the French in particular, pan-European cooperation would provide a means for keeping an eye on its traditional enemy, Germany. There was also a growing sense that economic rationalization and cooperation were needed to end wasteful competition and ease tensions between nations. Additionally, concern over the Soviet Union, which led to military cooperation through the establishment of NATO, aided the cause of European unity.

The first stage in this process took place in the realm of economic cooperation, with the establishment of the **Organization for European Economic Cooperation (OEEC)**, which had the task of handling the money provided by the United States through the Marshall Plan. The United States made it clear when providing the money that it did not want to see it used to revive unprofitable industries in order to salvage national pride, and the United States insisted that Europeans use the money in a cooperative manner. The OEEC also began the initial work on lowering tariffs and eliminating trade barriers among those states receiving assistance.

The next development was the creation in 1951 of the **European Coal and Steel Community (ECSC)**. The ECSC combined and administered the steel and coal resources of its member states: France, West Germany, Italy, Belgium, the Netherlands, and Luxemburg. The main architect of the ECSC, Frenchman **Robert Schuman**, stated that one byproduct of this form of economic cooperation was that "any war between France and Germany becomes not merely unthinkable, but materially impossible." The ECSC also provided certain models that were important for the future development of European unity, such as the establishment of a supranational assembly to guide the ECSC (which was renamed the **European Parliament** in 1962), a court of justice, and direct income for the Community in the form of taxes.

In 1957, the original members of the ECSC signed the **Treaty of Rome**, establishing the **European Economic Community** (more commonly referred to as the **Common Market**). The members of the EEC, who were joined by Britain, Ireland, and Denmark in 1973 in the first expansion of the Community, lifted almost all trade restrictions among member states. In 1986, in the first major revision to the Treaty of Rome, the **European Single Act** provided for the free movement among member nations of capital, labor, and such services as banking and insurance.

The **Maastricht Treaty** of 1992 led to the establishment of a common currency, the Euro, with banknotes and coins going into circulation in January 2002, with the exception of Denmark, Sweden, and most significantly the United Kingdom, which refused to give up the pound. The Maastricht Treaty also introduced new areas where there was supposed to be increased cooperation, such as in defense, justice, and environmental affairs, which resulted in a name change from the EEC to the **European Union (EU)**.

Recent and Future Expansion of the European Union

The European Union has undergone a number of expansions in its list of member states (the largest crop of entrants joined in 2004), notably with nations that were formerly members of the Warsaw Pact or part of the Soviet Union, such as the Czech Republic, Estonia, Hungary, Latvia, Lithuania, Poland, Slovakia, and Slovenia. Bulgaria and Romania joined in 2007, and Turkey entered into negotiations for membership back in 2005. Turkey's European Union bid has been controversial for a number of reasons. Some EU officials doubt that Turkey can meet economic targets required for membership, or they question Turkey's commitment to human rights. Some have expressed concern about admitting a Muslim state into the EU with a large population that would make it second only to Germany.

EU expansion has also led to the desire to make it work more efficiently, which led to the writing of a **European Constitution**, the caveat being that all EU members had to approve the constitution for it to go into effect. France, however, a nation that has been at the forefront of European cooperation, voted "no" in May 2005 in a national referendum. What this will mean for further European integration is not yet clear.

POST-WWII DEVELOPMENTS IN WESTERN EUROPEAN STATES

Great Britain

The postwar period in Great Britain began with what at the time was considered to be one of the greatest political upsets in electoral history—the replacement of Prime Minister Winston Churchill and his Conservative Party with the **Labour Party** and its leader, **Clement Attlee**. It probably shouldn't have come as such a surprise, because although many in Britain were deeply grateful to Churchill for the steely leadership he provided during the war, there was a sense that he was not the man to lead them in times of peace.

Economic and Social Reforms

Even while the war was in full swing, there was a sense that when the war ended, Britain had to move beyond the dismal economic and social conditions that had prevailed during the interwar years. **Sir William Beveridge**, a member of the Liberal Party, had produced in 1942 (at the request of the government) a report that recommended that all adults should pay a weekly contribution, and in return benefits would be paid to people who were sick, unemployed, retired, or widowed. For Beveridge, the benefit of such a system was that it would provide for a minimum standard of living "below which no one should be allowed to fall." The electoral triumph of the Labour Party was due to the belief within the British public that it was the party most committed to implementing this far-reaching plan for reform, and with its victory in 1945, Labour began the establishment of a cradle-to-grave social welfare program—the highlight being the establishment of the **National Health Service (NHS)**, which provided for a comprehensive system of free health care.

Nationalization of Industries

Attlee and the Labour party were also committed to a program of nationalization of major industries. Beginning in 1945, the government took control of the Bank of England, the railroads, and the electric, iron, and steel industries. This was not as revolutionary as it might appear, because in many cases, these industries had already been placed under government control during the war years. Fair compensation was paid to the existing owners, and company management (which some of the more radical members of the Labour Party wanted to see handled by the workers through committees) remained in the hands of professional managers, in many cases the same individuals who had led the firm prior to the takeover.

Economic conditions remained fairly grim in the immediate postwar years. Britain was now a major debtor to the United States, because its own gold and foreign currency reserves had been depleted to save the nation from the Nazi onslaught. The Labour party remained committed to sizeable military expenditures, because Britain still had large military commitments overseas, and the advent of the Cold War also affected spending. Although the standard of living improved for many people in the immediate postwar years due to the increase in social services, this period is generally referred to as the **"Age of Austerity"** and lasted until 1954, when the wartime rationing of butter and sugar finally came to an end.

By the 1951 general election, the Labour Party and the public were fairly exhausted from the pace of change, which provided a renewed opportunity for Churchill's Conservatives. Aside from reversing the nationalization of the iron and steel industries, the Conservatives did not return the remaining industries to private hands and continued to support the social service network implemented by the Labour Party. This has come to be known as the **"Politics of Consensus,"** because although the two major parties may have differed on details such as funding levels, they were in general agreement on the need to provide social services and that government should play a large role in the management of the economy.

Economic Decline

Although one can refer to a postwar **"economic miracle"** in Germany and Italy, such talk for Great Britain would be wide off the mark. Britain's economic growth by the 1950s was clearly less than that achieved by the nations of Western Europe. The reasons for **Britain's economic decline** in the postwar period remain controversial, but one can generally see factors such as the reliance on older factories, whereas plants in places like Germany were rebuilt with the latest technology following the destruction brought by the war. Britain also lacked the central economic planning that was to prove to be critical for French economic growth, and Britain had to deal with aggressive unions that wanted higher wages without agreeing to produce gains in productivity. Some scholars have even looked to cultural reasons for Britain's decline suggesting, for example, that the study of the sciences in British universities took a back seat to the pursuit of the humanities.

Violence in Ireland: Bloody Sunday
During these same years, the situation in **Northern Ireland** worsened, with the British government sending troops into the troubled province in 1969. On January 30, 1972, thirteen Catholics were killed when British soldiers fired on civil rights marchers. The day became known as **Bloody Sunday** and led to a renewed surge of violence by groups such as the Irish Republican Army that were opposed to the British presence in Northern Ireland.

Following a period of Conservative dominance in the period after 1951, the Labour Party re-emerged as the dominant political party in the period from 1964 to 1974. Although Prime Minister Harold Wilson was leading a party that would prove to be successful at the polls, he was not able to strengthen the position of Britain in the global economy.

Margaret Thatcher and the Post-Thatcher Years

In 1979, Prime Minister James Callaghan's Labour government proved unable to deal with a wave of strikes that negatively affected road transport and public services, known as the "winter of discontent." This provided an opportunity for the triumph of the Conservative Party and its leader **Margaret Thatcher**, who became Britain's first female prime minister. Thatcher had made it clear that she wanted to break with what she viewed as the failed policies of the past and stated, "I am not a consensus politician, I am a conviction politician." **Thatcherism**, the eponymous term for her economic policies, included tight control over the money supply to reduce inflation, sharp cuts in public spending, and a cut in taxes, particularly for higher earners.

Thatcher sought to make Britain more competitive in the global market by reducing the power of the trade unions and by reprivatizing those parts of the British economy still under the control of the government. Thatcher was a very divisive leader, and her career might have come to an early end if it had not received a boost following the successful war that Britain fought with Argentina in 1982 over the **Falkland Islands**. Thatcher ran into trouble during her third term when she tried to introduce market principles into the running of the NHS and education system, and her hostility to working toward further European integration created dissent within her own party. In 1990, she resigned and was replaced by **John Major**. Major continued with most of Thatcher's domestic policies, though perhaps without some of the vindictive gusto that she had brought to British politics. Because he was more pro-European than Thatcher, he signed the Maastricht Treaty.

In 1997, after being out of government for eighteen years, the Labour Party triumphed under its youthful leader **Tony Blair**. Blair, who had become the leader of his party in 1994, had moved Labour away from its socialist roots, creating what he referred to as "**New Labour**." Rather than renationalizing the economy, Labour under Blair focused on improving Britain's social services, reform of the House of Lords, and the devolution of power away from Westminster and toward regional parliaments in Wales and Scotland. Blair received a second term in 2001 and a third in 2005, although the margin of Labour's victory in the 2005 election was significantly reduced because of anger over Blair's support for the war in Iraq.

Blair resigned as Labour Leader in May of 2007, and Gordon Brown, who served as Chancellor of the Exchequer under Blair for many years, rose to become both leader of the Labour Party and prime minister of the United Kingdom. Brown served until 2010 when David Cameron (a Conservative party leader) became prime minister.

France

France in 1945 had to deal with the grim aftermath of what one writer has termed the "Strange Defeat" of 1940. France largely chose to deal with the difficult Vichy years by propagating certain myths, including the idea that France was a nation of resisters against German occupation, that few supported Marshal Pétain and Vichy, and that the tragic fate of the Jews in France was entirely the responsibility of the Germans. Marcel Ophuls's powerful documentary *The Sorrow and the Pity* (1969) helped open the door to questioning these national myths, although it remained several years before French television was willing to show the film. Under President **Jacques Chirac**, the nation finally began to address France's role in the deportation of 66,000 Jews to Germany, along with other issues involving collaboration activities during the war.

Charles de Gaulle, the leader of the French government-in-exile, expected to dominate political life in postwar France, but he stepped away from politics when the newly established **Fourth Republic** refused to establish the strong presidency that de Gaulle felt was needed if France was not going to repeat the mistakes of the politically contentious Third Republic. French political life was also transformed, if in a more positive manner, by the granting of the vote to women. It was left to the Fourth Republic to grapple with a series of colonial problems, including the disastrous defeat in Indochina in 1954 and in the same year a revolt that broke out in **Algeria**.

The crisis in Algeria, which led to fears that a military coup would take place in France itself, brought about the return of de Gaulle to politics, and he led the vote for a plebiscite in 1958 establishing the **Fifth Republic**, which contained the powerful presidency whose office de Gaulle now held. Although his enemies saw him as dictatorial, de Gaulle was committed to restoring France to a leading place on the global stage. To do this, he committed France to taking a leading role in Europe, which meant vetoing Britain's attempt to enter the Common Market in 1962.

To ensure that it could provide for its own defense, France refused to sign the **Limited Test Ban Treaty** and exploded its first hydrogen bomb in 1968. France also maintained an independent foreign policy marked by its withdrawal from NATO's unified command in 1966 and its recognition, over the strong objections of the United States, of the Communist government in China.

Economic Struggles

France's economy in the 1950s and 1960s made significant strides from the serious economic difficulties it faced at the end of the war. In 1945, five million men returned home from Germany and needed jobs, the transport system was shattered during the heavy fighting in the last year of the war, and the country had limited supplies of coal and food. This dire situation favored the **French Communist Party**, which had a good wartime resistance record (although it only turned against the German occupiers following the invasion of the Soviet Union in 1941) and appeared to offer answers to these economic problems. Although the Communists were part of the first postwar coalition government, they were pushed out of the coalition in 1947, in part with the support of the United States, which made it clear that economic assistance would not be forthcoming if the Communists remained in the government.

In that same year, France began the implementation of an economic program designed by **Jean Monnet**, who was also one of the founders of the European Community. The **Monnet Plan** established the Commissaritat General du Plan (CGP), which provided for nonpolitical technocrats to run the economy. With increased foreign investment and rational central planning, the French economy, which had traditionally lagged behind Germany and Great Britain, began to take off. This transformed life in France as newly prosperous consumers began to buy cars, televisions, and dishwashers. It also, however, created a sense that their unique way of life was being transformed by what its critics referred to as **Americanization**, embodied most directly by the newfound popularity of that most American of products, Coca-Cola.

By 1968, disenchantment among the young over what they considered to be the sterile course of French life, as well as anger over classrooms, laboratories, and libraries that were bursting at the seams as more students pursued higher education, led to student revolts at every major French university, with the most serious situation taking place in Paris. In May of that year, students forged an alliance with workers, but this soon petered out as the students' demand for a thorough reordering of French society clashed with the more limited demands of the workers for wage increases and better working conditions. Although de Gaulle survived this crisis, in the next year he resigned.

France continued to be led by members of the Gaullist party until the electoral victory in 1981 of Socialist leader **François Mitterrand**, the longest-serving president of France. A moderate within his party, Mitterrand focused on social reform programs and reducing unemployment rather than radical plans for the socialization of the French economy. Mitterrand, who was reelected in 1988, retired from politics in 1995 and was replaced in office by **Jacques Chirac**, the Gaullist mayor of Paris.

Chirac served two full terms as president of France for a total of twelve years, the second longest tenure in the job after Mitterand. He ran on a platform committed to healing social ills (such as racism and labor strikes), providing tax cuts, and instituting job programs. Unfortunately, social unrest grew in his second term with some of the worst rioting seen in France since the late 1960s. Chirac also came under fire during his presidency for several instances of corruption that took place while he was mayor of Paris and for general wastefulness in spending, particularly where his own palace services were concerned.

Conservative **Nicolas Sarkozy** succeeded Chirac in May of 2007, winning a runoff against Socialist Segolene Royal. He vowed to implement a controlled immigration policy and an ambitious development plan to modernize the country. After Sarkozy, Francois Hollande of the Socialist party took office in 2012 and serves as president still today.

Italy

The fall of Mussolini's government in 1943 presaged a violent civil war that lasted until the end of the Second World War. Because the Italian monarchy was tainted by its association with the Fascists, a referendum in 1946 led to the establishment of a republic. The **Christian Democrats** became the party of government, dominating political life in Italy until the 1990s. In Italy, unlike the rest of Western Europe, the Communists remained a significant opposition party. In part, this was due to the influence of **Antonio Gramsci** (1891–1937), one of the founders of the Italian Communist party, whose writings encouraged a measure of political flexibility that was certainly not found within the more doctrinaire French Communist Party.

Italy made outstanding economic progress in the 1950s and 1960s, to the point that it was referred to as the "**economic miracle**." In part, this was achieved through the large role played by the state in the Italian economy through the **Institute for Industrial Reconstruction** (IRI), which was created in 1931 during the Fascist years. The IRI controlled shipbuilding, airlines, metallurgy, and the chemical industry, with the automaker Fiat being the only large manufacturer to remain in private hands.

Italy benefited from its early commitment to the Common Market, as well as from the cheap labor supply provided by the 6 million southern Italians who moved to the north in the 1960s. Attempts were made to address the longstanding poverty of the south, with an interest in the "**southern question**" emerging as a peculiar byproduct of Mussolini's exile of political opponents to the south. This meant that a number of postwar Italian political leaders had a firsthand acquaintance with the economic plight of that region. Land reform broke up the large estates, and money was pumped into the region through a series of five-year plans, but to this day, there is a significant economic gap between north and south.

By the 1970s, economic problems were increasing, including high unemployment, inflation, and the loss of a staggering number of workdays to strikes. The Christian Democrats limped on as the party in power, in part because despite their own failings, there was seemingly no other option. A revival of the mafia took place in the south, while political terrorism from the extreme left led to frequent attacks on politicians, judges, and business leaders. The most brazen of these terrorist attacks took place in 1978 when the **Red Brigade** kidnapped former Prime Minster Aldo Moro and eventually murdered him when the government refused to negotiate his release.

Although Italy remains politically stable, frequent changes of government remain a part of the political landscape as do charges of corruption, which after years of being ignored, shook the Christian Democratic Party in the late 1990s. In 2006, questions regarding corruption led to the defeat of Prime Minister **Silvio Berlusconi**, a conservative media magnate who controls most of the major media outlets in Italy outside of government control. **Romano Prodi** of the Olive Tree party became prime minister in May of 2006, his second time assuming the position (first was in 1996). Since then Italy has had as prime minister Berlusconi again (2008-2011), Mario Monti (2011-2013), Enrico Letta (2013-2014), and Matteo Renzi (current).

Germany

The first years after the war were extremely difficult in Germany, as the nation dealt with the sheer magnitude of its defeat and the incredible destruction from the war; in 1947, industrial production was still only half the prewar level. Adding to the problems was the reality that if there was one place in Europe where Cold War tensions could flare up into actual fighting, then that location was **Berlin**, a city that was divided, like the country at large, into four occupation zones.

A series of crises would periodically flare up over the divided city, the first taking place in June 1948, when the United States and Britain introduced a new currency into their occupation zones without seeking Soviet approval. Stalin retaliated by **blockading** the city of Berlin, completely cutting off the city from the west. Why Stalin took this step is not entirely clear, but perhaps he felt that this was a way to push for negotiations on the status of the city. An odd quirk from the negotiations at Potsdam was that, although there was no written agreement on access to Berlin by rail, road, or water, there were three officially designated air corridors. Seeing this as an opportunity, U.S. General Clay once again showed personal initiative and began to send supplies by air, with President Truman soon offering his full support. The **Berlin Airlift** went on for ten-and-a-half months and came to an end in May 1949, when Stalin lifted the blockade with no preconditions.

A Divided Country: East and West Germany

Seizing on the momentum achieved by the successful airlift, in 1949, the United States, Great Britain, and France agreed to combine their zones to create the **Federal Republic of Germany**, with the city of Bonn as its capital. The Soviet Union responded several months later and decreed that its zone in eastern Germany would become the Communist-dominated **German Democratic Republic**. Possible reunification was suggested by Stalin in a note he sent in 1952 to the West German government, in which he implied that Germany could be reunified and exist as an unarmed and neutral state. There has been a historical debate over how sincere Stalin was in his offer, though he may have been willing to allow for German unification because he desperately wanted to forestall West German rearmament. In any event, the offer was rejected, and West Germany rearmed and entered NATO in 1955.

Germany would remain at the center of the Cold War, with the city of Berlin as the critical hotspot. In 1958, Soviet Premier Nikita Khrushchev gave an ultimatum to the West saying that they could stay six months and then had to pull out all their troops and allow Berlin to become a free city with access controlled by East Germany. President Eisenhower refused to budge and made it clear that he would launch another Berlin airlift if necessary.

The Building of the Berlin Wall

The next stage in the conflict over Berlin began at the ungodly hour of 2:00 A.M. on August 13, 1961, when East German border police began to string a barbed-wire barrier between East and West Berlin. This was followed over the next several days by the building of a concrete barrier, the infamous **Berlin Wall**. For the East German Communists, this was deemed to be necessary because they were suffering a serious brain drain as the educated elite were leaving the country in droves, with more than 2.5 million having passed to West Germany by 1949.

The reaction of the Western Allies was fairly mild, because putting up the wall did not impact what the West thought was essential to its Berlin policy: the presence of Western troops, free access to the city, and political self-determination for West Berliners. Kennedy's critics said he should have done something when the barrier was just barbed wire, but short of war, there was little to be done. As proof that there may be something to the old adage "Good fences make good neighbors," the building of the Berlin Wall proved beneficial, in that it meant that the constant crises over Berlin would now come to an end with the acceptance by both sides of a divided city.

Political, Social, and Economic Reforms

The early years in the history of the Federal Republic of Germany were dominated by **Konrad Adenauer**, who served as chancellor from 1949 to 1963 as the head of the **Christian Democratic Union** party. Adenauer, an anti-Nazi German conservative who had been mayor of Cologne in the Weimar Republic, greatly feared the Soviet Union and therefore preferred to see a West German state tied to the West rather than a unified Germany that was forced into neutrality. Adenauer's government also attempted to address the terrible crimes committed by the Germans during the Nazi period by paying compensation to Jewish victims of the Holocaust as well as making direct payments to the state of Israel.

Adenauer's government also ushered in a period of economic growth, aided in the immediate postwar years by the influx of millions of Germans who had fled west from Poland, Czechoslovakia, and East Germany. In the most dramatic example of a **postwar economic miracle**, the West German economy grew from $23 billion in 1950 to $103 billion in 1964. Equally significant, this newfound prosperity trickled down through the population so that workers experienced increased wages from higher productivity, which they used on hitherto-unimagined luxuries like new cars and foreign vacations. The main government architect of this economic boom, which was notably achieved without high inflation, was **Gerhard Ritter**, Adenauer's minister of economics and chancellor following Adenauer's retirement in 1961.

During the Adenauer/Ritter years, the **Social Democrats** looked like they were going to remain in a position of permanent opposition. Electoral success arrived through a combination of two elements: dropping the Marxist language of class struggle, which the party did in 1955, and the emergence of the charismatic **Willy Brandt** as the leader of the party. Brandt, who rose to national prominence as mayor of Berlin, became chancellor in 1969, the first time a Socialist led a German government since 1930.

Although remaining firmly tied to the West, Brandt felt it necessary to reach out to the Soviets and their satellite states in Eastern Europe. This policy of contact, known as *Ostpolitik*, led to the signing of treaties with the Soviet Union, Poland, and Czechoslovakia and provided for de facto recognition of the East German state. In a famous display of national contrition, Brandt, on a visit to Poland in 1970, knelt before a monument to those who fell during the Warsaw Ghetto Uprising. Despite the international acclaim that he received, including the awarding of a Nobel Prize in 1972, the end of Brandt's term as chancellor occurred swiftly in 1974, when a member of his staff was arrested as an East German spy.

Brandt's successor as chancellor was **Helmut Schmidt**, who despite having to face economic problems stemming from the oil crisis of 1973 was still able to lead the Social Democrats to an electoral victory in 1976. As in Great Britain and the United States, the early 1980s seemed to represent a surge in conservative politics, and in 1982, the CDU achieved an electoral comeback under **Helmut Kohl**.

German Reunification

It was Kohl, however, who would move with speed and determination to bring about **German reunification in 1990**. He also worked with French President Francois Mitterand to promote the Maastricht Treaty which created the European Union. Kohl's tenure as chancellor of Germany, at sixteen years, was longer than that of any German chancellor since Otto von Bismarck. The aura surrounding him eventually wore off amid continuing problems in the newly reunified Germany, including high unemployment. In 1998, the German electorate turned once again to the Social Democrats under the leadership of **Gerhard Schröder**.

Schröder had promised more jobs during the 1998 election, and during his first term, unemployment did go down, only to rise back up to the level he had inherited from Kohl and later to a record-breaking level. After narrowly winning reelection in 2002, in large part because of his strong opposition to the looming U.S.-led invasion of Iraq, Schröder introduced several reforms that many perceived as a dismantlement of the welfare state. These reforms were very unpopular with the core constituency of the Social Democrats. In July of 2005, Schröder intentionally lost a vote of confidence in the Bundestag (German Parliament), paving the way for early elections in September of that year.

Angela Merkel of the CDU became the first female chancellor of Germany in November of 2005 after striking a coalition deal with the Social Democrats. This deal was brought about by the extremely close election in September of that same year whereby no party received a majority of seats in the Bundestag. So far, the German economy under Merkel is booming and her approval rating is high. As any politician will tell you, however, what goes up can just as easily come down. Time will tell how successful Germany is in dealing with its tough domestic issues.

THE COLLAPSE OF THE COMMUNIST BLOC

Having suffered two foreign invasions in the twentieth century, the Soviet Union set as its priority the establishment of a system of satellite states in Eastern Europe. The Soviet Union created the Warsaw Pact in 1955 to establish military ties with its satellite states and the COMENCON to link their economies. From the start, however, there was tension.

East Germany and the Berlin Wall

In 1953, East German workers went to the streets first to criticize the government's plan to increase productivity, then later to demand greater political freedom. By 1961, life was so grim in East Germany that millions of individuals fled to the West, which led the Soviets to construct the **Berlin Wall**.

> **Reform in Hungary**
>
> In 1956, similar strikes in Poland set off an even more important movement for change in Hungary, where reform-minded Communists led by Imre Nagy took the helm of government and began a liberalizing process. The Hungarians wanted to create a multiparty system, pull themselves out of the Warsaw Pact, and reestablish Hungary as a neutral nation. By late 1956, the Soviets grew tired of such demands, which threatened the whole system of satellite states, and crushed the reform movement, killing thousands along the way.

Power Struggles in the Soviet Union

Within the Soviet Union, significant developments followed the death of Stalin in 1953. The winner of the power struggle for his replacement was **Nikita Khrushchev** (1894–1971), who, in a significant reversal from the previous regime, did not execute the losers in this political contest. At the Communist Party's twentieth national congress in 1956, Khrushchev, standing before a secret session, made a speech in which he attacked the many crimes of Stalin. Khrushchev claimed that Stalin's government had deviated from the political program of Marxist-Leninism, rather than being a natural outgrowth of it, and that the only reforms that would be acceptable would be those that stayed within the guidelines offered by Marxist-Leninism. Although Khrushchev made a successful visit to the United States in 1959, tensions between the two nations were heightened in the following year when the Soviet Union shot down an American U-2 spy plane over Russia. By October 1962, the two nuclear superpowers nearly went to war when the Soviets placed missiles in Cuba. President Kennedy's skillful handling of the crisis, however, allowed both nations to avoid the specter of a nuclear nightmare.

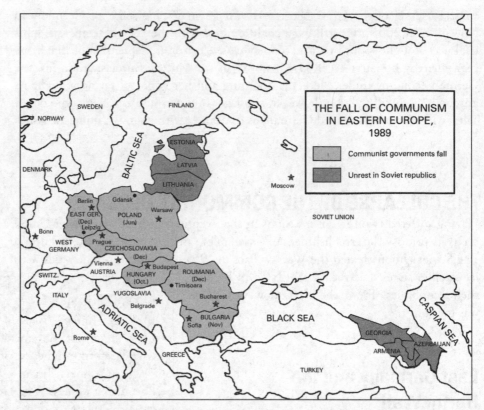

THE FALL OF COMMUNISM
IN EASTERN EUROPE,
1989

Communist governments fall

Unrest in Soviet republics

The Fall of Communism in Eastern Europe

The relative liberalization of the Khrushchev years came to an end with his forced retirement in 1964. His successor, Leonid Brezhnev (1906–1982), did not reinstate the terror of the Stalin years, but he did seek to once again strengthen the role of the party bureaucracy and the KGB and encouraged the further clampdown on reform in the satellite states.

By 1968, disaffection with this step backward led to the emergence of a reform movement in Czechoslovakia. The goal of this "**Prague Spring**" was to bring about a more humanistic socialism within certain limits, such as keeping the nation within the Soviet Bloc. Brezhnev still saw this as a threat to the entire Warsaw Pact and initiated what became known as the "**Brezhnev Doctrine**," declaring that the Soviet Union would support with all the means at its disposal (including military intervention) any established communist state in Eastern Europe that was threatened by internal strife. The reform movement was crushed and its leader, Alexander Dubček, was replaced by someone more to Brezhnev's liking.

Reform in Poland and Eastern Europe

The most significant challenge to the Brezhnev Doctrine came in Poland, a land whose people were deeply stirred when in 1978 Karol Wojtyla, a Polish Cardinal, was elected **Pope John Paul II**. Two years later, led by Lech Walesa, an electrician, a massive strike took place at the Lenin shipyard in Gdansk, where workers demanded the right to form an independent trade union. **Solidarity**, as the new union was called, survived the declaration of martial law and being outlawed by going underground, in part with the aid of the Catholic Church. By 1989, the Polish economy was in such a shambles that the government was forced to negotiate with Walesa and his union. Surprisingly, the negotiations resulted in the promise for multiparty elections, which, when they took place in that same year, resulted in the defeat of all Communist candidates.

When the reform-minded **Mikhail Gorbachev** (b. 1931) took charge of the Kremlin, he indicated his opposition to the "Brezhnev Doctrine." With reform looming overhead, 1989 proved to be one of the most remarkable years of the century, as Communist-led regimes peacefully collapsed in Hungary, Czechoslovakia, Bulgaria, and Albania. In East Germany, the collapse of the regime in that same year was followed in 1990 by the reunification of East and West Germany and the destruction of the Berlin Wall. Romania proved to be an exception to this peaceful transformation, as the violent dictator **Nicolae Ceausescu** (1918–1989) desperately tried to hold on to power. In the end, his government collapsed, and he and his wife, Elena, were executed on Christmas Day 1989.

The Collapse of the Soviet Union

As their satellite states underwent a complete political transformation, people within the Soviet Union expressed their desire for change. Disasters like the Soviet invasion of Afghanistan and the nuclear accident at Chernobyl revealed the deplorable state of affairs within the nation. Gorbachev wanted to limit the extent of this change; he accepted the need for *glasnost*, or openness in debate, as well as *perestroika*, an economic restructuring of the state, but he was no democrat and still wanted to see the Communist Party lead these reforms. Events, however, went beyond his control, and in 1990, the government was forced to allow the political participation of non-Communist parties. Nationalist movements throughout the Soviet Union also popped up, beginning with the declaration of independence by Lithuania, followed by the insistence of the Russian Republic, another Soviet state, that its laws superseded those of the Soviet Union.

By the end of 1990, Gorbachev appointed some hard-liners to government positions to make the prospect of future reform far less likely. Instead, the whole system collapsed. In part, this was the result of the rivalry between Gorbachev and **Boris Yeltsin** (1931–2007), who served as chairman of the Russian Parliament. In August 1991, hard-line communists decided that Gorbachev's policies were threatening the existence of the Communist Party and staged a coup while Gorbachev was on vacation, placing him under arrest in his Crimean home. This turned out to be the last gasp of the Soviet Union, as Yeltsin bravely defied the plotters when he stood on a tank outside the parliament building and led the resistance.

The coup failed and with it any hope of preserving Communist control. One by one, the assorted republics left the Soviet Union, and by the end of 1991, the Soviet Union was dissolved; soon after, Gorbachev resigned.

A New Russian Republic

In 1991, Yeltsin was elected president of the newly created Russian Federation with 57 percent of the vote amid heightened expectations among Russians following the end of the Soviet Union. Sadly, when he resigned from office in 1999, Yeltsin acknowledged that his time in office was a lost opportunity, and in his resignation speech, he went so far as to say to his nation, "I want to ask you for forgiveness, because many of our dreams have not been realized."

Beginning his first term in office, Yeltsin decided to move the economy rapidly from centralized state control to free-market capitalism, a policy strongly advocated by many foreign economists, including advisors from the International Monetary Fund. This policy, which supporters and skeptics both referred to as "shock treatment," was based on significant short-term economic dislocation followed by greater economic stability and expansion. Unfortunately, the pain proved even harsher than expected and was marked by the transfer of state assets to a handful of well-placed oligarchs and hyperinflation, which created turmoil for millions of Russians who depended on fixed state pensions. Official corruption and the emergence of vast mafia-style criminal organizations also became mainstays of the new Russian state and greatly contributed to a diminishment of Yeltsin's popularity.

The transition to political democracy was equally troubled. Conflict with the Congress of People's Deputies (the Parliament of the Russian Federation) over his economic policies brought about a series of confrontations with Parliament, leading to a serious crisis in October 1993 when the Congress began impeachment proceedings against the president. Yeltsin responded by ordering tanks to shell the building where the Congress met and ordered the legislature to be dissolved. Without a recalcitrant parliament to block his plans, Yeltsin was able to impose a new constitution providing enhanced power for the presidency and the establishment of the **Duma**, a new parliamentary body.

In 1996, Yeltsin surprised many Kremlin observers by running for reelection, despite having suffered several strokes and also having appeared drunk on public occasions. When his reelection seemed about to be derailed by a growing electoral threat from a resurgent Communist Party, Yeltsin turned to the business oligarchs who agreed to fund a lavish campaign for him in exchange for greater access to the remaining state assets, although the oligarchs were also fearful that the election of a Communist government would hinder their economic activities. Yeltsin comfortably won reelection, but except for working out a peace treaty that brought a brief end to the fighting with separatists in Chechnya, there were few other significant accomplishments during his second term.

Just prior to his resignation in December 1999, Yeltsin chose the relatively unknown Vladimir Putin as his prime minister. A former officer in the KGB, one of Putin's first acts upon assuming the presidency was to protect Yeltsin and his family from prosecution for corruption. Because other possible presidential candidates were surprised by the rapid promotion of Putin and the resignation of Yeltsin, Putin had a tremendous political advantage over his rivals and was easily elected to his own term as president in 2000.

In sharp contrast with Yeltsin, Putin has garnered significant popular support among Russians and he would have been easily reelected in 2004 even without his control over most media outlets. Part of his popularity stemmed from a rise in worldwide oil prices, which provided a huge boost to the Russian economy, although once again, Russia is in danger of repeating the Soviet mistake of the 1970s when it became too dependent on the proceeds from this one commodity.

Many Russians also embraced Putin's attempt to restore Russia to a higher place on the world stage. After a sharp military decline in the 1990s, Putin sought to restore Russia's military might, principally to ensure regional dominance. He has also at times made use of the sort of rhetoric denouncing the West that has not been used since the Cold War and ordered the resumption of regular patrols of strategic bombers, which were suspended in 1991.

In 2008, Putin was replaced as president by Dmitry Medvedev, a businessman and a young independent, widely regarded as Putin's puppet. Putin then moved to take the office of prime minister. In 2012, they swapped and currently Putin is back as president of Russia while Medvedev is the Prime Minister.

Democracy Under the Putin Presidency

Democracy, which never truly thrived under Yeltsin, has received further blows during Putin's presidency, such as in the aftermath of the Beslan massacre of September 2004, when Chechen terrorists seized control of a school leading to the death of more than three hundred hostages. The tragedy was used by Putin as an excuse for enacting a law that ended the practice of popular elections for governors in Russia's provinces, with the spurious claim that it would be more efficient to fight terror with a more centralized government. The suspicious deaths of several Russian journalists and the poisoning in London of former spy and Putin critic Alexander Litvinenko has further chilled the political climate in Russia.

Ethnic Warfare in the Former Yugoslavia

Uncertainty has been the hallmark of the former Yugoslavia. Its former leader, Josip Tito (1892–1980), led a successful resistance force against the Germans during the Second World War and after the war helped establish a Yugoslav state that avoided being tied to the Soviet Bloc. His strong leadership limited the intense ethnic rivalries within the country, but after he died in 1980, Slovenia and Croatia broke away from Yugoslavia to create their own states.

In 1992, a majority of the Muslim and Croat populations living in the Yugoslavian province of Bosnia wanted to follow suit. Bosnia's Serbs, however, refused to allow themselves to become part of a Bosnian state in which they would be a minority, and with the help of Yugoslavian President **Slobodan Milošević**, they carried out "**ethnic cleansing**," the forced removal, and, at times, genocidal murder, of Muslims and ethnic Bosnians in certain regions under their control. One of the last great atrocities of a century that has known so many was the Serb shelling of the Bosnian capital of Sarejevo, particularly the firing of shells on market days, when more people would be out on the streets. Such horrors led to the American-brokered **Dayton Accords** of 1995, which provided for a precarious peace for a time.

The next stage of the conflict in the Balkans centered on the Yugoslav province of **Kosovo**, a territory that the Serbs saw as the cradle of their national identity, stemming from their defeat in the Battle of Kosovo against the Ottoman Turks in 1389. In 1998, Milošević ordered an assault on Kosovo, using as his justification the attacks made on Serbs living in the province by the Kosovo Liberation Army (K.L.A.), a small militant group that wanted to see the creation of an independent Kosovo. When the Serbs refused to sign a treaty that would have granted the Kosovars greater autonomy, NATO in March 1999 launched an aerial bombardment on Serbia that lasted for 74 days. This was the first offensive action taken by NATO against a sovereign nation in the alliance's history and resulted in the withdrawal of Serbian troops from Kosovo.

For Milošević, this was the beginning of the end of his dominance over Yugoslavian politics. In 2000, he was forced to call new elections, which he lost to Vojislav Kostunica. While Milošević was reluctant to turn over the reins of government to Kostunica, his hand was forced when hundreds of thousands of Serbs went into the street to demand he honor the election results. Though initially President Kostunica said that he would not turn Milošević over to the **War Crimes Tribunal** in The Hague, he changed his mind in 2001 in order to receive badly needed economic assistance from the West—though the point wound up being moot when Milošević died of a heart attack while his trial was still ongoing in 2006.

In February 2007, the United Nations International Court of Justice (ICJ) found that there was no evidence linking Serbia under the rule of Slobodan Milošević to genocide and war crimes committed in the Bosnian War. However, the court did find that Milošević and others in Serbia did not do enough to prevent acts of genocide from occurring. Still today there is widespread disagreement and controversy over whether what occurred in this era was ethnic cleansing or genocide, or whether there is a significant difference between the two, and the ruling bodies (the International Criminal Tribunal of the Former Yugoslavia and the International Court of Justice) and courts have prosecuted numerous people involved in the warfare.

In January 2009 the European Parliament passed a resolution to commemorate July 11th as a day of remembrance and mourning of the 1995 Srebrenica genocide. That incident was a July 1995 killing of more than 8,000 Muslim men and boys and forcible deportation of nearly 25,000 women, children and elderly.

CHAPTER 7 TIMELINE

Year(s)	Event
1914	Assassination of Franz Ferninand (June 28)
1914	Austria-Hungary issues ultimatum to Serbia (July 23)
1914	Austria-Hungary declares war on Serbia (July 28)
1914	Russia begins mobilization (July 29)
1914	Germany declares war on Russia (August 1)
1914	Germany declares war on France (August 3)
1914	Germans defeat Russians at Tannenberg (August 26–30)
1914	First Battle of the Marne (September 5–10)
1914	Completion of the Panama Canal
1915	Gallipoli campaign begins (April 25)
1915	Sinking of the *Lusitania* (May 7)
1915	Germans begin attack on Verdun (February 21)
1916	British launch attack at the Somme (July 1)
1917	Zimmermann Telegram (January 19)
1917	Germany resumes unrestricted submarine warfare (February 1)
1917	Bolsheviks sign armistice with Germany (December 3)
1917	United States declares war on Germany (April 6)
1917	Provisional Government established in Russia (February)
1917	Bolshevik seizure of power (November)
1918	Worldwide influenza outbreak
1918	Female suffrage begins in Great Britain
1918	Germany Republic established after abdication of Kaiser Wilhelm II (November 10)
1918	Armistice brings the war to a close

1919	Treaty of Versailles
1919	Mussolini organizes first Fascist party
1919	Weimar Constitution established
1920	Formation of Communist International
1922	Mussolini becomes Prime Minister of Italy
1923	German hyperinflation
1923	Beer Hall Putsch
1924	Death of Lenin
1924	Dawes Plan
1925	Treaty of Lucarno
1928	First Soviet Five-Year Plan
1929	Beginning of collectivized farms in Soviet Union
1929	Lateran Accord between Mussolini and the Catholic Church
1929	Young Plan
1929	Stock market crash
1930	Nazis make huge electoral gains
1931	Bank failures
1932	Hindenburg defeats Hitler for the German presidency
1932	Nazis become largest party in Reichstag
1933	Hitler becomes Chancellor
1933	Reichstag fire
1933	Enabling Act
1933	Germany withdraws from League of Nations
1933	German boycott of Jewish businesses
1934	Beginning of the Great Terror in the Soviet Union

1934	Night of the Long Knives
1934	Hitler becomes Führer after death of Hindenburg
1935	Germany openly begins rearmament
1935	Italian invasion of Ethiopia
1935	Nuremberg Laws directed against German Jews
1936	Berlin Olympics
1936	German remilitarization of the Rhineland
1936	Beginning of the Spanish Civil War
1938	Germany absorbs Austria in Anschluss
1938	Munich Agreement leads to dismemberment of Czechoslovakia
1938	Kristallnacht (November 9)
1939	Nazi-Soviet nonaggression pact
1939	Invasion of Poland
1939	Britain and France declare war on Germany
1940	Fall of France
1940	Winston Churchill replaces Chamberlain as Prime Minister
1940	Battle of Britain (July–October)
1940	Germans begin Blitz on British cities (September to May 1941)
1941	Germany launches Operation Barbarossa
1941	Japanese attack on Pearl Harbor
1941	30,000 Jews killed at Babi Yar over two days
1941	Atlantic Charter
1942	German advance stopped at Stalingrad
1942	Battle of Midway (June)
1942	Wansee Conference organizes the Final Solution

1943	Battle of Kursk
1943	Allies land in Italy
1943	Mussolini's government fails
1943	Warsaw ghetto uprising
1944	Percentages Agreement between Churchill and Stalin
1944	D-Day
1944	Germans launch Battle of the Bulge (December 16)
1945	Yalta Conference (February 4–11)
1945	Hitler commits suicide (April 30)
1945	V-E Day (May 8)
1945	Victory of British Labour Party over Conservatives (July)
1945	Potsdam Conference (July 17–August 2)
1945	Atomic bomb dropped on Hiroshima (August 6)
1945	V-J Day (August 14)
1945	United Nations' charter is ratified (October)
1945	Nuremberg Trials for crimes against humanity begin (November)
1946	Establishment of French Fourth Republic
1946	Referendum establishes the Italian Republic
1946	Churchill delivers Iron Curtain speech at Westminster College
1947	George Kennan writes the "Long Telegram"
1947	Truman Doctrine
1947	Introduction of the Marshall Plan
1947	India and Pakistan become independent states
1948	Break between the Soviet Union and Yugoslavia
1948	Establishment of the State of Israel

1948	National Health Service established in Great Britain
1948	Soviet dominance in Eastern Europe solidified
1949	Formation of NATO
1949	Berlin Airlift leads to ending blockade after 11 months
1949	Establishment of the Federal Republic of Germany
1949	Establishment of Democratic Republic of Germany
1951	Establishment of the European Coal and Steel Community
1953	Death of Stalin
1954	French suffer defeat in Indochina
1954	Algerian revolt begins
1955	Establishment of the Warsaw Pact
1956	Soviets send in troops to put down Hungarian uprising
1957	Ghana declares its independence from Great Britain
1957	Signing of the Treaty of Rome establishing the EEC
1958	French plebiscite leads to creation of the Fifth Republic
1961	East Germany begins construction of the wall dividing Berlin
1962	France vetoes Britain's attempt to join the European Community
1962	Cuban missile crisis
1968	Wave of student protests in Europe and the United States
1968	Prague Spring
1969	Willy Brandt becomes German Chancellor
1972	Irish Troubles begin with the shooting of 13 Catholic peace marchers on "Bloody Sunday"
1973	Oil crisis
1978	Red Brigades kidnap and murder former Prime Minister Aldo Moro

1978	Papal election of John Paul II
1979	Margaret Thatcher becomes prime minister
1981	Francois Mitterand elected president of France
1985	Mikhail Gorbachev becomes leader of the Soviet Union
1989	End of Communist rule in Eastern Europe
1990	Reunification of Germany
1991	End of Soviet Union Boris Yeltsin elected president of newly created Russian Federation
1992	Maastricht Treaty
1992	Beginning of a series of violent conflicts in the former Yugoslavia
1997	Tony Blair becomes prime minister of Great Britain and Northern Ireland
1999	Vladimir Putin becomes president of Russian Federation
2002	Introduction of the euro
2004	Entry into NATO of former Warsaw Pact nations
2008	Dmitry Medvedev becomes president of Russian Federation (Putin becomes prime minister)
2010	David Cameron becomes prime minister of Great Britain and Northern Ireland
2012	Medvedev and Putin switch positions; Medvedev becomes prime minister and Putin becomes president

CHAPTER 7 REVIEW QUESTIONS

Try these questions to assess how well you understood and retained the information covered in the chapter. Answers and explanations are in Chapter 8.

1. During the first years of the Great Depression, governments responded to the economic crisis by

   (A) supporting the economic ideas of John Maynard Keynes
   (B) launching major public works projects
   (C) committing their countries to a laissez-faire economic policy
   (D) reducing their expenditures in order to balance their budgets

2. Mussolini attempted to improve the relationship between the Italian state and the Catholic Church by

   (A) mandating that all Italians attend mass
   (B) placing loyal Fascists in key clerical positions
   (C) emphasizing his own path towards religious belief
   (D) signing the Lateran Treaty, which resolved some of the longstanding issues between the Church and the Italian state

3. The British won a major propaganda victory at the start of the First World war because of

   (A) the sinking of the *Lusitania*
   (B) the Zimmerman Telegram
   (C) German atrocities in Belgium
   (D) the destruction by the Germans of major Parisian landmarks

4. The term "popular fronts" refers to the idea of

   (A) political parties of the center and the left working together to block the triumph of Fascism
   (B) Communism uniting with unions to oppose bourgeois governments
   (C) the elimination of class conflict
   (D) using German and Italian forces to support Spanish nationalists

5. The Nuremberg Trials of 1945–1946 were the first tests in international law of the concept of

   (A) collective guilt
   (B) the natural rights of victims
   (C) crimes against humanity
   (D) genocide

6. The Matignon Agreement in France (1936)

   (A) failed to lead to the forty-hour work week
   (B) provided the legal right for unions to organize and strike
   (C) led to the end of the Popular Front government
   (D) ended the informal practice of owner-employee cooperation stemming from the Great War

7. The British government had an impact on private life during the First World War in all of the following ways EXCEPT

   (A) the regulation of pub hours
   (B) rationing
   (C) conscription
   (D) billeting of soldiers in civilian residences

8. The Atlantic Charter was the founding document behind what entity?

   (A) The International Monetary Fund
   (B) The World Court
   (C) The European Union
   (D) The United Nations

9. The Percentages Agreement signed between Stalin and Churchill dealt with

   (A) Yugoslavia's future under Tito
   (B) the political future of Poland
   (C) spheres of influence in Eastern Europe
   (D) the question of postwar reparations

10. The Truman Doctrine came about as a direct result of

    (A) remaining issues from the Potsdam conference
    (B) the presence of Soviet troops in Poland
    (C) the issue of the status of Berlin
    (D) Britain's withdrawal from Greece

11. During the "Prague Spring" of 1968, Czechoslovakia attempted to

(A) break completely free from the influence of the Soviet Union
(B) end military links with the Warsaw Pact nations
(C) introduce a capitalist economy
(D) allow greater personal liberties

12. The German "economic miracle" was in part due to

(A) socialization of the means of production
(B) a labor force enlarged by Germans fleeing from the east
(C) a high degree of central planning
(D) limiting overseas investment

13. All of the following are true concerning the student revolts in Paris in 1968 EXCEPT

(A) they involved student organizations with differing ideological agendas
(B) they stemmed from overcrowding in French universities
(C) they helped spark a general strike by French workers
(D) they caused the fall of Charles de Gaulle's government

14. Mikhail Gorbachev's *perestroika* program

(A) ended the practice of central economic planning
(B) failed to improve the average Russian's standard of living
(C) provided the economic foundation for improved foreign ties with the West
(D) focused on heavy industry at the expense of consumer products

REFLECT

- For which content topics discussed in this chapter do you feel you have achieved sufficient mastery to answer multiple-choice questions correctly?

- For which content topics discussed in this chapter do you feel you have achieved sufficient mastery to discuss effectively in an essay or short answer?

- For which content topics discussed in this chapter do you feel you need more work before you can answer multiple-choice questions correctly?

- For which content topics discussed in this chapter do you feel you need more work before you can discuss effectively in an essay or short answer?

- What parts of this chapter are you going to re-review?

- Will you seek further help outside of this book (such as a teacher, tutor, or AP Students) on any of the content in this chapter—and, if so, on what content?

Chapter 8
Chapter Review Questions: Answers and Explanations

CHAPTER 4 REVIEW QUESTIONS

1. **B**   While medieval scholars read secondhand commentaries on ancient works, the humanists, inspired by the example of Petrarch, sought out the manuscripts in their original form. The other choices are closely associated with the humanists, so they cannot be correct.

2. **D**   Renaissance artists rejected the practice of hierarchical scaling, in which the size of figures in a composition is proportionate to their spiritual significance, in favor of a greater emphasis on realism. For example, Leonardo, in his *Last Supper*, emphasized Christ's significance not by rendering him as larger than his disciples, but by placing him at the center of the painting.

3. **D**   Pope Leo X made the assumption that since Luther was an Augustinian monk and Tetzel, the main seller of indulgences, was a Dominican, the *95 Theses* were simply a typical squabble between religious orders. Leo had not counted on the fact that the printing press would enable Luther to reach an audience far beyond his native city of Wittenberg. The lack of a more determined response by the Catholic Church in the early stages of the Reformation played a major role in the successful spread of Luther's ideas.

4. **C**   Luther had very little interest in social issues and was furious when German peasants tied some of his theological ideas to certain social goals such as the elimination of serfdom. His lack of interest in challenging the existing social order encouraged some German rulers to support his religious ideas because they didn't pose a challenge to their primacy in the social hierarchy.

5. **D**   In 1559, one year after coming to the throne, Elizabeth worked out a religious settlement that led to a formal break with Rome and the creation of a Church of England that emphasized middle-of-the-road Protestant beliefs.

6. **D**   While many were surprised by his decision, the 42-year-old Luther's marriage to Katharina von Bora emphasized his refusal to accept the need for clerical celibacy. By marrying the 26-year-old former nun and having six children, Luther placed the family, rather than the institutional Church, at the center of religious faith.

7. **B**   The majority of Florence's population of 60,000 in the fifteenth century was involved in the most important commodity produced in Florence, wool cloth, which it exported to the rest of Europe.

8. **C**   In 1498, Vasco da Gama, a Portuguese captain, reached the coast of India.

9. **B**   The year 1492 marked the final stage of the *Reconquista*, the long struggle by the Christian states in the north of the Spanish peninsula against the Muslims. In that year, Grenada, the last Islamic outpost in Spain, fell to the armies of Ferdinand and Isabella.

10. **D**   Bankrolled by a French monarchy that wished to see its rivals the Habsburgs weakened, Gustavus Adolphus entered the conflict in part to seek territorial gains for Sweden along the Baltic coast, but also to defend Protestant interests in the Empire that had recently come under attack following the issuing of the Edict of Restitution.

CHAPTER 5 REVIEW QUESTIONS

1. **B** After becoming King of France in 1589, Henry IV, a Calvinist, found that he was unable to gain control over Paris due to the strong Catholic sentiments of the inhabitants of the city. Never one to take his religious beliefs all too seriously, Henry decided it would be expeditious to convert to Catholicism in order to control the French capital.

2. **A** King Charles was able to rule without calling a Parliament so long as he kept his expenditures to a minimum. This proved to be impossible in 1640, when a rebellion broke out in Scotland following Charles's insistence on placing the *Book of Common Prayer* in Scottish churches. In order to raise an army to put down the rebellious Scots, Charles was forced to call his first Parliament in eleven years.

3. **D** While urban riots stemmed from a variety of causes, those disturbances that saw the extensive participation of journeymen and apprentices were often tied to their growing frustration over a glass ceiling that now limited their opportunities. With the guild method of production being replaced by large-scale production featuring capitalist entrepreneurs, the economically hard-pressed guilds were increasingly reluctant to see further competition and therefore limited the number of entrants into the ranks of guild master.

4. **A** While both rich and poor families in the early modern period can be viewed as an economic unit, there were significant gender differences within this unit. While men served in the "public" sphere, such as working the family's plot of land or handling commercial transactions, women were expected to remain exclusively tied to the "domestic" sphere by either doing the housework themselves or, if wealthier, supervising such activities.

5. **D** Medieval science consisted of a synthesis of Christian theology and classical authors. The Scientific Revolution would bring about a rejection of this synthesis in favor of a new brand of science in which the experimental method would predominate.

6. **D** In his *Concerning the Revolutions of the Celestial Spheres*, Copernicus hypothesized that the planets moved around the sun in perfect circles. It was Johannes Kepler, however, who was the first to explain that the planets moved in an elliptical orbit around the sun.

7. **A** After viewing the horrors of the English Revolution, Thomas Hobbes wrote *Leviathan* to show that men were naturally depraved and therefore required an absolutist state in order to rein in their evil passions.

8. **D** Women played an important role in the Enlightenment by sponsoring salons, where *philosophes* could speak on an informal basis with the elite of society.

9. **C** Deists such as Voltaire believe that God created the world but plays no additional role in overseeing his creation. Science must therefore be used to explain the workings of the universe.

10. **C** As surprising as it may seem, prior to the eighteenth century, children were viewed simply as smaller versions of adults (something that is quite apparent when looking at medieval images of Mary holding an infant Christ looking like an adult in miniature). The change in this perception owes a great deal to Rousseau's *Émile* and his description of three distinct stages on the road to adulthood: infancy, childhood, and adolescence.

11. **C** Angered by a 1791 report to the French Revolutionary government that stated women should receive an education geared only toward their domestic duties, Mary Wollstonecraft wrote her *Vindication of the Rights of Women* to support the French thinker Olympe de Gouges's *Declaration of the Rights of Women*, a document which the French Republican government had rejected.

12. **A** The members of the Third Estate realized that if voting was done by estate they would consistently be outvoted by the clergy and aristocracy. Therefore, they refused to show their credentials unless the King met all attendees of the Estates-General in a National Assembly, a new legislative body where there would be no further distinctions based on social class.

13. **B** The Bastille was traditionally the place where prisoners of conscience were kept for opposing the Bourbon monarchy. By 1789, the year the prison was stormed, it no longer housed political prisoners. Nevertheless, it still stood as a symbol of royal repression.

14. **B** The march of the women of Paris on Versailles was one of the turning points of the French Revolution since the march ended with Louis XVI and his family returning to Paris with the women. Paris was far more radical than any other locality in France, and with the King now within the confines of the city, the revolution would advance much further than if the King had remained at Versailles.

15. **B** After realizing that he could not defeat the British navy, Napoleon decided to wage economic war on Britain through his Continental System, which closed the European continent to British imports and exports.

16. **D** The Napoleonic Code enshrined one of the fundamental ideas of the French Revolution: There were no special rights based on social class and therefore everyone was responsible for the payment of taxes.

17. **D** The *sans-culottes*, who proudly wore pants rather than the silk breeches of wealthier Parisians, were members of the working class and played a vital role in the growing radicalization of the French Revolution. It was support from the *sans-culottes* that allowed the Jacobins to push the Girondins out of the National Assembly and assume control over the Revolutionary government.

18. **A** While abhorring what he felt was the anarchism of the French Revolution, Baron von Stein recognized that there were new forces being introduced into Europe by the power of nationalism. To that end, von Stein directly challenged one of the key rights of the Prussian Junkers—their exclusive hold over the officer corps—by placing members of the bourgeoisie within their ranks.

CHAPTER 6 REVIEW QUESTIONS

1. **D** The Corn Laws introduced high tariffs for wheat imported into Great Britain. While the law was hailed by the landed classes, who wanted to keep foreign grain out of the country so they could have exclusive rights to the British market, it was hated by the middle-class manufacturers, who believed that expensive bread forced them to pay higher wages. Getting rid of the Corn Laws was a sign that the middle class, which had entered Parliament as a result of the Great Reform Bill of 1832, was now a force to be reckoned with in British politics.

2. **C** While the middle-class liberals viewed the revolution as a means to securing political rights, the more radical workers hoped that the revolution would provide increased economic opportunities. Their demands led to the creation of national workshops that provided jobs for unemployed workers, this over the objections of the liberals, who viewed the workshops as a costly and unnecessary intrusion by the government into the economy.

3. **B** The Chartists believed that annual parliamentary elections were necessary in order to create a government more responsive to the needs of the people. This was the one point within the Six Acts of the People's Charter that was never implemented. Today, the life of a British parliament is five years, thanks to a law enacted in 2011. Before then, it was the prime minister who in effect called for elections.

4. **C** Belgium, like Great Britain, was blessed with a ready supply of coal and iron, as well as a stable government and a ready supply of merchant capital. With these advantages, it was able to become the first industrialized nation on the continent.

5. **B** With the advent of the Franco–Prussian War in 1870, Napoleon III was forced to remove from Rome the French troops who were protecting the city on behalf of the papacy. Following this withdrawal, Italian troops entered the city, which became the new capital of the Italian state.

6. **D** Collecting firsthand testimony from adults who began their working lives as child laborers in factories and mines, the Sadler Committee brought child labor to the attention of the British public. The investigations of the committee would eventually lead to the passage of the Factory Act in 1833.

7. **B** The emancipation decree signed by Tsar Alexander II in 1861 required the newly emancipated serfs to pay for their freedom in annual payments extending over fifty years. This practice was brought to an end as part of a series of concessions by the monarchy in the aftermath of the Revolution of 1905.

8. **C** In the second half of the nineteenth century, governments throughout Europe began to develop postal systems, reflecting such factors as increased literacy through the expansion of public schools and the ability to move large quantities of letters through an ever-increasing rail network. This clear-cut expansion of the role of government is the direct opposite of (C), which posits that European governments were stepping away from providing such services and expected private concerns to pick up the task.

9. **B**   The middle class was important in the second half of the nineteenth century not because it was new, but because it was newly powerful, replacing traditional aristocracy as the group that shaped public opinion, set the historical record, and guided society's values.

10. **D**   "Informal empire" refers to when a nation controls the economy and politics of another nation or territory. Prior to the expansion of direct colonial control in the period after 1870, nations such as Britain sought to secure their trading privileges without feeling the need to step in directly and rule. The situation in China serves as the best description of informal empire, since Britain, France, Germany, and other nations insisted on certain economic rights without directly controlling the vast Chinese state.

11. **C**   While the other items on the list were all invented in the second half of the nineteenth century, the power loom was invented in 1785 by Edmund Cartwright and was one of the most important inventions of the Early Industrial Revolution, not the Second Industrial Revolution.

12. **A**   All of these writers are considered to be part of the realist tradition in literature. Realism was a movement in the nineteenth century that focused on depicting the relatively ordinary lives of the middle and working classes without relying on traditional embellishments such as the romanticization of their subject.

13. **B**   While establishing the rules that European states needed to follow to show their control over the various parts of Africa, the Conference was initially called to deal with the status of the Congo, a territory that King Leopold II of Belgium was seeking to control for economic exploitation through the formation of what would eventually be known as the Congo Free State.

14. **D**   Thomas Cook's career as a travel agent began when he came up with the idea of providing travel arrangements for a group of fellow temperance advocates who were in need of transportation to a rally. By the 1860s, Cook was selling group tours to destinations such as Egypt, Italy, France, and Switzerland and introduced packaged foreign travel to the British middle class.

CHAPTER 7 REVIEW QUESTIONS

1. **D** When the economic slowdown began, governments responded by following the standard economic theory of the day and reducing their expenditures in order to balance their budgets. Unfortunately, this had the unintended consequence of making the depression far worse, as declines in both governmental and individual consumption dramatically shrunk the global economy.

2. **D** In 1929, Mussolini, an agnostic, decided to heal the long-term rift between the papacy and the Italian state. With the Lateran Treaty, Mussolini allowed the pope to become the ruler of Vatican City, a district in the heart of Rome, in exchange for the Church's recognition of Mussolini's Fascist government.

3. **C** In the early stages of the war, German atrocities in neutral Belgium provided the British with a powerful propaganda tool both for domestic consumption as well as for the important task of swaying American public opinion.

4. **A** Popular front governments were created in France and Spain as a reaction to the triumph of Fascism in Germany. Politicians of the left in both nations viewed the conflict between Communists and Social Democrats in Germany as having provided an opportunity for the ascendency of Hitler.

5. **C** The term "crimes against humanity" was originally found in the preamble to the 1907 Hague Convention on War. At the conclusion of the Second World War, the Allied states formed an International Military Tribunal charged with prosecuting Nazi war criminals. One of the charges against the accused, "crimes against humanity," was the category used to cover the murder of millions of civilians by the Nazis.

6. **B** The Matignon Agreements, named after the hotel where the French government, employers, and the trade unions met and signed the accord, took place in the aftermath of a damaging general strike. The Agreements, the crowning achievement of Leon Blum's Popular Front government, for the first time provided a guarantee for French unions to organize and to strike.

7. **D** The First World War was not fought on British territory; the fighting took place entirely on continental Europe. Soldiers at home were housed in bases for training, and the British government had no way to require foreign citizens to house its soldiers.

8. **D** Meeting in July 1941 for the first time on a ship off the coast of Newfoundland, Roosevelt and Churchill issued a joint proclamation in which they declared that the struggle against the Axis powers was to "ensure life, liberty, independence, and religious freedom and to preserve the rights of man and justice." The Atlantic Charter served as the foundation for the later establishment of the United Nations, a central postwar goal for Roosevelt.

9. **C** On his own initiative, Churchill traveled to Moscow in October 1944 in an attempt to get Stalin to accept some sort of role for the Western Allies in Eastern Europe. The name of the agreement comes from the numbers that Churchill had scribbled on the piece of paper that he gave to Stalin, listing the various percentages of control that each of the Allies might expect to have in the postwar period.

10. **D** When the Second World War ended, Britain had 40,000 troops in Greece and was providing the military and financial support that allowed for the survival of the Greek government in its struggle with a Communist insurgency. Due to its own dire financial situation, Great Britain informed the United States that it would withdraw from Greece at the end of March 1947. To fill the void left by the British, Truman went before Congress and requested money for the Greeks, using the justification that the United States needed to support any nation that was trying to avoid subjugation by Communists. This later became known as the Truman Doctrine.

11. **D** In 1968, the "Prague Spring," a movement in Czechoslovakia that sought not to overturn the Socialist system, but simply to allow greater personal liberties such as freedom of the press, was brutally put down when the leader of the Soviet Union, Leonid Brezhnev, decided that the reform movement was a threat to Soviet dominance in Eastern Europe.

12. **B** Millions of Germans expelled from Poland and Czechoslovakia were joined by millions of other Germans fleeing from the approaching Red Army in a mass migration into what later became established as West Germany. These individuals were to provide the low wage (but relatively skilled) workforce, which later proved essential for the expansion of the German economy in the 1950s.

13. **D** While the mass protests that hit France in the wake of the student revolt of May 1968 shook the government of Charles de Gaulle to its core, the parliamentary elections that took place the following month, in which the Gaullists won 358 of 487 seats, showed that de Gaulle still maintained the support of the majority of Frenchmen.

14. **B** *Perestroika* was an attempt to redirect the Soviet economy toward meeting consumer demand, but it was to do so within the continuing structure of central planning. This inability to break away from the limits of central planning led to the clear-cut failure of *perestroika* and a general decline in living standards.

Part VI
Practice Test 2

- Practice Test 2
- Practice Test 2: Answers and Explanations

Practice Test 2

AP® European History Exam

DO NOT OPEN THIS BOOKLET UNTIL YOU ARE TOLD TO DO SO.

At a Glance

Time
55 minutes
Number of Questions
55
Percent of Total Score
40%
Writing Instrument
Pencil required

Instructions

Section I, Part A, of this exam contains 55 multiple-choice questions. Fill in only the ovals for numbers 1 through 55 on your answer sheet. Because this section offers only four answer options for each question, do not mark the (E) answer circle for any question.

Indicate all of your answers to the multiple-choice questions on the answer sheet. No credit will be given for anything written in this exam booklet, but you may use the booklet for notes or scratch work. After you have decided which of the suggested answers is best, completely fill in the corresponding oval on the answer sheet. Give only one answer to each question. If you change an answer, be sure that the previous mark is erased completely. Here is a sample question and answer.

Sample Question   Sample Answer

Chicago is a   (A) ● (C) (D)
(A) state
(B) city
(C) country
(D) continent

Use your time effectively, working as quickly as you can without losing accuracy. Do not spend too much time on any one question. Go on to other questions and come back to the ones you have not answered if you have time. It is not expected that everyone will know the answers to all the multiple-choice questions.

Your total score on the multiple-choice section is based only on the number of questions answered correctly. Points are not deducted for incorrect answers or unanswered questions.

At a Glance

Time
50 minutes
Number of Questions
4
Percent of Total Score
20%
Writing Instrument
Pen with black or dark blue ink

Instructions

Section I, Part B of this exam consists of 4 short-answer questions. Write your responses on a separate sheet of paper.

This page intentionally left blank.

GO ON TO THE NEXT PAGE.

EUROPEAN HISTORY

SECTION I, Part A

Time—55 minutes

55 Questions

Directions: Each of the questions or incomplete statements below is followed by either four suggested answers or completions. Select the one that is best in each case and then fill in the appropriate letter in the corresponding space on the answer sheet.

Questions 1–4 refer to the following passage.

"The substitution of Plato for the scholastic Aristotle was hastened by contact with Byzantine scholarship. Already at the Council of Ferrera (1438), which nominally reunited the Eastern and Western churches, there was a debate in which the Byzantines maintained the superiority of Plato to Aristotle. Cosimo and Lorenzo de Medici were both addicted to Plato; Cosimo founded and Lorenzo continued the Florentine Academy, which was largely devoted to the study of Plato…The humanists of the time, however, were too busy acquiring knowledge of antiquity to be able to produce anything of value."

Bertrand Russell, British philosopher, *History of Western Philosophy,* 1946

1. In what way does this passage best exemplify the view of twentieth-century philosophers and thinkers?

   (A) Faced with an unprecedented number of social and technological changes, the twentieth century embraced innovation as one of the most valued characteristics of life.
   (B) Overwhelmed by the unprecedented number of social and technological changes, the twentieth century sought refuge in the longstanding traditions of the past.
   (C) After the devastation of World Wars I and II erased the possibility of finding a unified meaning to life, philosophers occupied themselves with finding small differences between the philosophies of past thinkers.
   (D) Nihilists typically find ways to doubt the postulations of those who came before them.

2. According to the information in the text, the schools founded by the Medici family most favored a philosophy known as

   (A) Neoclassicism
   (B) Scholasticism
   (C) Renaissance humanism
   (D) Neoplatonism

3. It can be inferred from the passage that the Council of Ferrera

   (A) laid the foundation for the Florentine Academy
   (B) permanently reconciled the differences between the Eastern and Western churches
   (C) accelerated the rediscovery of classical philosophy in Western Europe
   (D) allowed the Byzantines to learn from Florentine scholarship

4. The cultural diffusion described by Bertrand Russell most directly influenced the composition of which text?

   (A) *Oration on the Dignity of Man*
   (B) *The Decameron*
   (C) *Handbook of the Christian Knight*
   (D) *Utopia*

GO ON TO THE NEXT PAGE.

Questions 5–9 refer to the tables below.

D-Day Statistics

Unit	Allies	Germans	Ratio
Ground Troops	1 million	700,000	1.43:1
Replacements	120,000	20,000	6:1
Other Men	1.75 million	780,000	2.25:1
Total	2.87 million	1.5 million	1.92:1

Unit	Allies	Germans	Ratio
Tanks	5,500	1,400	3.93:1
Artillery	4,800	3,200	1.5:1
Others	2,000	800	2.5:1

Air Force	Bombers	Fighters	Total
RAF	624	2,172	2,796
USAAF	1,922	1,311	3,233
Luftwaffe	400	420	820
Ratio	6.4:1	8.3:1	7.4:1

5. The tables indicate which of the following about World War II?

   (A) Rescuing Europe from the Germans was out of the question until the arrival of the American forces.
   (B) Keen strategy was perhaps less important to military success than the amount of available resources.
   (C) German replacements had slowed to an unacceptable level.
   (D) The ratio of artillery to tanks didn't correlate with the eventual victory.

6. What might best explain the discrepancy between the number of fighter jets and bombers of the United States and the British?

   (A) The increased fuel efficiency of submarines at the time
   (B) A cultural preference for larger and smaller modes of transportation
   (C) The distance of North America from Europe versus the distance of Great Britain from Europe
   (D) Smaller production facilities in British factory towns

7. The large difference in the number of tanks between the Germans and the Allies was most probably due to what?

   (A) The presence of the Russian army in the Allied forces
   (B) The German tendency towards quality, not quantity, in manufacturing
   (C) The enormous production capabilities of the U.S.
   (D) Japanese purchase of raw materials from Germany, limiting the available production

8. In which unit did the Germans most closely match the Allies, according to the tables?

   (A) Ground Troops
   (B) Tanks
   (C) Artillery
   (D) Air Force

9. Which of the following statements about Germany could be supported by the data shown in the tables?

   (A) What Germany's military lacked in ground troops, it made up for in replacements.
   (B) Germany relied on its use of tanks more than it did any other unit.
   (C) D-Day accounted for the worst losses Germany experienced during World War II.
   (D) As opposed to aircraft producers in the Allied countries, Germany's aviation industry did not adequately meet the production needs requested by the generals.

GO ON TO THE NEXT PAGE.

Questions 10–14 refer to the cartoon below.

"And don't forget that your Kaiser will find a use for you—alive or dead."

Punch Magazine, 1917

10. The concept of "total war" as practiced by the kaiser in the sketch included all of the following EXCEPT

   (A) food rationing
   (B) women moving into factory production
   (C) propaganda
   (D) attacks specifically targeting civilians

11. The long-term impact of the event portrayed in the cartoon could best be seen through the

   (A) proliferation of governmental regulation of industry throughout Europe
   (B) end of European countries' imperial ambitions
   (C) demilitarization of Germany
   (D) end of the Kaiser's rule in Germany

12. One consequence that resulted from the situation depicted in the cartoon was

   (A) a rise in unemployment
   (B) a dramatic decline in food production
   (C) the prohibition of cannon usage
   (D) the decrease in funds available for the war effort

GO ON TO THE NEXT PAGE.

13. The perspective of the cartoonist is most likely influenced by his

    (A) experience in the Kaiser's army
    (B) experience working for the Kaiser
    (C) British citizenship
    (D) German citizenship

14. The cartoonist would be mostly likely to agree with which of the following statements?

    (A) The Kaiser's popularity was not limited to Germany.
    (B) During a time of war, the Kaiser was the best leader that Germany could hope for.
    (C) The Kaiser placed more value on the war effort than on the well being of his people.
    (D) The Kaiser's immorality ultimately led to his downfall.

GO ON TO THE NEXT PAGE.

Questions 15–19 refer to the passage below.

"After all the slaves had been brought together and severally marked with the letter G, the emperor's fifths and then Cortés' were deducted before we were aware of it; and, besides this, on the night preceding, the finest of the Indian females had been secretly set apart, so that when it came to a division among us soldiers, we found none left but old and ugly women…. Another soldier asked Cortés if the division he had made of the gold in Mexico was not a sufficient imposition, for, at first, he had merely spoken of 300,000 pesos, but when we were obliged to retreat from the city, it was estimated at 700,000 pesos. And now he was going to deprive the poor soldier, who had undergone so many hardships, and suffered from innumerable wounds, of this small remuneration, and not even allow him a pretty Indian female for a companion…

[Later], when Cortés learnt that there were still a great many bars of gold among the men, and heavy gambling in consequence, (for, according to the old saying, gold and love cannot lie long concealed,) he made known, under threats of severe punishment, that everyone should produce the gold he had obtained on the night of our retreat, of which one third was to be returned to him; but that anyone who refused to pay this, should have the whole taken from him. Many of our men refused downright to comply with this; yet Cortés managed to extort a good deal of it under the pretence of a loan…"

The Memoirs of the Conquistador Bernal Diaz del Castillo, 1568

15. As described by the author, the driving philosophy behind the *conquistadores'* search for gold was the economic policy known as

(A) protectionism
(B) laissez-faire
(C) mercantilism
(D) supply-side

16. Upon the return of Cortés's expedition, which of the following was a consequence of the actions described in the memoir?

(A) A decentralized political state
(B) A strengthened agricultural sector
(C) An increased rate of inflation
(D) Less tolerance for Jews and Muslims

17. The motivations described in the text are most similar to those of which explorer?

(A) Christopher Columbus
(B) Vasco de Gama
(C) Francisco Pizarro
(D) Bartholomew Dias

18. The events described in the passage most likely occurred in which modern-day country?

(A) Argentina
(B) South Africa
(C) Mexico
(D) Peru

19. The *encomienda* system, which is described in the text and was used during the colonization of the Americas to regulate the indigenous people, was NOT ended by which of the following?

(A) The protests of the Catholic missionaries against abuses of forced labor
(B) The lack of new land to assign to well-connected Spaniards and conquistadores
(C) The Spanish royal crown's desire to control the estates more directly
(D) An increase in the number of mestizos, who by law were forbidden from working on the *encomiendas*

GO ON TO THE NEXT PAGE.

Questions 20–24 refer to the cartoon below.

"The Devilfish in Egyptian Waters," 1882

20. Which was NOT a factor that led to the issue depicted in this cartoon?

   (A) A natural system of internal waterways that facilitated transportation of raw materials and finished goods
   (B) A natural barrier between England and possible invading armies from the European mainland
   (C) A long tradition of technological innovation
   (D) A top-down political system that implemented changes quickly and efficiently

21. The cartoon was created in reaction to Great Britain's ambitions following

   (A) the Suez Canal Crisis
   (B) the near war over Foshoda
   (C) the completion of construction by the Suez Canal Company
   (D) Russia's actions in the "great game."

22. The Primrose League's opinion of this cartoon would likely be one of

   (A) indifference, since they saw both the benefits and drawbacks of colonialism
   (B) displeasure at the cartoonists' critique of a noble pursuit
   (C) agreement with the criticisms offered by the cartoon
   (D) harsh condemnation for glorifying violent imperialism

23. A similar cartoon could be made about each of the following countries prior to 1890 EXCEPT

   (A) Netherlands
   (B) France
   (C) Belgium
   (D) Germany

24. This cartoon could be used as evidence to support the claim that

   (A) European lands were not immune to Great Britain's imperialism
   (B) Great Britain did not extend their imperial conquest to South Africa
   (C) the British Empire was limited to one hemisphere
   (D) Great Britain experienced little resistance to its colonial ambitions

GO ON TO THE NEXT PAGE.

Questions 25–29 refer to the passage below.

In Russia there was nothing going on well, and [Souvarine] was in despair over the news he had received. His old companions were all turning to the politicians; the famous Nihilists who made Europe tremble—sons of village priests, of the lower middle class, of tradesmen—could not rise above the idea of national liberation, and seemed to believe that the world would be delivered—when they had killed their despot...

"Foolery! They'll never get out of it with their foolery."

Then, lowering his voice still more, in a few bitter words he described his old dream of fraternity. He had renounced his rank and his fortune; he had gone among workmen, only in the hope of seeing at last the foundation of a new society of labour in common. All the sous in his pockets had long gone to the urchins of the settlement; he had been as tender as a brother with the colliers, smiling at their suspicion, winning them over by his quiet workmanlike ways and his dislike of chattering. But decidedly the fusion had not taken place.

His voice changed, his eyes grew bright, he fixed them on Étienne, directly addressing him:

"Now, do you understand that? These hatworkers at Marseilles who have won the great lottery prize of a hundred thousand francs have gone off at once and invested it, declaring that they are going to live without doing anything! Yes, that is your idea, all of you French workmen; you want to unearth a treasure in order to devour it alone afterwards in some lazy, selfish corner. You may cry out as much as you like against the rich, you haven't got courage enough to give back to the poor the money that luck brings you. You will never be worthy of happiness as long as you own anything, and your hatred of the bourgeois proceeds solely from an angry desire to be bourgeois yourselves in their place."

Émile Zola, French writer, *Germinal*, 1885

25. The conflict referred to in the final paragraph of the passage was best described in which book?

   (A) *On Liberty,* by John Stuart Mill
   (B) *The Communist Manifesto,* by Marx and Engels
   (C) *Protocols of the Elders of Zion*
   (D) *Looking Backward,* by Edward Bellamy

26. The radical movement known as anarchism, alluded to in the first paragraph, had been related to all of the following EXCEPT

   (A) the International Workingman's Association
   (B) Pierre-Joseph Proudhon
   (C) the Congress of Vienna
   (D) the Paris Commune

27. The passage displays the direct concern for the welfare of the working classes that was typically a part of which movement?

   (A) Capitalist
   (B) Scientific
   (C) Communist
   (D) Existentialist

28. In European industry, the mining industry as discussed in the passage grew in importance following the invention of

   (A) the water frame
   (B) the spinning jenny
   (C) the steam engine
   (D) the internal combustion engine

29. A nineteenth-century Russian historian evaluating this passage would probably be most interested in

   (A) the Russian interest in French culture
   (B) the spirit of camaraderie amongst the miners
   (C) the sense of continual class struggle
   (D) the need for *noblesse oblige*

GO ON TO THE NEXT PAGE.

Questions 30–34 refer to the passage below.

"In 1500 that work appeared which Erasmus had written after his misfortune at Dover, and had dedicated to Mountjoy, the *Adagiorum Collectanea*. It was a collection of about eight hundred proverbial sayings drawn from the Latin authors of antiquity and elucidated for the use of those who aspired to write an elegant Latin style. In the dedication Erasmus pointed out the profit an author may derive, both in ornamenting his style and in strengthening his argumentation, from having at his disposal a good supply of sentences hallowed by their antiquity. He proposes to offer such a help to his readers. What he actually gave was much more. He familiarized a much wider circle than the earlier humanists had reached with the spirit of antiquity.

Until this time the humanists had, to some extent, monopolized the treasures of classic culture, in order to parade their knowledge of which the multitude remained destitute, and so to become strange prodigies of learning and elegance. With his irresistible need of teaching and his sincere love for humanity and its general culture, Erasmus introduced the classic spirit, in so far as it could be reflected in the soul of a sixteenth-century Christian, among the people. Not he alone; but none more extensively and more effectively. Not among all the people, it is true, for by writing in Latin he limited his direct influence to the educated classes, which in those days were the upper classes.

Erasmus made current the classic spirit. Humanism ceased to be the exclusive privilege of a few. According to Beatus Rhenanus he had been reproached by some humanists, when about to publish the *Adagia*, for divulging the mysteries of their craft. But he desired that the book of antiquity should be open to all."

Johan Huizinga, twentieth-century Dutch philosopher, *Erasmus and the Age of Reformation*, 1924

30. Based on Huizinga's description of Erasmus's career, the contributions of Erasmus are most similar to those of

(A) Johannes Gutenberg
(B) Martin Luther
(C) Francesco Petrarch
(D) Christine de Pisan

31. What was the primary impact of "Humanism ceas[ing] to be the exclusive privilege of the few"?

(A) The populous demanded rights from the state.
(B) People could begin to question the Church on a wider scale.
(C) Latin replaced many of the vulgar languages throughout Europe.
(D) European literature stagnated due to widespread interest in the writings of antiquity.

32. Huizinga's apparent support of Erasmus' belief in the "book of antiquity" being "open to all" is most likely a product of

(A) the author's life as a member of twentieth-century Europe, which prized such characteristics
(B) the longevity of Erasmus' works
(C) the Dutch reverence for the works of Erasmus
(D) the typical unflinching support of one philosopher for another philosopher's work

33. The type of humanism attributed to Erasmus in this passage is most similar to what Southern Renaissance movement?

(A) Neoplatonism
(B) Antitrinitarianism
(C) Pietism
(D) Rationalism

34. According to Huizinga, Erasmus's legacy was more significant than that of earlier humanists because

(A) he had more support from the Church
(B) he wrote in a language that was understandable to the masses, unlike his predecessors
(C) he wrote exclusively about religious matters
(D) he valued educating the masses more than his predecessors had

GO ON TO THE NEXT PAGE.

Questions 35–39 refer to the image below.

William Hogarth, *Gin Lane,* 1751

35. Social reformers of the eighteenth century saw the exaggerations in Hogarth's work as reason to

    (A) morally improve the living habits of the underclass
    (B) feel deep revulsion against the working-class everywhere
    (C) take pleasure in seeing such joyfulness among the destitute
    (D) return society to a more natural, unhurried state of life

36. Hogarth primarily intended for this engraving to advocate for the passage of

    (A) the Act of Toleration
    (B) the Mutiny Act
    (C) the Act of Union
    (D) the Sale of Spirits Act

37. This piece of art can be best categorized as

    (A) Baroque
    (B) Romanticism
    (C) satire
    (D) single-point perspective

GO ON TO THE NEXT PAGE.

38. Which of the following would most directly have contributed to the scene depicted in the engraving?

   (A) Enclosure Acts
   (B) the Sadler Committee
   (C) Poor Laws
   (D) the Act of Settlement

39. Art critics would most likely criticize Hogarth's work for all of the following reasons EXCEPT its

   (A) emphasis on traditional portrayals of humans
   (B) use of stereotyped characters
   (C) attention to realistic detail
   (D) typical portraiture composition

GO ON TO THE NEXT PAGE.

Questions 40–44 refer to the passage below.

"**Buckingham Palace, 10th May 1839.**

    The Queen forgot to ask Lord Melbourne if he thought there would be any harm in her writing to the Duke of Cambridge that she really was fearful of fatiguing herself, if she went out to a party at Gloucester House on Tuesday, an Ancient Concert on Wednesday, and a ball at Northumberland House on Thursday, considering how much she had to do these last four days. If she went to the Ancient Concert on Wednesday, having besides a concert of her own here on Monday, it would be four nights of fatigue, really exhausted as the Queen is.

    But if Lord Melbourne thinks that as there are only to be English singers at the Ancient Concert, she ought to go, she could go there for one act; but she would much rather, if possible, get out of it, for it is a fatiguing time....

    As the negotiations with the Tories are quite at an end, and Lord Melbourne has been here, the Queen hopes Lord Melbourne will not object to dining with her on Sunday?"

The Letters of Queen Victoria, Volume 1 (of 3), 1837–1843:
A Selection from Her Majesty's Correspondence Between the Years 1837 and 1861

40. The long evenings of entertainment for Queen Victoria suggest what about the nature of the English monarchy in the nineteenth century?

    (A) That true political power lay elsewhere
    (B) That she was very fond of attending balls and concerts
    (C) That important political progress could only be made by attending social events
    (D) That with England's nineteenth-century economic success came more leisure time for the upper classes

41. The phrase "negotiations with the Tories" suggests that what historical transition had been made complete?

    (A) The switch from a liberal-dominated to a conservative-dominated Parliament
    (B) The conversion from male-dominated politics to female-dominated politics
    (C) The change from a divinely-ordained monarch to a constitutionally-approved monarch
    (D) An end to war and the creation of a lasting peace

42. A similar fondness for entertainment amongst the nobility was taken to its most outrageous degree in which of the following eras and places?

    (A) Sixteenth-century Spain
    (B) Seventeenth-century Netherlands
    (C) Eighteenth-century France
    (D) Nineteenth-century Prussia

43. Modern historians are noted for their tendency to portray leaders and historical figures as merely human, even flawed. What might such a historian find most notable about the queen's letter?

    (A) The odd capitalization of certain words
    (B) Her sense of duty to support English singers
    (C) Her referral to herself in the third-person
    (D) Admitting her exhaustion at having to attend so many social functions

44. Apart from a grueling social calendar, which of the following most challenged Queen Victoria during her reign from 1837 to 1901?

    (A) An English potato famine in 1845
    (B) An unprecedented onslaught of industrial, social, cultural, political, and scientific change
    (C) Constant military attacks from mainland Europe
    (D) A rapidly shrinking number of overseas colonies

GO ON TO THE NEXT PAGE.

Questions 45–49 refer to the maps below, which show the Soviet Union before (top) and during (bottom) the Cold War.

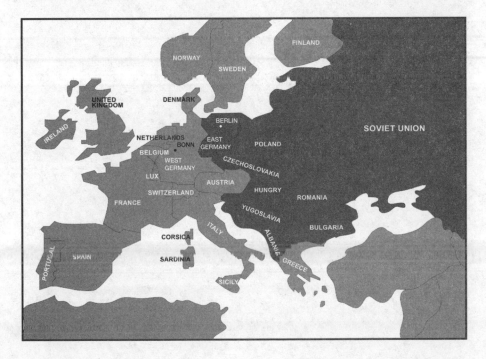

45. The post-World War II geographic expansion of the Soviet Union began with

    (A) the decision to expand to the Black Sea
    (B) the ten-month-long blockade of Berlin
    (C) the invasion of Afghanistan
    (D) the decision at the Conference at Yalta to divide Germany into four different zones

46. During the Cold War, Yugoslavia and Hungary were part of a treaty organization known as

    (A) NATO
    (B) the KGB
    (C) the Warsaw Pact
    (D) the Iron Curtain

GO ON TO THE NEXT PAGE.

47. Which of the following statements about the Soviet Union's influence is consistent with the Cold War map's border?

    (A) Stalin could not force his ideology on the Austrian president.
    (B) Finland largely held on to a command economy.
    (C) Greece and other Balkan nations maintained a strong alliance.
    (D) Czechoslovakia was able to maintain a free economy.

48. The only country in Eastern Europe that presented serious resistance to Soviet control was Poland. What was NOT a general reason for this?

    (A) The popular perception that Western powers had abandoned them to the Soviets
    (B) The questionable authenticity of the first postwar elections, in which communists won nearly all positions
    (C) A general agreement with Soviet tactics during the war
    (D) The reluctance to lose their identity as a country once again

49. Which of the following is NOT true regarding the divided Germany shown on the second map?

    (A) The capital of West Germany was located in East Germany.
    (B) West Germany experienced a postwar economic miracle.
    (C) Both East Germany and West Germany were allowed to rearm.
    (D) France had occupied West Germany.

GO ON TO THE NEXT PAGE.

Questions 50–52 refer to the painting below.

Johannes Vermeer, *The Music Lesson,* 1665

50. How does the content of Vermeer's painting depict a lifestyle that is different from that of the Southern Renaissance?

    (A) Art was often placed in homes, as they were commissioned by a new wealthy merchant class, rather than by church officials.
    (B) Music outside of the church was not central to Italian life, but was important to the Dutch middle class.
    (C) Dutch architecture was more ornate than that of Italy.
    (D) Dutch servants lived in the home, as opposed to the servants in Southern Europe.

51. The standard of living reflected in Vermeer's painting could be attributed to all of the following EXCEPT

    (A) cheap energy available from windmills and peat
    (B) Protestant and Jewish skilled craftsmen who immigrated to escape persecution in other lands
    (C) a thriving fruit-and-vegetable export industry
    (D) the establishment of the Dutch East India Company

52. *The Music Lesson* is indicative of the Golden Age of Dutch art, which often featured images of

    (A) the ancient world
    (B) royalty
    (C) saints
    (D) everyday life

GO ON TO THE NEXT PAGE.

Questions 53–55 refer to the passage below.

"XI. As the present sciences are useless for the discovery of effects, so the present system of logic is useless for the discovery of the sciences.

XIX. There are and can exist but two ways of investigating and discovering truth. The one hurries on rapidly from the senses and particulars to the most general axioms, and from them, as principles and their supposed indisputable truth, derives and discovers the intermediate axioms. This is the way now in use. The other constructs its axioms from the senses and particulars, by ascending continually and gradually, till it finally arrives at the most general axioms, which is the true but unattempted way.

XXII. Each of these two ways begins from the senses and particulars, and ends in the greatest generalities...

XXXVI. We have but one simple method of delivering our sentiments, namely, we must bring men to particulars and their regular series and order, and they must for a while renounce their notions, and begin to form an acquaintance with things."

Francis Bacon, English philosopher and essayist, *Novum Organum,* 1620

53. The method of inquiry elucidated by Francis Bacon in the passage is known as

(A) humanism
(B) deduction
(C) empiricism
(D) scientific socialism

54. How does the approach outlined in *Novum Organum* differ from the studies of the Renaissance era that preceded it?

(A) The Renaissance was anchored in Italy; the scientific era was barely noticed there.
(B) The Renaissance revered the natural teachings of classical authority; Bacon's writings sought to overturn them.
(C) The Renaissance was sponsored primarily by the Church, whereas scientific societies were sponsored mainly by wealthy merchants.
(D) The Renaissance featured a wild spirit of discovery, but the scientific pioneers were much more cautious in their pronouncements.

55. By the 1800s, the method of empirical reasoning reflected in the passage had undergone which of the following changes?

(A) It had weakened to the point of irrelevance.
(B) It had become a core principle of European culture.
(C) It had been refined and changed by so many people that it had become unrecognizable to those such as Bacon who had pioneered it.
(D) It had stagnated to the point that the common person had begun to search for a new organizing principle of life.

GO ON TO THE NEXT PAGE.

EUROPEAN HISTORY

SECTION I, Part B

Time—50 minutes

4 Questions

Directions: Read each question carefully and write your responses in the corresponding boxes on a separate sheet of paper.

Use complete sentences; an outline or bulleted list alone is not acceptable. On test day, you will be able to plan your answers in the exam booklet, but only your responses in the corresponding boxes on the free-response answer sheet will be scored.

1. Use the chart below and your knowledge of European history to answer all parts of the question that follows.

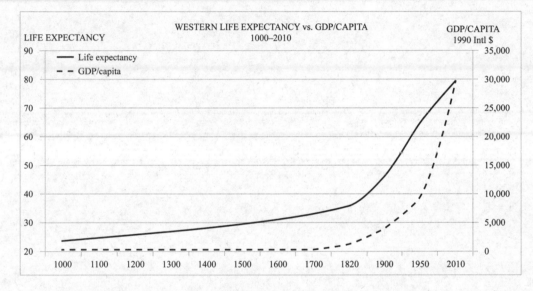

a) Describe ONE similarity between the First Industrial Revolution and the Second Industrial Revolution.
b) Describe ONE difference between the First Industrial Revolution and the Second Industrial Revolution.

GO ON TO THE NEXT PAGE.

2. Use your knowledge of European history to answer all parts of the question that follows.

   Historians have praised many philosophers for ushering in the Enlightenment. These philosophers include

   - John Locke
   - Thomas Hobbes
   - Adam Smith
   - René Descartes
   - David Hume

   a) Briefly explain why TWO of the thinkers on the list represent Enlightenment ideals.
   b) Briefly explain why ONE of the thinkers on the list does <u>not</u> represent Enlightenment ideals.

GO ON TO THE NEXT PAGE.

3. Use the following passage and your knowledge of European history to answer all parts of the question that follows.

"In this unholy work, to such extremes has their impiety, practised in all the arts of Satan, been carried, that it would seem almost impossible to confine it within bounds; and did we not rely on the splendid promises of the Saviour, who declared that he had 'built his Church on so solid a foundation, that the gates of hell should never prevail against it,' we should be filled with most alarming apprehension lest, beset on every side by such a host of enemies, assailed by so many and such formidable engines, the Church of God should, in these days, fall beneath their combined efforts. To omit those illustrious states which heretofore professed, in piety and holiness, the Catholic faith transmitted to them by their ancestors, but are now gone astray, wandering from the paths of truth, and openly declaring that their best claims of piety are founded on a total abandonment of the faith of their fathers: there is no region however remote, no place however securely guarded, no corner of the Christian republic, into which this pestilence has not sought secretly to insinuate itself."

The Catechism of the Council of Trent, 1566

a) Describe TWO figures to which the Council of Trent was reacting.
b) Explain ONE response of the Catholic Church to this challenge.

GO ON TO THE NEXT PAGE.

4. The map below shows the extent of the Holy Roman Empire in the year 1600. Use the map and your knowledge of European history to answer all parts of the question that follows.

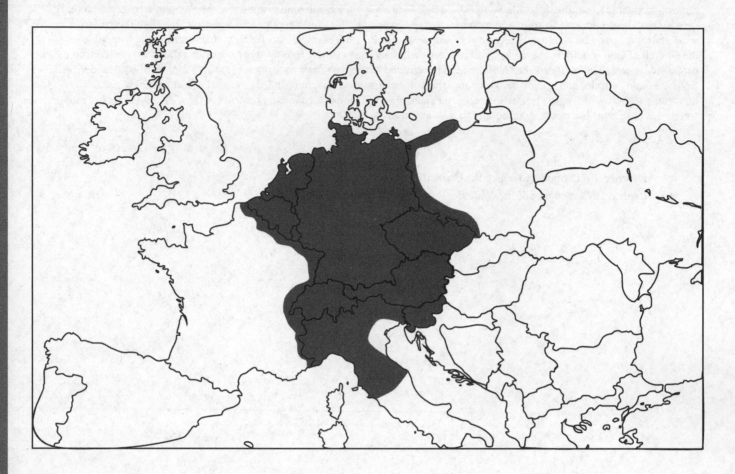

a)   Describe ONE religious conflict that weakened the Holy Roman Empire <u>before</u> 1600.
b)   Describe ONE religious conflict that weakened the Holy Roman Empire <u>after</u> 1600.

STOP
END OF SECTION I

IF YOU FINISH BEFORE TIME IS CALLED, YOU MAY CHECK YOUR WORK ON THIS SECTION.
DO NOT GO ON TO SECTION II UNTIL YOU ARE TOLD TO DO SO.

This page intentionally left blank.

AP® European History Exam

SECTION II: Free Response

DO NOT OPEN THIS BOOKLET UNTIL YOU ARE TOLD TO DO SO.

At a Glance

Total Time
1 hour, 30 minutes
Number of Questions
2
Percent of Total Score
40%
Writing Instrument
Pen with black or dark blue ink

Reading Period

Time
15 minutes (suggested).
Use this time to read the questions and plan your answer to Question 1, the document-based question.

Writing Period

Time
1 hour, 15 minutes

Question 1 (DBQ): Mandatory

Question 1 (DBQ)
Suggested Time
40 minutes
Percent of Total Score
25%

Question 2 or 3: Choose One Question

Answer either Question 2 or 3
Suggested Time
35 minutes
Percent of Total Score
15%

Instructions

The questions for Section II are printed in the Questions and Documents booklet. You may use that booklet to organize your answers and for scratch work, but you must write your answers in this Section II: Free Response booklet. No credit will be given for any work written in the Questions and Documents booklet.

The proctor will announce the beginning and end of the reading period. You are advised to spend the 15-minute period reading the question and planning your answer to Question 1, the document-based question. If you have time, you may also read Questions 2 and 3.

Section II of this exam requires answers in essay form. Write clearly and legibly. Circle the number of the question you are answering at the top of each page in this booklet. Begin each answer on a new page. Do not skip lines. Cross out any errors you make; crossed-out work will not be scored.

Manage your time carefully. The proctor will announce the suggested time for each part, but you may proceed freely from one part to the next. Go on to Question 2 or 3 if you finish Question 1 early. You may review your responses if you finish before the end of the exam is announced.

After the exam, you must apply the label that corresponds to the long-essay question you answered—Question 2 or 3. For example, if you answered Question 2, apply the label 2. Failure to do so may delay your score.

This page intentionally left blank.

GO ON TO THE NEXT PAGE.

EUROPEAN HISTORY

SECTION II

Total Time—1 hour, 30 minutes

Question 1 (Document-Based Question)

Suggested reading and writing time: 55 minutes

It is suggested that you spend 15 minutes reading the documents and 40 minutes writing your response.

Note: You may begin writing your response before the reading period is over.

Directions: Question 1 is based on the accompanying Documents 1–7. The documents have been edited for the purpose of this exercise.

In your response you should do the following.

* <u>Thesis:</u> Present a thesis that makes a historically defensible claim and responds to all parts of the question. The thesis must consist of one or more sentences located in one place, either in the introduction or the conclusion.

* <u>Argument Development:</u> Develop and support a cohesive argument that recognizes and accounts for historical complexity by explicitly illustrating relationships among historical evidence such as contradiction, corroboration, and/or qualification.

* <u>Use of the Documents:</u> Utilize the content of at least six of the documents to support the thesis or a relevant argument.

* <u>Sourcing the Documents:</u> Explain the significance of the author's point of view, author's purpose, historical context, and/or audience for at least four of the documents.

* <u>Contextualization:</u> Situate the argument by explaining the broader historical events, developments, or processes immediately relevant to the question.

* <u>Outside Evidence:</u> Provide an example or additional piece of specific evidence beyond those found in the documents to support or qualify the argument.

* <u>Synthesis:</u> Extend the argument by explaining the connections between the argument and ONE of the following.

    – A development in a different historical period, situation, era, or geographical area.

    – A course theme and/or approach to history that is not the focus of the essay (such as political, economic, social, cultural, or intellectual history).

    – A different discipline or field of inquiry (such as economics, government and politics, art history, or anthropology).

GO ON TO THE NEXT PAGE.

Question 1: Using the documents and your knowledge of European history, describe and evaluate the attitudes of those who saw Chartism as a revolutionary movement versus those who saw it as essentially moderate.

Document 1

Source: Minutes of the London Working Men's Association, May, 15, 1838.

Resolved, That the Members of the Working Men's Association fully concurring in the great principles of Universal Suffrage, Annual Parliaments, the Ballot, and all the other essentials to the free exercise of Man's political rights—and hearing that a meeting is to be held at Glasgow on the 21st of May in furtherance of those objects do request our Honorary Members Mr. Thos. Murphy and the Revd. Dr Wade to present to that meeting our pamphlet entitled the 'People's Charter' being the outline of an act to provide for the just representation of the people of Great Britain in the Commons House of Parliament— embracing the principles of Universal Suffrage, No Property Qualifications, Annual Parliaments, Equal Representation, Payment of Members, and Vote by [secret] Ballot prepared by a committee of twelve persons, six members of parliament and six members of the Working Men's Association.

Document 2

Source: Joseph Stevens, in a speech at a Chartist Rally in Manchester, September 1838.

This question of Universal Suffrage was a knife and fork question after all; this question was a bread and cheese question, notwithstanding all that had been said against it; and if any man ask him what he meant by Universal Suffrage, he would answer, that every working man in the land had a right to have a good coat to his back, a comfortable abode in which to shelter himself and his family, a good dinner upon his table, and as much wages for that work as would keep him in plenty, and afford him the enjoyment of all the blessings of life which a reasonable man could desire.

Document 3

Source: Article from a Chartist publication, May 1839.

It is also upon all sides agreed that this is a fearful remedy, which, like hazardous, extreme, and painful operations in surgery, is only to be brought into action in very extreme cases, when all ordinary courses of treatment have failed. Physical force is a thing not to be lightly had recourse to; it is the last remedy known to the Constitution…

Document 4

Source: Thomas Cooper, from his poem "The Lion of Freedom," written in honor of Chartist leader Feargus O'Connor, 1841.

> …The pride of the nation, he's noble and brave
> He's the terror of tyrants, the friend of the slave,
> The bright star of freedom, the nobles of men,
> We'll rally around him again and again.
>
> Though proud daring tyrants his body confined,
> They never could alter his generous mind;
> We'll hail our caged lion, now free from his den
> And we'll rally around him again and again…

GO ON TO THE NEXT PAGE.

Document 5

Source: Excerpt from *Leeds Mercury,* August 1842.

Last evening, a Chartist tea party and ball, as previously announced by placard were given in the Carpenters' Hall, by 'The committee for the erection of Hunt's monument.' The room and gallery were densely crowded, and an amateur band was in attendance. John Murray presided. After tea, the Rev. James Scholefield entered the room, and announced that Mr. Feargus O'Connor was unable to attend, as he was, in conjunction with other Chartists, engaged in considering what measures were best to be adopted in the present crisis [the call for a general strike].

Document 6

Source: Address of the Female Political Union, a Chartist organization, to their fellow countrywomen, February 1839.

Year after year have passed away, and even now our wishes have no prospect of being realized, our husbands are over wrought, our houses half furnished, our families ill-fed, and our children uneducated—the fear of want hangs over our heads, the scorn of the rich is pointed towards us; the brand of slavery is on our kindred, and we feel the degradation. We are a despised caste, our oppressors are not content with despising our feelings, but demand the control of our thoughts and wants!—want's bitter bondage binds us to their feet, we are oppressed because we are poor.

Document 7

Source: Letter from middle-class merchant to his wife, April 1848.

London is in a state of panic from the contemplated meeting of the Chartists, 200,000 strong on Monday; for myself, nothing that happened would in the least surprise me: I expect a revolution within two years: there may be one within three days. The Times is alarmed beyond all measure. I have it from good authority that the Chartists are determined to have their wishes granted.

END OF PART A

GO ON TO THE NEXT PAGE.

EUROPEAN HISTORY

Question 2 or Question 3

Suggested writing time: 35 minutes

Directions: Choose EITHER Question 2 or Question 3.

In your response you should do the following.

- **Thesis:** Present a thesis that makes a historically defensible claim and responds to the question. The thesis must consist of one or more sentences located in one place, either in the introduction or the conclusion.

- **Application of Historical Thinking Skills:** Develop and support an argument that applies the historical thinking skill of comparison.

- **Supporting the Argument with Evidence:** Utilize specific examples of evidence to fully and effectively substantiate the stated thesis or relevant argument.

- **Synthesis:** Extend the argument by explaining the connections between the argument and ONE of the following.

  – A development in a different historical period, situation, era, or geographical area.

  – A course theme and/or approach to history that is not the focus of the essay (such as political, economic, social, cultural, or intellectual history).

  – A different discipline or field of inquiry (such as economics, government and politics, art history, or anthropology).

Question 2: Compare the extent to which the term "enlightened absolutism" applied to certain rulers in Eastern Europe and Russia during the eighteenth century.

Question 3: Compare the domestic problems faced by TWO of the great European powers in the decade immediately prior to the outbreak of the First World War.

END OF EXAMINATION

Practice Test 2: Answers and Explanations

PRACTICE TEST 2 ANSWER KEY

1.	A	29.	C
2.	D	30.	C
3.	C	31.	B
4.	A	32.	A
5.	B	33.	A
6.	C	34.	D
7.	C	35.	A
8.	A	36.	D
9.	D	37.	C
10.	D	38.	A
11.	A	39.	D
12.	B	40.	A
13.	C	41.	C
14.	C	42.	C
15.	C	43.	D
16.	C	44.	B
17.	C	45.	D
18.	C	46.	C
19.	B	47.	A
20.	D	48.	C
21.	C	49.	A
22.	B	50.	A
23.	D	51.	C
24.	A	52.	D
25.	B	53.	C
26.	C	54.	B
27.	C	55.	B
28.	C		

PRACTICE TEST 2: ANSWERS AND EXPLANATIONS

Section I, Part A: Multiple Choice

1. **A**   Innovation has become an accepted and desired part of life, but it wasn't always so. The world of tradition transformed itself in the last years of the nineteenth century and the first half of the twentieth century, when massive world wars, radical scientific discoveries, and an utterly changed standard of living for all European people resulted in a new philosophy. Russell was radical in one other respect; he was one of Europe's first atheists as well.

2. **D**   The phrase "knowledge of antiquity" should've clued you into the right answer. Neoplatonism developed concurrently with Renaissance humanism, but it was different—a mystical theology based on The One (think *The Matrix*), *nous*, the world-soul, numerology, and celestial hierarchy. None of this is covered by Renaissance humanism. Neoclassicism was an eighteenth-century movement, and scholasticism was medieval.

3. **C**   The text states that there was an emphasis on the relative importance of Plato as opposed to Aristotle. Such conversation, as well as the bridging of Eastern European and Western European cultures at the Council of Ferrera, created a venue for the Greek classics to enter the minds of Western Europeans. Therefore, the correct answer is (C).

4. **A**   According to the text, the "substitution of Plato for the scholastic Aristotle was hastened by contact with Byzantine scholarship." Therefore, you should look for an answer that brings Plato to Italian culture. Italian Renaissance author Pico della Mirandola's *Oration on the Dignity of Man* provides a Platonic view of humanity by highlighting the potential of man. This is a perfect example of the cultural diffusion described by Bertrand Russell. The correct answer is (A).

5. **B**   Process of Elimination combined with some test-taking logic should tell you that the other answers are unsupported. A glance at the tables tells you that, materially, the Allied forces outweighed the German forces in every possible way. The word *perhaps* in (B) also tells you that it's a good answer—the College Board does love a good weasel word, signifying possibility, but not certainty.

6. **C**   Bombers were long-distance military planes. Given the distance from the U.S. to Europe—as well as the distance from our bases to various locations in the Pacific theater—it would be logical that the U.S. forces might have many more of those.

7. **C**   Choice (A) is the trap. While the Soviets had an enormous military, they didn't quite have the same production capabilities as the United States. Furthermore, they didn't participate in D-Day, busy as they were with their own eastern front battle against the German menace.

8. **A**   The most straightforward way to determine which German and Allied units are most closely matched is to look at the ratios in the tables. The ratio of Allied to German ground troops is 1.43 to 1. This is closer than the ratio for tanks (3.93 to 1), artillery (1.5 to 1), and air force (7.4 to 1).

9. **D**   It is clear from the table that Germany lagged far behind the Allies in terms of air force production. This data is consistent with the idea that German production lines did not keep up with the needs of the generals. Choice (D) is correct.

10. **D**   During World War I, the German populace experienced rationing, the entrance of women into the factories (to replace the men who were called to duty), and much propaganda urging them to fight for their country. English citizens experienced all of these things, too. Total war, however, did not mean the total annihilation of all citizens of your opponent's country. While civilians were certainly killed, the primary aim of military attacks remained enlisted personnel and centers of production.

11. **A**   The cartoon depicts the German Kaiser using all possible resources, including people, to win the Great War. (Remember to pay attention to the caption! This goes for any image on the exam that is accompanied by text.) This idea is referred to as "total war." In order to mobilize all resources, governments took control of certain industries. This action set the precedent in a number of countries for government regulation of industry—even during peacetime.

12. **B**   Because the cartoon is a commentary on the concept of total war, you should think about total war's consequences. One is that industries must focus their resources on winning the war and not necessarily domestic concerns. It was not uncommon for food shortages to arise on the home front due to this temporary change in priorities. Choice (B) is the answer.

13. **C**   The cartoon offers a critical view of the Kaiser's commitment to total war. This is perhaps due to the fact that the creator of the cartoon is British, which matches (C). The clue here is the caption—*Punch* magazine was a famous British satirical publication, which suggests the nationality of the artist.

14. **C**   Indicating that he would use his people dead or alive is not a ringing endorsement for the Kaiser's sense of empathy. The cartoon clearly intends to criticize this callous indifference, which aligns with (C).

15. **C**   The philosophy of mercantilism went through many phases, one of which was an early, primitive form known as bullionism. This holds one simple tenet—the more specie (gold and silver) your society possesses, the wealthier your society will be. This describes sixteenth-century Spain quite well. However, while this may seem superficially true, it doesn't take into account important variables such as productivity, favorable balance-of-trade, individual rights, and so on.

16. **C**   High inflation was caused by the influx of gold and silver from the Spanish treasure fleet from the New World, especially the silver from Potosí, Bolivia. Basically, there were too many people with too much money chasing too few goods. While inflation has been a fact of life in the West for many decades, even centuries, back then it was a shockingly new phenomenon, and the poor felt even poorer as they could no longer afford to purchase goods.

17. **C** This question requires you to have some knowledge about the individual goals and motivations of explorers during the Age of Exploration. According to the text, Cortés is motivated by the acquisition of gold. A similar motivation drove Pizzaro, (C), to South America and into the Incan Empire. The primary goal of Columbus, da Gama, and Dias was to find better routes for the spice trade.

18. **C** Hernán Cortés had briefly owned an encomienda in Hispañiola, but really is noted for conquering the Aztec Empire in modern-day Mexico. There is no other option that relates to his life. Be sure to associate Pizarro with Incas, Cabral with Brazil, Diaz with the Cape of Good Hope, da Gama with India, and Magellan with circumnavigation.

19. **B** Given the vast amounts of land in South America, Central America, and the Caribbean, there was hardly any shortage of land. Most encomiendas were assigned to former conquistadores as the Spanish crown's way of both rewarding their loyalty (despite being essentially mass murderers) and organizing the people in newly conquered lands. Interestingly, though, the Spanish crown never intended them to be permanent, and by the end of the century had assumed direct control over the encomiendas.

20. **D** England, as the most advanced representative democracy in Europe, the first to convert to a constitutional monarchy, took the lead in decentralizing political authority. While there was still a King and Queen, there had also been a prime minister since the early nineteenth century. Most other European countries retained harsher forms of centralized authority, and thus handicapped their own success.

21. **C** The title of the cartoon, "The Devilfish in Egyptian Waters," should indicate that it is referencing an event that took place in Egypt. This should eliminate (B) and (D), which involve Fashoda (in Eastern Africa) and Russia, respectively. This leaves (A) and (C), which both have to do with the Suez Canal. After the Suez Canal was completed in 1882, the British created a protectorate in Egypt to defend its pathway to its colonial holdings in India, which aligns with (C). The Suez Crisis, (A), refers to an event that took place much later, during the Cold War.

22. **B** If you remember that the Primrose League advocated for British imperialism, then you should have guessed that they would not be happy with a cartoon such as this, since it portrays imperial Great Britain as a menacing creature. The correct answer is (B).

23. **D** All of the countries listed in the answer choices except for Germany, (D), had significant imperial holdings. Germany, as you should recall, abstained from the imperial game due to Otto von Bismarck's indifference. He found European dominance much more appealing than imperialism.

24. **A** As an old saying goes, "the sun never sets on the British Empire." Great Britain had secured imperial holdings all over the globe, from India to Australia to Boersland (South Africa). Therefore, you can eliminate (B) and (C). The cartoon provides no evidence of countries either resisting or not resisting Imperial Britain, so (D) cannot be correct. The fact that the sea creature is holding on to Ireland should point you to (A).

25. **B** The word *bourgeois*, as well as the phrase "You will never be happy as long as you own anything" should've clued you in that the author is referring to redistribution of wealth via socialist means.

26. **C** The Congress of Vienna had existed to reorganize and stabilize Europe after the fall of Napoleon. Headed by Metternich, it was profoundly conservative by nature. That's a pretty far cry from anarchy.

27. **C** Communism primarily was concerned with the overturning the traditional owner/employee model of societal organization. You could make the argument that capitalism also cares about its workers, but only indirectly, given the invisible hand theory, and that a rising tide lifts all boats.

28. **C** The steam engine operated more efficiently on coal than on wood, and so with its invention, a new industry was created—coal mining. There were massive deposits in England, France, and Poland, and going down into the mines became the primary way for working-class people to make a living.

29. **C** Class struggle was on everybody's minds in the late nineteenth century owing to Marx and Engels. *Noblesse oblige* was a traditional way of taking care of the poorest in society, but that had been rejected a hundred years earlier. Choices (A) and (B) are off topic.

30. **C** Even though there are many similarities between Erasmus and Martin Luther, both of whom criticized the Catholic Church, the focus in this particular text is on Erasmus's ability to bring Latin and classical culture to the masses. The key sentence is at the end of the first paragraph: "He familiarized a much wider circle than the earlier humanists had reached with the spirit of antiquity." In this regard, Erasmus is quite similar to Francisco Petrarch, whose fascination with classical culture inspired the civic humanists. Therefore, the answer is (C).

31. **B** When humanism ceased to be the exclusive privilege of the few, people could study the Latin Bible as well as ancient texts of the classical era. This newfound knowledge would eventually enable people to begin questioning the laws and interpretations of the Catholic Church. Thus, (B) is the answer.

32. **A** As a product of the twentieth century, the author has consciously or unconsciously adopted the biases of his age, which includes a predilection for universal education and openness to various different points of view.

33. **A** In the passage, Huizinga writes, "Erasmus introduced the classic spirit, in so far as it could be reflected in the soul of a sixteenth-century Christian, among the people." It is evident that Erasmus understood classical texts to be consistent with his religion. Similarly, the Neoplatonists endeavored to use Platonic texts to better understand Christianity, making (A) the correct answer.

34. **D** According to Huizinga, "Until this time the humanists had...monopolized the treasures of classical culture." However, he then goes on to contrast these humanists with Erasmus, who had "an irresistible need of teaching." This indicates that, unlike earlier humanists, Erasmus made it a priority to spread his knowledge of classical culture. This best aligns with (D), which is the correct answer.

35. **A** The social reformers of the Victorian era were largely middle-class Christian women who decided that the lower classes lacked moral instruction, which alone would improve their lives. You can argue whether or not this was exactly true, but nonetheless it was in line with Biblical teachings. It also reflected a new class-consciousness in England, as the middle class had ballooned to a previously unknown size and strength.

36. **D** The title "Gin Lane," along with the destitute people pictured in the engraving, indicate that this piece of art comments on the problems associated with alcohol consumption. Since "spirits" refers to liquor, (D) is correct. Even if you have never heard of the Sale of Spirits Act, close analysis of the engraving coupled with Process of Elimination should help you get rid of the other answer choices, which have nothing to do with alcohol or destitution.

37. **C** Use question 35 to help you here, which established that the artist uses deliberate exaggeration for effect in this engraving. Deliberate exaggeration as an artistic device points to the piece's satirical purpose, which aligns with (C).

38. **A** The crowded city scene depicted in the engraving should bring to mind the Enclosure Acts, (A), which forced farmers off their lands and into the cities, resulting in overcrowding. This accelerated during the Industrial Revolution, as machines, rather than people, became a cheaper way for landowners to produce crops.

39. **D** Similar to what happened in the realm of science, twentieth-century European art was marked by the rejection of pretty much every aspect of traditional art up until that time. This includes recognizable human figures, evident character, and attention to minute details. However, since Hogarth's work wasn't portraiture, (D) isn't applicable.

40. **A** Indeed, by this time in English history, the monarchy was well on its way towards becoming a titular head-of-state. The power of Parliament had already been well established, and the office of the prime minister had become (in the persons of Disraeli and Gladstone) a new center of political power.

41. **C** The Tories were (and are) one of England's political parties, which hints at the idea of democracy and greater egalitarianism. This transition had occurred back in the turbulent seventeenth century, as the members of the famous Stuart dynasty struggled with the rise of representative democracy. This ultimately ended with the forcible abdication of James II, and the official creation by William and Mary of a constitutional monarchy.

42. **C** For outrageous behavior amongst nobility, nobody can beat the French under Louis XIV. A quick tour of the pleasure grounds at Versailles will show you how vain, pompous, self-absorbed, and weak the nobility had become under his reign. That was all by design, of course. Distracting the nobles with endless free parties allowed Louis XIV to assume power in their neglected states, which contributed to his absolute power.

43. **D** There is nothing in this letter as ordinary—and, you could say, as touching—as when the queen complains of her exhaustion. We've all felt tired. Modern historians, and modern entertainment, have seized upon the "ordinary lives of the powerful" meme for quite a while. It's a sign of the deeply egalitarian nature of our current society.

44. **B** With Britain enduring no military attacks from mainland Europe during this time period, and with the British Empire growing rapidly overseas, you can eliminate (C) and (D). There was a potato famine in 1845, but it was in Ireland, not England, so eliminate (A). You're left with the truth—in her unprecedented 64-year reign (the longest of any monarch on earth), Queen Victoria had to navigate through an equally unprecedented number of changes to English society.

45. **D** At the conference at Yalta, Roosevelt and Churchill divided Germany into four zones—U.S., English, French, and Soviet. Since the Soviets had marched into the country from the East, it made sense that they would control that portion. This was the beginning of East Germany and the Iron Curtain, and it marks the first formal postwar expansion of their land.

46. **C** Eastern European countries such as Yugoslavia and Hungary joined the Warsaw Pact, (C), an organization created as a direct answer to NATO. The Warsaw Pact was in part a Soviet military reaction to the integration of West Germany into NATO in 1955, but it was primarily motivated by Soviet desires to maintain control over military forces in Central and Eastern Europe.

47. **A** As indicated by the bottom map, while Eastern Europe fell under Soviet influence, Austria held its own (it is the lighter shade of gray). This observation is consistent with (A), as it suggests that Austria was able to resist Stalin. Since command economies are characteristic of communist systems, there is no evidence that Finland (also shaded the lighter gray on the map) had such an economy. Eliminate (B). Unlike the other Balkan countries on the map, Greece is a lighter shade of gray, so (C) can be eliminated. Choice (D) is also incorrect, as Czechoslovakia fell under Soviet influence (it is dark gray on the map) and therefore it's unlikely that it was able to maintain a free economy.

48. **C** Soviet tactics during World War II included rolling across Polish land, destroying its people, murdering 15,000 Polish officers in a forest (see Katyn massacre), and generally behaving even worse than the Germans that were occupying the country. No Pole would support these methods.

49. **A** Although West Berlin, entrenched in East Germany, was technically a part of West Germany, West Berlin was not the capital. The capital of West Germany was actually Bonn, a city firmly situated in West Germany. Therefore, the answer is (A).

50. **A** Northern European churches did not place the same emphasis on art as did southern European churches. Therefore, churches in the Netherlands did not commission artists to create works. However, the Netherlands in the seventeenth-century was a wealthy place. Private collectors were able to support the artists directly, so Dutch homes were not uncommon places to see art on display. The correct answer is therefore (A).

51. C   Process of Elimination should help you choose the correct answer. Since the Dutch were dominant in trade in the seventeenth century, (D) should have stood out to you as being possibly true. The Netherlands was a haven of religious tolerance; indeed, the Puritans who first settled America spent several years in the Netherlands preparing for their journey. Thus, (B) can be eliminated. You should vaguely associate the Netherlands with windmills, so you can get rid of (A) as well. Choice (C) is the answer.

52. D   The focus on the ancient world is more characteristic of the Italian Renaissance, so eliminate (A). Royalty commissioned art and thus increasingly became the subject of artwork when absolute monarchs began to rise, which is a bit later in European history than when this painting was created. Eliminate (B). The Dutch were not particularly concerned with religious imagery in art, so (C) does not work here. The mundane scene depicted in the painting should point you to (D), everyday life.

53. C   The arrival of empiricism was the hallmark of the scientific era. Francis Bacon was one of its earliest proponents, and the book that this passage is taken from, Novum Organum, was his attempt to unseat Aristotle, whose body of work was called the Organon. It was intended to be a catalog of everything that could be sensed. Perhaps unsurprisingly, he never finished it.

54. B   The Aristotlean worldview had been rediscovered by Italian traders as they entered into Arabic lands. This sparked the accomplishments of the Renaissance. However, the scientists of the time considered ancient natural science to be antiquated and irrational, and a poor method of searching for truth. Therefore, the answer here is (B).

55. B   The entire scientific explosion of the late nineteenth century—all the plodding laboratory work that was performed by Pasteur, Curie, and hundreds of other famous names—was based upon a belief in empirical thought. While (D) may have been tempting, the common person doesn't generally look for new organizing principles for life.

Section I, Part B: Short Answer

Question 1

Pinpoint the years from around 1760 to 1820 on the graph to locate the First Industrial Revolution, and 1840 to the late-nineteenth century for the Second Industrial Revolution to get a sense of the impact those revolutions had. Similarities abound between the two industrial revolutions, and you could've included any of the following:

- rapid technological advances

    o   First revolution: Mention Richard Arkwright, flying shuttle, spinning jenny, etc.

    o   Second revolution: steam engine, railroads, Henry Bessemer, etc.

- peasantry divorced from agriculture

- increased production, as evidenced by the graph

- continued rise of the merchant class

- improved health outcomes due to increased food production and medical innovations, as evidenced by the life expectancy data

Differences include any of the following:

- The Enclosure Acts and the putting-out system (or cottage industry) occurred in the first revolution. The peasants were reduced to doing piecework in their huts.

- The second revolution, by contrast, saw the massive movement of peasants into cities, and the beginning of work in factories.

Question 2

The first three thinkers (Locke, Hobbes, Smith) are most likely to be chosen to be representative of Enlightenment thought. Descartes is most likely *not* to represent Enlightenment thought, but you can make a case for Hobbes or Hume too. Here is a checklist of things you should've mentioned for each:

- Locke: strong individual = little government needed. The right to private property is sacred, *tabula rasa*, *Second Treatise on Government.*

- Hobbes: weak individual = strong government needed. *Leviathan.* Life in a state of nature is nasty, brutish, and short.

- Smith: invisible hand of the market guides society, *laissez faire*, *Wealth of Nations.*

- Descartes: deductive reasoning, mind/body split, systematic doubt, "I think; therefore, I am."

- David Hume: empiricism, radical rejection of all religion, relentless systematic doubt, sensory experience is everything, early psychologist.

Question 3

Despite the 1829 translation, you should remember that the Council of Trent was part of the sixteenth-century Counter-Reformation. It was the official dogmatic response to the Reformation.

- **Part (a):** Any of the famous Protestant Reformer figures would be appropriate here, including Desiderius Erasmus, Jan Hus, Martin Luther, Huldrych Zwingli, John Calvin, Thomas Cranmer, William Tyndale, and others.

- **Part (b):** The Counter Reformation had three components: the Council of Trent (which cannot be used, since it is the provided source material), the Spanish Inquisition, the Index of banned books, and the establishment of the Jesuit order as a manner of promoting good Catholic behavior to the world.

Question 4

The Holy Roman Empire was a loose, multiethnic conglomeration of principalities that existed from the early Middle Ages until its dissolution in the early 1800s. The questions zero in precisely on the religious history.

- **Part (a):** The religious conflict in general that gripped all of northern Europe in the 1500s was obviously the Protestant Reformation. You could've mentioned this alone, or you could've been more specific, discussing many of the figures mentioned above in part (a) of question 3. You also could've brought in specific events such as the *95 Theses*, the Diet of Worms, the Bibles printed in vernacular, or the Peace of Augsburg.

- **Part (b):** After 1600, there's really only one major event in European religious history: the Thirty Years' War (1618–1648). It devastated the Holy Roman Empire, both financially and politically, and left the territory divided into a Protestant north and Catholic south.

Section II, Part A: Document-Based Question (DBQ)

The Document-Based Question (DBQ) section begins with a suggested 15-minute reading period. During these 15 minutes, you'll want to do the following: (1) come up with some information not included in the given documents (your outside knowledge) to include in your essay, (2) get an overview of what each document means and the perspective of each author, (3) decide what opinion you are going to argue, and (4) write an outline of your essay.

This DBQ deals with the issue of Chartism and is asking you to determine whether Chartism should be viewed as a revolutionary movement or as a moderate movement. You will need to have some knowledge of British politics in the nineteenth century to handle this question and at least a little familiarity with Chartism, although don't be too concerned if your knowledge of Chartism is somewhat limited.

The first thing you want to do, BEFORE YOU LOOK AT THE DOCUMENTS, is to brainstorm for a minute or two. Try to list everything you know (from class or leisure reading or informational television programs) about both Chartism and British politics in the first half of the nineteenth century. This list will serve as your reference to the outside information you must provide to earn a top grade.

Next, read over the documents. As you read them, take notes in the margins and underline those passages that you are certain you are going to use in your essay. Make note of the opinions and position of the document's author. If a document reminds you of a piece of outside information, add that information to your brainstorming list. If you cannot make sense of a document or it argues strongly against your position, relax! You do not need to mention every document to score well on the DBQ.

Here is what you might see in the time you have to look over the documents.

The Documents

Document 1

This first document lays out the six points of the Charter. They are as follows:

1. universal suffrage
2. no property requirement for Members of Parliament
3. annual parliaments
4. equal representation (meaning that all areas of the nation would be equally represented)
5. payment of Members
6. vote by secret ballot

You'll notice that the document refers to the idea of the Charter providing for the "just representation of the people of Great Britain...," an indication that the goal is the political inclusion of working-class individuals rather than the complete overhaul of the system.

Document 2

This excerpt from a speech by Joseph Stevens given at a Chartist rally addresses one of the central issues behind the rise of Chartism. For Stevens, the Charter is all about providing people with the basic needs of life such as food and shelter. As a Chartist, Stevens believed that political rights were the means for British workers to achieve a better standard of living.

Document 3

This article, which appeared in a Chartist newspaper, appears to be aimed at those Chartists who were advocating the need for armed violence. While implying that it is within an Englishman's right to rebel and is, in fact, "the last remedy known to the Constitution," the article strongly rejects the use of physical force as an option in the current situation.

Interestingly, one of the arguments against the use of arms has little to do with morality and everything to do with the potential for success. The author points out that to succeed, armed revolts would have to be staged concurrently throughout the land, and that even if they are staged concurrently there would still be only a "slender chance" for success. Perhaps reluctantly, the author does concede that those who have arms should hold onto them, although they should be used only in self-defense.

Document 4

This document is a poem in honor of Feargus O'Connor. Besides noticing how nicely everything rhymes, you should be aware that the document refers to the earlier imprisonment of O'Connor, who, at the time the poem appeared in print, was free to continue with his labors on behalf of the Chartists.

Document 5

Document 5 contains a portion of a newspaper article detailing the events at a Chartist social gathering. It is important to note that the gathering consists of a tea party and ball, activities that clearly imitate the social activities of the upper classes and appear far from revolutionary. Feargus O'Connor (the same individual lionized in Document 4) was unable to attend the tea party because he and some of the other Chartists were busy debating whether to call for a general strike (certainly not many middle-class tea parties were interrupted for similar reasons).

Document 6

While male Chartists split over the question of whether the right to vote should be extended to women, women were actively engaged in the Chartist movement, both as a source of support for male Chartists and as active participants in their own right. This document, from a female Chartist organization, should be viewed in conjunction with Document 2, because, like the earlier document, it focuses on the economic hardships of working-class life, rather than placing a specific emphasis on the political struggle or women's rights within the Chartist movement.

Document 7

Make note that the author of this letter is a middle-class man and that the letter reveals some of the fears that his class must have felt about a working-class movement that they neither understood nor sympathized with. Also, the source for his information is the *Times*, the most important newspaper of the establishment and again not necessarily a source for genuine understanding of the Chartist movement.

Outside Information

We have already discussed much more than you could possibly write in only 40 minutes. Don't worry. You will not be expected to mention everything or even most of what we have covered in the section above. You will, however, be expected to include some outside information, that is, information not mentioned directly in the documents. The following is some outside information you might have used in your essay.

- The ostensible goal of Chartism was the passage of the "People's Charter," a document that called for universal suffrage for all men over the age of twenty-one, the end of property requirements for those holding seats in Parliament, annual parliamentary elections, equal electoral districts, and payment of those holding seats in Parliament. Chartists organized massive petitions that were presented on several occasions to the House of Commons, although the House of Commons did nothing to act on them. The largest and final petition was presented in 1848 with around 3 million signers.

- Five of the demands of the Chartists are today a part of the British constitution. The only one that has never been enacted was the idea of annual parliamentary elections, a radical idea that went back to the constitutional struggles of the seventeenth century. Today the maximum life of a parliament is five years thanks to the Fixed-Term Parliaments Act 2011. Before the passage of this act, Parliament could be dissolved only by royal proclamation. The changes enacted in 2011 were part of the Conservative–Liberal Democrat coalition agreement which was produced after the 2010 general election.

- The late 1830s and the 1840s were a particularly difficult period, one known to historians as the "hungry forties." Economic difficulties may account for the rise of Chartism, particularly if the movement is viewed as one whose primary goal was the establishment of political rights for working-class individuals so that they could have some say over the economic conditions that ruled their lives. Economic conditions may also account for the decline of Chartism after 1848, since these were years of growing economic prosperity and therefore may have led to an easing of political demands.

- Working-class individuals were angered over the passage of the Great Reform Bill (1832), which provided political rights for middle-class individuals, but ignored the rights of the working class. Additionally, there was a tremendous amount of working-class frustration with certain bills passed by this new "reformed" Parliament, including the 1834 Poor Law, which treated those suffering from poverty with great harshness.

- 1848 was a year of revolutionary activity throughout Europe. In France, the monarchy was replaced by a republic and revolutions spread across Europe. You should know from your studies of this period, however, that England and Russia were the two European states that were exempt from revolutionary activity in that year.

- There were two dominant factions within Chartism. The majority can be labeled "moral force" Chartists; they wanted to peacefully campaign for the passage of the "People's Charter." "Physical force" Chartists were a smaller faction found primarily in the cities of Northern England; they advocated the possible use of violence should their demands not be met. William Lovell was the leader of the moral force Chartists, while Feargus O'Connor was the main figure in the opposing faction.

- Chartism as a movement declined rapidly in the years after 1848. Working-class men increasingly looked to labor unions as a source for economic change rather than mass political movements, though working-class political activity did not disappear. The British political system would prove to be more flexible than many had imagined, and in 1867 male working-class householders received the vote, while in 1884 their counterparts in the countryside received the same.

Choosing a Thesis Statement

This DBQ is asking you to take sides in a debate. On the basis of the documents, a much stronger case could be provided for taking the position that Chartism should be viewed as a movement for political change that was *not* fundamentally revolutionary. Keep in mind that while there are strong historical arguments for taking the other side (and a number of books and articles have taken the position that Chartism *was* inherently revolutionary), you must base your argument primarily on the documents provided on the exam. The documents provided truly lean toward the nonrevolutionary aspects of the movement. Your thesis statement could be as follows: Though it inspired passion among both upper and lower classes in England, Chartism was undoubtedly a nonrevolutionary movement.

Planning Your Essay

Unless you read extremely quickly, you probably will not have time to write a detailed outline for your essay during the 15-minute reading period. However, it is worth taking several minutes to jot down a loose structure of your essay because it will actually save you time when you write. First, decide on your thesis and write it down in the test booklet. (There is usually some blank space below the documents.) Then, take a minute or two to brainstorm all the points you might put in your essay. Choose the strongest points and number them in the order you plan to present them. Lastly, note which documents and outside information you plan to use in conjunction with each point. If you organize your essay in advance of writing, the actual writing process will go much more smoothly. More important, you will not write yourself into a corner, suddenly finding yourself making a point you cannot support or heading toward a weak conclusion (or worse still, no conclusion at all).

For example, to deal with the issue of whether Chartism was revolutionary you might want to organize a brainstorm list like the following:

> *Political demands of the Chartists*
> *Six points of the Charter*
> *Economic issues*
> *Chartism and women*
> *Violence and nonviolence*
> *Hunger*
> *Actions taken by the Chartists*
> *End result of Chartist activities*

Next, you would want to figure out which of your brainstorm ideas could be the main idea of paragraph number one, which ones could be used as evidence to support a point, and which should be eliminated. You should probably begin your first paragraph with your thesis, and then discuss the specific political demands of the Chartists in an attempt to show that the Chartists were interested in being included in the British political system and were not seeking its destruction. You should mark the paragraph topic with a 1 to show that it's the theme of your first paragraph; then get more specific with a note if it's supporting evidence. In this case, your list might look like this:

> *Political demands of the Chartists*   *1*
> *Six points of the Charter*   *1-evidence*
> *Economic issues*
> *Chartism and women*
> *Violence and nonviolence*
> *Hunger*
> *Actions taken by the Chartists*
> *End result of Chartist activities*

If paragraph one is going to deal with the political demands of Chartism, you should certainly refer to Document 1 because it lays out the Chartist program. You might want to use your second paragraph to deal with the economic issues behind Chartism. This approach is a way to show that economic deprivation played a major role in leading working-class individuals toward political activity, not for the purposes of destroying British society, but to ensure that there was food on their tables. You could therefore make use of Documents

2 and 6, both of which deal with the economic deprivations behind Chartism. In this case your list would look like this:

Political demands of the Chartists	*1*
Six points of the Charter	*1-evidence*
Economic issues	*2*
Chartism and women	*2-evidence*
Violence and nonviolence	
Hunger	*2-evidence*
Actions taken by the Chartists	
End result of Chartist activities	

Proceed in this way until you have finished planning your strategy. Try to fit as many of the documents into your argument as you can, but do not stretch too far to fit one in. Don't be concerned, for example, if you can't find a use for the poem in honor of Feargus O'Connor. An obvious, desperate stretch will only hurt your grade. Also, remember that history is often intricate and that the readers of your exam want to see that you respect the intrinsic complexity behind many historical events.

Section II, Part B: Long Essay

Because you only have 35 minutes to plan and write this essay, you will not have time to work out elaborate arguments. That's okay; nobody is expecting you to read two questions, choose one, remember all the pertinent facts about the subject, formulate a brilliant thesis, and then write a perfect essay. Here are the steps you should follow. First, choose your question, brainstorm for two or three minutes, and edit your brainstorm ideas. Then, number the points you are going to include in your essay in the order you plan to present them. Finally, think of a simple thesis statement that allows you to discuss the points your essay will make.

Question 2—Enlightened Absolutism (Option 1)

> **Question 2:** Compare the extent to which the term "enlightened absolutism" applied to certain rulers in Eastern Europe and Russia during the eighteenth century.

About the Structure of Your Essay

In this essay, you will want to make a strong thesis statement, perhaps arguing that while those rulers who are labeled as "enlightened absolutists" often spoke about enlightened ideas, for the most part they failed to implement any substantive changes within their realms. On the other hand, you could list some of their actual achievements (such as in the area of religious toleration), while pointing out that powerful elements within their states such as the Church or nobility blocked any possibility for further reform. Most importantly, be sure to *compare* rulers of different countries and draw connections among them. The question makes it clear that comparison is the historical thinking skill you are being tested on.

Your essay should mention at least some of the following:

- Most of the leading writers of the Enlightenment, such as Voltaire and Diderot, wanted change to come about not through the advent of republics, but rather through "enlightened monarchs" who would seek to reform their ideas based on the concepts of enlightened reason.

- The monarchs whom historians are mostly referring to when using the term "Enlightened Absolutists" are Catherine the Great, the empress of Russia (1762–1796); Joseph II of Austria (1741–1790); and Frederick the Great, the King of Prussia (1740–1786).

- These Enlightened Absolutists certainly read the works of the leading writers of the Enlightenment. Frederick read Voltaire and was so impressed that he invited him to stay at his court. Catherine also read Voltaire, as well as Diderot, and when Diderot desperately needed money to get out of debt, Catherine bought his extensive library and then generously lent it back to him.

- Joseph of Austria was influenced by the Enlightenment's call for religious toleration. Joseph granted Jews the right to worship (though they had to pay special taxes for the privilege), while Protestants were given the right to hold positions at the court in Vienna. That spirit of tolerance didn't extend to all Enlightened Absolutists, as Frederick refused to grant similar rights to the Jews of his realm and Catherine did nothing to grant rights to religious minorities in Russia.

- Writers of the Enlightenment had discussed the need for humane treatment for the accused. Both Joseph and Frederick banned the use of judicial torture within their realms, while Frederick went so far as to ban capital punishment. Both rulers also relaxed the strict censorship that existed in their states, although at times they still banned works they considered critical of their rule.

- All three enlightened monarchs attempted to expand the number of individuals receiving an education, not so as to create freethinkers, but rather that they might have more trained individuals to serve as bureaucrats. Although none of the states implemented anything close to universal public education, they did greatly increase the number of individuals who went to school. These students, however, almost exclusively came from the higher classes.

- Frederick, in his youth, had toyed with the concept of enlightened statecraft based on just relations among states. However, when he saw the opportunity, he launched an unprovoked attack on the Habsburg territory of Silesia.

- Joseph of Austria ended the practice of owning serfs, although the newly freed peasants found that freedom came with the price of greatly increased taxes. Joseph discovered that further reform in the countryside was impossible due to the strong resistance of the nobility.

- None of these rulers took steps toward making their states constitutional monarchies. Catherine toyed with the idea of granting a constitution, but in the end, she and her fellow absolutists showed little interest in doing anything that would place actual limits on their power.

Question 3—Domestic Tensions on the Eve of World War I (Option 2)

Question 3: Compare the domestic problems faced by TWO of the great European powers in the decade immediately prior to the outbreak of the First World War.

About the Structure of Your Essay

The years immediately prior to World War I were notable for the domestic problems faced by the great powers: Germany, Austria-Hungary, Russia, France, Italy, and Great Britain. Since the question is asking you to deal with two of these states, it would be to your advantage to quickly consider a list of domestic concerns for each of these states and then decide which two states on your list look most promising when it comes to writing your actual essay. Like Question 2, this question requires you to compare the domestic problems of two countries, so be sure to draw explicit connections between them in the text of your essay.

Depending on which two nations you decide to focus on, your essay might mention some of the following points:

- On the surface, Germany was the great behemoth of Europe, possessing the strongest army, a growing navy, and an unmatched industrial base. Despite these apparent strengths, on the eve of the First World War, Germany was facing a potential political crisis, with more than one nationalistic politician stating that Germany needed a "blood cure" (war) to divert public attention. The constitution that Bismarck established for the new German state in 1871 did not create a constitutional monarchy along British lines. While the national Parliament, the Reichstag, was elected by universal male suffrage, its powers were severely restricted. The chief minister of the state, the chancellor, was selected by the kaiser and not dependent upon the support of the Reichstag.

  Despite being in many ways a conservative, militaristic society, Germany also had the largest Socialist party in all of Europe, and the Socialists were the single largest political party in the Reichstag by 1912. The problem was that while the party could bring hundreds of thousands of people out in the street for demonstrations and garner around a third of the popular vote, by itself it could not enact desperately needed political reform. The party rejected the revisionist Socialist views of Eduard Bernstein, who argued that a socialist state could be achieved without a violent revolution. Yet, the S. P. D., while clinging to revolutionary rhetoric, became a parliamentary party rather than a revolutionary one. Kaiser Wilhelm, however, remained convinced that the party was committed to the destruction of his state and lived in dread of the eventual day when the Socialists would put their revolutionary rhetoric into action.

  German Liberals, who perhaps should have been the leaders of the move to a genuine parliamentary system, found themselves split among a number of splinter parties as they argued over issues such as protective tariffs. Meanwhile, in the decade before the war, the right witnessed a surge in small parties that espoused beliefs that foreshadowed the program of the Nazi party.

  Germany faced other domestic problems on the eve of the war. Many Germans bemoaned the declining world of the independent farmers, who were being crushed by a decline in food prices, and of craftsmen, who were threatened by the rise of large industry. Small shopkeepers also were threatened by large department stores. All of these problems contributed to the rise of anti-Semitic parties, which deflected blame from the government and encouraged Germans to blame the negative changes that were coming to their lives on Jewish retailers and bankers. While not as considerable as that facing Austria-Hungary, Germany had its own nationality problem with many voicing concern that Polish families were buying farmland from impoverished Prussian Junkers, while the higher birthrate among Polish families portended a potential population explosion in the east. Meanwhile in Alsace and Lorraine, territories that Germany had seized as part of their victory in the Franco-Prussian War in 1871, a population that was ostensibly ethnically German would have preferred to substitute French rule for that of the heavy-handed Germans.

- In Austria-Hungary, the Emperor Franz-Joseph saw himself as the father of his people, but he couldn't have been a proud parent when considering the behavior of his "children." The Emperor saw his throne as being above the nationality problem and to some extent affection for the Emperor made this true. However, the aging Franz-Joseph (he was born in 1830) couldn't live forever, and there was a sense that his demise would soon be followed by the collapse of his empire. The establishment of the dual monarchy of Austria-Hungary in 1867 had not solved the nationality problem and, in some ways, had made it worse as other nationalities strove to match the status achieved by the Hungarians. Within Hungary, the Magyars, who made up half of the population, essentially ignored minority rights. With only five percent of the male population in Hungary allowed to vote, Magyar magnates controlled a political machine that ensured their dominance over the political and cultural life in the Hungarian kingdom. While there were those within the empire who were advocates of breaking the empire into a federation of nationalities, the grim reality in Hungary revealed that this would not solve the problem since each federation would have had its own nationality problem. The nationality question dominated all other issues within the empire and right on the eve of the war there was a major political problem in Bohemia over the question of whether to teach German or Czech in the public schools.

While the army and civil service were two institutions that were reasonably successful in providing some sense of common imperial identity, other attempts to match this success failed. Universal male suffrage, adopted in 1907, led to even greater conflict in the Austrian Parliament, the Reichsrat, as each nationality was represented by its various partisans. The institution itself was to become infamous for the unbelievably poor behavior of the parliamentary representatives as they cursed, threw things, and spit on their rivals. Eventually this tentative experiment in parliamentary rule was deemed a failure, and the Emperor shut down the Parliament at the beginning of the war.

Of all the seemingly implacable problems facing Austria-Hungary, it was the South Slav issue that was most pressing on the eve of the First World War. The establishment of an independent Serbian state in 1878 out of a former piece of the Ottoman Empire was not a major problem for Austria-Hungary except for the fact that it was a state built on the issue of nationality, in this case, a Serbian national identity. At the same time the Serbian state was born, Austria-Hungary took administrative control over the province of Bosnia, a territory that had a significant ethnic Serbian population. Relations between the two states were amicable until 1903 when the pro-Austrian Serbian dynasty was replaced by a group of army officers who wished to see Serbia pursue a more nationalistic program and ally themselves with their fellow Slavs in Russia. Ensuing tensions between Austria-Hungary and Serbia led to the so-called "Pig War," an economic war in which Austria-Hungary refused to import Serbia's main export—pigs. In 1908, Austria-Hungary broke an earlier promise it had made to Russia and formally incorporated Bosnia into the empire. This step was undertaken not out of a desire to add more Slavs to their already polyglot empire, but rather to forestall a possible expansion of Serbian power into the territory. The step infuriated the Russians, who, because they were just recovering from their war with Japan and the Revolution of 1905, were unable to respond with vigor, though they vowed that next time they would not stand down if there was a similar Austro-Hungarian provocation in the Balkans. By the summer of 1914, tensions between Austria-Hungary and Serbia were at a fever pitch, with Archduke Franz Ferdinand on his way to Sarajevo to inspect the army divisions that would be used for a potential invasion and occupation of Serbia.

- In the years before the war, Russia remained something of an enigma in that it combined political backwardness with an economy that was making impressive advances. The nation had begun to industrialize by the 1890s, and, on the eve of the First World War, the potential size of its economy was becoming apparent. In 1914, Russia was the fourth largest industrial power on Earth, having overtaken France. Rather than begin with smaller industrial concerns, Russian industrialization had occurred on a massive scale with gigantic factories sprouting up in the area in and around St. Petersburg, a city that was facing an acute housing shortage and sanitation problems. The booming economy in the years prior to the war also brought about a high rate of inflation and significant social tensions resulting from an exploited workforce, with a significant number of workdays lost to strikes. There was also serious unrest in the countryside, where many peasants continued to try to scrape by on inadequate land holdings and grappled with declining agricultural prices.

Politically, the tsarist system of royal absolutism seemed incredibly anachronistic at the start of the twentieth century. An unsuccessful war with Japan in 1904 would reveal the numerous failings of the political system and would help bring about the revolution of 1905. The tsarist state survived, but just barely, in part because the army stayed loyal, while the opposition to the tsar was scattered among many different groups. As a concession to those clamoring for change, Nicholas II was forced to accept a parliament, or Duma, but he treated it with disdain and by 1907 had packed it with sympathetic representatives. In order to restore its popularity following the Revolution, the government turned to anti-Semitism and nationalism as unifying forces, but even these proved problematic. As an empire that stretched across two continents populated by numerous peoples with different languages and cultures, Russia had a serious national identity problem.

- It can be argued that of all the great powers, France was in the best shape domestically on the eve of the war. Even so, the Third French Republic did face some significant domestic conflicts prior to the First World War, including the fact that many Frenchmen still questioned the legitimacy of the republic itself. The Third Republic that was officially created in 1875 was in some ways conceived by accident when it became clear that restoring the monarchy, a move many Frenchmen would have preferred, was fraught with difficulties. In the years that followed, prime ministers came and went but no single party was able to dominate the legislature. Unlike the other great European powers, French economic output was fairly stagnant in the decade prior to the war. As a result of this lack of growth, France encountered significant labor unrest with the number of work days lost to strikes increasing every year leading up to 1914.

The fallout from the Dreyfus affair, in which a Jewish officer had been falsely accused of selling military secrets to the Germans, overshadowed life in the Third Republic even after Dreyfus's pardon in September of 1899. *Action Française*, a right-wing newspaper, continued to push an anti-Semitic agenda, something that received a favorable response among a significant portion of the French populace, particularly as France's Jewish population increased with refugees escaping from the horrors of tsarist Russia. Other religious issues were equally contentious, such as the question of the role of the Catholic Church. Although church and state were officially separated in 1905, that decision continued to rankle the more religiously inclined. In the years immediately prior to the war, the Third Republic also debated if they should maintain a three-year military service commitment for French conscripts (to keep up with Germany's vastly larger population) as well as the controversial question of whether to introduce an income tax to pay for larger military expenditures and a minimal system of old-age pensions.

- The Italian economy was growing at a nice clip in the years prior to 1914, but the economy still could not keep up with the needs of a rapidly growing population. The industrialized north suffered from a wave of strikes, which, due to the relative weakness of the Italian trade union movement in comparison with its German or British counterparts, provided an opening for extremist groups. One such group was the Syndicalists, a group whose mission was to transform capitalist society through action by the working class, who threatened to use the tool of the general strike to bring down the capitalist system. Meanwhile, in the largely agricultural south of Italy, life had hardly changed since the eighteenth century; it was still a land of great estates and a hardworking, impoverished peasantry. The desperate poverty of the region would eventually lead to entire villages packing up and emigrating to the United States.

Parliamentary politics in Italy had never been a particularly enlightening sight, and, on the eve of the war, the entire system appeared to be breaking down. When Italy entered the war on the side of the Entente in 1915, the Parliament was not even consulted. As in France, there was a significant anti-clerical element in Italian politics. While the growing Catholic Center Party benefited from the papacy's continued refusal to recognize the Italian state, it came to realize that it would be useful to have a party that reflected Church desire in order to stop the passage of bills allowing for such things as divorce. As a possible way out of the political quagmire, the government turned its attention to imperial affairs, such as the worthless conquest of Libya in 1911. For more ardent Italian nationalists, this action was not enough, and they clamored for the conquest of *Italia irredenta* (unredeemed Italy); that is, areas occupied by ethnic Italians living under Austro-Hungarian rule.

- Great Britain was facing a number of significant issues on the eve of the First World War. On the front burner in the decade prior to the First World War was the question of the extension of suffrage to women. In the first half of the nineteenth century, Liberals often argued that voting should be limited to men of property, but once the vote was granted to working-class male householders in the reform bills of 1867 and 1884, it opened up the possibility of a further extensions to include women. In the second half of the century a number of women's suffrage societies emerged that worked for the vote through peaceful means, such as organizing petitions meant to influence Members of Parliament. By 1900, a new, more violent element emerged with the formation of the Women's Social and Political Union (W.S.P.U.), led by Emmeline Pankhurst. Pankhurst's group, often referred to as suffragettes, was quite different from the earlier suffrage societies in that the members felt justified in using means such as arson as a tool for bringing attention to the plight of women. When some suffragettes were arrested for violent acts, they staged hunger strikes in prison and brought negative publicity to the government of Liberal Prime Minister Herbert Asquith.

Great Britain struggled over the place of the unelected House of Lords in a nation that was increasingly heading towards democracy. The focal point for this struggle came in 1909 when the Liberals introduced a bill to provide for old-age pensions. In order to finance the plan, David Lloyd George, the Chancellor of the Exchequer, proposed raising income taxes, death duties, and taxing landed wealth. The bill passed the House of Commons, but stalled in the House of Lords, where the Lords broke with tradition for the first time in over two hundred years and rejected a money bill. As punishment for this unprecedented behavior, the Liberal government pushed a bill to limit the House of Lords' power to a suspending veto lasting two parliamentary sessions. When the House of Lords refused to pass a bill that would effectively strip it of its powers, Prime Minister Asquith threatened to have the King instantly create several hundred new lords in order to stack the upper house of Parliament and pass the bill. With this the House of Lords finally passed the bill.

Yet the most serious crisis facing the British government on the eve of the First World War was the question of Home Rule for Ireland. The Liberal Party had first broached the subject when Prime Minister William Gladstone introduced a Home Rule bill in 1884. The bill failed to win support among the party faithful and, in fact, led to a split within the Liberal Party that helped bring about a long period of Conservative dominance over British politics. By 1914, Asquith was ready to try again to bring about Home Rule. Fearing the domination of Catholics, the Protestants of Ulster began to take up arms to resist home rule, while the Catholic population began to arm in response. Civil war looked almost certain in Ireland, and, to make matters worse, some British army officers indicated that they would refuse to obey if ordered to disarm the Ulster Protestants.

The Princeton Review

Completely darken bubbles with a No. 2 pencil. If you make a mistake, be sure to erase mark completely. Erase all stray marks.

1.

YOUR NAME:
(Print)　　　Last　　　First　　　M.I.

SIGNATURE. _____　DATE: __/__/__

HOME ADDRESS: _____
(Print)　　　Number and Street

_____
City　　　State　　　Zip Code

PHONE NO.: _____

IMPORTANT: Please fill in these boxes exactly as shown on the back cover of your test book.

2. TEST FORM

3. TEST CODE

4. REGISTRATION NUMBER

5. YOUR NAME

First 4 letters of last name				FIRST INIT	MID INIT
A	A	A	A	A	A
B	B	B	B	B	B
C	C	C	C	C	C
D	D	D	D	D	D
E	E	E	E	E	E
F	F	F	F	F	F
G	G	G	G	G	G
H	H	H	H	H	H
I	I	I	I	I	I
J	J	J	J	J	J
K	K	K	K	K	K
L	L	L	L	L	L
M	M	M	M	M	M
N	N	N	N	N	N
O	O	O	O	O	O
P	P	P	P	P	P
Q	Q	Q	Q	Q	Q
R	R	R	R	R	R
S	S	S	S	S	S
T	T	T	T	T	T
U	U	U	U	U	U
V	V	V	V	V	V
W	W	W	W	W	W
X	X	X	X	X	X
Y	Y	Y	Y	Y	Y
Z	Z	Z	Z	Z	Z

6. DATE OF BIRTH

Month	Day	Year
JAN		
FEB	0 0	0 0
MAR	1 1	1 1
APR	2 2	2 2
MAY	3 3	3 3
JUN	4	4 4
JUL	5	5 5
AUG	6	6 6
SEP	7	7 7
OCT	8	8 8
NOV	9	9 9
DEC		

7. GENDER

MALE
FEMALE

The Princeton Review

1. A B C D E
2. A B C D E
3. A B C D E
4. A B C D E
5. A B C D E
6. A B C D E
7. A B C D E
8. A B C D E
9. A B C D E
10. A B C D E
11. A B C D E
12. A B C D E
13. A B C D E
14. A B C D E
15. A B C D E
16. A B C D E
17. A B C D E
18. A B C D E

19. A B C D E
20. A B C D E
21. A B C D E
22. A B C D E
23. A B C D E
24. A B C D E
25. A B C D E
26. A B C D E
27. A B C D E
28. A B C D E
29. A B C D E
30. A B C D E
31. A B C D E
32. A B C D E
33. A B C D E
34. A B C D E
35. A B C D E
36. A B C D E

37. A B C D E
38. A B C D E
39. A B C D E
40. A B C D E
41. A B C D E
42. A B C D E
43. A B C D E
44. A B C D E
45. A B C D E
46. A B C D E
47. A B C D E
48. A B C D E
49. A B C D E
50. A B C D E
51. A B C D E
52. A B C D E
53. A B C D E
54. A B C D E

55. A B C D E
56. A B C D E
57. A B C D E
58. A B C D E
59. A B C D E
60. A B C D E
61. A B C D E
62. A B C D E
63. A B C D E
64. A B C D E
65. A B C D E
66. A B C D E
67. A B C D E
68. A B C D E
69. A B C D E
70. A B C D E

The Princeton Review®

Completely darken bubbles with a No. 2 pencil. If you make a mistake, be sure to erase mark completely. Erase all stray marks.

1.

YOUR NAME: (Print)
Last   First   M.I.

SIGNATURE: _____ DATE: ___/___/___

HOME ADDRESS: (Print)
Number and Street

City   State   Zip Code

PHONE NO.: _____

IMPORTANT: Please fill in these boxes exactly as shown on the back cover of your test book.

2. TEST FORM
_____

3. TEST CODE

4. REGISTRATION NUMBER

5. YOUR NAME

First 4 letters of last name				FIRST INIT	MID INIT
A A A A				A	A
B B B B				B	B
C C C C				C	C
D D D D				D	D
E E E E				E	E
F F F F				F	F
G G G G				G	G
H H H H				H	H
I I I I				I	I
J J J J				J	J
K K K K				K	K
L L L L				L	L
M M M M				M	M
N N N N				N	N
O O O O				O	O
P P P P				P	P
Q Q Q Q				Q	Q
R R R R				R	R
S S S S				S	S
T T T T				T	T
U U U U				U	U
V V V V				V	V
W W W W				W	W
X X X X				X	X
Y Y Y Y				Y	Y
Z Z Z Z				Z	Z

6. DATE OF BIRTH

Month	Day		Year	
JAN				
FEB	0	0	0	0
MAR	1	1	1	1
APR	2	2	2	2
MAY	3	3	3	3
JUN		4	4	4
JUL		5	5	5
AUG		6	6	6
SEP		7	7	7
OCT		8	8	8
NOV		9	9	9
DEC				

3. TEST CODE (column values)

U A J U
1 B K 1
2 C L 2
3 D M 3
4 E N 4
5 F O 5
6 G P 6
7 H Q 7
8 I R 8
9

4. REGISTRATION NUMBER

U U U U U U U
0 0 0 0 0 0 0
1 1 1 1 1 1 1
2 2 2 2 2 2 2
3 3 3 3 3 3 3
4 4 4 4 4 4 4
5 5 5 5 5 5 5
6 6 6 6 6 6 6
7 7 7 7 7 7 7
8 8 8 8 8 8 8
9 9 9 9 9 9 9

7. GENDER
- MALE
- FEMALE

The Princeton Review®

1. A B C D E
2. A B C D E
3. A B C D E
4. A B C D E
5. A B C D E
6. A B C D E
7. A B C D E
8. A B C D E
9. A B C D E
10. A B C D E
11. A B C D E
12. A B C D E
13. A B C D E
14. A B C D E
15. A B C D E
16. A B C D E
17. A B C D E
18. A B C D E

19. A B C D E
20. A B C D E
21. A B C D E
22. A B C D E
23. A B C D E
24. A B C D E
25. A B C D E
26. A B C D E
27. A B C D E
28. A B C D E
29. A B C D E
30. A B C D E
31. A B C D E
32. A B C D E
33. A B C D E
34. A B C D E
35. A B C D E
36. A B C D E

37. A B C D E
38. A B C D E
39. A B C D E
40. A B C D E
41. A B C D E
42. A B C D E
43. A B C D E
44. A B C D E
45. A B C D E
46. A B C D E
47. A B C D E
48. A B C D E
49. A B C D E
50. A B C D E
51. A B C D E
52. A B C D E
53. A B C D E
54. A B C D E

55. A B C D E
56. A B C D E
57. A B C D E
58. A B C D E
59. A B C D E
60. A B C D E
61. A B C D E
62. A B C D E
63. A B C D E
64. A B C D E
65. A B C D E
66. A B C D E
67. A B C D E
68. A B C D E
69. A B C D E
70. A B C D E

NOTES

International Offices Listing

China (Beijing)
1501 Building A,
Disanji Creative Zone,
No.66 West Section of North 4th Ring Road Beijing
Tel: +86-10-62684481/2/3
Email: tprkor01@chol.com
Website: www.tprbeijing.com

China (Shanghai)
1010 Kaixuan Road
Building B, 5/F
Changning District, Shanghai, China 200052
Sara Beattie, Owner: Email: sbeattie@sarabeattie.com
Tel: +86-21-5108-2798
Fax: +86-21-6386-1039
Website: www.princetonreviewshanghai.com

Hong Kong
5th Floor, Yardley Commercial Building
1-6 Connaught Road West, Sheung Wan, Hong Kong
(MTR Exit C)
Sara Beattie, Owner: Email: sbeattie@sarabeattie.com
Tel: +852-2507-9380
Fax: +852-2827-4630
Website: www.princetonreviewhk.com

India (Mumbai)
Score Plus Academy
Office No.15, Fifth Floor
Manek Mahal 90
Veer Nariman Road
Next to Hotel Ambassador
Churchgate, Mumbai 400020
Maharashtra, India
Ritu Kalwani: Email: director@score-plus.com
Tel: + 91 22 22846801 / 39 / 41
Website: www.score-plus.com

India (New Delhi)
South Extension
K-16, Upper Ground Floor
South Extension Part–1,
New Delhi-110049
Aradhana Mahna: aradhana@manyagroup.com
Monisha Banerjee: monisha@manyagroup.com
Ruchi Tomar: ruchi.tomar@manyagroup.com
Rishi Josan: Rishi.josan@manyagroup.com
Vishal Goswamy: vishal.goswamy@manyagroup.com
Tel: +91-11-64501603/ 4, +91-11-65028379
Website: www.manyagroup.com

Lebanon
463 Bliss Street
AlFarra Building - 2nd floor
Ras Beirut
Beirut, Lebanon
Hassan Coudsi: Email: hassan.coudsi@review.com
Tel: +961-1-367-688
Website: www.princetonreviewlebanon.com

Korea
945-25 Young Shin Building
25 Daechi-Dong, Kangnam-gu
Seoul, Korea 135-280
Yong-Hoon Lee: Email: TPRKor01@chollian.net
In-Woo Kim: Email: iwkim@tpr.co.kr
Tel: + 82-2-554-7762
Fax: +82-2-453-9466
Website: www.tpr.co.kr

Kuwait
ScorePlus Learning Center
Salmiyah Block 3, Street 2 Building 14
Post Box: 559, Zip 1306, Safat, Kuwait
Email: infokuwait@score-plus.com
Tel: +965-25-75-48-02 / 8
Fax: +965-25-75-46-02
Website: www.scorepluseducation.com

Malaysia
Sara Beattie MDC Sdn Bhd
Suites 18E & 18F
18th Floor
Gurney Tower, Persiaran Gurney
Penang, Malaysia
Email: tprkl.my@sarabeattie.com
Sara Beattie, Owner: Email: sbeattie@sarabeattie.com
Tel: +604-2104 333
Fax: +604-2104 330
Website: www.princetonreviewKL.com

Mexico
TPR México
Guanajuato No. 242 Piso 1 Interior 1
Col. Roma Norte
México D.F., C.P.06700
registro@princetonreviewmexico.com
Tel: +52-55-5255-4495
+52-55-5255-4440
+52-55-5255-4442
Website: www.princetonreviewmexico.com

Qatar
Score Plus
Office No: 1A, Al Kuwari (Damas)
Building near Merweb Hotel, Al Saad
Post Box: 2408, Doha, Qatar
Email: infoqatar@score-plus.com
Tel: +974 44 36 8580, +974 526 5032
Fax: +974 44 13 1995
Website: www.scorepluseducation.com

Taiwan
The Princeton Review Taiwan
2F, 169 Zhong Xiao East Road, Section 4
Taipei, Taiwan 10690
Lisa Bartle (Owner): lbartle@princetonreview.com.tw
Tel: +886-2-2751-1293
Fax: +886-2-2776-3201
Website: www.PrincetonReview.com.tw

Thailand
The Princeton Review Thailand
Sathorn Nakorn Tower, 28th floor
100 North Sathorn Road
Bangkok, Thailand 10500
Thavida Bijayendrayodhin (Chairman)
Email: thavida@princetonreviewthailand.com
Mitsara Bijayendrayodhin (Managing Director)
Email: mitsara@princetonreviewthailand.com
Tel: +662-636-6770
Fax: +662-636-6776
Website: www.princetonreviewthailand.com

Turkey
Yeni Sülün Sokak No. 28
Levent, Istanbul, 34330, Turkey
Nuri Ozgur: nuri@tprturkey.com
Rona Ozgur: rona@tprturkey.com
Iren Ozgur: iren@tprturkey.com
Tel: +90-212-324-4747
Fax: +90-212-324-3347
Website: www.tprturkey.com

UAE
Emirates Score Plus
Office No: 506, Fifth Floor
Sultan Business Center
Near Lamcy Plaza, 21 Oud Metha Road
Post Box: 44098, Dubai
United Arab Emirates
Hukumat Kalwani: skoreplus@gmail.com
Ritu Kalwani: director@score-plus.com
Email: info@score-plus.com
Tel: +971-4-334-0004
Fax: +971-4-334-0222
Website: www.princetonreviewuae.com

Our International Partners

The Princeton Review also runs courses with a variety of partners in Africa, Asia, Europe, and South America.

Georgia
LEAF American-Georgian Education Center
www.leaf.ge

Mongolia
English Academy of Mongolia
www.nyescm.org

Nigeria
The Know Place
www.knowplace.com.ng

Panama
Academia Interamericana de Panama
http://aip.edu.pa/

Switzerland
Institut Le Rosey
http://www.rosey.ch/

All other inquiries, please email us at
internationalsupport@review.com